THE LANAHAN READINGS

in the

American Polity

THIRD EDITION

THE LANAHAN READINGS

in the

American Polity

THIRD EDITION

—

Ann G. Serow
Kingswood-Oxford School
Central Connecticut State University

Everett C. Ladd
The Roper Center for Public Opinion Research
University of Connecticut

LANAHAN PUBLISHERS, INC.

Baltimore

The text of this book was composed in Bembo with display type set in Garamond.
Composition by Bytheway Publishing Services.
Manufacturing by Victor Graphics, Inc.

ISBN 1-930398-03-4

LANAHAN PUBLISHERS, INC.
324 Hawthorn Road
Baltimore, MD 21210
1-866-345-1949 TOLL FREE

8   9   0

To Our Students

CONTENTS

Contents

PART THREE

Separation of Powers

PART FOUR

Federalism

PART FIVE

Congress

Contents

PART SIX

The Presidency

PART SEVEN

The Executive Branch

Contents

PART EIGHT

The Judiciary

PART NINE

Civil Liberties and Civil Rights

Contents

PART TEN

Public Opinion

PART ELEVEN

Interest Groups

Contents

PART TWELVE

Voting and Elections

Contents

PART THIRTEEN

Political Parties

PART FOURTEEN

The Media

PART FIFTEEN

Political Economy and Public Welfare

Contents xxi

PART SIXTEEN

America in a Changed World

PREFACE

The first edition of *The LANAHAN READINGS in The American Polity* began a happy new collaboration of the editors with LANAHAN PUBLISHERS, INC., and Donald W. Fusting, who founded this new publishing company in 1995. During the previous decade, we had worked closely and confidently with Don on two earlier versions of this book, *The American Polity Reader*, and we were pleased that the association would continue—in fact, quite pleased as it turned out: the second edition of *The LANAHAN READINGS* was assigned in nearly four hundred schools.

Launching another new edition of an established volume is still a big step. What matters to students using the volume, however, is what's between the covers. Here, readers of the new third edition will find in large measure both fundamental continuity in basic design and big changes in specific readings.

There's good reason for continuity. This book is designed to help undergraduates who are taking the basic American government course better understand their country's political system by providing essential readings on American ideas, constitutional system, core political institutions, public opinion, political competition, and policy debates. All of these readings have in fact shown exceptional continuity over time because they reflect the views and values of a society that is strikingly similar now at the beginning of the twenty-first century to what it was when the United States was founded in the late eighteenth century.

At first glance, this proposition might seem surprising. After all, in some regards the America we now inhabit differs greatly from that of George Washington, John Adams, and Thomas Jefferson. They traveled either on foot or, quite literally, by horsepower; we travel faster and more comfortably in automobiles and jet planes. They could communicate only face to face or through the written word; we have now gone beyond the telephone to the Internet. The average life expectancy in their day was thirty-three years; in ours, seventy-five—and so on is the process of change across so many of the physical dimensions of life.

But in social and political values, Americans in 1776 and now, in the twenty-first century, are similar people. That's true because America's founding brought the nation to modernity so abruptly and completely. It was a profound break from the aristocratic past that dominated European life—as indeed life in countries all around the world. The great French social commentator, Alexis de Tocqueville, grasped this fact more fully perhaps than anyone else and wrote what is still the most insightful book on American society, *Democracy in America* (Volume I, 1835 and Volume II, 1839). "The emigrants who colonized America at the beginning of the seventeenth century," Tocqueville wrote, "in some way separated the principle of democracy from all those other principles against which they contended when living in the heart of the old European societies, and transplanted that principle only on the shores of the New World." He did not study America, Tocqueville went on, "just to satisfy curiosity, however legitimate; I sought there lessons from which we might profit. . . . I accept that [democratic] revolution as an accomplished fact, or a fact that soon will be accomplished, and I selected of all the peoples experiencing it that nation in which it has come to the fullest and most peaceful completion. . . . I admit that I saw in America more than America; it was the shape of democracy itself which I sought, its inclinations, character, prejudices, and passions."

Now, over 160 years after Tocqueville wrote, America remains a democratic nation and an intensely individualist society—the latter encompassing much of what he understood when he used the term "democracy." This broad continuity in social values and social structure goes far to explain the institutional continuities we find in *The LANAHAN READINGS*.

The world of American politics keeps changing, nonetheless. Students need readings on the country's political institutions and its political competition that present the American polity in a fresh, contemporary form. So for the third edition of *The LANAHAN READINGS in The American Polity*, we have replaced about a quarter of the selections. Among the many new readings:

Robert Putnam, in *Bowling Alone*, looks at our "social capital" and the decline of civic association.

Barbara Sinclair makes intelligible for students the byzantine budget process in Congress in her *Unorthodox Lawmaking*.

David Gergen isolates the ingredients needed for presidential success in his *Eyewitness to Power*.

Robert Reich, in *Locked in the Cabinet*, opens the cabinet door just enough to let students see what a department head has to deal with.

David Yalof takes us through the travails of becoming a Supreme Court justice in his *Pursuit of Justices.*

Appellate Judge Richard Posner offers some thoughts on security versus civil liberties.

Frances Fox Piven and Richard Cloward retrace voting patterns once again in their *Why Americans Still Don't Vote.*

The political staff at the *Washington Post* gives an analysis of the controversial result of the 2000 presidential election.

Katharine Graham relays the excitement and constraints of investigating one of the biggest media stories in American politics—Watergate.

Benjamin Barber in *Jihad vs. McWorld* and Samuel Huntington in *The Clash of Civilizations* consider America's post-Cold War changed world.

To guide readers through these and all other selections, a brief description of each article appears in brackets below its listing in the Table of Contents. To help orient students, we continue to provide brief introductions to each article. In doing so, we can offer some political, and occasionally, historical and cultural background to the selections. To help students further, we again continue the process of writing footnotes not to dredge up obscure and unnecessary information, but to make clear those words, phrases, and allusions that students need defined or explained in order to understand the particular reading.

This third edition arrives with two changes in organization. First, because so many instructors assign readings on civil liberties and civil rights earlier in their courses, second edition Part Fourteen, "Civil Liberties and Civil Rights," has been moved up for the new third edition to the Part Nine position to follow the readings on the judiciary. Second, the sections on the political economy and public welfare (formerly Parts 15 and 16) are now combined into one section, Part Fifteen, "Political Economy and Public Welfare."

As with the first edition, Ann Serow has written the *Instructor's Guide and Quiz Book.* This ancillary gives instructors an ample amount of questions with which to test their students on each of the readings, and also, some further ideas on how the selections can be used. For example, there are a number of readings that can be set up in a point-counterpoint arrangement for instructors who might want to include this approach in their classroom.

Returning to our opening comments, we have been engaged in this project for well over a decade. We believe that the continuity of having the same team, author/editors and publishing editor, has helped keep the goals of the book in focus: This is a book for students of American government and the list of selections was made, and revised, for them. They, too, have contributed heavily to the reader-making process by their in-class comments. The selections can truly be said to have been class-tested. For this, we again dedicate The LANAHAN READINGS to these willing and observant participants, our students.

AGS
ECL

NOTE OF ACKNOWLEDGMENT   Much appreciation goes to our young political scientist-proofreaders for their many hours of assistance: Frank Saccomandi, Sara Hatch, Jonathan Goldstein, Michael Gladstone, Stephanie Nelson, Alicia LaPorte, Benjamin Nulsen, Elisabeth Chiniara, Brennan Berry, and Ashley Fleming, and to Professor Howard Sacks.

THE LANAHAN READINGS

in the

American Polity

THIRD EDITION

PART ONE

American Ideology

ALEXIS DE TOCQUEVILLE

From *Democracy in America*

In May of 1831, a fancily-dressed, young French aristocrat arrived in the United States to begin his "scientific" study of a new social and political phenomenon, American democracy. After nine months of traveling across the new nation, interviewing numerous Americans from all walks of life, Alexis de Tocqueville returned to France to write Democracy in America, *the single best source with which to begin our exploration of American government and politics. Tocqueville saw the United States as a unique nation. From the start, Americans were all equal. Some were richer and others were poorer, but all who were not indentured or enslaved had an equal opportunity from the start. This clearly was not the case in any other nineteenth-century nation. To the young visitor, this idea of equality was America's identifying mark, a most cherished, if elusive, national virtue.*

———

AFTER THE BIRTH of a human being his early years are obscurely spent in the toils or pleasures of childhood. As he grows up the world receives him, when his manhood begins, and he enters into contact with his fellows. He is then studied for the first time, and it is imagined that the germ of the vices and the virtues of his maturer years is then formed.

This, if I am not mistaken, is a great error. We must begin higher up; we must watch the infant in his mother's arms; we must see the first images which the external world casts upon the dark mirror of his mind; the first occurrences which he witnesses; we must hear the first words which awaken the sleeping powers of thought, and stand by his earliest efforts, if we would understand the prejudices, the habits, and the passions which will rule his life. The entire man is, so to speak, to be seen in the cradle of the child.

The growth of nations presents something analogous to this: they all bear some marks of their origin; and the circumstances which accompanied their birth and contributed to their rise affect the whole term of their being.

If we were able to go back to the elements of states, and to examine the oldest monuments of their history, I doubt not that we should discover in them the primal cause of the prejudices, the habits, the ruling passions, and, in short, of all that constitutes what is called the national character: we should there find the explanation of certain customs which now seem at variance with the prevailing manners; of such laws as conflict with established principles; and of such incoherent opinions as are here and there to be met with in society, like those fragments of broken chains which we sometimes see hanging from the vault of an edifice, and supporting nothing. This might explain the destinies of certain nations which seem borne on by an unknown force to ends of which they themselves are ignorant. But hitherto facts have been wanting to researches of this kind: the spirit of inquiry has only come upon communities in their latter days; and when they at length contemplated their origin, time had already obscured it, or ignorance and pride adorned it with truth-concealing fables.

America is the only country in which it has been possible to witness the natural and tranquil growth of society, and where the influence exercised on the future condition of states by their origin is clearly distinguishable. . . .

America, consequently, exhibits in the broad light of day the phenomena which the ignorance or rudeness of earlier ages conceals from our researches. Near enough to the time when the states of America were founded, to be accurately acquainted with their elements, and sufficiently removed from that period to judge of some of their results, the men of our own day seem destined to see further than their predecessors into the series of human events. Providence has given us a torch which our forefathers did not possess, and has allowed us to discern fundamental causes in the history of the world which the obscurity of the past concealed from them.

If we carefully examine the social and political state of America, after having studied its history, we shall remain perfectly convinced that not an opinion, not a custom, not a law, I may even say not an event, is upon record which the origin of that people will not explain. The readers of this book will find the germ of all that is to follow in the present chapter, and the key to almost the whole work.

The emigrants who came at different periods to occupy the territory now covered by the American Union, differed from each other in many respects; their aim was not the same, and they governed themselves on different principles.

These men had, however, certain features in common, and they were all placed in an analogous situation. The tie of language is perhaps the strongest and the most durable that can unite mankind. All the emigrants spoke the same tongue; they were all offsets from the same people. Born in a country which had been agitated for centuries by the struggles of faction, and in which all parties had been obliged in their turn to place themselves under the protection of the laws, their political education had been perfected in this rude school, and they were more conversant with the notions of right, and the principles of true freedom, than the greater part of their European contemporaries. At the period of the first emigrations, the parish system, that fruitful germ of free institutions, was deeply rooted in the habits of the English; and with it the doctrine of the sovereignty of the people. . . .

Another remark, to which we shall hereafter have occasion to recur, is applicable not only to the English, but to . . . all the Europeans who successively established themselves in the New World. All these European colonies contained the elements, if not the development, of a complete democracy. Two causes led to this result. It may safely be advanced that on leaving the mother country the emigrants had in general no notion of superiority one over another. The happy and the powerful do not go into exile, and there are no surer guaranties of equality among men than poverty and misfortune. It happened, however, on several occasions, that persons of rank were driven to America by political and religious quarrels. Laws were made to establish a gradation of ranks; but it was soon found that the soil of America was opposed to a territorial aristocracy. To bring that refractory land into cultivation, the constant and interested exertions of the owner himself were necessary; and when the ground was prepared, its produce was found to be insufficient to enrich a master and a farmer at the same time. The land was then naturally broken up into small portions, which the proprietor cultivated for himself. Land is the basis of an aristocracy, which clings to the soil that supports it; for it is not by privileges alone, nor by birth, but by landed property handed down from generation to generation, that an aristocracy is constituted. A nation may present immense fortunes and extreme wretchedness; but unless those fortunes are territorial there is no true aristocracy, but simply the class of the rich and that of the poor. . . .

In virtue of the law of partible inheritance, the death of every proprietor brings about a kind of revolution in the property; not only do his possessions change hands, but their very nature is altered; since they are parcelled into shares, which become smaller and smaller at each division. This is the direct and, as it were, the physical effect of the law. It follows, then, that in countries where equality of inheritance is established by law, property, and especially landed property, must have a tendency to perpetual diminution. . . .

. . . But the law of equal division exercises its influence not merely upon the property itself, but it affects the minds of the heirs, and brings their passions into play. These indirect consequences tend powerfully to the destruction of large fortunes, and especially of large domains. . . .

Great landed estates which have once been divided never come together again; for the small proprietor draws from his land a better revenue, in proportion, than the large owner does from his; and of course he sells it at a higher rate. The calculations of gain, therefore, which decide the rich man to sell his domain, will still more powerfully influence him against buying small estates to unite them into a large one.

What is called family-pride is often founded upon an illusion of self-love. A man wishes to perpetuate and immortalize himself, as it were, in his great-grandchildren. Where the *esprit de famille* ceases to act, individual selfishness comes into play. When the idea of family becomes vague, indeterminate, and uncertain, a man thinks of his present convenience; he provides for the establishment of his succeeding generation, and no more.

Either a man gives up the idea of perpetuating his family, or at any rate, he seeks to accomplish it by other means than that of a landed estate. . . .

I do not mean that there is any deficiency of wealthy individuals in the United States; I know of no country, indeed, where the love of money has taken stronger hold on the affections of men, and where a profounder contempt is expressed for the theory of the permanent equality of property. But wealth circulates with inconceivable rapidity, and experience shows that it is rare to find two succeeding generations in the full enjoyment of it. . . .

. . . The social condition of the Americans is eminently democratic; this was its character at the foundation of the Colonies, and it is still more strongly marked at the present day. . . .

America, then, exhibits in her social state an extraordinary phenomenon. Men are there seen on a greater equality in point of fortune and intellect, or, in other words, more equal in their strength, than in any other country of the world, or in any age of which history has preserved the remembrance.

The political consequences of such a social condition as this are easily deducible.

It is impossible to believe that equality will not eventually find its way into the political world as it does everywhere else. To conceive of men remaining for ever unequal upon a single point, yet equal on all others, is impossible; they must come in the end to be equal upon all. . . .

2

JAMES BRYCE

From *The American Commonwealth*

The Englishman James Bryce visited the United States in the 1880s, during the so-called Gilded Age. His topic in this excerpt is equality in America. Equality can be measured in several different ways, he says, by money, knowledge, position, and status. The first three measures of equality point up the obvious differences among the American people. But wealthy or poor, educated or not, highly-positioned or lowly, Bryce concludes, Americans regard one another as fundamentally equal as human beings. A fellow citizen may be more famous or more accomplished or more successful, "but it is not a reason for . . . treating him as if he were porcelain and yourself only earthenware." Is Bryce on target one hundred years later? What has happened to the idea of equality in America in the post-porcelain, post-earthenware age?

THE UNITED STATES are deemed all the world over to be preeminently the land of equality. This was the first feature which struck Europeans when they began, after the peace of 1815 had left them time to look beyond the Atlantic, to feel curious about the phenomena of a new society. This was the great theme of Tocqueville's description, and the starting point of his speculations; this has been the most constant boast of the Americans themselves, who have believed their liberty more complete than that of any other people, because equality has been more fully blended with it. Yet some philosophers say that equality is impossible, and others, who express themselves more precisely, insist that distinctions of rank are so inevitable, that however you try to expunge them, they are sure to reappear. Before we discuss this question, let us see in what senses the word is used.

First there is legal equality, including both what one may call passive or private equality, i.e. the equal possession of civil private rights by all inhabitants, and active or public equality, the equal possession by all of rights to a share in the government, such as the electoral franchise and eligibility to public office. Both kinds of political equality exist in America, in the amplest measure, and may be dismissed from the present discussion.

Next there is the equality of material conditions, that is, of wealth, and all that wealth gives; there is the equality of education and intelligence: there is the equality of social status or rank: and there is (what comes near to, but is not exactly the same as, this last) the equality of estimation, i.e. of the value which men set upon one another, whatever be the elements that come into this value, whether wealth, or education, or official rank, or social rank, or any other species of excellence. In how many and which of these senses of the word does equality exist in the United States? Not as regards material conditions. Till about the middle of last century there were no great fortunes in America, few large fortunes, no poverty. Now there is some poverty (though only in a few places can it be called pauperism), many large fortunes, and a greater number of gigantic fortunes than in any other country in the world. . . .

As respects education, the profusion of superior as well as elementary schools tends to raise the mass to a somewhat higher point than in Europe, while the stimulus of life being keener and the habit of reading more general, the number of persons one finds on the same general level of brightness, keenness, and a superficially competent knowledge of common facts, whether in science, history, geography, or literature, is extremely large. This general level tends to rise. But the level of exceptional attainment in that still relatively small though increasing class who have studied at the best native universities or in Europe, and who pursue learning and science either as a profession or as a source of pleasure, rises faster than does the general level of the multitude, so that in this regard also it appears that equality has diminished and will diminish further.

So far we have been on comparatively smooth and easy ground. Equality of wealth is a concrete thing; equality of intellectual possession and resource is a thing which can be perceived and gauged. Of social equality, of distinctions of standing and estimation in private life, it is far more difficult to speak, and in what follows I speak with some hesitation.

One thing, and perhaps one thing only, may be asserted with confidence. There is no rank in America, that is to say, no external and recognized stamp, marking one man as entitled to any social privileges, or to deference and respect from others. No man is entitled to think himself better than his fellows, or to expect any exceptional consideration to be shown by them to him. Except in the national capital, there is no such thing as a recognized order of precedence, either on public occasions or at a private party, save that yielded to a few official persons, such as the governor and chief judges of a State within that State, as well as to the President and Vice-President, the Speaker of the House, the Federal senators, the judges of the Supreme Federal Court, and the members of the President's cabinet everywhere through the Union. In fact, the idea of a regular "rule of precedence" displeases the Americans. . . .

The fault which Americans are most frequently accused of is the worship of wealth. The amazing fuss which is made about very rich men, the descriptions of their doings, the speculation as to their intentions, the gossip about their private life, lend colour to the reproach. He who builds up a huge fortune, especially if he does it suddenly, is no doubt a sort of hero, because an enormous number of men have the same ambition. Having done best what millions are trying to do, he is discussed, admired, and envied in the same way as the captain of a cricket eleven is at an English school, or the stroke of the university boat at Oxford or Cambridge. If he be a great financier, or the owner of a great railroad or a great newspaper, he exercises vast power, and is therefore well worth courting by those who desire his help or would avert his enmity. Admitting all this, it may seem a paradox to observe that a millionaire has a better and easier social career open to him in England than in America. Nevertheless there is a sense in which this is true. In America, if his private character be bad, if he be mean, or openly immoral, or personally vulgar, or dishonest, the best society may keep its doors closed against him. In England great wealth, skilfully employed, will more readily force these doors to open. For in England great wealth can, by using the appropriate methods, practically buy rank from those who bestow it; or by obliging persons whose position enables them to command fashionable society, can induce them to stand sponsors for the upstart, and force him into society, a thing which no person in America has the power of doing. To effect such a stroke in England the rich man must of course have stopped short of positive frauds, that is, of such frauds as could be proved in court. But he may be still distrusted and disliked by the *élite* of the commercial world, he may be vulgar and ill-educated, and indeed have nothing to recommend him except his wealth and his willingness to spend it in providing amusement for fashionable people. All this will not prevent him from becoming a baronet, or possibly a peer, and thereby acquiring a position of assured dignity which he can transmit to his offspring. The existence of a system of artificial rank enables a stamp to be given to base metal in Europe which cannot be given in a thoroughly republican country. The feeling of the American public towards the very rich is, so far as a stranger can judge, one of curiosity and wonder rather than of respect. There is less snobbishness shown towards them than in England. They are admired as a famous runner or jockey is admired, and the talents they have shown, say, in railroad management or in finance, are felt to reflect lustre on the nation. But they do not necessarily receive either flattery or social deference, and sometimes, where it can be alleged that they have won their wealth as the leading spirits in monopolistic combinations, they are made targets for attack, though they may have done nothing more than what other business men have attempted, with less ability and less success.

The persons to whom official rank gives importance are very few indeed, being for the nation at large only about one hundred persons at the top of the Federal Government, and in each State less than a dozen of its highest State functionaries. For these State functionaries, indeed, the respect shown is extremely scanty, and much more official than personal. A high Federal officer, a senator, or justice of the Supreme Court, or cabinet minister, is conspicuous while he holds his place, and is of course a personage in any private society he may enter; but less so than a corresponding official would be in Europe. A simple member of the House of Representatives is nobody. Even men of the highest official rank do not give themselves airs on the score of their position. Long ago, in Washington, I was taken to be presented to the then head of the United States army, a great soldier whose fame all the world knows. We found him standing at a desk in a bare room in the War Department, at work with one clerk. While he was talking to us the door of the room was pushed open, and there appeared the figure of a Western sight-seer belonging to what Europeans would call the lower middle class, followed by his wife and sister, who were "doing" Washington. Perceiving that the room was occupied they began to retreat, but the Commander-in-chief called them back. "Walk in, ladies," he said. 'You can look around. You won't disturb me; make yourselves at home." . . .

Perhaps the best way of explaining how some of the differences above mentioned, in wealth or official position or intellectual eminence, affect social equality is by reverting to what was called, a few pages back, equality of estimation—the idea which men form of other men as compared with themselves. It is in this that the real sense of equality comes out. In America men hold others to be at bottom exactly the same as themselves. If a man is enormously rich, or if he is a great orator, like Daniel Webster or Henry Ward Beecher, or a great soldier like Ulysses S. Grant, or a great writer like R. W. Emerson, or President, so much the better for him. He is an object of interest, perhaps of admiration, possibly even of reverence. But he is deemed to be still of the same flesh and blood as other men. The admiration felt for him may be a reason for going to see him and longing to shake hands with him, a longing frequent in America. But it is not a reason for bowing down to him, or addressing him in deferential terms, or treating him as if he were porcelain and yourself only earthenware.

3

LOUIS HARTZ

From *The Liberal Tradition in America*

Scholar Louis Hartz has used Alexis de Tocqueville's idea that Americans were "born equal" as a take-off point for his complicated philosophical analysis of the American political tradition. Citing the ideas of John Locke, Edmund Burke, and Jeremy Bentham, Hartz points to the many paradoxes evident in American thought: "pragmatism and absolutism, historicism and rationalism, optimism and pessimism, materialism and idealism, individualism and conformism." Underlying all these paradoxes is the ultimate one. Hartz argues that America, in many ways the most revolutionary nation in the world, never really had a revolution to attain the goal of equality. This paradox places the United States in a "strange relationship" with the nations that seek to emulate America's success.

———

THE ANALYSIS which this book contains is based on what might be called the storybook truth about American history: that America was settled by men who fled from the feudal and clerical oppressions of the Old World. If there is anything in this view, as old as the national folklore itself, then the outstanding thing about the American community in Western history ought to be the nonexistence of those oppressions, or since the reaction against them was in the broadest sense liberal, that the American community is a liberal community. We are confronted, as it were, with a kind of inverted Trotskyite law of combined development, America skipping the feudal stage of history as Russia presumably skipped the liberal stage. . . . One of the central characteristics of a nonfeudal society is that it lacks a genuine revolutionary tradition, the tradition which in Europe has been linked with the Puritan and French revolutions: that it is "born equal," as Tocqueville said. . . .

Surely, then, it is a remarkable force: this fixed, dogmatic liberalism of a liberal way of life. It is the secret root from which have sprung many of the most puzzling of American cultural phenomena. . . .

At bottom it is riddled with paradox. Here is a Lockian doctrine which in the West as a whole is the symbol of rationalism, yet in America the devotion to it has been so irrational that it has not even been recognized for what it is: liberalism. There has never been a "liberal movement" or a real "liberal party" in America: we have only had the American Way of Life, a nationalist articulation of Locke which usually does not know that Locke himself is involved; and we did not even get that until after the Civil War when the Whigs of the nation, deserting the Hamiltonian tradition, saw the capital that could be made out of it. This is why even critics who have noticed America's moral unity have usually missed its substance. Ironically, "liberalism" is a stranger in the land of its greatest realization and fulfillment. But this is not all. Here is a doctrine which everywhere in the West has been a glorious symbol of individual liberty, yet in America its compulsive power has been so great that it has posed a threat to liberty itself. Actually Locke has a hidden conformitarian germ to begin with, since natural law tells equal people equal things, but when this germ is fed by the explosive power of modern nationalism, it mushrooms into something pretty remarkable. One can reasonably wonder about the liberty one finds in Burke.

I believe that this is the basic ethical problem of a liberal society: not the danger of the majority which has been its conscious fear, but the danger of unanimity, which has slumbered unconsciously behind it: the "tyranny of opinion" that Tocqueville saw unfolding. . . . When Tocqueville wrote that the "great advantage" of the American lay in the fact that he did not have "to endure a democratic revolution," he advanced what was surely one of his most fundamental insights into American life. However, while many of his observations have been remembered but not followed up, this one has scarcely even been remembered. Perhaps it is because, fearing revolution in the present, we like to think of it in the past, and we are reluctant to concede that its romance has been missing from our lives. Perhaps it is because the plain evidence of the American revolution of 1776, especially the evidence of its social impact that our newer historians have collected, has made the comment of Tocqueville seem thoroughly enigmatic. But in the last analysis, of course, the question of its validity is a question of perspective. Tocqueville was writing with the great revolutions of Europe in mind, and from that point of view the outstanding thing about the American effort of 1776 was bound to be, not the freedom to which it led, but the established feudal structure it did not have to destroy. . . .

Thus the fact that the Americans did not have to endure a "democratic revolution" deeply conditioned their outlook on people elsewhere who did; and by helping to thwart the crusading spirit in them, it gave to the wild enthusiasms of Europe an appearance not only of analytic error but of unrequited love. Symbols of a world revolution, the Americans were not in truth world revolutionaries. There is no use complaining about the confusions implicit in this position, as Woodrow Wilson used to complain when he said that we had "no business" permitting the French to get the wrong impression about the American revolution. On both sides the reactions that arose were well-nigh inevitable. But one cannot help wondering about something else: the satisfying use to which our folklore has been able to put the incongruity of America's revolutionary role. For if the "contamination" that Jefferson feared, and that found its classic expression in Washington's Farewell Address, has been a part of the American myth, so has the "round the world" significance of the shots that were fired at Concord. We have been able to dream of ourselves as emancipators of the world at the very moment that we have withdrawn from it. We have been able to see ourselves as saviors at the very moment that we have been isolationists. Here, surely, is one of the great American luxuries that the twentieth century has destroyed. . . . When the Americans celebrated the uniqueness of their own society, they were on the track of a personal insight of the profoundest importance. For the nonfeudal world in which they lived shaped every aspect of their social thought: it gave them a frame of mind that cannot be found anywhere else in the eighteenth century, or in the wider history of modern revolutions. . . . The issue of history itself is deeply involved here. On this score, inevitably, the fact that the revolutionaries of 1776 had inherited the freest society in the world shaped their thinking in an intricate way. It gave them, in the first place, an appearance of outright conservatism. . . . The past had been good to the Americans, and they knew it. . . .

Actually, the form of America's traditionalism was one thing, its content quite another. Colonial history had not been the slow and glacial record of development that Bonald and Maistre loved to talk about.* On the contrary, since the first sailing of the *Mayflower*, it had been a story of new beginnings, daring enterprises, and explicitly stated principles— it breathed, in other words, the spirit of Bentham himself. The result was that the traditionalism of the Americans, like a pure freak of logic, often bore amazing marks of antihistorical rationalism. The clearest case of this undoubtedly is to be found in the revolutionary constitutions of 1776, which evoked, as Franklin reported, the "rapture" of European liberals everywhere. In America, of course, the concept of a written constitution, including many of the mechanical devices it embodied, was the end-product of a chain of historical experience that went back to the Mayflower

---

*Louis Bonald and Joseph de Maistre were prominent French conservative political theorists of the early nineteenth century. Both were inveterate enemies of the radical and rationalistic ideas associated with the French Revolution. They were leading figures in the European Reaction.—EDS.

Compact and the Plantation Covenants of the New England towns: it was the essence of political traditionalism. But in Europe just the reverse was true. The concept was the darling of the rationalists—a symbol of the emancipated mind at work. . . .

But how then are we to describe these baffling Americans? Were they rationalists or were they traditionalists? The truth is, they were neither, which is perhaps another way of saying that they were both. For the war between Burke and Bentham on the score of tradition, which made a great deal of sense in a society where men had lived in the shadow of feudal institutions, made comparatively little sense in a society where for years they had been creating new states, planning new settlements, and, as Jefferson said, literally building new lives.* In such a society a strange dialectic was fated to appear, which would somehow unite the antagonistic components of the European mind; the past became a continuous future, and the God of the traditionalists sanctioned the very arrogance of the men who defied Him.

This shattering of the time categories of Europe, this Hegelian-like revolution in historic perspective, goes far to explain one of the enduring secrets of the American character: a capacity to combine rock-ribbed traditionalism with high inventiveness, ancestor worship with ardent optimism. Most critics have seized upon one or the other of these aspects of the American mind, finding it impossible to conceive how both can go together. That is why the insight of Gunnar Myrdal is a very distinguished one when he writes: "America is . . . conservative. . . . But the principles conserved are liberal and some, indeed, are radical." Radicalism and conservatism have been twisted entirely out of shape by the liberal flow of American history. . . .

What I have been doing here is fairly evident: I have been interpreting the social thought of the American revolution in terms of the social goals *it did not need to achieve.* Given the usual approach, this may seem like a perverse inversion of the reasonable course of things; but in a world where the "canon and feudal law" are missing, how else are we to understand the philosophy of a liberal revolution? The remarkable thing about the "spirit of 1776," as we have seen, is not that it sought emancipation but that it sought it in a sober temper; not that it opposed power but that it opposed it ruthlessly and continuously; not that it looked forward to the

---

*Edmund Burke, an eighteenth-century English political theorist, is perhaps the most artful defender of tradition in the history of political theory. Jeremy Bentham, an English theorist of the late eighteenth and early nineteenth centuries, was as rationalistic as Burke was traditionalistic. While Burke generally saw virtues in inherited institutions, Bentham generally advocated their reform. —Eds.

future but that it worshiped the past as well. Even these perspectives, however, are only part of the story, misleading in themselves. The "free air" of American life, as John Jay once happily put it, penetrated to deeper levels of the American mind, twisting it in strange ways, producing a set of results fundamental to everything else in American thought. The clue to these results lies in the following fact: the Americans, though models to all the world of the middle class way of life, lacked the passionate middle class consciousness which saturated the liberal thought of Europe. . . .

But this is not all. If the position of the colonial Americans saved them from many of the class obsessions of Europe, it did something else as well: it inspired them with a peculiar sense of community that Europe had never known. . . . Amid the "free air" of American life, something new appeared: men began to be held together, not by the knowledge that they were different parts of a corporate whole, but by the knowledge that they were similar participants in a uniform way of life—by that "pleasing uniformity of decent competence" which Crèvecoeur loved so much. The Americans themselves were not unaware of this. When Peter Thacher proudly announced that "simplicity of manners" was the mark of the revolutionary colonists, what was he saying if not that the norms of a single class in Europe were enough to sustain virtually a whole society in America? Richard Hildreth, writing after the leveling impact of the Jacksonian revolution had made this point far more obvious, put his finger directly on it. He denounced feudal Europe, where "half a dozen different codes of morals," often in flagrant contradiction with one another, flourished "in the same community," and celebrated the fact that America was producing "one code, moral standard, by which the actions of all are to be judged. . . . " Hildreth knew that America was a marvelous mixture of many peoples and many religions, but he also knew that it was characterized by something more marvelous even than that: the power of the liberal norm to penetrate them all.

Now a sense of community based on a sense of uniformity is a deceptive thing. It looks individualistic, and in part it actually is. It cannot tolerate internal relationships of disparity, and hence can easily inspire the kind of advice that Professor Nettels once imagined a colonial farmer giving his son: "Remember that you are as good as any man—and also that you are no better." But in another sense it is profoundly anti-individualistic, because the common standard is its very essence, and deviations from that standard inspire it with an irrational fright. The man who is as good as his neighbors is in a tough spot when he confronts all of his neighbors combined. Thus William Graham Sumner looked at the other side of

Professor Nettels's colonial coin and did not like what he saw: "public opinion" was an "impervious mistress. . . . Mrs. Grundy held powerful sway and Gossip was her prime minister."

Here we have the "tyranny of the majority" that Tocqueville later described in American life; here too we have the deeper paradox out of which it was destined to appear. Freedom in the fullest sense implies both variety and equality. . . . At the bottom of the American experience of freedom, not in antagonism to it but as a constituent element of it, there has always lain the inarticulate premise of conformity. . . . American political thought, as we have seen, is a veritable maze of polar contradictions, winding in and out of each other hopelessly: pragmatism and absolutism, historicism and rationalism, optimism and pessimism, materialism and idealism, individualism and conformism. But, after all, the human mind works by polar contradictions; and when we have evolved an interpretation of it which leads cleanly in a single direction, we may be sure that we have missed a lot. The task of the cultural analyst is not to discover simplicity, or even to discover unity, for simplicity and unity do not exist, but to drive a wedge of rationality through the pathetic indecisions of social thought. In the American case that wedge is not hard to find. . . .

It is this business of destruction and creation which goes to the heart of the problem. For the point of departure of great revolutionary thought everywhere else in the world has been the effort to build a new society on the ruins of an old one, and this is an experience America has never had. We are reminded again of Tocqueville's statement: the Americans are "born equal."

That statement, especially in light of the strange relationship which the revolutionary Americans had with their admirers abroad, raises an obvious question. Can a people that is born equal ever understand peoples elsewhere that have become so? Can it ever lead them? . . . America's experience of being born equal has put it in a strange relationship to the rest of the world.

4

ROBERT PUTNAM

From *Bowling Alone*

In one of the most influential studies of the late twentieth century, social scientist Robert Putnam explains the importance of "social capital" in Americans' lives—the person-to-person contacts that create complex networks of relationships among citizens. These networks, especially as they tradition-ally existed in the many civic associations that permeated American towns and cities, have dramatically declined in number and relevance in recent decades, Putnam believes. He discusses the difference between social capital that is bonding and social capital that is bridging. Putnam concludes the excerpt by identifying reasons why Americans today are "bowling alone." It's a problem for citizens, he feels, because strong networks of interpersonal relationships lead to healthy, happy lives.

———

NO ONE IS LEFT from the Glenn Valley, Pennsylvania, Bridge Club who can tell us precisely when or why the group broke up, even though its forty-odd members were still playing regularly as recently as 1990, just as they had done for more than half a century. The shock in the Little Rock, Arkansas, Sertoma club, however, is still painful: in the mid-1980s, nearly fifty people had attended the weekly luncheon to plan activities to help the hearing- and speech-impaired, but a decade later only seven regulars continued to show up.

The Roanoke, Virginia, chapter of the National Association for the Advancement of Colored People (NAACP) had been an active force for civil rights since 1918, but during the 1990s membership withered from about 2,500 to a few hundred. By November 1998 even a heated contest for president drew only fifty-seven voting members. Black city councillor Carroll Swain observed ruefully, "Some people today are a wee bit compla-cent until something jumps up and bites them." VFW Post 2378 in Berwyn, Illinois, a blue-collar suburb of Chicago, was long a bustling "home away from home" for local veterans and a kind of working-class country club for the neighborhood, hosting wedding receptions and class reunions. By 1999, however, membership had so dwindled that it was a struggle just to pay taxes on the yellow brick post hall. Although numerous veterans of Vietnam and the post-Vietnam military lived in the area, Tom

Kissell, national membership director for the VFW, observed, "Kids today just aren't joiners."

The Charity League of Dallas had met every Friday morning for fifty-seven years to sew, knit, and visit, but on April 30, 1999, they held their last meeting; the average age of the group had risen to eighty, the last new member had joined two years earlier, and president Pat Dilbeck said ruefully, "I feel like this is a sinking ship." Precisely three days later and 1,200 miles to the northeast, the Vassar alumnae of Washington, D.C., closed down their fifty-first—and last—annual book sale. Even though they aimed to sell more than one hundred thousand books to benefit college scholarships in the 1999 event, co-chair Alix Myerson explained, the volunteers who ran the program "are in their sixties, seventies, and eighties. They're dying, and they're not replaceable." Meanwhile, as Tewksbury Memorial High School (TMHS), just north of Boston, opened in the fall of 1999, forty brand-new royal blue uniforms newly purchased for the marching band remained in storage, since only four students signed up to play. Roger Whittlesey, TMHS band director, recalled that twenty years earlier the band numbered more than eighty, but participation had waned ever since. Somehow in the last several decades of the twentieth century all these community groups and tens of thousands like them across America began to fade.

It wasn't so much that old members dropped out—at least not any more rapidly than age and the accidents of life had always meant. But community organizations were no longer continuously revitalized, as they had been in the past, by freshets of new members. . . .

. . . In recent years social scientists have framed concerns about the changing character of American society in terms of the concept of "social capital." By analogy with notions of physical capital and human capital—tools and training that enhance individual productivity—the core idea of social capital theory is that social networks have value. Just as a screwdriver (physical capital) or a college education (human capital) can increase productivity (both individual and collective), so too social contacts affect the productivity of individuals and groups.

Whereas physical capital refers to physical objects and human capital refers to properties of individuals, social capital refers to connections among individuals—social networks and the norms of reciprocity and trustworthiness that arise from them. In that sense social capital is closely related to what some have called "civic virtue." The difference is that "social capital" calls attention to the fact that civic virtue is most powerful when embedded in a dense network of reciprocal social relations. A society of many virtuous but isolated individuals is not necessarily rich in social capital. . . .

. . . [S]ocial capital has both an individual and a collective aspect—a private face and a public face. First, individuals form connections that benefit our own interests. One pervasive strategem of ambitious job seekers is "networking," for most of us get our jobs because of whom we know, not what we know—that is, our social capital, not our human capital. Economic sociologist Ronald Burt has shown that executives with bounteous Rolodex files enjoy faster career advancement. Nor is the private return to social capital limited to economic rewards. As Claude S. Fischer, a sociologist of friendship, has noted, "Social networks are important in all our lives, often for finding jobs, more often for finding a helping hand, companionship, or a shoulder to cry on."

If individual clout and companionship were all there were to social capital, we'd expect foresighted, self-interested individuals to invest the right amount of time and energy in creating or acquiring it. However, social capital also can have "externalities" that affect the wider community, so that not all the costs and benefits of social connections accrue to the person making the contact. As we shall see later . . . , a well-connected individual in a poorly connected society is not as productive as a well-connected individual in a well-connected society. And even a poorly connected individual may derive some of the spillover benefits from living in a well-connected community. If the crime rate in my neighborhood is lowered by neighbors keeping an eye on one another's homes, I benefit even if I personally spend most of my time on the road and never even nod to another resident on the street.

Social capital can thus be simultaneously a "private good" and a "public good." Some of the benefit from an investment in social capital goes to by-standers, while some of the benefit redounds to the immediate interest of the person making the investment. For example, service clubs, like Rotary or Lions, mobilize local energies to raise scholarships or fight disease at the same time that they provide members with friendships and business connections that pay off personally.

Social connections are also important for the rules of conduct that they sustain. Networks involve (almost by definition) mutual obligations; they are not interesting as mere "contacts." Networks of community engagement foster sturdy norms of reciprocity: I'll do this for you now, in the expectation that you (or perhaps someone else) will return the favor. "Social capital is akin to what Tom Wolfe called 'the favor bank' in his novel *The Bonfire of the Vanities*," notes economist Robert Frank.

It was, however, neither a novelist nor an economist, but Yogi Berra who offered the most succinct definition of reciprocity: "If you don't go to somebody's funeral, they won't come to yours."

Sometimes, as in these cases, reciprocity is *specific*: I'll do this for you if you do that for me. Even more valuable, however, is a norm of *generalized* reciprocity: I'll do this for you without expecting anything specific back from you, in the confident expectation that someone else will do something for me down the road. The Golden Rule is one formulation of generalized reciprocity. Equally instructive is the T-shirt slogan used by the Gold Beach, Oregon, Volunteer Fire Department to publicize their annual fund-raising effort: "Come to our breakfast, we'll come to your fire." "We act on a norm of specific reciprocity," the firefighters seem to be saying, but onlookers smile because they recognize the underlying norm of generalized reciprocity—the firefighters will come even if *you* don't. When Blanche DuBois depended on the kindness of strangers, she too was relying on generalized reciprocity.

A society characterized by generalized reciprocity is more efficient than a distrustful society, for the same reason that money is more efficient than barter. If we don't have to balance every exchange instantly, we can get a lot more accomplished. Trustworthiness lubricates social life. Frequent interaction among a diverse set of people tends to produce a norm of generalized reciprocity. Civic engagement and social capital entail mutual obligation and responsibility for action. As L. J. Hanifan and his successors recognized, social networks and norms of reciprocity can facilitate cooperation for mutual benefit. When economic and political dealing is embedded in dense networks of social interaction, incentives for opportunism and malfeasance are reduced. This is why the diamond trade, with its extreme possibilities for fraud, is concentrated within close-knit ethnic enclaves. Dense social ties facilitate gossip and other valuable ways of cultivating reputation—an essential foundation for trust in a complex society.

Physical capital is not a single "thing," and different forms of physical capital are not interchangeable. An eggbeater and an aircraft carrier both appear as physical capital in our national accounts, but the eggbeater is not much use for national defense, and the carrier would not be much help with your morning omelet. Similarly, social capital—that is, social networks and the associated norms of reciprocity—comes in many different shapes and sizes with many different uses. Your extended family represents a form of social capital, as do your Sunday school class, the regulars who play poker on your commuter train, your college roommates, the civic organizations to which you belong, the Internet chat group in which you participate, and the network of professional acquaintances recorded in your address book. . . .

Of all the dimensions along which forms of social capital vary, perhaps the most important is the distinction between *bridging* (or inclusive) and *bonding* (or exclusive). Some forms of social capital are, by choice or necessity, inward looking and tend to reinforce exclusive identities and homogeneous groups. Examples of bonding social capital include ethnic fraternal organizations, church-based women's reading groups, and fashionable country clubs. Other networks are outward looking and encompass people across diverse social cleavages. Examples of bridging social capital include the civil rights movement, many youth service groups, and ecumenical religious organizations.

Bonding social capital is good for undergirding specific reciprocity and mobilizing solidarity. Dense networks in ethnic enclaves, for example, provide crucial social and psychological support for less fortunate members of the community, while furnishing start-up financing, markets, and reliable labor for local entrepreneurs. Bridging networks, by contrast, are better for linkage to external assets and for information diffusion. Economic sociologist Mark Granovetter has pointed out that when seeking jobs — or political allies — the "weak" ties that link me to distant acquaintances who move in different circles from mine are actually more valuable than the "strong" ties that link me to relatives and intimate friends whose sociological niche is very like my own. Bonding social capital is, as Xavier de Souza Briggs puts it, good for "getting by," but bridging social capital is crucial for "getting ahead."

Moreover, bridging social capital can generate broader identities and reciprocity, whereas bonding social capital bolsters our narrower selves. In 1829 at the founding of a community lyceum in the bustling whaling port of New Bedford, Massachusetts, Thomas Greene eloquently expressed this crucial insight:

We come from all the divisions, ranks and classes of society . . . to teach and to be taught in our turn. While we mingle together in these pursuits, we shall learn to know each other more intimately; we shall remove many of the prejudices which ignorance or partial acquaintance with each other had fostered. . . . In the parties and sects into which we are divided, we sometimes learn to love our brother at the expense of him whom we do not in so many respects regard as a brother. . . . We may return to our homes and firesides [from the lyceum] with kindlier feelings toward one another, because we have learned to know one another better.

Bonding social capital constitutes a kind of sociological superglue, whereas bridging social capital provides a sociological WD-40. Bonding social capital, by creating strong in-group loyalty, may also create strong out-group antagonism, as Thomas Greene and his neighbors in New Bedford knew, and for that reason we might expect negative external effects to be more common with this form of social capital. Nevertheless, under many circumstances both bridging and bonding social capital can have powerfully positive social effects.

Many groups simultaneously bond along some social dimensions and bridge across others. The black church, for example, brings together people of the same race and religion across class lines. The Knights of Columbus was created to bridge cleavages among different ethnic communities while bonding along religious and gender lines. Internet chat groups may bridge across geography, gender, age, and religion, while being tightly homogeneous in education and ideology. In short, bonding and bridging are not "either-or" categories into which social networks can be neatly divided, but "more or less" dimensions along which we can compare different forms of social capital. . . .

Before October 29, 1997, John Lambert and Andy Boschma knew each other only through their local bowling league at the Ypsi-Arbor Lanes in Ypsilanti, Michigan. Lambert, a sixty-four-year-old retired employee of the University of Michigan hospital, had been on a kidney transplant waiting list for three years when Boschma, a thirty-three-year-old accountant, learned casually of Lambert's need and unexpectedly approached him to offer to donate one of his own kidneys.

"Andy saw something in me that others didn't," said Lambert. "When we were in the hospital Andy said to me, 'John, I really like you and have a lot of respect for you. I wouldn't hesitate to do this all over again.' I got choked up." Boschma returned the feeling: "I obviously feel a kinship [with Lambert]. I cared about him before, but now I'm really rooting for him." This moving story speaks for itself, but the photograph that accompanied this report in the *Ann Arbor News* reveals that in addition to their differences in profession and generation, Boschma is white and Lambert is African American. That they bowled together made all the difference. In small ways like this—and in larger ways, too—we Americans need to reconnect with one another. . . .

Something important happened to social bonds and civic engagement in America over the last third of the twentieth century. Before exploring why, let's summarize what we have learned.

During the first two-thirds of the century Americans took a more and more active role in the social and political life of their communities—

in churches and union halls, in bowling alleys and clubrooms, around committee tables and card tables and dinner tables. Year by year we gave more generously to charity, we pitched in more often on community projects, and (insofar as we can still find reliable evidence) we behaved in an increasingly trustworthy way toward one another. Then, mysteriously and more or less simultaneously, we began to do all those things less often.

We are still more civically engaged than citizens in many other countries, but compared with our own recent past, we are less connected. We remain interested and critical spectators of the public scene. We kibitz, but we don't play. We maintain a facade of formal affiliation, but we rarely show up. We have invented new ways of expressing our demands that demand less of us. We are less likely to turn out for collective deliberation—whether in the voting booth or the meeting hall—and when we do, we find that discouragingly few of our friends and neighbors have shown up. We are less generous with our money and (with the important exception of senior citizens) with our time, and we are less likely to give strangers the benefit of the doubt. They, of course, return the favor.

Not all social networks have atrophied. Thin, single-stranded, surf-by interactions are gradually replacing dense, multistranded, well-exercised bonds. More of our social connectedness is one shot, special purpose, and self oriented. As sociologist Morris Janowitz foresaw several decades ago, we have developed "communities of limited liability," or what sociologists Claude Fischer, Robert Jackson, and their colleagues describe more hopefully as "personal communities." Large groups with local chapters, long histories, multiple objectives, and diverse constituencies are being replaced by more evanescent, single-purpose organizations, smaller groups that "reflect the fluidity of our lives by allowing us to bond easily but to break our attachments with equivalent ease." Grassroots groups that once brought us face-to-face with our neighbors, the agreeable and disagreeable alike, are overshadowed by the vertiginous rise of staff-led interest groups purpose built to represent our narrower selves. Place-based social capital is being supplanted by function-based social capital. We are withdrawing from those networks of reciprocity that once constituted our communities. . . .

Let us sum up what we have learned about the factors that have contributed to the decline in civic engagement and social capital. . . .

First, pressures of time and money, including the special pressures on two-career families, contributed measurably to the diminution of our social and community involvement during these years. My best guess is that no more than 10 percent of the total decline is attributable to that set of factors.

Second, suburbanization, commuting, and sprawl also played a supporting role. Again, a reasonable estimate is that these factors together might account for perhaps an additional 10 percent of the problem.

Third, the effect of electronic entertainment—above all, television—in privatizing our leisure time has been substantial. My rough estimate is that this factor might account for perhaps 25 percent of the decline.

Fourth and most important, generational change—the slow, steady, and ineluctable replacement of the long civic generation by their less involved children and grandchildren—has been a very powerful factor. The effects of generational succession vary significantly across different measures of civic engagement—greater for more public forms, less for private *schmoozing*—but as a rough rule of thumb we concluded . . . that this factor might account for perhaps half of the overall decline. . . .

By virtually every conceivable measure, social capital has eroded steadily and sometimes dramatically over the past two generations. The quantitative evidence is overwhelming, yet most Americans did not need to see charts and graphs to know that something bad has been happening in their communities and in their country. Americans have had a growing sense at some visceral level of disintegrating social bonds. It is perhaps no coincidence that on the eve of the millennium the market for civic nostalgia was hotter than the market for blue-chip stocks. For example, newscaster Tom Brokaw's book profiling the heroic World War II generation got mixed reviews from critics yet was a runaway best-seller. In Los Angeles there was an on-again, off-again movement to rename the LAX airport after the actor Jimmy Stewart, a military hero in real life who brought civic heroes Jefferson Smith and George Bailey to the silver screen. American nostalgia in the late twentieth century is no run-of-the-mill, rosy-eyed remembrance of things past. It is an attempt to recapture a time when public-spiritedness really did carry more value and when communities really did "work." As we buy books and rename airports, we seem to be saying that at a profound level civic virtue and social capital do matter.

Are we right? Does social capital have salutary effects on individuals, communities, or even entire nations? Yes, an impressive and growing body of research suggests that civic connections help make us healthy, wealthy, and wise. Living without social capital is not easy, whether one is a villager in southern Italy or a poor person in the American inner city or a well-heeled entrepreneur in a high-tech industrial district.

If we are to believe that social capital benefits individuals and communities, we must first understand how social capital works its magic. High levels of trust and citizen participation operate through a variety of mechanisms to produce socially desirable outcomes. Obviously the mechanism(s) at work will vary by the circumstance and outcome in question. But in general social capital has many features that help people translate aspirations into realities.

First, social capital allows citizens to resolve collective problems more easily. Social scientists have long been concerned about "dilemmas" of collective action. Such dilemmas are ubiquitous, and their dynamics are straightforward. People often might all be better off if they cooperate, with each doing her share. But each individual benefits more by shirking her responsibility, hoping that others will do the work for her. Moreover, even if she is wrong and the others shirk, too, she is still better off than if she had been the only sucker. Obviously if every individual thinks that the others will do the work, nobody will end up taking part, and all will be left worse off than if all had contributed.

Supporting government through a tax system is a dilemma of collective action. So is limiting lawn sprinklers and long showers during arid summers. These and other coordination challenges go by various names — "collective-action problems," "the prisoner's dilemma," "the free-rider problem," and "the tragedy of the commons," to name a few. But they all share one feature: They are best solved by an institutional mechanism with the power to ensure compliance with the collectively desirable behavior. Social norms and the networks that enforce them provide such a mechanism.

Second, social capital greases the wheels that allow communities to advance smoothly. Where people are trusting and trustworthy, and where they are subject to repeated interactions with fellow citizens, everyday business and social transactions are less costly. There is no need to spend time and money making sure that others will uphold their end of the arrangement or penalizing them if they don't. Economists such as Oliver Williamson and political scientists such as Elinor Ostrom have demonstrated how social capital translates into financial capital and resource wealth for businesses and self-governing units. Indeed, the Nobel Prize-winning economist Kenneth Arrow has concluded, "Virtually every commercial transaction has within itself an element of trust, certainly any transaction conducted over a period of time. It can be plausibly argued that much of the economic backwardness in the world can be explained by a lack of mutual confidence."

A third way in which social capital improves our lot is by widening our awareness of the many ways in which our fates are linked. People who have active and trusting connections to others — whether family members, friends, or fellow bowlers — develop or maintain character traits that are good for the rest of society. Joiners become more tolerant, less cynical, and more empathetic to the misfortunes of others. When people lack connections to others, they are unable to test the veracity of their own views, whether in the give-and-take of casual conversation or in more formal deliberation. Without such an opportunity, people are more likely to be swayed by their worst impulses. It is no coincidence that random acts of violence, such as the 1999 spate of schoolyard shootings, tend to be committed by people identified, after the fact, as "loners."

The networks that constitute social capital also serve as conduits for the flow of helpful information that facilitates achieving our goals. For example, . . . many Americans—perhaps even most of us—get our jobs through personal connections. If we lack that social capital, economic sociologists have shown, our economic prospects are seriously reduced, even if we have lots of talent and training ("human capital"). Similarly, communities that lack civic interconnections find it harder to share information and thus mobilize to achieve opportunities or resist threats.

Social capital also operates through psychological and biological processes to improve individuals' lives. Mounting evidence suggests that people whose lives are rich in social capital cope better with traumas and fight illness more effectively. Social capital appears to be a complement, if not a substitute, for Prozac, sleeping pills, antacids, vitamin C, and other drugs we buy at the corner pharmacy. "Call me [or indeed almost anyone] in the morning" might actually be better medical advice than "Take two aspirin" as a cure for what ails us.

5

EVERETT CARLL LADD

From *The Ladd Report*

In his role as executive director of the Roper Center for Public Opinion Research at the University of Connecticut, Professor Everett Carll Ladd closely followed the data on many political and social aspects of America. Here he uses poll data to assess the popular thesis found in the work of Robert Putnam and other social scientists that citizens no longer take part in associations and groups as they once did but rather prefer to carry on private, individual-centered lives. Putnam termed this phenomenon "bowling alone." Ladd, however, finds the evidence quite contrary. While older groups may have lost membership, newer ones are thriving. Americans are more active than ever in joining together for civic, religious, and political goals. Ladd's example of the displacement of the PTA by other parent-teacher school organizations illustrates his interpretation of the richness of group activity in the United States and reveals how carefully data must be analyzed to arrive at valid conclusions.

———

THE UNITED STATES is an individualist democracy. "Let government do it" has never been our thing. We've counted on individuals doing it—by accepting responsibility for building and maintaining a good society.

Somewhat paradoxically, an individualist democracy is unusually dependent on harnessing collective or cooperative energies. Individual citizens can't manage a society—can't possibly address its manifold needs in any satisfactory fashion—through solitary labors. We must come together in associations large and small where we learn and practice *citizenship*. Our ideal has been and remains an America of active civic and social organizations, churches, philanthropies, and voluntarism—not just to help concretely with a myriad of social needs and problems but, even more important, to sustain vibrant community life. That the "me" will become too insistent, at the expense of the "we," is a persistent American worry. And engaging citizens in civic affairs is the persistent American answer to how a narrowly self-serving individualism can best be avoided.

No one has ever thought it would be easy, though. A "collectivist" individualism built around community engagement can release enormous civic energy, but it asks a lot of millions of citizens. It's not surprising that many in each succeeding generation of Americans have worried that vigorous community participation through groups and charities and voluntary service is somehow losing ground. . . .

These worries are very much evident today. The U.S. economy is hugely successful, but isn't "community" suffering even amidst these burgeoning material resources? Aren't we too transfixed by what *I need*, to make *me* happy, at the expense of what *we need*, as in our family life, for real individual fulfillment? Aren't we losing the level of confidence and trust in one another that's essential to the health of our democracy? Aren't we retreating into private pursuits, or to use a metaphor that has resonated in recent years, aren't we now increasingly "bowling alone"?

Polls pick up the current angst. For example, surveys taken by ABC News and the *Washington Post* regularly ask respondents if they think "things in this country are generally going in the right direction, or . . . have gotten pretty seriously off on the wrong track?" Much of the time large majorities answer that we're heading the wrong way: 57 percent

28 EVERETT CARLL LADD

said this in late summer 1997, even though the economy was doing nicely, compared with just 39 percent who thought the country was moving in the right direction. The *Los Angeles Times* had asked this same question in a 1995 survey and got similar results—55 percent said we were off on the wrong track, only 35 percent that things were on the whole moving positively. What's most instructive, when the newspaper's pollsters followed up by asking those who had said the country was somehow going the wrong way rather than progressing why they felt this way, 50 percent talked about crime, family breakdown, and a weakening of religious commitments and standards (while just 19 percent mentioned anything to do with the economy).

Such concerns are often expressed in terms of our "social capital" account. The traditional reference to capital involves economics, of course. My dictionary defines the term as "the wealth, whether in money or property, owned or employed in business . . . "; and as "any form of wealth employed or capable of being employed in the production of more wealth." Drawing on this root, "social capital" encompasses any form of citizens' civic engagement employed or capable of being employed to address community needs and problems and, in general, to enhance community life. The Great Social Capital Debate addresses this question: Are we spending down our supply of social capital? Many think that the balance is now dangerously low and worry about the consequences.

Are we right to so worry? In the pages that follow I will argue that the answer is yes from one important perspective, but an emphatic no from another. Social capital *is* crucial, and it's undergoing some major changes of form. But at the same time, an extensive record shows that we're building up our supply of social capital, not depleting it. . . .

I was waiting in line for a cup of coffee at a gourmet coffee wagon near my office when a hand patted my back and a voice boomed out: "So what do you think about 'Bowling Alone'?"

It was a distinguished colleague, not in the social sciences, who had just finished reading commentary on Robert Putnam's work, in particular on the argument advanced in his famous article ["Bowling Alone"]. It wasn't exactly the spot for an extended seminar on America's "social capital." I replied briefly that while I agreed entirely with Putnam (and many others) that the health of the country's associational life and individual participation in civic affairs is of vital importance, I didn't think Putnam was right in claiming that the data show civic decline. "Well, I don't know about the data," my friend replied, "but what he has to say feels right to me, right here." At that he gently patted his abdomen.

The Ladd Report wasn't written primarily as a response to Robert Putnam. Though his essays have received enormous attention, "bowling alone" has seemed to many a powerfully evocative metaphor for a set of worries—diffuse but substantial—about the health of contemporary citizenship. My University of Connecticut colleague is hardly alone in feeling that America's participatory civic life has fallen into sad disrepair. Instead of the nation of joiners so often celebrated in the past, we are, in this view, fast becoming a nation of loners. "Bowling alone" has become the widely accepted shorthand for these concerns. I take issue with Robert Putnam's essay, but only as one among many voices making similar claims. . . .

America's associational life is extensive, diverse, and decentralized—which makes it hard to sort out trends. As I've struggled with the data, I've often felt like I'm drowning in a sea of anecdotes. There are so many different stories—and inevitably they don't all point in the same direction. These difficulties acknowledged, the debate over the health of civic America should be resolved by systematic empirical determination. I believe . . . that, taken together, the available data provide a reasonably clear picture of trends in our civic engagement—and that the trends show it extending, not contracting, as it finds new forms and outlets. . . .

Theda Skocpol thinks that the idea of a vigorous citizenry addressing social needs and problems outside of government is simply "Tocqueville romanticism." It's possible, of course, to present civic engagement in sentimental and unrealistic terms, but Tocqueville didn't romanticize things. He did observe that the United States of his day displayed a level and vigor in associational activity surpassing anything in Europe. "Americans of all ages, all conditions, and all dispositions constantly form associations," he wrote. "They have not only commercial and manufacturing companies, in which all take part, but associations of a thousand other kinds, religious, moral, serious, futile, general or restricted, enormous or diminutive." He thought that one type of American association that he called "intellectual and moral" was especially important. The United States had lots of groups pursuing political and economic interests, but Europe, too, had experience with groups such as these. It was in its churches, of great denominational diversity, and other groups committed to social improvement that America stood out. . . .

Tocqueville saw political democracy growing out of experience acquired in the great variety of civil associations—many entirely nonpolitical. "The greater the multiplicity of small affairs, the more do men, even without knowing it, acquire facility in prosecuting great undertakings in common. Civil associations, therefore, facilitate political associations." An individualist democracy requires that many people be trained to participate and accept responsibility for social outcomes. Even when they entirely lack political objectives, then, small groups are a kind of school of democracy.

National political institutions, notably political parties, in their turn provide essential democratic education for narrowly based community organizations. The latter always run the risk of becoming too assertive of their own immediate objectives, too unwilling to compromise. Broad-based political parties teach people that they must join with many others of diverse views if they are to succeed in advancing general programs. "Thus political life makes the love and practice of association more general; it imparts a desire of union and teaches the means of combination to numbers of men who otherwise would have always lived apart. . . . "

Tocqueville's final major argument about Americans' civic engagement was that, somewhat paradoxically, it was spurred, not diminished, by the strength of their individualism. Unless ordinary citizens have an expansive sense of their rights and responsibilities, and are reasonably confident that their society is organized in a way that lets them really make a difference, they are unlikely to bestir themselves. Tocqueville concluded that individualist Americans believed they were obliged to make personal effort on behalf of social amelioration—and that their society was congenial to such efforts. Individuals *should* participate, and when they do *it works*.

Though individualism may become too narrowly self-serving, without a strong, self-confident individualism an expansive idea of citizenship is impossible. This citizen accepts partial ownership and responsibility for the health of his/her society—which can't be exercised passively. There is no need to introduce "romantic" or utopian standards. Tocqueville's argument is simply that active, voluntary participation by large segments of the populace is needed if individualist democracy is to work. . . .

As I will argue, civic engagement in America is high and in fact increasing. There is good reason for the trend: It is easier to be an engaged citizen in the Information Economy than in an Industrial Economy. Writing in the early 1970s, Daniel Bell described the emergence of the United States (and other economically advanced countries) into a broad new era. He contrasted this emergent "postindustrial" society with its predecessor, arguing that whereas "industrial society is the coordination of machines and men for the production of goods," postindustrial society is "organized around knowledge." The key developments defining postindustrialism, Bell concluded, are "the exponential growth and branching of science, the rise of a new intellectual technology, the creation of systematic research through R&D budgets, and . . . the codification of theoretical knowledge." The technological revolutions of the postindustrial age have also dramatically expanded wealth. Thus postindustrialism extends the resources for civic participation. It increases dramatically the proportion of the public given advanced educational skills and new communications tools. It frees broad segments of the populace from grinding physical toil. By extending material abundance, it widens the range of individual choice and invites millions to explore civic life in ways previously out of reach for them. . . .

One reason the idea of declining civic engagement has seemed plausible is easy to see: Many older groups have in fact lost ground. Robert Putnam notes that membership or participation is down significantly in Lions Clubs, Shriners, Jaycees, Elks, Masons, the League of Women Voters, the Federation of Women's Clubs, the PTA, labor unions . . . and bowling leagues. Of course, membership is down even more dramatically in the Grand Army of the Republic (GAR), easily the largest social/civic group in post–Civil War America; and in the Anti-Saloon League, an association which energized millions of Protestant Americans in towns across the country in an effort, for a time successful, to make prohibition the law of the land.

Granted, the factors that caused the demise of the GAR and the Anti-Saloon League predated by many decades the drop in Jaycees and Elks. But groups have always come and gone, for many reasons. Membership declines become worrisome only when they're widespread, or if limited, when the groups in retreat are highly important civically and aren't being satisfactorily replaced. If the PTA lost half its members and other parent-teacher associations did not fill the gap, or if the PTA's decline reflected a growing unwillingness of parents to join with others in support of school programs and improvements beyond what's good for Amy and Christopher, that would point to a troubling loss of social capital in at least one key area. But, is that the case?

We will see . . . that there has been in fact no loss of parental engagement in school affairs. And this reflects the general pattern. Important changes are occurring in group life—but not decline. Many civic groups in America are further decentralizing. "Devolution" has come to them far more forcefully than to government. In addition, lots of new groups have emerged, crowding out some of the players of earlier eras. Environmental organizations are one example of groups on the rise. Soccer leagues are another. Churches, long a primary part of the country's associational experience, continue to evolve in response to changing styles of religious expression and social needs. . . .

Of all of the assertions of a decline in civic participation made in recent years, one of the most troubling is that involving the National Congress of Parents and Teachers. Data provided by the organization's national headquarters in Chicago show that the number of parents in local chapters plunged from the early sixties through the early eighties. Membership reached a high of 12.1 million in 1962 and then began falling off, slowly at first but rapidly in the late 1960s and throughout the 1970s. It reached a modern-day low in 1981 of just 5.3 million — a drop in just twenty years of 6.8 million parents. . . . Since most of us agree with Robert Putnam that "parental involvement in the educational process represents a particularly productive form of social capital," the PTA's experience deserves examination.

A few factors immediately give pause to the idea that PTA's membership troubles reflect an erosion of social capital. For one thing, note what's happened since the early 1980s. PTA membership nationally has by no means regained anything approaching its high mark, but it has climbed by roughly 1.7 million (1982 to 1996). If the steep decline of the earlier years is a disheartening indicator of eroding social capital, then the substantial gains in recent years should be a heartening sign of recovery. More important, a number of national surveys showed parental involvement in school affairs high and, if anything, increasing over the span when PTAs were declining.

The real reason PTA membership fell off wasn't that parents stopped participating; *rather, they associated increasingly with groups other than the PTA.* That is, they substituted other groups for the same basic functions. This was a big deal for the PTA, and for those who believe that its lobbying efforts are important. But it has nothing to do with developments in civic America. Months after I began puzzling over the PTA story, I discussed it with Harry O'Neill of Roper Starch Worldwide. He noted that in the New Jersey community where he lived, the local parent-teacher groups had decided not to disband but to disaffiliate from the national PTA — largely to keep for local use the large portion of dues going to the national and state headquarters. When I related O'Neill's assessment to my wife, she reminded me that when she was an officer of our local Mansfield, Connecticut, PTA in the late sixties, the group voted to become independent — calling itself a parent-teacher organization, or PTO.

The PTA's loss in O'Neill's New Jersey hometown, and in Connecticut, certainly did not represent a lessening of parental involvement. But how typical, in fact, were parents' decisions in these two communities of what was happening across the United States? Highly so, it turns out. In the 1960s and 1970s, huge numbers of local parent-teacher groups disaffiliated from the national PTA. They then took on a great variety of different names, but a large majority became PTOs. . . .

. . . [B]y the mid-1990s, less than one-fourth of all public and private K–12 schools had PTA affiliates—ranging from lows of just 4 percent of schools in Massachusetts, 7 percent in Wyoming, 8 percent in Vermont, and 9 percent in Nebraska to highs of 48 percent in Virginia, 51 percent in Maryland, and 72 percent in Utah. On its face it was unlikely that in education-conscious Massachusetts only one school in twenty-five had a parent-teacher group. Something else had to be happening.

There's a political argument over the cause of the PTA's decline. Critics of the organization charge it with becoming a "lapdog of the teachers' unions." According to them, the National Education Association and the American Federation of Teachers have, in effect, taken over the PTA and shaped its political agenda. This has allegedly turned off large numbers of parents. It's clear that many prominent education activists are mad at the PTA for its stands on issues like vouchers and school choice— which the PTA opposes vigorously. But for many parents, "controlling things ourselves right here in town" and keeping all the dues money for local use are probably more important factors leading them to disaffiliate.

How many of the schools without PTAs in fact have no parent-teacher organization at all, or at least none in which parents are much engaged? That was a hard question to answer because no one collects data on PTOs or other unaffiliated parent-teacher groups. We had to conduct our own survey. Covering all fifty states was not possible given our resources, but doing a careful study in a couple of states was. I picked Connecticut— my home state, the country's most affluent, and one with high education levels and a highly urban population. For the other state I picked Kansas, in the agricultural Midwest, which has a demographic profile sharply different from Connecticut's in income, educational background, ethnicity, and occupation. In both these states we drew a random 10 percent sample of all state-accredited private and public schools and contacted their principals' or superintendents' offices. We then conducted telephone interviews to find out what (if any) parent-teacher organizations operated in these schools. We received outstanding cooperation from local officials and completed interviews at more than 90 percent of the schools in our original samples.

We found that virtually all the schools had parent-teacher associations that officials said were active. These officials described concretely the work being done. Their descriptions of the activities belie any claim that we have entered an era of "schooling alone." In both states the preponderance of the parent-teacher groups aren't affiliated with the PTA (or for that matter, with any other body). By far the largest share of unaffiliates call themselves PTOs, but in Connecticut, with numerous Catholic schools, "Home and School Associations" are also common. In Kansas some groups call themselves "Parents in Education" and "Parent-Teacher Groups" (Tables 1 and 2).

"PTA" is still a shorthand reference for the entire range of parent-teacher organizations. In fact, the PTA isn't the primary association of parents and teachers any longer; it's now a minority player. But because "PTA" is still the widely accepted shorthand, we have had the confusing case of surveys showing enhanced levels of "PTA involvement" in school affairs, even though formal membership in the organization was declining, or holding at levels far below 1960s highs. Surveys taken by the Gallup Organization for Phi Delta Kappa found the proportion of parents of public school children saying they had attended "a PTA meeting" over the past school year up from 36 percent in 1983 to 49 percent in 1994. . . .

It's impossible to measure precisely the extent and variety of parents' engagement in school affairs—whether working with their own children individually or coming together with others in organized activity—to examine curriculum issues, complain about educational programs, or enhance the schools' social and recreational life. Still, it's striking that not one set of systematic data shows a decline in parental involvement, while many show increases. If there's an empirical case for the argument that America's social capital is eroding, the experience of parents and schools doesn't provide it. Instead, the PTO story makes the case for the existence of expansive, energetic local engagement. . . .

The American ideology is commonly described in terms of a far-reaching individualism, and while that's valid, unless carefully qualified it's also misleading. The drift and consequences of American individualism are collectivist, though certainly not of a state-centered variety. It's a collectivism of citizenship. The value of each individual's shareholding depends upon the beliefs and behavior of millions of others. A sense of ownership encourages us to make sweeping claims of our rights, and to accept responsibility for the nation's health—and yet in both areas to feel vulnerable. We Americans have been less inclined than our counterparts in other democracies to turn to government for answers—in part because we've sensed that only the quality of our shared citizenship, expressed through a vast array of self-formed and self-managed groups, can sustain the type of societal life to which we aspire. . . .

Table 1 · But It's Not that Parent-Teacher Groups
Are in Decline: In Connecticut, Most Parents' Groups
Active in Schools Aren't PTA-Affiliated

AUTHOR'S NOTE: Staff of the Roper Center reached a random sample of 115
K–8, state-accredited schools—public and private—in Connecticut. There are in
all 1,066 such schools; we drew a random 10% sample. Principals' and superintendents' offices were then contacted for each selected school and asked what forms
of parent-teacher organizations operated in their schools. What follows are the
distributions given in these telephone interviews.

	N	%
PTA	26	23
All independent, nonaffiliated groups	87	76
PTO	54	47
Home and School Association*	13	11
PAC (Parents and Children)	2	2
Other	18	16
No formal group	1	1
Refused	1	1
Total N = 115		

*"Home and School Association" is the Catholic school equivalent of PTO. "Other"
includes 18 organizations each found in only one of 18 schools. Examples—"Parent Activity
Club," "Principal's Advisory Committee," "Parents' Association," "Parent Council," etc.

AND THESE PARENT-TEACHER GROUPS ARE ACTIVE:
WHAT THEY DO

	N	%
In-School Volunteers		
General classroom and office help	68	59
Library volunteers	36	31
Computer room volunteers	18	16
Reading/literacy volunteers	10	9
Lunch room volunteers	9	8
Fund-Raising (book fairs, magazine drives, bake sales, fairs, etc.)	46	40
Field Trips	23	20
Social/Cultural/Charity Events and Activities (plays, dances, arts programs, concerts, environmental programs)	21	18
Senior Citizen Volunteers (senior literacy volunteers, grandparents' programs, retired people as classroom volunteers)	9	8

Note: Adds to more than 100% due to multiple responses.

Table 2 · IN KANSAS, THE STORY IS MUCH THE SAME

AUTHOR'S NOTE: Staff of the Roper Center reached a random sample of 81 K–8, state-accredited schools—public and private—in Kansas. There are in all 792 such schools; we drew a random 10% sample. Principals' and superintendents' offices were then contacted for each selected school and asked what forms of parent-teacher organizations operated in their schools. What follows are the distributions given in these telephone interviews.

	N	%
PTA	21	26
All independent, nonaffiliated groups	50	62
PTO	27	33
Home and School Association*	4	5
Site Council	4	5
Booster Club	2	2
Other	13	16
No formal group	8	10
Refused	2	2
Total N = 81		

*"Home and School Association" is the Catholic school equivalent of PTO. "Other" includes 13 organizations each found in only one of 13 schools. Examples—"Parents Always Support Schools," "Parents in Education," "Parent, Student, Teacher Organization," "Parent-Teacher Group," etc.

THE GROUPS ARE ACTIVE: WHAT THEY DO

	N	%
In-School Volunteers		
General classroom and office help	75	93
Library volunteers	13	16
Computer room volunteers	8	10
Reading/literacy volunteers	17	21
Lunch room volunteers	10	12
Fund-Raising (book fairs, magazine drives, bake sales, fairs, etc.)	44	54
Field Trips	32	40
Social/Cultural/Charity Events and Activities (plays, dances, arts programs, concerts, environmental programs)	43	53
Senior Citizen Volunteers (senior literacy volunteers, grandparents' programs, retired people as classroom volunteers)	3	4

Note: Adds to more than 100% due to multiple responses.

Shortcomings in citizens' performance are a recurring lament—and sometimes, it must be said, for good reason. . . .

Present-day worries about the depletion of vital social capital are the latest expression of this persistent American anxiety: that too many citizens—on whom the quality of our individualist democracy depends— may not be up to the job. Recessions and depressions have caused social pain and prompted national doubts, but it's the sense of broad moral decline or insufficiency that has really shaken us in every era. The triggering events this time around are well known and deeply disturbing: a surge in rates of violent crime and drug abuse; of illegitimacy, divorce, and single-parent households—and implicated in all these a corruption of their childhood for all too many kids. Some related developments, such as the widespread use of abortion to end unwanted pregnancies, are intensely controversial; many others, though, are uniformly regretted. All saw sharp increases in their incidence in the latter half of the 1960s and early 1970s; and while there has been some recent improvement, none have returned to their pre-1960 levels.

A great many analysts locate the roots of these developments in the strong new currents that roiled our historic individualism in the quarter-century or so after World War II, leaving aspects of it altered. But here agreement breaks down. Some critics see contemporary individualism almost as the villain—as seriously, if not fatally, flawed. Robert Bellah and his colleagues argue, for example, that the self-imposed restraints that once tamed individualism in its biblical and republican forms have been weakened in today's "expressive" mutation, leaving a radically narrow and often destructive sense of individual autonomy. Mary Ann Glendon, writing from a public law perspective, believes that a narrow, unnecessarily exclusionist emphasis on individual rights has diminished the society's capacity to attend satisfactorily to *responsibilities*, as opposed to *entitlements*. She sees America as being "set apart from rights discourse in other liberal democracies by its starkness and simplicity, its prodigality in bestowing the rights label, its legalistic character, its exaggerated absoluteness, its hyperindividualism, its insularity, and its silence with respect to personal, civic, and collective responsibilities." . . .

Liberal individualism continues, however, to have strong defenders. Jeffrey Hayes and S. M. Lipset take issue with communitarians who argue "that norms of responsibility to the collective whole should somehow be 'emphasized' in order to 'counterbalance' the destructive tide of individualism and selfishness in modern America. But the scale is not out of whack. Social developments in America have always been wrought with complicated contradictions, successes and failures. The way to ensure that we avoid moral decay is not to alter the culture, but rather to illuminate the ways in which we can use the moral tools with which our individualistic culture provides us so that we can fix the social problems generated by the underside of individualism." I strongly agree.

If the public now showed signs of abandoning its historic inclination to join with others to meet common needs; if positive energy applied to social improvement were dissipating—leaving narrowly self-serving impulses, always present, ever more ascendant—we would in fact be facing a crisis of American citizenship. That's why it's so important for us to get the facts on social capital. The levels of engagement of individual citizens in associational activities documented here—involving millions of kids in the physical training, competition, and friendships of soccer leagues; enhancing and enjoying our natural environment; supporting school programs in almost every city and town; helping the elderly and the infirm; sustaining vigorous community religious life; etc.—clearly refute claims that individualism's "dark side" is becoming predominant.

There *is* a dark side. Tocqueville saw it more than a century and a half ago. Hayes and Lipset are right that the big contemporary challenge isn't between individualism and communitarianism, but rather between competing impulses that have always inhered in America's individualist philosophy. There isn't any viable alternative in the United States to a far-reaching individualism. The answer to its deficiencies can only be a more elevated sense of what individuals can accomplish when they accept the responsibilities of citizenship and work together more constructively.

There's no magic formula for achieving this, but surely we have lots of resources. The "nation of joiners, volunteers, and givers" idea isn't myth; the foundation built from past experience is pretty strong. What's more, present trends are encouraging. Contemporary socioeconomic developments are adding to the supply of civic resources. In today's postindustrial, knowledge-based economy, far more Americans than ever before are getting educations that help confer the skills needed for active participation. The old neighborhoods of tight physical propinquity are far less important than they used to be, but better systems of information exchange and transportation have created a great variety of new and more inclusive communities of social interaction. Greater affluence and freedom from harsh physical labor probably haven't made our lives any less stressful, but they do give more of us a chance to choose among forms of community engagement. . . .

Contemporary America hasn't dissipated the country's historic reserve of social capital. We really do have a chance to pass on to succeeding generations a richer supply than any predecessor enjoyed. And for all the hand-wringing, lots of Americans understand this. The record examined here hasn't been compiled by a public that's given up on the demands of citizenship.

6

CORNEL WEST

From *Race Matters*

The opening pages of Professor Cornel West's book tell an unforgettable story of the pervasiveness of racism in the United States. Think about it the next time you wait for a taxi. In an America that promises a chance for life, liberty, and the pursuit of happiness to all its citizens, "race matters," West contends. He challenges all Americans to change their thinking about race: the problems of African Americans are not their problems but American problems. West identifies the issues that threaten to disrupt the fabric of the nation—economic, social, political, spiritual—and he suggests a broad outline for solutions.

THIS PAST SEPTEMBER my wife, Elleni, and I made our bi-weekly trek to New York City from Princeton. I was in good spirits. My morning lecture on the first half of Plato's *Republic* in my European Cultural Studies course had gone well. And my afternoon lecture on W. E. B. Du Bois's *The Souls of Black Folk* in my Afro-American Cultural Studies course had left me exhausted yet exhilarated. Plato's powerful symbolism of Socrates' descent to the great port of Piraeus—the multicultural center of Greek trade and commerce and the stronghold of Athenian democracy—still rang in my ears. And Du Bois's prescient pronouncement—"The problem of the twentieth century is the problem of the color line"—haunted me. In a mysterious way, this classic twosome posed the most fundamental challenges to my basic aim in life: to speak the truth to power with love so that the quality of everyday life for ordinary people is enhanced and white supremacy is stripped of its authority and legitimacy. Plato's profound—yet unpersuasive—critique of Athenian democracy as inevitably corrupted by the ignorance and passions of the masses posed one challenge, and Du Bois's deep analysis of the intransigence of white supremacy in the American democratic experiment posed another.

As we approached Manhattan, my temperature rose, as it always does when I'm in a hurry near the Lincoln Tunnel. How rare it is that I miss the grinding gridlock—no matter the day or hour. But this time I drove right through and attributed my good luck to Elleni. As we entered the city, we pondered whether we would have enough time to stop at Sweetwater's (our favorite place to relax) after our appointments. I dropped my wife off for an appointment on 60th Street between Lexington and Park avenues. I left my car—a rather elegant one—in a safe parking lot and stood on the corner of 60th Street and Park Avenue to catch a taxi. I felt quite relaxed since I had an hour until my next engagement. At 5:00 P.M. I had to meet a photographer who would take the picture for the cover of this book on the roof of an apartment building in East Harlem on 115th Street and 1st Avenue. I waited and waited and waited. After the ninth taxi refused me, my blood began to boil. The tenth taxi refused me and stopped for a kind, well-dressed, smiling female fellow citizen of European descent. As she stepped in the cab, she said, "This is really ridiculous, is it not?"

Ugly racial memories of the past flashed through my mind. Years ago, while driving from New York to teach at Williams College, I was stopped on fake charges of trafficking cocaine. When I told the police officer I was a professor of religion, he replied "Yeh, and I'm the Flying Nun. Let's go, nigger!" I was stopped three times in my first ten days in Princeton for driving too slowly on a residential street with a speed limit of twenty-five miles per hour. (And my son, Clifton, already has similar memories at the tender age of fifteen.) Needless to say, these incidents are dwarfed by those like Rodney King's beating* or the abuse of black targets of the FBI's COINTELPRO† efforts in the 1960s and 1970s. Yet the memories cut like a merciless knife at my soul as I waited on that godforsaken corner. Finally I decided to take the subway. I walked three long avenues, arrived late, and had to catch my moral breath as I approached the white male photographer and white female cover designer. I chose not to dwell on this everyday experience of black New Yorkers. And we had a good time talking, posing, and taking pictures.

*In 1992, four Los Angeles policemen were charged in criminal court with using unnecessary force in the arrest of Rodney King, a black man whom they had stopped while he was driving.—EDS.

†COINTELPRO was the FBI's "counterintelligence program," conducted over decades but most active in the 1960s. FBI Director J. Edgar Hoover used COINTELPRO to investigate and harass Americans whose activities were considered by the bureau to be subversive: socialist and communist sympathizers; anti-Vietnam War protestors; and especially, black citizens active in the civil rights movement. The press was instrumental in uncovering COINTELPRO's secret machinations in the mid-1970s.—EDS.

When I picked up Elleni, I told her of my hour spent on the corner, my tardy arrival, and the expertise and enthusiasm of the photographer and designer. We talked about our fantasy of moving to Addis Ababa, Ethiopia—her home and the site of the most pleasant event of my life. I toyed with the idea of attending the last day of the revival led by the Rev. Jeremiah Wright of Chicago at Rev. Wyatt T. Walker's Canaan Baptist Church of Christ in Harlem. But we settled for Sweetwater's. And the ugly memories faded in the face of soulful music, soulful food, and soulful folk.

As we rode back to Princeton, above the soothing black music of Van Harper's Quiet Storm on WBLS, 107.5 on the radio dial, we talked about what *race* matters have meant to the American past and of how much race *matters* in the American present. And I vowed to be more vigilant and virtuous in my efforts to meet the formidable challenges posed by Plato and Du Bois. For me, it is an urgent question of power and morality; for others, it is an everyday matter of life and death. . . .

What happened in Los Angeles in April of 1992 was neither a race riot nor a class rebellion.* Rather, this monumental upheaval was a multiracial, trans-class, and largely male display of justified social rage. For all its ugly, xenophobic resentment, its air of adolescent carnival, and its downright barbaric behavior, it signified the sense of powerlessness in American society. Glib attempts to reduce its meaning to the pathologies of the black underclass, the criminal actions of hoodlums, or the political revolt of the oppressed urban masses miss the mark. Of those arrested, only 36 percent were black, more than a third had full-time jobs, and most claimed to shun political affiliation. What we witnessed in Los Angeles was the consequence of a lethal linkage of economic decline, cultural decay, and political lethargy in American life. Race was the visible catalyst, not the underlying cause.

The meaning of the earthshaking events in Los Angeles is difficult to grasp because most of us remain trapped in the narrow framework of the dominant liberal and conservative views of race in America, which with its worn-out vocabulary leaves us intellectually debilitated, morally disempowered, and personally depressed. The astonishing disappearance of the event from public dialogue is testimony to just how painful and distressing a serious engagement with race is. Our truncated public discussions of race suppress the best of who and what we are as a people because they

---

*Rioting occurred in Los Angeles after a jury, made up of white citizens, acquitted the policemen who had been accused in the beating of Rodney King.—EDS.

fail to confront the complexity of the issue in a candid and critical manner. The predictable pitting of liberals against conservatives, Great Society Democrats against self-help Republicans, reinforces intellectual parochialism and political paralysis.

The liberal notion that more government programs can solve racial problems is simplistic—precisely because it focuses *solely* on the economic dimension. And the conservative idea that what is needed is a change in the moral behavior of poor black urban dwellers (especially poor black men, who, they say, should stay married, support their children, and stop committing so much crime) highlights immoral actions while ignoring public responsibility for the immoral circumstances that haunt our fellow citizens.

The common denominator of these views of race is that each still sees black people as a "problem people," in the words of Dorothy I. Height, president of the National Council of Negro Women, rather than as fellow American citizens with problems. Her words echo the poignant "unasked question" of W. E. B. Du Bois, who, in *The Souls of Black Folk* (1903), wrote:

They approach me in a half-hesitant sort of way, eye me curiously or compassionately, and then instead of saying directly, How does it feel to be a problem? they say, I know an excellent colored man in my town. . . . Do not these Southern outrages make your blood boil? At these I smile, or am interested, or reduce the boiling to a simmer, as the occasion may require. To the real question, How does it feel to be a problem? I answer seldom a word.

Nearly a century later, we confine discussions about race in America to the "problems" black people pose for whites rather than consider what this way of viewing black people reveals about us as a nation.

This paralyzing framework encourages liberals to relieve their guilty consciences by supporting public funds directed at "the problems"; but at the same time, reluctant to exercise principled criticism of black people, liberals deny them the freedom to err. Similarly, conservatives blame the "problems" on black people themselves—and thereby render black social misery invisible or unworthy of public attention.

Hence, for liberals, black people are to be "included" and "integrated" into "our" society and culture, while for conservatives they are to be "well behaved" and "worthy of acceptance" by "our" way of life. Both fail to see that the presence and predicaments of black people are neither additions to nor defections from American life, but rather *constitutive elements of that life.*

To engage in a serious discussion of race in America, we must begin not with the problems of black people but with the flaws of American society—flaws rooted in historic inequalities and longstanding cultural stereotypes. How we set up the terms for discussing racial issues shapes our perception and response to these issues. As long as black people are viewed as a "them," the burden falls on blacks to do all the "cultural" and "moral" work necessary for healthy race relations. The implication is that only certain Americans can define what it means to be American—and the rest must simply "fit in."

The emergence of strong black-nationalist sentiments among blacks, especially among young people, is a revolt against this sense of having to "fit in." The variety of black-nationalist ideologies, from the moderate views of Supreme Court Justice Clarence Thomas in his youth to those of Louis Farrakhan today, rest upon a fundamental truth: white America has been historically weak-willed in ensuring racial justice and has continued to resist fully accepting the humanity of blacks. As long as double standards and differential treatment abound—as long as the rap performer Ice-T is harshly condemned while former Los Angeles Police Chief Daryl F. Gates's antiblack comments are received in polite silence, as long as Dr. Leonard Jeffries's anti-Semitic statements are met with vitriolic outrage while presidential candidate Patrick J. Buchanan's anti-Semitism receives a genteel response—black nationalisms will thrive.

Afrocentrism, a contemporary species of black nationalism, is a gallant yet misguided attempt to define an African identity in a white society perceived to be hostile. It is gallant because it puts black doings and sufferings, not white anxieties and fears, at the center of discussion. It is misguided because—out of fear of cultural hybridization and through silence on the issue of class, retrograde views on black women, gay men, and lesbians, and a reluctance to link race to the common good—it reinforces the narrow discussions about race.

To establish a new framework, we need to begin with a frank acknowledgment of the basic humanness and Americanness of each of us. And we must acknowledge that as a people—*E Pluribus Unum*—we are on a slippery slope toward economic strife, social turmoil, and cultural chaos. If we go down, we go down together. The Los Angeles upheaval forced us to see not only that we are not connected in ways we would like to be but also, in a more profound sense, that this failure to connect binds us even more tightly together. The paradox of race in America is that our common destiny is more pronounced and imperiled precisely when our divisions are deeper. The Civil War and its legacy speak loudly here.

And our divisions are growing deeper. Today, eighty-six percent of white suburban Americans live in neighborhoods that are less than 1 percent black, meaning that the prospects for the country depend largely on how its cities fare in the hands of a suburban electorate. There is no escape from our interracial interdependence, yet enforced racial hierarchy dooms us as a nation to collective paranoia and hysteria—the unmaking of any democratic order.

The verdict in the Rodney King case which sparked the incidents in Los Angeles was perceived to be wrong by the vast majority of Americans. But whites have often failed to acknowledge the widespread mistreatment of black people, especially black men, by law enforcement agencies, which helped ignite the spark. The verdict was merely the occasion for deep-seated rage to come to the surface. This rage is fed by the "silent" depression ravaging the country—in which real weekly wages of all American workers since 1973 have declined nearly 20 percent, while at the same time wealth has been upwardly distributed.

The exodus of stable industrial jobs from urban centers to cheaper labor markets here and abroad, housing policies that have created "chocolate cities and vanilla suburbs" (to use the popular musical artist George Clinton's memorable phrase), white fear of black crime, and the urban influx of poor Spanish-speaking and Asian immigrants—all have helped erode the tax base of American cities just as the federal government has cut its supports and programs. The result is unemployment, hunger, homelessness, and sickness for millions.

And a pervasive spiritual impoverishment grows. The collapse of meaning in life—the eclipse of hope and absence of love of self and others, the breakdown of family and neighborhood bonds—leads to the social deracination and cultural denudement of urban dwellers, especially children. We have created rootless, dangling people with little link to the supportive networks—family, friends, school—that sustain some sense of purpose in life. We have witnessed the collapse of the spiritual communities that in the past helped Americans face despair, disease, and death and that transmit through the generations dignity and decency, excellence and elegance.

The result is lives of what we might call "random nows," of fortuitous and feeling moments preoccupied with "getting over"—with acquiring pleasure, property, and power by any means necessary. (This is not what Malcolm X meant by this famous phrase.) Post-modern culture is more and more a market culture dominated by gangster mentalities and self-destructive wantonness. This culture engulfs all of us—yet its impact on the disadvantaged is devastating, resulting in extreme violence in everyday life. Sexual violence against women and homicidal assaults by young black men on one another are only the most obvious signs of this empty quest for pleasure, property, and power.

Last, this rage is fueled by a political atmosphere in which images, not ideas, dominate, where politicians spend more time raising money than debating issues. The functions of parties have been displaced by public polls, and politicians behave less as thermostats that determine the climate of opinion than as thermometers registering the public mood. American politics has been rocked by an unleashing of greed among opportunistic public officials—who have followed the lead of their counterparts in the private sphere, where, as of 1989, 1 percent of the population owned 37 percent of the wealth and 10 percent of the population owned 86 percent of the wealth—leading to a profound cynicism and pessimism among the citizenry.

And given the way in which the Republican Party since 1968 has appealed to popular xenophobic images—playing the black, female, and homophobic cards to realign the electorate along race, sex, and sexual-orientation lines—it is no surprise that the notion that we are all part of one garment of destiny is discredited. Appeals to special interests rather than to public interests reinforce this polarization. The Los Angeles upheaval was an expression of utter fragmentation by a powerless citizenry that includes not just the poor but all of us.

What is to be done? How do we capture a new spirit and vision to meet the challenges of the post-industrial city, post-modern culture, and post-party politics?

First, we must admit that the most valuable sources for help, hope, and power consist of ourselves and our common history. As in the ages of Lincoln, Roosevelt, and King, we must look to new frameworks and languages to understand our multilayered crisis and overcome our deep malaise.

Second, we must focus our attention on the public square—the common good that undergirds our national and global destinies. The vitality of any public square ultimately depends on how much we *care* about the quality of our lives together. The neglect of our public infrastructure, for example—our water and sewage systems, bridges, tunnels, highways, subways, and streets—reflects not only our myopic economic policies, which impede productivity, but also the low priority we place on our common life.

The tragic plight of our children clearly reveals our deep disregard for public well-being. About one out of every five children in this country lives in poverty, including one out of every two black children and two out of every five Hispanic children. Most of our children—neglected by overburdened parents and bombarded by the market values of profit-hungry corporations—are ill-equipped to live lives of spiritual and cultural quality. Faced with these facts, how do we expect ever to constitute a vibrant society?

One essential step is some form of large-scale public intervention to ensure access to basic social goods—housing, food, health care, education, child care, and jobs. We must invigorate the common good with a mixture of government, business, and labor that does not follow any existing blueprint. After a period in which the private sphere has been sacralized and the public square gutted, the temptation is to make a fetish of the public square. We need to resist such dogmatic swings.

Last, the major challenge is to meet the need to generate new leader-ship. The paucity of courageous leaders—so apparent in the response to the events in Los Angeles—requires that we look beyond the same elites and voices that recycle the older frameworks. We need leaders—neither saints nor sparkling television personalities—who can situate themselves within a larger historical narrative of this country and our world, who can grasp the complex dynamics of our peoplehood and imagine a future grounded in the best of our past, yet who are attuned to the frightening obstacles that now perplex us. Our ideals of freedom, democracy, and equality must be invoked to invigorate all of us, especially the landless, propertyless, and luckless. Only a visionary leadership that can motivate "the better angels of our nature," as Lincoln said, and activate possibilities for a freer, more efficient, and stable America—only that leadership de-serves cultivation and support.

This new leadership must be grounded in grass-roots organizing that highlights democratic accountability. Whoever *our* leaders will be as we approach the twenty-first century, their challenge will be to help Americans determine whether a genuine multiracial democracy can be created and sustained in an era of global economy and a moment of xenophobic frenzy.

Let us hope and pray that the vast intelligence, imagination, humor, and courage of Americans will not fail us. Either we learn a new language of empathy and compassion, or the fire this time will consume us all.*

---

*In *The Fire Next Time* (1963), African–American writer James Baldwin quotes a black slave's prophecy, found in a song recreated from the Bible, "God gave Noah the rainbow sign, no more water, the fire next time!"—EDS.

7

MICHAEL KAMMEN

From *People of Paradox*

Thinking about the United States, its history, culture, and politics, as a paradox is one of the most useful ways to tie together all the themes and facts in American government. Historian Michael Kammen offers a sometimes-fanciful, sometimes-profound analysis of the many paradoxes that riddle American life. Citizens expect their leaders to be "Everyman and Superman," he perceptively observes. Kammen takes on the difficult issue of the American melting pot; he substitutes the metaphor of a "super-highway" to explain nicely the country and its people. He points out paradoxes in all aspects of American life, ending with a poetic vision of the super-highway, along the side of the road, at Thanksgiving. Many scholars and thinkers are quoted in Kammen's piece, but his top source opens the selection: "We have met the enemy and he is us," cartoon character Pogo recognizes.

———

> We have met the enemy and he is us.
>
> POGO

. . . OUR INHERITANCE has indeed been bitter-sweet, and our difficulty in assessing it just now arises from the fact that American institutions have had too many uncritical lovers and too many unloving critics. We have managed to graft pride onto guilt—guilt over social injustice and abuses of power—and find that pride and guilt do not neutralize each other, but make many decisions seem questionable, motives suspect, and consciences troubled.

Perhaps so many American shibboleths seem to generate their very opposites because they are often half-truths rather than the wholesome verities we believe them to be. Perhaps we ought to recall Alice in Wonderland playing croquet against herself, "for this curious child was very fond of pretending to be two people. 'But it's no use now,' thought poor Alice, 'to pretend to be two people! Why, there's hardly enough of me left to make one respectable person!'" . . .

This dualistic state of mind may be found also in the domestic political values subscribed to by most Americans. We are comfortable believing in both majority rule and minority rights, in both consensus and freedom, federalism and centralization. It may be perfectly reasonable to support majority rule with reservations, or minority rights with certain other reservations. But this has not been our method. Rather, we have tended to hold contradictory ideas in suspension and ignore the intellectual and behavioral consequences of such "doublethink." . . .

Americans have managed to be both puritanical and hedonistic, idealistic and materialistic, peace-loving and war-mongering, isolationist and interventionist, conformist and individualist, consensus-minded and conflict-prone. "We recognize the American," wrote Gunnar Myrdal in 1944, "wherever we meet him, as a practical idealist." . . .

Americans expect their heroes to be Everyman and Superman simultaneously. I once overheard on an airplane the following fragment of conversation: "He has none of the virtues I respect, and none of the vices I admire." We cherish the humanity of our past leaders: George Washington's false teeth and whimsical orthography, Benjamin Franklin's lechery and cunning. The quintessential American hero wears both a halo *and* horns.

Because our society is so pluralistic, the American politician must be all things to all people. Dwight Eisenhower represented the most advanced industrial nation, but his chief appeal rested in a naive simplicity which recalled our pre-industrial past. Robert Frost once advised President Kennedy to be as much an Irishman as a Harvard man: "You have to have both the pragmatism and the idealism." The ambivalent American is ambitious and ambidextrous; but the appearance of ambidexterity—to some, at least—suggests the danger of double-dealing and deceit. The story is told of a U.S. senator meeting the press one Sunday afternoon. "How do you stand on conservation, Senator?" asked one panelist. The senator squirmed. "Well, I'll tell you," he said. "Some of my constituents are for conservation, and some of my constituents are against conservation, and I stand foresquare behind my constituents." . . .

Raymond Aron, the French sociologist, has remarked that a "dialectic of plurality and conformism lies at the core of American life, making for the originality of the social structure, and raising the most contradictory evaluations." Americans have repeatedly reaffirmed the social philosophy of individualism, even making it the basis of their political thought. Yet they have been a nation of joiners and have developed the largest associations and corporations the world has ever known. Nor has American respect for the abstract "individual" always guaranteed respect for particular persons.

There is a persistent tension between authoritarianism and individualism in American history. The genius of American institutions at their best has been to find a place and a use for both innovators and consolidators, rebellious dreamers and realistic adjudicators. "America has been built on a mixture of discipline and rebellion," writes Christopher Jencks, "but the balance between them has constantly shifted over the years." Our individualism, therefore, has been of a particular sort, a collective individualism. Individuality is not synonymous in the United States with singularity. When Americans develop an oddity they make a fad of it so that they may be comfortable among familiar oddities. Their unity, as Emerson wrote in his essay on the New England Reformers, "is only perfect when all the uniters are isolated."

How then can we adequately summarize the buried historical roots of our paradoxes, tensions, and biformities? The incongruities in American life are not merely fortuitous, and their stimuli appear from the very beginning. "America was always promises," as Archibald MacLeish has put it. "From the first voyage and the first ship there were promises." Many of these have gone unfulfilled—an endless source of ambiguity and equivocation. . . .

Above all other factors, however, the greatest source of dualisms in American life has been unstable pluralism in all its manifold forms: cultural, social, sequential, and political. *E pluribus unum* is a misbegotten motto because we have *not* become one out of many. The myth of the melting pot is precisely that: a myth. Moreover, our constitutional system seems to foster fragmentation of power while our economic-technological system seems to encourage consolidation of power. Thus the imperatives of pluralism under conditions of large-scale technology commonly conflict with principles and practices of constitutional democracy. . . .

It has been the impulse of our egalitarianism to make all men American and alike, but the thrust of our social order and intolerance to accentuate differences among groups. We have achieved expertise at both xenophobia and self-hate! At several stages of our history, population growth has outstripped institutional change. The result in many cases has been violence, vigilante movements, or economic unrest, all with the special coloration of unstable pluralism. Because there are significant variations in state laws regulating economic enterprise, taxation, and welfare payments, people and corporations move to tax-sheltered states and to those with the most generous welfare provisions. In this way mobility becomes a function of pluralism.

I do not argue that pluralism is a peculiarly American phenomenon. But I do believe that unstable pluralism on a scale of unprecedented proportion is especially American. . . .

There is a sense in which the super-highway is the most appropriate American metaphor. We have vast and anonymous numbers of people rushing individually (but simultaneously) in opposite directions. In between lies a no-man's-land, usually landscaped with a barrier of shrubs and trees, so that we cannot see the road to Elsewhere, but cannot easily turn back either. Indeed, the American experience in some spheres has moved from unity to diversity (e.g., denominationalism), while in other areas it has flowed in the opposite direction, from diversity to unity (e.g., political institutions). Along both roads we have paused from time to time in order to pay substantially for the privilege of traveling these thoroughfares.

There have always been Americans aware of unresolved contradictions between creed and reality, disturbed by the performance of their system and culture. Told how much liberty they enjoy, they feel less free; told how much equality they enjoy, they feel less equal; told how much progress they enjoy, their environment seems even more out of control. Most of all, told that they should be happy, they sense a steady growth in American unhappiness. Conflicts *between* Americans have been visible for a very long time, but most of us are just beginning to perceive the conflicts *within* us individually.

It is a consequence of some concern that our ambiguities often appear to the wider world as malicious hypocrisies. As when we vacillate, for example, between our missionary impulse and our isolationist instinct. From time to time we recognize that the needs of national security and the furtherance of national ideals may both be served by our vigorous but restrained participation in world affairs. At other times these two desiderata tug in opposite directions. However much we desperately want to be understood, we are too often misunderstood. . . .

Because of our ambivalent ambiance, we are frequently indecisive. "I cannot be a crusader," remarked Ralph McGill, "because I have been cursed all my life with the ability to see both sides." Our experience with polarities provides us with the potential for flexibility and diversity; yet too often it chills us into sheer inaction, or into contradictory appraisals of our own designs and historical development. Often we are willing to split the difference and seek consensus. "It is this intolerable paradox," James Reston writes, "of being caught between the unimaginable achievements of men when they cooperate for common goals, and their spectacular failures when they divide on how to achieve the simple decencies of life, that creates the present atmosphere of division and confusion." . . .

We have reached a moment in time when the national condition seems neither lifeless nor deathless. It's like the barren but sensuous serenity of the natural world in late autumn, before Thanksgiving, containing the promise of rebirth and the potential for resurrection. On bare branches whose leaves have fallen, buds bulge visibly in preparation for spring. Along the roadside, goldenrod stands sere and grizzled, and the leafless milkweed with its goosehead pods strews fluff and floss to every breeze, thereby seeding the countryside with frail fertility. The litter of autumn becomes the mulch, and then the humus, for roots and tender seeds. So it was, so it has been, and so it will be with the growth of American Civilization.

8

ROBERT BELLAH AND OTHERS

From *Habits of the Heart*

American ideology touches more than just government and politics. It also guides the nation's social, economic, religious, and cultural life. It is fitting, therefore, that an important comment on American ideology comes from the discipline of sociology. Robert Bellah and his colleagues borrow Alexis de Tocqueville's phrase "habits of the heart" to explore the place of individualism in American life. The authors concede that individualism is the single most important ingredient in the nation's values, illustrating it with the symbol of cowboy-heroes Shane and the Lone Ranger. But, they contend, individualism cannot exist without being balanced by a sense of community.

INDIVIDUALISM lies at the very core of American culture. Every one of the four traditions we have singled out is in a profound sense individualistic. There is a biblical individualism and a civic individualism as well as a utilitarian and an expressive individualism. Whatever the differences among the traditions and the consequent differences in their understandings of individualism, there are some things they all share, things that are basic to American identity. We believe in the dignity, indeed the sacredness, of the individual. Anything that would violate our right to think for ourselves, judge for ourselves, make our own decisions, live our lives as we see fit, is not only morally wrong, it is sacrilegious. Our highest and noblest aspirations, not only for ourselves, but for those we care about, for our society and for the world, are closely linked to our individualism. Yet, as we have been suggesting repeatedly in this book, some of our deepest problems both as individuals and as a society are also closely linked to our individualism. We do not argue that Americans should abandon individualism—that would mean for us to abandon our deepest identity. But individualism has come to mean so many things and to contain such contradictions and paradoxes that even to defend it requires that we analyze it critically, that we consider especially those tendencies that would destroy it from within. . . .

The question is whether an individualism in which the self has become the main form of reality can really be sustained. What is at issue is not simply whether self-contained individuals might withdraw from the public sphere to pursue purely private ends, but whether such individuals are capable of sustaining either a public *or* a private life. If this is the danger, perhaps only the civic and biblical forms of individualism—forms that see the individual in relation to a larger whole, a community and a tradition—are capable of sustaining genuine individuality and nurturing both public and private life. . . .

America is also the inventor of that most mythic individual hero, the cowboy, who again and again saves a society he can never completely fit into. The cowboy has a special talent—he can shoot straighter and faster than other men—and a special sense of justice. But these characteristics make him so unique that he can never fully belong to society. His destiny is to defend society without ever really joining it. He rides off alone into the sunset like Shane,* or like the Lone Ranger moves on accompanied only by his Indian companion. But the cowboy's importance is not that he is isolated or antisocial. Rather, his significance lies in his unique, individual virtue and special skill and it is because of those qualities that society needs and welcomes him. Shane, after all, starts as a real outsider, but ends up with the gratitude of the community and the love of a woman and a boy. And while the Lone Ranger never settles down and marries the local schoolteacher, he always leaves with the affection and gratitude of the people he has helped. It is as if the myth says you can be a truly good person, worthy of admiration and love, only if you resist fully joining the group. But sometimes the tension leads to an irreparable break. Will Kane, the hero of *High Noon*, abandoned by the cowardly townspeople, saves them from an unrestrained killer, but then throws his sheriff's badge in the dust and goes off into the desert with his bride. One is left wondering where they will go, for there is no longer any link with any town. . . .

[T]he cowboy . . . tell[s] us something important about American individualism. The cowboy . . . can be valuable to society only because he is a completely autonomous individual who stands outside it. To serve society, one must be able to stand alone, not needing others, not depending

*Shane is the gunfighter-hero of the 1953 western film *Shane*.—EDS.

on their judgment, and not submitting to their wishes. Yet this individualism is not selfishness. Indeed, it is a kind of heroic selflessness. One accepts the necessity of remaining alone in order to serve the values of the group. And this obligation to aloneness is an important key to the American moral imagination. Yet it is part of the profound ambiguity of the mythology of American individualism that its moral heroism is always just a step away from despair. . . .

. . . The inner tensions of American individualism add up to a classic case of ambivalence. We strongly assert the value of our self-reliance and autonomy. We deeply feel the emptiness of a life without sustaining social commitments. Yet we are hesitant to articulate our sense that we need one another as much as we need to stand alone, for fear that if we did we would lose our independence altogether. The tensions of our lives would be even greater if we did not, in fact, engage in practices that constantly limit the effects of an isolating individualism, even though we cannot articulate those practices nearly as well as we can the quest for autonomy. . . .

. . . It is now time to consider what a self that is not empty would be like—one that is constituted rather than unencumbered, one that has, let us admit it, encumbrances, but whose encumbrances make connection to others easier and more natural. Just as the empty self makes sense in a particular institutional context—that of the upward mobility of the middle-class individual who must leave home and church in order to succeed in an impersonal world of rationality and competition—so a constituted self makes sense in terms of another institutional context, what we would call, in the full sense of the world, community.

Communities, in the sense in which we are using the term, have a history—in an important sense they are constituted by their past—and for this reason we can speak of a real community as a "community of memory," one that does not forget its past. In order not to forget that past, a community is involved in retelling its story, its constitutive narrative, and in so doing, it offers examples of the men and women who have embodied and exemplified the meaning of the community. These stories of collective history and exemplary individuals are an important part of the tradition that is so central to a community of memory. . . .

Examples of such genuine communities are not hard to find in the United States. There are ethnic and racial communities, each with its own story and its own heroes and heroines. There are religious communities that recall and reenact their stories in the weekly and annual cycles of their ritual year, remembering the scriptural stories that tell them who they are and the saints and martyrs who define their identity. There is the national community, defined by its history and by the character of its representative leaders from [early colonist] John Winthrop to [civil rights leader] Martin Luther King, Jr. Americans identify with their national community partly because there is little else that we all share in common but also partly because America's history exemplifies aspirations widely shared throughout the world: the ideal of a free society, respecting all its citizens, however diverse, and allowing them all to fulfill themselves. Yet some Americans also remember the history of suffering inflicted and the gap between promise and realization, which has always been very great. At some times, neighborhoods, localities, and regions have been communities in America, but that has been hard to sustain in our restless and mobile society. Families can be communities, remembering their past, telling the children the stories of parents' and grandparents' lives, and sustaining hope for the future—though without the context of a larger community that sense of family is hard to maintain. Where history and hope are forgotten and community means only the gathering of the similar, community degenerates into lifestyle enclave. The temptation toward that transformation is endemic in America, though the transition is seldom complete.

People growing up in communities of memory not only hear the stories that tell how the community came to be, what its hopes and fears are, and how its ideals are exemplified in outstanding men and women; they also participate in the practices—ritual, aesthetic, ethical—that define the community as a way of life. We call these "practices of commitment" for they define the patterns of loyalty and obligation that keep the community alive. And if the language of the self-reliant individual is the first language of American moral life, the languages of tradition and commitment in communities of memory are "second languages" that most Americans know as well, and which they use when the language of the radically separate self does not seem adequate. . . . Sometimes Americans make a rather sharp dichotomy between private and public life. Viewing one's primary task as "finding oneself" in autonomous self-reliance, separating oneself not only from one's parents but also from those larger communities and traditions that constitute one's past, leads to the notion that it is in oneself, perhaps in relation to a few intimate others, that fulfillment is to be found. Individualism of this sort often implies a negative view of public life. The impersonal forces of the economic and political worlds are what the individual needs protection against. In this perspective, even occupation, which has been so central to the identity of Americans in the past, becomes instrumental—not a good in itself, but only a means to the attainment of a rich and satisfying private life. But on the basis of what we have seen in our observation of middle-class American life, it would seem that this quest for purely private fulfillment is illusory: it often ends in emptiness instead. On the other hand, we found many people . . . for whom private fulfillment and public involvement are not antithetical. These people evince an individualism that is not empty but is full of content drawn from an active identification with communities and traditions. Perhaps the notion that private life and public life are at odds is incorrect. Perhaps they are so deeply involved with each other that the impoverishment of one entails the impoverishment of the other. Parker Palmer is probably right when he says that "in a healthy society the private and the public are not mutually exclusive, not in competition with each other. They are, instead, two halves of a whole, two poles of a paradox. They work together dialectically, helping to create and nurture one another."

Certainly this dialectical relationship is clear where public life degenerates into violence and fear. One cannot live a rich private life in a state of siege, mistrusting all strangers and turning one's home into an armed camp. A minimum of public decency and civility is a precondition for a fulfilling private life. On the other hand, public involvement is often difficult and demanding. To engage successfully in the public world, one needs personal strength and the support of family and friends. A rewarding private life is one of the preconditions for a healthy public life.

For all their doubts about the public sphere, Americans are more engaged in voluntary associations and civic organizations than the citizens of most other industrial nations. In spite of all the difficulties, many Americans feel they must "get involved." In public life as in private, we can discern the habits of the heart that sustain individualism and commitment, as well as what makes them problematic. . . .

The communities of memory of which we have spoken are concerned in a variety of ways to give a qualitative meaning to the living of life, to time and space, to persons and groups. Religious communities, for example, do not experience time in the way the mass media present it—as a continuous flow of qualitatively meaningless sensations. The day, the week, the season, the year are punctuated by an alternation of the sacred and the profane. Prayer breaks into our daily life at the beginning of a meal, at the end of the day, at common worship, reminding us that our utilitarian pursuits are not the whole of life, that a fulfilled life is one in which God and neighbor are remembered first. Many of our religious traditions recognize the significance of silence as a way of breaking the incessant flow of sensations and opening our hearts to the wholeness of being. And our republican tradition, too, has ways of giving form to time, reminding us on particular dates of the great events of our past or of the heroes who helped to teach us what we are as a free people. Even our private family life takes on a shared rhythm with a Thanksgiving dinner or a Fourth of July picnic.

In short, we have never been, and still are not, a collection of private individuals who, except for a conscious contract to create a minimal government, have nothing in common. Our lives make sense in a thousand ways, most of which we are unaware of, because of traditions that are centuries, if not millennia, old. It is these traditions that help us to know that it does make a difference who we are and how we treat one another.

PART TWO

The Constitution and American Democracy

9

RICHARD HOFSTADTER

From *The American Political Tradition*

Richard Hofstadter, one of the nation's leading historians, explores the real thoughts and motivations behind the men whom all schoolchildren have been taught to revere as Founding Fathers. Hofstadter's classic work points out the ambivalence of those who wrote the Constitution: they viewed human beings as selfish and untrustworthy, yet they strongly believed in the importance of self-government. The founders' ambivalence toward democracy led them to design the political system the United States still lives with today, one in which each interest (or branch or layer of government or economic class or region . . .) would be checked and balanced by competing interests. Hofstadter goes on to interpret what the near-sacred idea of liberty meant to the founders. Liberty was not really related to democracy, he contends, but rather ensured the freedom to attain and enjoy private property. To make this idea clearer, test the author's thesis against the current political debate over health care or social security reform.

. . . THE MEN who drew up the Constitution in Philadelphia during the summer of 1787 had a vivid Calvinistic sense of human evil and damnation and believed with Hobbes that men are selfish and contentious. They were men of affairs, merchants, lawyers, planter-businessmen, speculators, investors. Having seen human nature on display in the marketplace, the courtroom, the legislative chamber, and in every secret path and alleyway where wealth and power are courted, they felt they knew it in all its frailty. To them a human being was an atom of self-interest. They did not believe in man, but they did believe in the power of a good political constitution to control him.

This may be an abstract notion to ascribe to practical men, but it follows the language that the Fathers themselves used. General Knox, for example, wrote in disgust to Washington after the Shays Rebellion that Americans were, after all, "men—actual men possessing all the turbulent passions belonging to that animal." Throughout the secret discussions at the Constitutional Convention it was clear that this distrust of man was first and foremost a distrust of the common man and democratic rule. . . .

And yet there was another side to the picture. The Fathers were intellectual heirs of seventeenth-century English republicanism with its opposition to arbitrary rule and faith in popular sovereignty. If they feared the advance of democracy, they also had misgivings about turning to the extreme right. Having recently experienced a bitter revolutionary struggle with an external power beyond their control, they were in no mood to follow Hobbes to his conclusion that any kind of government must be accepted in order to avert the anarchy and terror of a state of nature. . . .

Unwilling to turn their backs on republicanism, the Fathers also wished to avoid violating the prejudices of the people. "Notwithstanding the oppression and injustice experienced among us from democracy," said George Mason, "the genius of the people is in favor of it, and the genius of the people must be consulted." Mason admitted "that we had been too democratic," but feared that "we should incautiously run into the opposite extreme." James Madison, who has quite rightfully been called the philosopher of the Constitution, told the delegates: "It seems indispensable that the mass of citizens should not be without a voice in making the laws which they are to obey, and in choosing the magistrates who are to administer them." James Wilson, the outstanding jurist of the age, later appointed to the Supreme Court by Washington, said again and again that the ultimate power of government must of necessity reside in the people. This the Fathers commonly accepted, for if government did not proceed from the people, from what other source could it legitimately come? To adopt any other premise not only would be inconsistent with everything they had said against British rule in the past but would open the gates to an extreme concentration of power in the future. . . .

If the masses were turbulent and unregenerate, and yet if government must be founded upon their suffrage and consent, what could a Constitution-maker do? One thing that the Fathers did not propose to do, because they thought it impossible, was to change the nature of man to conform with a more ideal system. They were inordinately confident that they knew what man always had been and what he always would be. The eighteenth-century mind had great faith in universals. . . .

. . . It was too much to expect that vice could be checked by virtue; the Fathers relied instead upon checking vice with vice. Madison once objected during the Convention that Gouverneur Morris was "forever inculcating the utter political depravity of men and the necessity of opposing one vice and interest to another vice and interest." And yet Madison himself in the *Federalist* number 51 later set forth an excellent statement of the same thesis:

Ambition must be made to counteract ambition. . . . It may be a reflection on human nature that such devices should be necessary to control the abuses of government. But what is government itself, but the greatest of all reflections on human nature? If men were angels, no government would be necessary. . . . In framing a government which is to be administered by men over men, the great difficulty lies in this: you must first enable the government to control the governed; and in the next place oblige it to control itself.

. . . If, in a state that lacked constitutional balance, one class or one interest gained control, they believed, it would surely plunder all other interests. The Fathers, of course, were especially fearful that the poor would plunder the rich, but most of them would probably have admitted that the rich, unrestrained, would also plunder the poor. . . .

In practical form, therefore, the quest of the Fathers reduced primarily to a search for constitutional devices that would force various interests to check and control one another. Among those who favored the federal Constitution three such devices were distinguished.

The first of these was the advantage of a federated government in maintaining order against popular uprisings or majority rule. In a single state a faction might arise and take complete control by force; but if the states were bound in a federation, the central government could step in and prevent it. . . .

The second advantage of good constitutional government resided in the mechanism of representation itself. In a small direct democracy the unstable passions of the people would dominate lawmaking; but a representative government, as Madison said, would "refine and enlarge the public views by passing them through the medium of a chosen body of citizens." . . .

The third advantage of the government . . . [was that] each element should be given its own house of the legislature, and over both houses there should be set a capable, strong, and impartial executive armed with the veto power. This split assembly would contain within itself an organic check and would be capable of self-control under the governance of the executive. The whole system was to be capped by an independent judiciary. The inevitable tendency of the rich and the poor to plunder each other would be kept in hand. . . .

It is ironical that the Constitution, which Americans venerate so deeply, is based upon a political theory that at one crucial point stands in direct antithesis to the mainstream of American democratic faith. Modern American folklore assumes that democracy and liberty are all but identical, and when democratic writers take the trouble to make the distinction, they usually assume that democracy is necessary to liberty. But the Founding Fathers thought that the liberty with which they were most concerned was menaced by democracy. In their minds liberty was linked not to democracy but to property.

What did the Fathers mean by liberty? What did Jay mean when he spoke of "the charms of liberty"? Or Madison when he declared that to destroy liberty in order to destroy factions would be a remedy worse than the disease? Certainly the men who met at Philadelphia were not interested in extending liberty to those classes in America, the Negro slaves and the indentured servants, who were most in need of it, for slavery was recognized in the organic structure of the Constitution and indentured servitude was no concern of the Convention. Nor was the regard of the delegates for civil liberties any too tender. It was the opponents of the Constitution who were most active in demanding such vital liberties as freedom of religion, freedom of speech and press, jury trial, due process, and protection from "unreasonable searches and seizures." These guarantees had to be incorporated in the first ten amendments because the Convention neglected to put them in the original document. Turning to economic issues, it was not freedom of trade in the modern sense that the Fathers were striving for. Although they did not believe in impeding trade unnecessarily, they felt that failure to regulate it was one of the central weaknesses of the Articles of Confederation, and they stood closer to the mercantilists than to Adam Smith. Again, liberty to them did not mean free access to the nation's unappropriated wealth. At least fourteen of them were land speculators. They did not believe in the right of the squatter to occupy unused land, but rather in the right of the absentee owner or speculator to preempt it.

The liberties that the constitutionalists hoped to gain were chiefly negative. They wanted freedom from fiscal uncertainty and irregularities in the currency, from trade wars among the states, from economic discrimination by more powerful foreign governments, from attacks on the creditor class or on property, from popular insurrection. They aimed to create a government that would act as an honest broker among a variety of propertied interests, giving them all protection from their common enemies and preventing any one of them from becoming too powerful. The Convention was a fraternity of types of absentee ownership. All property should be permitted to have its proportionate voice in government. Individual property interests might have to be sacrificed at times, but only for the community of propertied interests. Freedom for property would result in liberty for men—perhaps not for all men, but at least for all worthy men. Because men have different faculties and abilities, the Fathers believed, they acquire different amounts of property. To protect property is only to protect men in the exercise of their natural faculties. Among the many liberties, therefore, freedom to hold and dispose [of] property is paramount. Democracy, unchecked rule by the masses, is sure to bring arbitrary redistribution of property, destroying the very essence of liberty. . . .

A cardinal tenet in the faith of the men who made the Constitution was the belief that democracy can never be more than a transitional stage in government, that it always evolves into either a tyranny (the rule of the rich demagogue who has patronized the mob) or an aristocracy (the original leaders of the democratic elements). . . .

What encouraged the Fathers about their own era, however, was the broad dispersion of landed property. The small land-owning farmers had been troublesome in recent years, but there was a general conviction that under a properly made Constitution a *modus vivendi* could be worked out with them. The possession of moderate plots of property presumably gave them a sufficient stake in society to be safe and responsible citizens under the restraints of balanced government. Influence in government would be proportionate to property: merchants and great landholders would be dominant, but small property-owners would have an independent and far from negligible voice. It was "politic as well as just," said Madison, "that the interests and rights of every class should be duly represented and understood in the public councils," and John Adams declared that there could be "no free government without a democratical branch in the constitution." . . .

. . . At the very beginning contemporary opponents of the Constitution foresaw an apocalyptic destruction of local government and popular institutions, while conservative Europeans of the old regime thought the young American Republic was a dangerous leftist experiment. Modern critical scholarship, which reached a high point in Charles A. Beard's *An Economic Interpretation of the Constitution of the United States*, started a new turn in the debate. The antagonism, long latent, between the philosophy of the Constitution and the philosophy of American democracy again came into the open. Professor Beard's work appeared in 1913 at the peak of the Progressive era, when the muckraking fever was still high; some readers tended to conclude from his findings that the Fathers were selfish reactionaries who do not deserve their high place in American esteem. Still more recently, other writers, inverting this logic, have used Beard's facts to praise the Fathers for their opposition to "democracy" and as an argument for returning again to the idea of a "republic."

In fact, the Fathers' image of themselves as moderate republicans

standing between political extremes was quite accurate. They were im-
pelled by class motives more than pietistic writers like to admit, but they
were also controlled, as Professor Beard himself has recently emphasized,
by a statesmanlike sense of moderation and a scrupulously republican
philosophy. Any attempt, however, to tear their ideas out of the eighteenth-
century context is sure to make them seem starkly reactionary. Consider,
for example, the favorite maxim of John Jay: "The people who own the
country ought to govern it." To the Fathers this was simply a swift
axiomatic statement of the stake-in-society theory of political rights, a
moderate conservative position under eighteenth-century conditions of
property distribution in America. Under modern property relations this
maxim demands a drastic restriction of the base of political power. A large
portion of the modern middle class—and it is the strength of this class
upon which balanced government depends—is propertyless; and the urban
proletariat, which the Fathers so greatly feared, is almost one half the
population. Further, the separation of ownership from control that has
come with the corporation deprives Jay's maxim of twentieth-century
meaning even for many propertied people. The six hundred thousand
stockholders of the American Telephone & Telegraph Company not only
do not acquire political power by virtue of their stock-ownership, but
they do not even acquire economic power: they cannot control their own
company.

     From a humanistic standpoint there is a serious dilemma in the philoso-
phy of the Fathers, which derives from their conception of man. They
thought man was a creature of rapacious self-interest, and yet they wanted
him to be free—free, in essence, to contend, to engage in an umpired
strife, to use property to get property. They accepted the mercantile image
of life as an eternal battleground, and assumed the Hobbesian war of each
against all; they did not propose to put an end to this war, but merely to
stabilize it and make it less murderous. They had no hope and they offered
none for any ultimate organic change in the way men conduct themselves.
The result was that while they thought self-interest the most dangerous
and unbrookable quality of man, they necessarily underwrote it in trying
to control it. . . .

IO

JAMES MADISON

The Federalist 10

This is the most important reading in an American government class. Along with its companion, Federalist 51 *(coming in the next section of the book), James Madison's* Federalist 10 *is the first and last word on U.S. government and politics. In it, he takes up the idea of "faction," by which he means any single group (especially the mob-like majority, but perhaps even a tiny minority) that tries to dominate the political process. Can faction be removed from politics? No, he admits, for a variety of reasons that deeply illuminate his assessment of the American people. But faction can be controlled by a republican (representative) system. Madison favored a large and diverse nation; if there were many groups, no one faction would ever be able to dominate. Signing these papers Publius, Madison, along with Alexander Hamilton and John Jay, wrote eighty-four essays collectively known as* The Federalist Papers, *which were published in several New York newspapers on behalf of the ratification of the new Constitution in 1787. James Madison's genius is revealed not only in the workable system of government he helped create for America, but also in his vision of the United States in the future, very much as it is today.*

No. 10: Madison

AMONG the numerous advantages promised by a well-constructed Union, none deserves to be more accurately developed than its tendency to break and control the violence of faction. The friend of popular governments never finds himself so much alarmed for their character and fate as when he contemplates their propensity to this dangerous vice. He will not fail, therefore, to set a due value on any plan which, without violating the principles to which he is attached, provides a proper cure for it. The instability, injustice, and confusion introduced into the public councils have, in truth, been the mortal diseases under which popular governments have everywhere perished, as they continue to be the favorite and fruitful topics from which the adversaries to liberty derive their most specious declamations. The valuable improvements made by the American constitutions on the popular models, both ancient and modern, cannot certainly be too much admired; but it would be an unwarrantable partiality to contend that they have as effectually obviated the danger on this side, as was wished and expected. Complaints are everywhere heard from our most considerate and virtuous citizens, equally the friends of public and private faith and of public and personal liberty, that our governments are too unstable, that the public good is disregarded in the conflicts of rival parties, and that measures are too often decided, not according to the rules of justice and the rights of the minor party, but by the superior force of an interested and overbearing majority. However anxiously we may wish that these complaints had no foundation, the evidence of known facts will not permit us to deny that they are in some degree true. It will be found, indeed, on a candid review of our situation, that some of the distresses under which we labor have been erroneously charged on the operation of our governments; but it will be found, at the same time, that other causes will not alone account for many of our heaviest misfortunes; and, particularly, for that prevailing and increasing distrust of public engagements and alarm for private rights which are echoed from one end of the continent to the other. These must be chiefly, if not wholly, effects of the unsteadiness and injustice with which a factious spirit has tainted our public administration.

By a faction I understand a number of citizens, whether amounting to a majority or minority of the whole, who are united and actuated by some common impulse of passion, or of interest, adverse to the rights of other citizens, or to the permanent and aggregate interests of the community.

There are two methods of curing the mischiefs of faction: the one, by removing its causes; the other, by controlling its effects.

There are again two methods of removing the causes of faction: the one, by destroying the liberty which is essential to its existence; the other, by giving to every citizen the same opinions, the same passions, and the same interests.

It could never be more truly said than of the first remedy that it was worse than the disease. Liberty is to faction what air is to fire, an aliment without which it instantly expires. But it could not be a less folly to abolish liberty, which is essential to political life, because it nourishes faction than it would be to wish the annihilation of air, which is essential to animal life, because it imparts to fire its destructive agency.

The second expedient is as impracticable as the first would be unwise. As long as the reason of man continues fallible, and he is at liberty to exercise it, different opinions will be formed. As long as the connection subsists between his reason and his self-love, his opinions and his passions will have a reciprocal influence on each other; and the former will be objects to which the latter will attach themselves. The diversity in the faculties of men, from which the rights of property originate, is not less an insuperable obstacle to a uniformity of interests. The protection of these faculties is the first object of government. From the protection of different and unequal faculties of acquiring property, the possession of different degrees and kinds of property immediately results; and from the influence of these on the sentiments and views of the respective proprietors ensues a division of the society into different interests and parties.

The latent causes of faction are thus sown in the nature of man; and we see them everywhere brought into different degrees of activity, according to the different circumstances of civil society. A zeal for different opinions concerning religion, concerning government, and many other points, as well of speculation as of practice; an attachment to different leaders ambitiously contending for pre-eminence and power; or to persons of other descriptions whose fortunes have been interesting to the human passions, have, in turn, divided mankind into parties, inflamed them with mutual animosity, and rendered them much more disposed to vex and oppress each other than to co-operate for their common good. So strong is this propensity of mankind to fall into mutual animosities that where no substantial occasion presents itself the most frivolous and fanciful distinctions have been sufficient to kindle their unfriendly passions and excite their most violent conflicts. But the most common and durable source of factions has been the various and unequal distribution of property. Those who hold and those who are without property have ever formed distinct interests in society. Those who are creditors, and those who are debtors, fall under a like discrimination. A landed interest, a manufacturing interest, a mercantile interest, a moneyed interest, with many lesser interests, grow up of necessity in civilized nations, and divide them into different classes, actuated by different sentiments and views. The regulation of these various and interfering interests forms the principal task of modern legislation and involves the spirit of party and faction in the necessary and ordinary operations of government.

No man is allowed to be a judge in his own cause, because his interest would certainly bias his judgment, and, not improbably, corrupt his integrity. With equal, nay with greater reason, a body of men are unfit to be both judges and parties at the same time; yet what are many of the most important acts of legislation but so many judicial determinations, not indeed concerning the rights of single persons, but concerning the rights of large bodies of citizens? And what are the different classes of legislators but advocates and parties to the causes which they determine?

Is a law proposed concerning private debts? It is a question to which the creditors are parties on one side and the debtors on the other. Justice ought to hold the balance between them. Yet the parties are, and must be, themselves the judges; and the most numerous party, or in other words, the most powerful faction must be expected to prevail. Shall domestic manufacturers be encouraged, and in what degree, by restrictions on foreign manufacturers? are questions which would be differently decided by the landed and the manufacturing classes, and probably by neither with a sole regard to justice and the public good. The apportionment of taxes on the various descriptions of property is an act which seems to require the most exact impartiality; yet there is, perhaps, no legislative act in which greater opportunity and temptation are given to a predominant party to trample on the rules of justice. Every shilling with which they overburden the inferior number is a shilling saved to their own pockets.

It is in vain to say that enlightened statesmen will be able to adjust these clashing interests and render them all subservient to the public good. Enlightened statesmen will not always be at the helm. Nor, in many cases, can such an adjustment be made at all without taking into view indirect and remote considerations, which will rarely prevail over the immediate interest which one party may find in disregarding the rights of another or the good of the whole.

The inference to which we are brought is that the *causes* of faction cannot be removed and that relief is only to be sought in the means of controlling its *effects*.

If a faction consists of less than a majority, relief is supplied by the republican principle, which enables the majority to defeat its sinister views by regular vote. It may clog the administration, it may convulse the society; but it will be unable to execute and mask its violence under the forms of the Constitution. When a majority is included in a faction, the form of popular government, on the other hand, enables it to sacrifice to its ruling passion or interest both the public good and the rights of other citizens. To secure the public good and private rights against the danger of such a faction, and at the same time to preserve the spirit and the form of popular government, is then the great object to which our inquiries are directed. Let me add that it is the great desideratum by which alone this form of government can be rescued from the opprobrium under which it has so long labored and be recommended to the esteem and adoption of mankind.

By what means is this object attainable? Evidently by one of two only. Either the existence of the same passion or interest in a majority at the same time must be prevented, or the majority, having such coexistent passion or interest, must be rendered, by their number and local situation, unable to concert and carry into effect schemes of oppression. If the impulse and the opportunity be suffered to coincide, we well know that neither moral nor religious motives can be relied on as an adequate control. They are not found to be such on the injustice and violence of individuals, and lose their efficacy in proportion to the number combined together, that is, in proportion as their efficacy becomes needful.

From this view of the subject it may be concluded that a pure democracy, by which I mean a society consisting of a small number of citizens, who assemble and administer the government in person, can admit of no cure for the mischiefs of faction. A common passion or interest will, in almost every case, be felt by a majority of the whole; a communication and concert results from the form of government itself; and there is nothing to check the inducements to sacrifice the weaker party or an obnoxious individual. Hence it is that such democracies have ever been spectacles of turbulence and contention; have ever been found incompatible with personal security or the rights of property; and have in general been as short in their lives as they have been violent in their deaths. Theoretic politicians, who have patronized this species of government, have erroneously supposed that by reducing mankind to a perfect equality in their political rights, they would at the same time be perfectly equalized and assimilated in their possessions, their opinions, and their passions.

A republic, by which I mean a government in which the scheme of representation takes place, opens a different prospect and promises the cure for which we are seeking. Let us examine the points in which it varies from pure democracy, and we shall comprehend both the nature of the cure and the efficacy which it must derive from the Union.

The two great points of difference between a democracy and a republic are: first, the delegation of the government, in the latter, to a small number of citizens elected by the rest; secondly, the greater number of citizens and greater sphere of country over which the latter may be extended.

The effect of the first difference is, on the one hand, to refine and enlarge the public views by passing them through the medium of a chosen body of citizens, whose wisdom may best discern the true interest of their country and whose patriotism and love of justice will be least likely to sacrifice it to temporary or partial considerations. Under such a regulation it may well happen that the public voice, pronounced by the representatives of the people, will be more consonant to the public good than if pronounced by the people themselves, convened for the purpose. On the other hand, the effect may be inverted. Men of factious tempers, of local prejudices, or of sinister designs, may, by intrigue, by corruption, or by other means, first obtain the suffrages, and then betray the interests of the people. The question resulting is, whether small or extensive republics are most favorable to the election of proper guardians of the public weal; and it is clearly decided in favor of the latter by two obvious considerations.

In the first place it is to be remarked that however small the republic may be the representatives must be raised to a certain number in order to guard against the cabals of a few; and that however large it may be they must be limited to a certain number in order to guard against the confusion of a multitude. Hence, the number of representatives in the two cases not being in proportion to that of the constituents, and being proportionally greatest in the small republic, it follows that if the proportion of fit characters be not less in the large than in the small republic, the former will present a greater option, and consequently a greater probability of a fit choice.

In the next place, as each representative will be chosen by a greater number of citizens in the large than in the small republic, it will be more difficult for unworthy candidates to practise with success the vicious arts by which elections are too often carried; and the suffrages of the people being more free, will be more likely to center on men who possess the most attractive merit and the most diffusive and established characters.

It must be confessed that in this, as in most other cases, there is a mean, on both sides of which inconveniencies will be found to lie. By enlarging too much the number of electors, you render the representative too little acquainted with all their local circumstances and lesser interests; as by reducing it too much, you render him unduly attached to these, and too little fit to comprehend and pursue great and national objects. The federal Constitution forms a happy combination in this respect; the great and aggregate interests being referred to the national, the local and particular to the State legislatures.

The other point of difference is the greater number of citizens and extent of territory which may be brought within the compass of republican than of democratic government; and it is this circumstance principally which renders factious combinations less to be dreaded in the former than in the latter. The smaller the society, the fewer probably will be the distinct parties and interests composing it; the fewer the distinct parties and interests, the more frequently will a majority be found of the same party; and the smaller the number of individuals composing a majority, and the smaller the compass within which they are placed, the more easily will they concert and execute their plans of oppression. Extend the sphere and you take in a greater variety of parties and interests; you make it less probable that a majority of the whole will have a common motive to invade the rights of other citizens; or if such a common motive exists, it will be more difficult for all who feel it to discover their own strength and to act in unison with each other. Besides other impediments, it may be remarked that, where there is a consciousness of unjust or dishonorable purposes, communication is always checked by distrust in proportion to the number whose concurrence is necessary.

Hence, it clearly appears that the same advantage which a republic has over a democracy in controlling the effects of faction is enjoyed by a large over a small republic—is enjoyed by the Union over the States composing it. Does this advantage consist in the substitution of representatives whose enlightened views and virtuous sentiments render them superior to local prejudices and to schemes of injustice? It will not be denied that the representation of the Union will be most likely to possess these requisite endowments. Does it consist in the greater security afforded by a greater variety of parties, against the event of any one party being able to outnumber and oppress the rest? In an equal degree does the increased variety of parties comprised within the Union increase this security? Does it, in fine, consist in the greater obstacles opposed to the concert and accomplishment of the secret wishes of an unjust and interested majority? Here again the extent of the Union gives it the most palpable advantage.

The influence of factious leaders may kindle a flame within their particular States but will be unable to spread a general conflagration through the other States. A religious sect may degenerate into a political faction in a part of the Confederacy; but the variety of sects dispersed over the entire face of it must secure the national councils against any danger from that source. A rage for paper money, for an abolition of debts, for an equal division of property, or for any other improper or wicked project, will be less apt to pervade the whole body of the Union than a particular member of it, in the same proportion as such a malady is more likely to taint a particular county or district than an entire State.

In the extent and proper structure of the Union, therefore, we behold a republican remedy for the diseases most incident to republican government. And according to the degree of pleasure and pride we feel in being republicans ought to be our zeal in cherishing the spirit and supporting the character of federalists.   *Publius*

II

MICHAEL KAMMEN

From A Machine That Would Go of Itself

Written at the time of the bicentennial of the United States Constitution, historian Michael Kammen's book is of interest to those seeking greater depth on the evolution of the nation's basic document. Kammen traces the shifts in thought about the Constitution's interpretation, from that of a "machine" that once put in motion would function steadily and unchangingly forever, to a more fluid and malleable plan. Particularly memorable is his analogy of a 1966 "Star Trek" episode, "The Omega Glory," in which we see Captain Kirk and the crew of the Enterprise *grappling with the same questions that we ask today about the Constitution.*

————◆————

THE [metaphor], the notion of a constitution as some sort of machine or engine, had its origins in Newtonian science. Enlightened philosophers, such as David Hume, liked to contemplate the world with all of its components as a great machine. Perhaps it was inevitable, as politics came to be regarded as a science during the 1770s and '80s, that leading revolutionaries in the colonies would utilize the metaphor to suit their purposes. In 1774 Jefferson's *Summary View* mentioned "the great machine of government." . . .

Over the next one hundred years such imagery did not disappear. But neither did it notably increase; and hardly anyone expressed apprehension about the adverse implications of employing mechanistic metaphors. Occasionally an observer or enthusiast might call the Constitution "the best national machine that is now in existence" (1794); or, at the Golden Jubilee in 1839, John Quincy Adams could comment that "fifty years have passed away since the first impulse was given to the wheels of this political machine."

James Fenimore Cooper uttered one of the few expressions of concern couched in this language between 1787 and 1887. "The boldest violations of the Constitution are daily proposed by politicians in this country," he observed in 1848, "but they do not produce the fruits which might be expected, because the nation is so accustomed to work in the harness it has placed on itself, that nothing seems seriously to arrest the movement of the great national car." Although his metaphors are ridiculously muddled, the message is clear enough. Exactly forty years later James Russell Lowell articulated this same apprehension much more cogently in an address to the Reform Club of New York. The pertinent passage marks the apogee of the metaphor, and remains today as profound a warning as it was in 1888.

After our Constitution got fairly into working order it really seemed as if we had invented a machine that would go of itself, and this begot a faith in our luck which even the civil war itself but momentarily disturbed. Circumstances continued favorable, and our prosperity went on increasing. I admire the splendid complacency of my countrymen, and find something exhilarating and inspiring in it. We are a nation which has *struck ile* [sic], but we are also a nation that is sure the well will never run dry. And this confidence in our luck with the absorption in material interests, generated by unparalleled opportunity, has in some respects made us neglectful of our political duties.

That statement epitomizes not merely the main historical theme of this book, but the homily that I hope to convey as well. Machine imagery lingered on for fifty years, casually used by legal scholars, journalists, civics textbooks, even great jurists like Holmes, and by Franklin D. Roosevelt in his first inaugural address. On occasion, during the 1920s and '30s especially, conservatives would declare that the apparatus, being more than adequate, should not be tampered with, whereas reformers insisted that "the machinery of government under which we live is hopelessly antiquated" (a word they loved) and therefore "should be overhauled."

In the quarter century that followed Lowell's 1888 lament, a cultural transition took place that leads us to the last of the major constitutional metaphors. We may exemplify it with brief extracts from three prominent justices: Holmes, who wrote in 1914 that "the provisions of the Constitution are not mathematical formulas . . . they are organic living institutions"; Cardozo, who observed in 1925 that "a Constitution has an organic life"; and Frankfurter, who declared in 1951 that "the Constitution is an organism."

Unlike the other analogies that have been discussed, which were not mutually exclusive, this shift was not merely deliberate but intellectually aggressive at times. The quarter century is punctuated by the declarations of two political scientists deeply involved in public affairs. At the close of the 1880s, A. Lawrence Lowell wrote that "a political system is not a mere machine which can be constructed on any desired plan. . . . It is far more than this. It is an organism . . . whose various parts act and react upon one another." In 1912, when Woodrow Wilson ran for the presidency, a key passage in his campaign statement, *The New Freedom*, elaborated upon Lowell's assertion. "The makers of our Federal Constitution," in Wilson's words, "constructed a government as they would have constructed an orrery,*—to display the laws of nature. Politics in their thought was a variety of mechanics. The Constitution was founded on the law of gravitation. The government was to exist and move by virtue of the efficacy of 'checks and balances.'"

Lowell and Wilson had obviously responded to the same current of cultural change; but they were not attempting to be intellectually trendy by explaining government in terms of evolutionary theory. The word-concept they both used in condemning a Newtonian notion of constitutionalism was "static." Wilson spelled out the implications: "Society is a living organism and must obey the laws of life, not of mechanics; it must develop. All that progressives ask or desire is permission—in an era when 'development,' 'evolution,' is the scientific word—to interpret the Constitution according to the Darwinian principle; all they ask is recognition of the fact that a nation is a living thing and not a machine." . . .

I would describe the basic pattern of American constitutionalism as one of *conflict within consensus.* At first glance, perhaps, we are more likely to notice the consensus. . . .

The volume of evidence is overwhelming that our constitutional conflicts have been consequential, and considerably more revealing than the consensual framework within which they operate. When Americans have been aware of the dynamic of conflict within consensus, most often they have regarded it as a normative pattern for a pluralistic polity. . . .

There is . . . a . . . closely linked aspect of American constitutionalism about which there has been no consensus: namely, whether our frame of government was meant to be fairly unchanging or flexible. Commentators are quick to quote Justice Holmes's "theory of our Constitution. It is an experiment, as all life is an experiment." Although much less familiar, and less eloquent, more Americans have probably shared this sentiment, written in 1936 by an uncommon common man, the chief clerk in the Vermont Department of Highways: "I regard the Constitution as of too much value to be experimented with."

The assumption that our Constitution is lapidary has a lineage that runs, among the justices, from Marshall and Taney to David J. Brewer and George Sutherland. It has been the dominant assumption for most of our history, and provided the basis for Walter Bagehot, Lord Bryce, and others to regard the U.S. Constitution as "rigid" by comparison with the British. The idea that adaptability was desirable emerged gradually during the mid-nineteenth century, appeared in some manuals aimed at

*An apparatus for representing the motions . . . of the planets. . . .

a popular audience by the 1880s, and achieved added respectability in 1906 when Justice Henry Billings Brown spoke at a dinner in his honor. The Constitution, he said, "should be liberally interpreted—interpreted as if it were intended as the foundation of a great nation, and not merely a temporary expedient for the united action of thirteen small States. . . . Like all written Constitutions, there is an underlying danger in its inflexibility." For about a generation that outlook slowly gained adherents, until the two contradictory views were essentially counterpoised in strength by the 1930s.

Meanwhile, a third position appeared during the early decades of the twentieth century—one that might be considered a compromise because it blended facets of the other two. This moderately conservative, evolutionary position was expressed in 1903 by James Ford Rhodes, a nationalistic businessman-turned-historian. The Constitution, in his mind, "is rigid in those matters which should not be submitted to the decision of a legislature or to a popular vote without checks which secure reflection and a chance for the sober second thought, [yet] it has proved flexible in its adaptation to the growth of the country." . . .

Admittedly, our strict constructionists have on occasion stretched the Constitution, as Jefferson did in 1803 to acquire the vast Louisiana Territory. Lincoln, Wilson, and FDR each stood accused of ignoring constitutional restraints; yet each one could honestly respond that, within the framework of a Constitution intended to be flexible in an emergency, his goal had been to preserve the Union, to win a war fought for noble goals, or to overcome the worst and most prolonged economic disaster in American history. In each instance their constitutional critics spoke out clearly, a national debate took place, and clarification of our constitutional values occurred. Sometimes that clarification has come from the Supreme Court; sometimes from a presidential election campaign; sometimes from a combination of the two; and sometimes by means of political compromise. Each mode of resolution is a necessary part of our democratic system. I am led to conclude that Americans have been more likely to read and understand their Constitution when it has been controversial, or when some group contended that it had been misused, than in those calmer moments when it has been widely venerated as an instrument for all time. . . .

During the later 1950s, Robert M. Hutchins and his colleagues at the Center for the Study of Democratic Institutions, located in Santa Barbara, California, began to discuss the desirability of far-reaching constitutional changes. In 1964, following a series of seminars modestly entitled "Drafting a New Constitution for the United States and the World,"

Hutchins invited Rexford G. Tugwell, once a member of FDR's "Brain Trust," to direct a reassessment of the Constitution. Tugwell accepted and spent two years conferring with hundreds of jurists, politicians, and scholars. . . .

During the 1970s the Center's primary concerns shifted away from constitutionalism; Tugwell's two major volumes (1974 and 1976) received little attention aside from scholarly journals. When Tugwell died in 1979 at the age of eighty-eight, the *New York Times*'s appreciative editorial did not even mention the revised constitution on which he labored for more than a decade. The *Times* apparently did not regard it as a fitting culmination for a distinguished career in scholarship and public service.

The negligible impact of this seasoned planner's constitutional vision provides a striking contrast with an extremely tradition-oriented interpolation of the U.S. Constitution in science fiction. One popular episode of the television series "Star Trek," written in 1966, received hundreds of reruns during the many years when Tugwell labored over his revision. Millions of Americans watched "The Omega Glory" and recognized its affirmation of the good old Constitution that continued to function even though space, time, and ignorance shrouded its meaning.

Reducing the saga to its ideological essence, Captain Kirk and the starship *Enterprise* land on a planet where the inhabitants are guided by a Prime Directive that must not be violated. Those inhabitants are called Yangs (presumably the descendants of colonizers once known as Yanks), and possess "a worn parchment document" that is "the greatest of holies." Kirk and his crew encounter a bizarre political situation that is not so very different from the one criticized by James Russell Lowell in 1888. The Yangs worship "freedom" but do not understand what it means. Through the ages it has become a ritualized "worship word." The Yangs believe that their ancestors must have been very superior people; they swear an oath to abide by all regulations in the Prime Directive; and they can recite the opening lines of the Prime Directive, but "without meaning."

Following a primitive court scene, complete with jury, it becomes clear that institutions of justice are amazingly resilient—capable of enduring even though their rationale has suffered badly from neglect and amnesia. At the culmination Captain Kirk informs the Yangs that they revere a sacred document without understanding what it is all about. Kirk faces Cloud William, chief of the Yangs, and explains the meaning of the Prime Directive's preamble. Enlightenment then occurs and the great question— is the Prime Directive still operative, and does it apply to this planet?—

achieves a satisfactory resolution. To use the language of yesteryear, "constitutional morality" would surely be restored.

Unlike Rexford Tugwell's new constitution, which kept "emerging" for so long that after a while no one cared, "Star Trek" had a constitutional homily with a happy ending. Americans like happy endings. Hence many younger Americans can still narrate "The Omega Glory" (Old Glory? Ultimate Glory?) flawlessly. How much of the homily got through, however, is another matter. . . .

Ultimately, however, for better and for worse, it is ideological conflict that most meaningfully calls attention to the Constitution. We are then reminded that all Americans do not agree about the most appropriate division of authority: federalism tilting toward states' rights or federalism leaning toward national authority? We are then reminded that we still have broad and strict constructionists, followers of Hamilton and followers of Madison. And we are then reminded that we have had two complementary but divergent modes of constitutional interpretation: a tradition of conflict within consensus. . . .

It is instructive to recall that the founders did not expect their instrument of government to achieve utopia: "merely" national cohesion, political stability, economic growth, and individual liberty. Despite abundant setbacks and imperfections, much of that agenda has been fulfilled for a great many Americans. During the past generation social justice got explicitly added to the agenda as a high priority, and the American Constitution, interpreted by the Supreme Court, was adapted accordingly. For a society to progress toward social justice within a constitutional framework, even by trial and error, is a considerable undertaking. To do so in good faith, more often than not, is equally commendable. If from time to time we require the assistance of gadflies, what flourishing political culture does not? Senator Lowell P. Weicker of Connecticut, for example, has played that role rather well on occasion. As he thundered in 1981, during debate over a legislative amendment to endorse organized prayer in public schools: "To my amazement, any time the word constitutionalism comes up it's looked upon as a threat. A threat! It shouldn't be; it's what holds us all together."

That has been true more often than not. Perhaps those who feel threatened by constitutionalism do not fully understand it. People frequently feel threatened by the unfamiliar. Perhaps it has not been fully understood because it has not been adequately explained. Perhaps it has perplexed us because aspects of its meaning have changed over time. Back in 1786 Benjamin Rush believed it "possible to convert men into republican machines. This must be done if we expect them to perform their parts properly in the great machine of the government of the state." His contemporaries not only took Rush at his word, but regarded the conversion of men into republican machines as a national imperative. . . .

More than a century later, Woodrow Wilson presented a piece of wisdom that tacked the other way. Call it constitutional revisionism if you like. He declared that if the real government of the United States "had, in fact, been a machine governed by mechanically automatic balances, it would have had no history; but it was not, and its history has been rich with the influences and personalities of the men who have conducted it and made it a living reality." Walter Lippmann chose to quote that sentence in 1913 when he wrote *A Preface to Politics*. But he promptly added that "only by violating the very spirit of the constitution have we been able to preserve the letter of it." What Lippmann had in mind was the role played by that palpable reality the Progressives called "invisible government": political parties, interest groups, trade unions, and so on.

Lippmann's remark was not meant to be as cynical as it might sound. It reflects the Progressive desire to be realistic and tough-minded. It also reflects the fact that Americans have been profoundly ambivalent in their feelings about government. Then, too, it reflects the discovery by three overlapping generations of Americans—represented by James Russell Lowell, Wilson, and Lippmann—that the U.S. Constitution is not, and was not meant to be, a machine that would go of itself.

Above all, Lippmann wanted to build upon his excerpt from Wilson and establish the point that there has been more to the story of constitutionalism in American culture than the history of the Constitution itself. The latter is a cherished charter of institutions and a declaration of protections. The former, constitutionalism, embodies a set of values, a range of options, and a means of resolving conflicts within a framework of consensus. It has supplied stability and continuity to a degree the framers could barely have imagined.

12

C. WRIGHT MILLS

From *The Power Elite*

C. Wright Mills's book The Power Elite *stands as a classic in political science. In it he offers one answer to the question "Who rules America?" A three-part elite rules, he believes, composed of corporate, political, and military leaders. These sectors of American life are connected, creating an "interlocking" power structure with highly centralized decision-making. Mills considers a conspiracy theory to account for the power elite's control, but rejects it for something much more frightening. Average Americans are like "trusting children" who rely on the power elite to run things smoothly and well. Today, a half-century after Mills wrote, his ideas seem a bit ultra-dramatic and overstated. Still, Mills offers a warning about power in America that is timeless, one that many people believe is true.*

THE POWERS of ordinary men are circumscribed by the every-day worlds in which they live, yet even in these rounds of job, family, and neighborhood they often seem driven by forces they can neither understand nor govern. "Great changes" are beyond their control, but affect their conduct and outlook none the less. The very framework of modern society confines them to projects not their own, but from every side, such changes now press upon the men and women of the mass society, who accordingly feel that they are without purpose in an epoch in which they are without power.

But not all men are in this sense ordinary. As the means of information and of power are centralized, some men come to occupy positions in American society from which they can look down upon, so to speak, and by their decisions mightily affect, the everyday worlds of ordinary men and women. They are not made by their jobs; they set up and break down jobs for thousands of others; they are not confined by simple family responsibilities; they can escape. They may live in many hotels and houses, but they are bound by no one community. They need not merely "meet the demands of the day and hour"; in some part, they create these demands, and cause others to meet them. Whether or not they profess their power, their technical and political experience of it far transcends that of the underlying population. What Jacob Burckhardt said of "great men," most Americans might well say of their elite: "They are all that we are not."

The power elite is composed of men whose positions enable them to transcend the ordinary environments of ordinary men and women; they are in positions to make decisions having major consequences. Whether they do or do not make such decisions is less important than the fact that they do occupy such pivotal positions: their failure to act, their failure to make decisions, is itself an act that is often of greater consequence than the decisions they do make. For they are in command of the major hierarchies and organizations of modern society. They rule the big corporations. They run the machinery of the state and claim its prerogatives. They direct the military establishment. They occupy the strategic command posts of the social structure, in which are now centered the effective means of the power and the wealth and the celebrity which they enjoy.

The power elite are not solitary rulers. Advisers and consultants, spokesmen and opinion-makers are often the captains of their higher thought and decision. Immediately below the elite are the professional politicians of the middle levels of power, in the Congress and in the pressure groups, as well as among the new and old upper classes of town and city and region. Mingling with them, in curious ways which we shall explore, are those professional celebrities who live by being continually displayed but are never, so long as they remain celebrities, displayed enough. If such celebrities are not at the head of any dominating hierarchy, they do often have the power to distract the attention of the public or afford sensations to the masses, or, more directly, to gain the ear of those who do occupy positions of direct power. More or less unattached, as critics of morality and technicians of power, as spokesmen of God and creators of mass sensibility, such celebrities and consultants are part of the immediate scene in which the drama of the elite is enacted. But that drama itself is centered in the command posts of the major institutional hierarchies.

The truth about the nature and the power of the elite is not some secret which men of affairs know but will not tell. Such men hold quite various theories about their own roles in the sequence of event and decision. Often they are uncertain about their roles, and even more often they allow their fears and their hopes to affect their assessment of their own power. No matter how great their actual power, they tend to be less acutely aware of it than of the resistances of others to its use. Moreover, most American men of affairs have learned well the rhetoric of public relations, in some cases even to the point of using it when they are alone, and thus coming to believe it. The personal awareness of the actors is only one of the several sources one must examine in order to understand the higher circles. Yet many who believe that there is no elite, or at any rate none of any consequence, rest their argument upon what men of affairs believe about themselves, or at least assert in public.

There is, however, another view: those who feel, even if vaguely, that a compact and powerful elite of great importance does now prevail in America often base that feeling upon the historical trend of our time. They have felt, for example, the domination of the military event, and from this they infer that generals and admirals, as well as other men of decision influenced by them, must be enormously powerful. They hear that the Congress has again abdicated to a handful of men decisions clearly related to the issue of war or peace. They know that the bomb was dropped over Japan in the name of the United States of America, although they were at no time consulted about the matter. They feel that they live in a time of big decisions; they know that they are not making any. Accordingly, as they consider the present as history, they infer that at its center, making decisions or failing to make them, there must be an elite of power.

On the one hand, those who share this feeling about big historical events assume that there is an elite and that its power is great. On the other hand, those who listen carefully to the reports of men apparently involved in the great decisions often do not believe that there is an elite whose powers are of decisive consequence.

Both views must be taken into account, but neither is adequate. The way to understand the power of the American elite lies neither solely in recognizing the historic scale of events nor in accepting the personal awareness reported by men of apparent decision. Behind such men and behind the events of history, linking the two, are the major institutions of modern society. These hierarchies of state and corporation and army constitute the means of power; as such they are now of a consequence not before equaled in human history—and at their summits, there are now those command posts of modern society which offer us the sociological key to an understanding of the role of the higher circles in America.

Within American society, major national power now resides in the economic, the political, and the military domains. Other institutions seem off to the side of modern history, and, on occasion, duly subordinated to these. No family is as directly powerful in national affairs as any major corporation; no church is as directly powerful in the external biographies of young men in America today as the military establishment; no college is as powerful in the shaping of momentous events as the National Security

Council. Religious, educational, and family institutions are not autonomous centers of national power; on the contrary, these decentralized areas are increasingly shaped by the big three, in which developments of decisive and immediate consequence now occur.

Families and churches and schools adapt to modern life; governments and armies and corporations shape it; and, as they do so, they turn these lesser institutions into means for their ends. Religious institutions provide chaplains to the armed forces where they are used as a means of increasing the effectiveness of its morale to kill. Schools select and train men for their jobs in corporations and their specialized tasks in the armed forces. The extended family has, of course, long been broken up by the industrial revolution, and now the son and the father are removed from the family, by compulsion if need be, whenever the army of the state sends out the call. And the symbols of all these lesser institutions are used to legitimate the power and the decisions of the big three.

The life-fate of the modern individual depends not only upon the family into which he was born or which he enters by marriage, but increasingly upon the corporation in which he spends the most alert hours of his best years; not only upon the school where he is educated as a child and adolescent, but also upon the state which touches him throughout his life; not only upon the church in which on occasion he hears the word of God, but also upon the army in which he is disciplined.

If the centralized state could not rely upon the inculcation of nationalist loyalties in public and private schools, its leaders would promptly seek to modify the decentralized educational system. If the bankruptcy rate among the top five hundred corporations were as high as the general divorce rate among the thirty-seven million married couples, there would be economic catastrophe on an international scale. If members of armies gave to them no more of their lives than do believers to the churches to which they belong, there would be a military crisis.

Within each of the big three, the typical institutional unit has become enlarged, has become administrative, and, in the power of its decisions, has become centralized. Behind these developments there is a fabulous technology, for as institutions, they have incorporated this technology and guide it, even as it shapes and paces their developments.

The economy—once a great scatter of small productive units in autonomous balance—has become dominated by two or three hundred giant corporations, administratively and politically interrelated, which together hold the keys to economic decisions.

The political order, once a decentralized set of several dozen states with a weak spinal cord, has become a centralized, executive establishment which has taken up into itself many powers previously scattered, and now enters into each and every crany of the social structure.

The military order, once a slim establishment in a context of distrust fed by state militia, has become the largest and most expensive feature of government, and, although well versed in smiling public relations, now has all the grim and clumsy efficiency of a sprawling bureaucratic domain.

In each of these institutional areas, the means of power at the disposal of decision makers have increased enormously; their central executive powers have been enhanced; within each of them modern administrative routines have been elaborated and tightened up.

As each of these domains becomes enlarged and centralized, the consequences of its activities become greater, and its traffic with the others increases. The decisions of a handful of corporations bear upon military and political as well as upon economic developments around the world. The decisions of the military establishment rest upon and grievously affect political life as well as the very level of economic activity. The decisions made within the political domain determine economic activities and military programs. There is no longer, on the one hand, an economy, and, on the other hand, a political order containing a military establishment unimportant to politics and to money-making. There is a political economy linked, in a thousand ways, with military institutions and decisions. On each side of the world-split running through central Europe and around the Asiatic rimlands, there is an ever-increasing interlocking of economic, military, and political structures. If there is government intervention in the corporate economy, so is there corporate intervention in the governmental process. In the structural sense, this triangle of power is the source of the interlocking directorate that is most important for the historical structure of the present.

The fact of the interlocking is clearly revealed at each of the points of crisis of modern capitalist society—slump, war, and boom. In each, men of decision are led to an awareness of the interdependence of the major institutional orders. In the nineteenth century, when the scale of all institutions was smaller, their liberal integration was achieved in the automatic economy, by an autonomous play of market forces, and in the automatic political domain, by the bargain and the vote. It was then assumed that out of the imbalance and friction that followed the limited decisions then possible a new equilibrium would in due course emerge. That can no longer be assumed, and it is not assumed by the men at the top of each of the three dominant hierarchies.

For given the scope of their consequences, decisions—and indecisions—in any one of these ramify into the others, and hence top decisions

tend either to become co-ordinated or to lead to a commanding indecision. It has not always been like this. When numerous small entrepreneurs
made up the economy, for example, many of them could fail and the
consequences still remain local; political and military authorities did not
intervene. But now, given political expectations and military commitments, can they afford to allow key units of the private corporate economy
to break down in slump? Increasingly, they do intervene in economic
affairs, and as they do so, the controlling decisions in each order are
inspected by agents of the other two, and economic, military, and political
structures are interlocked.

At the pinnacle of each of the three enlarged and centralized domains,
there have arisen those higher circles which make up the economic, the
political, and the military elites. At the top of the economy, among the
corporate rich, there are the chief executives; at the top of the political
order, the members of the political directorate; at the top of the military
establishment, the elite of soldier-statesmen clustered in and around the
Joint Chiefs of Staff and the upper echelon. As each of these domains
has coincided with the others, as decisions tend to become total in their
consequence, the leading men in each of the three domains of power—
the warlords, the corporation chieftains, the political directorate—tend
to come together, to form the power elite of America. . . .

The conception of the power elite and of its unity rests upon the
corresponding developments and the coincidence of interests among economic, political, and military organizations. It also rests upon the similarity
of origin and outlook, and the social and personal intermingling of the
top circles from each of these dominant hierarchies. This conjunction of
institutional and psychological forces, in turn, is revealed by the heavy
personnel traffic within and between the big three institutional orders, as
well as by the rise of go-betweens as in the high-level lobbying. The
conception of the power elite, accordingly, does *not* rest upon the assumption that American history since the origins of World War II must be
understood as a secret plot, or as a great and co-ordinated conspiracy of
the members of this elite. The conception rests upon quite impersonal
grounds.

There is, however, little doubt that the American power elite—which
contains, we are told, some of "the greatest organizers in the world"—
has also planned and has plotted. The rise of the elite, as we have already
made clear, was not and could not have been caused by a plot; and the
tenability of the conception does not rest upon the existence of any
secret or any publicly known organization. But, once the conjunction of

structural trend and of the personal will to utilize it gave rise to the power elite, then plans and programs did occur to its members and indeed it is not possible to interpret many events and official policies of the fifth epoch without reference to the power elite. "There is a great difference," Richard Hofstadter has remarked, "between locating conspiracies *in* history and saying that history *is*, in effect, a conspiracy . . . "

The structural trends of institutions become defined as opportunities by those who occupy their command posts. Once such opportunities are recognized, men may avail themselves of them. Certain types of men from each of the dominant institutional areas, more far-sighted than others, have actively promoted the liaison before it took its truly modern shape. They have often done so for reasons not shared by their partners, although not objected to by them either; and often the outcome of their liaison has had consequences which none of them foresaw, much less shaped, and which only later in the course of development came under explicit control. Only after it was well under way did most of its members find themselves part of it and become gladdened, although sometimes also worried, by this fact. But once the co-ordination is a going concern, new men come readily into it and assume its existence without question.

So far as explicit organization—conspiratorial or not—is concerned, the power elite, by its very nature, is more likely to use existing organizations, working within and between them, than to set up explicit organizations whose membership is strictly limited to its own members. But if there is no machinery in existence to ensure, for example, that military and political factors will be balanced in decisions made, they will invent such machinery and use it, as with the National Security Council. Moreover, in a formally democratic polity, the aims and the powers of the various elements of this elite are further supported by an aspect of the permanent war economy: the assumption that the security of the nation supposedly rests upon great secrecy of plan and intent. Many higher events that would reveal the working of the power elite can be withheld from public knowledge under the guise of secrecy. With the wide secrecy covering their operations and decisions, the power elite can mask their intentions, operations, and further consolidation. Any secrecy that is imposed upon those in positions to observe high decision-makers clearly works for and not against the operations of the power elite.

There is accordingly reason to suspect—but by the nature of the case, no proof—that the power elite is not altogether "surfaced." There is nothing hidden about it, although its activities are not publicized. As an elite, it is not organized, although its members often know one another, seem quite naturally to work together, and share many organizations in common. There is nothing conspiratorial about it, although its decisions are often publicly unknown and its mode of operation manipulative rather than explicit.

It is not that the elite "believe in" a compact elite behind the scenes and a mass down below. It is not put in that language. It is just that the people are of necessity confused and must, like trusting children, place all the new world of foreign policy and strategy and executive action in the hands of experts. It is just that everyone knows somebody has got to run the show, and that somebody usually does. Others do not really care anyway, and besides, they do not know how. So the gap between the two types gets wider.

13

RICHARD ZWEIGENHAFT
G. WILLIAM DOMHOFF

From *Diversity in the Power Elite*

In the previous excerpt, C. Wright Mills presented his interpretation of who holds power in America: a small elite. Mills wrote his classic book decades ago. Richard Zweigenhaft and G. William Domhoff revisit Mills's thesis by examining the composition of today's power elite—assuming, of course, that there is such an elite. The authors offer a fascinating account of Jews, women, blacks, Latinos, Asian Americans, and gay men and lesbians in the elite, including many personal stories of powerful individuals. The excerpt here looks at corporate women and African-American men in the military. Yes, the elite looks different today, but no, it is not really so different than when Mills wrote.

INJUSTICES BASED ON race, gender, ethnicity, and sexual orientation have been the most emotional and contested issues in American society since the end of the 1960s, far exceeding concerns with social class, and rivaled only by conflicts about abortion. These issues are now subsumed under the umbrella terms *diversity* and *multiculturalism*, and they have been written about extensively from the perspectives of both the aggrieved and those at the middle and lower levels of the social ladder who resist any changes.

. . . [W]e look at multiculturalism from a new angle: we examine its impact on the small group at the top of American society that we call the power elite—those who own and manage large banks and corporations, finance the political campaigns of conservative Democrats and virtually all Republicans at the state and national levels, and serve in government as appointed officials and military leaders. We ask whether the decades of pressure from civil rights groups, feminists, and gay and lesbian rights activists has resulted in a more culturally diverse power elite. If it has, what effects has this new diversity had on the functioning of the power elite and on its relation to the rest of society? . . .

According to many commentators, the higher circles in the United States had indeed become multicultural by the late 1980s and early 1990s. Some went even further, saying that the old power elite had been pushed aside entirely. The demise of the "old" power elite was the theme of such books as Nelson Aldrich's *Old Money* and Robert Christopher's *Crashing the Gates*, the latter emphasizing the rise of ethnic minorities. There have also been wide-eyed articles in mainstream magazines, such as one in the late 1980s in *U.S. News and World Report* entitled "The New American Establishment," which celebrated a new diversity at the top, claiming that "new kinds of men and women" have "taken control of institutions that influence important aspects of American life." School and club ties are no longer important, the article announced; the new role of women was highlighted with a picture of some of the "wise women" who had joined the "wise men" who dominated the old establishment.

Then, in July 1995, *Newsweek* ran a cover story on "The Rise of the Overclass," featuring a gallery of one hundred high-tech, media, and Wall Street stars, women as well as men, minorities as well as whites, who supposedly come from all rungs of the social ladder. The term *overclass* was relatively new, but the argument—that the power elite was dead, superseded by a diverse meritocratic elite—was not. . . .

Since the 1870s the refrain about the new diversity of the governing circles has been closely intertwined with a staple of American culture created by Horatio Alger Jr., whose name has become synonymous with upward mobility in America. Born in 1832 to a patrician family—Alger's father was a Harvard graduate, a Unitarian minister, and a Massachusetts state senator—Alger graduated from Harvard at the age of nineteen. There followed a series of unsuccessful efforts to establish himself in various careers. Finally, in 1864 Alger was hired as a Unitarian minister in Brewster, Massachusetts. Fifteen months later, he was dismissed from this position for homosexual acts with boys in the congregation.

Alger returned to New York, where he soon began to spend a great deal of time at the Newsboys' Lodging House, founded in 1853 for footloose youngsters between the ages of twelve and sixteen and home to many youths who had been mustered out of the Union Army after serving as drummer boys. At the Newsboys' Lodging House Alger found his literary niche and his subsequent claim to fame: writing books in which poor boys make good. His books sold by the hundreds of thousands in the last third of the nineteenth century, and by 1910 they were enjoying annual sales of more than one million in paperback.

The deck is not stacked against the poor, according to Horatio Alger. When they simply show a bit of gumption, work hard, and thereby catch a break or two, they can become part of the American elite. The persistence of this theme, reinforced by the annual Horatio Alger Awards to such well-known personalities as Ronald Reagan, Bob Hope, and Billy Graham (who might not have been so eager to accept them if they had known of Alger's shadowed past), suggests that we may be dealing once again with a cultural myth. In its early versions, of course, the story concerned the great opportunities available for poor white boys willing to work their way to the top. More recently, the story has featured black Horatio Algers who started in the ghetto, Latino Horatio Algers who started in the barrio, Asian-American Horatio Algers whose parents were immigrants, and female Horatio Algers who seem to have no class backgrounds—all of whom now sit on the boards of the country's largest corporations.

But is any of this true? Can anecdotes and self-serving autobiographical accounts about diversity, meritocracy, and upward social mobility survive a more systematic analysis? Have very many women and previously excluded minorities made it to the top? Has class lost its importance in shaping life chances?

. . . [W]e address these and related questions within the framework provided by the iconoclastic sociologist C. Wright Mills in his hard-hitting classic *The Power Elite*, published in 1956 when the media were in the midst of what Mills called the Great American Celebration. In spite of the Depression of the 1930s, Americans had pulled together to win World War II, and the country was both prosperous at home and influential abroad. Most of all, according to enthusiasts, the United States had become a relatively classless and pluralistic society, where power belonged to the people through their political parties and public opinion. Some groups certainly had more power than others, but no group or class had too much. The New Deal and World War II had forever transformed the corporate-based power structure of earlier decades.

Mills challenged this celebration of pluralism by studying the social backgrounds and career paths of the people who occupied the highest positions in what he saw as the three major institutional hierarchies in postwar America—the corporations, the executive branch of the federal government, and the military. He found that almost all the members of this leadership group, which he called the power elite, were white Christian males who came from "at most, the upper third of the income and occupational pyramids," despite the many Horatio Algeresque claims to the contrary. . . .

The power elite depicted by C. Wright Mills was, without doubt, an exclusively male preserve. On the opening page of *The Power Elite*—a book with no preface, no introduction, no acknowledgments, just a direct plunge into the opening chapter—Mills stated clearly that "the power elite is composed of men whose positions enable them to transcend the ordinary environments of ordinary men and women." Although there were some women in the corporate, political, and military worlds, very few were in or near the higher circles that constituted the power elite. Are they there now? If so, how substantial and how visible is their presence? When did they arrive, and how did they get there? What are their future prospects? . . .

In 1990, Elizabeth Dole, then secretary of labor, initiated a department-level investigation into the question of whether or not there was a "glass ceiling" blocking women and minorities from the highest ranks of U.S. corporations. When the report was issued by the Federal Glass Ceiling Commission in 1995, comments by the white male managers who had been interviewed and surveyed supported the earlier claims that upper management was willing to accept women and minorities only if they were not too different. As one manager explained, "What's important is comfort, chemistry, relationships, and collaborations. That's what makes a shop work. When we find minorities and women who think like we do, we snatch them up."

Terry Miyamoto, an Asian-American labor relations executive at U.S. West, Inc., a telecommunications company that ranked number 62 on the Fortune 500 list in 1995, uses the term "comfort zone" to make the same point about "chemistry" and reducing "uncertainty": "You need to build relationships," she said, "and you need to be pretty savvy. And for a woman or a person of color at this company, you have to put in more effort to get into this comfort zone."

Much has been made of the fact that men have traditionally been socialized to play competitive team sports and women have not. In *The Managerial Woman*, Margaret Hennig and Anne Jardim argue that the experience of having participated in competitive team sports has provided men with many advantages in the corporate world. Playing on sports teams teaches boys such things as how to develop their individual skills in the context of helping the team to win, how to develop cooperative goal-oriented relationships with teammates, how to focus on winning, and how to deal with losing. "The experience of most little girls," they wrote, "has no parallel." Although the opportunities for young women to participate in competitive sports have increased dramatically in recent years, including team sports like basketball and soccer, few such opportunities were available when most women now in higher management in U.S. corporations were young.

Just as football is often identified as the classic competitive and aggressive team sport that prepares men for the rough and tumble (and hierarchical) world of the corporation, an individual sport—golf—is the more convivial but still competitive game that allows boys to play together, shoot the breeze, and do business. As Marcia Chambers shows in *The Unplayable Lie*, the golf course, and especially the country club, can be as segregated by sex as the football field. Few clubs bar women, but some clubs do not allow women to vote, sit on their governing boards, or play golf on weekend mornings.

Many women managers are convinced that their careers suffer because of discrimination against them by golf clubs. In a study of executives who manage "corporate-government affairs," Denise Benoit Scott found that the women in such positions "share meals with staff members and other government relations officials but never play golf." In contrast, men in such positions "play golf with a broad range of people in business and government, including legislators and top corporate executives." As one of the women she interviewed put it: "I wish I played golf. I think golf is the key. If you want to make it, you have to play golf."

Similarly, when the editors of *Executive Female* magazine surveyed the top fifty women in line-management positions (in sales, marketing, production, and general management with a direct impact on the company's bottom line), they asked them why more women had not made it to the "upper reaches of corporate America." The most frequently identified problem was the "comfort factor"—that the men atop their corporations wanted others around them with whom they were comfortable, and that generally meant other men similar to themselves. One of the other most frequently identified problems, not unrelated to the comfort factor, was the exclusion from "the social networks—the clubs, the golf course— where the informal networking that is so important to moving up the ladder often takes place."

Based on the interviews they conducted for *Members of the Club*, Dawn-Marie Driscoll and Carol Goldberg also conclude that there is an important connection between golf and business. Both Driscoll and

Goldberg have held directorships on major corporate boards. They establish their insider status at the beginning of their book: "We are both insiders. We always have been and probably always will be." In a section entitled "The Link That Counts," they explain how they came to realize the importance of golf: "We heard so many stories about golf that we began to pay more attention to the interaction between golf and business. We realized the importance of golf had been right in front of our eyes all the time, but because neither of us played golf, we had missed it as an issue for executive women. But golf is central to many business circles."

A few months before Bill Clinton was elected president, his future secretary of energy had some pertinent comments about the importance of fitting into corporate culture and the relevance of playing golf. "Without losing your own personality," said Hazel O'Leary, then an executive vice president at Northern States Power in Minnesota, "it's important to be part of the prevailing corporate culture. At this company, it's golf. I've resisted learning to play golf all my life, but I finally had to admit I was missing something that way." She took up golf.

There is evidence that the golf anxiety expressed by women executives has its counterpart in the attitudes held by male executives: in its 1995 report, the Federal Glass Ceiling Commission found that many white male executives "fretted" that minorities and women did not know how to play golf.

Whether or not playing golf is necessary to fit in, it is clear that women who make it into the corporate elite must assimilate sufficiently into the predominantly male culture to make it into the comfort zone. . . .

. . . [W]e told of Midshipman Leonard Kaplan's being "sent to Coventry"—which meant that no one spoke to him during his entire four years at the Naval Academy. Benjamin O. Davis Jr., the first black to graduate from the U.S. Military Academy in the twentieth century, had a parallel experience during his four years at that institution. After he had been at West Point for a short time, there was a knock on his door announcing a meeting in the basement in ten minutes. Davis painfully recalls that meeting and its long-term effects in the autobiography he wrote almost sixty years later:

As I approached the assembly where the meeting was in progress, I heard someone ask, "What are we going to do about the nigger?" I realized then that the meeting was about me, and I was not supposed to attend. I turned on my heel and double-timed back to my room.

From that meeting on, the cadets who roomed across the hall, who had been friendly earlier, no longer spoke to me. In fact, no one spoke to me except in the line of duty. Apparently, certain upperclass cadets had determined that I was getting along too well at the Academy to suit them, and they were going to enforce an old West Point tradition—"silencing"—with the object of making my life so unhappy that I would resign. Silencing had been applied in the past to certain cadets who were considered to have violated the honor code and refused to resign. In my case there was no question of such a violation; I was to be silenced solely because cadets did not want blacks at West Point. Their only purpose was to freeze me out.

Except for the recognition ceremony at the end of plebe year, I was silenced for the entire four years of my stay at the Academy.

Davis stuck it out at West Point and graduated near the top of his class. Even after graduation in 1936, his classmates (among them William Westmoreland, from a wealthy textile family in South Carolina) continued their silent treatment of him for years. In fact, for the next fifteen years, as his assignments took him to different locations in the United States and around the world, not only did his classmates continue to give him the silent treatment, but they and their wives also shunned Davis's wife. . . .

Still, a retired black general has become one of the best-known and most admired Americans. It was a major breakthrough in 1989 when Colin Powell was named chairman of the Joint Chiefs of Staff. And, indeed, Powell's ascendance to the top of the military hierarchy has had as much impact for civilians as for soldiers. According to Moskos and Butler, "the elevation of Colin Luther Powell to the chairmanship of the Joint Chiefs of Staff in 1989 was an epic event in American race relations, whose significance has yet to be fully realized."

Powell's parents were both Jamaican immigrants, a fact he makes much of. . . . While a student at the City College of New York, Powell joined ROTC, and when he graduated in 1958, he was commissioned as a second lieutenant. Powell has emphasized that he "found himself" in ROTC: "Suddenly everything clicked. . . . I had found something I was good at. . . . For the first time, in the military I always knew exactly what was expected of me." Equally important, the military had become a place where blacks could do well. "I had an intuitive sense that this was a career which was beginning to open up for blacks," says Powell. "You could not name, in those days, another profession where black men routinely told white men what to do and how to do it."

Powell rose through the ranks. He served as a junior officer in Vietnam, then held a series of command and staff jobs. In 1972 he became a White House Fellow; noting that race worked to his advantage in this appointment, he said to a friend, "I was lucky to be born black." Four years later, Jimmy Carter appointed Clifford Alexander as secretary of the army, and the number of black generals tripled while Alexander held that position. "My method was simple," Alexander revealed. "I just told everyone that I would not sign the goddam promotion list unless it was fair." In 1979, at the age of forty-two, Colin Powell achieved the rank of general. By 1987 he had become national security adviser under Reagan, and in 1989, under Bush, he became the first black—and the youngest man ever—to be chairman of the Joint Chiefs of Staff. After the Gulf War, polls consistently indicated that Powell was among the most admired people in America. . . .

The power elite has been strengthened because diversity has been achieved primarily by the selection of women and minorities who share the prevailing perspectives and values of those already in power. The power elite is not "multicultural" in any full sense of the concept, but only in terms of ethnic or racial origins. This process has been helped along by those who have called for the inclusion of women and minorities without any consideration of criteria other than sex, race, or ethnicity. Because the demand was strictly for a woman on the Supreme Court, President Reagan could comply by choosing a conservative upper-class corporate lawyer, Sandra Day O'Connor. When pressure mounted to have more black justices, President Bush could respond by appointing Clarence Thomas, a conservative black Republican with a law degree from Yale University. It is yet another irony that appointments like these served to undercut the liberal social movements that caused them to happen.

It is not surprising, therefore, that when we look at the business practices of the women and minorities who have risen to the top of the corporate world, we find that their perspectives and values do not differ markedly from those of their white male counterparts. When Linda Wachner, one of the few women to become CEO of a *Fortune*-level company, the Warnaco Group, concluded that one of Warnaco's many holdings, the Hathaway Shirt Company, was unprofitable, she decided to stop making Hathaway shirts and to sell or close down the factory. It did not matter to Wachner that Hathaway, which started making shirts in 1837, was one of the oldest companies in Maine, that almost all of the five hundred employees at the factory were working-class women, or even that the workers had given up a pay raise to hire consultants to teach them to work more effectively and, as a result, had doubled their productivity. The bottom-line issue was that the company was considered unprofitable, and the average wage of the Hathaway workers, $7.50 an hour, was thought to be too high. (In 1995 Wachner was paid $10 million in salary and stock, and Warnaco had a net income of $46.5 million.) "We did need to do the right thing for the company and the stockholders," explained Wachner.

Nor did ethnic background matter to Thomas Fuentes, a senior vice president at a consulting firm in Orange County, California, a director of Fleetwood Enterprises, and chairman of the Orange County Republican Party. Fuentes targeted fellow Latinos who happened to be Democrats when he sent uniformed security guards to twenty polling places in 1988 "carrying signs in Spanish and English warning people not to vote if they were not U.S. citizens." The security firm ended up paying $60,000 in damages when it lost a lawsuit stemming from this intimidation.

We also recall that the Fanjuls, the Cuban-American sugar barons, have had no problem ignoring labor laws in dealing with their migrant labor force, and that the Sakioka family illegally gave short-handled hoes to its migrant farm workers. These people were acting as employers, not as members of ethnic groups. That is, members of the power elite of both genders and all ethnicities have practiced class politics, making it possible for the power structure to weather the challenge created by the social movements that began in the 1960s.

Those who challenged Christian white male homogeneity in the power structure during the 1960s not only sought to create civil rights and new job opportunities for men and women who had previously been mistreated, important though these goals were. They also hoped that new perspectives in the boardrooms and the halls of government would bring greater openness throughout the society. The idea was both to diversify the power elite and to shift some of its power to previously excluded groups and social classes. The social movements of the 1960s were strikingly successful in increasing the individual rights and freedoms available to all Americans, especially African Americans. As we have shown, they also created pressures that led to openings at the top for individuals from groups that had previously been excluded.

But as the concerns of social movements, political leaders, and the courts came to focus more and more on individual rights, the emphasis on social class and "distributive justice" was lost. The age-old American commitment to individualism, reinforced at every turn by members of the power elite, won out over the commitment to greater equality of income and wealth that had been one strand of New Deal liberalism and a major emphasis of left-wing activists in the 1960s.

We therefore have to conclude on the basis of our findings that the diversification of the power elite did not generate any changes in an underlying class system in which the top 1 percent have 45.6 percent of all financial wealth, the next 19 percent have 46.7 percent, and the bottom 80 percent have 7.8 percent. The values of liberal individualism embedded in the Declaration of Independence, the Bill of Rights, and the civic culture were renewed by vigorous and courageous activists, but despite their efforts the class structure remains a major obstacle to individual fulfillment for the overwhelming majority of Americans. This fact is more than an irony. It is a dilemma. It combines with the dilemma of race to create a nation that celebrates equal opportunity but is, in reality, a bastion of class privilege and conservatism.

14

ROBERT DAHL

From *Who Governs?* and from *A Preface to Democratic Theory*

In any city in the United States—like New Haven, Connecticut—as in the entire nation, political power is no longer in the hands of a few people as it once was early in American history. Nor is power spread evenly among all citizens. Influential political theorist Robert Dahl presents here the classic statement of pluralism: the dispersion of power among many groups of people. Dahl differentiates the "political stratum," made up of interested and involved citizens, from the "apolitical stratum," those who do not take an active part in government. These two segments of society are vastly different in their degree of involvement, yet they are closely tied together in many ways in a pluralist system. At least in theory, anyone can enter the political stratum where numerous interest groups compete and bargain for their goals. Public policy is made by "the steady appeasement of relatively small groups." Because of this "strange hybrid," Dahl contends, pluralism is the best way to describe how power is distributed in America.

IN A POLITICAL SYSTEM where nearly every adult may vote but where knowledge, wealth, social position, access to officials, and other resources are unequally distributed, who actually governs?

The question has been asked, I imagine, wherever popular government has developed and intelligent citizens have reached the stage of critical self-consciousness concerning their society. It must have been put many times in Athens even before it was posed by Plato and Aristotle.

The question is peculiarly relevant to the United States and to Americans. In the first place, Americans espouse democratic beliefs with a fervency and a unanimity that have been a regular source of astonishment to foreign observers . . . [such as] Tocqueville and Bryce. . . .

In the course of the past two centuries, New Haven has gradually changed from oligarchy to pluralism. Accompanying and probably causing this change—one might properly call it a revolution—appears to be a profound alteration in the way political resources are distributed among the citizens of New Haven. This silent socioeconomic revolution has not substituted equality for inequality so much as it has involved a shift from cumulative inequalities in political resources—to use an expression introduced a moment ago—to noncumulative or dispersed inequalities. This point will grow clearer as we proceed. . . .

In the political system of the patrician oligarchy, political resources were marked by a cumulative inequality: when one individual was much better off than another in one resource, such as wealth, he was usually better off in almost every other resource—social standing, legitimacy, control over religious and educational institutions, knowledge, office. In the political system of today, inequalities in political resources remain, but they tend to be *noncumulative*. The political system of New Haven, then, is one of *dispersed inequalities*. . . .

Within a century a political system dominated by one cohesive set of leaders had given way to a system dominated by many different sets of leaders, each having access to a different combination of political resources. It was, in short, a pluralist system. If the pluralist system was very far from being an oligarchy, it was also a long way from achieving the goal of political equality advocated by the philosophers of democracy and incorporated into the creed of democracy and equality practically every American professes to uphold.

An elite no longer rules New Haven. But in the strict democratic sense, the disappearance of elite rule has not led to the emergence of rule by the people. Who, then, rules in a pluralist democracy? . . .

One of the difficulties that confronts anyone who attempts to answer the question, "Who rules in a pluralist democracy?" is the ambiguous relationship of leaders to citizens.

Viewed from one position, leaders are enormously influential— so influential that if they are seen only in this perspective they might well be considered a kind of ruling elite. Viewed from another position, however, many influential leaders seem to be captives of their constituents. Like the blind men with the elephant, different analysts have meticulously examined different aspects of the body politic and arrived at radically different conclusions. To some, a pluralistic democracy with dispersed inequalities is all head and no body; to others it is all body and no head. . . .

Two additional factors help to account for this obscurity. First, among all the persons who influence a decision, some do so more directly than others in the sense that they are closer to the stage where concrete alternatives are initiated or vetoed in an explicit and immediate way. Indirect influence might be very great but comparatively difficult to observe and weigh. Yet to ignore indirect influence in analysis of the distribution of influence would be to exclude what might well prove to be a highly significant process of control in a pluralistic democracy.

Second, the relationship between leaders and citizens in a pluralistic democracy is frequently reciprocal: leaders influence the decisions of constituents, but the decisions of leaders are also determined in part by what they think are, will be, or have been the preferences of their constituents. Ordinarily it is much easier to observe and describe the distribution of influence in a political system where the flow of influence is strongly in one direction (an asymmetrical or unilateral system, as it is sometimes called) than in a system marked by strong reciprocal relations. In a political system with competitive elections, such as New Haven's, it is not unreasonable to expect that relationships between leaders and constituents would normally be reciprocal. . . .

In New Haven, as in other political systems, a small stratum of individuals is much more highly involved in political thought, discussion, and action than the rest of the population. These citizens constitute the political stratum.

Members of this stratum live in a political subculture that is partly but not wholly shared by the great majority of citizens. Just as artists and intellectuals are the principal bearers of the artistic, literary, and scientific skills of a society, so the members of the political stratum are the main bearers of political skills. If intellectuals were to vanish overnight, a society would be reduced to artistic, literary, and scientific poverty. If the political stratum were destroyed, the previous political institutions of the society would temporarily stop functioning. In both cases, the speed with which the loss could be overcome would depend on the extent to which the elementary knowledge and basic attitudes of the elite had been diffused. In an open society with widespread education and training in civic attitudes, many citizens hitherto in the apolitical strata could doubtless step into roles that had been filled by members of the political stratum. However, sharp discontinuities and important changes in the operation of the political system almost certainly would occur.

In New Haven, as in the United States, and indeed perhaps in all pluralistic democracies, differences in the subcultures of the political and the apolitical strata are marked, particularly at the extremes. In the political stratum, politics is highly salient; among the apolitical strata, it is remote. In the political stratum, individuals tend to be rather calculating in their choice of strategies; members of the political stratum are, in a sense, relatively rational political beings. In the apolitical strata, people are notably less calculating; their political choices are more strongly influenced by inertia, habit, unexamined loyalties, personal attachments, emotions, transient impulses. In the political stratum, an individual's political beliefs tend to fall into patterns that have a relatively high degree of coherence and internal consistency; in the apolitical strata, political orientations are disorganized, disconnected, and unideological. In the political stratum, information about politics and the issues of the day is extensive; the apolitical strata are poorly informed. Individuals in the political stratum tend to participate rather actively in politics; in the apolitical strata citizens rarely go beyond voting and many do not even vote. Individuals in the political stratum exert a good deal of steady, direct, and active influence on government policy; in fact some individuals have a quite extraordinary amount of influence. Individuals in the apolitical strata, on the other hand, have much less direct or active influence on policies.

Communication within the political stratum tends to be rapid and extensive. Members of the stratum read many of the same newspapers and magazines; in New Haven, for example, they are likely to read the *New York Times* or the *Herald Tribune*, and *Time* or *Newsweek*. Much information also passes by word of mouth. The political strata of different communities and regions are linked in a national network of communications. Even in small towns, one or two members of the local political stratum usually are in touch with members of a state organization, and certain members of the political stratum of a state or any large city maintain relations with members of organizations in other states and cities, or with national figures. Moreover, many channels of communication not designed specifically for political purposes — trade associations, professional associations, and labor organizations, for example — serve as a part of the network of the political stratum.

In many pluralistic systems, however, the political stratum is far from being a closed or static group. In the United States the political stratum does not constitute a homogeneous class with well-defined class interests. In New Haven, in fact, the political stratum is easily penetrated by anyone whose interests and concerns attract him to the distinctive political culture of the stratum. It is easily penetrated because (among other reasons) elections and competitive parties give politicians a powerful motive for expanding their coalitions and increasing their electoral followings.

In an open pluralistic system, where movement into the political stratum is easy, the stratum embodies many of the most widely shared values and goals in the society. If popular values are strongly pragmatic, then the political stratum is likely to be pragmatic; if popular values prescribe reverence toward the past, then the political stratum probably shares that reverence; if popular values are oriented toward material gain and personal advancement, then the political stratum probably reflects these values; if popular values are particularly favorable to political, social, or economic equality, then the political stratum is likely to emphasize equality. The apolitical strata can be said to "govern" as much through the sharing of common values and goals with members of the political stratum as by other means. However, if it were not for elections and competitive parties, this sharing would—other things remaining the same—rapidly decline.

Not only is the political stratum in New Haven not a closed group, but its "members" are far from united in their orientations and strategies. There are many lines of cleavage. . . .

Because of the ease with which the political stratum can be penetrated, whenever dissatisfaction builds up in some segment of the electorate party politicians will probably learn of the discontent and calculate whether it might be converted into a political issue with an electoral payoff. If a party politician sees no payoff, his interest is likely to be small; if he foresees an adverse effect, he will avoid the issue if he can. As a result, there is usually some conflict in the political stratum between intellectuals, experts, and others who formulate issues, and the party politicians themselves, for the first group often demands attention to issues in which the politicians see no profit and possibly even electoral damage.

The independence, penetrability, and heterogeneity of the various segments of the political stratum all but guarantee that any dissatisfied group will find spokesmen in the political stratum, but to have a spokesman does not insure that the group's problems will be solved by political action. Politicians may not see how they can gain by taking a position on an issue; action by government may seem to be wholly inappropriate; policies intended to cope with dissatisfaction may be blocked; solutions may be improperly designed; indeed, politicians may even find it politically profitable to maintain a shaky coalition by keeping tension and discontent alive and deflecting attention to irrelevant "solutions" or alternative issues. . . .

. . . In devising strategies for building coalitions and allocating rewards, one must take into account a large number of different categories of citizens. It would be dangerous to formulate strategies on the assumption that most or all citizens can be divided into two or three categories, for a successful political coalition necessarily rests upon a multiplicity of groups and categories. . . .*

. . . I defined the "normal" American political process as one in which there is a high probability that an active and legitimate group in the population can make itself heard effectively at some crucial stage in the process of decision. To be "heard" covers a wide range of activities, and I do not intend to define the word rigorously. Clearly, it does not mean that every group has equal control over the outcome.

In American politics, as in all other societies, control over decisions is unevenly distributed; neither individuals nor groups are political equals. When I say that a group is heard "effectively" I mean more than the simple fact that it makes a noise; I mean that one or more officials are not only ready to listen to the noise, but expect to suffer in some significant way if they do not placate the group, its leaders, or its most vociferous members. To satisfy the group may require one or more of a great variety of actions by the responsive leader: pressure for substantive policies, appointments, graft, respect, expression of the appropriate emotions, or the right combination of reciprocal noises.

Thus the making of governmental decisions is not a majestic march of great majorities united upon certain matters of basic policy. It is the steady appeasement of relatively small groups. . . .

To be sure, reformers with a tidy sense of order dislike it. Foreign observers, even sympathetic ones, are often astonished and confounded by it. Many Americans are frequently dismayed by its paradoxes; indeed, few Americans who look upon our political process attentively can fail, at times, to feel deep frustration and angry resentment with a system that on the surface has so little order and so much chaos.

For it is a markedly decentralized system. Decisions are made by endless bargaining; perhaps in no other national political system in the world is bargaining so basic a component of the political process. In an age when the efficiencies of hierarchy have been re-emphasized on every continent, no doubt the normal American political system is something of an anomaly, if not, indeed, at times an anachronism. For as a means

*At this point, the excerpt from *Who Governs?* ends, and *A Preface to Democratic Theory* begins. —EDS.

to highly integrated, consistent decisions in some important areas — foreign policy, for example — it often appears to operate in a creaking fashion verging on total collapse.

Yet we should not be too quick in our appraisal, for where its vices stand out, its virtues are concealed to the hasty eye. Luckily the normal system has the virtues of its vices. With all its defects, it does nonetheless provide a high probability that any active and legitimate group will make itself heard effectively at some stage in the process of decision. This is no mean thing in a political system.

It is not a static system. The normal American system has evolved, and by evolving it has survived. It has evolved and survived from aristocracy to mass democracy, through slavery, civil war, the tentative uneasy reconciliation of North and South, the repression of Negroes and their halting liberation; through two great wars of worldwide scope, mobilization, far-flung military enterprise, and return to hazardous peace; through numerous periods of economic instability and one prolonged depression with mass unemployment, farm "holidays," veterans' marches, tear gas, and even bullets; through two periods of postwar cynicism, demagogic excesses, invasions of traditional liberties, and the groping, awkward, often savage, attempt to cope with problems of subversion, fear, and civil tension.

Probably this strange hybrid, the normal American political system, is not for export to others. But so long as the social prerequisites of democracy are substantially intact in this country, it appears to be a relatively efficient system for reinforcing agreement, encouraging moderation, and maintaining social peace in a restless and immoderate people operating a gigantic, powerful, diversified, and incredibly complex society.

This is no negligible contribution, then, that Americans have made to the arts of government — and to that branch, which of all the arts of politics is the most difficult, the art of democratic government.

PART THREE

Separation of Powers

15

JAMES MADISON

The Federalist 51

In Federalist 10, an earlier selection, one of the Constitution's designers, James Madison, explained his fear of "faction"—any single group that tries to dominate the political process—and why faction cannot be removed from politics. Madison's solution was to accept factions, but control them. Federalist 10 offered a republican (representative) government and a large, diverse nation with many factions as effective controls. In No. 51 he continues, citing the structural features that characterize American government. Power will be separated among different departments, or branches, of government, independent from one another. Then, power will be divided between the national and state levels, a system called federalism. Madison's philosophy for government is here in this essay too: "Ambition must be made to counteract ambition." Don't miss that paragraph, since it contains warnings that resonate across the centuries.

———

No. 51: Madison

TO WHAT EXPEDIENT, then, shall we finally resort, for maintaining in practice the necessary partition of power among the several departments as laid down in the Constitution? The only answer that can be given is that as all these exterior provisions are found to be inadequate the defect must be supplied, by so contriving the interior structure of the government as that its several constituent parts may, by their mutual relations, be the means of keeping each other in their proper places. Without presuming to undertake a full development of this important idea I will hazard a few general observations which may perhaps place it in a clearer light, and enable us to form a more correct judgment of the principles and structure of the government planned by the convention.

In order to lay a due foundation for that separate and distinct exercise of the different powers of government, which to a certain extent is admitted on all hands to be essential to the preservation of liberty, it is evident that each department should have a will of its own; and consequently should be so constituted that the members of each should have as little agency as possible in the appointment of the members of the others. Were this principle rigorously adhered to, it would require that all the appointments for the supreme executive, legislative, and judiciary magistracies should be drawn from the same fountain of authority, the people, through channels having no communication whatever with one another. Perhaps such a plan of constructing the several departments would be less difficult in practice than it may in contemplation appear. Some difficulties, however, and some additional expense would attend the execution of it. Some deviations, therefore, from the principle must be admitted. In the constitution of the judiciary department in particular, it might be inexpedient to insist rigorously on the principle: first, because peculiar qualifications being essential in the members, the primary consideration ought to be to select that mode of choice which best secures these qualifications; second, because the permanent tenure by which the appointments are held in that department must soon destroy all sense of dependence on the authority conferring them.

It is equally evident that the members of each department should be as little dependent as possible on those of the others for the emoluments annexed to their offices. Were the executive magistrate, or the judges, not independent of the legislature in this particular, their independence in every other would be merely nominal.

But the great security against a gradual concentration of the several powers in the same department consists in giving to those who administer each department the necessary constitutional means and personal motives to resist encroachments of the others. The provision for defense must in this, as in all other cases, be made commensurate to the danger of attack. Ambition must be made to counteract ambition. The interest of the man must be connected with the constitutional rights of the place. It may be a reflection on human nature that such devices should be necessary to control the abuses of government. But what is government itself but the greatest of all reflections on human nature? If men were angels, no government would be necessary. If angels were to govern men, neither external nor internal controls on government would be necessary. In framing a government which is to be administered by men over men, the great difficulty lies in this: you must first enable the government to control the governed; and in the next place oblige it to control itself. A dependence on the people is, no doubt, the primary control on the government; but experience has taught mankind the necessity of auxiliary precautions.

This policy of supplying, by opposite and rival interests, the defect of better motives, might be traced through the whole system of human affairs, private as well as public. We see it particularly displayed in all the subordinate distributions of power, where the constant aim is to divide and arrange the several offices in such a manner as that each may be a check on the other—that the private interest of every individual may be a sentinel over the public rights. These inventions of prudence cannot be less requisite in the distribution of the supreme powers of the State.

But it is not possible to give to each department an equal power of self-defense. In republican government, the legislative authority necessarily predominates. The remedy for this inconveniency is to divide the legislature into different branches; and to render them, by different modes of election and different principles of action, as little connected with each other as the nature of their common functions and their common dependence on the society will admit. It may even be necessary to guard against dangerous encroachments by still further precautions. As the weight of the legislative authority requires that it should be thus divided, the weakness of the executive may require, on the other hand, that it should be fortified. An absolute negative on the legislature appears, at first view, to be the natural defense with which the executive magistrate should be armed. But perhaps it would be neither altogether safe nor alone sufficient. On ordinary occasions it might not be exerted with the requisite firmness, and on extraordinary occasions it might be perfidiously abused. May not this defect of an absolute negative be supplied by some qualified connection between this weaker department and the weaker branch of the stronger department, by which the latter may be led to support the constitutional rights of the former, without being too much detached from the rights of its own department?

If the principles on which these observations are founded be just, as I persuade myself they are, and they be applied as a criterion to the several State constitutions, and to the federal Constitution, it will be found that if the latter does not perfectly correspond with them, the former are infinitely less able to bear such a test.

There are, moreover, two considerations particularly applicable to the federal system of America, which place that system in a very interesting point of view.

First. In a single republic, all the power surrendered by the people is submitted to the administration of a single government; and the usurpations are guarded against by a division of the government into distinct and separate departments. In the compound republic of America, the power surrendered by the people is first divided between two distinct governments, and then the portion allotted to each subdivided among distinct and separate departments. Hence a double security arises to the rights of the people. The different governments will control each other, at the same time that each will be controlled by itself.

Second. It is of great importance in a republic not only to guard the society against the oppression of its rulers, but to guard one part of the society against the injustice of the other part. Different interests necessarily exist in different classes of citizens. If a majority be united by a common interest, the rights of the minority will be insecure. There are but two methods of providing against this evil: the one by creating a will in the community independent of the majority—that is, of the society itself; the other, by comprehending in the society so many separate descriptions of citizens as will render an unjust combination of a majority of the whole very improbable, if not impracticable. The first method prevails in all governments possessing an hereditary or self-appointed authority. This, at best, is but a precarious security; because a power independent of the society may as well espouse the unjust views of the major as the rightful interests of the minor party, and may possibly be turned against both parties. The second method will be exemplified in the federal republic of the United States. Whilst all authority in it will be derived from and dependent on the society, the society itself will be broken into so many parts, interests and classes of citizens, that the rights of individuals, or of the minority, will be in little danger from interested combinations of the majority. In a free government the security for civil rights must be the same as that for religious rights. It consists in the one case in the multiplicity of interests, and in the other in the multiplicity of sects. The degree of security in both cases will depend on the number of interests and sects; and this may be presumed to depend on the extent of country and number of people comprehended under the same government. This view of the subject must particularly recommend a proper federal system to all the sincere and considerate friends of republican government, since it shows that in exact proportion as the territory of the Union may be formed into more circumscribed Confederacies, or States, oppressive combinations of a majority will be facilitated; the best security, under the republican forms, for the rights of every class of citizen, will be diminished; and consequently the stability and independence of some member of the government, the only other security, must be proportionally increased. Justice is the end of government. It is the end of civil society. It ever has been and ever will be pursued until it be obtained, or until liberty be lost in the pursuit. In a society under the forms of which the stronger faction can readily unite and oppress the weaker, anarchy may as truly be said to reign as in a state of nature, where the weaker individual is not secured against the violence of the stronger; and as, in the latter state, even the stronger individuals are prompted, by the uncertainty of their condition, to submit to a government which may protect the weak as well as themselves; so, in the former state, will the more powerful factions or parties be gradually induced, by a like motive, to wish for a government which will protect all parties, the weaker as well as the more powerful. It can be little doubted that if the State of Rhode Island was separated from the Confederacy and left to itself, the insecurity of rights under the popular form of government within such narrow limits would be displayed by such reiterated oppressions of factious majorities that some power altogether independent of the people would soon be called for by the voice of the very factions whose misrule had proved the necessity of it. In the extended republic of the United States, and among the great variety of interests, parties, and sects which it embraces, a coalition of a majority of the whole society could seldom take place on any other principles than those of justice and the general good; whilst there being thus less danger to a minor from the will of a major party, there must be less pretext, also, to provide for the security of the former, by introducing into the government a will not dependent on the latter, or, in other words, a will independent of the society itself. It is no less certain than it is important, notwithstanding the contrary opinions which have been entertained, that the larger the society, provided it lie within a practicable sphere, the more duly capable it will be of self-government. And happily for the *republican cause*, the practicable sphere may be carried to a very great extent by a judicious modification and mixture of the *federal principle*.   *Publius*

16

WOODROW WILSON

From *Congressional Government*

Before becoming president of the United States, Woodrow Wilson was governor of New Jersey. Previously, he had been the president of Princeton University and, earlier still, a professor of political science. In his 1885 doctoral writings, Wilson criticizes the fragmentation of power and lack of clear accountability in the American structure of government. The dilution of the national government's authority by state governments excites Wilson's ire, too. He sympathizes with the president's position because of its weakness relative to Congress at the time. Wilson's strongest negative judgment is saved for congressional committees, which he considered major impediments to getting the nation's business accomplished efficiently. Wilson the political scientist makes a good case against the gridlock inherent in the framers' separation of powers design. One wonders whether the beleaguered President Wilson re-read his own scholarly treatise in 1919, at the end of World

War I, when Senator Henry Cabot Lodge led the Foreign Relations
Committee in blocking the passage of the Versailles Treaty based on Wilson's
Fourteen Points and containing his League of Nations.

————

I KNOW OF few things harder to state clearly and within reasonable compass than just how the nation keeps control of policy in spite of these hide-and-seek vagaries of authority. Indeed, it is doubtful if it does keep control through all the roundabout paths which legislative and executive responsibility are permitted to take. It must follow Congress somewhat blindly; Congress is known to obey without altogether understanding its Committees: and the Committees must consign the execution of their plans to officials who have opportunities not a few to hoodwink them. At the end of these blind processes is it probable that the ultimate authority, the people, is quite clear in its mind as to what has been done or what may be done another time? Take, for example, financial policy,—a very fair example, because, as I have shown, the legislative stages of financial policy are more talked about than any other congressional business, though for that reason an extreme example. If, after appropriations and adjustments of taxation have been tardily and in much tribulation of scheming and argument agreed upon by the House, the imperative suggestions and stubborn insistence of the Senate confuse matters till hardly the Conference Committees themselves know clearly what the outcome of the disagreements has been; and if, when these compromise measures are launched as laws, the method of their execution is beyond the view of the Houses, in the semi-privacy of the departments, how is the comprehension—not to speak of the will—of the people to keep any sort of hold upon the course of affairs? There are no screws of responsibility which they can turn upon the consciences or upon the official thumbs of the congressional Committees principally concerned. Congressional Committees are nothing to the nation; they are only pieces of the interior mechanism of Congress. To Congress they stand or fall. And, since Congress itself can scarcely be sure of having its own way with them, the constituencies are manifestly unlikely to be able to govern them. As for the departments, the people can hardly do more in drilling them to unquestioning obedience and docile efficiency than Congress can. Congress is, and must be, in these matters the nation's eyes and voice. If it cannot see what goes wrong and cannot get itself heeded when it commands, the nation likewise is both blind and dumb.

This, plainly put, is the practical result of the piecing of authority, the cutting of it up into small bits, which is contrived in our constitutional system. Each branch of the government is fitted out with a small section of responsibility, whose limited opportunities afford to the conscience of each many easy escapes. Every suspected culprit may shift the responsibility upon his fellows. Is Congress rated for corrupt or imperfect or foolish legislation? It may urge that it has to follow hastily its Committees or do nothing at all but talk; how can it help it if a stupid Committee leads it unawares into unjust or fatuous enterprises? Does administration blunder and run itself into all sorts of straits? The Secretaries hasten to plead the unreasonable or unwise commands of Congress, and Congress falls to blaming the Secretaries. The Secretaries aver that the whole mischief might have been avoided if they had only been allowed to suggest the proper measures; and the men who framed the existing measures in their turn avow their despair of good government so long as they must intrust all their plans to the bungling incompetence of men who are appointed by and responsible to somebody else. How is the schoolmaster, the nation, to know which boy needs the whipping?

Moreover, it is impossible to deny that this division of authority and concealment of responsibility are calculated to subject the government to a very distressing paralysis in moments of emergency. There are few, if any, important steps that can be taken by any one branch of the government without the consent or cooperation of some other branch. Congress must act through the President and his Cabinet; the President and his Cabinet must wait upon the will of Congress. There is no one supreme, ultimate head—whether magistrate or representative body—which can decide at once and with conclusive authority what shall be done at those times when some decision there must be, and that immediately. Of course this lack is of a sort to be felt at all times, in seasons of tranquil rounds of business as well as at moments of sharp crisis; but in times of sudden exigency it might prove fatal,—fatal either in breaking down the system or in failing to meet the emergency. Policy cannot be either prompt or straightforward when it must serve many masters. It must either equivocate, or hesitate, or fail altogether. It may set out with clear purpose from Congress, but get waylaid or maimed by the Executive.

If there be one principle clearer than another, it is this: that in any business, whether of government or of mere merchandising, *somebody must be trusted*, in order that when things go wrong it may be quite plain who should be punished. In order to drive trade at the speed and with the success you desire, you must confide without suspicion in your chief clerk, giving him the power to ruin you, because you thereby furnish him with a motive for serving you. His reputation, his own honor or disgrace, all his own commercial prospects, hang upon your success. And human nature is much the same in government as in the dry-goods trade. *Power and strict accountability for its use* are the essential constituents of good government. A sense of highest responsibility, a dignifying and elevating sense of being trusted, together with a consciousness of being in an official station so conspicuous that no faithful discharge of duty can go unacknowledged and unrewarded, and no breach of trust undiscovered and unpunished, — these are the influences, the only influences, which foster practical, energetic, and trustworthy statesmanship. The best rulers are always those to whom great power is entrusted in such a manner as to make them feel that they will surely be abundantly honored and recompensed for a just and patriotic use of it, and to make them know that nothing can shield them from full retribution for every abuse of it.

It is, therefore, manifestly a radical defect in our federal system that it parcels out power and confuses responsibility as it does. The main purpose of the Convention of 1787 seems to have been to accomplish this grievous mistake. The "literary theory" of checks and balances is simply a consistent account of what our constitution-makers tried to do; and those checks and balances have proved mischievous just to the extent to which they have succeeded in establishing themselves as realities. It is quite safe to say that were it possible to call together again the members of that wonderful Convention to view the work of their hands in the light of the century that has tested it, they would be the first to admit that the only fruit of dividing power had been to make it irresponsible. . . .

It was something more than natural that the Convention of 1787 should desire to erect a Congress which would not be subservient and an executive which could not be despotic. And it was equally to have been expected that they should regard an absolute separation of these two great branches of the system as the only effectual means for the accomplishment of that much desired end. It was impossible that they could believe that executive and legislature could be brought into close relations of cooperation and mutual confidence without being tempted, nay, even bidden, to collude. How could either maintain its independence of action unless each were to have the guaranty of the Constitution that its own domain should be absolutely safe from invasion, its own prerogatives absolutely free from challenge? "They shrank from placing sovereign power anywhere. They feared that it would generate tyranny; George III had been a tyrant to them, and come what might they would not make a George III." They would conquer, by dividing, the power they so much feared to see in any single hand. . . .

The natural, the inevitable tendency of every system of self-government like our own and the British is to exalt the representative body, the people's parliament, to a position of absolute supremacy. . . . Our Constitution, like every other constitution which puts the authority to make laws and the duty of controlling the public expenditure into the hands of a popular assembly, practically sets that assembly to rule the affairs of the nation as supreme overlord. But, by separating it entirely from its executive agencies, it deprives it of the opportunity and means for making its authority complete and convenient. The constitutional machinery is left of such a pattern that other forces less than that of Congress may cross and compete with Congress, though they are too small to overcome or long offset it; and the result is simply an unpleasant, wearing friction which, with other adjustments, more felicitous and equally safe, might readily be avoided. . . .

The dangers of this serious imperfection in our governmental machinery have not been clearly demonstrated in our experience hitherto; but now their delayed fulfillment seems to be close at hand. The plain tendency is towards a centralization of all the greater powers of government in the hands of the federal authorities, and towards the practical confirmation of those prerogatives of supreme overlordship which Congress has been gradually arrogating to itself. The central government is constantly becoming stronger and more active, and Congress is establishing itself as the one sovereign authority in that government. In constitutional theory and in the broader features of past practice, ours has been what Mr. Bagehot has called a "composite" government.* Besides state and federal authorities to dispute as to sovereignty, there have been within the federal system itself rival and irreconcilable powers. But gradually the strong are overcoming the weak. If the signs of the times are to be credited, we are fast approaching an adjustment of sovereignty quite as "simple" as need be. Congress is not only to retain the authority it already possesses, but is to be brought again and again face to face with still greater demands upon its energy, its wisdom, and its conscience, is to have ever-widening duties and responsibilities thrust upon it, without being granted a moment's opportunity to look back from the plough to which it has set its hands.

The sphere and influence of national administration and national legislation are widening rapidly. Our populations are growing at such a rate that one's reckoning staggers at counting the possible millions that may have a home and a work on this continent ere fifty more years shall

*Walter Bagehot (1826–1877), British economist, political theorist, and journalist, wrote *The English Constitution*, a book that had great influence on the young Woodrow Wilson. The idealized picture of the virtues of the British polity that informs *Congressional Government* is straight out of Bagehot.—EDS.

have filled their short span. The East will not always be the centre of national life. The South is fast accumulating wealth, and will faster recover influence. The West has already achieved a greatness which no man can gainsay, and has in store a power of future growth which no man can estimate. Whether these sections are to be harmonious or dissentient depends almost entirely upon the methods and policy of the federal government. If that government be not careful to keep within its own proper sphere and prudent to square its policy by rules of national welfare, sectional lines must and will be known; citizens of one part of the country may look with jealousy and even with hatred upon their fellow-citizens of another part; and faction must tear and dissension distract a country which Providence would bless, but which man may curse. The government of a country so vast and various must be strong, prompt, wieldy, and efficient. Its strength must consist in the certainty and uniformity of its purposes, in its accord with national sentiment, in its unhesitating action, and in its honest aims. It must be steadied and approved by open administration diligently obedient to the more permanent judgments of public opinion; and its only active agency, its representative chambers, must be equipped with something besides abundant powers of legislation.

As at present constituted, the federal government lacks strength because its powers are divided, lacks promptness because its authorities are multiplied, lacks wieldiness because its processes are roundabout, lacks efficiency because its responsibility is indistinct and its action without competent direction. It is a government in which every officer may talk about every other officer's duty without having to render strict account for not doing his own, and in which the masters are held in check and offered contradiction by the servants. Mr. Lowell has called it "government by declamation." Talk is not sobered by any necessity imposed upon those who utter it to suit their actions to their words. There is no day of reckoning for words spoken. The speakers of a congressional majority may, without risk of incurring ridicule or discredit, condemn what their own Committees are doing; and the spokesmen of a minority may urge what contrary courses they please with a well-grounded assurance that what they say will be forgotten before they can be called upon to put it into practice. Nobody stands sponsor for the policy of the government. A dozen men originate it; a dozen compromises twist and alter it; a dozen offices whose names are scarcely known outside of Washington put it into execution. . . .

An intelligent observer of our politics has declared that there is in the United States "a class, including thousands and tens of thousands of the best men in the country, who think it possible to enjoy the fruits of good government without working for them." Every one who has seen beyond the outside of our American life must recognize the truth of this; to explain it is to state the sum of all the most valid criticisms of congressional government. Public opinion has no easy vehicle for its judgments, no quick channels for its action. Nothing about the system is direct and simple. Authority is perplexingly subdivided and distributed, and responsibility has to be hunted down in out-of-the-way corners. So that the sum of the whole matter is that the means of working for the fruits of good government are not readily to be found. The average citizen may be excused for esteeming government at best but a haphazard affair, upon which his vote and all of his influence can have but little effect. How is his choice of a representative in Congress to affect the policy of the country as regards the questions in which he is most interested, if the man for whom he votes has no chance of getting on the Standing Committee which has virtual charge of those questions? How is it to make any difference who is chosen President? Has the President any very great authority in matters of vital policy? It seems almost a thing of despair to get any assurance that any vote he may cast will even in an infinitesimal degree affect the essential courses of administration. There are so many cooks mixing their ingredients in the national broth that it seems hopeless, this thing of changing one cook at a time.

The charm of our constitutional ideal has now been long enough wound up to enable sober men who do not believe in political witchcraft to judge what it has accomplished, and is likely still to accomplish, without further winding. The Constitution is not honored by blind worship. The more open-eyed we become, as a nation, to its defects, and the prompter we grow in applying with the unhesitating courage of conviction all thoroughly-tested or well-considered expedients necessary to make self-government among us a straightforward thing of simple method, single, unstinted power, and clear responsibility, the nearer will we approach to the sound sense and practical genius of the great and honorable statesmen of 1787. And the first step towards emancipation from the timidity and false pride which have led us to seek to thrive despite the defects of our national system rather than seem to deny its perfection is a fearless criticism of that system. When we shall have examined all its parts without sentiment, and gauged all its functions by the standards of practical common sense, we shall have established anew our right to the claim of political sagacity; and it will remain only to act intelligently upon what our opened eyes have seen in order to prove again the justice of our claim to political genius.

17

JAMES STERLING YOUNG

From *The Washington Community: 1800–1828*

Numerous books and articles have been written about the early years of American government, right after the Constitution was ratified. It seems that scholars have left nothing uncovered in their exploration of that crucial era. But historian James Young succeeds in finding a most unusual angle, one that has great significance for students of American government. He relates the physical living arrangements in early Washington to the separation of powers embodied in the Constitution. Young describes the swamp that delineated parts of the town. He recounts stories about the boardinghouses where legislators lived and sometimes argued vehemently. Young's depiction of House and Senate floor activity can certainly match today's C-SPAN for excitement. Early Washington, D.C., established a clear precedent for the future: many interests were represented, but cooperation was minimal. As Young observes, "Some government!"

DESOLATE IN SURROUNDING, derogatory in self-image, the governmental community was also distinctive for the extraordinary manner in which the personnel chose to situate themselves in Washington—the social formations into which they deployed on the terrain. The settlement pattern of a community is, in a sense, the signature that its social organization inscribes upon the landscape, defining the groups of major importance in the life of the community and suggesting the relationships among them. In the case of the early Washington community that signature is very clear.

The members did not, in their residential arrangements, disperse uniformly or at random over the wide tract of the intended city. Nor did they draw together at any single place. The governmental community rather inscribed itself upon the terrain as a series of distinct subcommunities, separated by a considerable distance, with stretches of empty land between them. Each was clustered around one of the widely separated public buildings; each was a self-contained social and economic entity. The personnel of the governmental community segregated themselves, in short, into distinct groups, and formed a society of "we's" and "they's." . . .

From data gathered in an 1801 survey, listing the location of houses completed and under construction in the capital, it is possible to reconstruct the settlement pattern of the early governmental community with reasonable accuracy. . . .

Members of the different branches of government chose to situate themselves close by the respective centers of power with which they were affiliated, seeking their primary associations in extra-official life among their fellow branch members.

Despite its relative civilization, old Georgetown attracted few members of government as residents, and most of those who stayed there moved as soon as they could find quarters in Washington, nearer to their places of work. . . .

At the opposite end of the city, about five miles from Georgetown, near the Capitol but separated from it by a dense swamp, was the village of the armed forces. . . .

. . . Commercialization failing, the environs became the site of the congressional burying ground, a poorhouse, and a penitentiary with an arsenal "near, much too near" it, thus associating by coresidence the men and matériel of war with the dead, the indigent, and the incorrigible. The settlement was generally shunned by civilian members of the government as a place to live, and high-ranking military and naval officers also forsook it eventually to take up residence in the executive sector.

The chief centers of activity were the village community of the executives and the village community of the legislators, lying "one mile and a half and seventeen perches" apart as the crow flies, on the "great heath" bisected by the River Tiber.

Senators and Representatives lived in the shadow of the Capitol itself, most of them in knots of dwellings but a moment's walk from their place of meeting. . . .

The knolltop settlement of legislators was a complete and self-contained village community from beginning to end of the Jeffersonian era. Neither work nor diversion, nor consumer needs, nor religious needs required them to set foot outside it. Eight boardinghouses, a tailor, a shoemaker, a washerwoman, a grocery store, and an oyster house served the congressional settlement in 1801. Within three years a notary, an ironmonger, a saddle maker, several more tailors and bootmakers, a liquor store, bookstores, stables, bakery, and taverns had been added. In twenty years' time the settlement had increased to more than two thousand people and the Capitol was nearly surrounded by brick houses "three stories high, and decent, without being in the least elegant," where the lawmakers lodged during the session. An itinerant barber served the community, shuttling between the scattered villages of the capital on horseback, and a nearby bathhouse catered to congressional clientele. Legislators with families could send their children to school on the Hill. The members had their own congressional library and their own post office, dispatching and receiving mail—which was distributed on the floor of the Senate and the House daily—without leaving the Hill. Page boys, doorkeepers, sergeants-at-arms, and other ancillary personnel for Congress were supplied from the permanent population of Capitol Hill—mainly the boardinghouse proprietors and their families. . . . The settlement pattern of early Washington clearly reveals a community structure paralleling the constitutional structure of government itself. The "separation of powers" became a separation of persons, and each of the branches of government became a self-contained, segregated social system within the larger governmental establishment. Legislators with legislators, executives with executives, judges with judges, the members gathered together in their extraofficial as well as in their official activities, and in their community associations deepened, rather than bridged, the group cleavages prescribed by the Constitution.

Why did the rulers make this highly contrived, unconventional legal structure into their community structure at Washington? . . . A key factor contributing to social segregation by branch affiliation is suggested by the consistency between such behavior and community attitudes about power and politicians. In the absence of any extrinsic forces compelling the rulers to segregate in community life, patterned avoidance between executives, legislators, and judges indicates that they felt a stronger sense of identification with their constitutional roles than with other more partisan roles they may have had in the community. Social segregation on the basis of branch affiliation suggests, in other words, that the rulers generally considered themselves executives, legislators, or judges first, and politicians or party members second. Such a preference for nonpartisan, constitutionally sanctioned roles fully accords with, and tends to confirm the authenticity of, the members' disparaging image of politicians. Their decided preference for associating with fellow branch members in extraofficial life is also precisely the sort of social behavior that was foreshadowed by the attitudes they held concerning power. Power-holders acculturated to antipower values would, it was predicted, be attracted toward behaviors and associations which were sanctioned by the Constitution. By subdividing into separate societies of executives, legislators, and judges, the rulers could not have more literally translated constitutional principles of organization into social realities nor afforded themselves greater security from reproach in this aspect of their community life at Washington. When one sees, moreover, the remarkable consistency between the organizational precepts of the Constitution of 1787 and the community plan of 1791, on the one hand, and, on the other hand, the actual community structure of the governing politicians from 1800 to 1828, one must presume a consistency also in the attitudes from which these principles of organization originally derived, namely, attitudes of mistrust toward political power.

Whatever the underlying causes, here was a community of power-holders who preferred and who sanctioned, in their extraofficial life, a structural configuration that had been designed explicitly to check power. Here was a community of rulers who chose, among all the alternatives of social organization open to them, precisely the one most prejudicial to their capacity to rule. . . . Power made a community of cultural strangers. And power, shared, was hardly a thing to bind strangers together.

To achieve political accord among men of such disparate interests and different acculturation would not have been an easy task even under the most auspicious circumstances. For those gathered to govern on Capitol Hill in the Jeffersonian era, the circumstances were anything but auspicious.

To the political cleavages inherent in any representative assembly were added the deeper social tensions that are generated when men of widely diverging beliefs and behaviors are thrust upon each other in everyday living. Close-quarters living gave rise to personal animus even between "men whose natural interests and stand in society are in many respects similar. . . . The more I know of [two New England Senators] the more I am impressed with the idea how unsuited they are ever to co-operate," commented a fellow lodger; "never were two substances more completely adapted to make each other explode." As social intimacy bared the depth of their behavioral differences, tolerance among men from different regions was strained to the breaking point. Political coexistence with the South and the frontier states was hard enough for New Englanders to accept. Social coexistence was insufferable with slaveholders "accustomed to speak in the tone of masters" and with frontiersmen having "a license of tongue incident to a wild and uncultivated state of society. With men of such states of mind and temperament," a Massachusetts delegate protested, "men educated in . . . New England . . . could have little pleasure in intercourse, less in controversy, and of course no sympathy." Close scrutiny of their New England neighbors in power could convince southerners, in their turn, that there was "not one [who] possesses the slightest tie of common interest or of common feeling with us," planters and gentlemen cast among men "who raised 'beef and pork, and butter and cheese, and potatoes and cabbages'" and carried on "a paltry trade in potash and codfish." Cultural antipathies, crowded barracks, poor rations, and separation from families left at home combined to make tempers wear thin as the winters wore on, leading to sporadic eruptions of violence. In a sudden affray at the table in Miss Shields's boardinghouse, Randolph, "pouring out a glass of wine, dashed it in Alston's face. Alston sent a decanter at his head in return, and these and similar missiles continued to fly to and fro, until there was much destruction of glass ware." The chambers of the Capitol themselves witnessed more than one scuffle, and, though it was not yet the custom for legislators to arm themselves when legislating, pistols at twenty paces cracked more than once in the woods outside the Capitol.

To those who would seek political agreement in an atmosphere of social tensions, the rules of proceeding in Congress offered no aid at all. On the contrary, contentiousness was encouraged by Senate and House rules which gave higher precedence to raising questions than to deciding them and which guaranteed almost total freedom from restraint to the idiosyncratic protagonist. . . . "Political hostilities are waged with great vigour," commented another observer, "yet both in attack and defence there is evidently an entire want both of discipline and organization. There is no concert, no division of duties, no compromise of opinion. . . . Any general system of effective co-operation is impossible."

The result was a scene of confusion daily on the floor of House and Senate that bore no resemblance to the deliberative processes of either the town meeting or the parliamentary assemblies of the Old World. Congress at work was Hyde Park* set down in the lobby of a busy hotel — hortatory outcry in milling throngs, all wearing hats as if just arrived or on the verge of departure, variously attired in the fashions of faraway places. Comings and goings were continual — to the rostrum to see the clerk, to the anterooms to meet friends, to the Speaker's chair in a sudden surge to hear the results of a vote, to the firesides for hasty caucuses and strategy-planning sessions. Some gave audience to the speaker of the moment; some sat at their desks reading or catching up on correspondence; some stood chatting with lady friends, invited on the floor; others dozed, feet propped high. Page boys weaved through the crowd, "little Mercuries" bearing messages, pitchers of water for parched throats, bundles of documents, calling out members' names, distributing mail just arrived on the stagecoach. Quills scratched, bond crackled as knuckles rapped the sand off wet ink, countless newspapers rustled. Desk drawers banged, feet

*Hyde Park, in London, has a corner reserved for those in the public who wish to stand up in front of the crowd and offer their views on various issues. At any moment of the day, Hyde Park is filled with raucous, boisterous argument on every subject under the sun. — EDS.

shuffled in a sea of documents strewn on the floor. Bird dogs fresh from the hunt bounded in with their masters, yapping accompaniment to contenders for attention, contenders for power. Some government! . . .

What emerges from a community study of Capitol Hill is, therefore, a social system which gave probably greater sanction and encouragement to constituency-oriented behavior than any institutional norms or organizational features of the modern Congress. . . . Constituency-oriented behavior, in other words, justified the possession of power in a context of personal and national values which seems to have demanded justification for the possession of power. . . .

As a system for the effective representation of citizen interests the social system of Capitol Hill has probably never been surpassed in the history of republican government. But a fragmented social system of small blocs, more anarchic than cohesive, seems hardly to meet the minimal requirements for a viable system of managing social conflict, for performing "the regulation of . . . various and interfering interests" which the author of *The Federalist*, No. 10 acknowledged to be "the principal task of modern legislation." Far from serving as an institution for the management of conflict, the little democracy on the Hill seems more likely to have acted as a source of conflict in the polity. An ironic and provocative judgment is thus suggested by the community record of Capitol Hill: at a time when citizen interest in national government was at its lowest point in history the power-holders on the Potomac fashioned a system of surpassing excellence for representing the people and grossly deficient in the means for governing the people.

18

DAVID BRADY
CRAIG VOLDEN

From *Revolving Gridlock*

Political scientists David Brady and Craig Volden offer a complex but fascinating analysis of gridlock, the failure of the Congress and the president to be able to achieve major changes in policy. Gridlock can occur not only when there is divided government—when the presidency and the Congress are controlled by different political parties—but also, surprisingly, when the president and the legislature are of the same party. The reason for this, Brady and Volden argue, is that the real cause of gridlock lies with "supermajorities," the number of senators needed to end a filibuster (three-fifths) and

the number of legislators needed to override a presidential veto (two-thirds
of each chamber). In other words, a party's simple majority status is not
enough to ensure control. This excerpt is difficult to grasp with a quick
reading, so go slowly. It also demands some basic knowledge of the workings
of the legislative process.

————

AS THE 103RD CONGRESS (1993–1994) ground to a close, political columnists, television commentators, Senators and Representatives, as well as the President, bemoaned the lack of progress on health care, campaign finance reform, and environmental legislation. "The worst Congress in over fifty years" and "gridlock dominates" proclaimed newspaper headlines and stories. The election of a Democratic President and Democratic majorities in the House and Senate in 1992 had heralded the end of both divided government and policy gridlock. The Democratic campaign of 1992 had featured gridlock as an issue, and the early passage of family leave and the reconciliation budget was trumpeted as the end of policy gridlock. Yet by January 1994 the story began to shift, as health care and other legislation was deeply mired in the congressional labyrinth. Political scientists, columnists, Washington insiders, and other observers began to characterize the 103rd Congress as overtly partisan and controlled by "special interests"; the filibuster in the Senate was seen as largely responsible for the lack of legislative action. By early October both parties were pointing fingers, trying to interpret the inaction in ways that forwarded their own electoral purposes. Democrats, including the President, blamed Republicans for the gridlock; whereas Republicans, sensing victory in the 1994 elections, tried to make President Clinton the issue and thus the election a referendum on his performance. Congress as an institution was held in ever lower esteem, and the turnover of the 1994 elections brought in the first Republican Congress in forty years.

The newly elected Republican majority in Congress pushed through some of the reforms defined by their Contract with America—ending unfunded mandates, enacting a line-item veto, and, in the House, passing a balanced budget amendment. By April, Congress enjoyed its highest approval ratings in over twenty years, Speaker Newt Gingrich was riding high in the opinion polls, and Americans saw Republicans as the party of action, fully capable of balancing the budget. Yet within seven months all this had changed. Congress's approval rating had shrunk to about 20 percent; Speaker Gingrich's approval rating had fallen to 30 percent; President Clinton's popularity was over 50 percent for the first time in more than a year; and the government was operating on a continuing resolution (after a seven-day shutdown) while the President and the Republican Congress negotiated a new budget deal that was far to the left of the one originally passed by Congress.

What accounts for the "failure" of unified government in the 103rd Congress to break gridlock? Why, given a mandate in the 104th Congress, couldn't the Republicans have their way on policy? In the following . . . we shall attempt to define gridlock and to explain why gridlock characterized both the unified government of the 103rd Congress and the divided government of the 104th. The explanation will not focus on the role of special interests, political parties, or the media, and it does not rely heavily on presidential leadership. This is not to say that these variables don't play a role in making public policy—clearly they do. Nevertheless, our explanation for gridlock focuses on two primary factors: (1) the preferences of members of Congress regarding particular policies, and (2) supermajority institutions—the Senate filibuster and the presidential veto. . . .

The idea is really quite straightforward. When considering the U.S. Congress, instead of thinking of which party is in control, think of the members as arrayed from left to right—liberal to conservative. The further left a member is positioned, the more that member favors increased government activity on health care, the environment, education, and so on. The further right one moves, the more the members favor less government activity on health care, the environment, and education; these members thus favor lower taxes. Given this ordering of preferences, what does it take to achieve a policy change? . . .

Because in some legislation a minority of members can block a majority, the gridlock region (the range of status quo policies that is nearly impossible to change) can be sizable. Consider the filibuster as allowed by Rule XXII in the Senate. That rule, roughly, allows forty-one determined Senators to dominate floor activity so as to prohibit a bare majority from enacting its legislation. Such supermajoritarian institutions are common in state legislatures and in many foreign legislatures. The idea is that in some matters 50 percent is not enough to make fundamental changes, so rules requiring a supermajority are used. . . .

. . . [H]ow many voters are needed to move the policy—one-half (a simple majority), three-fifths (to break a filibuster), or two-thirds (to override a veto)—determines policy. Thus if the preferences of key members of Congress remain similar from one administration to the next, the party of the President won't tell us much about policy results. In addition to the distribution of preferences, supermajority institutional rules, specifically the Senate filibuster and the presidential veto (or threat to veto), also affect policy. . . .

The first institutional feature of note is the filibuster. The Senate has always been known for its slow and deliberate consideration of issues. In particular, a Senator, once given the floor, can continue to speak for extended periods of time. When a Senator's right to hold the floor indefinitely is utilized to slow or stop the advancement of a bill, the action is commonly referred to as a filibuster. The filibuster gained particular notoriety during the passage of civil rights bills in the 1950s and 1960s. In one instance, Strom Thurmond of South Carolina, speaking out against civil rights legislation, held the floor for twenty-four hours and eighteen minutes. Obviously, filibusters could keep the Senate from acting on important legislation. As a result, the Senate has over time adopted rules limiting the use of the filibuster. Of great significance is Senate Rule XXII, allowing for a cloture vote to end debate. To invoke cloture, sixty Senators must agree that the issue has been sufficiently discussed and that the Senate should continue on with its business, often leading to a vote on the bill being filibustered. The cloture rule thus limits the power of any small group of Senators who wish to talk an issue to death. But it still allows a minority to have significant power over an issue. If forty-one Senators wish to kill a bill through a filibuster, they can do so by voting against cloture. This institutional feature thus can have a great impact on policy outcomes. . . .

It should not be assumed that this model rests on the *observance* of filibusters and vetoes. The mere *threat* of a veto or a filibuster is often enough to kill a bill or to force it to be altered so as to override a veto or to gain sufficient votes for cloture. Successful vetoes and filibusters might actually be quite rare. Because time and effort are scarce commodities in Congress, it would be easier for the majority and the leadership to abandon a bill early on than to lose it to a filibuster or veto. However, in some circumstances politicians may wish to go down swinging. Opponents can raise the issue of repeated sustained vetoes, such as those in the Bush presidency, as an example of the President and his party causing gridlock. And Democrats could claim that the repeated filibusters by Bob Dole and other conservatives in the 103rd Congress were "obstructionist." Of course, on the other side of the coin, during the 1994 elections Republicans effectively claimed that the Democrats were poor at policymaking, unable to pass major legislation even with control of Congress and the presidency. . . .

. . . Our argument was that it is not parties that cause gridlock; rather, it is preferences of the members of the House and Senate in combination with supermajoritarian institutions like Senate Rule XXII that cause gridlock. . . .

If the preferences of key members of Congress essentially drive policies, what further conclusions can we draw? The first is that the President's powers are generally overrated by some scholars and the media, and that Congress ultimately determines policy results. Gridlock objectively means that neither conservative nor liberal Presidents can pull or push policy far away from where Congress wants it. Unified government gridlock simply means that policy change will be held back by the filibuster . . . , rather than by the members needed to override a veto. In short, in order to get any kind of legislation from budgets to civil rights acts passed, Republican Presidents are forced to move their proposals to the left whereas Democratic Presidents must move theirs right. Second, since policy is maintained within a narrow band controlled by moderate Democrats and Republicans, gridlock occurs under both unified and divided government. Third, the key to understanding what will happen to today's proposed policies is [:] . . . If they are to pass, policy proposals must be modified to accommodate these key members. . . .

In addition, not only is there a lack of consensus in the Congress, there is a lack of consensus among the public about what should be done. "The budget should be balanced while taxes are cut and expenses increased" is a classic example of the American public's contradictory views on policy. It is hard to determine whether voters are inherently unrealistic or whether they have been induced to be unrealistic. Consider the budget problem. The public (a majority of respondents in various surveys) believes that we can reduce taxes, increase expenditures (in different areas, depending on the respondent's particulars), and have a balanced budget all at the same time. One view drawn from such results is that the public is uninformed, irrational, and/or unrealistic. A counter to this would be: What should we expect from a public that has for decades been told that solving the budget problem will be painless? From Jimmy Carter's energy crises as "the moral equivalent of war" to Walter Mondale's pledge to raise taxes, to George Bush breaking his opposing pledge of "no new taxes," politicians who admitted that pain was involved in problem solving have not fared well at the polls. Politicians from LBJ (with his Great Society) to Ronald Reagan (with his Morning in America) who focused on the positive have done much better at the polls. In short, politicians often tell the public that problems can be solved without pain. Whether right or wrong, the 1996 campaign for the presidency took Social Security and Medicare off the table as policy areas vulnerable to change. Both parties' candidates spent considerable time assuring citizens that they were better able to protect these entitlements than their opponents. President Clinton had a real advantage over Dole on this issue, forcing Dole to claim time and again that Medicare would be safe under him. After twenty years of being told that budget problems can be solved without cutting middle-class entitlements or raising middle-class taxes, the public may well have begun to believe it. . . .

. . . We believe . . . that an inability to override vetoes or end filibusters is a further testimony to the lack of policy consensus in the United States.

This is not to say that we are not troubled by policy gridlock. . . . The revolving gridlock theory predicts that often the majority view is tempered by the need to secure supermajorities, and by the complexity of the issues. Where the will of the majority is continually thwarted by diverse preferences and supermajority institutions, the public may turn to elections to align politicians' preferences. But when politicians are already representing diverse district preferences, gridlock continues. Gridlock thus represents a lack of policy consensus regarding the difficult decisions we ask our representatives to make. Whether caused by complex issues or supermajority institutions, the political wrangling and subsequent inability to break gridlock leaves the public feeling dissatisfied.

The predicament of contemporary politics in America could be relieved by lowering public expectations about what the government is able to achieve, given the diversity of views held by Americans and the complexity of the problems with which the country is faced.

PART FOUR

Federalism

19

JAMES MADISON

From *The Federalist* 39 and 46

Ratification of the Constitution in 1787 required delicate and persuasive diplomacy. The Articles of Confederation, flawed as they were in allowing virtually no centralized governmental power, did give each state the near-total independence valued after their experiences as English colonies. The proponents of the new Constitution had to convince the states to adopt a new structure of government that would strengthen national power. In Nos. 39 and 46, Madison first discusses the importance of representative government. Then he turns to the "bold and radical innovation" that both divided and shared power between the national government and the state governments—what we today call federalism. The approval of the Constitution was to be by the people of the states, and once in operation, the government would be both national and federal. But, Madison explained, the American people would be the ultimate repository of power. State governments would always claim the citizenry's top loyalty, unless the people chose otherwise. Publius argued successfully in the great American tradition of compromise; there was something for everyone in the Constitution.

No. 39: Madison

... THE FIRST QUESTION that offers itself is whether the general form and aspect of the government be strictly republican. It is evident that no other form would be reconcilable with the genius of the people of America; with the fundamental principles of the Revolution; or with that honorable determination which animates every votary of freedom to rest all our political experiments on the capacity of mankind for self-government. If the plan of the convention, therefore, be found to depart from the republican character, its advocates must abandon it as no longer defensible.

What, then, are the distinctive characters of the republican form? ...

If we resort for a criterion to the different principles on which different forms of government are established, we may define a republic to be, or at least may bestow that name on, a government which derives all its powers directly or indirectly from the great body of the people, and is administered by persons holding their offices during pleasure for a limited

period, or during good behavior. It is *essential* to such a government that
it be derived from the great body of the society, not from an inconsiderable
proportion or a favored class of it; otherwise a handful of tyrannical nobles,
exercising their oppressions by a delegation of their powers, might aspire
to the rank of republicans and claim for their government the honorable
title of republic. It is *sufficient* for such a government that the persons
administering it be appointed, either directly or indirectly, by the people;
and that they hold their appointments by either of the tenures just specified;
otherwise every government in the United States, as well as every other
popular government that has been or can be well organized or well
executed, would be degraded from the republican character. According
to the constitution of every State in the Union, some or other of the
officers of government are appointed indirectly only by the people. According to most of them, the chief magistrate himself is so appointed.
And according to one, this mode of appointment is extended to one of
the co-ordinate branches of the legislature. According to all the constitutions, also, the tenure of the highest offices is extended to a definite
period, and in many instances, both within the legislative and executive
departments, to a period of years. According to the provisions of most
of the constitutions, again, as well as according to the most respectable
and received opinions on the subject, the members of the judiciary department are to retain their offices by the firm tenure of good behavior. . . .

"But it was not sufficient," say the adversaries of the proposed Constitution, "for the convention to adhere to the republican form. They ought
with equal care to have preserved the *federal* form, which regards the
Union as a *Confederacy* of sovereign states; instead of which they have
framed a *national* government, which regards the Union as a *consolidation*
of the States." And it is asked by what authority this bold and radical
innovation was undertaken? . . .

First.—In order to ascertain the real character of the government, it
may be considered in relation to the foundation on which it is to be
established; to the sources from which its ordinary powers are to be drawn;
to the operation of those powers; to the extent of them; and to the
authority by which future changes in the government are to be introduced.

On examining the first relation, it appears, on one hand, that the
Constitution is to be founded on the assent and ratification of the people
of America, given by deputies elected for the special purpose; but, on
the other, that this assent and ratification is to be given by the people,
not as individuals composing one entire nation, but as composing the
distinct and independent States to which they respectively belong. It is
to be the assent and ratification of the several States, derived from the

supreme authority in each State—the authority of the people themselves. The act, therefore, establishing the Constitution will not be a *national* but a *federal* act.

That it will be a federal and not a national act, as these terms are understood by the objectors—the act of the people, as forming so many independent States, not as forming one aggregate nation—is obvious from this single consideration: that it is to result neither from the decision of a *majority* of the people of the Union, nor from that of a *majority* of the States. It must result from the *unanimous* assent of the several States that are parties to it, differing not otherwise from their ordinary dissent than in its being expressed, not by the legislative authority, but by that of the people themselves. . . . Each State, in ratifying the Constitution, is considered as a sovereign body independent of all others, and only to be bound by its own voluntary act. In this relation, then, the new Constitution will, if established, be a *federal* and not a *national* constitution.

The next relation is to the sources from which the ordinary powers of government are to be derived. The House of Representatives will derive its powers from the people of America; and the people will be represented in the same proportion and on the same principle as they are in the legislature of a particular State. So far the government is *national*, not *federal*. The Senate, on the other hand, will derive its powers from the States as political and coequal societies; and these will be represented on the principle of equality in the Senate, as they now are in the existing Congress. So far the government is *federal*, not *national*. The executive power will be derived from a very compound source. The immediate election of the President is to be made by the States in their political characters. The votes allotted to them are in a compound ratio, which considers them partly as distinct and coequal societies, partly as unequal members of the same society. . . . From this aspect of the government it appears to be of a mixed character, presenting at least as many *federal* as *national* features. . . . The idea of a national government involves in it not only an authority over the individual citizens, but an indefinite supremacy over all persons and things, so far as they are objects of lawful government. Among a people consolidated into one nation, this supremacy is completely vested in the national legislature. Among communities united for particular purposes, it is vested partly in the general and partly in the municipal legislatures. In the former case, all local authorities are subordinate to the supreme; and may be controlled, directed, or abolished by it at pleasure. In the latter, the local or municipal authorities form distinct and independent portions of the supremacy, no more subject, within their respective spheres, to the general authority than the general authority is subject to them, within its own sphere. In this relation, then, the proposed government cannot be deemed a *national* one; since its jurisdiction extends to certain enumerated objects only, and leaves to the several States a residuary and inviolable sovereignty over all other objects. . . .

If we try the Constitution by its last relation to the authority by which amendments are to be made, we find it neither wholly *national* nor wholly *federal*. Were it wholly national, the supreme and ultimate authority would reside in the *majority* of the people of the Union; and this authority would be competent at all times, like that of a majority of every national society to alter or abolish its established government. Were it wholly federal, on the other hand, the concurrence of each State in the Union would be essential to every alteration that would be binding on all. The mode provided by the plan of the convention is not founded on either of these principles. In requiring more than a majority, and particularly in computing the proportion by *States*, not by *citizens*, it departs from the national and advances towards the *federal* character; in rendering the concurrence of less than the whole number of States sufficient, it loses again the *federal* and partakes of the *national* character.

The proposed Constitution, therefore, even when tested by the rules laid down by its antagonists, is, in strictness, neither a national nor a federal Constitution, but a composition of both. In its foundation it is federal, not national; in the sources from which the ordinary powers of the government are drawn, it is partly federal and partly national; in the operation of these powers, it is national, not federal; in the extent of them, again, it is federal, not national; and, finally in the authoritative mode of introducing amendments, it is neither wholly federal nor wholly national.   *Publius*

No. 46: Madison

. . . I proceed to inquire whether the federal government or the State governments will have the advantage with regard to the predilection and support of the people. Notwithstanding the different modes in which they are appointed, we must consider both of them as substantially dependent on the great body of the citizens of the United States. I assume this position here as it respects the first, reserving the proofs for another place. The federal and State governments are in fact but different agents and trustees of the people, constituted with different powers and designed for different purposes. The adversaries of the Constitution seem to have lost sight of the people altogether in their reasonings on this subject; and to have viewed these different establishments not only as mutual rivals and enemies, but as uncontrolled by any common superior in their efforts to usurp the authorities of each other. These gentlemen must here be reminded of their error. They must be told that the ultimate authority, wherever the derivative may be found, resides in the people alone, and that it will not depend merely on the comparative ambition or address of the different governments whether either, or which of them, will be able to enlarge its sphere of jurisdiction at the expense of the other. Truth, no less than decency, requires that the event in every case should be supposed to depend on the sentiments and sanction of their common constituents. . . .

Many considerations, besides those suggested on a former occasion, seem to place it beyond doubt that the first and most natural attachment of the people will be to the governments of their respective States. . . .

If . . . the people should in future become more partial to the federal than to the State governments, the change can only result from such manifest and irresistible proofs of a better administration as will overcome all their antecedent propensities. And in that case, the people ought not surely to be precluded from giving most of their confidence where they may discover it to be most due; but even in that case the State governments could have little to apprehend, because it is only within a certain sphere that the federal power can, in the nature of things, be advantageously administered.   *Publius*

20

DANIEL ELAZAR

From *American Federalism*

American government has been based on a system of federalism since the Constitution was ratified. Yet, over two centuries, change and flexibility have marked American federalism; the national and state governments have shared power in different ways, to different degrees, with different roles. In the mid-1990s, for example, there is much talk in Washington about moving more governmental programs and policy decisions back to the state level, away from central government edicts. Professor Daniel Elazar offers a classic piece on federalism in which he defends the importance of state governments, even at a time when the national government seemed to dominate. Elazar points to the innovative ideas developed at the state level. He recognizes the states' importance as managers of government programs. Elazar is right on target for today, viewing American federalism as an ever-changing "partnership" between Washington, D.C., and the state capitals.

———

THE SYSTEM of state-federal relations . . . is not the neat system often pictured in the textbooks. If that neat system of separate governments performing separate functions in something akin to isolation is used as the model of what federalism should be to enable the states to maintain their integrity as political systems, then the states are in great difficulty indeed. If, however, the states have found ways to function as integral political systems—civil societies, if you will—within the somewhat chaotic system of intergovernmental sharing that exists, then they are, as the saying goes, in a different ball game. . . . We have tried to show that the states are indeed in a different ball game and as players in that game are not doing badly at all. Viewed from the perspective of that ball game, the strength and vitality of the states—and the strength and vitality of the American system as a whole—must be assessed by different standards from those commonly used.

In the first place, the states exist. This point is no less significant for its simplicity. The fact that the states survive as going concerns (as distinct from sets of historical boundaries used for the administration of centrally directed programs) after thirty-five years of depression, global war, and then cold war, which have all functioned to reduce the domestic freedom necessary to preserve noncentralized government, is in itself testimony to their vitality as political institutions. . . . Every day, in many ways, the states are actively contributing to the achievement of American goals and to the continuing efforts to define those goals.

Consequently, it is a mistake to think that national adoption of goals shared by an overwhelming majority of the states is simply centralization. To believe that is to deny the operation of the dynamics of history within a federal system. Any assessment of the states' position in the federal union must be made against a background of continuous social change. It is no more reasonable to assume that the states have lost power vis-à-vis the federal government since 1789 because they can no longer maintain established churches than it is to believe that white men are no longer as free as they were in that year because they can no longer own slaves. An apparent loss of freedom in one sphere may be more than made up by gains in another. Massachusetts exercises more power over its economy today than its governors ever hoped to exercise over its churches five generations ago. National values change by popular consensus and *all* governments must adapt themselves to those changes. The success of the states is that they have been able to adapt themselves well.

Part of the states' adaptation has been manifested in their efforts to improve their institutional capabilities to handle the new tasks they have assumed. In the twentieth century, there has been an extensive and continuing reorganization of state governments leading to increased executive responsibility, greater central budgetary control, and growing expertise of state personnel (whose numbers are also increasing). . . .

There has also been a great and continuing increase in the states' supervision of the functions carried out in their local subdivisions. The states' role in this respect has grown as fast as or faster than that of the federal government and is often exercised more stringently, a possibility enhanced by the constitutionally unitary character of the states. The states' supervision has been increased through the provision of technical aid to their localities, through financial grants, and through control of the power to raise (or authorize the raising of) revenue for all subdivisions.

In all this, though, there remains one major unsolved problem, whose importance cannot be overemphasized: that of the metropolitan areas. By and large, the states have been unwilling or unable to do enough to meet metropolitan problems, particularly governmental ones. Here, too, some states have better records than others but none have been able to deal with metropolitan problems comprehensively and thoroughly. It is becoming increasingly clear that—whatever their successes in the past—the future role of the states will be determined by their ability to come to grips with those problems.

A fourth factor that adds to the strength and vitality of the states is the manner in which state revenues and expenditures have been expanding since the end of World War II. . . .

Still a fifth factor is the continuing role of the states as primary managers of great programs and as important innovators in the governmental realm. Both management and innovation in education, for example, continue to be primary state responsibilities in which outside aid is used to support locally initiated ideas.

Even in areas of apparent state deficiencies, many states pursue innovative policies. Much publicity has been generated in recent years that reflects upon police procedures in certain states; yet effective actions to eliminate the death penalty have been confined to the state level. The states have also been active in developing means for releasing persons accused of crimes on their own recognizance when they cannot afford to post bail, thus reducing the imprisonment of people not yet convicted of criminal activity.

Because the states are political systems able to direct the utilization of the resources sent their way, federal grants have served as a stimulus to the development of state capabilities and, hence, have helped enhance their strength and vitality. Federal grants have helped the states in a positive way by broadening the programs they can offer their citizens and strengthening state administration of those programs. Conversely, the grants have prevented centralization of those programs and have given the states the ability to maintain their position despite the centralizing tendencies of the times.

For this reason, and because the concerns of American politics are universal ones, there is relatively little basic conflict between the federal government and the states or even between their respective interests. Most of the conflicts connected with federal-state relations are of two kinds: (1) conflicts between interests that use the federal versus state argument as a means to legitimize their demands or (2) low-level conflicts over the best way to handle specific cooperative activities. There are cases, of course, when interests representing real differences are able to align themselves with different levels of government to create serious federal-state conflict. The civil rights question in its southern manifestation is today's example of that kind of situation.

Finally, the noncentralized character of American politics has served to strengthen the states. Noncentralization makes possible intergovernment cooperation without the concomitant weakening of the smaller partners by giving those partners significant ways in which to preserve their integrity. This is because a noncentralized system functions to a great extent through bargaining and negotiation. Since its components are relatively equal in their freedom to act, it can utilize only a few of the hierarchical powers available in centralized systems. In essence, its general government can only use those powers set forth in the fundamental compact between the partners as necessary to the maintenance of the system as a whole. Stated baldly, congressional authorization of new federal programs is frequently no more than a license allowing federal authorities to begin negotiations with the states and localities. . . .

In the last analysis, the states remain viable entities in a federal system that has every tendency toward centralization present in all strong governments. They remain viable because they exist as civil societies with political systems of their own. They maintain that existence because the American political tradition and the Constitution embodying it give the states an important place in the overall fabric of American civil society. The tradition and the Constitution remain viable because neither Capitol Hill nor the fifty state houses have alone been able to serve all the variegated interests on the American scene that compete equally well without working in partnership.

The states remain vital political systems for larger reasons as well as immediate ones, reasons that are often passed over unnoticed in the public's concern with day-to-day problems of government. These larger reasons are not new; though they have changed in certain details, they remain essentially the same as in the early days of the Union.

The states remain important in a continental nation as reflectors of sectional and regional differences that are enhanced by the growing social and economic complexity of every part of the country, even as the older cultural differences may be diminished by modern communications. They remain important as experimenters and innovators over a wider range of fields than ever before, simply because government at every level in the United States has been expanding. The role of the states as recruiters of political participants and trainers of political leaders has in no way been diminished, particularly since the number of political offices of every kind seems to be increasing at least in proportion to population growth.

In at least two ways, traditional roles of the states have been enhanced by recent trends. They have become even more active promoters and administrators of public services than ever before. In part, this is simply because governments are doing more than they had in the past, but it is also because they provide ways to increase governmental activity while maintaining noncentralized government. By handling important programs at a level that can be reached by many people, the contribute to the maintenance of a traditional interest of democratic politics, namely, the maximization of local control over the political and administrative decision-makers whose actions affect the lives of every citizen in ever-increasing ways.

As the population of the nation increases, the states become increasingly able to manage major governmental activities with the competence and expertise demanded by the metropolitan–technological frontier. At the same time, the federal government becomes further removed from popular pressures simply by virtue of the increased size of the population it must serve. The states may well be on their way to becoming the most "manageable" civil societies in the nation. Their size and scale remain comprehensible to people even as they are enabled to do more things better.

In sum, the virtue of the federal system lies in its ability to develop and maintain mechanisms vital to the perpetuation of the unique combination of governmental strength, political flexibility, and individual liberty, which has been the central concern of American politics. The American people are known to appreciate their political tradition and the Constitution. Most important, they seem to appreciate the partnership, too, in some unreasoned way, and have learned to use all its elements to reasonably satisfy their claims on government.

21

DAVID OSBORNE

From *Laboratories of Democracy*

Earlier in the twentieth century, Supreme Court Justice Louis Brandeis called state governments "laboratories of democracy." States were where new policy ideas were first developed and tried out. Yet, after President Franklin Roosevelt's New Deal in the 1930s, state governments hardly seemed to be where the action was in government. A strong national government dominated American politics—until recently. Public policy specialist David Osborne looks at the way reinvigorated state governments have taken the lead in developing innovative ideas today. In this excerpt, he focuses on former Arizona governor—later Clinton administration Interior secretary— Bruce Babbitt, who transformed Arizona's old politics-as-usual state govern-ment into a modern, forward-looking one. Osborne's book is the prelude to Reinventing Government, *which carries further his idea of a "new paradigm" for "entrepreneurial" government.*

FRANKLIN ROOSEVELT once said of the New Deal, "Practi-cally all the things we've done in the federal government are like things Al Smith did as governor of New York." There was surprising honesty in Roosevelt's remark, though he might have credited other states as well. Many of FDR's initiatives—including unemployment compensation, massive public works programs, deposit insurance, and social security— were modeled on successful state programs. The groundwork for much of the New Deal social agenda was laid in the states during the Progressive Era.

A similar process is under way today, particularly in the economic arena. The 1980s have been a decade of enormous innovation at the state level. For those unfamiliar with state politics—and given the media's relentless focus on Washington, that includes most Americans—the spe-cifics are often startling. While the Reagan administration was denouncing government intervention in the marketplace, governors of both parties were embracing an unprecedented role as economic activists. Over the past decade, they have created well over 100 public investment funds, to make loans to and investments in businesses. Half the states have set up public venture capital funds; others have invested public money in the creation of private financial institutions. At least 40 states have created programs to stimulate technological innovation, which now number at least 200. Dozens of states have overhauled their public education systems. Tripartite business-labor-government boards have sprung up, often with the purpose of financing local committees dedicated to restructuring labor-management relations. A few states have even launched cooperative efforts with management and labor to revitalize regional industries.

Why this sudden burst of innovation at the state level? Just 25 years ago, state governments were widely regarded as the enemies of change, their resistance symbolized by George Wallace in the schoolhouse door.* The answer has to do with the profound and wrenching economic transition the United States has experienced over the past two decades. In the 1980s, a fundamentally new economy has been born. With it has come a series of new problems, new opportunities, and new challenges. In the states, government has responded.

The notion that America has left the industrial era behind is now commonplace. Some call the new age the "postindustrial era," some the "information age," others the "era of human capital." But most agree that the fundamental organization of the American and international economies that prevailed for three decades after World War II has changed. The United States has evolved from an industrial economy built upon assembly-line manufacturing in large, stable firms to a rapidly changing, knowledge-intensive economy built upon technological innovation.

The most obvious symptoms of this transition are idle factories, dislocated workers, and depressed manufacturing regions. Less obvious are the problems that inhibit our ability to innovate: a poorly educated and trained work force; adversarial relations between labor and management; inadequate supplies of risk capital; and corporate institutions that lag behind their foreign competitors in the speed with which they commercialize the fruits of their research, adopt new production technologies, and exploit foreign markets.

Jimmy Carter was elected just as the public began to sense that something had gone wrong with the American economy. Like other national politicians of his day, he only dimly perceived the emerging realities of the new economy. Ronald Reagan owed his election to the deepening

---

*George Wallace was the governor of Alabama in 1963, when the federal government forced the state to integrate its schools following the Supreme Court's 1954 *Brown v. Board of Education* decision. President Kennedy mobilized the Alabama National Guard, despite the governor's defiance of the desegregation decree. Governor Wallace gave a speech against desegregation at the schoolhouse door before the guard ushered African–American students into the building. — EDS.

economic crisis, but his solution was to reach back to the free-market myths of the preindustrial era. He had the luxury to do so because he governed an enormously diverse nation, in which rapid growth along both coasts balanced the pain experienced in the industrial and agricultural heartland.

Most governors have not had that luxury. When unemployment approached 13 percent in Massachusetts, or 15 percent in Pennsylvania, or 18 percent in Michigan, governors had to respond. They could not afford to wait for the next recovery, or to evoke the nostrums of free-market theory.

The same dynamic occurred during the last great economic transformation: the birth of our industrial economy. The Progressive movement, which originated at the state and local level, grew up in response to the new problems created by rapid industrialization: the explosion of the cities, the emergence of massive corporate trusts, the growth of urban political machines, the exploitation of industrial labor.* Many Progressive reforms introduced in the cities or states were gradually institutionalized at the federal level—culminating in the New Deal.

This reality led Supreme Court Justice Louis Brandeis to coin his famous phrase, "laboratories of democracy." One of America's leading Progressive activists during the early decades of the twentieth century, Brandeis viewed the states as laboratories in which the Progressives could experiment with new solutions to social and economic problems. Those that worked could be applied nationally; those that failed could be discarded.

Brandeis's phrase captured the peculiar, pragmatic genius of the federal system. As one approach to government—one political paradigm—wears thin, its successor is molded in the states, piece by piece. The process has little to do with ideology and everything to do with trial-and-error, seat-of-the-pants pragmatism. Part of the beauty, as Brandeis pointed out, is that new ideas can be tested on a limited scale—to see if they work, and to see if they sell—before they are imposed on the entire nation.

Today, at both the state and local levels, we are in the midst of a new progressive era. Just as the state and local Progressivism of Brandeis's day

---

*Progressivism was a movement that developed during the first two decades of the twentieth century advocating reform at all levels of government. Well-known as progressives were Governor Robert La Follette of Wisconsin and President Theodore Roosevelt, who ran as a Progressive in the 1912 presidential election. Progressives wanted to clean up urban government, throw out party bosses, and place more power in the hands of ordinary voters through referendum and the direct primary. In journalism, the Muckrakers uncovered political corruption, exploitative working conditions, corporate greed, and consumer abuse as targets for Progressive reform.—EDS.

foreshadowed the New Deal, the state and local experimentation of the 1980s may foreshadow a new national agenda. . . .

Life in Arizona is something few Americans raised east of the Mississippi would recognize. Two-thirds of all state residents were born elsewhere. Half arrived in the last fifteen years. Every fall a third of the students in the typical Phoenix school district are new. In 1986, 61 new shopping centers were completed or under way in the Phoenix metropolitan area.

In the mid-1980s, Phoenix was the nation's fastest growing city; Arizona one of its fastest growing states. At the current pace, the Phoenix area will double its population of 1.9 million—nearly half the state total—within 15 years. Every year this mushrooming metropolis—an endless expanse of one-story, suburban-style homes and shopping centers—gobbles up thousands of acres of desert in a race for the horizon. At 400 square miles, it now covers more ground than New York City.

This explosive growth has transformed a dusty, sparsely populated frontier state into a land of the modern, Sunbelt metropolis. Arizona was the last of the contiguous 48 states to join the union, in 1912. By 1940, it had only 500,000 people, spread out in small, desert towns and over vast Indian reservations. Phoenix had only 65,000 people. But World War II brought military bases and defense plants, and the postwar boom brought air conditioning and air travel. Suddenly Arizona's location and climate were advantages, rather than disadvantages. The defense contractors, aerospace companies, and electronics manufacturers poured in, bringing an army of young engineers and technicians with their wives and their children. This was the Eisenhower generation—raised during the depression, hardened by World War II, anxious for the security of a job, a home, and a future for their children. With their crew cuts and their conservatism, they transformed Arizona from a sleepy, almost southern Democratic state into a bastion of Sunbelt Republicanism.

Before the Republican takeover in the 1950s, the farmers, the mining companies, and the bankers had run the state. Copper, cotton, and cattle were king. "It used to be that there were five or six men who would sit around a luncheon table at the old Arizona Club and pretty much decide on how things were going to be," says Jack Pfister, general manager of the Salt River Project, the state's largest water and power utility. "Some legislators were said to wear a copper collar."

At first, the new suburban middle class did not change this arrangement a great deal. Real estate developers, the new millionaires on the block, joined the club. But even as the Republicans cemented their control in the 1960s, rural legislators held onto the reins of seniority—and thus power. State government was tiny, the governor a figurehead. And the new suburbanites embraced the frontier ethos in which the old Arizona had taken such pride. Ignoring the fact that without major government investments—in military bases, defense plants, and dams—Arizona would still be a rural backwater, they believed their newfound prosperity was the product of untrammeled free enterprise. Beginning in 1952, they voted Republican in every presidential election. They had little truck with Washington. In the 1950s, Arizona declined to participate in the federal Interstate Highway System; in the 1960s, it turned down medicaid. As local people still say with a hint of pride, Arizona is the last preserve of the lone gun slinger.

The combination of explosive growth and a frontier mentality created problems very different from those encountered by the other states profiled in this book. "In the East, you have old cities, old infrastructure, and a fight for economic survival," says Republican Senator Anne Lindemann. "Here, we're trying to control the growth as best we can."

This process was not without its lessons for the rest of the nation, however. Because Arizona is a desert, with a fragile ecosystem, its rapid growth threw into sharp relief the most serious environmental problems of the postindustrial era—particularly those involving water and toxic chemicals. And because the political climate makes public resources so scarce, the struggle to cope with the social problems created by a modern economy stimulated a degree of creativity rarely seen in a conservative state.

The task of dragging Arizona into the modern era fell to Bruce Babbitt, who by the time he left office in 1987 had changed the very nature of the governorship. A lanky, scholarly type whose habitual slouch and thoughtful manner hide an enormous drive, Babbitt looks like a cross between Donald Sutherland and Tom Poston. He has sandy hair, a lined face that has begun to sag with the wear of 14 years in politics, and large, pale eyes that bulge out from behind his eyebrows when he scowls. In a small group, when he is in his natural, analytic mode, Babbitt can be brilliant. On a dais, when he tries to sound like a politician, his body stiffens, his eyes bulge, and he does a good imitation of Don Knotts.

Despite his weakness as a public speaker, Babbitt captivated the Arizona electorate. He was elected in 1978 with 52 percent of the vote, re-elected four years later, during a recession, with 62 percent. Summing up the Babbitt years, the *Arizona Republic*, a conservative newspaper, called him the "take-charge governor." "He is without a doubt the smartest, quickest elected official I have ever met," an environmental activist told me, in a comment echoed by many others. "Babbitt plays it on the precipice," added a state senator. "He is constantly pushing this state forward, and he has an uncanny ability to pull it off." . . .

Traditionally, the governor's office in Arizona had been extremely weak. Arizona was perhaps the only state in the union in which a governor would consider the ambassadorship to Argentina a step up. State government was run by a small group of senior legislators and their staffs, who brought out the governor for ceremonial occasions. The notion that a governor might try to set an agenda for the state, or dare to veto a bill, never crossed most politicians' minds.

Babbitt immediately set out to change that. Six weeks into his term he vetoed two bills on the same day—then timed his veto message for the evening news, knocking the wind out of a planned override. The legislature reacted with shock. "Our idea of an activist governor was one who met with us once a month to seek our advice," said Alfredo Gutierrez. "This guy called us daily to tell us what he wanted to do."

Babbitt vetoed 21 bills in 1979, 30 more over the next two years. His total of 114 vetoes in nine years was more than double the record set by Arizona's first governor, who served for 13 years. "My business friends used to complain that we had a weak governor," says Jack Pfister. "After Babbitt was in there about two or three years, you never heard anybody complain about that again. What he demonstrated was that it was more the individual than the structure of the office itself." . . .

In Arizona, the economic problem has been too much growth, not too little. Ever since Motorola built an R&D center for military electronics in Phoenix in 1948, high-tech manufacturers have flocked to the state. They have been lured—many of them from nearby California—by the cheap land, the cheap labor, and the desert climate, all of which make Arizona perfect for manufacturing precision electronics. As time passed, the only problems they experienced arose from the state's failure to keep up with their growth.

The most pressing problem, aside from water, was the higher education system. Arizona State University, the major school in the Phoenix area, was known for big-time sports and big-time parties. *Playboy* once named it the nation's number one party school. Its engineering and business schools were second rate. As the high-tech industries boomed, they began having trouble recruiting engineers—many of whom wanted to update their education every three to five years to remain on top of their fields—because of the poor reputation of ASU's engineering school. In 1978, industry leaders created an advisory committee to work with the school and took their case to the governor.

Babbitt stole their thunder. His friend Pat Haggerty, the founder and then chairman of Texas Instruments, had convinced him that sustained high-tech growth depended upon top-quality higher education and research institutions. He interrupted the committee presentation, told them about Haggerty, and instructed them to think big. "I'm not interested in being behind short-term or small-time budget increases," he said. "Come back to me with a sweeping multiyear program, and I'll support you."

The advisory committee drew up a five-year plan calling for $32 million in new investments in the engineering school—from industry, from the federal government, and from the state. (As it worked out, industry raised $18.5 million, the federal government contributed about $8 million, and the state provided about $28 million.) With both the governor and the business community pushing the package, the legislature embraced it. Between 1979 and 1984, the College of Engineering and Applied Science built a 120,000-square-foot Engineering Research Center, installed $15 million worth of new equipment, hired 65 new faculty, moved from $1 million a year in research to $9.4 million, and set up a continuing education program that included televised classes beamed right into local plants and offices. In 1984, the National Academy of Sciences ranked ASU's Mechanical Engineering and Electrical Engineering departments second and third in the nation, respectively, in improvement over the previous five years.

In July 1985, the advisory committee and the engineering school adopted a second five-year plan. This one called for $62 million in new money, split among industry, the federal government, and the state. The goal was to move the school into the top ten in the nation.

ASU also launched a university research park. It decided to allow professors to own their own companies, to spend 20 percent of their time working in industry, and to keep a portion of the patent rights on their discoveries. The Babbitt administration played a role in both developments. Babbitt also pushed through a new Disease Control Research Commission, to fund medical research.

Throughout this period, Babbitt worked hard to convince the public that investment in its universities was critical. "In earlier, less complex times, universities were nice to have but not essential to economic growth," he said in a 1983 speech to a high-technology symposium he organized. "When Arizona's first great industry, copper, developed in the late nineteenth century, the main ingredient for success was a strong back and a lot of courage in the face of drought. Then came tourism; its principal ingredients were sunshine and hospitality.

"Now, in 1983, high technology is our growth industry, and the essential resource to sustain high technology cannot be mined from the hills or grown in our soil or derived from hospitality. The main ingredient of the new high-technology evolution is education, in the form of well-educated citizens with strong scientific and technical skills. . . . Universities and colleges are now an economic asset as important to our economic future as copper ore, farms, banks, factories, and airlines." . . .

If traditional liberalism was the thesis and Reagan conservatism was its antithesis, the developments in America's state capitols offer the glimmerings of a new synthesis—a paradigm that may foreshadow the *next* realignment of American politics, as progressivism foreshadowed New Deal liberalism. The thesis, in its purist form, viewed the private sector as the problem and government as the solution. The antithesis, again in its extreme form, viewed government as the problem and the private sector as the solution. The synthesis redefines the nature of both the problem and its solution. It defines the problem as our changing role in the international marketplace. It defines the solution as new roles for and new relationships between our national institutions—public sector and private, labor and management, education and business. The fundamental goal is no longer to create—or eliminate—government programs; it is to use government to change the nature of the marketplace. To boil it down to a slogan, if the thesis was government as solution and the antithesis was government as problem, the synthesis is government as partner.

The new paradigm can be described as a series of interdependent assumptions about political reality, which together form a coherent way of thinking about our problems. The first assumption is that economic growth must be our major priority, but that it can be combined with equity, environmental protection, and other social goals. Whereas interest-group liberals put their social goals first, and Reagan conservatives put growth first, many governors are beginning to understand that in the new economy, growth *requires* equity and environmental protection.

Second, and perhaps most important, the new breed of governor assumes that the real solutions lie in changing the structure of the marketplace. By the late 1960s, many liberals had come to view the market as the problem; often they saw government as a way to overcome or replace the market. If the market would not build low-income housing, government would. If the market would not bring capital into Appalachia, government would. Reagan conservatives, in contrast, wanted government out of the marketplace—a logical contradiction, given that government sets the rules that allow the marketplace to operate. Today both Democratic and Republican governors understand that the market is far more powerful than government—that government cannot "overcome" or "replace" it. But they also understand that government *shapes* the market. To solve problems, they change the rules of the marketplace, or they use government to channel the market in new directions.

A related assumption has to do with attitudes toward government bureaucracies. Today's governors search for nonbureaucratic solutions to problems; if reshaping the marketplace will not suffice, they turn to third-sector organizations. They believe that many of the large, centralized government programs created in the past—medicaid, medicare, welfare, housing programs—have been inefficient and wasteful (often because government had to buy off the private sector, as in the case of medicare and medicaid). . . .

The fourth assumption is that in the newly competitive global economy, our governments have in a sense bumped up against their fiscal limits. Every governor portrayed in this book has taken great pains to make it clear to the electorate that he is not a big spender. . . .

The fifth assumption flows from the fiscal climate: if public resources are relatively scarce, they must be *invested*, not merely spent. Interest-group liberals responded to many problems, as Ronald Reagan likes to say, by "throwing money at them." If people were poor, the solution was higher welfare grants, more food stamps, greater housing subsidies. Reagan and his followers responded to the same problems by taking money away. The failure of both approaches has created a deep ambivalence within the American public, and a desire for a third path. When public opinion polls ask voters if welfare spending should be increased, they overwhelmingly say no. When polls ask if we have a responsibility to improve the plight of the poor, they overwhelmingly say yes. This seeming contradiction actually has a compelling logic: voters want solutions, but not the ones the two parties have traditionally offered.

The governors are gradually working out new ways to address these problems, by investing in the capacities of poor people and poor communities. "I think the American people don't want to simply break with our commitment to improve the lives of the poor; they don't want to throw all that away," says Art Hamilton, the black minority leader of the Arizona House. "But they don't want to have to pay for all the Great Society madness. People don't believe that the welfare system is designed to put itself out of business; that's what bothers a lot of the people I talk to. If the system were designed to lift people from where they are to where their potential can take them, I think people would gladly support that system." . . .

The new paradigm also involves new assumptions about the proper roles of federal, state, and local governments. The New Deal was a time in which America finally accepted bigness: big business, big labor, and big

government. An economy dominated by large, stable, mass-production industries required large, centralized institutions in all three areas. Today, however, our economy is decentralizing. Mass production is moving offshore,
and smaller, more automated, more flexible manufacturing operations are
thriving in the United States. In the service sector small businesses are prolif-
erating, and in both sectors the entrepreneurial process is accelerating. In
1985, seven times as many new businesses were formed as in 1950. . . .

   If current state trends do foreshadow national politics, these principles—growth with equity, a focus on market solutions, a search for nonbureaucratic methods, fiscal moderation, investment rather than spending,
redistribution of opportunity rather than outcomes, and a new federalism—provide a rough outline of the next political paradigm.

22

United States v. Lopez

*In 1995, the Supreme Court took a dramatic step in reinterpreting federal-
ism, the division of power between the national government and the state
governments. Federalism has been interpreted and reinterpreted a number of
times in U.S. history. Mostly, since the late 1930s, the national government's
powers have been expanded. In 1990, the Gun-Free School Zones Act—
a federal law prohibiting the possession of a firearm within a school zone—
became law. Two years later, a senior in a Texas high school was accused
of violating the act by bringing a gun to school and thereby engaging in a
form of interstate commerce. According to the act, the federal government
was authorized to prosecute the student under its power to regulate interstate
commerce. In a 5–4 decision, the Court ruled that bringing a gun to school
was not an act that came under the federal government's interstate commerce
powers; the guns-in-school issue belonged at the state and local level. Writing
the majority opinion, Chief Justice William Rehnquist mentioned his
reliance on the Constitution's "enumerated" powers as a guide to what the
national government may control, in contrast to the many other powers left
for the states.*

————

United States v. Lopez
115 S. Ct. 1624 (1995)

Chief Justice REHNQUIST delivered the opinion of the Court.
   In the Gun-Free School Zones Act of 1990, Congress made it a

federal offense "for any individual knowingly to possess a firearm at a place that the individual knows, or has reasonable cause to believe, is a school zone." . . . The Act neither regulates a commercial activity nor contains a requirement that the possession be connected in any way to interstate commerce. We hold that the Act exceeds the authority of Congress "to regulate Commerce . . . among the several States. . . . " U.S. Const., Art. I, § 8, cl. 3.

On March 10, 1992, respondent, who was then a 12th-grade student, arrived at Edison High School in San Antonio, Texas, carrying a concealed .38 caliber handgun and five bullets. Acting upon an anonymous tip, school authorities confronted respondent, who admitted that he was carrying the weapon. He was arrested and charged under Texas law with firearm possession on school premises. . . . The next day, the state charges were dismissed after federal agents charged respondent by complaint with violating the Gun-Free School Zones Act of 1990. 18 U.S.C. § 922(q). . . .

We start with first principles. The Constitution creates a Federal Government of enumerated powers. See U.S. Const., Art. I., § 8. As James Madison wrote, "the powers delegated by the proposed Constitution to the federal government are few and defined. Those which are to remain in the State governments are numerous and indefinite." . . .

The Constitution delegates to Congress the power "to regulate Commerce with foreign Nations, and among the several States, and with the Indian Tribes." U.S. Const., Art. I, § 8, cl. 3. The Court, through Chief Justice Marshall, first defined the nature of Congress' commerce power in *Gibbons v. Ogden*. . . .

. . . In [*NLRB v.*] *Jones & Laughlin Steel*, the Court warned that the scope of the interstate commerce power "must be considered in the light of our dual system of government and may not be extended so as to embrace effects upon interstate commerce so indirect and remote that to embrace them, in view of our complex society, would effectually obliterate the distinction between what is national and what is local and create a completely centralized government." . . . Since that time, the Court has heeded that warning and undertaken to decide whether a rational basis existed for concluding that a regulated activity sufficiently affected interstate commerce. . . .

. . . We conclude, consistent with the great weight of our case law, that the proper test requires an analysis of whether the regulated activity "substantially affects" interstate commerce.

We now turn to consider the power of Congress, in the light of this framework, to enact § 922(q). The first two categories of authority may be quickly disposed of: § 922(q) is not a regulation of the use of the channels of interstate commerce, nor is it an attempt to prohibit the interstate transportation of a commodity through the channels of commerce; nor can § 922(q) be justified as a regulation by which Congress has sought to protect an instrumentality of interstate commerce or a thing in interstate commerce. Thus, if § 922(q) is to be sustained, it must be under the third category as a regulation of an activity that substantially affects interstate commerce.

First, we have upheld a wide variety of congressional Acts regulating intrastate economic activity where we have concluded that the activity substantially affected interstate commerce. Examples include the regulation of intrastate coal mining . . . restaurants utilizing substantial interstate supplies . . . inns and hotels catering to interstate guests . . . and production and consumption of home-grown wheat. . . . These examples are by no means exhaustive, but the pattern is clear. Where economic activity substantially affects interstate commerce, legislation regulating that activity will be sustained. . . .

Section 922(q) is a criminal statute that by its terms has nothing to do with "commerce" or any sort of economic enterprise, however broadly one might define those terms. Section 922 (q) is not an essential part of a larger regulation of economic activity, in which the regulatory scheme could be undercut unless the intrastate activity were regulated. It cannot, therefore, be sustained under our cases upholding regulations of activities that arise out of or are connected with a commercial transaction, which viewed in the aggregate, substantially affects interstate commerce. . . .

Although as part of our independent evaluation of constitutionality under the Commerce Clause we of course consider legislative findings, and indeed even congressional committee findings, regarding effect on interstate commerce . . . the Government concedes that "neither the statute nor its legislative history contains express congressional findings regarding the effects upon interstate commerce of gun possession in a school zone." . . .

The Government's essential contention, *in fine*, is that we may determine here that § 922(q) is valid because possession of a firearm in a local school zone does indeed substantially affect interstate commerce. . . . The Government argues that possession of a firearm in a school zone may result in violent crime and that violent crime can be expected to affect the functioning of the national economy in two ways. First, the costs of violent crime are substantial. . . . Second, violent crime reduces the willingness of individuals to travel to areas within the country that are perceived to be unsafe. . . . The Government also argues that the presence of guns in schools poses a substantial threat to the educational process by threatening the learning environment. A handicapped educational process, in turn, will result in a less productive citizenry. That, in turn, would have an adverse effect on the Nation's economic well-being. As a result, the Government argues that Congress could rationally have concluded that § 922(q) substantially affects interstate commerce.

We pause to consider the implications of the Government's arguments. The Government admits, under its "cost of crime" reasoning, that Congress could regulate not only all violent crime, but all activities that might lead to violent crime, regardless of how tenuously they relate to interstate commerce. . . . Similarly, under the Government's "national productivity" reasoning, Congress could regulate any activity that it found was related to the economic productivity of individual citizens: family law (including marriage, divorce, and child custody), for example. Under the theories that the Government presents in support of § 922(q), it is difficult to perceive any limitation on federal power, even in areas such as criminal law enforcement or education where States historically have been sovereign. Thus, if we were to accept the Government's arguments, we are hard-pressed to posit any activity by an individual that Congress is without power to regulate. . . .

For instance, if Congress can, pursuant to its Commerce Clause power, regulate activities that adversely affect the learning environment, then *a fortiori*, it also can regulate the educational process directly. Congress could determine that a school's curriculum has a "significant" effect on the extent of classroom learning. As a result, Congress could mandate a federal curriculum for local elementary and secondary schools because what is taught in local schools has a significant "effect on classroom learning," . . . and that, in turn, has a substantial effect on interstate commerce. . . .

. . . We do not doubt that Congress has authority under the Commerce Clause to regulate numerous commercial activities that substantially affect interstate commerce and also affect the educational process. That authority, though broad, does not include the authority to regulate each and every aspect of local schools. . . .

To uphold the Government's contentions here, we would have to pile inference upon inference in a manner that would bid fair to convert congressional authority under the Commerce Clause to a general police power of the sort retained by the States. Admittedly, some of our prior cases have taken long steps down that road, giving great deference to congressional action. . . . The broad language in these opinions has suggested the possibility of additional expansion, but we decline here to proceed any further. To do so would require us to conclude that the Constitution's enumeration of powers does not presuppose something not enumerated . . . and that there never will be a distinction between what is truly national and what is truly local. . . . This we are unwilling to do.

For the foregoing reasons the judgment of the Court of Appeals is *Affirmed.*

PART FIVE

Congress

23

DAVID MAYHEW

From *Congress: The Electoral Connection*

Congressional scholar David Mayhew admits from the start that his explanation for the motivation of members of Congress is one-dimensional: they are "single-minded seekers of reelection." While Mayhew's thesis is intentionally narrow and his examples a bit out-of-date (none of the members cited in the excerpt is still in the House), reelection remains a primary motivator for congressional behavior. To attain reelection, representatives use three strategies. They advertise, so that their names are well-known. They claim credit for goodies that flow to their districts. And they take positions on political issues. Mayhew's theme, illustrated with amusing examples, may seem cynical, but it is doubtlessly realistic. Perhaps his analysis should have been fair warning to members of Congress about the public's growing disillusionment with the national legislature.

. . . I SHALL CONJURE UP a vision of United States congressmen as single-minded seekers of reelection, see what kinds of activity that goal implies, and then speculate about how congressmen so motivated are likely to go about building and sustaining legislative institutions and making policy. . . .

I find an emphasis on the reelection goal attractive for a number of reasons. First, I think it fits political reality rather well. Second, it puts the spotlight directly on men rather than on parties and pressure groups, which in the past have often entered discussions of American politics as analytic phantoms. Third, I think politics is best studied as a struggle among men to gain and maintain power and the consequences of that struggle. Fourth — and perhaps most important — the reelection quest establishes an accountability relationship with an electorate, and any serious thinking about democratic theory has to give a central place to the question of accountability. . . .

Whether they are safe or marginal, cautious or audacious, congressmen must constantly engage in activities related to reelection. There will be differences in emphasis, but all members share the root need to do things — indeed, to do things day in and day out during their terms. The next step here is to present a typology, a short list of the *kinds* of activities congressmen find it electorally useful to engage in. . . .

One activity is *advertising*, defined here as any effort to disseminate one's name among constituents in such a fashion as to create a favorable image but in messages having little or no issue content. A successful congressman builds what amounts to a brand name, which may have a generalized electoral value for other politicians in the same family. The personal qualities to emphasize are experience, knowledge, responsiveness, concern, sincerity, independence, and the like. Just getting one's name across is difficult enough; only about half the electorate, if asked, can supply their House members' names. It helps a congressman to be known. "In the main, recognition carries a positive valence; to be perceived at all is to be perceived favorably." A vital advantage enjoyed by House incumbents is that they are much better known among voters than their November challengers. They are better known because they spend a great deal of time, energy, and money trying to make themselves better known. There are standard routines—frequent visits to the constituency, nonpolitical speeches to home audiences, the sending out of infant care booklets and letters of condolence and congratulation. . . .

Some routines are less standard. Congressman George E. Shipley (D., Ill.) claims to have met personally about half his constituents (i.e. some 200,000 people). For over twenty years Congressman Charles C. Diggs, Jr. (D., Mich.) has run a radio program featuring himself as a "combination disc jockey–commentator and minister." Congressman Daniel J. Flood (D., Pa.) is "famous for appearing unannounced and often uninvited at wedding anniversaries and other events." Anniversaries and other events aside, congressional advertising is done largely at public expense. Use of the franking privilege has mushroomed in recent years; in early 1973 one estimate predicted that House and Senate members would send out about 476 million pieces of mail in the year 1974, at a public cost of $38.1 million—or about 900,000 pieces per member with a subsidy of $70,000 per member. By far the heaviest mailroom traffic comes in Octobers of even-numbered years. There are some differences between House and Senate members in the ways they go about getting their names across. House members are free to blanket their constituencies with mailings for all boxholders; senators are not. But senators find it easier to appear on national television—for example, in short reaction statements on the nightly news shows. Advertising is a staple congressional activity, and there is no end to it. For each member there are always new voters to be apprised of his worthiness and old voters to be reminded of it.

A second activity may be called *credit claiming*, defined here as acting so as to generate a belief in a relevant political actor (or actors) that one is personally responsible for causing the government, or some unit thereof, to do something that the actor (or actors) considers desirable. The political logic of this, from the congressman's point of view, is that an actor who believes that a member can make pleasing things happen will no doubt wish to keep him in office so that he can make pleasing things happen in the future. The emphasis here is on individual accomplishment (rather than, say, party or governmental accomplishment) and on the congressman as doer (rather than as, say, expounder of constituency views). Credit claiming is highly important to congressmen, with the consequence that much of congressional life is a relentless search for opportunities to engage in it.

Where can credit be found? . . . For the average congressman the staple way of doing this is to traffic in what may be called "particularized benefits." . . .

In sheer volume the bulk of particularized benefits come under the heading of "casework" — the thousands of favors congressional offices perform for supplicants in ways that normally do not require legislative action. High school students ask for essay materials, soldiers for emergency leaves, pensioners for location of missing checks, local governments for grant information, and on and on. Each office has skilled professionals who can play the bureaucracy like an organ — pushing the right pedals to produce the desired effects. But many benefits require new legislation, or at least they require important allocative decisions on matters covered by existent legislation. Here the congressman fills the traditional role of supplier of goods to the home district. It is a believable role; when a member claims credit for a benefit on the order of a dam, he may well receive it. Shiny construction projects seem especially useful. . . .

The third activity congressmen engage in may be called *position taking*, defined here as the public enunciation of a judgmental statement on anything likely to be of interest to political actors. The statement may take the form of a roll call vote. The most important classes of judgmental statements are those prescribing American governmental ends (a vote cast against the war; a statement that "the war should be ended immediately") or governmental means (a statement that "the way to end the war is to take it to the United Nations"). . . .

The ways in which positions can be registered are numerous and often imaginative. There are floor addresses ranging from weighty orations to mass-produced "nationality day statements." There are speeches before home groups, television appearances, letters, newsletters, press releases, ghostwritten books, *Playboy* articles, even interviews with political scientists. . . . Outside the roll call process the congressman is usually able to tailor his positions to suit his audiences. . . .

. . . On a controversial issue a Capitol Hill office normally prepares two form letters to send out to constituent letter writers—one for the pros and one (not directly contradictory) for the antis. Handling discrete audiences in person requires simple agility, a talent well demonstrated in this selection from a Nader profile*:

"You may find this difficult to understand," said Democrat Edward R. Roybal, the Mexican-American representative from California's thirtieth district, "but sometimes I wind up making a patriotic speech one afternoon and later on that same day an anti-war speech. In the patriotic speech I speak of past wars but I also speak of the need to prevent more wars. My positions are not inconsistent; I just approach different people differently." Roybal went on to depict the diversity of crowds he speaks to: one afternoon he is surrounded by balding men wearing Veterans' caps and holding American flags; a few hours later he speaks to a crowd of Chicano youths, angry over American involvement in Vietnam. Such a diverse constituency, Roybal believes, calls for different methods of expressing one's convictions.

Indeed it does.

24

RICHARD FENNO

From *Home Style*

Stated simply, political scientist Richard Fenno had a wonderful idea for a book. Instead of studying members of Congress at work in Washington, D.C., on the House floor, legislating, he researched them in what has always seemed their most obscure, out-of-the-spotlight moments. At home, in their districts, very little was known about legislators until Fenno's work. He opens with the psychological concept of "presentation of self," a technique designed to "win trust" from constituents. Fenno makes mention of the important "delegate" and "trustee" models of representation. Legislators do not explain every detail of their policy positions to the voters, rather, they want voters to trust them enough to allow them "voting leeway" back in Washington.

---

*Ralph Nader is a public-interest activist who has dedicated himself to protecting the American people against both governmental and private industry wrong-doing. One of Nader's best known campaigns came in the 1960s against General Motors, whose Chevrolet Corvair, Nader claimed, was "unsafe at any speed." In the 1996 and 2000 presidential elections, he ran as a third-party candidate.—EDS.

MOST HOUSE MEMBERS spend a substantial proportion of their working lives "at home." Even those in our low frequency category return to their districts more often than we would have guessed. Over half of that group go home more than once a month. What, then, do representatives do there? Much of what they do is captured by Erving Goffman's idea of *the presentation of self*. That is, they place themselves in "the immediate physical presence" of others and then "make a presentation of themselves to others." Goffman writes about the ordinary encounters between people "in everyday life." But, the dramaturgical analogues he uses fit the political world, too. Politicians, like actors, speak to and act before audiences from whom they must draw both support and legitimacy. Without support and legitimacy, there is no political relationship.

In all his encounters, says Goffman, the performer will seek to control the response of others to him by expressing himself in ways that leave the correct impressions of himself with others. His expressions will be of two sorts—"the expressions that he gives and the expression that he gives off." The first are mostly verbal; the second are mostly nonverbal. Goffman is particularly interested in the second kind of expression—"the more theatrical and contextual kind"—because he believes that the performer is more likely to be judged by others according to the nonverbal than the verbal elements of his presentation of self. Those who must do the judging, Goffman says, will think that the verbal expressions are more controllable and manipulable by the performer. And they will, therefore, read his nonverbal "signs" as a check on the reliability of his verbal "signs." Basic to this reasoning is the idea that, of necessity, every presentation has a largely "promissory character" to it. Those who listen to and watch the presentation cannot be sure what the relationship between themselves and the performer really is. So the relationship must be sustained, on the part of those watching, by inference. They "must accept the individual on faith." In this process of acceptance, they will rely heavily on the inferences they draw from his nonverbal expressions—the expressions "given off."

Goffman does not talk about politicians; but politicians know what Goffman is talking about. The response they seek from others is political support. And the impressions they try to foster are those that will engender political support. House member politicians believe that a great deal of their support is won by the kind of individual self they present to others, i.e., to their constituents. More than most other people, they consciously try to manipulate it. Certainly, they believe that what they say, their verbal expression, is an integral part of their "self." But, with Goffman, they place special emphasis on the nonverbal, "contextual" aspects of their presentation. At the least, the nonverbal elements must be consistent with the verbal ones. At the most, the expressions "given off" will become the basis for constituent judgment. Like Goffman, members of Congress are willing to emphasize the latter because, with him, they believe that their constituents will apply a heavier discount to what they say than to how they say it or to how they act in the context in which they say it. In the members' own language, constituents want to judge you "as a person." The comment I have heard most often during my travels is: "he's a good man" or "she's a good woman," unembossed by qualifiers of any sort. Constituents, say House members, want to "size you up" or "get the feel of you" "as a person," or "as a human being." And the largest part of what House members mean when they say "as a person" is what Goffman means by expressions "given off." Largely from expressions given off comes the judgment: "he's a good man," "she's a good woman."

So members of Congress go home to present themselves as a person and to win the accolade: "he's a good man," "she's a good woman." With Goffman, they know there is a "promissory character" to their presentation. And their object is to present themselves as a person in such a way that the inferences drawn by those watching will be supportive. The representatives' word for these supportive inferences is *trust*. It is a word they use a great deal. When a constituent trusts a House member, the constituent is saying something like this: "I am willing to put myself in your hands temporarily; I know you will have opportunities to hurt me, although I may not know when those opportunities occur; I assume— and I will continue to assume until it is proven otherwise—that you will not hurt me; for the time being, then, I'm not going to worry about your behavior." The ultimate response House members seek is political support. But the instrumental response they seek is trust. The presentation of self—that which is given in words and given off as a person—will be calculated to win trust. "If people like you and trust you as individual," members often say, "they will vote for you." So trust becomes central to the representative-constituent relationship. For their part, constituents must rely on trust. They must "accept on faith" that the congressman is what he says he is and will do what he says he will do. House members, for their part, are quite happy to emphasize trust. It helps to allay the uncertainties they feel about their relationship with their supportive constituencies. If members are uncertain as to how to work for support directly, they can always work indirectly to win a degree of personal trust that will increase the likelihood of support or decrease the likelihood of opposition.

Trust is, however, a fragile relationship. It is not an overnight or a one-time thing. It is hard to win; and it must be constantly renewed and

rewon. "Trust," said one member, "is a cumulative thing, a totality thing.
. . . You do a little here and a little there." So it takes an enormous amount
of time to build and to maintain constituent trust. That is what House
members believe. And that is why they spend so much of their working
time at home. Much of what I have observed in my travels can be explained
as a continuous and continuing effort to win (for new members) and to
hold (for old members) the trust of supportive constituencies. Most of
the communication I have heard and seen is not overtly political at all.
It is, rather, part of a ceaseless effort to reenforce the underpinnings of
trust in the congressman or the congresswoman as a person. Viewed from
this perspective, the archetypical constituent question is not "What have
you done for me lately?" but "How have you looked to me lately?" In
sum, House members make a strategic calculation that helps us understand
why they go home so much. *Presentation of self enhances trust; enhancing
trust takes time; therefore, presentation of self takes time. . . .*

Explaining Washington activity, as said at the outset, includes justifying
that activity to one's constituents. The pursuit of power, for example, is
sometimes justified with the argument that the representative accumulates
power not for himself but for his constituents. In justifying their policy
decisions, representatives sometimes claim that their policy decisions follow not what they want but what their constituents want. Recall the
member who justified his decision not to support his own highway bill
with the comment, "I'm not here to vote my own convictions. I'm here
to represent my people." Similarly, the member who decided to yield to
his constituent's wishes on gun control said, "I rationalize it by saying
that I owe it to my constituents if they feel that strongly about it." But
this is not a justification all members use. The independent, issue-oriented
Judiciary Committee member mentioned earlier commented (privately)
with heavy sarcasm,

All some House members are interested in is "the folks." They think "the folks"
are the second coming. They would no longer do anything to displease "the
folks" than they would fly. They spend all their time trying to find out what "the
folks" want. I imagine if they get five letters on one side and five letters on
the other side, they die.

An alternative justification, of course, is that the representative's policy
decisions are based on what he thinks is good public policy, regardless of
what his constituents want. As the Judiciary Committee member told his
constituents often, "If I were sitting where you are, I think what I would
want is to elect a man to Congress who will exercise his best judgment
on the facts when he has them all." At a large community college gathering

in the heart of his district, a member who was supporting President Nixon's Vietnam policy was asked, "If a majority of your constituents signed a petition asking you to vote for a date to end the war, would you vote for it?" He answered,

It's hard for me to imagine a majority of my constituents agreeing on anything. But if it did happen, then no, I would not vote for it. I would still have to use my own judgment—especially where the security of the country is involved. You can express opinions. I have to make the decision. If you disagree with my decisions, you have the power every two years to vote me out of office. I listen to you, believe me. But, in the end, I have to use my judgment as to what is in your best interests.

He then proceeded to describe his views on the substantive question.

To political scientists, these two kinds of policy justification are very familiar. One is a "delegate" justification, the other a "trustee" justification. The two persist side by side because the set of constituent attitudes on which each depends also exist side by side. Voters, that is, believe that members of Congress should follow constituents' wishes; and voters also believe that members of Congress should use their own best judgment. They want their representatives, it has been said, to be "common people of uncommon judgment." Most probably, though we do not know, voters want delegate behavior on matters most precious to them and trustee behavior on all others. Nonetheless, both kinds of justification are acceptable as a general proposition. Both are legitimate, and in explaining their Washington activity members are seeking to legitimate that activity. They use delegate and trustee justifications because both are legitimating concepts.

If, when they are deciding how to vote, House members think in terms of delegates and trustees, it is because they are thinking about the terms in which they will explain (i.e., justify or legitimate) that vote back home if the need to do so arises. If members never had to legitimate any of their policy decisions back home, they would stop altogether talking in delegate or trustee language. . . .

Members elaborate the linkage between presentation and explanation this way: There are at most only a very few policy issues on which representatives are constrained in their voting by the views of their reelection constituencies. They may not *feel* constrained, if they agree with those views. But that is beside the point; they are constrained nevertheless. On the vast majority of votes, however, representatives can do as they wish—provided only that they can, when they need to, explain their votes to the satisfaction of interested constituents. The ability to get explanations accepted at home is, then, the essential underpinning of a member's voting leeway in Washington.

So the question arises: How can representatives increase the likelihood that their explanations will be accepted at home? And the answer House members give is: They can win and hold constituent trust. The more your various constituencies trust you, members reason, the less likely they are to require an explanation of your votes and the more likely they are to accept your explanation when they do ask for it. The winning of trust, we have said earlier, depends largely on the presentation of self. Presentation of self, then, not only helps win votes at election time. It also makes voting in Washington easier. So members of Congress make a strategic calculation: *Presentation of self enhances trust; trust enhances the acceptability of explanations; the acceptability of explanations enhances voting leeway; therefore, presentation of self-enhances voting leeway. . . .*

The traditional focus of political scientists on the policy aspects of representation is probably related to the traditional focus on activity in the legislature. So long as concentration is on what happens in Washington, it is natural that policymaking will be thought of as the main activity of the legislature and representation will be evaluated in policy terms. To paraphrase Woodrow Wilson, it has been our view that Congress in Washington is Congress at work, while Congress at home is Congress on exhibition. The extrapolicy aspects of representational relationships have tended to be dismissed as symbolic—as somehow less substantial than the relationship embodied in a roll call vote in Washington—because what goes on at home has not been observed. For lack of observation, political scientists have tended to downgrade home activity as mere errand running or fence mending, as activity that takes the representative away from the important things—that is, making public policy in Washington. As one small example, the "Tuesday to Thursday Club" of House members who go home for long weekends—have always been criticized out of hand, on the assumption, presumably, that going home and doing things there was, ipso facto, bad. But no serious inquiry was ever undertaken into what they did there or what consequences—other than their obvious dereliction of duty—their home activity might have had. Home activity has been overlooked and denigrated and so, therefore, have those extra policy aspects of representation which can only be studied at home.

Predictably, the home activities described in this book will be regarded by some readers as further evidence that members of Congress spend too little of their time "on the job"—that is, in Washington, making policy. However, I hope readers will take from the book a different view—a view that values both Washington and home activity. Further, I hope readers will entertain the view that Washington and home activities may even be mutually supportive. Time spent at home can be time spent in developing leeway for activity undertaken in Washington. And that leeway in Washington should be more valued than the sheer number of contact hours spent there. If that should happen, we might then ask House members not to justify their time spent at home, but rather to justify their use of the leeway they have gained therefrom—during the legislative process in Washington. It may well be that a congressman's behavior in Washington is crucially influenced by the pattern of support he has developed at home, and by the allocational, presentational, and explanatory styles he displays there. To put the point most strongly, perhaps we can never understand his Washington activity without also understanding his perception of his various constituencies and the home style he uses to cultivate their support. . . .

25

RICHARD DAVIS

From *The Web of Politics*

In the first half of Richard Davis's study about the effect of the Internet on politics, he looks at the debate about whether the Web will bring more average Americans into the political process. It can, he finds, but it hasn't yet. Most Americans do not utilize the potential that technology offers for citizen education and participation. However, the future holds great promise. Who does utilize the Internet effectively for political purposes? Davis explains how members of Congress, through home pages and e-mail, make themselves better known to their constituents. Mentioning classic studies of Congress, Davis concludes that the Internet functions largely to keep incumbents incumbent.

———

ACCORDING TO THE predictions concerning its political role, the Internet holds great promise. *Newsweek* columnist Howard Fineman called it, "the new Louisiana Purchase, an uncharted west." The political role of new communication technology has been termed a "great transformation."

The Internet is viewed as a vehicle for educating individuals, stimulating citizen participation, measuring public opinion, easing citizen access to government officials, offering a public forum, simplifying voter registration, and even facilitating actual voting. It has been termed a "powerful technology for grassroots democracy" and one that by "facilitating discussion and collective action by citizens, strengthens democracy." It also has been called potentially "the most powerful tool for political organizing developed in the past fifty years." Some organizations are already attempting to implement Web-based voter information and participation systems. Books, like *How to Access the Federal Government on the Internet 1997*, *Environmental Guide to the Internet*, and *Politics on the Net*, have appeared to guide Internet users to sites of interest to them in order to facilitate their roles as active citizens.

Even more grandly, according to some observers, the Internet is imbued with a capability to restructure relations between people on the planet and solve vexing economic, social, and political problems. Repeatedly, Vice President Al Gore has painted a bright future with the Internet, or "Global Information Infrastructure," as a worldwide communications device:

These highways . . . will allow us to share information, to connect, and to communicate as a global community. From these connections we will derive robust and sustainable economic progress, strong democracies, better solutions to global and local environmental challenges, improved health care, and—ultimately—a greater sense of shared stewardship of our small planet.

The Global Information Infrastructure will help educate our children and allow us to exchange ideas within a community and among nations. It will be a means by which families and friends will transcend the barriers of time and distance. It will make possible a global information marketplace, where consumers can buy or sell products.

As the Internet spokesperson for the Clinton administration, Gore claimed that the knowledge received from the information superhighway would "spread participatory democracy," thus granting people access to information essential for participating in a representative democracy. He envisioned a global conversation "in which everyone who wants can have his or her say." Gore's statement reflects a widespread appellation for the Internet as the ultimate democracy because "no computer is 'above' any other . . . neither IBM nor the White House has any special advantage over a 15-year-old clever enough to set up his own connection. Class, hierarchy, and even physical location count for nothing on the Internet."

Similarly, President Clinton views the Internet as "our new town square." "The day is coming when every home will be connected to it (the Internet) and it will be just as normal a part of our life as a telephone and a television." And Senator John Ashcroft of Missouri suggests the

information age "redefines the way citizens can communicate and participate in our democracy. As Washington resists change, new technologies
and the Internet are providing new avenues for people to be involved in
changing government."

The claims of proponents of an Internet revolution in political participation can be sorted into three categories: citizen information, interaction
between citizens and government, and policy making.

The most common promise of the Internet is twofold: an increase in
information readily available to the average citizen, and more individual
control over what information is received. Combined, these two promise
true citizen awareness. Political scientist Anthony Corrado concludes that
the result may well be "a revitalized democracy characterized by a more
active and informed citizenry." And Howard Fineman has opined: "Access
to political information is being radically democratized."

Undoubtedly, the Web has already made accessible to users extensive
amounts of information in electronic form. Previously, access to this
material would have required extensive research and long hours in libraries.
Furthermore, the future bodes well for more information appearing, much
of which could be useful for political purposes.

The extent of such information currently available for free on the
Net is astounding: data on PAC contributions to candidates for federal
office; the voting records of individual members of Congress; the full
texts of legislation, executive agreements, treaties, and speeches; transcripts
of press conferences, and on and on. This is in addition to the plethora
of news media sources that are now available online.

Citizens armed with such information, it is claimed, will then be
able to interact intelligently with government officials to articulate their
concerns. Such electronic interaction is already becoming a common
feature of communication between elected officials and interested constituents. On January 13, 1994, Vice President Al Gore was the first federal
government official to conduct an online news conference with Internet
users. Other officials, including presidential candidates and state officials,
have conducted similar sessions.

According to former PBS president Lawrence Grossman, the Internet
is making the previously passive into political activists: "In kitchens, living
rooms, dens, bedrooms, and workplaces throughout the nation, citizens
have begun to apply such electronic devices to political purposes, giving
those who use them a degree of empowerment they never had before."

Perhaps the greatest expectation of the Internet is its promise to
help average citizens affect policy. Involvement by common citizens, it is

predicted, will alter the policy-making process, thus enabling the citizenry to instantaneously communicate their wishes to their representatives. "By pushing a button, typing on-line, or talking to a computer, they will be able to tell their president, senators, members of Congress, and local leaders what they want them to do and in what priority order."

In response to criticism that this kind of democratic participation is dangerous, proponents argue that, if properly informed, the citizenry are capable of serving in such a role. The solution is not to undo technology, but to educate the public to perform their essential democratic tasks. . . .

The above scenario is appealing in an age of intense cynicism about the common person's ability to affect policy. Yet, plainly the realities of political participation intrude. These lofty predictions assume something quite unusual—dramatic changes in human behavior. Anthony Corrado admits that the success of new technology as a democratic tool depends on "the willingness of significant numbers of citizens to take advantage of these extraordinary new tools to engage in meaningful political discourse, become better informed voters, and get more involved in civic life."

However, there is no evidence such a change will occur. The scenario of an active, informed electorate gathering information and expressing opinions electronically is accurate for some individuals—those who are already politically interested and motivated. For that group, the Internet will be a tremendous boon in the process of collecting information, interacting with policy makers, and, indeed, shaping policy.

But for the majority who are less politically interested, this scenario is unreal. These people will not be more likely, just because of a technological innovation, to suddenly acquire an interest in politics and follow the above scenario. As Russell Neuman has noted, "the mass citizenry, for most issues, simply will not take the time to learn more or understand more deeply, no matter how inexpensive or convenient further learning may be." . . .

For proponents of direct democracy (or at least more responsiveness to public will), the Internet has come not a moment too soon. They believe unrepresentative elected officials and unaccountable judges and bureaucrats have wasted time squabbling among themselves, corrupted the public trust, and thwarted public will, all of which has dramatically demonstrated the need for public involvement.

As a consequence of the Internet, it is predicted that mediating institutions in the process of translating public will into public policy will be forced to step aside, or at the very least, act clearly under the thumb of the public. These institutions, such as the president, Congress, the bureaucracy, the judicial branch, and state and local governments, will possess less autonomy to make independent decisions, since public opinion will be readily known through electronic votes, either binding or, at the least, strongly advisory.

Will this vision of the future actually occur? Will the Internet replace these mediating institutions with direct public decision making, or at the least, plebiscitary votes directly pointed at policy makers and ignored only at the policy maker's peril?

The answer is a resounding "no." In fact, instead of being displaced by the Internet, politicians will utilize it to maintain and reinforce existing power. They already have been, and yet will be, engaged in an accommodation process designed to employ the Internet as a tool for pursuing the same objectives they have sought through other public communication mechanisms. And they will succeed in doing so.

These objectives include personal reelection, general public approval, and specific public support for policy agendas. The Internet has the potential of helping them achieve those objectives, perhaps to an even greater extent than was true before the Internet came along. . . .

The online presence of individual members has now progressed far beyond e-mail addresses. Members of Congress now have individually distinctive home pages complete with background information and committee assignments, as well as a listing of legislation either sponsored or cosponsored by the member. . . .

While "homestyle" has been conducted through the news media (such as interviews, press conferences, and press releases) as well as personal contact, the Internet raises the possibility for another vehicle for homestyle. At first glance, the Internet may not be the appropriate vehicle for communicating homestyle. Members' Web sites are not exactly "in the district" since they actually occupy cyberspace, nor is it really possible for a member to tailor their Web site exclusively to the constituency since anyone anywhere can see it.

However, in another sense the Internet seems the perfect vehicle for member communication to their districts. The member can be in the district without actually being there. The member can communicate messages without having to rely on local news media, party organizations, or even his or her own staff. Moreover, the message communicated is an unfiltered one. . . .

. . . Members employ the Web as a vehicle to advertise themselves. Nearly all placed on their sites personal narrative biographies, often emphasizing their roots among their constituents as well as their past legislative accomplishments. Representative J.D. Hayworth (R-AZ)'s stresses that "J.D. goes home almost every weekend to his Arizona district, meeting with constituents and spending time with his family." . . .

Members sometimes discuss their families. The Web biography of Representative Richard Armey (R-TX) relates that Armey and his wife "attend Lewisville Bible Church. They have five children. Armey is an avid bass fisherman and believes in the restorative powers of fishing, where he can put aside the pressures of work and spend time with his wife and children." The biography is accompanied by a photograph of Armey kissing a fish. One of the few openly gay members of Congress, Representative Barney Frank (D-MA) mentions on his site that he lives with his gay partner.

The Web, then, is a vehicle for helping representatives to convey a less formal portrait of themselves, particularly one that conforms to the expectations of the district. In other words, they communicate homestyle. . . .

Like constituency mailings, press releases, and speeches on C-SPAN, the Internet provides yet another venue for favorable attention to the member. Members are not going to offer negative information about themselves on their own sites. Nor are constituents apt to find negative information about the vast majority of members in many other places without more searching than most people care to engage in. Theoretically, the constituent could conduct her or his own research. Political activists are finding the Internet an invaluable tool for such research, but few constituents will go to such lengths. Therefore, rather than reallocating power away from the elected member of Congress, the Internet is far more likely to reinforce it.

26

IRWIN GERTZOG

From *Congressional Women*

*Over the past twenty years, there has been a significant increase in the
number of women elected to the House of Representatives. Because so many
women were elected, 1992 is sometimes called "The Year of the Woman."
So is the House still seen as a "male institution"? In this piece, Irwin
Gertzog compares the perceptions of the 1978 congresswomen with those
of their 1993 counterparts. Incorporating some very telling quotes, Gertzog
reveals what has changed and what has not changed at the House.*

INTERVIEWS WITH THIRTY-THREE female Representatives,
twelve male Representatives, and ten staff members during the 103rd
Congress revealed both continuities and changes in the level of congresswomen's integration into the House. The most important continuity is
that the House was still perceived as a "male institution" by almost all
respondents. The most important changes were a product of the marked
increase of women in the House and of the more liberated social orientations of the men with whom they were serving. . . .

Among the forty-five members interviewed, forty-one affirmed the
"male" character of the House. Some justifications for this characterization
were related to those offered earlier. The House was male because such
amenities as toilets, the gym, and the swimming pool were less accessible
to women. It was male because elevator operators, Capitol Hill police,
and parking lot attendants could not bring themselves to treat congresswomen as House members, and because repeated slights, though often
trivial, had a cumulative effect. It was male because the daily schedule,
which often called for evening sessions, and the foreshortened weekly
schedule were inconvenient for female members whose household, spousal, and child care concerns competed with their legislative responsibilities.
These schedules, said one congresswoman, are determined by "male leaders who believe that members have wives" to take care of their families.
A few first-term congresswomen mentioned the small number of female
Representatives to explain House "maleness." However much they were
impressed by gains following the 1992 election, they found 11 percent
female membership little different from the 4 percent present in 1978.

Most respondents adopted variations on that theme, however, offering explanations that were heard less often in 1978, when the painfully small size of the female contingent obscured other fundamental disparities. The House was male, they said, because there were no women among top leaders of either party; because none chaired a standing committee; because no more than one token woman was ordinarily appointed to fill vacancies on Boards and Commissions; and because women were often denied recognition for legislative successes by committee chairs who became principal sponsors of the measures at the eleventh hour, only after women had done the spade work necessary to place them on the agenda. "Look at the photographs taken at bill-signing ceremonies," said one senior congresswoman. "The figures in the foreground are committee chairmen, with the women who were instrumental in passing the bill either relegated to the background or absent."

A large majority of 1993 respondents alluded to the "male culture of the House" to explain the chamber's gender imbalances, just as so many Representatives had in 1978. One congresswoman noted:

Most men are more comfortable dealing with other men than they are with women, and they prefer to work with one another. There is a congeniality among men that does not include women and a congeniality among women that excludes men. Differences between us extend beyond "comfort levels" to the issues each group thinks are important.

From the point of view of some congresswomen, the difference was reflected in the way men and women defined themselves as human beings. "Being a congressman is central to most males' sense of self," said one first-term, female Representative. "Congresswomen," she continued, "define themselves as much by their family and kids as where they happen to work, and I am more excited when my daughter calls me 'mommy' than when someone else calls me 'the honorable.'"

These gender differences affected the day-to-day interactions female and male House members had with one another. Inasmuch as many older, influential congressmen continued to be uncomfortable with women and were disinclined to work with them, the relationships they established with female lawmakers were strained, perfunctory, and unproductive. Several congresswomen described interactions with male Representatives during which they were not taken seriously, "half-listened to," or advised, through body language, that they "didn't know what they were talking about." Two anecdotes, one told by a first-term congresswoman, the other by a veteran, highlight the difficulties female members encounter. The newcomer allowed that women have not been completely ignored, as was once the case, but they are sometimes treated with subtle disdain. She said:

Men are not comfortable with us. In the cloak room, for example, a first-term woman will say "hello" to a congressman and he will be polite and say "hello," but soon dismiss her. But when that same congressman is greeted by a first-term male, he will be outgoing and friendly, sustaining the conversation. I understand that women have not spent much time in the cloak room, but I will make it a point to go there as often as possible in the future.

The second woman described a set of circumstances occurring repeatedly in subcommittee deliberations.

The men have louder voices and they talk over you, more interested in what they have to say than what you have to contribute. At some point you will make what you think is a worthwhile point, but no one will acknowledge it. It's as if you hadn't opened your mouth. Ten minutes later the same observation will be made by a male, and the others will say "what a good idea" as if they had never heard it before. We will just have to shout and be more aggressive.

The cloak room was singled out by many congresswomen as a vivid expression of the institution's "male" identity.

The more overt forms of discrimination described in 1978 continued into the 1990s, although with less frequency. Among the four forms detailed by Kirkpatrick and observed in the House in 1978, three— linguistic discrimination, overprotective or flirtatious behavior, and insulting remarks—were mentioned by members of the 103rd Congress. Their occurrence, while unusual, was not rare.

Male members occasionally referred to the "gentlemen of the House" and employed other locutions suggesting an all-male chamber. Some were accused of using women's first names during committee sessions while referring to congressmen by title and surname. Early in her first term, Californian Maxine Waters stopped a subcommittee meeting dead in its tracks when the chair, Representative Joseph Gaydos, called her "Maxine," after using formal titles when calling upon males. The African-American congresswoman described the encounter as follows:

I'd never met the man before in my life, and he turned to me and said "Maxine." I stopped right in the middle of that committee meeting and said "Just a minute. What are the rules around here? We must be consistent. If he's Congressman Barton, then I'm Congresswoman Waters."

This fractious exchange is a reflection of what might be a more deeply rooted division in the House. . . . Nevertheless, it is an example of discriminatory linguistic conventions that continue to be employed, even if heard less often than was once the case. By the 1990s, male members were more likely to use such terms as "Madam Chairwoman" when referring to a female presiding officer, and "my colleague," and "the member from California," terms they would use as a matter of course when referring to male members.

Patronizing behavior, described so vividly by earlier congresswomen, had also survived, even if manifested less frequently. Most male members, particularly junior congressmen, had had experience enough with professional women to treat them as colleagues. Such terms as "dear" or "young lady," let alone "honey," as they were once applied to congresswomen were infrequently uttered, although Marjorie Margolies-Mezvinsky describes an incident during which a committee chair responded to a congresswoman's request for the floor by saying "Well, young lady, what would you want?" At the same time, exaggerated politeness and condescension continued to be exhibited on Capitol Hill. One congressman told a first-term female colleague how "pleasing" all the new women were and how "they certainly brightened up the place." "The subtext of his remark," she said later, "was why else were we elected except to be pleasing and brighten up the place." And a young Democratic congresswoman publicly condemned unwanted sexual attention she had received from a male Representative. She said: "A colleague of mine complimented me on my appearance and then said he was going to chase me around the House floor. Because he was not my boss I was not intimidated, but I was offended and I was embarrassed."

The corps of unreconstructed congressmen who, in 1978, were described as "macho SOBs," whose image of female colleagues did not extend beyond prevailing stereotypes, who were flagrantly insensitive to public issues central to women's concerns and who were scornful of almost any professional activity in which women engaged, was also present in 1993, albeit diminished in size. Representatives recalled a dozen or more instances when they were embarrassed by the behavior of mostly senior congressmen toward women. These men were described as "insensitive," "vulgar," "insulting" or "sexist." One congressman recalled the committee chairman who appeared at orientation session for newly elected members and spent the afternoon "leering" at the congresswomen and commenting with coarse humor on their "good looks" and "nice bodies." According to this informant, nothing was said or done about the situation because no one wanted to tangle with a committee chairman.

Another informant described the strikingly insensitive behavior of a senior Democrat following a roll call vote. The vote was on an amendment to allow Medicaid funds to pay for mammograms annually—a preferred schedule for older women—rather than biennially, as had been stipulated in the original measure. When the amendment was defeated, a disappointed congresswoman was approached by a male opponent in the debate. In a sorry attempt at humor, he said "All is not lost. Poor women can still have one breast tested this year, the other breast tested next year."

The difficulty some men had in taking women professionals seriously was reflected in the comment of a highly respected Republican congressman to a National Public Television audience. He remarked that after the 1992 election "There are so many women in Congress now that it looks like a mall." Realizing that not everyone present appreciated his comment, he quickly denied authorship of the "joke," stating lamely that it did not originate with him, and adding "I am just repeating what other members of Congress are saying." . . .

Some of the incidents revealed a resistant, deeply rooted male chauvinism, even misogyny, among a small group of mostly senior males. Although almost all knew enough to avoid flagrantly sexist remarks, unusual events sometimes stripped away a fragile veneer of civility. One such event was the 1991 Clarence Thomas confirmation hearings before the Senate Judiciary Committee at which Anita Hill testified. Feelings about race, sexuality, ideology, and party advantage conjoined to raise emotions to extraordinary heights. After watching the televised hearings with a group of male Republicans, one of their colleagues reported that he was appalled by the blatantly sexist remarks made by men he believed were "above those kind of comments." "If a woman were present they would not have talked that way," he said. "The vulgar remarks about Anita Hill's sexuality shocked me. I had no idea that these men had such retrograde attitudes, and maybe it took the atmosphere of the Thomas hearings to trigger gutter values that they are usually able to mask."

Virtually all congresswomen interviewed in 1993 knew that some of their male colleagues were "beyond redemption," but, like most of their 1970s predecessors, they could not be bothered thinking about them as obstacles to their legislative effectiveness. One third-term woman observed that even talking about these men in an interview was unproductive—a waste of time because it means "we are not talking about issues that are really important." And a female Republican remarked:

So much of life is reflected in the personal attitudes that you bring to a situation. I have tried to think positively and not let obstacles of this kind stand in my way. I want to establish a reputation as a hard-working, knowledgeable, conscientious, problem-solving, substantive person. I can't change the attitudes of some of these men but neither can I let these attitudes affect what I do. . . .

The most visible change affecting female integration into the House in 1993 was their increase from twenty-eight in the 102nd Congress to forty-seven in the 103rd. Other, related changes were sparked by the unprecedented increase.

The large turnover in House members in 1992 left a correspondingly large number of vacancies on coveted standing committees and on influential party instrumentalities. Democratic and Republican leaders had little choice but to fill many of these vacancies with women. Some informants said these leaders went out of their way to showcase female members. They were sensitive to the arrival of twenty-four new women, said some, and fearful that they would lose partisan advantage if they gave inadequate attention to female members' concerns. Such highly valued committees as Appropriations and Energy and Commerce were staffed with unprecedented numbers of women. So were party policy committees and the Whip networks. Veteran women capitalized on the high turnover and the seniority system, vaulting five or more positions up their committee ladders, poised to become senior and ranking members of key subcommittees. They now had unprecedented access to influential House-Senate conference committees. And this was just the beginning of an advantageous positioning process. Said one senior male Democrat, "No amount of male chauvinism can hold back a woman who occupies a top subcommittee position and who works hard at her job. She is an integral part of the process whether people like it or not."

Increased numbers were particularly helpful for Democratic women. Twenty-one first-term Democrats joined fifteen female party holdovers to produce a critical mass of votes which could, if cast as a unit on selected issues, hold the balance of power. Female ubiquity was especially apparent among the sixty-four Democratic first-termers, one-third of whom were women. The latter used their clout to help elect African-American Eva Clayton of North Carolina President of the Democratic class for the first session of the 103rd Congress.

The augmented numbers would not have produced as much change if the new women were not as experienced or as talented as they were. With most having served in state legislatures and on city or county councils, the female class of 1993 had already built reputations as able lawmakers, and as creative, caring public servants. They were capable, confident women, prepared to work hard, take their lumps and, said one senior congresswoman, "They do not say 'poor me' when they fail to achieve their goals." Official Washington could not ignore these "agents of change." The electorate had sent them to Washington to purge government of waste and corruption and they were conscious of their mandate. Floridian Tillie Fowler and Utah's Karen Shepherd became co-leaders of their respective parties' efforts to reform the House. In the meantime, the new congresswomen drew strength from their numbers and from highly visible, conscious attempts by the Clinton administration to appoint women to key executive branch positions. As one senior Republican put it, "women were now being judged by their dialectical more than their decorative contributions to government."

But the "decorative" was not being ignored. To punctuate their presence, congresswomen dressed in bright, feminine colors, and the pinks and reds and oranges and orchids and apricots and fuchsias accentuated the drabness of dark-suited congressmen when President Clinton came to the House for a televised speech to a joint session of Congress. Said one congresswoman: "We didn't necessarily plan it that way but each of us decided independently that we were going to make a visual statement and we wanted tens of millions of people to see that this was a start of a new era for the representation of women." Twenty-two of the twenty-four new women joined the Congressional Caucus for Women's Issues soon after they arrived. Caucus members and non-members, Democrats and Republicans, entered into an unprecedented network of mentoring relationships, with their conviviality occasionally crossing party lines. Said one senior Republican woman, "Can you imagine Democratic and Republican men arranging to break bread with one another?"

Whereas the partisan division between males was largely unbridgeable in the 103rd Congress, the social orientations of female and male Representatives were converging. This development was hastened by the wholesale replacement of older by younger men in the 1992 election. One second-term Democrat remarked on the shift in attitudes toward women held by recently elected congressmen. He said:

My generation has been trained differently. We have become accustomed to dealing with women in professional situations. We have come to accept basic premises of the women's movement. Consequently, the proliferation of women in Congress poses no adjustment problems for us.

And several Representatives detected greater circumspection by senior congressmen in relationships established with congresswomen. Said one, "a few members of the old guard have concluded that the political liabilities of insensitivity are prohibitive."

Changes associated with increased numbers, with assignments to more valued committees, with more comprehensive networking and mentoring relationships among women, with women's greater visibility, and with new cohorts of socially aware male colleagues all had a profound effect on the level of female integration into the House. Whereas informants in 1978 frequently referred to women's exclusion from formal and informal House groups, few did so in 1993. . . .

Turnover and generational change among congressmen diminished even if it did not end the open, raw hostility exhibited by some males toward congresswomen. Many of the new men were hypersensitive to the feelings of female colleagues, and contemporary congresswomen recalled fewer examples of unconscious sexism than had their predecessors. Male behavior changed markedly after the Clarence Thomas hearings. The Navy's apologies following vulgar depictions of Congresswoman Pat Schroeder in skits produced in the wake of the Tailhook scandal also had an impact. And references which gratuitously called attention to gender differences among members, once common, became occasional. . . .

. . . The Clinton administration made women's concerns an integral part of the national agenda and feminist constituencies were better mobilized than they had been. Furthermore, many congressmen felt comfortable sponsoring feminist legislation, and congresswomen were emboldened by their numbers to determine priorities in terms of their own experience. As one senior Democratic congressman said, "For the first time it is possible to be a feminist and a 'House insider' at the same time."

27

MAURILIO VIGIL

From *Hispanics in Congress*

The 1990 and 2000 censuses recorded a dramatic increase in the number of Americans who categorize themselves as Hispanic. Along with this population growth will come congressional elections producing many new Hispanic members of the House of Representatives. Maurilio Vigil looks at the past, present, and future of Hispanics in Congress, emphasizing their organizing group, the Congressional Hispanic Caucus (CHC). The CHC has much potential for success. But it may be limited in effectiveness, Vigil notes, by the vast differences among Hispanics, who include Mexican Americans, Puerto Ricans, Cubans, and others, all across the country, each group often holding different partisan and issue positions.

TODAY'S CONGRESS WOULD, no doubt, seem alien to the authors of the Constitution, for it has evolved and changed in ways that differ markedly from that body which first convened in New York on April 1, 1789. Nevertheless, the basic structure of Congress continues to operate in much the same way as the framers planned it.

One of the basic elements of Congress that has remained true is the idea or concept that a representative should reflect the people he/she represents. In 1789, Anti-Federalist Robert Yates said that "the term, representative, implies that a person chosen for this purpose should resemble those who appoint them" and also that "for an assembly to be a true likeness of the people of any country, they must be considerably numerous." Yates went on to point out that the United States, albeit young at the time, was made up of a number of classes of people and that to have proper representation of them, all groups should have the opportunity of choosing their best informed to represent them. John Adams echoed this sentiment when he said that a representative legislature "should be an exact portrait, in miniature, of the people at large." Whether Adams' and Yates' views can be seen as a reflection of the founding fathers' perception of the ideal "representative" or of the ideal "Congress," they do show that the founders appreciated the value of diversity among representatives in the American Congress.

While the founders espoused diversity, it was of course meant in the narrowest of terms, for women and Blacks were absent from the early Congresses due to legal impediments.

Still, one of the most important features of the American Congress is that it has been made up of individuals who are as diverse as the people they represent. Hispanics are an ethnic minority who were never formally denied membership in the U.S. Congress. It may come as some surprise that Hispanics have been represented in the American Congress as early as the 1820s and almost continuously since the 1850s.

If the U.S. Congress of today were an "exact portrait in miniature of the people at large" of Adams' conception, there would be thirty Hispanics in the U.S. House of Representatives and seven in the U.S. Senate.

The 103rd Congress, which convened in January, 1993, welcomed the largest class of Hispanic Congresspersons in history. Eight new Hispanic members entered the U.S. House of Representatives and their overall number increased from ten to seventeen. Counting the two nonvoting members from Puerto Rico (Carlos Romero-Barcelo) and the Virgin Islands (Ron de Lugo), Hispanics number nineteen in the House, the largest delegation of Hispanics ever. Nevertheless, Hispanics, who constitute 9 percent of the United States population, are still underrepresented in the U.S. House with 4.4 percent of the membership. Hispanics have not been represented in the U.S. Senate since the defeat of Senator Joseph M. Montoya in 1976.

The span of time between 1822, when the first Hispanic, Joseph Marion Hernández, took his seat in Congress and January, 1993, when the record number of Hispanics were present, is but a small footnote in the history of the United States Congress, but it is a major chapter in the history of the Hispanic people in the United States. That chapter not only reflects the evolution and development of Hispanics in American society, but also relates a record of distinguished service among a number of Hispanics who emerged from modest backgrounds to the highest centers of political power in the greatest democracy on earth. . . .

In addition to the normal patterns of interaction among members of Congress such as partisanship and state delegations, Congress has developed various policy groups that provide opportunity for interpersonal contact among select congresspersons who have some other characteristic and policy interests in common. The first ethnic group to form a policy group were Blacks, who formed the Congressional Black Caucus (CBC) in 1969.

The Congressional Hispanic Caucus (CHC) was organized in December, 1976 by the five Hispanics then serving in the U.S. House of Representatives. Why the CHC had not been formed earlier remains a mystery, since most of the original members had been in Congress since the 1960s. Perhaps it was the formation and early success of the Black Caucus and the prompting of Herman Badillo, who entered Congress in 1970, that caused Hispanics to form their own caucus. The objectives of the caucus were to advance the interests of Hispanics through public policies and to enhance public awareness of Hispanic issues and problems. It was envisioned a bipartisan group of Congressmen with a common commitment to develop a united Congressional effort on behalf of Hispanic Americans.

The stated purposes of the Caucus were "to monitor legislation and other government activity that affects Hispanics" and "to develop programs and other activities that would increase opportunities for Hispanics to participate in and contribute to the American political system." Most importantly, the CHC was founded in order "to reverse the national pattern of neglect, exclusion and indifference suffered for decades by Spanish-speaking citizens of the U.S.," and to fulfill the need for the development of "a national policy on the Spanish-speaking". . . .

In 1993, as indicated before, seven new Hispanics entered the 103rd Congress bringing the total number of Hispanics to seventeen and all but two, Henry Gonzalez of Texas, and Matthew Martinez of California, became active in the CHC. José Serrano was selected as chairperson and the increased numbers promised to revitalize the Caucus. Almost immediately, the cohesiveness of the larger Caucus was tested as Congress debated the North American Free Trade Agreement (NAFTA)*, an issue of great importance to Hispanic Americans. Beyond the generic issues of expanded trade, business development and jobs, some analysts viewed NAFTA as a policy that would, if approved, bring the United States closer to the Hispanic countries of Latin America. On the other hand, if it was rejected it would create a wider barrier between the United States and those countries. NAFTA thus presented the CHC, if it could act as a unified bloc, with the opportunity of being at the vanguard of one of the most important American policy decisions relating to the Hispanic world. CHC unity was particularly important after it became apparent that the Congressional Black Caucus was overwhelmingly opposed to the accord.

After one of the most dramatic and bitter congressional battles of the 103rd Congress, NAFTA was approved. The CHC, like the Democratic majority in the House, was bitterly divided over the issue. Nine of the Hispanics supported NAFTA and eight opposed it. In fact, the issue split the Hispanics along regional and ethnic sub-group lines as the nine supporters of the measure were Mexican-Americans from the southwestern states and the opponents included the two Puerto Ricans from New York, the three Cubans from Florida and New Jersey and a Mexican-American from Chicago. Henry Gonzales (Texas) and Marty Martinez (California) were the only Mexican-Americans from the southwest who opposed it.

The fact that Congressman Bill Richardson, a former chairperson of the CHC and a Deputy Majority Whip in the House, was one of the two "point men" who orchestrated the successful vote in support of the Clinton administration, helped sway some of his Hispanic colleagues, but did not convert the others. The various reasons given for Hispanic Congressional opposition to NAFTA again reflected the diversity of the CHC. Democratic Congresspersons from Illinois, New York and New Jersey represent urban industrial centers with large working class populations who could be adversely affected by the loss of unskilled jobs. Indeed,

*The North American Free Trade Agreement (NAFTA) treaty took effect on January 1, 1994. Debate in the country and in Congress during 1993 revealed the sharp divisions of opinion on NAFTA. Its purpose was to eliminate all trade restrictions among the United States, Canada, and Mexico. The treaty was supported by so-called free traders. Opponents of NAFTA believed that American workers would lose jobs to lower-wage Mexican laborers. —EDS.

the most intensive opposition to NAFTA came from organized labor. Cuban-American Congressmen opposed NAFTA because of their unhappiness with Mexican immigration policy. The Puerto Rican congresspersons were also concerned that NAFTA would weaken the United States' 936 program which gives U.S. companies tax breaks as inducements to invest in Puerto Rico. The division within the CHC caused by the NAFTA could have future consequences for unity as well, as Mexican-American congresspersons, bitter over the negative vote of their colleagues could retaliate in such future votes as expansion of tax breaks for corporations doing business in Puerto Rico or economic assistance and trade with Cuba if relations are normalized between the U.S. and that country. . . .

Still some progress has been made by the Caucus in laying the basis for a collective national leadership of Hispanics. A permanent CHC staff is in place and has begun to perform a variety of services for member Congressmen and Hispanics. This staff will likely push for greater cooperation among Hispanic Congressmen and their staffs. A method of financing CHC activities has been established with the annual banquet held during Hispanic Heritage week in September. A CHC institute to coordinate the Caucus educational programs and other activities has been created and the CHC has gained visibility among Hispanic organizations and is recognized for its policy-making orientations in Washington. Moreover, the CHC Washington staff and the CHC Institute have begun to serve as a clearinghouse for collecting and disseminating information on Hispanics. It also provides information on educational scholarships and fellowship programs for Hispanics.

The additional Hispanic Congresspersons who joined the CHC in the 103rd Congress did offer some prospect for the revitalization of the Caucus. The increased numbers made the Caucus "more visible and [it] will have a louder voice" as new member Frank Tejeda pointed out. Certainly the diversification of the Caucus (both geographically and by cultural group) with new members from Illinois (Gutíerrez), New Jersey (Menéndez), New York (Serrano and Velásquez), Florida (Ros-Lehtinen and Díaz-Bolart) and Arizona (Pastor) as well as the new members from California and Texas provided a greater ideological and regional mix that more accurately reflects the diversity of America's Hispanic population.

Until 1990, most Hispanics in Congress were Mexican-Americans from the Southwest. Today they include Mexican-Americans from the Southwest and Midwest, Puerto Ricans from New York and Cubans from Florida and New Jersey.

The ideological and partisan division of the Caucus will continue to be evident, with the Republicans from Florida (Ros-Lehtinen and Díaz-Balart) and Texas (Bonilla) more clearly juxtaposed to the remaining Caucus members who are liberal to moderate Democrats. And, not all Hispanic Congressmen are members of the Caucus. Henry Gonzales from Texas and Matthew "Marty" Martinez continue to boycott the Caucus in the 104th Congress. Nevertheless, as Solomon Ortiz (D. Texas) said, "there will be some issues that divide us, but there are more issues like education, housing and jobs that unite us." The new Chairman of the Caucus, José Serrano from New York, although a liberal Democrat, promised in 1993 to "lead the Caucus by consensus . . . on very emotional issues that we disagree on, we just won't go into them in the Caucus." . . .

The inability of the CHC to present a united front on a variety of issues deprives it of a very important strategic tool. The voting power of the Caucus, because of its small size in members, is insignificant, except in very close roll-call votes. Rather, unity is important because of its potential influence on the other 418 Congressmen, some of whom have sizable Hispanic constituencies or who may be sensitive to Hispanic concerns.

It is unlikely that all the members of the Hispanic Caucus will achieve consensus on all or even the most important issues to Hispanics. It is more likely that the different personalities, partisanship and political ideologies, constituency interests and personal agendas of the individual members, will undermine the unity of the Hispanic Caucus. However, the extent to which the individual members can rise above these differences and come together, on the basis of common, cultural, linguistic and surname characteristics, will determine the collective future of Hispanics in American politics. . . .

If the progress achieved by Hispanics in the past two decades is any indication, the prospects for Hispanics in the Congresses of the future appear bright. The advances of the 1980s and 1990s can be attributed to a combination of factors including continued Hispanic migration to the United States; the continued concentration of Hispanics in urban areas of industrial and sunbelt states; the passage and implementation of the 1965 Voting Rights Act and in particular, the amendments of 1975 and 1982; the effect of favorable court decisions which have enabled or even mandated the creation of minority-majority districts; the continued activism of Hispanic leaders and organizations which have lobbied for the creation of Hispanic-majority districts; and perhaps most importantly, the willingness of Hispanic voters to register and vote for their own Hispanic candidate when the opportunity presents itself.

Still, Hispanics remain underrepresented in Congress, and as was the case in 1992, their Congressional gains were far short of what they could have been, given their population increases. Only a more concerted effort by Hispanic leaders and organizations will assure that Hispanics secure their fair share of representation in the future.

28

PAUL STAROBIN

Pork: A Time-Honored Tradition Lives On

Journalist Paul Starobin's look at congressional "pork" updates a classic subject. Pork, a project that a representative can secure for her or his district, has been a central part of congressional politics from the start. In times past, pork was easier to notice — edifices like canals, highways, bridges — as well as less controversial. The United States needed these infrastructure improvements, and the money was available for a generous pork barrel. Today, pork carries a different connotation. Starobin lists the new forms that pork takes in the "post-industrial" era. Modern pork projects don't look like those of the past. And the pork barrel, while as popular as always, isn't nearly as deep as it once was. Legislators are under pressure to cut, not spend, and pork is a perfect target. But what is pork? Some other district's waste-treatment plant.

POLITICAL PORK. Since the first Congress convened two centuries ago, lawmakers have ladled it out to home constituencies in the form of cash for roads, bridges and sundry other civic projects. It is a safe bet that the distribution of such largess will continue for at least as long into the future.*

Pork-barrel politics, in fact, is as much a part of the congressional scene as the two parties or the rules of courtesy for floor debate. . . .

---

*The interesting, little-known, and ignominious origin of the term "pork barrel" comes from early in American history, when a barrel of salt pork was given to slaves as a reward for their work. The slaves had to compete among themselves to get their piece of the handout. —EDS.

And yet pork-barrel politics always has stirred controversy. Critics dislike seeing raw politics guiding decisions on the distribution of federal money for parochial needs. They say disinterested experts, if possible, should guide that money flow.

And fiscal conservatives wonder how Congress will ever get a handle on the federal budget with so many lawmakers grabbing so forcefully for pork-barrel funds. "Let's change the system so we don't have so much porking," says James C. Miller III, director of the White House Office of Management and Budget (OMB). Miller says he gets complaints on the order of one a day from congressional members taking issue with OMB suggestions that particular "pork" items in the budget are wasteful.

But pork has its unabashed defenders. How, these people ask, can lawmakers ignore the legitimate demands of their constituents? When a highway needs to be built or a waterway constructed, the home folks quite naturally look to their congressional representative for help. Failure to respond amounts to political suicide.

"I've really always been a defender of pork-barreling because that's what I think people elect us for," says Rep. Douglas H. Bosco, D-Calif.

Moreover, many accept pork as a staple of the legislative process, lubricating the squeaky wheels of Congress by giving members a personal stake in major bills. . . .

Not only does the flow of pork continue pretty much unabated, it seems to be spreading to areas that traditionally haven't been subject to pork-barrel competition. Pork traditionally was identified with public-works projects such as roads, bridges, dams and harbors. But, as the economy and country have changed, lawmakers have shifted their appetites to what might be called "post-industrial" pork. Some examples:

• *Green Pork.* During the 1960s and 1970s, when dam-builders fought epic struggles with environmentalists, "pork-barrel" projects stereotypically meant bulldozers and concrete. But many of today's projects are more likely to draw praise than blame from environmentalists. The list includes sewer projects, waste-site cleanups, solar energy laboratories, pollution-control research, parks and park improvements and fish hatcheries, to name a few. . . .

• *Academic Pork.* Almost no federal funds for construction of university research facilities are being appropriated these days, except for special projects sponsored by lawmakers for campuses back home. Many of the sponsors sit on the Appropriations committees, from which they are well positioned to channel such funds. . . .

• *Defense Pork.* While the distribution of pork in the form of defense contracts and location of military installations certainly isn't new, there's no question that Reagan's military buildup has expanded opportunities for lawmakers to practice pork-barrel politics. . . .

This spread of the pork-barrel system to new areas raises a question: What exactly is pork? Reaching a definition isn't easy. Many people consider it wasteful spending that flows to a particular state or district and is sought to please the folks back home.

But what is wasteful? One man's boondoggle is another man's civic pride. Perhaps the most sensible definition is that which a member seeks for his own state or district but would not seek for anyone else's constituency.

Thus, pork goes to the heart of the age-old tension between a lawmaker's twin roles as representative of a particular area and member of a national legislative body. In the former capacity, the task is to promote the local interest; in the latter it is to weigh the national interest. . . .

Like other fraternities, the system has a code of behavior and a pecking order. It commands loyalty and serves the purpose of dividing up federal money that presumably has to go somewhere, of helping re-elect incumbents and of keeping the wheels of legislation turning. . . .

When applied with skill, pork can act as a lubricant to smooth passage of complex legislation. At the same time, when local benefits are distributed for merely "strategic" purposes, it can lead to waste. . . .

Just about everyone agrees that the budget crunch has made the competition to get pet projects in spending legislation more intense. Demand for such items has not shrunk nearly as much as the pool of available funds.

29

JOHN ELLWOOD
ERIC PATASHNIK

In Praise of Pork

Pork-barrel spending is high on Americans' list of gripes against Congress. "Asparagus research and mink reproduction" typify the wasteful spending that seems to enrich congressional districts and states while bankrupting the nation. John Ellwood and Eric Patashnik take a different view. Pork is not the real cause of the nation's budget crisis, they feel. In fact, pork projects may be just what members of the House and Senate need to be able to satisfy constituents in order to summon the courage to vote for real, significant, painful budget cuts.

———

IN A WHITE HOUSE address . . . [in] March [1992], President Bush challenged Congress to cut $5.7 billion of pork barrel projects to help reduce the deficit.* Among the projects Bush proposed eliminating were such congressional favorites as funding for asparagus research, mink reproduction, and local parking garages. The examples he cited would be funny, said the President, "if the effect weren't so serious." . . .

Such episodes are a regular occurrence in Washington. Indeed, since the first Congress convened in 1789 and debated whether to build a lighthouse to protect the Chesapeake Bay, legislators of both parties have attempted to deliver federal funds back home for capital improvements and other projects, while presidents have tried to excise pork from the congressional diet. . . .

In recent years, public outrage over government waste has run high. Many observers see pork barrel spending not only as a symbol of an out-of-control Congress but as a leading cause of the nation's worsening budget deficit. To cite one prominent example, *Washington Post* editor Brian Kelly claims in his recent book, *Adventures in Porkland: Why Washington Can't Stop Spending Your Money,* that the 1992 federal budget alone contains $97 billion of pork projects so entirely without merit that they could be "lopped out" without affecting the "welfare of the nation."

Kelly's claims are surely overblown. For example, he includes the lower prices that consumers would pay if certain price supports were withdrawn, even though these savings (while certainly desirable) would for the most part not show up in the government's ledgers. Yet reductions in pork barrel spending have also been advocated by those who acknowledge that pork, properly measured, comprises only a tiny fraction of total federal outlays. For example, Kansas Democrat Jim Slattery, who led the battle in the House in 1991 against using $500,000 in federal funds to turn Lawrence Welk's birthplace into a shrine, told *Common Cause Magazine,* "it's important from the standpoint of restoring public confidence in Congress to show we are prepared to stop wasteful spending," even if the cuts are only symbolic.

*The "pork-barrel" refers to congressional spending on projects that bring money and jobs to particular districts throughout America, thereby aiding legislators in their reelection bids. The interesting, little-known, and ignominious origin of the term "pork barrel" comes from early in American history, when a barrel of salt pork was given to slaves as a reward for their work. The slaves had to compete among themselves to get their piece of the handout.—EDS.

In a similar vein, a recent *Newsweek* cover story, while conceding that "cutting out the most extreme forms of pork wouldn't eliminate the federal deficit," emphasizes that doing so "would demonstrate that Washington has the political will to reform its profligate ways."

The premise of these statements is that the first thing anyone—whether an individual consumer or the United States government—trying to save money should cut out is the fluff. As *Time* magazine rhetorically asks: "when Congress is struggling without much success to reduce the federal budget deficit, the question naturally arises: is pork *really* necessary?"

Our answer is yes. We believe in pork not because every new dam or overpass deserves to be funded, nor because we consider pork an appropriate instrument of fiscal policy (there are more efficient ways of stimulating a $5 trillion economy). Rather, we think that pork, doled out strategically, can help to sweeten an otherwise unpalatable piece of legislation.

No bill tastes so bitter to the average member of Congress as one that raises taxes or cuts popular programs. Any credible deficit-reduction package will almost certainly have to do both. In exchange for an increase in pork barrel spending, however, members of Congress just might be willing to bite the bullet and make the politically difficult decisions that will be required if the federal deficit is ever to be brought under control.

In a perfect world it would not be necessary to bribe elected officials to perform their jobs well. But, as James Madison pointed out two centuries ago in *Federalist* 51, men are not angels and we do not live in a perfect world. The object of government is therefore not to suppress the imperfections of human nature, which would be futile, but rather to harness the pursuit of self-interest to public ends.

Unfortunately, in the debate over how to reduce the deficit, Madison's advice has all too often gone ignored. Indeed, if there is anything the major budget-reform proposals of the last decade (Gramm-Rudman, the balanced-budget amendment, an entitlement cap*) have in common, it is that in seeking to impose artificial limits on government spending without offering anything in return, they work against the electoral interests of congressmen instead of with them—which is why these reforms have been so vigorously resisted.

---

*Many attempts have been made in past years to lower the deficit. In 1985, the Gramm-Rudman-Hollings law set dollar–limit goals for deficit reduction, to be followed by automatic percentage cuts; however, many programs were exempted. A 1995 balanced-budget amendment passed the House, but failed to get two-thirds of the Senate's approval. Entitlement caps would seek to limit the total amount the federal government could pay out in programs such as Medicare, Medicaid, Social Security, and food stamps.—Eds.

No reasonable observer would argue that pork barrel spending has always been employed as a force for good or that there are no pork projects what would have been better left unbuilt. But singling out pork as the culprit for our fiscal troubles directs attention away from the largest sources of budgetary growth and contributes to the illusion that the budget can be balanced simply by eliminating waste and abuse. While proposals to achieve a pork-free budget are not without superficial appeal, they risk depriving leaders trying to enact real deficit-reduction measures of one of the most effective coalition-building tools at their disposal.

In order to appreciate why congressmen are so enamored of pork it is helpful to understand exactly what pork is. But defining pork is not as easy as it sounds. According to *Congressional Quarterly*, pork is usually considered to be "wasteful" spending that flows to a particular state or district in order to please voters back home. Like beauty, however, waste is in the eye of the beholder. As University of Michigan budget expert Edward M. Gramlich puts it, "one guy's pork is another guy's red meat." To a district plagued by double-digit unemployment, a new highway project is a sound investment, regardless of local transportation needs.

Some scholars simply define pork as any program that is economically inefficient—that is, any program whose total costs exceed its total benefits. But this definition tars with the same brush both real pork and programs that, while inefficient, can be justified on grounds of distributional equity or in which geographic legislative influence is small or nonexistent.

A more promising approach is suggested by political scientist David Mayhew in his 1974 book, *Congress: The Electoral Connection*. According to Mayhew, congressional life consists largely of "a relentless search" for ways of claiming credit for making good things happen back home and thereby increasing the likelihood of remaining in office. Because there are 535 congressmen and not one, each individual congressman must try to "peel off pieces of governmental accomplishment for which he can believably generate a sense of responsibility." For most congressmen, the easiest way of doing this is to supply goods to their home districts.

From this perspective, the ideal pork barrel project has three key properties. First, benefits are conferred on a specific geographical constituency small enough to allow a single congressman to be recognized as the benefactor. Second, benefits are given out in such a fashion as to lead constituents to believe that the congressman had a hand in the allocation. Third, costs resulting from the project are widely diffused or otherwise obscured from taxpayer notice.

Political pork, then, offers a congressman's constituents an array of benefits at little apparent cost. Because pork projects are easily distinguished by voters from the ordinary outputs of government, they provide an incumbent with the opportunity to portray himself as a "prime mover" who deserves to be reelected. When a congressman attends a ribbon-cutting ceremony for a shiny new building in his district, every voter can *see* that he is accomplishing something in Washington. . . .

"It's outrageous that you've got to have such political payoffs to get Congress to do the nation's business," says James Miller, OMB director under Ronald Reagan. Miller's outrage is understandable but ultimately unproductive. Human nature and the electoral imperative being what they are, the pork barrel is here to stay.

But if pork is a permanent part of the political landscape, it is incumbent upon leaders to ensure that taxpayers get something for their money. Our most effective presidents have been those who have linked the distribution of pork to the achievement of critical national objectives. When Franklin Roosevelt discovered he could not develop an atomic bomb without the support of Tennessee Senator Kenneth McKellar, chairman of the Appropriations Committee, he readily agreed to locate the bomb facility in Oak Ridge. By contrast, our least effective presidents—Jimmy Carter comes to mind—have either given away plum projects for nothing or waged hopeless battles against pork, squandering scarce political capital and weakening their ability to govern in the process.

The real value of pork projects ultimately lies in their ability to induce rational legislators into taking electorally risky actions for the sake of the public good. Over the last ten years, as the discretionary part of the budget has shrunk, congressmen have had fewer and fewer opportunities to claim credit for directly aiding their constituents. As Brookings scholar R. Kent Weaver has argued, in an era of scarcity and difficult political choices, many legislators gave up on trying to accomplish anything positive, focusing their energies instead on blame avoidance. The result has been the creation of a political climate in which elected officials now believe the only way they can bring the nation back to fiscal health is to injure their own electoral chances. This cannot be good for the future of the republic.

Politics got us into the deficit mess, however, and only politics can get us out. According to both government and private estimates, annual deficits will soar after the mid-1990s, and could exceed $600 billion in 2002 if the economy performs poorly. Virtually every prominent mainstream economist agrees that reducing the deficit significantly will require Congress to do what it has been strenuously trying to avoid for more than a decade—rein in spending for Social Security, Medicare, and other popular, middle-class entitlement programs. Tax increases may also be necessary. From the vantage point of the average legislator, the risk of electoral retribution seems enormous.

If reductions in popular programs and increases in taxes are required to put our national economic house back in order, the strategic use of pork to obtain the support of key legislators for these measures will be crucial. . . .

. . . [T]he president should ignore the advice of fiscal puritans who would completely exorcise pork from the body politic. Favoring legislators with small gifts for their districts in order to achieve great things for the nation is an act not of sin but of statesmanship. To be sure, determining how much pork is needed and to which members it should be distributed is difficult. Rather than asking elected officials to become selfless angels, however, we would ask of them only that they be smart politicians. We suspect Madison would agree that the latter request has a far better chance of being favorably received.

30

BARBARA SINCLAIR

From *Unorthodox Lawmaking*

When the Republicans won a majority in the House of Representatives and the Senate in 1994, for the first time in many decades, they had promised voters big changes in government. Barbara Sinclair, an authority on Congress, recounts in great detail how the 1995 budget-making process illustrated the complex and frustrating task facing the new leadership. Conflict was multidimensional: between House and Senate, and between the legislative branch and the Democratic president Bill Clinton. In the end, Sinclair notes, the Republican majority did enact significant policy changes, but they also endured heavy criticism for the government shutdowns that occurred during the process. This "Republican Revolution" happened less than a decade ago, but it is instructive to notice that many of the names Sinclair cites—Speaker Gingrich, Chairman Kasich, Senators Dole and Gramm, President Clinton—are now gone from the scene. Still, the controversial legacy of the 1994 congressional election continues today.

DURING THE 1994 ELECTIONS Republicans promised that, were the voters to make them the congressional majority, they would balance the budget in seven years and enact a host of major policy changes. House Republicans had formalized a number of their promises in their Contract with America, which they pledged to bring to a vote within the first 100 days of the 104th Congress.

In early January 1995 the new Republican majorities in the House and Senate confronted a monumental task in delivering on their promises. Balancing the budget (without touching social security or reducing defense spending, as they had promised) would require restructuring and vastly reducing large, complex federal programs such as Medicare, Medicaid, and farm programs. House Republicans had included a big tax cut in the Contract; fulfilling that promise would, of course, make balancing the budget that much harder. The Contract committed House Republicans to revamping federal welfare programs, especially Aid to Families with Dependent Children (AFDC), and Senate Republicans too were dedicated to that task. To deliver on their campaign promises, Republicans had to make a myriad of highly significant and extraordinarily complex policy decisions, many of which would inflict pain on constituents and thus be extremely controversial, and they had to do so quickly. House Republicans believed they had to bring all the Contract items to the floor within the promised 100 days, but even the full two years of a Congress is not much time to thoroughly overhaul large numbers of programs that have developed over decades.

Furthermore, Republicans faced enacting such far-reaching policy change with narrow margins of control in both chambers and a hostile president in the White House. The radical character of the Republicans' agenda ensured that the battle over its enactment would be hard fought and that opponents would attempt to stop them using all available weapons. Certainly, opponents would appeal to the court of public opinion and attempt to make voting for the components of the program prohibitively expensive in reelection terms for many Republicans. Given the ideological gulf between President Bill Clinton and congressional Republicans, the president with his veto and his bully pulpit would be one of those opponents.

The budget process provided the primary procedural tool through which Republicans would attempt to enact their agenda. Without it, the "Republican revolution" of a balanced budget in seven years would have had no chance whatsoever; the Republican congressional leaders knew that getting a large number of major and often painful changes through both chambers and past the president as separate bills was a hopeless task. The budget process allowed packaging, it provided protection against the Senate filibuster, and, combined with an adept strategy, it might make it possible to force Clinton to sign the legislation. . . .

Fulfilling the Contract: Welfare Reform and Tax Cuts

Tax cuts and welfare reform, which were both in the Contract, would eventually become part of the reconciliation bill. To meet the 100-day deadline, however, House Republicans had to bring them up before the budget resolution was ready. Welfare reform legislation was referred to the committees on Ways and Means, Economic and Educational Opportunities, and Agriculture, which reported their provisions by early March. Under strict instructions from the party leadership, Republican committee leaders had pushed the measures through their committees with limited debate and on largely party-line votes. The leadership then combined the provisions from the three committees, making alterations where that seemed advisable. The welfare reform bill ended welfare as an entitlement and turned the responsibility over to the states. The federal government would give the states block grants to fund welfare, but the federal contribution would be less than it would have been under AFDC, so the legislation saved money.

The bill was brought to the floor under a tight rule that barred votes on several amendments that would have split Republicans. For example, "pro-life" Republicans, who feared that cutting off benefits to teenaged unwed mothers would encourage abortion, were denied a chance to offer amendments deleting such provisions. The rule was narrowly approved, but then the bill passed on a 234–199 party-line vote.

Welfare reform passed on March 24; the tax bill followed on April 5. . . .

Fulfilling the promise of bringing to the floor all of the Contract items in the first 100 days left the new Republican majority in the House with little time for anything else, so the budget process began late. The budget resolution is supposed to be passed by April 15, a deadline seldom met, though it was in 1993; in 1995 the House Budget Committee did not report its resolution until May 11.

John R. Kasich of Ohio, the new chair of the Budget Committee and a part of the Republican leadership's inner circle, had not been idle. Knowing that making cuts of the magnitude necessary to balance the budget would require restructuring and in some cases abolishing programs, not just marginally trimming spending, he had set up in January a number of working groups to develop proposals. By including top Republicans from the authorizing and appropriations committees with Budget Committee members, he hoped to reach consensus on specific policy changes to reduce spending. Policy at this level, however, is not in the Budget Committee's jurisdiction; the committee is supposed to propose broad guidelines that are then filled in by other committees. A number of Republican committee leaders objected to Kasich's overstepping, and to keep peace within the Republican Party Speaker Gingrich had to tell him to back off. . . .

Drafting the Budget Resolution

The chairman of the Senate Budget Committee, Pete V. Domenici, R-N.M., beat his House counterpart to the mark. In early April the outlines of Domenici's budget plan began to emerge. Initially unwilling to commit himself to offering a budget plan that would lead to a balanced budget in seven years because he feared his colleagues lacked the political will to pass such a plan, Domenici changed his mind and made clear he would submit such a plan. He had at first intended to propose a plan that made a down payment toward balance but decided such a plan would bring much of the pain but none of the gain that a balanced budget plan would. That a balanced budget plan, particularly under the ground rules the Republicans had established during the elections, would entail real pain was evident; although Domenici's plan included no tax cuts, getting to a balanced budget without raising taxes, touching social security, or reducing defense required huge cuts in Medicare, Medicaid, and other entitlement programs, as well as in appropriations for discretionary domestic programs.

Domenici had intended to formally unveil the plan and start markup on May 1, but the difficulty of amassing sufficient support delayed action. Majority Leader Bob Dole of Kansas and Budget Committee member Phil Gramm of Texas, both running for the Republican presidential nomination, were unhappy with the lack of a big tax cut in the Domenici proposal. Gramm and some like-minded colleagues threatened to withhold their support from any budget resolution that lacked substantial tax cuts. The cuts in Medicare immediately became controversial, making a lot of Republicans nervous. A public opinion poll released in late April showed that 62 percent of those questioned did not want Congress to cut Medicare to reduce the deficit. Democrats had been charging that the Republicans' proposed cuts would gut Medicare, and their criticism had begun to take hold. "There's a lot of queasiness here," Domenici said. "I'm queasy myself."

Senate and House Republicans jointly planned a public relations counteroffensive on Medicare. A report by the Medicare trustees released in early April gave them ammunition: the report predicted that the Medicare hospital insurance trust fund would go bankrupt by 2002 unless changes were made. Republicans trumpeted the report and altered their rhetoric. No longer were they cutting Medicare to balance the budget; they were reforming it to save it from going broke. Congressional Republicans also tried to lure the president into giving them cover on Medicare cuts, demanding that he, as the country's highest leader, present his own plan to save Medicare. Clinton refused to take the bait. Instead he criticized Republicans for being so tardy with their budget resolution and excoriated them for cutting programs for the elderly to pay for tax cuts for the wealthy. "I will not support proposals to slash these programs, to undermine their integrity, to pay for tax cuts for people who are well-off," Clinton said at a White House conference on the problems of aging. . . .

On June 13 President Clinton on national television unveiled a new budget that reached balance in ten years. The budget that Clinton had submitted to Congress in early 1995 had included no deficit reduction beyond that approved in the 1993 budget deal. Clinton knew that the Republicans' big electoral victory in 1994 and the fact that the budget resolution does not require the president's signature severely reduced his influence during the early parts of the budget process. Having gotten no credit for the deficit reduction that he and congressional Democrats enacted in 1993, Clinton also had no intention of providing political cover to Republicans for the big and painful cuts that balancing the budget would entail. When the budget committees reported out their budget plans, the administration had strongly criticized the priorities they incorporated and had warned that, were they incorporated into law, the president would exercise his veto.

Given the ambitiousness and painfulness of the task, it was by no means certain in early 1995 that Republicans would be able to come up with a budget resolution that met their targets. When both chambers passed such a resolution, the strategic situation for the president changed. If Republicans did, in fact, send him a reconciliation bill that led to a balanced budget in seven years—still not a certainty but considerably more likely—Clinton would be in a weak position if he had no credible budget of his own. To prepare for that eventuality, Clinton proposed his plan.

When different parties control the presidency and Congress, the strategy that most effectively furthers the president's political goals may conflict with that best for the congressional members of his party. Congressional Democrats who believed they were making large political gains by criticizing the Republicans' budget plan were furious with Clinton for proposing a budget plan that cut spending on popular programs; Clinton had pulled the rug out from under them, they believed, by blurring the differences between the parties and taking the spotlight off the Republicans' heartless spending cuts and big tax breaks for the wealthy.

Resolving House-Senate Differences

The conference between the House and the Senate had begun June 8. Although there were many differences to resolve, the biggest issue and the most difficult problem was the tax cut. Not only did the two chambers have substantially different provisions, but this was an issue on which many Republicans held passionate beliefs. Even before the budget resolution came to the Senate floor, eight Senate Republicans had written Majority Leader Dole expressing their opposition to a tax cut of the size the House supported. In the House seventy-nine Republicans signed a letter threatening to withhold their support from the conference report if it "significantly" diminished the House-approved tax cuts. Senator Gramm warned that he, too, would oppose a budget plan without big tax cuts.

After two weeks of tough bargaining among congressional Republicans (Democrats having been relegated to the sidelines), Speaker Gingrich and Majority Leader Dole reached an agreement on taxes. With the Fourth of July recess approaching and most other differences already resolved, the two top leaders agreed to a $245 billion tax cut. To a very considerable extent, the House won. Three factors worked to the advantage of the House. The House Republicans' iron commitment to a big tax cut made senators realize that only a long and bloody war of attrition was likely to budge the House conferees. Because Senate rules prevent movement on appropriations bills until a budget resolution has been approved, the Senate was more eager than the House to complete action. Bob Dole's presidential ambitions made him especially eager to get quick agreement on a resolution that included a big tax cut. Conservative Republicans who make up the bulk of the primary electorate strongly favored big tax cuts. If the process dragged on, Dole would look like an ineffective leader.

On June 29 both chambers approved the conference report. . . .

Republicans were ecstatic about what they had accomplished. "We are changing directions," said Domenici, the elated Senate Budget Committee chairman. "It is the framework to change the fiscal policy of America and to change the way the federal government operates." They were determined to finish the job, Republicans said, no matter how recalcitrant Clinton was. "This is a revolution," declared moderate Republican representative Christopher Shays of Connecticut, vowing to refuse to raise the debt ceiling if Clinton did not agree to a balanced budget. "We are prepared to shut the government down in order to solve this problem," proclaimed House Budget Committee chairman Kasich.

Shooting with Real Bullets: Reconciliation

As difficult as enacting the budget resolution had been, a bigger and more politically difficult task lay ahead. The budget resolution is a blueprint; by its passage the Congress had promised to make the changes in law necessary to reach balance in the federal budget by 2002. Now Republicans had to deliver; as Bob Dole had said at the same stage in the budget process in 1993, "From now on we're shooting with real bullets."

The budget resolution committed Congress to making savings of $894 billion over seven years. It instructed twelve House and eleven Senate committees to change law under their jurisdictions so as to meet spending targets. Much of the savings were slated to come from entitlement programs: $270 billion from Medicare, $182 billion from Medicaid, and $175 billion from other mandatory spending programs such as food stamps, farm subsidies, welfare, and federal pensions. The committees of jurisdiction were free to decide just how to reach these targets, but the magnitude of the required savings dictated a major restructuring of the programs.

The budget resolution also prescribed $190 billion in savings in nondefense discretionary spending, which funds all those government activities—from the federal courts to Head Start to national park maintenance—that are not entitlements. The budget resolution contained a multitude of suggestions for how these cuts could be made. The budget committees had proposed closing down whole departments, agencies, and programs. Such specifics just provide guidance; they are not binding. The appropriations committees would be responsible for deciding how to make the cuts. Given the magnitude of the cuts—about 10 percent in the first year—drastic changes would be required.

About the only pleasant task mandated by the reconciliation instructions was for the taxing committees to cut taxes by $245 billion; however, given the disagreements within the Republican Party about whether a sizable tax cut made political and policy sense, even that task promised to be difficult. And finally, all this had to be done in a very short period of time. The thirteen appropriations bills are supposed to be enacted by October 1, the beginning of the federal government's fiscal year. The budget resolution instructed the committees to report their provisions for the reconciliation bill by September 22. . . .

Resolving the differences between the House and Senate bills was a task of formidable scope. The bills, after all, dealt with hundreds of issues and programs. Agriculture, Medicare, Medicaid, and welfare were expected to present the trickiest problems. The two chambers' provisions on agricultural programs were very far apart. Medicare is a politically sensitive program, and the two bills made cuts in different ways. At issue on Medicaid was the formula for distributing funds to the states, always a potentially divisive matter. Both Medicaid and welfare involved highly charged ideological issues—guaranteed coverage for certain groups and cutting off funds to teenaged mothers, for example.

Tax provisions were also a potential source of conflict. After the budget resolution specified a tax cut of $245 billion, the House did not rewrite its original $353 billion bill but sent it to conference with instructions that the size of the tax cut be reduced there; among the many differences in the two chambers' bills was the income ceiling for the $500-per-child tax credit.

In addition to being faced with many tough issues, the negotiators were constrained by the numerous promises that had been made during the effort to pass the bill. In both chambers the leaders had over and over again promised members concerned with some provision that "we'll fix it in conference."

Countering this formidable set of problems was the momentum passing the legislation in both chambers had created. Members had made a host of difficult decisions; they had put their careers on the line; if no agreement were reached it would all be for naught. And, given that important deadlines had already been missed, more long delay was likely to hurt the Republican Party's image. The leaders were determined to get a bill to the president before Thanksgiving. . . .

Why Nonincremental Change?

"This is what they said we could never do," crowed House Budget Committee chairman John Kasich after the House approved the reconciliation bill. Congressional Republicans had passed a bill of enormous scope and consequence, one that significantly shrank the size and responsibilities of the federal government and restructured some of the biggest and most complex federal programs including Medicare, which because of its popularity with the middle class had long been considered untouchable.

In our system of government, political scientists agree, nonincremental policy change is difficult to effect; when that policy change entails pain for major constituency groups, elected representatives are even less inclined to make the necessary decisions. So why were Republicans able to pass a reconciliation bill that did represent nonincremental change?

A part of the answer lies in the fact that there were powerful organized interests that did, in fact, benefit mightily from the bill. Business interests in particular gained, especially but not only from the tax provisions. Conversely, the biggest losers, the poor, are neither powerful nor organized. The political circumstances that the 1994 elections created were, however, crucial. Republicans in 1995 were able to stay united and pass legislation radically redirecting policy because their leaders skillfully exploited the sense of mandate the election results produced and because they had the congressional budget process available as a tool.

The 1994 elections brought into the House, and to a lesser extent into the Senate, a group of new members who were strongly committed to effecting policy change; the seventy-three-member strong House freshman Republican class joined a sizable group of sophomore Republicans that shared its fervent ideological belief in budget balancing, tax cutting, and government downsizing. They and many more senior House Republicans as well believed that the 1994 elections had mandated them to make major changes in government; their signing of the Contract with America, of course, heightened and focused that belief. Furthermore, the voter cynicism about Congress, which they had so effectively exploited, meant they had to deliver, Republicans realized; if they failed to keep their promises, voters were likely to punish them. The Republican leadership, especially in the House, brilliantly capitalized on such fears to keep its members unified. Over and over the leaders emphasized that, if they hoped to retain their congressional majorities, Republicans had to keep their promises, had to show they could govern, and doing so meant passing a balanced budget plan.

As the process moved forward and members went on the record with more and more difficult decisions, the prospect of receiving no political or policy payoff became increasingly unthinkable; any member responsible for failure had to know his party colleagues would make him pay dearly. The fear of voter retribution for coming up empty influenced moderate Republicans who had qualms about specific policy changes and hardliners who abhorred all compromise. "The last time I checked, every single Republican enjoyed being in the majority," remarked moderate Sherwood Boehlert, R-N.Y. "So I think that's going to weigh heavily on the minds of some people who might be cantankerous and find the plan unacceptable for one or two or three reasons." . . .

Politics and procedure had relegated President Clinton to the sidelines during much of the budget process. Convinced that the 1994 elections had given them a mandate that superseded any Clinton may have had and finding nothing of value in either of the budget plans Clinton had proposed, Republicans had proceeded on their own. Since the budget resolution does not require the president's signature, Republicans were not forced to take Clinton's preferences into account. The president, however, can veto the reconciliation bill, and Republicans knew they could not muster the votes to override.

As Republicans were crafting their bill, President Clinton made clear that he strongly opposed many of its provisions. The bill, Clinton argued, cut much too deeply in Medicaid, Medicare, welfare, education, and the environment; ending poor people's entitlement to health care under Medicaid and slashing the earned-income tax credit for the working poor while providing huge tax cuts to the well off were unacceptable.

Bargaining Chips and Strategy

If, as he had repeatedly threatened, Clinton vetoed the reconciliation bill, Republicans would have to bargain with him; otherwise the legislation on which they had spent so much of their first year in power would die. Yet the differences between their position and Clinton's were enormous and reflected basic philosophical disagreement about the appropriate role of government. Reconciliation legislation is not in the strict sense "must-pass" legislation, and this put the Republicans at a disadvantage. To be sure, when the Congress passes a budget resolution with reconciliation instructions, it promises to pass a reconciliation bill, and if it does not the Congress looks ineffective. Furthermore, most Republicans were convinced that public judgment of their performance would rest on their enacting legislation that balanced the budget in seven years as they had promised. Thus, congressional Republicans considered the bill to be must-pass legislation. Failure of a reconciliation bill does not, however, entail direct and concrete negative consequences of the sort that pressure an opposition party president to sign it.

Republicans controlled the fate of true must-pass legislation that they could use to shore up their bargaining position. To provide the funds necessary to keep the government functioning, appropriations legislation has to be passed every year; otherwise large chunks of the government must shut down. Perhaps even more of a weapon, Congress must periodically pass legislation raising the debt ceiling so that the federal government can borrow the funds necessary to pay its debts; if borrowing authority runs out, the federal government would have to default on its obligations, a course potentially disastrous for the economy and the credibility of the United States. From very early in the year, Republicans had been contemplating using these measures as bargaining tools. They hoped that public opinion, which they were convinced strongly supported a balanced budget, would provide the main pressure on Clinton to agree to a deal to their liking. If that failed, they had a backup plan: the threat of shutting down the federal government or bringing it to the brink of default.

All thirteen appropriations bills are supposed to be enacted by October 1, the beginning of the new fiscal year. In 1995 the process was far behind schedule, slowed by the time the House had spent on the Contract, the big cuts that the appropriations committees were required to make, and legislative "riders." With the party leadership orchestrating the effort, House Republicans, eager to make changes in law quickly, attached controversial legislative provisions—known as "riders"—to appropriations bills. Intended to protect the provisions from a presidential veto, the strategy in many cases made House-Senate agreement on the bills excruciatingly difficult. Compared with hard-line House Republicans, moderate Senate Republicans were much less enthusiastic about hamstringing the Environmental Protection Agency, imposing new restrictions on abortion, or effectively barring liberal interest groups from lobbying.

By late September only two of thirteen appropriations bills had been cleared for the president. Not wanting to call attention to their inability to meet deadlines, congressional Republicans agreed with the president on a continuing (appropriations) resolution (CR) to fund government programs for forty-four days. . . .

The Early Rounds and the First Government Shutdown

Both sides knew that the time when they would have to talk to each other was fast approaching. Leon Panetta, then White House chief of staff, and Pete Domenici, the chairman of the Senate Budget Committee, had been meeting informally for months trying to find common ground in preparation for serious talks. On November 1 President Clinton and the Republican leadership met for two hours at the White House to discuss budget issues including the debt limit. Republicans reiterated that any agreement must balance the budget in seven years according to conservative CBO estimates; House Republicans would not vote for anything less, Speaker Gingrich declared. Clinton made it clear he would not cave in as many Republicans seem to have hoped. "If you're determined to undermine the government's role in things I believe in, you'll have to put someone else in that chair," the president said, pointing to his big leather chair. Although both sides called the meeting useful, no agreements were reached.

Implementing their strategy of using must-pass legislation to pressure the president into an agreement, congressional Republicans passed a continuing resolution and a debt ceiling increase, including in both pieces of legislation provisions the president strongly opposed. The debt limit bill prohibited the administration from using a financial strategy that the secretary of the Treasury was considering to avoid default, and it would have plunged the U.S. government into default as soon as the temporary increase ran out on December 12, thus forcing Clinton to agree with Republicans on a plan by then. The House version had also included a provision abolishing the Commerce Department, but that was stripped out of the bill at the insistence of Senate Republican moderates. The continuing resolution contained deep cuts, especially for Clinton's priorities, and prevented a decrease as current law dictated in Medicare premiums. On November 13 Clinton vetoed both bills as he had said he would.

In a final attempt to avert a government shutdown, Clinton sent Panetta to the Hill to confer with Gingrich and Dole; however, when Panetta insisted that congressional Democrats be included in the talks, the Republican leaders refused, and no negotiations took place. On November 14 the federal government shut down. Only two of the regular appropriations bills had been signed into law by the president, though Congress had completed several others; more than half, including such large and contentious bills as the one funding the departments of Labor, Education, and Health and Human Services were unfinished, many hung up by House-Senate disagreements. A number of appropriations bills were under veto threat.

Under law, "essential" government services (law enforcement, for example) continue even if appropriations bills are not passed; but all other services and programs not yet funded have to close down. About 800,000 federal employees were sent home all across the country; national parks were shut; the Small Business Administration stopped processing loan requests; new applicants for social security were out of luck, though the checks (an entitlement and not funded by appropriations) continued to go out. . . .

On November 19 President Clinton and Republican leaders announced an agreement to end the six-day shutdown. To their surprise, Republicans found the public blaming them rather than the president by a 2-to-1 margin. Threats of defection by significant numbers of congressional Democrats put Clinton under pressure as well. After Clinton's vetoes, Republicans had brought to the floor a continuing resolution without the extraneous provisions in the previous one but with a provision committing the president and Congress to a budget balanced in seven years using CBO numbers; in both chambers a substantial number of Democrats had joined Republicans in support. With both sides concerned about prolonging the shutdown, the talks that had proceeded by fits and starts bore fruit.

The deal struck on November 19 and incorporated in a continuing resolution passed the next day funded the government until December 15 and bound the president and Congress to enacting a budget that the CBO certified as balanced by 2002 and that, at the same time, protected future generations, ensured Medicare solvency, reformed welfare, and provided adequate funding for Medicaid, education, agriculture, national defense, veterans, and the environment.

Disagreement about what the agreement meant surfaced almost immediately. . . .

With the talks again stalled, Republicans refused to approve another short-term continuing resolution, and the government shut down again. . . .

When Congress returned in early January, the government shutdown had lasted far longer than any before. Although several more appropriations bills had become law before the second shutdown started, six were still outstanding. The press was full of articles about the harm the shutdown might cause—preparation of next year's flu vaccine was being hindered, for example—and of the suffering of federal employees. The public was blaming Republicans far more than the president for the impasse. . . .

The curtain finally came down on the 1995 budget battle in late April when Congress passed and Clinton signed an omnibus appropriations bill to fund the nine departments and dozens of agencies covered by the five regular appropriations bills never enacted. After fourteen continuing resolutions and two government shutdowns, the government was finally funded for the fiscal year ending October 1, 1996. . . .

Using the budget process, the new Republican majorities managed to cut domestic appropriations by 9 percent over the previous year, a very considerable achievement from their perspective. They failed in their much more ambitious attempt to cut spending for, and fundamentally restructure, the big entitlement programs, especially Medicare and Medicaid. . . .

The procedures and practices of unorthodox lawmaking are . . . just tools. They are by no means sufficient to produce fundamental change in policy direction. Summits are, in fact, a procedure of last resort. The president and Congress agree to try to settle their differences through a summit when more orthodox procedures have failed. The American governmental system of separate institutions sharing power has a status quo bias; making major policy changes is difficult and usually requires compromise. Sometimes the philosophical differences between the president and the congressional majority are so great that what one considers a reasonable compromise the other regards as selling out. When this happens, significant policy change is unlikely unless the actor advocating change can marshal strong public support and thereby make holding out too costly in electoral terms for the other actor. In fact, in the summer of 1996, Republicans scored an impressive victory when President Clinton signed a welfare overhaul bill. Although Clinton had extracted significant compromise, the legislation ended welfare as an entitlement and, in other provisions as well, bore a clear Republican stamp. This was a case in which the Republicans were backed by a strong public desire for policy change; Clinton and many other Democrats feared the electoral consequences of killing the legislation. On the budget, Republicans had hoped that public support for a balanced budget in the abstract would translate into strong public pressure on Clinton to make a deal on their terms. Instead, the Democrats' warnings that the Republicans' plan would cut Medicare, education, and environmental protection proved more persuasive. When Clinton won the battle for public opinion, Republicans lost their chance of winning the policy war.

31

DAVID PRICE

From *The Congressional Experience*

From a political science classroom at Duke University in Durham, North Carolina, to the U.S. House of Representatives, David Price describes his background, his decision to run for office, and his concerns for the future of the Congress. Price reveals his typical daily schedule as a representative. He discusses his distaste for "Congress-bashing," the favorite pastime of members

*of the Congress. Price condemns the "hot-button attack politics" campaigning
style that has pushed issues aside and created a negative cynical tone in
American politics.*

*In November 1994, Rep. David Price (D–NC) lost his seat in the
House of Representatives to his Republican challenger. Then in November,
1996, Price won back his seat.*

——————

ON NOVEMBER 4, 1986, I was elected to the U.S. House of
Representatives from the Fourth District of North Carolina, a five-county
area that includes the cites of Raleigh, Chapel Hill, and Asheboro. Many
thoughts crowded in on me on election night, but one of the most vivid
was of that spring evening in 1959 when I had first set foot in the part
of North Carolina I was now to represent. At the time, I was a student
at Mars Hill, a junior college in the North Carolina mountains a few
miles from my home in the small town of Erwin, Tennessee. I had taken
an eight-hour bus ride from Mars Hill to Chapel Hill to be interviewed
for a Morehead Scholarship, a generous award that subsequently made it
possible for me to attend the University of North Carolina (UNC). I was
awed by the university and nervous about the interview; thinking back
on some of the answers I gave the next morning ("Would you say Cecil
Rhodes was an imperialist?" "I believe so"), I still marvel that I won the
scholarship. But I did, and the next two years were among the most
formative and exciting of my life.

I went north in 1961 to divinity school and eventually to graduate
school and a faculty appointment in political science at Yale University.
But the idea of returning to the Raleigh-Durham-Chapel Hill area of
North Carolina exerted a continuing tug on me, particularly as I decided
on a teaching career and thought about where I would like to put down
personal and academic roots. Fortunately, my wife, Lisa, also found the
idea agreeable, despite her budding political career as a member of New
Haven's Board of Aldermen. Therefore, when I received an offer to join
the political science faculty at Duke University and also to help launch
the university's Institute of Policy Sciences and Public Affairs, I jumped
at the opportunity. In mid-1973, we moved with our two children—
Karen, three, and Michael, one—to Chapel Hill. Though we were delighted with the community and the job and saw the move as a long-
term one, I would have been incredulous at the suggestion that within
fourteen years I would represent the district in Congress. . . .

Among some voters—and occasionally among congressional colleagues—my academic background has represented a barrier to be over-

come. But usually it has not. My district, it is claimed, has the highest number of Ph.D.'s per capita of any comparable area in the country. Certainly, with eleven institutions of higher education and the kind of people who work in the Research Triangle Park, I have some remarkably literate constituents. I sometimes reflect ambivalently on this as I contemplate the piles of well-reasoned letters on every conceivable issue that come into my office. Yet the electoral advantages are considerable. During my first campaign, we polled to test public reactions to my academic affiliation and background, expecting to downplay them in the campaign. Instead, we found highly positive associations and ended up running a television ad that featured me in the classroom! . . .

Becoming a member of the House shakes up not only family life but also the roles and routines associated with one's previous career. I took a special interest, naturally, in [political scientist Richard] Fenno's* interview with a freshman senator who had been a college professor. "Life in the Senate," he said, "is the antithesis of academic life." I would not put it quite that way: Such a view seems both to exaggerate the orderliness and tranquility of modern academic life and to underestimate the extent to which one can impose a modicum of order on life in the Congress. Still, few jobs present as many diverse and competing demands as does service in Congress.

Consider, for example, my schedule for two rather typical days in the spring of 1991, reprinted here without change except for the deletion of some personal names and the addition of a few explanatory notes. By this time, I had moved to the Appropriations Committee from the three committees on which I sat during my first term, so the hearing schedule was less demanding; nonetheless, the Agriculture Appropriations Subcommittee held hearings on each of these two days. I also testified on a North Carolina environmental matter before a subcommittee of which I was not a member. The Budget Study Group and the Mainstream Forum, two of the informal organizations with which I am affiliated, held meetings, and the Prayer Breakfast, an informal fellowship group, met, as usual, on Thursday morning. I had several scheduled media interviews and probably a number of unscheduled press calls as well. There were a number of party meetings and activities: The Democratic Caucus met to discuss the

*Richard Fenno's most well-known book is his 1978 *Home Style*. It represented a whole new way to study Congress. He followed certain representatives as they returned home, to their districts, to meet with constituents. Fenno found that members of Congress try to build "trust" among the voters so that more "leeway" exists for members in their congressional voting. Much of Fenno's work involved interviewing and observing members of Congress as individuals, to gain insight into their behavior as elected officials. —EDS.

Typical Member's Daily Schedule in Washington

Wednesday, April 10, 1991

8:00 A.M.	Budget Study Group—Chairman Leon Panetta, Budget Committee, room 340 Cannon Building
8:45 A.M.	Mainstream Forum Meeting, room 2344 Rayburn Building
9:15 A.M.	Meeting with Consulting Engineers Council of N.C. from Raleigh about various issues of concern
9:45 A.M.	Meet with N.C. Soybean Assn. representatives re: agriculture appropriations projects
10:15 A.M.	WCHL radio interview (by phone)
10:30 A.M.	Tape weekly radio show—budget
11:00 A.M.	Meet with former student, now an author, about intellectual property issue
1:00 P.M.	Agriculture Subcommittee Hearing—Budget Overview and General Agriculture Outlook, room 2362 Rayburn Building
2:30 P.M.	Meeting with Chairman Bill Ford and southern Democrats re: HR-5, Striker Replacement Bill, possible amendments
3:15 P.M.	Meet with Close-Up students from district on steps of Capitol for photo and discussions
3:45 P.M.	Meet with Duke professor re: energy research programs
4:30 P.M.	Meet with constituent of Kurdish background re: situation in Iraq
5:30–7:00 P.M.	Reception—Sponsored by National Assn. of Home Builders, honoring new president Mark Tipton from Raleigh, H-328 Capitol
6:00–8:00 P.M.	Reception—Honoring retiring Rep. Bill Gray, Washington Court Hotel
6:00–8:00 P.M.	Reception–Sponsored by Firefighters Assn., room B-339 Rayburn Building
6:00–8:00 P.M.	Reception—American Financial Services Assn., Gold Room

Thursday, April 11, 1991

8:00 A.M.	Prayer Breakfast—Rep. Charles Taylor to speak, room H-130 Capitol
9:00 A.M.	Whip meeting, room H-324 Capitol
10:00 A.M.	Democratic Caucus Meeting, Hall of the House, re: budget
10:25 A.M.	UNISYS reps. in office (staff, DP meets briefly)
10:30 A.M.	Firefighters from Raleigh re: Hatch Act Reform, Manufacturer's Presumptive Liability, etc.

TYPICAL MEMBER'S DAILY SCHEDULE IN WASHINGTON (*continued*)

11:00 A.M.	American Business Council of the Gulf Countries re: rebuilding the Gulf, improving competitiveness in Gulf market
11:15 A.M.	Whip Task Force meeting re: Budget Resolution, room H-114 Capitol
12:00 P.M.	Speech—One Minute on House floor re: budget
12:30 P.M.	Party Effectiveness Lunch—re: banking reform, room H-324 Capitol
1:00 P.M.	Agriculture Subcommittee Hearing—Inspector General Overview and the Office of the General Counsel, room 2362 Rayburn Building
3:00 P.M.	Testify at Oceanography Subcommittee Hearing re: naval vessel waste disposal on N.C. Outer Banks, room 1334 Longworth Building
3:30 P.M.	Speak to Duke public policy students re: operations of Congress, room 188 Russell Building
5:00 P.M.	Interview with Matthew Cross, WUNC stringer re: offshore drilling
6:45 P.M.	Depart National Airport for Raleigh-Durham

pending budget resolution; a whip's task force was organized to mobilize Democrats behind the resolution; the caucus held a "party effectiveness" luncheon open to all members to discuss a major pending issue; and I participated in a caucus-organized set of one-minute speeches at the beginning of the House session. The other items are self-explanatory— meetings with North Carolina groups on issues of concern, talks to student groups, and various receptions that substituted for dinner or at least provided enough sustenance to take me through the evening of editing letters and reading in my office. And of course, the schedule does not capture the numerous trips to the House floor for votes, the phone calls, and the staff conferences scattered throughout every day.

These schedules list only events I actually attended; they also reflect the rules of thumb by which my staff and I keep life from getting even more hectic. In general, I talk with groups about pending legislation only when there is a North Carolina connection; most Washington groups are well aware that their delegations need to include at least one representative from the district. I also generally skip receptions at the end of the day unless constituents are to be there or a colleague has asked me to attend.

This sheer busyness in Washington and at home as well surpasses what almost all members have experienced in their previous careers and requires specific survival techniques. Most important, you must set priorities— separate those matters in which you want to invest considerable time and energy from those you wish to handle perfunctorily or not deal with personally at all. Confronted with three simultaneous subcommittee hearings, a member often has a choice: pop in on each of the three for fifteen minutes or choose one and remain long enough to learn and contribute something. It is also essential to delegate a great deal to staff and to develop a good mutual understanding within the office as to when the member's personal direction and attention are required. But there are no management techniques on earth that could make a representative's life totally predictable or controllable or that could convert a congressional office into a tidy bureaucracy. A member (or aide) who requires that kind of control—who cannot tolerate, for example, being diverted to talk to a visiting school class or to hear out a visiting delegation of homebuilders or social workers—is simply in the wrong line of work.

. . . Former Congressman Bob Eckhardt (D–Texas) suggested that every member of Congress performs three functions: lawmaker, ombudsman, and educator. This last function, as I have shown, may be closely related to the first: Lawmakers who wish to do more than simply defer to the strongest and best-organized interests on a certain matter must give some attention to explaining their actions and educating their constituents, helping them place the issue in broader perspective or perhaps activating alternative bases of support. And the extent to which a member is willing and able to undertake such explanations is ethically as well as politically significant.

Here, I turn to another facet of the legislators' educative role: their portrayal of Congress itself. On traveling with House members around their districts, Richard Fenno noted that the greatest surprise for him was the extent to which each one "polished his or her individual reputation at the expense of the institutional reputation of Congress":

In explaining what he was doing in Washington, every one of the eighteen House members took the opportunity to picture himself as different from, and better than, most of his fellow members in Congress. No one availed himself of the opportunity to educate his constituents about Congress as an institution—not in any way that would "hurt a little." To the contrary, the members' process of differentiating themselves from the Congress as a whole only served, directly or indirectly, to downgrade the Congress.

This was in the mid-1970s, and every indication is that such tactics have become even more prevalent as Congress-bashing by advocacy groups and in the media has intensified. "We have to differentiate me from the rest of those bandits down there in Congress," Fenno heard a member say to a campaign strategy group. " 'They are awful, but our guy is wonderful' — that's the message we have to get across."

So much for the traditional norm of institutional patriotism! Opinion polls regularly reveal that public officials in general and Congress in particular rank low in public esteem, an evaluation reinforced by the recent spate of ethics charges in both houses but rooted much more deeply in our country's history and political culture. Every indication is that we members reinforce such an assessment by distancing ourselves from any responsibility for the institution's functioning. And we are phenomenally successful at it, matching a 30 percent approval rate for Congress with a 95+ percent reelection rate for ourselves.

My point is not that a member should defend Congress, right or wrong. I understand very well the disadvantages of being put on the defensive about Congress's ethical problems — pointing out that only a small number of members are involved, for example, or that Ethics Committee proceedings are generally bipartisan and fair — although I believe many of these defenses have merit. Rather, I am speaking of a more general tendency to trash the institution. It is often tempting — but I believe, also deceptive and irresponsible — to pose as the quintessential outsider, carping at accommodations that have been reached on a given issue as though problems could simply be ignored, cost-free solutions devised, or the painful necessities of compromise avoided. Responsible legislators will communicate to their constituencies not only the assembly's failings but also what it is fair and reasonable to expect, what accommodations they would be well advised to accept, and so forth. In the past, institutional patriotism has too often taken an uncritical form, assuming that whatever the process produces must be acceptable. But self-righteous, anti-institutional posturing is no better. The moral quixotism to which reelection-minded legislators are increasingly prone too often serves to rationalize their own nonproductive legislative roles and to perpetuate public misperceptions of the criteria one can reasonably apply to legislative performance.

Therefore, although it may be politically profitable to "run *for* Congress by running *against* Congress," the implications for the institution's effectiveness and legitimacy are ominous. As Fenno concluded, "The strategy is ubiquitous, addictive, cost-free, and foolproof. . . . In the short run, everybody plays and nearly everybody wins. Yet the institution bleeds from 435 separate cuts. In the long run, therefore, somebody may lose.

... Congress may lack public support at the very time when the public needs Congress the most." ...

My job keeps me very busy and flying, as they say, "close to the ground"—attending to myriad details in dealing with constituents, tracking appropriations, and all the rest. I sometimes feel that I had a better overview of the current state of American politics and even of certain broad policy questions before I was elected than I do now. I have, however, been in a position to observe some alarming trends in our politics and to develop strong convictions about our need to reverse them. I will therefore conclude with a few thoughts on the ominous gap that has opened up between campaigning and governing. ... It is in the nature of political campaigns to polarize and to oversimplify, but the negative attacks and distortions have increased markedly. And the link between what candidates say in their campaign advertisements and the decisions they make once in office has become more and more tenuous. ...

This trend has been reinforced by the new technology of campaign advertising and fund-raising; thirty-second television ads and direct mail financial solicitations, for example, put a premium on hard-hitting, oversimplified appeals and the pushing of symbolic hot buttons. The trend has also been both cause and effect of the modern emergence of cultural and value questions, like abortion, race, patriotism, and alternative lifestyles, that lend themselves to symbolic appeals. Republican candidates in particular have found in these issues a promising means of diverting voters' attention from economic and quality-of-life concerns and of driving divisive wedges in the Democratic coalition.

The growing gap between campaigning and governing also bespeaks a certain public alienation and cynicism. Voters complain about the nastiness and irrelevance of campaign advertising, and my campaigns have demonstrated that such tactics can effectively be turned against an opponent. But voters who find little to encourage or inspire them in politics are nonetheless tempted to vote in anger or in protest, inclinations that modern campaign advertising exploits very effectively. As E. J. Dionne suggested, the decline of the "politics of remedy"—that is, politics that attempts "to solve problems and resolve disputes"—seems to have created a vicious cycle:

Campaigns have become negative in large part because of a sharp decline in popular faith in government. To appeal to an increasingly alienated electorate, candidates and their political consultants have adopted a cynical stance which, they believe with good reason, plays into popular cynicism about politics and thus wins them votes. But cynical campaigns do not resolve issues. They do not lead to "remedies." Therefore, problems get worse, the electorate becomes *more* cynical—and so does the advertising.

Responsibility for our descent into attack politics, increasingly divorced from the major problems faced by the American people, is widely shared—by journalists, interest groups, campaign consultants, and the viewing, voting public. Members of Congress are hardly helpless—or blameless—before these trends. For one thing, our defensiveness in the face of tough votes is often exaggerated; members frequently underestimate their ability to deflect attacks or to deal effectively with hostile charges. All of us feel occasionally that "I'd rather vote against this than to have to explain it," but we should worry if we find ourselves taking this way out too often or on matters of genuine consequence. It is our *job* to interpret and explain difficult decisions, and with sufficient effort, we can usually do so successfully.

We also have some choices about the kind of campaigns we run. By making campaign tactics themselves an issue, we can heighten public awareness of and resistance to distorted and manipulative appeals. Above all, we can tighten the link between what we say in our own campaigns and what we have done and intend to do in office. This is not a plea for dull campaigns; on the contrary, it is our duty to arouse people's concern and anger about areas of neglect, to convince them that we can do better, to inspire them to contribute to the solution. Most people believe that politics and politicians ought to have something constructive to offer in the realms of education, housing, health care, economic development, environmental protection, and other areas of tangible concern. Our task is to get to work on these major challenges in both campaigning *and* governing in a credible way that inspires confidence and enthusiasm. As that happens, hot-button attack politics will increasingly be seen as the sham that it is.

PART SIX

The Presidency

32

RICHARD NEUSTADT

From *Presidential Power and the Modern Presidents*

From this often-read book comes the classic concept of presidential power as "the power to persuade." Richard Neustadt observed the essence of presidential power when working in the executive branch during Franklin Roosevelt's term as president. He stayed to serve under President Truman. It is said that President Kennedy brought Presidential Power *with him to the White House, and Neustadt worked briefly for JFK. The first half of the excerpt, in which he shows how presidents' well-developed personal characteristics permit successful persuasive abilities, comes from the book's first edition. The excerpt's closing pages reflect Neustadt's recent musings on the nation, on world affairs, and on the challenges presidents face.*

——————

IN THE EARLY summer of 1952, before the heat of the campaign, President [Harry] Truman used to contemplate the problems of the general-become-President should [Dwight David] Eisenhower win the forthcoming election. "He'll sit here," Truman would remark (tapping his desk for emphasis), "and he'll say, 'Do this! Do that!' *And nothing will happen.* Poor Ike—it won't be a bit like the Army. He'll find it very frustrating."

Eisenhower evidently found it so. "In the face of the continuing dissidence and disunity, the President sometimes simply exploded with exasperation," wrote Robert Donovan in comment on the early months of Eisenhower's first term. "What was the use, he demanded to know, of his trying to lead the Republican Party. . . . " And this reaction was not limited to early months alone, or to his party only. "The President still feels," an Eisenhower aide remarked to me in 1958, "that when he's decided something, that *ought* to be the end of it . . . and when it bounces back undone or done wrong, he tends to react with shocked surprise."

Truman knew whereof he spoke. With "resignation" in the place of "shocked surprise," the aide's description would have fitted Truman. The former senator may have been less shocked than the former general, but he was no less subjected to that painful and repetitive experience: "Do this, do that, and nothing will happen." Long before he came to talk of Eisenhower he had put his own experience in other words: "I sit here all day trying to persuade people to do the things they ought to have sense enough to do without my persuading them. . . . That's all the powers of the President amount to."

In these words of a President, spoken on the job, one finds the essence of the problem now before us: "powers" are no guarantee of power; clerkship is no guarantee of leadership. The President of the United States has an extraordinary range of formal powers, of authority in statute law and in the Constitution. Here is testimony that despite his "powers" he does not obtain results by giving orders — or not, at any rate, merely by giving orders. He also has extraordinary status, ex officio, according to the customs of our government and politics. Here is testimony that despite his status he does not get action without argument. Presidential power is the power to persuade. . . .

The limits on command suggest the structure of our government. The Constitutional Convention of 1787 is supposed to have created a government of "separated powers." It did nothing of the sort. Rather, it created a government of separated institutions *sharing* powers. "I am part of the legislative process," Eisenhower often said in 1959 as a reminder of his veto. Congress, the dispenser of authority and funds, is no less part of the administrative process. Federalism adds another set of separated institutions. The Bill of Rights adds others. Many public purposes can only be achieved by voluntary acts of private institutions; the press, for one, in Douglass Cater's phrase, is a "fourth branch of government." And with the coming of alliances abroad, the separate institutions of a London, or a Bonn, share in the making of American public policy.

What the Constitution separates our political parties do not combine. The parties are themselves composed of separated organizations sharing public authority. The authority consists of nominating powers. Our national parties are confederations of state and local party institutions, with a headquarters that represents the White House, more or less, if the party has a President in office. These confederacies manage presidential nominations. All other public offices depend upon electorates confined within the states. All other nominations are controlled within the states. The President and congressmen who bear one party's label are divided by dependence upon different sets of voters. The differences are sharpest at the stage of nomination. The White House has too small a share in nominating congressmen, and Congress has too little weight in nominating presidents for party to erase their constitutional separation. Party links are stronger than is frequently supposed, but nominating processes assure the separation.

The separateness of institutions and the sharing of authority prescribe the terms on which a President persuades. When one man shares authority with another, but does not gain or lose his job upon the other's whim, his willingness to act upon the urging of the other turns on whether he conceives the action right for him. The essence of a President's persuasive task is to convince such men that what the White House wants of them is what they ought to do for their sake and on their authority. (Sex matters not at all; for *man* read *woman*.)

Persuasive power, thus defined, amounts to more than charm or reasoned argument. These have their uses for a President, but these are not the whole of his resources. For the individuals he would induce to do what he wants done on their own responsibility will need or fear some acts by him on his responsibility. If they share his authority, he has some share in theirs. Presidential "powers" may be inconclusive when a President commands, but always remain relevant as he persuades. The status and authority inherent in his office reinforce his logic and his charm. . . .

A President's authority and status give him great advantages in dealing with the men he would persuade. Each "power" is a vantage point for him in the degree that other men have use for his authority. From the veto to appointments, from publicity to budgeting, and so down a long list, the White House now controls the most encompassing array of vantage points in the American political system. With hardly an exception, those who share in governing this country are aware that at some time, in some degree, the doing of *their* jobs, the furthering of *their* ambitions, may depend upon the President of the United States. Their need for presidential action, or their fear of it, is bound to be recurrent if not actually continuous. Their need or fear is his advantage.

A President's advantages are greater than mere listing of his "powers" might suggest. Those with whom he deals must deal with him until the last day of his term. Because they have continuing relationships with him, his future, while it lasts, supports his present influence. Even though there is no need or fear of him today, what he could do tomorrow may supply today's advantage. Continuing relationships may convert any "power," any aspect of his status, into vantage points in almost any case. When he induces other people to do what he wants done, a President can trade on their dependence now and later.

The President's advantages are checked by the advantages of others. Continuing relationships will pull in both directions. These are relationships of mutual dependence. A President depends upon the persons whom he would persuade; he has to reckon with his need or fear of them. They too will possess status, or authority, or both, else they would be of little use to him. Their vantage points confront his own; their power tempers his. . . .

The power to persuade is the power to bargain. Status and authority yield bargaining advantages. But in a government of "separated institutions sharing powers," they yield them to all sides. With the array of vantage points at his disposal, a President may be far more persuasive than his logic or his charm could make him. But outcomes are not guaranteed by his advantages. There remain the counter pressures those whom he would influence can bring to bear on him from vantage points at their disposal. Command has limited utility; persuasion becomes give-and-take. It is well that the White House holds the vantage points it does. In such a business any President may need them all—and more. . . .

When a President confronts divergent policy advisers, disputing experts, conflicting data, and uncertain outlooks, yet must choose, there plainly *are* some other things he can do for himself besides consulting his own power stakes. But there is a proviso—provided he has done that first and keeps clear in his mind how much his prospects may depend on his authority, how much on reputation, how much on public standing. In the world Reagan inhabited where reputation and prestige are far more intertwined than they had been in Truman's time, or even LBJ's, this proviso is no easy test of presidential expertise. It calls for a good ear and a fine eye. . . .

But when a President turns to others, regardless of the mode, he is dependent on their knowledge, judgment, and good will. If he turns essentially to one, alone, he puts a heavy burden on that other's knowledge. If he chooses not to read or hear details, he puts an even greater burden on the other's judgment. If he consents, besides, to secrecy from everyone whose task in life is to protect his flanks, he courts deep trouble. Good will should not be stretched beyond endurance. In a system characterized by separated institutions sharing powers, where presidential interests will diverge in some degree from those of almost everybody else, that suggests not stretching very far. . . .

Personally, I prefer Presidents . . . more skeptical than trustful, more curious than committed, more nearly Roosevelts than Reagans. I think the former energize our governmental system better and bring out its defects less than do the latter. Reagan's years did not persuade me otherwise, in spite of his appeal on other scores. Every scandal in his wake, for instance, must owe something to the narrow range of his convictions and the breadth of his incuriosity, along with all that trust. A President cannot abolish bad behavior, but he sets a tone, and if he is alert to possibilities he can set traps, and with them limits. Reagan's tone, apparently, was heard by all too many as "enrich yourselves," while those few traps deregulation spared appear to have been sprung and left unbaited for the most part. But this book has not been written to expound my personal preferences. Rather it endeavors to expose the problem for a President of either sort who seeks to buttress prospects for his future influence while making present choices—"looking toward tomorrow from today," as I wrote at the start. For me that remains a crucial enterprise. It is not, of course, the only thing a President should put his mind to, but it is the subject to which I have put my own throughout this book. It remains crucial, in my view, not simply for the purposes of Presidents, but also for the products of the system, whether effective policy, or flawed or none. Thus it becomes crucial for us all.

We now stand on the threshold of a time in which those separated institutions, Congress and the President, share powers fully and uncomfortably across the board of policy, both foreign and domestic. From the 1940s through the 1960s—"midcentury" in this book's terms—Congress, having been embarrassed at Pearl Harbor by the isolationism it displayed beforehand, gave successive Presidents more scope in defense budgeting and in the conduct of diplomacy toward Europe and Japan than was the norm between the two world wars. Once the Cold War had gotten under way, and then been largely militarized after Korea, that scope widened. With the onset of the missile age it deepened. Should nuclear war impend, the President became the system's final arbiter. Thus I characterized JFK against the background of the Cuban missile crisis. But by 1975 the denouement of Watergate and that of Vietnam, eight months apart, had put a period to what remained of congressional reticence left over from Pearl Harbor. And the closing of the Cold War, now in sight though by no means achieved, promises an end to nuclear danger as between the Soviet Union and the United States. Threats of nuclear attack could well remain, from Third World dictators or terrorists, but not destruction of the Northern Hemisphere. So in the realm of military preparations— even, indeed, covert actions—the congressional role waxes as the Cold War wanes, returning toward normality as understood in Franklin Roosevelt's first two terms.

In a multipolar world, crisscrossed by transnational relations, with economic and environmental issues paramount, and issues of security reshaped on regional lines, our Presidents will less and less have reason to seek solace in foreign relations from the piled-up frustrations of home affairs. Their foreign frustrations will be piled high too.

Since FDR in wartime, every President including Bush has found the role of superpower sovereign beguiling: personal responsibility at once direct and high, issues at once gripping and arcane, opposite numbers frequently intriguing and well-mannered, acclaim by foreign audiences echoing well at home, foreign travel relatively glamorous, compared with home, interest groups less clamorous, excepting special cases, authority always stronger, Congress often tamer. But the distinctions lessen—compare Bush's time with Nixon's to say nothing of Eisenhower's—and we should expect that they will lessen further. Telecommunications, trade, aid, banking and stock markets combined with AIDS and birth control and hunger, topped off by toxic waste and global warming—these are not the stuff of which the Congress of Vienna* was made, much less the summits of yore. Moreover, Europeans ten years hence, as well as Japanese, may not resemble much the relatively acquiescent "middle powers" we grew used to in the 1960s and 1970s. Cooperating with them may come to seem to Presidents no easier than cooperating with Congress. Our friends abroad will see it quite the other way around: How are they to cooperate with our peculiar mix of separated institutions sharing powers? Theirs are ordered governments, ours a rat race. Complaints of us by others in these terms are nothing new. They have been rife throughout this century. But by the next, some of the chief complainants may have fewer needs of us, while ours of them grow relatively greater, than at any other time since World War II. In that case foreign policy could cease to be a source of pleasure for a President. By the same token, he or she would have to do abroad as on the Hill and in Peoria: Check carefully the possible effects of present choices on prospective reputation and prestige— thinking of other governments and publics quite as hard as those at home. It is not just our accustomed NATO and Pacific allies who may force the pace here, but the Soviet Union, if it holds together, and potentially great powers—China, India, perhaps Brazil—as well as our neighbors, north and south.

From the multicentered, interdependent world now coming into being, environmentally endangered as it is, Presidents may look back on the Cold War as an era of stability, authority, and glamour. They may yearn for the simplicity they see in retrospect, and also for the solace. Too bad. The job of being President is tougher when incumbents have to struggle for effective influence in foreign and domestic spheres at once, with their command of nuclear forces losing immediate relevance, and the American

*After the 1814 defeat of the French leader Napoleon by Russia, Prussia, Austria, and Britain, these great powers met in Vienna, Austria, to ensure that the future of Europe would be peaceful. At the Congress of Vienna, they created a "balance of power" system so that no single European nation could dominate the continent.—EDS.

economy shorn of its former clout. There are, however, compensations, one in particular. If we outlive the Cold War,* the personal responsibility attached to nuclear weapons should become less burdensome for Presidents themselves, while contemplation of their mere humanity becomes less haunting for the rest of us. To me that seems a fair exchange.

33

ARTHUR SCHLESINGER

From *The Imperial Presidency*

Historian Arthur Schlesinger coined one of the most famous and often-quoted political phrases, used not just in academe but in the real world of government too. The demise of Richard Nixon, because of the Watergate scandal, inspired Schlesinger to look back in U.S. history to locate the roots of the tremendous power that the executive had accumulated. His observations led him to develop the idea of an "imperial Presidency," with all the connotations that phrase carries. The author believes that the imperial presidency initially evolved for a clear and identifiable reason; it then grew due to other secondary factors. Certain presidents—Roosevelt and especially Kennedy—garner praise from Schlesinger for their judicious use of imperial powers. Other presidents he condemns. Schlesinger's discussion of Richard Nixon, the ultimate imperial president as well as its destroyer, is a frank and unvarnished critique of the man who turned the imperial presidency homeward, against the American people. After Nixon left office, the phrase was little-used, until President Bush responded to the terrorist attacks of September 11, 2001.

———

IN THE LAST YEARS presidential primacy, so indispensable to the political order, has turned into presidential supremacy. The constitutional Presidency—as events so apparently disparate as the Indochina War and the Watergate affair showed—has become the imperial Presidency and threatens to be the revolutionary Presidency.

---

*The Cold War refers to the hostility that existed between the United States and the Soviet Union from the end of World War II until recent times. The Cold War involved many forms of hostility: democracy versus communism; America's NATO allies versus the Soviet Union's Warsaw Pact military partners; the threat of nuclear war; economic competition; the dividing of Third World nations into pro-U.S. and pro-Soviet camps. With the demise of communism in Eastern Europe and the disintegration of the Soviet Union, the Cold War era has ended.—EDS.

This book . . . deals essentially with the shift in the *constitutional* balance—with, that is, the appropriation by the Presidency, and particularly by the contemporary Presidency, of powers reserved by the Constitution and by long historical practice to Congress.

This process of appropriation took place in both foreign and domestic affairs. Especially in the twentieth century, the circumstances of an increasingly perilous world as well as of an increasingly interdependent economy and society seemed to compel a larger concentration of authority in the Presidency. It must be said that historians and political scientists, this writer among them, contributed to the rise of the presidential mystique. But the imperial Presidency received its decisive impetus, I believe, from foreign policy; above all, from the capture by the Presidency of the most vital of national decisions, the decision to go to war.

This book consequently devotes special attention to the history of the war-making power. The assumption of that power by the Presidency was gradual and usually under the demand or pretext of emergency. It was as much a matter of congressional abdication as of presidential usurpation. . . .

The imperial Presidency was essentially the creation of foreign policy. A combination of doctrines and emotions—belief in permanent and universal crisis, fear of communism, faith in the duty and the right of the United States to intervene swiftly in every part of the world—had brought about the unprecedented centralization of decisions over war and peace in the Presidency. With this there came an unprecedented exclusion of the rest of the executive branch, of Congress, of the press and of public opinion in general from these decisions. Prolonged war in Vietnam strengthened the tendencies toward both centralization and exclusion. So the imperial Presidency grew at the expense of the constitutional order. Like the cowbird, it hatched its own eggs and pushed the others out of the nest. And, as it overwhelmed the traditional separation of powers in foreign affairs, it began to aspire toward an equivalent centralization of power in the domestic polity.

. . . We saw in the case of Franklin D. Roosevelt and the New Deal that extraordinary power flowing into the Presidency to meet domestic problems by no means enlarged presidential authority in foreign affairs. But we also saw in the case of FDR and the Second World War and Harry S. Truman and the steel seizure that extraordinary power flowing into the Presidency to meet international problems could easily encourage Presidents to extend their unilateral claims at home. . . . Twenty years later, the spillover effect from Vietnam coincided with indigenous developments that were quite separately carrying new power to the Presidency.

For domestic as well as for international reasons, the imperial Presidency was sinking roots deep into the national society itself.

One such development was the decay of the traditional party system. . . . For much of American history the party has been the ultimate vehicle of political expression. Voters inherited their politics as they did their religion. . . . By the 1970s ticket-splitting had become common. Independent voting was spreading everywhere, especially among the young. Never had party loyalties been so weak, party affiliations so fluid, party organizations so irrelevant.

Many factors contributed to the decline of parties. The old political organizations had lost many of their functions. The waning of immigration, for example, had deprived the city machine of its classical clientele. The rise of civil service had cut off the machine's patronage. The New Deal had taken over the machine's social welfare role. Above all, the electronic revolution was drastically modifying the political environment. Two electronic devices had a particularly devastating impact on the traditional structure of politics — television and the computer. . . .

As the parties wasted away, the Presidency stood out in solitary majesty as the central focus of political emotion, the ever more potent symbol of national community. . . .

At the same time, the economic changes of the twentieth century had conferred vast new powers not just on the national government but more particularly on the Presidency. . . .

. . . The managed economy, in short, offered new forms of unilateral power to the President who was bold enough to take action on his own. . . .

. . . The imperial presidency, born in the 1940s and 1950s to save the outer world from perdition, thus began in the 1960s and 1970s to find nurture at home. Foreign policy had given the President the command of peace and war. Now the decay of the parties left him in command of the political scene, and the Keynesian revelation placed him in command of the economy. At this extraordinary historical moment, when foreign and domestic lines of force converged, much depended on whether the occupant of the White House was moved to ride the new tendencies of power or to resist them.

For the American Presidency was a peculiarly personal institution. It remained, of course, an agency of government, subject to unvarying demands and duties no matter who was President. But, more than most agencies of government, it changed shape, intensity and ethos according to the man in charge. . . . The management of the great foreign policy crisis of the Kennedy years — the Soviet attempt to install nuclear missiles in Cuba—came as if in proof of the proposition that the nuclear age left no alternative to unilateral presidential decision. . . .

. . . Time was short, because something had to be done before the bases became operational. Secrecy was imperative. Kennedy took the decision into his own hands, but it is to be noted that he did not make it in imperial solitude. The celebrated Executive Committee became a forum for exceedingly vigorous and intensive debate. Major alternatives received strong, even vehement, expression. Though there was no legislative consultation, there was most effective executive consultation. . . . But, even in retrospect, the missile crisis seems an emergency so acute in its nature and so peculiar in its structure that it did in fact require unilateral executive decision.

Yet this very acuteness and peculiarity disabled Kennedy's action in October 1962 as a precedent for future Presidents in situations less acute and less peculiar. For the missile crisis was unique in the postwar years in that it *really* combined all those pressures of threat, secrecy and time that the foreign policy establishment had claimed as characteristic of decisions in the nuclear age. Where the threat was less grave, the need for secrecy less urgent, the time for debate less restricted—i.e., in all other cases—the argument for independent and unilateral presidential action was notably less compelling.

Alas, Kennedy's action, which should have been celebrated as an exception, was instead enshrined as a rule. This was in great part because it so beautifully fulfilled both the romantic ideal of the strong President and the prophecy of split-second presidential decision in the nuclear age. The very brilliance of Kennedy's performance appeared to vindicate the idea that the President must take unto himself the final judgments of war and peace. The missile crisis, I believe, was superbly handled, and could not have been handled so well in any other way. But one of its legacies was the imperial conception of the Presidency that brought the republic so low in Vietnam. . . .

. . . Johnson talked to, even if he too seldom listened to, an endless stream of members of Congress and the press. He unquestionably denied himself reality for a long time, especially when it came to Vietnam. But in the end reality broke through, forcing him to accept unpleasant truths he did not wish to hear. Johnson's personality was far closer than Truman's to imperial specifications. But the fit was by no means perfect. . . .

Every President reconstructs the Presidency to meet his own psychological needs. Nixon displayed more monarchical yearnings than any of his predecessors. He plainly reveled in the ritual of the office, only regretting that it could not be more elaborate. What previous President, for example, would have dreamed of ceremonial trumpets or of putting the White House security force in costumes to rival the Guards at Buckingham Palace? Public ridicule stopped this. But Nixon saw no problem about using federal money, under the pretext of national security, to adorn his California and Florida estates with redwood fences, golf carts, heaters and wind screens for the swimming pool, beach cabanas, roof tiling, carpets, furniture, trees and shrubbery. . . . Nixon's fatal error was to institute within the White House itself a centralization even more total than that he contemplated for the executive branch. He rarely saw most of his so-called personal assistants. If an aide telephoned the President on a domestic matter, his call was switched to Haldeman's office.* If he sent the President a memorandum, Haldeman decided whether or not the President would see it. "Rather than the President telling someone to do something," Haldeman explained in 1971, "I'll tell the guy. If he wants to find out something from somebody, I'll do it."

Presidents like Roosevelt and Kennedy understood that, if the man at the top confined himself to a single information system, he became the prisoner of that system. Therefore they pitted sources of their own against the information delivered to them through official channels. They understood that contention was an indispensable means of government. But Nixon, instead of exposing himself to the chastening influence of debate, organized the executive branch and the White House in order to shield himself as far as humanly possible from direct question or challenge—i.e., from reality. . . .

As one examined the impressive range of Nixon's initiatives—from his appropriation of the war-making power to his interpretation of the appointing power, from his unilateral determination of social priorities to his unilateral abolition of statutory programs, from his attack on legislative privilege to his enlargement of executive privilege, from his theory of impoundment to his theory of the pocket veto, from his calculated disparagement of the cabinet and his calculated discrediting of the press to his carefully organized concentration of federal management in the White House—from all this a larger design ineluctably emerged. It was hard to know whether Nixon, whose style was banality, understood consciously where he was heading. He was not a man given to political philosophizing. But he was heading toward a new balance of constitutional powers, an audacious and imaginative reconstruction of the American Constitution.

*Robert Haldeman headed Richard Nixon's White House staff. He was a stern gatekeeper (the president wished it so) before his resignation in the face of the exploding Watergate scandals during the spring of 1973. He was subsequently convicted of criminal charges and imprisoned for his role in Watergate.—EDS.

He did indeed contemplate, as he said in 1971 State of the Union message, a New American Revolution. But the essence of this revolution was not, as he said at the time, power to the people. The essence was power to the Presidency. . . . His purpose was probably more unconscious than conscious; and his revolution took direction and color not just from the external circumstances pressing new powers on the Presidency but from the needs and drives of his own agitated psyche. This was the fatal flaw in the revolutionary design. For everywhere he looked he saw around him hideous threats to the national security—threats that, even though he would not describe them to Congress or the people, kept his White House in constant uproar and warranted in his own mind a clandestine presidential response of spectacular and historic illegality. If his public actions led toward a scheme of presidential supremacy under a considerably debilitated Constitution, his private obsessions pushed him toward the view that the Presidency could set itself, at will, *above* the Constitution. It was this theory that led straight to Watergate. . . .

Secrecy seemed to promise government three inestimable advantages: the power to withhold, the power to leak and the power to lie. . . .

The power to withhold held out the hope of denying the public the knowledge that would make possible an independent judgment on executive policy. The mystique of inside information—"if you only knew what we know"—was a most effective way to defend the national-security monopoly and prevent democratic control of foreign policy. . . .

The power to leak meant the power to tell the people what it served the government's purpose that they should know. . . .

The power to withhold and the power to leak led on inexorably to the power to lie. The secrecy system instilled in the executive branch the idea that foreign policy was no one's business save its own, and uncontrolled secrecy made it easy for lying to become routine. It was in this spirit that the Eisenhower administration concealed the CIA operations it was mounting against governments around the world. It was in this spirit that the Kennedy administration stealthily sent the Cuban brigade to the Bay of Pigs* and stealthily enlarged American involvement in Vietnam. It was in this spirit that the Johnson administration Americanized the Vietnam War, misrepresenting one episode after another to Congress and the peo-

*In 1961, President John F. Kennedy accepted responsibility for the disaster at the Bay of Pigs in Cuba. Over a thousand Cuban exiles, trained by the U.S. Central Intelligence Agency (CIA), tried to land in Cuba to overthrow the communist government of Fidel Castro. The invasion was a complete failure, forcing Kennedy to reassess his foreign policy approach, especially toward Latin America.—EDS.

ple—Tonkin Gulf, the first American ground force commitment, the bombing of North Vietnam, My Lai and the rest.*

The longer the secrecy system dominated government, the more government assumed the *right* to lie. . . .

God, it has been well said, looks after drunks, children and the United States of America. However, given the number, the brazen presumption and the clownish ineptitude of the conspirators, if it had not been Watergate, it would surely have been something else. For Watergate was a symptom, not a cause. Nixon's supporters complained that his critics were blowing up a petty incident out of all proportion to its importance. No doubt a burglary at Democratic headquarters was trivial next to a mission to Peking. But Watergate's importance was not simply in itself. Its importance was in the way it brought to the surface, symbolized and made politically accessible the great question posed by the Nixon administration in every sector—the question of presidential power. The unwarranted and unprecedented expansion of presidential power, because it ran through the whole Nixon system, was bound, if repressed at one point, to break out at another. This, not Watergate, was the central issue. . . . Watergate did stop the revolutionary Presidency in its tracks. It blew away the mystique of the mandate and reinvigorated the constitutional separation of powers. If the independent judiciary, the free press, Congress and the executive agencies could not really claim too much credit as institutions for work performed within them by brave individuals, nonetheless they all drew new confidence as institutions from the exercise of power they had forgotten they possessed. The result could only be to brace and strengthen the inner balance of American democracy. . . .

If the Nixon White House escaped the legal consequences of its illegal behavior, why would future Presidents and their associates not suppose themselves entitled to do what the Nixon White House had done? Only

*The Tonkin Gulf incident involved two alleged attacks on American ships in the waters off the coast of Vietnam in 1964. President Lyndon Johnson may have exaggerated the extent of the attacks to gain support for widening the war. In response to the incident, the Senate voted 88 to 2 and the House of Representatives 416 to 0 to allow the president significant latitude in the use of American forces in Vietnam. No formal declaration of war was ever made concerning Vietnam, but the Gulf of Tonkin Resolution became the executive branch's "blank check" to expand the conflict. The 1968 My Lai massacre was a turning point in American public opinion concerning the Vietnam War. U.S. soldiers killed over a hundred Vietnamese villagers. One lieutenant was tried and convicted for the slaughter that had happened because of the inability of American troops to distinguish between enemy soldiers and civilians. Some Americans believed that those higher up in the military, not just Lieutenant William Calley, should have been prosecuted for the massacre.—EDS.

condign punishment would restore popular faith in the Presidency and deter future Presidents from illegal conduct—so long, at least, as Watergate remained a vivid memory. We have noted that corruption appears to visit the White House in fifty-year cycles. This suggests that exposure and retribution inoculate the Presidency against its latent criminal impulses for about half a century. Around the year 2023 the American people would be well advised to go on the alert and start nailing down everything in sight.

34

THOMAS CRONIN
MICHAEL GENOVESE

From *The Paradoxes of the American Presidency*

The United States as a nation of paradoxes is a theme frequently used to explain the contradictions found throughout American life. In an earlier selection (#7), Michael Kammen called Americans "people of paradox." Here, political scientists Thomas Cronin and Michael Genovese use the concept of paradox to explore the many images that citizens hold of their president. Each image they describe is accompanied by a contrary image. For example, Cronin and Genovese note, the president is supposed to be an average person just like us, while simultaneously being outstanding and extraordinary. With such paradoxical expectations of a president, is it any wonder that Americans judge the executive so harshly?

———

THE MIND SEARCHES FOR answers to the complexities of life. We often gravitate toward simple explanations for the world's mysteries. This is a natural way to try and make sense out of a world that seems to defy understanding. We are uncomfortable with contradictions so we reduce reality to understandable simplifications. And yet, contradictions and clashing expectations are part of life. "No aspect of society, no habit, custom, movement, development, is without cross-currents," says historian Barbara Tuchman. "Starving peasants in hovels live alongside prosperous landlords in featherbeds. Children are neglected and children are loved." In life we are confronted with paradoxes for which we seek meaning. The same is true for the American presidency. We admire presidential power, yet fear it. We yearn for the heroic, yet are also inherently suspicious of it. We demand dynamic leadership, yet grant only limited powers to the president. We want presidents to be dispassionate analysts and listeners, yet they must also be decisive. We are impressed with presidents who have great self-confidence, yet we dislike arrogance and respect those who express reasonable self-doubt.

How then are we to make sense of the presidency? This complex, multidimensional, even contradictory institution is vital to the American system of government. The physical and political laws that seem to constrain one president, liberate another. What proves successful in one, leads to failure in another. Rather than seeking one unifying theory of presidential politics that answers all our questions, we believe that the American presidency might be better understood as a series of paradoxes, clashing expectations and contradictions.

Leaders live with contradictions. Presidents, more than most people, learn to take advantage of contrary or divergent forces. Leadership situations commonly require successive displays of contrasting characteristics. Living with, even embracing, contradictions is a sign of political and personal maturity.

The effective leader understands the presence of opposites. The aware leader, much like a first-rate conductor, knows when to bring in various sections, knows when and how to turn the volume up and down, and learns how to balance opposing sections to achieve desired results. Effective presidents learn how to manage these contradictions and give meaning and purpose to confusing and often clashing expectations. The novelist F. Scott Fitzgerald once suggested that, "The test of a first-rate intelligence is the ability to hold two opposed ideas in the mind at the same time." Casey Stengel, long-time New York Yankee manager and occasional (if accidental) Zen philosopher, captured the essence of the paradox when he noted, "Good pitching will always stop good hitting, and vice versa."

Our expectations of, and demands on, the president are frequently so contradictory as to invite two-faced behavior by our presidents. Presidential powers are often not as great as many of us believe, and the president gets unjustly condemned as ineffective. Or a president will overreach or resort to unfair play while trying to live up to our demands.

The Constitution is of little help. The founders purposely left the presidency imprecisely defined. This was due in part to their fears of both the monarchy and the masses, and in part to their hopes that future presidents would create a more powerful office than the framers were able to do at the time. They knew that at times the president would have to move swiftly and effectively, yet they went to considerable lengths to avoid enumerating specific powers and duties in order to calm the then widespread fear of monarchy. After all, the nation had just fought a war against executive tyranny. Thus the paradox of the invention of the presidency: To get the presidency approved in 1787 and 1788, the framers had to leave several silences and ambiguities for fear of portraying the office as an overly centralized leadership institution. Yet when we need central leadership we turn to the president and read into Article II of the Constitution various prerogatives or inherent powers that allow the president to perform as an effective national leader.

Today the informal and symbolic powers of the presidency account for as much as the formal, stated ones. Presidential powers expand and contract in response to varying situational and technological changes. The powers of the presidency are thus interpreted so differently that they sometimes seem to be those of different offices. In some ways the modern presidency has virtually unlimited authority for almost anything its occupant chooses to do with it. In other ways, a president seems hopelessly ensnarled in a web of checks and balances.

Presidents and presidential candidates must constantly balance conflicting demands, cross pressures, and contradictions. It is characteristic of the American mind to hold contradictory ideas without bothering to resolve the conflicts between them. Perhaps some contradictions are best left unresolved, especially as ours is an imperfect world and our political system is a complicated one, held together by countless compromises. We may not be able to resolve many of these clashing expectations. Some of the inconsistencies in our judgments about presidents doubtless stem from the many ironies and paradoxes of the human condition. While difficult, at the least we should develop a better understanding of what it is we ask of our presidents, thereby increasing our sensitivity to the limits and possibilities of what a president can achieve. This might free presidents to lead and administer more effectively in those critical times when the nation has no choice but to turn to them. Whether we like it or not, the vitality of our democracy depends in large measure upon the sensitive interaction of presidential leadership with an understanding public willing to listen and willing to provide support. Carefully planned innovation is nearly impossible without the kind of leadership a competent and fair-minded president can provide.

The following are some of the paradoxes of the presidency. Some are cases of confused expectations. Some are cases of wanting one kind of presidential behavior at one time, and another kind later. Still others stem from the contradiction inherent in the concept of democratic leadership, which on the surface at least, appears to set up "democratic" and "leadership" as warring concepts. Whatever the source, each has implications for presidential performance and for how Americans judge presidential success and failure. . . .

Paradox #1. Americans demand powerful, popular presidential leadership that solves the nation's problems. Yet we are inherently suspicious of strong centralized leadership and especially the abuse of power and therefore we place significant limits on the president's powers.

We admire power but fear it. We love to unload responsibilities on our leaders, yet we intensely dislike being bossed around. We expect impressive leadership from presidents, and we simultaneously impose constitutional, cultural, and political restrictions on them. These restrictions often prevent presidents from living up to our expectations. . . .

Presidents are supposed to follow the laws and respect the constitutional procedures that were designed to restrict their power, yet still they must be powerful and effective when action is needed. For example, we approve of presidential military initiatives and covert operations when they work out well, but we criticize presidents and insist they work more closely with Congress when the initiatives fail. We recognize the need for secrecy in certain government actions, but we resent being deceived and left in the dark—again, especially when things go wrong, as in Reagan's Iranian arms sale diversions to the Contras.

Although we sometimes do not approve of the way a president acts, we often approve of the end results. Thus Lincoln is often criticized for acting outside the limits of the Constitution, but at the same time he is forgiven due to the obvious necessity for him to violate certain constitutional principles in order to preserve the Union. FDR was often flagrantly deceptive and manipulative not only of his political opponents but also of his staff and allies. FDR even relished pushing people around and toying with them. But leadership effectiveness in the end often comes down to whether a person acts in terms of the highest interests of the nation. Most historians conclude Lincoln and Roosevelt were responsible in the use of presidential power, to preserve the Union, to fight the depression and nazism. Historians also conclude that Nixon was wrong for acting beyond the law in pursuit of personal power. . . .

Paradox #2. We yearn for the democratic "common person" and also for the uncommon, charismatic, heroic, visionary performance.

We want our presidents to be like us, but better than us. We like to think America is the land where the common sense of the common person reigns. Nourished on a diet of Frank Capra's "common-man-as-hero" movies, and the literary celebration of the average citizen by authors such as Emerson, Whitman, and Thoreau, we prize the common touch. The plain-speaking Harry Truman, the up-from-the-log-cabin "man or woman of the people," is enticing. Few of us, however, settle for anything but the best; we want presidents to succeed and we hunger for brilliant, uncommon, and semiregal performances from presidents. . . .

It is said the American people crave to be governed by a president who is greater than anyone else yet not better than themselves. We are inconsistent; we want our president to be one of the folks yet also something special. If presidents get too special, however, they get criticized and roasted. If they try to be too folksy, people get bored. We cherish the myth that anyone can grow up to be president, that there are no barriers and no elite qualifications, but we don't want someone who is too ordinary. Would-be presidents have to prove their special qualifications—their excellence, their stamina, and their capacity for uncommon leadership. Fellow commoner, Truman, rose to the demands of the job and became an apparently gifted decision maker, or so his admirers would have us believe.

In 1976 Governor Jimmy Carter seemed to grasp this conflict and he ran as local, down-home, farm-boy-next-door makes good. The image of the peanut farmer turned gifted governor contributed greatly to Carter's success as a national candidate and he used it with consummate skill. Early in his presidential bid, Carter enjoyed introducing himself as peanut farmer *and* nuclear physicist, once again suggesting he was down to earth but cerebral as well.

Ronald Reagan illustrated another aspect of this paradox. He was a representative all-American—small-town, midwestern, and also a rich celebrity of stage, screen, and television. He boasted of having been a Democrat, yet campaigned as a Republican. A veritable Mr. Smith goes to Washington, he also had uncommon star quality. Bill Clinton liked us to view him as both a Rhodes scholar and an ordinary saxophone-playing member of the high school band from Hope, Arkansas; as a John Kennedy and even an Elvis figure; and also as just another jogger who would stop by for a Big Mac on the way home from a run in the neighborhood. . . .

Paradox #3. We want a decent, just, caring, and compassionate president, yet we admire a cunning, guileful, and, on occasions that warrant it, even a ruthless, manipulative president.

There is always a fine line between boldness and recklessness, between strong self-confidence and what the Greeks called "hubris," between dogged determination and pigheaded stubbornness. Opinion polls indicate people want a just, decent, and intellectually honest individual as our chief executive. Almost as strongly, however, the public also demands the quality of toughness.

We may admire modesty, humility, and a sense of proportion, but most of our great leaders have been vain and crafty. After all, you don't get to the White House by being a wallflower. Most have aggressively sought power and were rarely preoccupied with metaphysical inquiry or ethical considerations.

Franklin Roosevelt's biographers, while emphasizing his compassion for the average American, also agree he was vain, devious, and manipulative and had a passion for secrecy. These, they note, are often the standard weaknesses of great leaders. Significant social and political advances are made by those with drive, ambition, and a certain amount of brash, irrational self-confidence. . . .

Perhaps Dwight Eisenhower reconciled these clashing expectations better than recent presidents. Blessed with a wonderfully seductive, benign smile and a reserved, calming disposition, he was also the disciplined, strong, no-nonsense five-star general with all the medals and victories to go along with it. His ultimate resource as president was this reconciliation of decency and proven toughness, likability alongside demonstrated valor. Some of his biographers suggest his success was at least partly due to his uncanny ability to appear guileless to the public yet act with ample cunning in private. . . .

One of the ironies of the American presidency is that those characteristics we condemn in one president, we look for in another. Thus a supporter of Jimmy Carter's once suggested that Sunday school teacher Carter wasn't "rotten enough," "a wheeler-dealer," "an s.o.b."—precisely the virtues (if they can be called that) that Lyndon Johnson was most criticized for a decade earlier. President Clinton was viewed as both a gifted Southern Baptist–style preacher by some of his followers and a man who was character challenged, by opponents. . . .

Paradox #4. We admire the "above politics" nonpartisan or bipartisan approach, yet the presidency is perhaps the most political office in the American system, a system in which we need a creative entrepreneurial master politician.

The public yearns for a statesman in the White House, for a George Washington or a second "era of good feelings"—anything that might prevent partisanship or politics as usual in the White House. Former French President Charles de Gaulle once said, "I'm neither of the left nor of the right nor of the center, but above." In fact, however, the job of president demands that the officeholder be a gifted political broker, ever attentive to changing political moods and coalitions. . . .

Presidents are often expected to be above politics in some respects while being highly political in others. Presidents are never supposed to act with their eyes on the next election, yet their power position demands they must. They are neither supposed to favor any particular group or party nor wheel and deal and twist too many arms. That's politics and that's bad! Instead, a president is supposed to be "president of all the people," above politics. A president is also asked to lead a party, to help fellow party members get elected or reelected, to deal firmly with party barons, interest group chieftains, and congressional political brokers. His ability to gain legislative victories depends on his skills at party leadership and on the size of his party's congressional membership. Jimmy Carter once lamented that "It's very difficult for someone to serve in this office and meet the difficult issues in a proper and courageous way and still maintain a combination of interest-group approval that will provide a clear majority at election time."

To take the president out of politics is to assume, incorrectly, that a president will be generally right and the public generally wrong, that a president must be protected from the push and shove of political pressures. But what president has always been right? Over the years, public opinion has usually been as sober a guide as anything else on the political waterfront. And, lest we forget, having a president constrained and informed by public opinion is what democracy is all about.

The fallacy of antipolitics presidencies is that only one view of the national interest is tenable, and a president may pursue that view only by ignoring political conflict and pressure. Politics, properly conceived, is the art of accommodating the diversity and variety of public opinion to meet public goals. Politics is the task of building durable coalitions and majorities. It isn't always pretty. "The process isn't immaculate and cannot always be kid-gloved. A president and his men must reward loyalty and punish opposition; it is the only way." . . .

Paradox #5. We want a president who can unify us, yet the job requires taking firm stands, making unpopular or controversial decisions that necessarily upset and divide us.

Closely related to paradox #4, paradox #5 holds that we ask the president to be a national unifier and a *harmonizer* while at the same time the job requires priority setting and *advocacy* leadership. The tasks are near opposites. . . .

Our nation is one of the few in the world that calls on its chief executive to serve as its symbolic, ceremonial head of state *and* as its political head of government. Elsewhere, these tasks are spread around. In some nations there is a monarch and a prime minister; in others there are three visible national leaders—a head of state, a premier, and a powerful party chief.

In the absence of an alternative office or institution, we demand that our president act as a unifying force in our lives. Perhaps it all began with George Washington, who so artfully performed this function. At least for a while he truly was above politics, a unique symbol of our new nation. He was a healer, a unifier, and an extraordinary man for several seasons. Today we ask no less of our presidents than that they should do as Washington did, and more.

We have designed a presidential job description, however, that often forces our contemporary presidents to act as national dividers. Presidents must necessarily divide when they act as the leaders of their political parties, when they set priorities to the advantage of certain goals and groups at the expense of others, when they forge and lead political coalitions, when they move out ahead of public opinion and assume the role of national educators, when they choose one set of advisers over another. A president, as a creative executive leader, cannot help but offend certain interests. When Franklin Roosevelt was running for a second term, some garment workers unfolded a great sign that said, "We love him for the enemies he has made." Such is the fate of a president on an everyday basis; if presidents choose to use power they will lose the goodwill of those who preferred inaction. . . .

Paradox #6. We expect our presidents to provide bold, visionary, innovative, *programmatic* leadership and at the same time to *pragmatically* respond to the will of public opinion majorities; that is to say, we expect presidents to lead and to follow, to exercise "democratic leadership."

We want both pragmatic and programmatic leadership. We want principled leadership and flexible, adaptable leaders. *Lead us,* but also *listen to us.*

Most people can be led only where they want to go. "Authentic leadership," wrote James MacGregor Burns, "is a collective process." It emerges from a sensitivity or appreciation of the motives and goals of both followers and leaders. The test of leadership, according to Burns, "is the realization of intended, real change that meets people's enduring needs." Thus a key function of leadership is "to engage followers, not merely to activate them, to commingle needs and aspirations and goals in a common enterprise, and in the process to make better citizens of both leaders and followers."

We want our presidents to offer leadership, to be architects of the future and to offer visions, plans, and goals. At the same time we want them to stay in close touch with the sentiments of the people. We want a certain amount of innovation, but we resist being led too far in any one direction.

We expect vigorous, innovative leadership when crises occur. Once a crisis is past, however, we frequently treat presidents as if we didn't need or want them around. We do expect presidents to provide us with bold, creative, and forceful initiatives "to move us ahead," but we resist radical new ideas and changes and usually embrace "new" initiatives only after they have achieved some consensus.

Most of our presidents have been conservatives or at best "pragmatic liberals." They have seldom ventured much beyond the crowd. They have followed public opinion rather than shaped it. John F. Kennedy, the author of the much-acclaimed *Profiles in Courage*, was often criticized for presenting more profile than courage. He avoided political risks where possible. Kennedy was fond of pointing out that he had barely won election in 1960 and that great innovations should not be forced on the public by a leader with such a slender mandate. President Kennedy is often credited with encouraging widespread public participation in politics, but he repeatedly reminded Americans that caution is needed, that the important issues are complicated, technical, and best left to the administrative and political experts. Seldom did Kennedy attempt to change the political context in which he operated. Instead he resisted, "the new form of politics emerging with the civil rights movement: mass action, argument on social fundamentals, appeals to considerations of justice and morality. Moving the American political system in such a direction would necessarily have been long range, requiring arduous educational work and promising substantial political risk."

Kennedy, the pragmatist, shied away from such an unpragmatic undertaking. . . .

Paradox #7. Americans want powerful, self-confident presidential leadership. Yet we are inherently suspicious of leaders who are arrogant, infallible, and above criticism.

We unquestionably cherish our three branches of government with their checks and balances and theories of dispersed and separated powers. We want our presidents to be successful and to share their power with their cabinets, Congress, and other "responsible" national leaders. In theory, we oppose the concentration of power, we dislike secrecy, and we resent depending on any one person to provide all of our leadership.

But Americans also yearn for dynamic, aggressive presidents—even if they do cut some corners. We celebrate the gutsy presidents who make a practice of manipulating and pushing Congress. We perceive the great presidents to be those who stretched their legal authority and dominated the other branches of government. It is still Jefferson, Jackson, Lincoln, and the Roosevelts who get top billing. Whatever may have been the framers' intentions for the three branches, most experts now agree that most of the time, especially in crises, our system works best when the presidency is strong and when we have a self-confident, assertive president.

There is, of course, a fine line between confidence and arrogance, between firmness and inflexibility. We want presidents who are not afraid to exert their will, but at what point does this become antidemocratic, even authoritarian? . . .

Paradox #8. What it takes to become president may not be what is needed to govern the nation.

To win a presidential election takes ambition, money, luck, and masterful public relations strategies. It requires the formation of an electoral coalition. To govern a democracy requires much more. It requires the formation of a *governing* coalition, and the ability to compromise and bargain.

"People who win primaries may become good presidents—but 'it ain't necessarily so'" wrote columnist David Broder. "Organizing well is important in governing just as it is in winning primaries. But the Nixon years should teach us that good advance men do not necessarily make trustworthy White House aides. Establishing a government is a little more complicated than having the motorcade run on time."

Ambition (in heavy doses) and stiff-necked determination are essential for a presidential candidate, yet too much of either can be dangerous. A candidate must be bold and energetic, but in excess these characteristics can produce a cold, frenetic candidate. To win the presidency obviously requires a single-mindedness, yet our presidents must also have a sense of proportion, be well-rounded, have a sense of humor, be able to take a joke, and have hobbies and interests outside the realm of politics.

To win the presidency many of our candidates (Lincoln, Kennedy, and Clinton come to mind) had to pose as being more progressive or even populist than they actually felt; to be effective in the job they are compelled to appear more cautious and conservative than they often want to be. One of Carter's political strategists said, "Jimmy campaigned liberal but governed conservative." And as Bill Clinton pointed out toward the end of his first year in office, "We've all become Eisenhower Republicans." . . .

We often also want both a "fresh face," an outsider, as a presidential candidate *and* a seasoned, mature, experienced veteran who knows the corridors of power and the back alleyways of Washington. That's why Colin Powell fascinated so many people. Frustration with past presidential performances leads us to turn to a "fresh new face" uncorrupted by Washington's politics and its "buddy system" (Carter, Reagan, Clinton).

But inexperience, especially in foreign affairs, has sometimes led to blunders by the outsiders. . . .

Paradox #9. The presidency is sometimes too strong, yet other times too weak.

Presidents are granted wide latitude in dealing with events abroad. At times, presidents can act unilaterally, without the express consent of Congress. While the constitutional grounds for such action may be dubious, the climate of expectations allows presidents to act decisively abroad. This being the case, the public comes to think the president can do the same at home. But this is usually not the case. A clashing expectation is built into the presidency when strength in some areas is matched with weakness in other areas.

It often seems that our presidency is *always too strong* and *always too weak.* Always too powerful given our worst fears of tyranny and our ideals of a "government by the people." Always too strong, as well, because it now possesses the capacity to wage nuclear war (a capacity that doesn't permit much in the way of checks and balances and deliberative, participatory government). But always too weak when we remember nuclear proliferation, the rising national debt, the budget deficit, lingering discrimination, poverty, and the clutch of other fundamental problems yet to be solved.

The presidency is always too strong when we dislike the incumbent. Its limitations are bemoaned, however, when we believe the incumbent is striving valiantly to serve the public interest as we define it. The Johnson presidency vividly captured this paradox: many who believed he was too strong in Vietnam also believed he was too weak to wage his War on Poverty. Others believed just the opposite. . . .

Ultimately, being paradoxical does not make the presidency incomprehensible. Can we rid the presidency of all paradoxes? We couldn't, even if we wanted to do so. And anyway, what is wrong with some ambiguity? It is in embracing the paradoxical nature of the American presidency that we may be able to arrive at understanding. And with understanding may come enlightened or constructive criticism. This is the basis for citizen democracy.

35

CRAIG RIMMERMAN

From *The Rise of the Plebiscitary Presidency*

Scholars who examine American presidents look not only at individuals who have held the position but also at trends that mark different interpretations of the office. Here, Professor Craig Rimmerman builds on Theodore Lowi's concept of the "plebiscitary presidency," in which the president seeks to govern through the direct support of the American people. Likewise, citizens view the plebiscitary presidency as the focal point of government activity. Rimmerman believes this view to be vastly different from the Constitution's intent. He traces changes in the executive's power through several phases, mentioning the contributions of prominent scholars to an understanding of the presidency. From Presidents Roosevelt to Bush and to candidate Perot, Rimmerman asks his readers to consider carefully the consequences of such an exalted and unrealistic vision of presidential power.

———

THE CONSTITUTIONAL framers would undoubtedly be disturbed by the shift to the presidentially centered government that characterizes the modern era. Their fear of monarchy led them to reject the concept of executive popular leadership. Instead, they assumed that the legislative branch would occupy the central policymaking role and would be held more easily accountable through republican government.

Congress has failed, however, to adhere to the framers' intentions and has abdicated its policymaking responsibility. The legislature, with support from the Supreme Court, has been all too willing to promote the illusion of presidential governance by providing the executive with new sources of power, including a highly developed administrative apparatus, and by delegating authority for policy implementation to the executive through vague legislative statutes. . . .

The president-centered government of the modern, plebiscitary era draws much of its power and legitimacy from the popular support of the citizenry, support that is grounded in the development of the rhetorical presidency and the exalted role of the presidency in the American political culture. Theodore Lowi is surely on target when he identifies "the refocusing of mass expectations upon the presidency" as a key problem of presidential governance since Franklin Delano Roosevelt and as a problem associated with the rise of the plebiscitary presidency.

The plebiscitary presidency is characterized by the following: presidential power and legitimacy emanates from citizen support as measured through public opinion polls; in the absence of coherent political parties, presidents forge a direct link to the masses through television; and structural barriers associated with the Madisonian governmental framework make it difficult for presidents to deliver on their policy promises to the citizenry. The framers of the Constitution would hardly have approved of these developments, for they had no intention of establishing a popularly elected monarch. Moreover, the nature of the governmental framework that they created actually prevents occupants of the Oval Office from meeting the heightened citizen expectations associated with the plebiscitary presidency in terms of concrete public policy, especially in the domestic policy arena. This has become particularly clear in the modern era as presidents confront a more fragmented and independent legislature, a decline in the importance of the political party as a governing and coalition-building device, an increase in the power of interest groups and political action committees that foster policy fragmentation, and a bureaucracy that resists centralized coordination. . . .

Throughout much of the nineteenth century, a passive president in domestic policymaking was deemed both acceptable and desirable. Congress took the lead in formulating public policy initiatives and expressed outright hostility toward presidential suggestions that particular legislation should be introduced. In fact, early in the nineteenth century it was commonly believed that the president should not exercise the veto to express policy preferences. The president's primary responsibility was to faithfully execute the laws passed by Congress. For the occupants of the Oval Office in the traditional period, the Constitution imposed "strict limitations on what a President could do." The constitutional separation of powers was taken seriously by all parties, and the prevailing view regarding the proper role of government was "the best government governed least." As opposed to the presidential government of the modern period, the traditional era was characterized by congressional leadership in the policy process.

In the foreign policy arena, however, the president did establish himself through the war-making power. Yet even here the president was restrained when compared to the occupants of the Oval Office in the twentieth century. A prevailing view in the nineteenth century was that the president should avoid involvement with foreign nations, although negotiation with foreign countries was occasionally required. The first president to travel abroad on behalf of the United States was Theodore Roosevelt. Prior to the twentieth century, some members of Congress even argued that the president lacked the necessary legal authority to travel in this manner.

Presidential speechmaking also reflected the largely symbolic chief-of-state roles played by presidents in the traditional era. Jeffrey Tulis's content analysis of presidential speeches reveals that presidents rarely gave the kind of official popular speeches that characterize speech-making in the modern era. When speeches were given, they were considered "unofficial," and they rarely contained policy pronouncements. Tulis concludes that William McKinley's rhetoric was representative of the century as a whole: "Expressions of greeting, inculcations of patriotic sentiment, attempts at building 'harmony' among the regions of the country, and very general, principled statements of policy, usually expressed in terms of the policy's consistency with that president's understanding of republicanism." Virtually all presidents of the time adhered to the same kind of presidential speechmaking. The only exception was Andrew Johnson, who attempted to rally support for his policies in Congress through the use of fiery demagoguery. Johnson's "improper" rhetoric fueled his impeachment charge; yet it is this same kind of rhetoric that today is accepted as "proper" presidential rhetoric.

The reserved role played by the president in the nineteenth century was clearly in keeping with the intention of the constitutional framers. . . .

. . . Yet as the United States headed into its second full century, this situation was to change, as congressional government began to yield to the presidentially centered form of governance that has characterized the modern period.

Students of the presidency have identified a number of factors that have led to the development of the modern, personal, plebiscitary presidency as we know it today. The personal presidency is "an office of tremendous personal power drawn from the people—directly through Congress and the Supreme Court—and based on the new democratic theory that the presidency with all powers is the necessary condition for governing a large, democratic nation. Its development is rooted in changes in presidential rhetoric, the efforts of the progressive reformers of the early twentieth century, the Great Depression and Franklin Delano Roosevelt's New Deal, the role of Congress in granting the executive considerable discretionary power, and Supreme Court decisions throughout the twentieth century that have legitimated the central role that the president should play in the domestic and foreign policy arenas. . . .

Presidential scholars have contributed to the presidentially centered government and the accompanying citizen expectations of presidential performance that characterize the development of presidential power since Franklin Roosevelt. The "cult of the presidency," "textbook presidency," or "savior model" was developed in response to FDR's leadership during the Great Depression, and it prevailed through the presidency of John F. Kennedy. Underlying this "cult" or model approach is a firm commitment to the presidency as a strong office and to the desirability of this condition for the political system as a whole. Political science texts written during this period concluded approvingly that the presidency was growing larger, while gaining more responsibilities and resources. The use of laudatory labels, such as "the Wilson years," "the Roosevelt revolution," "the Eisenhower period," and "the Kennedy Camelot years" also fostered the cult of the presidency and reinforced the notion that the president is the key figure in the American political system. . . .

Perhaps no other work contributed more to the development of this approach that Richard Neustadt's *Presidential Power*, which was first published in 1960. Representing a sharp break with the legalistic and constitutional approach that had dominated presidential scholarship up until that time, *Presidential Power* reinforced the notion that strong presidential leadership should be linked to good government. Neustadt eschewed strict legalistic interpretations of presidential power and instead conceived of power in the following way: "'Power' I defined as personal influence on governmental action. This I distinguished sharply—a novel distinction then—from formal powers vested in the Presidency." For Neustadt, the Franklin Delano Roosevelt activist presidency was the ideal model for presidential leadership and the exercise of power. Future presidents, according to Neustadt, should be evaluated on the basis of how well they achieved the standards set by Roosevelt. Like presidential scholars of his time and many since, Neustadt rejected the framers' view that the Congress should be the chief policymaking branch and that the president should be constrained by numerous checks and balances. Instead, Neustadt spoke of "separated institutions sharing powers."

As Neustadt and other scholars embraced a presidentially centered form of government, they failed to recognize the consequences of imposing a new interpretation of the political order on a governmental framework rooted in Madisonian principles. One such consequence has been that as presidents attempt to meet the heightened expectations associated with the modern presidency, they are sometimes driven to assert presidential prerogative powers in ways that threaten both constitutional and democratic principles. The Johnson and Nixon presidencies, in particular, provided empirical evidence to support this concern. In response, presidential scholars embraced a new model for evaluating presidential power: "the imperial presidency."

Concerns about excessive presidential power were articulated in light of Lyndon Johnson's legislative victories in the 1960s, Johnson's and Nixon's decisionmaking in the Vietnam War, the Nixon/Kissinger Cambodian debacle, and the Nixon presidency's disgrace in the wake of Watergate.* Presidential scholars began to question whether presidential strength would necessarily lead to the promotion of the general welfare. Scholars spoke of the pathological presidency, reinforcing many of the constitutional framers' fears regarding the consequences of concentrating excessive powers in the executive.

Writing in this vein and responding to presidential excesses in the conduct of the Vietnam War and the Watergate scandal, Arthur Schlesinger, Jr., developed the concept of the "imperial presidency." Schlesinger recognized that the system of checks and balances needed vigorous action by one of the three branches if the stalemate built into the system was to be overcome. Schlesinger believed that the presidency was best equipped to fill this role. Rather than rejecting centralized presidential power per se, he spoke of presidential abuses: "In the last years presidential primacy, so indispensable to the political order, has turned into presidential supremacy. The constitutional Presidency—as events so apparently disparate as the Indochina War and the Watergate affair showed—has become the imperial Presidency and threatens to be the revolutionary Presidency." Schlesinger placed much of the blame for the imperial presidency on presidential excesses in foreign policy. . . . Truman, Kennedy, Johnson, and Nixon interpreted the Constitution to permit the president to commit American combat troops unilaterally, and the prolonged Vietnam War encouraged foreign policy centralization and the use of secrecy. The imperial presidency, or "the presidency as satan model," can also be applied to the Nixon administration's domestic activities, including wiretapping, the use of impoundments, executive branch reorganization for political purposes, and expansive interpretations of executive privilege.

Schlesinger's analysis is an important contribution to the study of presidential power because it recognizes the limitations imposed by the framers and the potentially negative consequences of the plebiscitary presidency. . . .

The plebiscitary presidency has been a key source of presidential

---

*Set in motion by strong presidents, these three episodes—the prolonging of the war in Vietnam, the bombing of Vietnam's neutral neighbor, Cambodia, and a presidential administration's heavy involvement in and coverup of the burglary of the Democratic Party's Watergate Hotel–based election headquarters—all greatly divided the nation.—EDS.

power since 1933. For presidents such as Ford and Carter, however, the heightened expectations associated with the personal, plebiscitary presidency have also led to citizen unhappiness and characterizations of presidential failure. The Carter presidency, in particular, reinforced elements of the plebiscitary presidency. As a "trustee" president, Jimmy Carter reinforced the notion that as the elected representative of all the people, "the president must act as the counterforce to special interests" and provide the leadership necessary in setting the policy agenda and introducing "comprehensive policy proposals." Charles Jones makes a persuasive case that Carter's vision of the trustee presidency was anathema to a Congress that had just passed a series of reforms designed to tame the imperial Nixon presidency. When Carter tried to introduce unpopular energy conservation policies and cut back "unnecessary dams and water projects" because they represented the "worst examples of the pork-barrel," he challenged Congress and the American people to reject politics as usual. In this sense, he was displaying a style of presidential leadership unseen in recent years, one that reinforced the plebiscitary presidency while at the same time challenging some of the assumptions on which it is based. Unlike his immediate predecessors and successors, Carter at least tried to heighten the level of dialogue around resource scarcity concerns. He soon learned, however, that his unwillingness to cultivate congressional support for his policies and his call for a shared sacrifice on the part of the American people undermined the plebiscitary foundations of the modern presidency. His 1980 presidential challenger understood Carter's problems quite well and was determined not to repeat them. Ronald Reagan's campaign and governing strategies accepted and extended the plebiscitary presidency. This helps to account for his victories in both 1980 and 1984. . . .

In the American political system, presidents perform two roles that in other countries are often filled by separate individuals. As head of the nation, the president is required to play a unifying role of the kind played by monarchs in Britain, Norway, and the Netherlands or by presidents in France, Germany, and Austria. In addition, presidents serve as political leaders, "a post held in these other nations by a prime minister or chancellor." This dual role virtually guarantees that American presidents will occupy the central political and cultural role as the chief spokesperson for the American way of life. Political scientists, historians, and journalists have all reinforced and popularized the view that the presidency is an office of overwhelming symbolic importance.

Only recently have political scientists begun to challenge this perspective and discuss the negative consequences of such hero worship in a country that purports to adhere to democratic principles. Barbara Hinckley captures these issues well in her recent analysis:

> It is the magic of symbolism to create illusion. But illusion has costs that must be considered by journalists, teachers of politics, and future presidents. Is the nation best served by carrying on the symbolism or by challenging it? Should the two contradictory pictures, in a kind of schizophrenic fashion, be carried on together? If so, what line should be drawn and what accommodation made between the two? The questions are compounded by the peculiar openness of the office to changing interpretations. By definition, all institutions are shaped by the expectations of relevant actors. The presidency is particularly susceptible to such influence.

As we have seen in our study of the Reagan and Bush presidencies, presidents attempt to build on their symbolic importance to enhance their public opinion ratings and to extend the plebiscitary presidency. The upshot of this activity over the past sixty years is that the public equates the president with the nation and the values associated with American exceptionalism. A president, such as Jimmy Carter, who attempts to challenge traditional elements of presidential symbolism and demystify the trappings of the White House, is treated with disdain by the public, the press, and to a certain extent by political scientists. . . .

This book suggests that Presidents Reagan and Bush turned to foreign policy when they encountered difficulties in translating their domestic campaign promises into concrete public policy and in meeting the demands of the plebiscitary presidency. Presidents who are caught between citizens' expectations and the constraints of the Madisonian policymaking process* look to the foreign policy arena in an effort to promote the values associated with American exceptionalism.

Any of the examples discussed . . . provide ample opportunity to explore these themes. The Iran-Contra affair,† in particular, raises compelling questions regarding presidential power in the foreign policy arena. In light of the aggrandizement of presidential power that characterized the Vietnam War period and Watergate and the resulting congressional response, it is important to ask students why a president and/or his staff would employ some of the same strategies in dealing with Congress, the media, and the American people. The role of covert activities in a democracy also deserves considerable attention.

---

*James Madison's plan for American government limits each branch by checking and balancing the power of one branch against another.—EDS.

†During President Reagan's administration, members of his National Security Council (NSC) were charged with secretly selling arms to Iran in order to fund anti-communist Nicaraguan Contra activities.—EDS.

If scholars of the presidency are truly concerned with developing a pedagogy and presidential evaluation scheme rooted in critical education for citizenship, then their students must be asked to consider why so little questioning generally occurs regarding the role of the president in committing American troops to war. The Persian Gulf war was a case in point.* It begged for serious discussion, reflection, debate, and questioning about the Bush administration's foreign policy decisionmaking. Some argued that those who dissented from the president's foreign policy strategy were un-American and unpatriotic and were trying to undermine the troops who were already in the Middle East. In fact, if citizens fail to question a president's decisionmaking, then they are giving the president virtually unchecked power to do what he wants with their lives. The failure to question a president abdicates all of the principles of a meaningful and effective democracy and embraces the dictates of an authoritarian and totalitarian regime. This is, of course, the logical consequence of the plebiscitary presidency.

Alexis de Tocqueville spoke of a blind and unreflective patriotism that characterized the American citizenry during the nineteenth century. He would surely see evidence of such patriotism in America today. There is little doubt that such patriotism can be connected to the relationship of the citizenry to the state and the office of the presidency. No modern president can expect to succeed without the support of the public. Yet this support must be grounded in a firm rejection of the unrealistic notion of presidential power. Citizens who respond to the presidency in a highly personalized and reverential manner are likely to be disappointed by presidential performance and are also likely to embrace political passivity and acquiescence in the face of presidential power. In the words of Benjamin Barber, "democratic politics thus becomes a matter of what leaders do, something that citizens watch rather than something they do." As this book has pointed out, Ronald Reagan and George Bush heightened these expectations even further by using techniques that emphasize the plebiscitary, personal character of the modern presidency. Ross Perot's 1992 presidential campaign was firmly rooted in plebiscitary principles. His proposals for nation-wide town meetings and an electronic democracy scheme reflected support for government by plebiscite. To Perot, running

*The Persian Gulf War occurred within a two-month period in early 1991. Backed by House and Senate resolutions of support—not an actual declaration of war—President Bush sent U.S. troops to the Persian Gulf as part of a multination coalition to force Iraqi President Saddam Hussein's military out of Kuwait. The United States experienced quick and dramatic success, with CNN's coverage bringing the war directly to Americans daily. Years later, questions remained about the long-term effectiveness of the military strikes in weakening the Iraqi threat.—EDS.

as an outsider, anti-establishment candidate, such a plan was desperately needed to challenge the gridlock growing out of the Madisonian policy process and two party system. His proposals also enabled him to emphasize his own leadership abilities and claim that he had the necessary leadership and entrepreneurial abilities to break governmental paralysis. In doing so, Perot reinforced the direct line between the presidency and the American people. Any course on the presidency should examine Perot's government-by-plebiscite proposals and the broader implications of his apparent willingness to bypass the congressional policy process and the two party system. The amount of attention and popularity that Perot's campaign garnered in a short period of time suggests once again that the plebiscitary presidency is an important explanatory construct. It also encourages political scientists to study, with renewed vigor, the relationship between the presidency and the citizenry.

For many students, the presidency is the personification of democratic politics and, as a result, monopolizes "the public space." This view impedes the development of the meaningful and effective participation needed by citizens as they attempt to control decisions that affect the quality and direction of their lives. Presidential scholars have been developing a more realistic understanding of the changing sources of presidential power and how individual presidents have used these powers through the years. We would also do well to consider Murray Edelman's claim that "leadership is an expression of the inadequate power of followers in their everyday lives." This is particularly important as we begin to evaluate the Bush presidency. It is also the first step toward challenging the plebiscitary presidency and achieving a more realistic and successful presidency, one that is grounded in principles of democratic accountability and the development of citizenship.

36

RICHARD POSNER

From *An Affair of State*

In addition to being a U.S. Court of Appeals judge, Richard Posner is a law professor who tackles some of the most controversial and compelling issues in American government. On the impeachment of President Bill Clinton, Posner weighs the tremendous damage done to America's governmental institutions against the ability of those institutions to carry on the day-to-day tasks of smoothly running a huge superpower. Posner's theme is that many individuals—the president, the independent counsel who investigated him—were revealed as less than admirable people. Likewise, organizations involved in aspects of the impeachment process acted badly. This episode, however, taught Americans what they already knew: the nation can make it through this kind of crisis without permanent scars.

THE YEAR-LONG political, legal, constitutional, and cultural struggle that began on January 21, 1998, when the world learned that Independent Counsel Kenneth Starr was investigating charges that President Clinton had committed perjury and other crimes of obstruction of justice (primarily subornation of perjury and witness tampering) in an effort to conceal a sexual affair with a young White House worker named Monica Lewinsky, is the most riveting chapter of recent American history. The investigation culminated on December 19, 1998, in the impeachment of President Clinton by the House of Representatives for perjury before a grand jury and for obstruction of justice. It was only the second impeachment of a U.S. President. The first was the impeachment of Andrew Johnson 130 years earlier, although in 1974 Richard Nixon would have been impeached and convicted had he not resigned after the House Judiciary Committee recommended his impeachment to the full House. On January 7, 1999, the Senate trial of President Clinton began. Truncated and anticlimactic—indeed, a parody of legal justice—the trial ended on February 12 with the President's acquittal. With this, the end of the main legal phase of the struggle that began on January 21 of last year, the record of events . . . was complete, though the aftershocks (such as Juanita Broaddrick's rape charge and Lewinsky's television interview and book) continue. . . .

The public life of the nation in 1998 and the first six weeks of 1999 was dominated by President Clinton's struggle to retain his office. The struggle was deeply and not merely pruriently or dramatically interesting, though it *was* high drama—Wagnerian in intensity and protraction, with wonderful actors, the Clintons, in the lead roles, a supporting cast of hundreds, dramatic revelations aplenty (the tapes, the dress, the sex lives of Republican Congressmen), a splendid libretto by Kenneth Starr, a Greek chorus of television commentators; plus hapless walk-ons, clandestine comings and goings, betrayals, suspense, reversals of fortune, hints of violence (supplied by the Clinton haters), a May-December romance as it might be depicted by an Updike or a Cheever, a doubling and redoubling of plot, a *Bildungsroman*, even allegorical commentary (the movies *Primary Colors* and *Wag the Dog*) and a touch of comic opera (Chief Justice Rehnquist's costume out of *Iolanthe*). It was the ultimate Washington novel, the supreme and never to be equaled expression of the genre and the proof that truth is indeed stranger than fiction.

But putting its entertainment value to one side, are we better or worse off for the experience? It is too soon to tell; it is especially premature to say that we are worse off.

We are surely better off in some respects. We have learned a lot about the mischief of the independent counsel law and about the pitfalls of Presidential impeachment. Unlike other recent nonfiction entertainments (the death of Princess Diana for example, or John Glenn's reentry into outer space), the ordeal of Clinton's Presidency has gotten people thinking seriously about important issues—issues of law, morality, constitutional structure, public opinion, and political behavior. It has thus made people more civic minded, although one cannot know how long the civic lessons will be remembered. It has also contributed to a franker public discourse on matters of sex, which I think is good. The idea that it has loosened parental control over their children's moral development is unproven and implausible. Young children do not understand what Clinton and Lewinsky did, and teenagers understand without being told. It is too soon to tell whether oral sex will become a more popular sexual practice as a result of the incessant public discussion of the President's taste for it, but, if so, it would not be the end of the world; offensive though the practice is to some religious people, it is, at least, securely contraceptive and only rarely a conduit for disease. Phone sex is better yet on these dimensions, though I imagine that William Bennett would fall off his chair if he read a page of *Vox*. If some people have been encouraged by Clinton's survival in office to commit perjury and obstruction of justice, others, for whom these crimes had no resonance or visibility, have learned that one can get into a lot of trouble by committing them. The stripping away of the privacy not only of Clinton and Monica Lewinsky but of a number of the supporting characters in the Clinton-Lewinsky drama, including several Republican House members, may have neutralized scandal-mongering as an electoral tactic by revealing that a high percentage of politicians have skeletons in their closet, and may thus have contributed to a refocusing of electoral competition on substantive issues.

The drama has demonstrated the resilience of the American government. For despite everything, government ticked along in its usual way through thirteen months of so-called crisis. No doubt there was distraction. But the idea that the federal government (which is by no means the whole of American government) was *seriously* deflected from a productive engagement with international financial or political issues, or domestic crises such as Social Security and health insurance, is unsupported. Some of the problems that the government was asked to solve, or at least to make progress toward solving, in 1998 are insoluble by the federal (perhaps any) government; some are not problems; some were addressed in the usual way. Others would have been pushed to the back burner anyway in the twilight years of a lame-duck President facing a Congress both houses of which are controlled by the opposition at a time when peace and prosperity and at least a temporary abatement of some of the nation's most acute social problems, coupled with the toll that scandal and scandal-mongering have taken of public confidence in government, disincline the American people to support active government. Clinton, a proponent of active government, by his antic behavior damaged public faith in it. We have learned that the President of the United States, like Tolstoy's Napoleon, is to a certain extent a cork floating on the ocean rather than the moon controlling the tides. We have also learned about the strength of weakness. International terrorists may have maintained a lower than usual profile during Clinton's struggle for survival, knowing that Clinton was eager to demonstrate strength and change the subject (*Wag the Dog*). I do think that the Supreme Court was playing with fire when by the combined effect of its decisions in *Morrison** and *Jones* it exposed the President and

*The 1997 Supreme Court ruling in *Clinton v. Jones* decreed that Paula Jones could sue President Bill Clinton for sexual harassment, based on a 1991 incident. The Court ruling stated that defending himself in the suit would not mar the president's ability to function in his role as chief executive. Ultimately, Jones accepted a monetary settlement, ending the case. *Morrison v. Olson* (1988) was a case in which the Supreme Court held as constitutional the law allowing a judge-appointed independent counsel to investigate members of the executive branch or Congress. Critics of the law argued that it violated separation of powers, particularly the executive branch's ability to enforce the law, but the Court disagreed. The independent counsel law expired in 1999, after much political controversy had surrounded its use. — EDS.

the nation to the ordeal that began on January 21, 1998; but a lucky conjunction of circumstances has spared the nation from the worst consequences.

Resilient our institutions may be, meaning they can take a lot of punishment; but they are also flawed. The crisis of Clinton's Presidency, like the Vietnam War decades earlier, revealed feet of clay in a number of departments of the American Establishment—the media pundits (though not the working journalists), the political consultants and forecasters, the public intellectuals, the Washington bar, Supreme Court Justices, the members of Congress, the White House groupies and toadies, and, above all, the President. But it has done so at a time when we can learn the lessons at relatively low cost because we are in a period of calm between the crises that punctuate history.

We have learned that powerful, intelligent, articulate, well-educated, and successful people who would like us to submit to their leadership whether political or intellectual are, much of the time, fools, knaves, cowards, and blunderers, just like the rest of us. That is to say, they are ordinary people, with all the ordinary vices, whom luck, or specialized, compartmentalized talents have propelled into positions of power or influence in which they preen and strut until some unexpected event strips away their masks, demolishes their carefully constructed, imperturbable-seeming public selves, and exposes them in their full ordinariness and inadequacy.

We have learned that professionalism, whether in law, scholarship, or politics, is no guarantor of being able to cope with novel challenges. Rather the opposite. The tendency of professionalism is to a productive narrowness. The professional masters the proven techniques for dealing with a familiar category of problems. When something comes along to knock him out of his groove—in the case of the Clinton-Lewinsky business a political, legal, and cultural phenomenon without precedents to steer by—the limitedness of his professional skills, training, and experience is revealed.

We have learned that too much law can be a bad thing. We do not need to be able to sue our Presidents during their term of office, and we do not need an independent counsel law.

The mystique of the Presidency became a casualty of the narration in the Starr Report and of the public interrogation of the President by a grand jury before a global audience. It is one thing to know in the abstract, as everyone does, that Presidents have bodies and private lives that include bodily functions, have private embarrassments and lapses of taste (a President who collects *frogs*?) and character flaws aplenty, and make egregious errors of judgment. It is another thing to know in riveting and exact detail the normally hidden and in this case disreputable private life of the very President we have now, not some dim historical figure, so that when Joan Didion speaks cuttingly of the President as embodying "the familiar predatory sexuality of the provincial adolescent" and remarks "the reservoir of self-pity, the quickness to blame the narrowing of the eyes, as in a wildlife documentary, when things did not go his way," there is no one to deny the justness of her observations. Her reference to wildlife is apt. Animals have no privacy.

The mystique of the Presidency was damaged, maybe destroyed; but the mystique of the other branches of the federal government was not compensatorily enhanced—indeed was also damaged. The role of the courts will be remembered for the fiasco of *Morrison v. Olson* and *Clinton vs. Jones*, and for the stripes on Chief Justice Rehnquist's robe; and we have learned that the Senate of the United States, no less than the House of Representatives, is too politicized an organ of government to play the judicial role in Presidential impeachment that the Constitution assigned it.

The role of the courts in the fiasco will soon be forgotten; and no one who knows Congress could have thought it a judicial body. The most abiding effect of what I have called the ultimate Washington novel may be to make it difficult to take Presidents seriously, as superior people, for the same reason that an even greater novel, *The Remembrance of Things Past*, made it impossible by dint of its riveting detail to take aristocrats seriously as superior people. For those who think that authority depends on mystery, the shattering of the Presidential mystique has been a disaster for which Clinton ought of rights to have paid with his job. They may be right about the dependence of effective political leadership on mystique. My guess is that they are wrong, that Americans have reached a level of political sophistication at which they can take in stride the knowledge that the nation's political and intellectual leaders are their peers, and not their paragons. The nation does not depend on the superior virtue of one man.

37

DAVID GERGEN

From *Eyewitness to Power*

The title of David Gergen's book is apt since he served as an advisor to four presidents: Nixon, Ford, Reagan, and Clinton. Gergen sets forth a series of measures designed to evaluate a president's capacity for success. He then applies them to recent presidents as well as some not so recent, reminding students of government that a good basic background in U.S. history is a prerequisite for political science. Using Abigail Adams as his source, Gergen writes that "great crises usually bring forth great leaders," a principle that is being continually tested in the office of the President of the United States.

———

SOON AFTER A NEW PRESIDENT takes office, someone usually has a quiet word in his ear: "Did you know that there is still room up there on Mount Rushmore for one more face? At least a small profile." There isn't, in fact; the sixty-foot slabs are taken. But every president tries mightily to win a place equal to the four men remembered there.

In the eyes of historians, none of our recent occupants has come close. Following a tradition started by his father, Arthur Schlesinger, Jr., surveyed thirty-two fellow historians in December 1996, asking them to rate the presidents. Washington, Lincoln, and Franklin Roosevelt once again swept the boards. Jefferson, Jackson, Polk, Teddy Roosevelt, Wilson, and Truman were considered "near great." What was striking was the decline since Truman. His three successors—Eisenhower, Kennedy, and Johnson— barely made it into the top half of the class, scoring "above average." All six presidents thereafter were in the bottom half. Ford, Carter, Reagan, Bush, and Clinton were marked "below average," and Nixon was deemed a "failure."

If that's the case, why should we bother to look for lessons of leadership among recent presidents? For starters, that may not be the case—or at least not for long. As Schlesinger himself has written, presidential reputations wax and wane. Truman and Eisenhower have risen significantly in esteem since leaving office. The same will almost surely happen with Reagan (especially if more conservatives begin writing history), and signs of nostalgia are already popping up around Ford and Bush. Even Clinton may rise in historical estimation.

The larger point is that we need to face reality: it's a lot tougher for anyone to lead the country today than it was in the first half of the twentieth century. Expectations of what a president can accomplish have escalated dramatically, while his capacity for action has diminished even more. A White House today must keep its eye on half a dozen trouble spots around the world and help to steer an international economy, all the while taking responsibility for violence in schools and monitoring research into the human genome. Something is bound to go wrong somewhere, and when it does, a hungry press corps will give relentless chase and partisans in Congress will march cabinet secretaries to Capitol Hill. "It must be realized," Machiavelli wrote, "that there is nothing more difficult to plan, more uncertain of success, or more dangerous to manage than the establishment of a new order of government." And that was long before lobbyists could spend millions on grassroots campaigns to block a president. Not since 1986 has Congress passed bipartisan, blockbuster legislation—the reform of the tax code. No wonder the queue is short for Mount Rushmore.

But that's all the more reason to study the experiences of our recent presidents—to see what worked, what failed, and what can be learned by their successors. Understanding the past is essential to mastering the future. The next twenty years or so will be crucial in shaping the twenty-first century. As the forces of democratic capitalism sweep the world and as technology and science hold out new promise, we may be on the threshold of a new golden age. What could make the difference is the quality of our leadership, starting in the presidency. We need men and women in that job and in the White House who know what it takes to mobilize the energies of the country and can apply themselves with wisdom. There are no off-the-shelf manuals for presidents, but there are rich lessons to be gleaned from past experience.

I do not pretend here to have the final word on any of the four presidents [Nixon, Ford, Reagan, and Clinton] I have served. Their private papers will not be fully opened for some years, and even then will not give us a complete picture. President Kennedy was once sent an inquiry asking him to join a group of historians in assessing past presidents. He exploded in irritation. "How the hell can they know?" he said. "They've never had to sit here, reading all the cables, listening to people all day about these problems." He had a point. The most any of us can offer is our best sense of the picture.

My sense is that even if we do not know the details, certain broad conclusions about leadership can be drawn from recent presidents. . . .

In my judgment, there are seven keys to responsible and effective leadership in the White House. They apply whether the administration is Democratic or Republican, liberal or conservative. In fact, they apply as well to leaders of most other organizations—CEOs, university presidents, military generals, and heads of nonprofit institutions.

1. Leadership Starts from Within

Richard Nixon and Bill Clinton were the two most gifted presidents of the past thirty years. Each was inordinately bright, well read, and politically savvy. Each reveled in power. Nixon was the best strategist in the office since Eisenhower and possibly since Woodrow Wilson; Clinton was the best tactician since Lyndon Johnson and possibly Franklin Roosevelt. Yet each was the author of his own downfall. Nixon let his demons gain ascendance, and Clinton could not manage the fault lines in his character. They were living proof that before mastering the world, a leader must achieve self-mastery. Or, as Heraclitus put it more succinctly, "Character is destiny."

The inner soul of a president flows into every aspect of his leadership far more than is generally recognized. His passions in life usually form the basis for his central mission in office. Nixon's search for a "lasting structure of peace" grew out of his dream of becoming a world statesman, just as the hardscrabble youth of LBJ led to his pursuit of a Great Society. We know, too, that the character of a leader heavily influences his decision-making—both how and what he decides. Ford's pardon of Nixon grew out of his own decency. Reagan showed us the degree to which personality shapes rhetoric as well as the ability of a president to work with Congress and the press. In Nixon and Clinton, we saw that the character of a president also determines the character of his White House—that the men and women around him take their cues from the man in the center. Finally—and most importantly—the character of a president determines the integrity of his public life.

In his small classic, *On Leadership*, John W. Gardner assembles a list of fourteen personal attributes that he believes are important for leaders, public and private. He draws from his own experience as well as from scholars in the field such as Ralph Stogdill, Bernard Bass, and Edwin P. Hollander. A president certainly needs a high measure of all the qualities that Gardner lists: physical vitality; intelligence and judgment-in-action; a willingness to accept responsibilities; task competence; an understanding of followers and their needs; skill in dealing with people; a need to achieve; a capacity to motivate; courage and steadiness; a capacity to win and hold trust; a capacity to manage and set priorities; confidence; assertiveness; and an adaptability of approach.

Of these, integrity is the most important for a president. As former senator Alan Simpson said in introducing Gerald Ford at Harvard a year ago: "If you have integrity, nothing else matters. If you don't have integrity, nothing else matters."

People can reasonably debate how virtuous a public leader must be in private life. Some believe that if a politician has erred in his adult life—by committing adultery, for example—he should be disqualified from high office: "If his wife can't trust him, we can't either." But experience suggests that this standard sets the bar higher than we need or should expect. Consider Franklin Roosevelt. Twenty years after he died, Americans learned for the first time that the Roosevelts did not have a perfect marriage. FDR was a father of five when he had a passionate affair with Lucy Mercer that nearly destroyed his marriage. He broke off the relationship, but it was Lucy, not Eleanor, who was with him on the day of his fatal stroke, and as Doris Kearns Goodwin points out, Eleanor bore the burden of the affair for over forty years. Despite this relationship—and perhaps others—FDR emerged as the greatest president of the twentieth century.

How can one resolve these dilemmas about private virtue? There is no easy or simple answer. The rule that journalists used to apply before the new era of sensationalism has always seemed best to me: when a politician's private life interferes with the way he conducts himself in public, we should draw the line. If he drinks too much, is licentious, uses hard drugs, gambles himself into debt—those go too far. Otherwise, we should show greater tolerance and respect for human foibles. Bill Clinton went over the line not because he had sexual relations but because he engaged a White House intern in the Oval Office and then blatantly lied about it.

While there is room for disagreement about private life, there can be none about the conduct of public life. To govern, a president must have the trust of the public and people within the system. And trust does not come with the job anymore; it must be earned. It is thus vital that a president be truthful and accountable for his actions and insist that his staff meet the same rigorous standards. The government has a right to remain silent on matters of sensitivity, but no right to lie—unless the survival of the nation is at stake—and no right to mislead through excessive spin. Those who preach otherwise do violence to democratic principles.

Beyond personal integrity, it is especially important that the nation's chief executive rank high in what political scientist Everett Carll Ladd called "presidential intelligence"—that ineffable blend of knowledge, judgment, temperament, and faith in the future that leads to wise decisions and responsible leadership. It is dangerous, of course, to have a president who is ignorant of the world and of history. But if brains were the only criterion, Nixon, Carter, and Clinton would have been our best presidents of recent years. Rather, as we saw with Reagan, it is a combination of core competence and emotional intelligence that is a better predictor of effectiveness.

Equally important for presidential leadership is courage. No one can succeed in today's politics unless he or she is prepared to fall on a sword in a good cause. Nixon would never have opened the door to China if he lacked guts, nor would Reagan have survived a bullet and hastened the end of the Cold War, nor would Clinton have ended the deficits and secured the passage of NAFTA. Courage must be tempered by prudence, of course—something that was lacking in the Clinton health care plan— but the *sine qua non* of leadership is inner strength.

2. A Central, Compelling Purpose

Just as a president must have strong character, he must be of clear purpose. He must tell the country where he is heading so he can rally people behind him. Lincoln's purpose was to save the Union, FDR's to end the Depression and then to win the war. People could say in a single sentence what their presidencies were all about. Among recent executives, only Reagan was clear about his central goals—to reduce taxes, reduce spending, cut regulations, reduce the deficit, and increase the defense budget. By campaigning on those goals, he not only won a mandate but also made substantial progress toward their achievement (with the conspicuous exception of the budget deficit). By contrast, consider Ford, Carter, Bush, and Clinton. They had high hopes, too, but never articulated a central, compelling purpose for their presidencies, and they all suffered as a result.

A president's central purpose must also be rooted in the nation's core values. They can be found in the Declaration of Independence. As G. K. Chesterton famously observed, "America is the only nation in the world that is founded on a creed. That creed is set forth with dogmatic and even theological lucidity in the Declaration of Independence." All of our greatest presidents have gone there for inspirational strength. Lincoln said he never had a political sentiment that did not spring from it. It was not intended to be a statement of who we are but of what we dream of becoming, realizing that the journey never ends. It is our communal vision. That's why a president, unlike a CEO, need not reinvent the national vision upon taking office. He should instead give fresh life to the one we have, applying it to the context of the times, leading the nation forward to its greater fulfillment. The reason Martin Luther King was so powerful when he declared "I have a dream," was that he was standing at the Lincoln Memorial challenging us to carry out the promises of the Declaration.

Presidents depart from the nation's core values at their peril. The Clintons' health care plan failed in large part because it went against the grain. By contrast, FDR knew his Social Security plan was a sharp departure from past tradition but cleverly structured it so that the government did not pay for it out of general revenues; rather he designed it so that people "saved" for their own future. Making the plan consistent with core values was the secret to its passage.

3. A Capacity to Persuade

For most of the country's history, it didn't matter much whether a president could mobilize the public. From Jefferson until Wilson, the annual State of the Union was a written report to Congress. Even through Truman and Eisenhower, it was more important to be a good broker among interests than a good speaker. Television changed everything. Kennedy and Reagan now stand out in the public mind as the most memorable speakers of the late twentieth century because they were masters of the medium. They both had a capacity to persuade a mass audience through television, and in Reagan's case, he turned it into a powerful weapon to achieve his legislative goals.

If anything, the danger today is that presidents blab on so much that their audiences tune out. George Bush actually gave more public talks per year than Reagan, and Clinton has delivered more than both of them combined. In 1997, Clinton delivered 545 public speeches. He is unusually good at explaining complex public policy issues in simple terms that connect with his audiences, so that in any given forum, he is highly effective. But overexposure has dulled his impact.

4. An Ability to Work within the System

A common mistake among political consultants today is to believe that the only thing that counts in governing anymore is public persuasion. Television has become an indispensable tool for leadership, but as Reagan's success showed, it is still important that a president and his team be effective in working with other elements of our democratic system. Congress remains a coequal branch of government, and the press acts like one.

In effect, a president should see himself as the center of a web. Surrounding him are six different institutional forces with whom he must form successful working relationships, whether by cooperation, charm, or persuasion. The public, Congress, and the press are obviously the most critical. But there are other players who must also be approached with political savvy: foreign powers, domestic interest groups, and domestic elites. All of these outside players expect to have a place at his table and to share in decision-making; most of them will put their own needs first. No one in the twentieth century was better at juggling these many groups than Franklin Roosevelt. He was, as James MacGregor Burns wrote, both the lion and the fox, and that accounted in large measure for his extraordinary success.

Among recent executives, it is surprising how often that lesson has been lost. Nixon, Carter, and Clinton all seemed to thumb their nose at institutions like Congress, the press, and the political elite of Washington. It is difficult enough to govern in today's climate, but they managed to make it almost impossible by doubling the resistance to their agendas. Future presidents ought to go to school on FDR's success in the New Deal, Harry Truman's passage of the Marshall Plan, LBJ's victories in the civil rights bills of 1964 and 1965, and Reagan's passage of his economic program.

5. A Sure, Quick Start

If contemporary experience has taught us anything, surely it is the need for a president to "hit the ground running." The difference between Reagan's quick start and Clinton's stumbles put one on the path toward a succession of legislative triumphs and the other on the road to a debacle in health care and a loss of Congress. Had Clinton not been as agile as he was in recovering in late 1993 and then again in 1995–1996, he would have been a one-term president. As it was, he never became the transformational figure he had hoped.

In most institutions, the power of a leader grows over time. A CEO, a university president, the head of a union, acquire stature through the quality of their long-term performance. The presidency is just the opposite: power tends to evaporate quickly. It's not that a president must rival Franklin Roosevelt in his First Hundred Days, but his first months in office—up to the August recess of Congress—are usually the widest window of opportunity he will have, even if he serves two full terms. That's why he has to move fast.

Achieving a smooth, successful start is more arduous than it looks. Those who have been well schooled in national life have a definite advantage. FDR, LBJ, and Reagan knew how to pull the levers of power before they got to the White House; Carter and Clinton had to learn on the job. The campaign itself must also be focused on governing. By giving voters a clear sense of what they wanted to do in office, LBJ in 1964 and Reagan in 1980 both won mandates that greatly strengthened their hands in the months that followed. By contrast, Reagan never sought a mandate in the 1984 campaign, and his second term never matched his first. A well-run transition is a less appreciated but equally important element. Had Clinton settled down in the eleven weeks between his election and inauguration, he would have arrived in Washington with a more experienced White House team, a game plan for his first weeks in office, and a storehouse of personal energy. He lacked all three.

6. Strong, Prudent Advisers

When George Washington was preparing his third annual message to Congress, as biographer Richard Brookhiser has pointed out, he first took suggestions from James Madison and Thomas Jefferson. He then asked Alexander Hamilton to draw up a first draft, which went back to Madison for a rewrite. Not a bad lot.

The Washington experience underscores a repeated lesson from presidential history. The best presidents are ones who surround themselves with the best advisers. Lincoln wrote down the names of his potential cabinet on the night of his election and from them recruited a team that rivaled Washington's. Teddy Roosevelt, Franklin Roosevelt, Harry Truman—all were noted for the quality of the people around them. Of the presidents I have served, Reagan started with the best White House operation, and Ford wound up with the best cabinet. In each instance, one could see a palpable difference in the dynamics of their leadership.

In the future, we are likely to see the First Lady or the First Man exercise an ever-larger influence upon the political thinking of the president. Hillary Clinton is the first woman in the post with a professional degree, but she will be far from the last. The trend should be a welcome one: a president needs a friend in whom he can confide his private thoughts, and if that person is also an empathic, educated helpmate, all the better. The only caveat is whether the two keep their roles strictly separated. The Clinton experience should be lesson enough.

7. Inspiring Others to Carry On the Mission

One of the most instructive books about the leadership of Franklin Roosevelt starts with his death. Historian William Leuchtenburg shows that the next eight presidents after him all lived in his shadow. Three of them—Truman, Kennedy, and Johnson—were Democrats who consciously set out to complete the New Deal. Two—Eisenhower and Nixon—were Republicans who accepted it and even added on to it. In fact, Nixon was in many ways the last of the New Deal presidents. Even Reagan, who rejected the Great Society, didn't want to disturb the work of his first political hero and adopted much of his leadership style.

The point is that the most effective presidents create a living legacy, inspiring legions of followers to carry on their mission long after they are gone. Among contemporary presidents, only Reagan has come close to doing that. While he never built a coalition to match FDR's, he put a stamp upon his party and upon the nation's political culture that shapes it still.

As political scientist Stephen Skowronek has demonstrated, there is a pattern to the way presidents like Jefferson, Jackson, Lincoln, FDR, and Reagan have created a new politics. In each case, they came into power by knocking down an old orthodoxy and in its place built what is now popularly called "a new paradigm." Roosevelt gave the boot to laissez-faire and put government at the helm of the economy. Reagan shifted the balance away from a government-centered system and embraced an entrepreneurial culture. They also built new political movements and created cadres of loyal followers who would pick up their banner when they fell. Inevitably, they also left behind an agenda of unfinished work that subsequent presidents tried to complete.

Today's politics is ripe for a president to come into office and offer "a new paradigm." There may not be an old orthodoxy to knock down; no single regime of ideas is now dominant. But the winds of change are blowing so hard that voters are eager to find a leader who will set forth a clear, steady path into the future. The next president who does that successfully will also be the next to have a living legacy.

There are . . . a good many other lessons that recent experience suggests about leadership, but the seven enumerated here seem fundamental. They are the principles upon which to build. They do not guarantee success. Certainly, they offer no guarantee of producing a new candidate for Mount Rushmore. Great crises usually bring forth great leaders, as Abigail Adams once observed, and, for now, neither war nor depression is looming. But these principles do hold out the promise that if they are followed, the nation might once again enjoy a steady stream of presidents who are strong, honest, and effective. Who can ask for more? We might just find that new golden age.

38

BRADLEY PATTERSON

From *The White House Staff*: [Chief of Staff]

Drawing on many examples, Bradley Patterson paints a detailed picture of one of the least public but most important positions in Washington, D.C. The president's chief of staff is in charge of every aspect of the White House office, from the mundane to the weighty. Patterson is a long-time observer of the inside political scene in the nation's capital, and he brings to his prescription for the chief of staff a vast knowledge both of the individuals who have held the job and of the executive branch. The chief of staff must be all things to the president, Patterson feels, but he must be careful in the process not to become isolated and alienated from the numerous people whose requests he has to reject on behalf of his boss.

————

IT SEEMED AS IF two traditions were in the making: Republican presidents, following the Eisenhower model, emplaced chiefs of staff in their White Houses; Democratic presidents, aghast at the Nixon experience, shunned the idea. The second "tradition" came to a halt with Clinton. As presidential scholar James Pfiffner succinctly put it: "A chief of staff is essential in the modern White House."

. . . Beyond the chief of staff, there is only the president to try to knit his administration into a coherent set of institutions—and the president has vastly graver, and "undelegatable," responsibilities. The chief of staff is *system manager*: boss of none, but overseer of everything.

Does a new president understand this?

One former aide believes that a new chief executive often has a misconception:

[Presidents] always treat chiefs of staff incorrectly. They . . . think of chiefs of staff as nothing more than foremen, hired hands basically. Whereas chiefs of staff and everybody else think of [them] as exalted kinds of rulers with great power. So I think presidents need to think more about staff functions—how the White House operates, how it's going to operate, and the kind of people they choose to be around them. They don't seem to have that sense of history about them. It's like staff history is below them.

Thirty-eight years of experience—nineteen White House chiefs of staff—have, in this author's view, demonstrated a number of principles for effectiveness in fulfilling that central responsibility.

A chief of staff needs to be familiar with the unique pressures and pitfalls of public life in Washington. This means recognizing—and being comfortable with the existence of—the contravening authorities and forces from the vigorously competing centers of power in the nation and in the nation's capital: the cabinet departments, Congress, the courts, the press, the lobbyists, professional societies, interest groups, and the international community. The more successful chiefs of staff have had some thorough experience in one or more of those institutions. Former chief of staff Leon Panetta emphasized: "You really need to have somebody in that position who has some experience in Washington. It's just absolutely essential. The president can have somebody close to him, but it better be somebody who has some experience with what Washington is about, because that person has to make sure that the president isn't making any obvious mistakes."

The chief of staff needs to have firm, four-way support: not only from the president but from the first lady, the vice president, and the vice president's spouse as well. Nagging doubts or lack of confidence on the part of any of these four will eat away at the chief of staff's stature and authority. The wise chief will stay in especially close communication with the vice president and the two spouses. But communication is one thing; responsibility is another. In the end, the chief of staff has only one boss.

The chief of staff should be someone who is not only close to the president but also very familiar with those who operated the campaign. Most of the campaigners will have their hearts set on positions in Washington, hopefully on the White House staff. The incoming chief of staff must be able to distinguish effectiveness in campaigning from effectiveness in the business of governing—and give preference to those who share the president's political ideology rather than to factional advocates who are not necessarily on the same "policy wavelength" as the president.

The chief of staff has comprehensive control over the activities of the White House staff. Comments Panetta:

I had some military background—which was probably of even greater value than any kind of management background you have when you take a position like that. The role of a chief of staff is more like a battlefield commander: you've got a mission to accomplish, and you have to, sometimes, fight your way through a lot of incoming fire to make sure that the mission is done, but you need to have everybody knowing exactly what he or she has to do, in order to accomplish the mission. . . . It was very important to establish that the chief of staff had control.

But what does "control" mean? One Clinton staff chief allegedly tried to keep most of the policy balls bouncing on his own desk: he acted as the budget director, the legislative liaison head, the economic and domestic policy principal—and was the major White House spokesman. He handled all those functions superbly, it was acknowledged, but how long can such concentration be sustained? Another Clinton chief of staff preferred delegation: each senior presidential staffer was given goals, objectives, and guidelines—and then held firmly accountable for achieving them. "You have to empower people!" he said.

Former president George Bush would advise a president: "Get someone [with whom] you are totally comfortable. He/She must be a strong manager. Must be able to inspire confidence and loyalty in the rest of the staff. Must have had enough experience in some phase of life to walk in the White House door with a certain respect level already in place."

None of the policy centers of the White House—including the National Security Council apparat and the offices of the first lady and the vice president— can be allowed to work independently of the rest of the institution. In the Clinton White House, the national security adviser and the vice president's and the first lady's chiefs of staff all attended the chief of staff's senior staff meetings. The chief of staff attended the NSC principals' (cabinet-level) meetings and the intelligence briefings with the president. If even the most sensitive national security issue is being presented to the president, the national security adviser and the chief of staff jointly go into the Oval Office.

Chief of Staff John Podesta described his relationship with national security adviser Samuel (Sandy) Berger: "The one person I do not view, from a policy perspective, as reporting 'through me' is Sandy. I think it works better that way. I am not only comfortable with that; I think that is the better model. As long as we get along. He runs almost every big decision by me; I don't feel left out by him. He can keep a deeper sense of what is going on in his world; I keep a deeper sense of what is going on in my world—and we are pretty well integrated."

All presentations to the president are subject to the chief of staff's review. Issues—particularly those involving differences of opinion—are first vetted around the chief's table. The chief must ask: Is this an open process? Are the right people here? Have we asked the right questions? Are all the key options included? Has the "underbrush" been cleared out and the issues reduced to their core substance? Can consensus be reached on the lesser, "compromisable" differences?

The chief of staff controls the president's schedule. And the look-ahead period is not days but weeks — often, in fact, months. As for the schedule on a given day, the chief of staff's goal is to keep the focus on *the* principal event, ensuring that activities that would compete with news of that principal happening are downplayed or pushed aside. On policy issues awaiting discussion with the president, the chief of staff determines priorities: Which matters require attention and in what order?

The chief of staff controls the president's doorway. Who is invited to meetings and who is not? There may be some hurt feelings, but temporarily bruised egos are a small price to pay for conserving the president's absolutely invaluable time.

Review, by the chief of staff's office, of all papers that come out of the president's office is as important as scrutiny of those that come in. The president's scribbles and marginal comments are likely to be as important as the check marks in the decision box.

The chief will set up a special system for controlling the White House responses to congressional mail that contains important policy questions. Are budgetary issues being raised that require advice from the Office of Management and Budget? Constitutional ones? Is litigation possible? (The counsel must be consulted.) Who will draft the response? Have all the necessary clearances been obtained? Who will sign the outgoing letter?

The chief of staff may wish to have two or three deputy chiefs of staff. One perhaps will specialize in national security issues, another in management and operations matters, a third in domestic or economic questions. The various White House policy units may be divvied up to report on their work to the appropriate deputy *first* — before the chief of staff and the president get involved. Can such sequencing of reporting procedures be put in place without attenuating the relationships between the chief of staff and the principal White House assistants? The three most recent Clinton chiefs of staff all used this system with apparent success.

The chief of staff cannot avoid dealing with Congress. In fact, he may spend a great deal of time negotiating on the Hill on the president's behalf. The chief will likely have to take calls from governors and meet with the leaders of advocacy groups. As the chief does so, however, he always keeps the appropriate White House colleagues — legislative, intergovernmental, public liaison — closely informed and involved. The effective chief sets a firm practice: other staff members are not to be "disempowered." (Such wide-ranging extramural responsibilities are yet another reason that the contemporary White House chief of staff has deputies: to help create time for the chief to handle such external duties and not shirk his own responsibilities to the president.)

Perhaps the chief of staff's most sensitive judgment call is deciding where to draw the line: when to take an issue to the president and when to settle it before it gets that far. Podesta reflects:

I think I have a regulator that says to me, even if the president is likely to be with the consensus of his advisers, I will still have to take it into the Oval Office. There is a level of importance which, even if there is consensus, requires that the decision be signed off by the president. I think Berger would probably agree with that, from the national security viewpoint. He takes care of a lot of issues over in his office. But there is a certain level of decision which you can't just inform the president about; you really have to have his input. He may say, "I don't have a strong view; you decide." Which he will often do, if everybody is on the same page. "We'll just decide it here."

Podesta's predecessor, Erskine Bowles, expressed similar sentiments:

I made a lot of budget decisions that some people would probably have taken, on balance, right in to the president. But the president made it clear to me that he wanted me to do things like that, and the reason is: everyone has individual strengths and weaknesses. I don't have the vision; I can't dream like Bill Clinton. I can't see the things he can see. . . . But I am a doer; I can get things done. I am a negotiator; I can take tough positions and say no. The president would never say, "Erskine, you go out and make this final decision and just bring me the answer." At the same time, I didn't seek permission every time I did something. We would decide in advance what the ground rules were, what he wanted done and what I thought was practical. We would decide together: "This is what we have to have; it's going to be really tough." My job then was to "go to it." If he didn't like what I had negotiated, I expected him to let me know, which he would, quite clearly. At the same time, whether the results were positive or negative, good or bad, the president had to know it all.

Readers will instantly appreciate what a thin line this is—and will recognize how easily an egotistical chief of staff could be tempted to get into the habit of walling off staff or cabinet pleaders with the dictum "Take it from me: the president has decided!" when in fact the chief, rather than the president, was the decisionmaker.

In the decisionmaking process, the chief of staff is always an honest broker. But only an honest broker? By no means. Presidents expect their chiefs of staff to hold, and to express, their own independent judgments about any issue in the Oval Office neighborhood. They must do so, however, without using their stature and their proximity to give their own arguments an "edge" over competing contentions from other staffers or cabinet disputants.

The chief of staff must be possessed of the exceptional sensitivity to recognize a presidential command that is given in unthinking anger, frustration, or exhaustion—and to lay it aside. Scholar Fred Greenstein quotes Eisenhower: "I told my staff . . . once in a while you people have just got to be my safety-valve. So I'll get you in here and I will let go, but this is for you and your knowledge and your knowledge only. Now I've seen these people going out, and I've gotten a little extreme, a little white, but pretty soon one of them comes in and laughs and says, 'Well, you were in good form this morning, Mr. President.'"

Former presidential assistants Bob Haldeman and Joseph Califano both describe similar experiences. When Nixon issued an intemperate instruction on one occasion, Haldeman remembered: "I said nothing more, then stepped out of the office and placed the order immediately on my mental 'no action ever' shelf." President Johnson had the same habit, and Califano used the same response. Califano commented: "After three years of serving on his White House staff, he would have expected me to have some sense of how to measure his true meaning when he spoke in anger." (It is the author's belief that in May of 1993, when faced with what appeared to be a directive from on high to fire the staff of the White House Travel Office, OMA director David Watkins should have emulated the Haldeman practice.)

The chief of staff or one of the deputy chiefs of staff goes on each presidential journey as principal manager of the overall odyssey, since a presidential trip, particularly one overseas, presents a very special challenge for White House preparers and coordinators.

For nearly half a century it has been the chief of staff's responsibility to convene White House staff meetings. Harry S. Truman was the last president to do so personally. Under President Clinton, Chief of Staff Podesta inaugurated what he called strategic management team meetings, a daily morning gathering of the legislative, domestic, economic policy, and national security heads with the deputy chiefs of staff, the director and deputy director of the OMB, the secretary and deputy secretary of Treasury, and a few other senior staff. One could almost have called the group the "White House Executive Committee."

Because of the chief of staff 's stature and proximity to the president, invitations for media appearances—speeches, Sunday television talk shows—pour in. True, the chief is one of those in the White House best positioned to speak for the president—but any chief, even today, remembers Louis Brownlow's long-ago admonition to President Roosevelt: White House staff officers must have a "passion for anonymity." The need to explain or defend a president's actions may be almost overwhelming on some occasions, and a chief may be a spectacularly lucid and persuasive spokesperson. *Each chief of staff and each president will come to their own agreement on how public the chief's persona should be.* The author's personal preference is to give greater weight to Brownlow's advice.

The chief of staff must continually build bridges to the cabinet. While it is the fundamental thesis of this book that policy development and coordination are becoming more and more centralized in the White House staff, there is a risk in this development. Some cabinet secretaries, especially those with narrower and more specialized policy and operational responsibilities—and thus less contact with the White House—may tend to feel isolated, perhaps even alienated. *Locked in the Cabinet*, the memoir of former secretary of labor Robert Reich, evidences this sentiment:

The Secretary of Transportation phones to ask me how I discover what's going on at the White House. I have no clear answer. . . . The decision-making "loop" depends on physical proximity to B—who's whispering into his ear most regularly, whose office is closest to the Oval, who's sitting or standing next to him when a key issue arises. . . . One of the best techniques is to linger in the corridors of the West Wing after a meeting, picking up gossip. Another good place is the executive parking lot between the West Wing and the Old Executive Office Building, where dozens of White House staffers tromp every few minutes. In this administration you're either in the loop or you're out of the loop, but more likely you don't know where the loop is, or you don't even know there *is* a loop.

The chief of staff's antennae must be attuned to pick up such alienation—early.

Concerned that the 1998–99 scandal investigations and impeachment proceedings had led cabinet members to have "gotten kind of distant," Podesta began a series of breakfasts at the White House for small groups of cabinet secretaries. "Seven or eight at a time," he said, "just to kick things around, listen to them, let them tell me what was going on." A former assistant to Chief of Staff Bowles emphasized:

One of the challenges for our office was to act as a nexus, and to remember to keep everyone in the fold, and aware of what was going on in different parts of the White House. It is so big and there are so many different things taking place. There is a certain level of paranoia when you reach certain levels of power in government—in which everybody wants to know what everybody else is doing. The family—the organization—in my mind works better when people understand what's taking place. For the chief of staff to collect information is important, but so is it for the chief of staff to share information.

The chief of staff, finally, runs one more risk: that of becoming insensitive to the perquisites and privileges that necessarily accompany his status. The use of limousines and planes, proximity to the president, the toleration of what may be the chief's personal rudeness, the alacritous attention of subordinates—have gone to the heads of some. Over the years of their incumbency, having had to say no to so many supplicants (including members of Congress) will have added up to a paucity of close friends and a host of enemies. If the chief of staff—a Sherman Adams, a Donald Regan, a John Sununu—makes a stupid, even if unintentional slip, there may be only one friend left: and if he, the president, is embarrassed by the error, there is only the sad and sometimes precipitous exit. Would that the electronics wizards could invent a pocket-size "egometer" that would measure a chief of staff's ego, calculate his insensitivity index—and beep a warning! . . .

PART SEVEN

The Executive Branch

39

HUGH HECLO

From *A Government of Strangers*

To understand Hugh Heclo's intricate analysis of power inside the executive branch, students of American government must first know who the players are. Presidents select a small number (a few thousand) of high-level people to head the executive branch agencies. Among those appointments are cabinet secretaries, undersecretaries, assistant secretaries, and the like. The rest of those who work in the executive branch are civil servants, chosen for government jobs by merit exams, and they remain in government service for many years, even decades. They are the bureaucrats who provide continuity. Appointees come and go—as do presidents—but bureaucrats remain. Heclo identifies the often-unseen tension between a president's appointees and the bureaucrats. Be sure to pay particular attention to his discussion of the "iron triangle," one of the most interesting yet invisible forces in American government.

———

EVERY NEW ADMINISTRATION gives fresh impetus to an age-old struggle between change and continuity, between political leadership and bureaucratic power. Bureaucrats have a legitimate interest in maintaining the integrity of government programs and organizations. Political executives are supposed to have a broader responsibility: to guide rather than merely reflect the sum of special interests at work in the executive branch.

The search for effective political leadership in a bureaucracy of responsible career officials has become extraordinarily difficult in Washington. In every new crop of political appointees, some will have had government experience and a few will have worked together, but when it comes to group commitment to political leadership in the executive branch they constitute a government of strangers. And yet the fact remains that whether the President relies mainly on his White House aides or on his cabinet officials, someone is supposed to be mastering the bureaucracy "out there." For the President, his appointees, and high-ranking bureaucrats, the struggle to control the bureaucracy is usually a leap into the dark.

Despite a host of management and organization studies, Washington exposés and critiques of bureaucracy, very little information is available about the working world and everyday conduct of the top people in government. Even less is known about the operational lessons that could be drawn from their experiences. Congress is widely thought to have lost power to the executive branch, but congressional rather than executive behavior remains a major preoccupation in political research. Observers acknowledge that no president can cope with more than a tiny fraction of the decisionmaking in government, yet we know far more about a president's daily social errands than about the way vital public business is conducted by hundreds of political appointees and several thousand top bureaucrats who take executive actions in the name of the United States government—which is to say, in the name of us all. . . .

If popular impressions are any guide, few job titles are more suspect than "politician" and "bureaucrat." Periodic polls have shown that while most parents might want their offspring to become president, they dislike the notion of their becoming politicians. No pollster has dared to ask Americans what they would think of their children growing up to become Washington bureaucrats.

Yet in many ways the American form of government depends not only on a supply of able politicians and bureaucrats, but even more on a successful interaction between these two unpopular groups. . . .

. . . The administrative machinery in Washington represents a number of fragmented power centers rather than a set of subordinate units under the President. As many observers have noted, the cracks of fragmentation are not random but run along a number of well-established functional specialties and program interests that link particular government bureaus, congressional committees, and interest groups. People in the White House are aware of these subgovernments but have no obvious control over them. They seem to persist regardless of government reorganizations or, perhaps more to the point, they are able to prevent the reorganizations that displease them. In coping with these Washington subgovernments, the real lines of defense and accommodation are out in the departments, with their mundane operations of personnel actions, program approval, budget requests, regulation writing, and all the rest. These are the unglamorous tools with which political leaders in the agencies either help create a broader approach to the conduct of the public's business or acquiesce to the prevailing interest in business as usual. . . .

. . . Political executives who try to exercise leadership within government may encounter intense opposition that they can neither avoid nor reconcile. At such times some agency officials may try to undermine the efforts of political executives. Any number of reasons—some deplorable, some commendable—lie behind such bureaucratic opposition. Executive politics involves people, and certain individuals simply dislike each other and resort to personal vendettas. Many, however, sincerely believe in their bureau's purpose and feel they must protect its jurisdiction, programs, and budget at all costs. Others feel they have an obligation to "blow the whistle" as best they can when confronted with evidence of what they regard as improper conduct. In all these cases the result is likely to strike a political executive as bureaucratic subversion. To the officials, it is a question of higher loyalty, whether to one's self-interests, organization, or conscience.

The structure of most bureaucratic sabotage has been characterized as an "iron triangle" uniting a particular government bureau, its relevant interest group, and congressional supporters. The aims may be as narrow as individual profiteering and empire-building. Or they may be as magnanimous as "public interest" lobbies, reformist bureaucrats, and congressional crusaders all claiming somewhat incongruously to represent the unrepresented. There are alliances with fully developed shapes (e.g., the congressional sponsors of a program, the bureaucrats executing it, and its private clients or suppliers) and those made up of only a few diverse lines (e.g., a civil servant looking forward to post-retirement prospects with a particular lobby association or a congressman unconcerned about a bureaucrat's policy aims but aware that his specific favors can help win reelection). Some bureaucratic entrepreneurs initiate their own outside contacts; others have been pushed into becoming involved in outside alliances by former political appointees.

The common features of these subgovernments are enduring mutual interests across the executive and legislative branches and between the public and private sectors. However high-minded the ultimate purpose, the immediate aim of each alliance is to become "self-sustaining in control of power in its own sphere." The longer an agency's tradition of independence, the greater the political controversy surrounding its subject matter, and the more it is allied with outside groups, the more a new appointee can expect sub rosa opposition to develop to any proposed changes. If political leadership in the executive branch is to be more than the accidental sum of these alliances and if political representation is to be less arbitrary than the demands of any group that claims to speak for the unrepresented, then some conflict seems inevitable between higher political leaders and the subgovernments operating within their sphere.

Often sabotage is unrecognizable because of the virtually invisible ways civil servants can act in bad faith toward political executives. In addition to the bureaucracy's power of withholding needed information and services, there are other means. Like a long-married couple, bureaucrats and those in their networks can often communicate with a minimum of words: "If congressional staffs I trust call up and ask me, I might tell them. But I can also tell them I don't agree with the secretary by offering just technical information and not associating myself with the policy."

An official who does not want to risk direct dealings with Congress can encourage a private interest group to go to the agency's important appropriations and legislative committees, as one political executive discovered: "When we tried to downgrade the . . . bureau, its head was opposed, and he had a friend in a lobby group. After they got together rumblings started from the appropriations committee. I asked [the committee chairman] if he had a problem with this reorganization, and he said, 'No, you have the problem because if you touch that bureau I'll cut your job out of the budget.'" An experienced bureaucrat may not be able to make the decision, but he can try to arrange things to create the reaction he wants. "A colleague of mine," said a supergrade,* "keeps a file on field offices that can be abolished and their political sensitivity. Depending on who's pressing for cuts, he'll pull out those that are politically the worst for that particular configuration." The everyday relationships between people with specialized interests can shade effortlessly into subversion: "You know what it's like," said a bureau chief. "You've known each other and will have a drink complaining about what's happening and work up some little strategy of your own to do something about it." Or bureaucrats can work to get their way simply by not trying to know what is happening. One assistant secretary reported how his career subordinates agreed there might be mismanagement in the regional offices, "but they also said they didn't know what these offices were doing and so there wasn't enough information to justify doing what I wanted." Ignorance may not be bliss, but it can be security.

Political appointees can sometimes encounter much more vigorous forms of sabotage. These range from minor needling to massive retaliation. Since information is a prime strategic resource in Washington, the passing of unauthorized messages outside channels often approaches an art form. There are routine leaks to build credit and keep channels open for when they might be needed, positive leaks to promote something, negative leaks to discredit a person or policy, and counterleaks. There is even the daring reverse leak, an unauthorized release of information apparently for one reason but actually accomplishing the opposite.†

There is no lack of examples in every administration. A political

*Though not an official title, a "supergrade" would be a government civil servant in the upper levels of the bureaucracy.—EDS.
†One recent example involved a presidential assistant rather than a bureaucrat. While jockeying with another staff member, the assistant leaked a disclosure of his own impending removal from the West Wing. The opponent, who obviously stood the most to gain from

executive may discover that an agency subordinate "has gone to Congress and actually written the rider to the legislation that nullified the changes we wanted." A saboteur confided that "no one ever found it was [a division chief] who prepared the list showing which lobbyist was to contact which senator with what kind of argument." Still another official reported he had "seen appointees kept waiting in the outer office while their subordinate bureau officials were in private meetings with the congressional staff members." But waiting lines lack finesse. The telephone can be used with more delicacy, particularly after office hours: "The night before the hearings [a bureaucrat] fed the questions to the committee staff and then the agency witnesses spent the next two days having to reveal the information or duck the questions and catch hell." A young staff civil servant described how his superior operated:

I used to sit in [the bureau chief's] office after 6 P.M. when all the important business got done. He'd call up a senator and say, "Tom, you know this program that you and I got through a while back? Well, there's no crisis, but here are some things I'd like to talk to you about." He'd hang up and get on the phone to [a House committee chairman] and say, "I've been talking with Tom about this issue, and I'd like to bring you in on it." Hell, you'd find [the bureau chief] had bills almost drafted before anybody else in the executive branch had ever heard about them.

Encountering such situations, a public executive becomes acutely aware that experience as a private manager provides scant guidance. As one corporate executive with a six-figure salary said, "The end-runs and preselling were incredible. To find an equivalent you'd have to imagine some of your division managers going to the executive board or a major stockholder behind your back." Learning to deal with sabotage is a function of an executive's political leadership, not his private management expertise.

How do political executives try to deal with bureaucratic sabotage? . . . One approach is simply to ignore bureaucratic sabotage. Since the damage that may be done can easily cripple an executive's aims, diminish his reputation, and threaten his circles of confidence, those adopting this strategy can be presumed to have abdicated any attempt at political leadership in the Washington bureaucracy.

A second approach, especially favored by forceful managers, is to try to root out the leakers and prevent any recurrence. But political executives

---

the story, was naturally asked to confirm or deny the report. Since he was not yet strong enough to accomplish such a removal, the opponent had to deny responsibility for the leak and its accuracy, thereby inadvertently strengthening the position of the presidential assistant who first leaked the story.

usually discover that this straightforward approach has considerable disadvantages. For one thing, it is extremely time-consuming and difficult to actually investigate acts of subversion and pin down blame. For another thing, there are few effective sanctions to prevent recurrences. Moreover, a search for the guilty party can easily displace more positive efforts and leadership initiatives an executive needs to make in dealing with the bureaucracy. Even if it were possible, trying to censor bureaucratic contacts would probably restrict the informal help these outside relationships provide, as well as the harm they do. And in the end any serious sabotage will probably be buttressed by some mandate from Congress; punishing the saboteurs can be seen as an assault on legislative prerogatives and thus invite even sterner retribution. It is circumstances such as these that led an experienced undersecretary to conclude:

> Of course you can't be a patsy, but by and large you've got to recognize that leaks and end-runs are going to happen. You can spend all your time at trying to find out who's doing it, and if you do, then what? [One of my colleagues] actually tried to stop some of his bureaucrats from accepting phone calls from the press. They did stop accepting the calls, but they sure as hell returned them quickly. In this town there are going to be people running behind your back, and there's not much you can do to stop it.

However, while academics write about the iron triangle as if it were an immutable force, prudent political executives recognize that although they cannot stop bureaucratic sabotage, neither are they helpless against it. They can use personnel sanctions where misconduct can be clearly proven. But far more important, they can work to counteract sabotage with their own efforts—strengthening their outside contacts, extending their own lines of information and competitive analysis, finding new points of countertension. In general, experienced political executives try to use all their means of self-help and working relations so as to reshape the iron triangles into more plastic polygons.

To deal with sabotage, wise political appointees try to render it more obvious:

> I make it clear that all the information and papers are supposed to move through me. It increases your work load tremendously, and maybe you don't understand everything you see, but everyone knows I'm supposed to be in on things and that they are accepting risks by acting otherwise.

They try to counteract unwanted messages with their own accounts to the press and others. The more the agency's boat is leaking, "the more you go out and work the pumps. You can't plug all the leaks, but you can make sure to get your side of the story out."

Political executives also make use of timing to deal with sabotage:

I put in a one-year fudge factor for an important change. That's because I know people are going to be doing end-runs to Congress. This year lets congressmen blow off steam, and for another thing it shows me where the sensitive spots are so I can get busy trying to work out some compromises—you know, things that can serve the congressmen's interest as well as mine.

Substantial results can be achieved by bringing new forces into play, dealing not with just one alliance but creating tests of strengths among the triangles:

It's like when officials were getting together with the unions and state administrators to get at some committee chairman. I hustled out to line up governors and show the congressmen that state administrators weren't speaking for all of state government.

Washington offers more opportunities to search for allies than is suggested by any simple image of political executives on one side and bureaucratic opponents on the other. Political appointees may be "back-doored" by other appointees, higher bureaucrats by lower bureaucrats. Fights may be extended to involve some appointees and bureaucrats versus others. As the leader of one faction put it, "Often a guy preselling things on the Hill is hurting people elsewhere, making it tougher for them to get money and approval and straining their relations. I use this fact to get allies."

A political executive who works hard at outside contacts will discover what subversives may learn too late: that many groups are fickle allies of the bureaucracy. This has seemed especially true as Congress has increased its own bureaucracy of uncoordinated staffs. A veteran bureaucrat described the risks run by would-be saboteurs:

Everybody you might talk to weighs the value of the issue to them against the value of keeping you alive for the next time. I've seen [a congressman] ruin many a good civil servant by getting a relationship going with him and then dropping him to score points off the agency brass. Now, too, there are more Hill staffers running around telling appointees, "Hey, these guys from your department said this and that. How about it?" Then the appointee will go back to the agency and raise hell for the bureaucrat.

Thus the political executives' own positive efforts are the necessary— if not always a sufficient—condition for combating sabotage. Since some bureaucratic subversion is an ever-present possibility and since punishment is difficult, the government executives' real choice is to build and use their political relationships or forfeit most other strategic resources for leadership.

40

ROBERT REICH

From *Locked in the Cabinet*

University professor Robert Reich was appointed to President Clinton's cabinet in 1993 to be his Secretary of Labor. Writing with all the candor and humor that is Reich's trademark, he tells first about his selection of a deputy to serve under him and a chief of staff to run the office. Reich gives readers three important criteria he considered and then concludes, "I'm flying blind." His daily schedule is packed, and he is motivated to escape from the "bubble" and actually tour the vast buildings of the Labor Department. Finally, Reich offers an instructive anecdote about an idea developed by an obscure civil servant in the department, an idea that turns out to be a real winner and becomes an important new government policy.

February 1, [1993] Washington

I INTERVIEW TWENTY people today. I have to find a deputy secretary and chief of staff with all the management skills I lack. I also have to find a small platoon of assistant secretaries: one to run the Occupational Safety and Health Administration (detested by corporations, revered by unions); another to be in charge of the myriad of employment and job training programs (billions of dollars), plus unemployment insurance (billions more); another to police the nation's pension funds (four trillion dollars' worth); another to patrol the nation's nine million workplaces to make sure that young children aren't being exploited, that workers receive at least a minimum hourly wage plus time and a half for overtime, that sweatshops are relegated to history.

The Department of Labor is vast, its powers seemingly endless. With a history spanning the better part of the twentieth century—involving every major controversy affecting American workers—it issues thousands of regulations, sends vast sums of money to states and cities, and sues countless employers. I can barely comprehend it all. It was created in 1913 with an ambitious mission: *Foster, promote, and develop the welfare of the wage earners of the United States, improve their working conditions, and advance their opportunities for profitable employment.* That about sums it up.

And yet here I am assembling my team before I've even figured it all out. No time to waste. Bill will have to sign off on my choices, then each of them will be nitpicked for months by the White House staff and the FBI, and if they survive those hurdles each must be confirmed by the Senate.

If I'm fast enough out of the starting gate, my team might be fully installed by June. If I dally now and get caught in the traffic jam of subcabinet nominations from every department, I might not see them for a year. And whenever they officially start, add another six months before they have the slightest idea what's going on.

No other democracy does it this way. No private corporation would think of operating like this. Every time a new president is elected, America assembles a new government of 3,000 or so amateurs who only sometimes know the policies they're about to administer, rarely have experience managing large government bureaucracies, and almost never know the particular piece of it they're going to run. These people are appointed quickly by a president-elect who is thoroughly exhausted from a year and a half of campaigning. And they remain in office, on average, under two years—barely enough time to find the nearest bathroom. It's a miracle we don't screw it up worse than we do.

Part of my problem is I don't know exactly what I'm looking for and I certainly don't know how to tell whether I've found it. Some obvious criteria:

1. *They should share the President-elect's values.* But how will I know they do? I can't very well ask, "Do you share the President's values?" and expect an honest answer. Even if they contributed money to the campaign, there's no telling. I've heard of several middle-aged Washington lawyers so desperate to escape the tedium of law practice by becoming an assistant secretary for Anything That Gets Me Out of Here that they've made whopping contributions to both campaigns.

2. *They should be competent and knowledgeable about the policies they'll administer.* Sounds logical, but here again, how can I tell? I don't know enough to know whether someone *else* knows enough. "What do you think about the Employee Retirement Income Security Act?" I might ask, and an ambitious huckster could snow me. "I've thought a lot about this," he might say, "and I've concluded that Section 508(m) should be changed because most retirees have 307 accounts which are treated by the IRS as Subchapter 12 entities." Uttered with enough conviction, bullshit like this could sweep me off my feet.

3. *They should be good managers.* But how to find out? Yesterday I phoned someone about a particular job candidate's management skills, at

her suggestion. He told me she worked for him and was a terrific manager. "Terrific?" I repeated. "Wonderful. The best," he said. "You'd recommend her?" I asked. "Absolutely. Can't go wrong," he assured me. I thanked him, hung up the phone, and was enthusiastic for about five minutes, until I realized how little I had learned. How do I know *he* recognizes a good manager? Maybe he's a lousy manager himself and has a bunch of bozos working for him. Why should I trust that he's more interested in my having her on *my* team than in getting her off his?

I'm flying blind.

February 2 Washington

I've made two of the most important decisions I'll make in this job: the choices of deputy secretary and chief of staff.

The deputy runs the day-to-day operations of the department, allowing me to deal with everyone on the outside — Congress, the White House, the press, the unions, the business lobbies, community groups, and the rest of the world. The chief of staff runs *me* — my chief aide in dealing with this galaxy. Both jobs call for fast wits and hard heads. If they don't do their jobs well, deputy secretaries and chiefs of staff spend all their time carrying around the Washington equivalent of giant pooper-scoopers. They've got to clean up the shit.

For deputy I've chosen Tom Glynn. He used to run the subway system in Boston, now he's a vice president of Brown University, in charge of administration and finance. Ted Kennedy thinks the world of him. The unions like him. Staffers on the campaign say he was helpful. I've checked with every single one of his former employers, a number of people who have worked *for* him, and several whom we know in common (and whose judgment I trust). Everyone describes him in the same way: a superb administrator who can play politics like a pool hall champ. They say he's tough, cunning, disciplined, and doesn't suffer fools.

I never met Tom before I interviewed him. He's my age, gray-haired, blue-eyed, and wiry, with narrow shoulders. He has an Irish pug nose and a tiny mouth, which scarcely moves when he talks. And he doesn't talk much. His responses to my questions were never more than five words, but they were always sufficient. The man is economical, if nothing else. But I liked what I heard. His answers were sharp, insightful. And he had good questions for *me*. He actually wanted to know what I intended to *accomplish*. We talked about goals!

I wouldn't say he makes me comfortable. He's not a teddy bear. He doesn't smile much. I'd be more comfortable with someone like me—a short Jewish academic who likes to indulge in political-economic theory and grand historic visions. But I have to tell myself that the choice of deputy isn't about comfort. That's the mistake made by too many who move into positions like mine: They want to replicate themselves. Or they bring in old friends. It seems safer that way—after all, you know what you're getting and you can count on their loyalty—but it's also more dangerous, because an old friend or someone who shares the same personality traits isn't likely to be able to see what you can't see or do what you can't do. You share the same disabilities. I need someone who *isn't* like me. And that means a hard-ass who will hold people accountable, demand results, and fire them if they don't produce. With me in charge of day-to-day operations, people would be holding hands in a big circle, expressing their innermost feelings.

Tom's Irish and Catholic. He made the subways run on time. He understands power and how to wield it. He knows that the most efficient route within a vast bureaucracy within the vastness of politics is never a straight line, and he knows how to find the precise angle that will set the billiard ball into a sequence of collisions ending up with the right ball in the right pocket. Yet he also cares about America, and about social justice. As a young man he was a community organizer and social worker. His first job in government involved public welfare. He has a passion for helping people out of poverty.

Tom has two children, both of them girls, somewhat younger than Adam and Sam. His wife also works in government and is eager to come to Washington.

For chief of staff I've picked Kitty Higgins. What Tom lacks in direct experience with Congress and the White House, Kitty makes up for. Twenty years ago, she was a clerk-typist in the Labor Department, a GS-6 at the very bottom of the ladder. She worked her way up to a policy job in the Carter White House, followed by twelve years on the Hill as legislative assistant to several Dems and finally chief administrator for Congressman Sandy Levin of Michigan (who wrote me a four-page letter, in his own hand, gushing about Kitty's talents). She was the key staffer behind the last major piece of job-training legislation to move through Congress in the early 1980s. I've made a dozen calls about her, and the verdict is unanimous: Few people know Washington as well, and how to maneuver in it. She knows where the levers are, which ones I need to pull and when.

Kitty is middle-aged, stout, with a large round face and short brown hair. She's a widow with two teenage sons, of whom she's very proud.

In contrast to Tom, she talks and laughs easily. Even with her weight, she moves quickly, and because she uses her arms and hands to accentuate whatever she's saying, she gives the impression of being in constant motion. She has a good sense of humor and a twinkle in her eye. Her annual St. Patrick's Day party is a Washington fixture. People tell me she's a strong manager, but I think she'll take some of the rough edges off Tom's tough-ass management style. Another Irish pol, she loves the game of politics. And like Tom, she's also interested in the substance. She's devoted most of her adult life to the cause of helping working people make something more of their lives.

Tom Glynn. Kitty Higgins. They're both big gambles. My gut tells me they're the right people. . . .

March 2 Washington

This afternoon, I mount a small revolution at the Labor Department. The result is chaos.

Background: My cavernous office is becoming one of those hermetically sealed, germ-free bubbles they place around children born with immune deficiencies. Whatever gets through to me is carefully sanitized. Telephone calls are prescreened, letters are filtered, memos are reviewed. Those that don't get through are diverted elsewhere. Only Tom, Kitty, and my secretary walk into the office whenever they want. All others seeking access must first be scheduled, and have a sufficient reason to take my precious germ-free time.

I'm scheduled to the teeth. Here, for example, is today's timetable:

6:45 A.M.	Leave apartment
7:10 A.M.	Arrive office
7:15 A.M.	Breakfast with MB from the *Post*
8:00 A.M.	Conference call with Rubin
8:30 A.M.	Daily meeting with senior staff
9:15 A.M.	Depart for Washington Hilton
9:40 A.M.	Speech to National Association of Private Industry Councils
10:15 A.M.	Meet with Joe Dear (OSHA enforcement)
11:15 A.M.	Meet with Darla Letourneau (DOL budget)
12:00	Lunch with JG from National League of Cities
1:00 P.M.	CNN interview (taped)
1:30 P.M.	Congressional leadership panel
2:15 P.M.	Congressman Ford
3:00 P.M.	NEC budget meeting at White House
4:00 P.M.	Welfare meeting at White House
5:00 P.M.	National Public Radio interview (taped)
5:45 P.M.	Conference call with mayors

6:15 P.M.	Telephone time
7:00 P.M.	Meet with Maria Echeveste (Wage and Hour)
8:00 P.M.	Kitty and Tom daily briefing
8:30 P.M.	National Alliance of Business reception
9:00 P.M.	Return to apartment.

I remain in the bubble even when I'm outside the building—ushered from place to place by someone who stays in contact with the front office by cellular phone. I stay in the bubble after business hours. If I dine out, I'm driven to the destination and escorted to the front door. After dinner, I'm escorted back to the car, driven to my apartment, and escorted from the car, into the apartment building, into the elevator, and to my apartment door.

No one gives me a bath, tastes my food, or wipes my bottom—at least not yet. But in all other respects I feel like a goddamn two-year-old. Tom and Kitty insist it has to be this way. Otherwise I'd be deluged with calls, letters, meetings, other demands on my time, coming from all directions. People would force themselves on me, harass me, maybe even threaten me. The bubble protects me.

Tom and Kitty have hired three people to handle my daily schedule (respond to invitations, cull the ones that seem most promising, and squeeze all the current obligations into the time available), one person to ready my briefing book each evening so I can prepare for the next day's schedule, and two people to "advance" me by making sure I get where I'm supposed to be and depart on time. All of them now join Tom and Kitty as guardians of the bubble.

"How do you decide what I do and what gets through to me?" I ask Kitty.

"We have you do and see what you'd choose if you had time to examine all the options yourself—sifting through all the phone calls, letters, memos, and meeting invitations," she says simply.

"But how can you possibly *know* what I'd choose for myself?"

"Don't worry," Kitty says patiently. "We know."

They have no way of knowing. We've worked together only a few weeks. Clare and I have lived together for a quarter century and even she wouldn't know.

I trust Tom and Kitty. They share my values. I hired them because I sensed this, and everything they've done since then has confirmed it. But it's not a matter of trust.

The *real* criterion Tom and Kitty use (whether or not they know it or admit it) is their own experienced view of what a secretary of labor with my values and aspirations *should* choose to see and hear. They transmit to me through the bubble only those letters, phone calls, memoranda, people, meetings, and events which they believe *someone like me* ought to have. But if I see and hear only what "someone like me" should see and hear, no original or out-of-the-ordinary thought will ever permeate the bubble. I'll never be surprised or shocked. I'll never be forced to rethink or reevaluate anything. I'll just lumber along, blissfully ignorant of what I *really* need to see and hear—which are things that don't merely confirm my preconceptions about the world.

I make a list of what I want them to transmit through the bubble henceforth:

1. The angriest, meanest ass-kicking letters we get from the public every week.

2. Complaints from department employees about anything.

3. Bad news about fuck-ups, large and small.

4. Ideas, ideas, ideas: from department employees, from outside academics and researchers, from average citizens. Anything that even resembles a good idea about what we should do better or differently. Don't screen out the wacky ones.

5. Anything from the President or members of Congress.

6. A random sample of calls or letters from real people outside Washington, outside government—people who aren't lawyers, investment bankers, politicians, or business consultants; people who aren't professionals; people without college degrees.

7. "Town meetings" with department employees here at headquarters and in the regions. "Town meetings" in working-class and poor areas of the country. "Town meetings" in community colleges, with adult students.

8. Calls and letters from business executives, including those who hate my guts. Set up meetings with some of them.

9. Lunch meetings with small groups of department employees, randomly chosen from all ranks.

10. Meetings with conservative Republicans in Congress.

I send the memo to Tom and Kitty. Then, still feeling rebellious and with nothing on my schedule for the next hour (the NEC meeting scheduled for 3:00 was canceled) I simply walk out of the bubble. I sneak out of my big office by the back entrance and start down the corridor.

I take the elevator to floors I've never visited. I wander to places in the department I've never been. I have spontaneous conversations with employees I'd never otherwise see. *Free at last.*

Kitty discovers I'm missing. It's as if the warden had discovered an escape from the state pen. The alarm is sounded: Secretary loose! Secretary escapes from bubble! Find the Secretary! Security guards are dispatched.

By now I've wandered to the farthest reaches of the building, to corridors never before walked by anyone ranking higher than GS-12. I visit the mailroom, the printshop, the basement workshop. The hour is almost up. Time to head back. But which way? I'm at the northernmost outpost of the building, in bureaucratic Siberia. I try to retrace my steps but keep coming back to the same point in the wilderness.

I'm lost.

In the end, of course, a security guard finds me and takes me back to the bubble. Kitty isn't pleased. "You shouldn't do that," she says sternly. "We were worried."

"It was good for me." I'm defiant.

"We need to know where you *are*." She sounds like the mother of a young juvenile delinquent.

"Next time give me a beeper, and I'll call home to see if you need me."

"You *must* have someone with you. It's not safe."

"This is the Labor Department, not Bosnia."

"You might get lost."

"That's *ridiculous*. How in hell could someone get *lost* in this building?"

She knows she has me. "You'd be surprised." She smiles knowingly and heads back to her office. . . .

March 14 *Washington*

Tom and Kitty suggest I conduct a "town meeting" of Labor Department employees here at headquarters—give them an opportunity to ask me questions and me a chance to express my views. After all, I've been here almost eight weeks and presumably have a few answers and one or two views.

Some of the other senior staff think it unwise. They point to the risk of gathering thousands of employees together in one place with access to microphones. The cumulative frustrations from years of not being listened to by political appointees could explode when exposed to the open air, like a dangerous gas. Gripes, vendettas, personal slights, hurts, malfeasance, nonfeasance, mistreatments, slurs, lies, deceptions, frauds. Who knows what might be in that incendiary mix?

Secretaries of labor have come and gone, usually within two years. Assistant secretaries, even faster. Only a tiny fraction of Labor Department employees are appointed to their jobs because of who's occupying the White House. The vast majority are career employees, here because they got their jobs through the civil service. Most of them will remain here for decades, some for their entire careers. They have come as lawyers, accountants, economists, investigators, clerks, secretaries, and custodians. Government doesn't pay as well as the private sector, but the jobs are more secure. And some have come because they believe that public service is inherently important.

But for years they've been treated like shit. Republican appointees were often contemptuous of or uninterested in most of what went on here. The Reagan and Bush administrations didn't exactly put workplace issues at the top of their agenda. In fact, Reagan slashed the department's budget and reduced the number of employees by about a quarter. His first appointee as secretary of labor was a building contractor.

The career people don't harbor much more trust for Democrats. It's an article of faith among civil servants that political appointees, of whatever party, care only about the immediate future. They won't be here years from now to implement fully their jazzy ideas, or to pick up the pieces if the ideas fall apart. Career civil servants would prefer not to take short-term risks. They don't want headlines. Even if the headlines are positive, headlines draw extra attention, and in Washington attention can be dangerous.

There is a final reason for their cynicism. Career civil servants feel unappreciated by politicians. Every presidential candidate since Carter has run as a Washington "outsider," against the permanent Washington establishment. Almost every congressional and senatorial candidate decries the "faceless bureaucrats" who are assumed to wield unaccountable power. Career civil servants are easy targets. They can't talk back. This scapegoating parallels the public's mounting contempt for Washington. In opinion polls conducted during the Eisenhower administration, about seventy-five percent of the American public thought that their government "could be trusted to act in the public interest most of the time." In a recent poll, only twenty-five percent expressed similar sentiments. But career civil servants aren't to blame. The disintegration has come on the heels of mistakes and improprieties by political leaders—Vietnam, Watergate, the Iran-*contra* imbroglio, the savings-and-loan scandal. And it accelerated as the nation emerged from five decades of Depression, hot war, and cold war—common experiences that forced us to band together and support a strong government—into a global economy without clear borders or evil empires.

Our "town meeting" is set for noon. A small stage is erected on one side of a huge open hall on the first floor of the department. The hall is about the size of football field. On its walls are paintings of former secretaries of labor.

I walk in exactly at noon. Nervous (Wasn't President James Garfield assassinated by a disgruntled civil servant?)

The hall is jammed with thousands of people. Many are sitting on folding chairs, tightly packed around the makeshift stage. Others are standing. Several hundred are standing on risers around the outer perimeter, near the walls. Is it legal for so many employees to be packed so tightly in one place? Tomorrow's Washington *Post*: Labor Secretary Endangers Workers. Subhead: Violates the Occupational Safety and Health Act.

I make my way up to the small stage and face the crowd. I don't want to speak from behind a lectern, because to see over it I'd have to stand on a stool and would look ridiculous. So I hold the microphone. The crowd quiets.

"Hello."

"Hello!" they roar back in unison. Laughter. A good start, anyway.

"I've been here less than eight weeks and I've met several of you personally, but I wanted to have a chance to talk with you about the Labor Department and what I hope we can accomplish together."

"Praise the Lord!" from a large black woman in the front row. More laughter. This is either going to be a revival meeting or a complete farce, or both.

"Look, I know you've seen a lot of secretaries of labor come and go, but I intend to be here at least four years."

The place erupts in applause.

"You know as well as I do that working people in America have been getting a raw deal for years. Half of all workers haven't had a raise in more than a decade. And there's a growing number of people who are working full-time but who are still poor. Some of their jobs are unsafe. Some don't get paid what they're owed. Some are discriminated against because they're women or because their skin isn't white. Some don't get the pensions that are promised them. Most want to do better but don't have the skills they need to succeed in this new economy."

"Amen!" The woman in the first row again. Laughter.

"So I want to ask every one of you to do your job. It's more important than ever."

More applause, whoops, whistles. I feel like a preacher. No, more like the general of a liberating army come to free the prisoners of war.

"And I need you to help me do *my* job. You know what needs to be fixed. You know what we do here that's stupid and dumb."

Laughter and applause.

"And you know how we can do better, how we can serve the public better." I'm in full swing now. "You have the answers. I don't. I want your ideas. Starting tomorrow, I'm establishing a hot line which you can use to get me your ideas directly through e-mail. Or, if you wish, you can just write them down. I promise you that I'll consider every one of your suggestions."

"Bullshit." A voice from the back of the hall.

The hall is suddenly deadly quiet. The years of bitterness are about to tumble out.

I look toward the voice. "Yeah, I know it sounds like bullshit. You've probably heard that one before. They tell you they want your suggestions but they don't listen, and nothing changes."

"Amen" from the front row. Nervous laughter.

"Okay, let's start right now. Give me an idea you've been cooking for years that nobody's listened to. I'll make a decision on it right now, or I'll write it down and report back. Can someone give me a pen and pad?" They're handed me.

I can see Tom and Kitty out of the corner of my eye, standing in the shadows and whispering to each other. They probably think I've gone mad.

"Who's first?" I scan the crowd—left, center, right. No hands. I'm back in the classroom, first class of the semester. I've asked the question, but no one wants to break the ice. They have plenty to say, but no one dares. So I'll do what I always do: I'll just stand here silently, smiling, until someone gets up the courage. I can bear the silence.

I wait. Thirty seconds. Forty-five seconds. A minute. Thousands of people here, but no sound. They seem startled. I know they have all sorts of opinions about what should be done. They share them with each other every day. But have they ever shared them directly with the Secretary?

Finally, one timid hand in the air. I point to her. "Yes! You! What's your name?" All eyes on her. The crowd explodes into rumbles, murmurs, and laughs, like a huge lung exhaling. A cordless mike is passed to her.

"Connie," she answers, nervously.

I move to the front of the stage so I can see Connie better. "Which agency do you work in, Connie?"

"Employment Standards."

"What's your idea?"

Connie's voice is unsteady, but she's determined. "Well, I don't see why we need to fill out time cards when we come to work and when we leave. It's silly and demeaning."

Applause. Connie is buoyed by the response, and her voice grows stronger. "I mean, if someone is dishonest they'll just fill in the wrong times anyway. Our supervisors know when we come and go. The work has to get done. Besides, we're professionals. Why treat us like children?"

I look over at Tom. He shrugs his shoulders: Why not?

"Okay, done. Starting tomorrow, no more time cards."

For a moment, silence. The audience seems stunned. Then a loud roar of approval that breaks into wild applause. Many who were seated stand and cheer.

What have I done? I haven't doubled their salaries or sent them on all-expenses-paid vacations to Hawaii. All I did was accept a suggestion that seemed reasonable. But for people who have grown accustomed to being ignored, I think I just delivered an important gift.

The rest of the meeting isn't quite as buoyant. Some suggestions I reject outright (a thirty-five-hour workweek). Others I write down and defer for further consideration. But I learn a great deal. I hear ideas I never would have thought of. One thin and balding man from the Employment and Training Administration has a commonsensical one: When newly unemployed people register for unemployment insurance, why not determine whether their layoff is likely to be permanent or temporary — and if permanent, get them retraining and job-placement services right away instead of waiting until their benefits almost run out? He has evidence this will shorten the average length of unemployment and save billions of dollars. I say I'll look into it. . . .

August 14 *Washington*

Millions of jobless Americans have used up their unemployment insurance. That's because the whole unemployment insurance system was designed when most job losers were *temporarily* laid off until the economy picked up and their companies rehired them. Six months was about how long that took, and so that's how long the benefits last. But most of today's unemployed won't ever get their old jobs back. The economy is picking up, yet they're still unemployed after six months. Companies have used the recession to downsize, rightsize, restructure, reengineer, or whatever euphemism suits them for permanently *firing*.

This is why we have to change the old unemployment insurance system into a *reemployment* system. Rather than sit around collecting unemployment benefits for six months, job losers should start preparing for new jobs right away. If they have outmoded skills, they should get information about what new skills are in demand, and low-cost loans or vouchers to help pay for retraining. They should get unemployment benefits while they retrain, even beyond six months if necessary, but people should get *no* benefits unless they're preparing for a new job. Since most can't afford fancy private "outplacement" services, they also should get help searching for a job. And all this should be available at the same place they pick up the unemployment check—one-stop shopping.

How to pull this off? . . .

September 20 Washington

Tom tells me that calls are pouring in from members of Congress demanding that unemployment benefits be extended beyond their normal six months. "We've got to find several billion dollars, quick," says Tom. But I don't know where to find the money other than taking it out of job counseling and training—which would be nuts.

"We *won't* extend unemployment benefits if it means less money for finding new jobs!" I'm defiant.

"I don't think you have a choice," says Tom. "People just don't believe there're new jobs out there. All they know is they had a job. They think it's coming back eventually, and they need money to live on in the meantime."

Kitty rushes in. "I've got it!"

"What?"

"The *answer*. Remember the fellow at the department town meeting who had the idea for fixing the unemployment system?"

"Vaguely." I recall a tall, hollow-eyed career employee who spoke toward the end.

"He suggested that when newly unemployed people apply for unemployment insurance they're screened to determine whether their layoff is temporary or permanent—and if *permanent* they immediately get help finding a new job. *Well* . . . " Kitty pauses to catch her breath. "I spoke with him at some length this morning. His name is Steve Wandner. Seems that a few years ago he ran a pilot project for the department, trying his idea out. Get *this*: Where he tried it, the average length of unemployment dropped two to four weeks! The poor guy has been trying to sell the idea since then, but no one has ever listened."

"I don't get it. How does this help us?"

"Think of it! Do what he did all over the country, and cut the average length of unemployment two to four weeks. This saves the government $400 million a year in unemployment benefits. That's $2 billion over the next five years, if you need help with the math."

"I understand the math. I just don't understand the *point*. So what? That's money saved in the *future*. How does that get us the money we need now?"

Kitty stares at me with her usual what-is-this-man-doing-as-a-cabinet-member expression. "If we can show that we'll save this money over the next five years, we can use it *now* to offset extra unemployment benefits. It's like extra *cash!*" She lunges toward a stack of paper on the corner of my desk and tosses the entire pile into the air. "Manna *from heaven!*"

"I still don't get it. And by the way, you're making a mess."

Kitty is excited, but she talks slowly, as if to a recent graduate of kindergarten. "Try to *understand*. The federal budget law requires that if you want to spend more money, you've got to get the money from somewhere else. Right? One place you can get it is from future savings, but only if the Congressional Budget Office believes you. Follow me?"

"I think so."

"Now comes our brilliant geek from the bowels of the Labor Department with *proof* that we can save around $2 billion during the next five years. And the true *beauty* of it" — Kitty beams — "is that this reform brings us a step closer to what *you've* been talking about. We get a law providing emergency extra unemployment benefits—$2 billion worth—covering the next few months. And *at the same time* we permanently change the whole system so that it's more focused on finding new jobs. It's a twofer! A win-win! Nobody can vote against it! I *love* it!"

I look at Tom. "Is she right?"

"Yup." Tom is impressed.

Kitty begins to dance around the office. She is the only person I have ever met who can fall in love with proposed legislation. . . .

November 24 *The White House*

B sits at his elaborately carved desk in the Oval Office before the usual gaggle of cameras and spotlights. Clustered tightly around him in order to get into the shot are five smiling senators and ten smiling House members. B utters some sentences about why people who have lost their jobs shouldn't have to worry that their unemployment benefits will run out. He signs the bill into law. The congressmen applaud. He stands and shakes each of their hands. The spotlights go out and the cameras are packed away. The whole thing takes less than five minutes.

Kitty is here, smiling from ear to ear. I congratulate her.

Against a far wall, behind the small crowd, I see Steve Wandner, the hollow-eyed Labor Department employee who first suggested the idea that was just signed into law. I made sure Steve was invited to this signing ceremony. I walk over to where he's standing.

"Good job." I extend my hand.

He hesitates a moment. "I never thought . . . ." His voice trails off.

"I want to introduce you to the President."

Steve is reluctant. I pull his elbow and guide him toward where B is chatting energetically with several members of Congress who still encircle him. They're talking football—big men, each over six feet, laughing, telling stories, bonding. It's a veritable huddle. We wait on the periphery.

Several White House aides try to coax the group out of the Oval. It's early in the day, and B is already hopelessly behind schedule. Steve wants to exit, but I motion him to stay put.

The herd begins to move. I see an opening. "Mr. President!" B turns, eyes dancing. He's having fun. It's a good day: signing legislation, talking sports. It's been a good few months: the budget victory, the Middle East peace accord, the NAFTA victory. He's winning, and he can feel it. And when B is happy, the happiness echoes through the White House like a sweet song.

"Come here, pal." B draws me toward him and drapes an arm around my shoulders. I feel like a favorite pet.

"Mr. President, I want you to meet the man who came up with the idea for today's legislation." I motion Steve forward.

With his left arm still around my shoulders, B extends his right hand to Steve, who takes it as if it were an Olympic trophy.

"Good work," is all B says to Steve, but B's tight grip and his fleeting you-are-the-only-person-in-the-world-who-matters gaze into Steve's eyes light the man up, giving him a glow I hadn't thought possible.

It's over in a flash. B turns away to respond to a staffer who has urgently whispered something into his ear. But Steve doesn't move. The hand that had been in the presidential grip falls slowly to his side. He stares in B's direction. The afterglow remains.

I have heard tales of people who are moved by a profound religious experience, whose lives of torment or boredom are suddenly transformed, who actually *look* different because they have found Truth and Meaning. Steve Wandner—the gangly, diffident career bureaucrat who has traipsed to his office at the Labor Department every workday for twenty years, slowly chipping away at the same large rock, answering to the same career executives, coping with silly demands by low-level political appointees to do this or that, seeing the same problems and making the same suggestions and sensing that nothing will ever really change—has now witnessed the impossible. His idea has become the law of the land.

He will return to the Labor Department and continue to chip away at rocks in his small corner of the bureaucracy. But I doubt he'll ever be the same. And his glow will light up his small part of the Labor Department for weeks, perhaps years. Maybe he and a few others will even begin using the pronouns "we" and "us" when describing what the Labor Department does.

I doubt B and the assembled senators and congressmen have any clue about the modest reform they put in place today. To them it was simply a matter of getting some more money to extend unemployment benefits to several thousand people who are still out of work. And the media certainly don't get it: I doubt there will be a single news story.

But from now on, whenever people report to an unemployment office to receive benefits, they'll be screened to determine whether their layoff is temporary or permanent. And if it's permanent, they'll be given immediate access to whatever retraining, job counseling, and job search assistance is on hand. Because of this, many will find a new job faster than they would have otherwise. Steve stood up at our town meeting eight months ago and offered his idea. He had offered it many times before, but no one with any power to implement it had ever really heard it. Now—because he stood up, because Kitty remembered and followed up—it's the law. Whatever I may accomplish as a cabinet secretary, I'll always be especially proud of today's small victory. . . .

41

ROBERT TRATTNER

From *The 2000 Prune Book*

Floods, fires, hurricanes, tornadoes, volcanoes—these are natural disasters that occur within the United States frequently and unexpectedly. Man-made disasters happen too: September 11. FEMA, the Federal Emergency Management Agency, is the executive branch agency charged with aiding state and local governments deal with disasters that are great in magnitude. The head of FEMA is a presidential appointee who must receive Senate advice and consent before taking on the position. In this excerpt, Robert Trattner, writing for the Council on Excellence in Government, describes the qualifications for the job and the responsibilities it entails. The case study of FEMA is particularly interesting since in 2002 President George Bush recommended that FEMA be moved into the cabinet-level Department of Homeland Security. Trattner begins the selection by explaining where presidential appointees fit in the structure of the executive branch. He has titled his work the "prune book," a variation on the actual "plum book." Looking good is insufficient for a presidential appointee; results are what count.

THIS IS THE SIXTH BOOK in a series that began in the presidential election year of 1988. Drawing directly on the experience of people who know government best, it attempts, first, to show what good leadership in the upper appointed ranks of the federal executive branch is really about. Then it discusses several dozen jobs and types of jobs at those levels in which such leadership is indispensable. . . .

Members of the Council for Excellence in Government, most of them veterans of service in senior appointed federal positions, chose the positions discussed in this edition. Their task was to peruse and discuss together the universe of some 700 jobs filled by presidential appointment, identify those they judged to be most critical, and select a manageable number for inclusion in the book. . . .

The Council adheres to the simple truth that relevant experience is a critical criterion in finding the right person for a job with a high degree of responsibility and trust in the conduct of public business. Experience is by no means the only necessary ingredient. But it deserves as much consideration by presidents, cabinet officers, and White House personnel officials as any of the others. To emphasize this point, we chose the *Prune* title to contrast the content of *Prune* books with that of a sought-after congressional publication—*Policy and Supporting Positions*—issued at the end of each presidential election year. Known more widely as the Plum Book (explanations for this vary), it is basically a list of several thousand executive branch positions filled by presidential appointment, among them the several hundred requiring Senate confirmation.

Plum Books say nothing—that is not their purpose—about the experience that informed observers might deem necessary to handle the jobs effectively. In creating a resource that would do this and more, the Council wanted to remind readers and users of the inestimable value of experience: the quality developed through work, study, observation, practice, and the accumulation of on-site knowledge. A plum may look good on the outside, but it offers no guarantee that its content will satisfy. A prune wins no beauty prizes, but it has been around a while and has, as they say, the scars to prove it. It leaves no doubt that you will get what you see. That's what experience will do for you. And that's what *Prune Books* try to reflect. . . .

Many men and women who take appointed leadership jobs in a new administration have managed enterprises of one kind or another in their earlier careers. But most have not done so in the federal government. While there are some similarities between the two, the differences are far more important.

In fact, an administration's high-level political leaders inhabit a bracing landscape unlike any other. At their home base, appointees operate in the equivalent of a vast forest that echoes with the multiple tasks of governing—issues and goals, policy and action. On the upcountry slopes of the Congress, they negotiate the sometimes-fierce crosswinds of money, prerogative, and politics that deeply affect what they can achieve. Meanwhile, waves of watchful media beat steadily against the shores of this domain, now and again flooding the forest or sweeping an appointee (or an administration) out to sea. Surrounding the entire region lie the great plains of the people, who view what they see and hear with a mixture of hope and doubt.

Each main feature of this world—the executive branch, the legislature, the press, the public—tests the management skills of presidential appointees in distinctive ways. Those who can handle it are best equipped to lead the way to what every administration prizes most—the results it is setting out to get. Those who can't or don't want to play in that league will have a harder time achieving anything notable—and may even fail.

This chapter focuses the firsthand insights of dozens of qualified people on these leadership challenges and the management issues that are involved. Nothing they have to say makes any claim to originality—no secret gospels, no revelations, no strokes of genius. Rather, theirs are the collected nonpartisan voices of common sense, realism, and experience. They have all been around the track; they speak usefully and with authority. They are cabinet secretaries, other veterans of executive branch appointment, former members of the Congress, professional congressional staffers, journalists who cover government and individuals who teach or write about it, and knowledgeable political hands. Some have labored in more than one of these areas. . . .

What follows draws liberally from what these seasoned individuals said at leadership conferences for new presidential appointees that were convened jointly by the White House and the Council for Excellence in Government in 1997, 1998, and 1999; and from interviews with the occupants of the appointive jobs profiled elsewhere in this book. Largely through their eyes, we'll look at each sector of that diversified terrain where appointees toil. But first, brief comments from five of them that suggest the basic leadership tasks involved.

Former presidential appointee, about the executive branch:

It's hard for people in the private sector and even academia to understand how hard it is to get things done in Washington, how dense a thicket of constraints surrounds you. Constraints put in place by Congress, by budgetary limits, by campaign promises, constituency groups, the Administrative Procedures Act, the Constitution, all kinds of reasons why you can't do something you need to do, why you can't advance a perfectly reasonable piece of your agenda.

Former member of the House of Representatives, about the Congress:

All legislative powers are vested in Congress. Not most, not some, not domestic, but all legislative power is vested in Congress, and members of Congress take that seriously. Congress is much more ideological than the public generally is, and much more ideological than most members of the executive branch. Members of Congress are political. They are expected to be political. The role of Congress is to be the forum in which differing points of view are debated, thought out, and one or the other prevails.

Head of an agency, about the media:

You've got to understand that almost nobody in Washington is paying attention to your issue, regardless of how essential it is. You've got to break through the background clutter. You have to educate the media about your agency and its objectives. As a starter, better you invest an hour educating a reporter than try to get a story out.

Senior White House staffer, about the public:

It's really important nowadays that you explain why what you do in government is relevant to people's lives. It used to be self-evident, because there were a lot more tensions and everything "the government" did was seen as relevant. Generally now it's seen as irrelevant, and you have to make your case.

Political consultant, about the public:

What is truly lacking in so many people in government is that they don't bother to develop an understanding of where the public is. I've always believed that almost nothing in government is do-able if the public doesn't want it. There are times when members of Congress or presidents actually lead for a while. But in the main, what gets done here is done because there's a reasonable group of people out there that thinks it's important. . . .

What is successful leadership in an administration in Washington? Is it designing policy? Making decisions? Issuing instructions? Giving a speech? Spending money?

Hardly. Such activities are essential; they're what most political managers routinely do. By themselves, they don't amount to strong, productive leadership. A lot of people in government today recognize that, but it's useful to make the point for each new administration. Leading successfully really means getting something tangible, something visible, for the money and effort invested. In a word, results.

In private business, as is so often repeated, the bottom line—profit or loss—makes it relatively easy to judge results. In government, it's harder. Much that looks like a result really isn't. When public leaders think they've gone the last hard mile, crossed the finish line, they often haven't.

Suppose the Federal Aviation Administration is investing millions to protect the health of air travelers by developing a climate control system for passenger jets that doesn't distribute airborne bacteria around the cabin. It plans the project, puts the job out to bid, spends the funds, convenes a lot of interagency consultation, tells the media about it. But those aren't results, only steps along the way. Not until the prototype is built, tested successfully, and demonstrated to airframe builders and airline executives is any real result in hand. Not until airlines are convinced they should install the new system—or are required to by regulation—has the FAA gone the full route by ensuring that passengers benefit from it.

Or take the actual decision by the Internal Revenue Service to allow electronic filing of tax returns. Announcing the plan, getting the technology designed, hiring the personnel—again, those were just way stations. Certainly, they added up to a lot more than just a visible intention to make the change. But they were not yet a real result. That came when people could actually go on line, send their returns to the IRS, and see them accepted, safe and sound, as advertised.

The first lesson of leading within an agency, then, is to pursue ends, not means. It's not how much money you spend, how many meetings you call, how many policy papers you put out, how many times you testify on Capitol Hill. It is not input, or even output. It is what the professionals like to call desired outcomes. It's results.

Focus on outcomes, not on input. It's so easy to get caught up in getting the process right and getting the regulations just perfect and anticipating everything that might go wrong, but failing to notice that no real people were touched by what you did.

Part of the problem in going after results is the understandable attraction for appointees of the world of policymaking. Policy, after all, is what guides most of their work. It seems like the most important aspect of a leadership position. It requires creativity, design skill, the art of negotiating—loftier assets, to some, than the ability to run things, and it seemingly is more likely to earn recognition and prestige. Again, however, policy-making alone doesn't bring results.

A lot of us come to Washington and want to be engaged in high policy. If we just get the policy right, everything will be different. I would suggest just the opposite. We spend much more time on policy than is needed, and so little on implementation. In the end you're going to be judged on what actually happens, not on whether there is a new declaration of direction and a nice event at the White House.

Why are better results the executive branch's most critical assignment? It is not just their enormous intrinsic value for the national well-being. It is also because there are increasingly workable ways to measure results—that is, to measure performance. The Government Performance and Results Act, passed in 1993, was only the beginning. Tools to measure are becoming more precise. They are beginning to find more acceptance among the decisionmakers who appropriate money for government programs. That means executive branch managers will be facing ever-strengthening mandates from the Congress to get better results for the resources they use.

Yet the most convincing reason why results matter can be found in national opinion surveys. Just about every poll in sight shows persistent, widespread public disenchantment with government (though not with government's potential). Government today turns large numbers of Americans off. A majority thinks of it, not as our government, but as the government; according to a June 1999 Council for Excellence in Government Hart/Teeter national poll, only one in four believes Washington works for the public interest. But most people continue to believe that it can. They want better results from government. And that, in the end, is probably the most urgent mandate of all. . . .

Final point: If results come first, the reasons that bring talented people to seek selection by a chief of state for high office also demand intense focus. The last burden any administration needs is someone who has joined up primarily to enhance a career. Personal goals are important; they clearly have a place; an effective stint in government will serve them. But almost without exception, people whose careers need little boost from public service make the best appointees—among other reasons, because personal ambition is unlikely to interfere with clear thinking or clear judgment.

Here, therefore, are the thoughts of a former White House official who had a broader opportunity than most to see this principle in operation:

"Motivation is very important for the mission of your agency. If you don't believe in it, if you don't believe it will make a difference in the lives of ordinary people, stop doing it. Go do something else. Because if you don't believe in it, it's going to show to everybody. Everybody will notice that you're there more for the ride than for the goal." . . .

FEDERAL EMERGENCY MANAGEMENT AGENCY

Director
Executive Level II
Presidential appointment with Senate confirmation

RECOMMENDED SKILLS AND EXPERIENCE   The only person to head the Federal Emergency Management Agency with any prior experience in this field is James Lee Witt, who led the Arkansas Office of Emergency Services before becoming FEMA's director in the spring of 1993. That might partly explain the agency's reputation before he arrived as a backwater institution incapable of effective performance. It stands to reason, in any case, that Witt's successor should be an excellent manager with significant firsthand exposure to the requirements of emergency preparedness and response to natural and manmade disaster.

For that background, it hardly needs pointing out, the best places to look are clearly the offices of emergency response in the states and localities, which run the bulk of such efforts in this country. Candidates for the job should have at least some of the specific expertise (budget management, flood insurance, intergovernment coordination) and skills (political sensitivity, community and media relations) that will allow them to get a running start. More than usually, this is a job where it pays handsomely to have direct experience, not just political compatibility, in the driver's seat.

INSIGHT   What is "emergency management"? As redefined by today's FEMA, it is a four-part process that begins with preparedness for emergencies and disasters and continues through response and recovery to mitigation—easing or eliminating the long-term effects on people and property. It is the director's job to coordinate these elements, including the work that up to thirty federal agencies may contribute as well as activities, in any given emergency, of the American Red Cross and other voluntary agencies. The agency's chief also supervises the National Flood Insurance Program and the U.S. Fire Administration.

FEMA's turnaround (outlined elsewhere in this book), from laughing stock in 1993 to frontline success, has often been set out as an example of creative leadership, of reinvention, of outreach to customers, of sheer resolve to make things work on the part of an agency in the process of rebirth. It was, in fact, all of those things. It was a question of replacing "very serious stove piping" with "a flatter, more functional organization," Witt says. It was identifying those parts of the agency that needed elimination, "reestablishing areas we felt would be the focal point for where we wanted to go." It was bringing together senior career managers for three days at the beginning to set new priorities and "rework our mission statement." It was telling highly skeptical members of the Congress, governors, county officials, and mayors—one by one—that FEMA now meant business. And, over time, it was a question of providing the evidence.

There was a lot more. What Witt expresses now is the hope that "when I leave, we'll have institutionalized a lot of the changes we've made and that they will be continued for some time." An example of what he means is the appointment of disaster assistance employees, nonpermanent workers assigned to FEMA headquarters and regions who are temporarily activated to meet surge requirements during emergencies. Another, with broad implications, is a new approach to reducing disaster damage that bases preventive actions largely on local decision, brings in the private sector, and involves long-range planning and investment in prevention steps. Known as Project Impact, it is a nationwide public and private prevention partnership that, Witt says, has aroused substantial congressional support. In ten years, he predicts, it will make "a significant difference in lives saved, jobs saved, and reduction of the devastation we normally see in communities."

When the impact of a calamity—a flood, say, or an earthquake—outruns the ability of local and state governments to cope, presidents declare a major disaster and FEMA takes over. It activates its own response and coordinates it with all other federal, state, local, and nongovernment entities that, depending on the nature of the emergency, may have pieces of the action. The range of immediate response activity is great: the provision of food, water, shelter, and electric power and the operation of fire, evacuation, and medical services. Later come the early steps to help individuals and institutions recover and rebuild and, in the case of flood disaster, the management of insurance claims in any of the 18,000 communities that participate in the federal flood insurance program. FEMA also runs an extensive public communications program, one of whose key purposes is to keep people abreast of situations that pose real or potential threats, advise them of what is being done on their behalf, and tell them where to get help.

Perhaps even more important—in the context of Project Impact—

are FEMA's preparation and prevention responsibilities before emergencies occur. Again, the scope is extensive—running a variety of training or education programs for citizens and emergency professionals alike, promoting the use of land and of smart building codes to minimize damage, helping communities develop plans for continuation of essential government services, urging businesses to design their own emergency management plans and showing them how, and furnishing research support for local fire and medical teams.

For added understanding of FEMA's world, consider the following FEMA-supplied facts and figures:

• As of May 2000, close to 180 presidentially declared disasters had occurred during Witt's time at the agency. They affected 3,655 counties in fifty states. Among these episodes were the country's most costly flood, the most costly earthquake, and a dozen hurricanes that inflicted damage. Since the late 1980s, more than 500 people have been killed in events of this kind.

• All fifty states and eight U.S. territories are vulnerable to floods. Even though hard-to-predict chance floods occur only 1 percent of the time every year, FEMA estimates that more than nine million homes and other properties are at risk.

• U.S. coasts are hit by an average of five hurricanes every three years. Eighteen states on the east and gulf coasts are at greatest risk.

• Tornadoes, which affect nearly all states, are responsible for the greatest property damage in the central part of the country. Overall, severe windstorms are a major cause of U.S. fatalities and property loss.

• The United States has about sixty-five volcanoes, active or potentially active. When Mount St. Helens blew in 1980, it killed sixty people and caused $1.5 billion in damage.

• This country has one of the highest rates of loss from fire among industrialized countries, in terms of both death and financial loss. In many areas, valuable real estate is exposed to frequent urban and forest fires.

• To this list can be added landslides that occur in every state and endanger 40 percent of the population and the rapidly expanding threat of manmade incidents like the release of toxic materials. The worrying possibility of terrorist attacks poses problems of another order of magnitude.

At its headquarters and ten regional offices, FEMA employs a full-time staff of 2,400 and about 7,000 disaster assistance employees. For fiscal year 2001, the agency asked the Congress for budget authority of $971 million and $2.6 billion in emergency contingency funds. Looking back, Witt thinks his work on the Hill in the early days was a central factor in revitalizing FEMA. "The one-on-one meetings with different committee members were the most critical factor. We basically said, this is what we have done to reorganize, these are the priorities we've set, and these are our goals and the drivers of our budget. They had that blueprint of what we wanted to do and where we were going. They could see it and their staffs could see it." Witt adds, however, that the twenty-six congressional committees to which FEMA reports represent a heavy burden in time and effort. He favors "refocusing" the committees and cutting the multi-plicity of oversight.

In media relations, Witt resolved early to "be up front and truthful. If they request something, we're going to give it to them, whether it's good or bad. We're going to be flat honest with them." The improvement in press coverage of FEMA, in fact, was one of the notable features of the agency's comeback. "The media has been very, very good," Witt says today. "We've had some negative stories. But they've been fair."

At the outset of his tenure, he recalls, "I don't think Congress knew what mitigation and prevention were. Now they talk about it, want to do more of it. I don't think they or state and local officials will let it slow down. And that's really going to increase what we can do in that area." He identifies key future tasks for FEMA as (1) better preparation for the impacts of terrorist activity and (2) "dramatically" cutting the costs of disasters—getting people, communities, and states to assume more respon-sibility for how they build and where they develop. The job of protecting the environment will be "huge" as U.S. population shifts in the direction of the coasts. Many people don't understand that if they protect the environment and "build better and safer," then the environment in turn will protect them. "There's a lot more to FEMA," Witt adds, "than just emergency management."

42

DAVID OSBORNE
TED GAEBLER

From *Reinventing Government*

The bureaucratic rules surrounding the Defense Department's Sicilian bowl-ing alley exemplify the inefficiency, waste, and absurdity often present in government regulations today. Critics David Osborne and Ted Gaebler want Americans to "reinvent government," to make it responsive to the needs of Americans in the twenty-first century. With financial resources tight and the effectiveness of government programs under attack, Osborne and Gaebler suggest a model for entrepreneurial government, as they term it. Their ideas have been widely acclaimed by public officials, but are less easily applied.

WE HAVE CHOSEN an audacious title for this book. We know that cynicism about government runs deep within the American soul. We all have our favorite epithets: "It's close enough for government work." "Feeding at the public trough." "I'm from the government and I'm here to help." "My friend doesn't work; she has a job with the government."

Our governments are in deep trouble today. This book is for those who are disturbed by that reality. It is for those who care about govern-ment—because they work in government, or work with government, or study government, or simply want their governments to be more effective. It is for those who know something is wrong, but are not sure just what it is; for those who have glimpsed a better way, but are not sure just how to bring it to life; for those who have launched successful experiments, but have watched those in power ignore them; for those who have a sense of where government needs to go, but are not quite sure how to get there. It is for the seekers.

If ever there were a time for seekers, this is it. The millennium approaches, and change is all around us. Eastern Europe is free; the Soviet empire is dissolving; the cold war is over. Western Europe is moving toward economic union. Asia is the new center of global economic power. From Poland to South Africa, democracy is on the march.

The idea of reinventing government may seem audacious to those who see government as something fixed, something that does not change. But in fact governments constantly change. At one time, government armories manufactured weapons, and no one would have considered letting private businesses do something so important. Today, no one would think of letting government do it.

At one time, no one expected government to take care of the poor; the welfare state did not exist until Bismarck created the first one in the 1870s.* Today, not only do most governments in the developed world take care of the poor, they pay for health care and retirement pensions for every citizen.

At one time, no one expected governments to fight fires. Today, no government would be without a fire department. In fact, huge controversies erupt when a government so much as contracts with a private company to fight fires.

At one time, governments were active investors in the private economy, routinely seeding new businesses with loans and grants and equity investments. The federal government actually gave 9.3 percent of all land in the continental United States to the railroads, as an inducement to build a transcontinental system. Today, no one would dream of such a thing.

We last "reinvented" our governments during the early decades of the twentieth century, roughly from 1900 through 1940. We did so, during the Progressive Era and the New Deal, to cope with the emergence of a new industrial economy, which created vast new problems and vast new opportunities in American life. Today, the world of government is once again in great flux. The emergence of a postindustrial, knowledge-based, global economy has undermined old realities throughout the world, creating wonderful opportunities and frightening problems. Governments large and small, American and foreign, federal, state, and local, have begun to respond.

Our purpose in writing this book is twofold: to take a snapshot of governments that have begun this journey and to provide a map to those who want to come along. When Columbus set off 500 years ago to find a new route to bring spices back from the Orient, he accidentally bumped into a New World. He and the explorers who followed him—Amerigo Vespucci and Sir Francis Drake and Hernando de Soto—all found different

---

*In the 1870s and 1880s, German Chancellor Otto von Bismarck instituted a series of laws designed to provide some financial security for German workers. Germany established a sickness fund that included limited medical coverage, along with accident benefits for disabled workers and pensions for retired laborers. Government, employers, and employees all contributed. —EDS.

pieces of this New World. But it was up to the map makers to gather all these seemingly unrelated bits of information and piece together a coherent map of the newly discovered continents.

In similar fashion, those who are today reinventing government originally set off to solve a problem, plug a deficit, or skirt a bureaucracy. But they too have bumped into a new world. Almost without knowing it, they have begun to invent a radically different way of doing business in the public sector. Just as Columbus never knew he had come upon a new continent, many of today's pioneers—from governors to city managers, teachers to social workers—do not understand the global significance of what they are doing. Each has touched a part of the new world; each has a view of one or two peninsulas or bays. But it will take others to gather all this information and piece together a coherent map of the new model they are creating. . . .

We are, of course, responsible for the ultimate shape of the map we have drawn. As such, we feel a responsibility to make explicit the underlying beliefs that have driven us to write this book—and that have no doubt animated its conclusions.

First, we believe deeply in government. We do not look at government as a necessary evil. All civilized societies have some form of government. Government is the mechanism we use to make communal decisions: where to build a highway, what to do about homeless people, what kind of education to provide for our children. It is the way we provide services that benefit all our people: national defense, environmental protection, police protection, highways, dams, water systems. It is the way we solve collective problems. Think of the problems facing American society today: drug use; crime; poverty; homelessness; illiteracy; toxic waste; the specter of global warming; the exploding cost of medical care. How will we solve these problems? By acting collectively. How do we act collectively? Through government.

Second, we believe that civilized society cannot function effectively without effective government—something that is all too rare today. We believe that industrial-era governments, with their large, centralized bureaucracies and standardized, "one-size-fits-all" services, are not up to the challenges of a rapidly changing information society and knowledge-based economy.

Third, we believe that the people who work in government are not the problem; the systems in which they work are the problem. We write not to berate public employees, but to give them hope. At times it may sound as if we are engaged in bureaucrat-bashing, but our intention is to bash *bureaucracies*, not bureaucrats. We have known thousands of civil servants

through the years, and most—although certainly not all—have been responsible, talented, dedicated people, trapped in archaic systems that frus-
trate their creativity and sap their energy. We believe these systems can
be changed, to liberate the enormous energies of public servants—and
to heighten their ability to serve the public.

*Fourth, we believe that neither traditional liberalism nor traditional conservatism
has much relevance to the problems our governments face today.* We will not
solve our problems by spending more or spending less, by creating new
public bureaucracies or by "privatizing" existing bureaucracies. At some
times and in some places, we do need to spend more or spend less, create
new programs or privatize public functions. But to make our governments
effective again we must *reinvent* them.

Finally, we believe deeply in equity—in equal opportunity for all Americans.
Some of the ideas we express in this book may strike readers as inequitable.
When we talk about making public schools compete, for instance, some
fear that the result would be an even less equitable education system than
we have today. But we believe there are ways to use choice and competition
to *increase* the equity in our school system. And we believe passionately
that increased equity is not only right and just, but critical to our success
as a nation. In today's global marketplace, America cannot compete effectively if it wastes 25 percent of its human resources.

We use the phrase *entrepreneurial government* to describe the new model
we see emerging across America. . . .

Bob Stone works in America's archetypal bureaucracy, the Department
of Defense. As deputy assistant secretary of defense for installations, he
has at least theoretical authority over 600 bases and facilities, which house
4.5 million people and consume $100 billion a year. Soon after he was
promoted to the job, in 1981, Stone visited an air base in Sicily. "We
have 2,000 airmen there, and they're out in the middle of nowhere," he
says:

No families, no towns. They are an hour and a half drive over a horrible mountain
road from a Sicilian city of 20,000—and when you get there there's not much
to do. So most of our bases have bowling alleys, and we built a bowling alley at
this base. I visited them two or three weeks after the bowling center opened.
They took me in and they started showing me plans—they're going to take out
this wall and add six more lanes over there. I thought, "Gee, you've been open
for a couple of weeks, and you're going to tear the place apart and expand it?
Why is that?"

"Well," they told me, "there's this rule that says, if you have 2,000 troops, you're allowed to construct eight lanes." [You can get a waiver to build more—but only after you can prove you need them.] I got the book and that *is* what it says: 1,000 troops, four lanes; 2,000 troops, eight lanes. And it's true if you're in the wilds of Sicily, with no families, or in the northern part of Greenland, where you can't even go outdoors for most of the year.

The rule book Stone refers to covered 400 pages. The rules governing the operation of military housing covered 800 pages. Personnel rules for civilian employees covered another 8,800 pages. "My guess is that *a third* of the defense budget goes into the friction of following bad regulations—doing work that doesn't have to be done," Stone says. Engineers in New Mexico write reports to convince people in Washington that their roofs leak. Soldiers trek halfway across their bases to the base chemist when the shelf life of a can of spray paint expires, to have it certified for another year. The Department of Defense (DOD) pays extra for special paint, but because it takes longer to establish its specifications than it takes companies to improve their paint, DOD employees pay a premium for paint that is inferior to paint available at their local store.

"This kind of rule has two costs," Stone says. "One is, we've got people wasting time. But the biggest cost—and the reason I say it's a third of the defense budget—is it's a message broadcast to everybody that works around this stuff that it's a crazy outfit. 'You're dumb. We don't trust you. Don't try to apply your common sense.'"

Stone cut the rules governing military base construction from 400 pages down to 4, those governing housing from 800 to 40. Then he decided to go farther. In an experiment straight out of *In Search of Excellence*, he decided to turn one base, called a Model Installation, free from these rules and regulations. If the commander would commit to radically improving his installation, Stone would do his best to get any rules that were standing in his way waived. The principle was simple: let the base commander run the base his way, rather than Washington's way. A corollary was also important: if he saved money in the process, he didn't have to give it back. He could keep it to spend on whatever he felt was most important.

Forty commanders volunteered for the experiment. In the first two years, they submitted more than 8,000 requests for waivers or changes in regulations. Stone can tell stories about them for hours. In the air force, for instance, airmen use complex electronic test kits to check Minuteman missiles. When a kit fails, they sent it to Hill Air Force Base in Utah for repair. Meanwhile, the missile is put off alert—typically for 10 days. An airman at Whiteman Air Force Base got approval to fix the test kits himself—and suddenly Whiteman didn't have a Minuteman missile off alert for more than three hours.

Throughout Defense, people buy by the book. Stone holds up a simple steam trap, which costs $100. "When it leaks," he says, "it leaks $50 a week worth of steam. The lesson is, when it leaks, replace it quick. But it takes us a year to replace it, because we have a system that wants to make sure we get the very best buy on this $100 item, and maybe by waiting a year we can buy the item for $2 less. In the meantime, we've lost $3,000 worth of steam." Under the Model Installations program, commanders requested authority to buy things on their own. An entire army command requested permission to let craftsmen decide for themselves when spray paint cans should be thrown away, rather than taking them to the base chemist. Five air force bases received permission to manage their own construction, rather than paying the Corps of Engineers to do it. Shaken by the threat of competition, the corps adopted a new goal: to be "leaders in customer care."

The Model Installations experiment was so successful that in March 1986, Deputy Secretary of Defense William Howard Taft IV directed that it be applied to all defense installations. Stone and his staff then developed a budget experiment modeled on Visalia's system. Normal installation budgets, first drawn up *three years in advance*, include hundreds of specific line items. The Unified Budget Test allowed commanders to ignore the line items and shift resources as needs changed.

In its first year, the test revealed that 7 to 10 percent of the funding locked into line items was in the wrong account, and that when commanders could move it around, they could significantly increase the performance of their troops. The army compared the results at its two participating bases with normal bases and concluded that in just one year, the Unified Budget increased performance by 3 percent. The long-term impact would no doubt be greater. According to Stone and his colleagues, "Senior leaders in the Services have estimated that if all the unnecessary constraints on their money were removed, they could accomplish their missions with up to 10 percent less money." But in a $100 billion installations budget, even 3 percent is $3 billion. . . .

Over the past five years, as we have journeyed through the landscape of governmental change, we have sought constantly to understand the underlying trends. We have asked ourselves: What do these innovative, entrepreneurial organizations have in common? What incentives have they changed, to create such different behavior? What have they done which, if other governments did the same, would make entrepreneurship the norm and bureaucracy the exception?

The common threads were not hard to find. Most entrepreneurial governments promote *competition* between service providers. They *empower* citizens by pushing control out of the bureaucracy, into the community. They measure the performance of their agencies, focusing not on inputs but on *outcomes*. They are driven by their goals—their *missions*—not by their rules and regulations. They redefine their clients as *customers* and offer them choices—between schools, between training programs, between housing options. They *prevent* problems before they emerge, rather than simply offering services afterward. They put their energies into *earning* money, not simply spending it. They *decentralize* authority, embracing participatory management. They prefer *market* mechanisms to bureaucratic mechanisms. And they focus not simply on providing public services, but on *catalyzing* all sectors—public, private, and voluntary—into action to solve their community's problems.

We believe that these ten principles, which we describe at length in the next ten chapters, are the fundamental principles behind this new form of government we see emerging: the spokes that hold together this new wheel. Together they form a coherent whole, a new model of government. They will not solve all of our problems. But if the experience of organizations that have embraced them is any guide, they will solve the major problems we experience with bureaucratic government. . . .

Most of our leaders still tell us that there are only two ways out of our repeated public crises: we can raise taxes, or we can cut spending. For almost two decades, we have asked for a third choice. We do not want less education, fewer roads, less health care. Nor do we want higher taxes. We want better education, better roads, and better health care, for the same tax dollar.

Unfortunately, we do not know how to get what we want. Most of our leaders assume that the only way to cut spending is to eliminate programs, agencies, and employees. Ronald Reagan talked as if we could simply go into the bureaucracy with a scalpel and cut out pockets of waste, fraud, and abuse.

But waste in government does not come tied up in neat packages. It is marbled throughout our bureaucracies. It is embedded in the very way we do business. It is employees on idle, working at half speed—or barely working at all. It is people working hard at tasks that aren't worth doing, following regulations that should never have been written, filling out forms that should never have been printed. It is the *$100 billion* a year that Bob Stone estimates the Department of Defense wastes with its foolish overregulation.

Waste in government is staggering, but we cannot get at it by wading through budgets and cutting line items. As one observer put it, our governments are like fat people who must lose weight. They need to eat less and exercise more; instead, when money is tight they cut off a few fingers and toes.

To melt the fat, we must change the basic incentives that drive our governments. We must turn bureaucratic institutions into entrepreneurial institutions, ready to kill off obsolete initiatives, willing to do more with less, eager to absorb new ideas.

The lessons are there: our more entrepreneurial governments have shown us the way. Yet few of our leaders are listening. Too busy climbing the rungs to their next office, they don't have time to stop and look anew. So they remain trapped in old ways of looking at our problems, blind to solutions that lie right in front of them. This is perhaps our greatest stumbling block: the power of outdated ideas. As the great economist John Maynard Keynes once noted, the difficulty lies not so much in developing new ideas as in escaping from old ones.

The old ideas still embraced by most public leaders and political reporters assume that the important question is *how much* government we have—not *what kind* of government. Most of our leaders take the old model as a given, and either advocate more of it (liberal Democrats), or less of it (Reagan Republicans), or less of one program but more of another (moderates of both parties).

But our fundamental problem today is not too much government or too little government. We have debated that issue endlessly since the tax revolt of 1978, and it has not solved our problems. Our fundamental problem is that we have *the wrong kind of government.* We do not need more government or less government, we need *better* government. To be more precise, we need better *governance.*

PART EIGHT

The Judiciary

43

ALEXANDER HAMILTON

From *The Federalist* 78

The 1787 Federalist Papers *have been quoted extensively in earlier sections of this book. The most famous selections belong to James Madison, writing about separation of powers and federalism. The Federalist actually had three authors: Madison, Alexander Hamilton, and John Jay. In No. 78, Hamilton expounded on the judicial branch. He makes a strong case for an independent judiciary, separate from the legislative and executive branches. He discusses the lifetime appointment of federal judges. Hamilton was a strong proponent of the courts' power, and as such, he believed that the Supreme Court should have the right to declare an act of Congress unconstitutional. This enormous power, termed judicial review, is explained and justified here by Hamilton, although it was not explicitly stated in the Constitution. In 1803, Chief Justice John Marshall established the precedent for the Supreme Court's use of judicial review in the landmark* Marbury v. Madison *case. The year after Marshall's decision, Alexander Hamilton was killed in a duel with Vice-President Aaron Burr.*

No. 78: Hamilton

WE PROCEED now to an examination of the judiciary department of the proposed government. . . .

Whoever attentively considers the different departments of power must perceive that, in a government in which they are separated from each other, the judiciary, from the nature of its functions, will always be the least dangerous to the political rights of the Constitution; because it will be least in a capacity to annoy or injure them. The executive not only dispenses the honors but holds the sword of the community. The legislature not only commands the purse but prescribes the rules by which the duties and rights of every citizen are to be regulated. The judiciary, on the contrary, has no influence over either the sword or the purse; no direction either of the strength or of the wealth of the society, and can take no active resolution whatever. It may truly be said to have neither FORCE nor WILL but merely judgment; and must ultimately depend upon the aid of the executive arm even for the efficacy of its judgments.

This simple view of the matter suggests several important consequences. It proves incontestably that the judiciary is beyond comparison the weakest of the three departments of power;* that it can never attack with success either of the other two; and that all possible care is requisite to enable it to defend itself against their attacks. It equally proves that though individual oppression may now and then proceed from the courts of justice, the general liberty of the people can never be endangered from that quarter; I mean so long as the judiciary remains truly distinct from both the legislature and the executive. For I agree that "there is no liberty if the power of judging be not separated from the legislative and executive powers." And it proves, in the last place, that as liberty can have nothing to fear from the judiciary alone, but would have everything to fear from its union with either of the other departments; that as all the effects of such a union must ensue from a dependence of the former on the latter, notwithstanding a nominal and apparent separation; that as, from the natural feebleness of the judiciary, it is in continual jeopardy of being overpowered, awed, or influenced by its co-ordinate branches; and that as nothing can contribute so much to its firmness and independence as permanency in office, this quality may therefore be justly regarded as an indispensable ingredient in its constitution, and, in a great measure, as the citadel of the public justice and the public security.

The complete independence of the courts of justice is peculiarly essential in a limited Constitution. By a limited Constitution, I understand one which contains certain specified exceptions to the legislative authority; such, for instance, as that it shall pass no bills of attainder, no *ex post facto* laws, and the like. Limitations of this kind can be preserved in practice no other way than through the medium of courts of justice, whose duty it must be to declare all acts contrary to the manifest tenor of the Constitution void. Without this, all the reservations of particular rights or privileges would amount to nothing.

Some perplexity respecting the rights of the courts to pronounce legislative acts void, because contrary to the Constitution, has arisen from an imagination that the doctrine would imply a superiority of the judiciary to the legislative power. It is urged that the authority which can declare the acts of another void must necessarily be superior to the one whose acts may be declared void. As this doctrine is of great importance in all the American constitutions, a brief discussion of the grounds on which it rests cannot be unacceptable.

There is no position which depends on clearer principles than that

---

*The celebrated Montesquieu, speaking of them, says: "Of the three powers above mentioned, the JUDICIARY is next to nothing." — *Spirit of Laws*, Vol. I, page 186.

every act of a delegated authority, contrary to the tenor of the commission under which it is exercised, is void. No legislative act, therefore, contrary to the Constitution, can be valid. To deny this would be to affirm that the deputy is greater than his principal; that the servant is above his master; that the representatives of the people are superior to the people themselves; that men acting by virtue of powers may do not only what their powers do not authorize, but what they forbid.

If it be said that the legislative body are themselves the constitutional judges of their own powers and that the construction they put upon them is conclusive upon the other departments it may be answered that this cannot be the natural presumption where it is not to be collected from any particular provisions in the Constitution. It is not otherwise to be supposed that the Constitution could intend to enable the representatives of the people to substitute their *will* to that of their constituents. It is far more rational to suppose that the courts were designed to be an intermediate body between the people and the legislature in order, among other things, to keep the latter within the limits assigned to their authority. The interpretation of the laws is the proper and peculiar province of the courts. A constitution is, in fact, and must be regarded by the judges as, a fundamental law. It therefore belongs to them to ascertain its meaning as well as the meaning of any particular act proceeding from the legislative body. If there should happen to be an irreconcilable variance between the two, that which has the superior obligation and validity ought, of course, to be preferred; or, in other words, the Constitution ought to be preferred to the statute, the intention of the people to the intention of their agents.

Nor does this conclusion by any means suppose a superiority of the judicial to the legislative power. It only supposes that the power of the people is superior to both, and that where the will of the legislature, declared in its statutes, stands in opposition to that of the people, declared in the Constitution, the judges ought to be governed by the latter rather than the former. They ought to regulate their decisions by the fundamental laws rather than by those which are not fundamental. . . .

If, then, the courts of justice are to be considered as the bulwarks of a limited Constitution against legislative encroachments, this consideration will afford a strong argument for the permanent tenure of judicial offices, since nothing will contribute so much as this to that independent spirit in the judges which must be essential to the faithful performance of so arduous a duty.

This independence of the judges is equally requisite to guard the Constitution and the rights of individuals from the effects of those ill humors which the arts of designing men, or the influence of particular conjunctures, sometimes disseminate among the people themselves, and which, though they speedily give place to better information, and more deliberate reflection, have a tendency, in the meantime, to occasion dangerous innovations in the government, and serious oppressions of the minor party in the community. Though I trust the friends of the proposed Constitution will never concur with its enemies in questioning that fundamental principle of republican government which admits the right of the people to alter or abolish the established Constitution whenever they find it inconsistent with their happiness; yet it is not to be inferred from this principle that the representatives of the people, whenever a momentary inclination happens to lay hold of a majority of their constituents incompatible with the provisions in the existing Constitution would, on that account, be justifiable in a violation of those provisions; or that the courts would be under a greater obligation to connive at infractions in this shape than when they had proceeded wholly from the cabals of the representative body. Until the people have, by some solemn and authoritative act, annulled or changed the established form, it is binding upon themselves collectively, as well as individually; and no presumption, or even knowledge of their sentiments, can warrant their representatives in a departure from it prior to such an act. But it is easy to see that it would require an uncommon portion of fortitude in the judges to do their duty as faithful guardians of the Constitution, where legislative invasions of it had been instigated by the major voice of the community.

But it is not with a view to infractions of the Constitution only that the independence of the judges may be an essential safeguard against the effects of occasional ill humors in the society. These sometimes extend no farther than to the injury of the private rights of particular classes of citizens, by unjust and partial laws. Here also the firmness of the judicial magistracy is of vast importance in mitigating the severity and confining the operation of such laws. It not only serves to moderate the immediate mischiefs of those which may have been passed but it operates as a check upon the legislative body in passing them; who, perceiving that obstacles to the success of an iniquitous intention are to be expected from the scruples of the courts, are in a manner compelled, by the very motives of the injustice they meditate, to qualify their attempts. This is a circumstance calculated to have more influence upon the character of our governments than but few may be aware of. The benefits of the integrity and moderation of the judiciary have already been felt in more States than one; and though they may have displeased those whose sinister expectations they may have disappointed, they must have commanded the esteem and applause of all the virtuous and disinterested. Considerate men of every description ought to prize whatever will tend to beget or fortify that temper in the courts; as no man can be sure that he may not be tomorrow the victim of a spirit of injustice, by which he may be a gainer today. And every man must now feel that the inevitable tendency of such a spirit is to sap the foundations of public and private confidence and to introduce in its stead universal distrust and distress. . . .   *Publius*

44

EUGENE ROSTOW

The Democratic Character of Judicial Review

Written nearly half a century ago, this classic article by legal scholar Eugene Rostow remains the most important analysis written on the theory behind the Supreme Court's power. Judicial review, the ability of the Court to declare an act of Congress or the executive or a state law unconstitutional, may seem on the surface to be "antidemocratic." A handful of lifetime appointees determine the meaning of the Constitution and whether a law passed by Congress and signed by the president is valid. In precise terms and using complex reasoning, Rostow defends the Supreme Court's use of judicial review as being the essence of the American democratic system. In his words, "The political proposition underlying the survival of the power is that there are some phases of American life which should be beyond the reach of any majority, save by constitutional amendment." Rostow's argument is based on what is meant by a democracy. To add a bit to Rostow's explanation, the United States is a "polity" in which the majority rules with protections guaranteed for individuals and minorities. The judiciary ensures that the minority is protected from "tyranny of the majority." Notice the title of this reader.

THE IDEA that judicial review is undemocratic is not an academic issue of political philosophy. Like most abstractions, it has far-reaching practical consequences. I suspect that for some judges it is the mainspring of decision, inducing them in many cases to uphold legislative and executive action which would otherwise have been condemned. Particularly in the multiple opinions of recent years, the Supreme Court's self-searching often boils down to a debate within the bosoms of the Justices over the appropriateness of judicial review itself.

The attack on judicial review as undemocratic rests on the premise that the Constitution should be allowed to grow without a judicial check. The proponents of this view would have the Constitution mean what the President, the Congress, and the state legislatures say it means. . . .

It is a grave oversimplification to contend that no society can be democratic unless its legislature has sovereign powers. The social quality of democracy cannot be defined by so rigid a formula. Government and politics are after all the arms, not the end, of social life. The purpose of the Constitution is to assure the people a free and democratic society. The final aim of that society is as much freedom as possible for the individual human being. The Constitution provides society with a mechanism of government fully competent to its task, but by no means universal in its powers. The power to govern is parcelled out between the states and the nation and is further divided among the three main branches of all governmental units. By custom as well as constitutional practice, many vital aspects of community life are beyond the direct reach of government—for example, religion, the press, and, until recently at any rate, many phases of educational and cultural activity. The separation of powers under the Constitution serves the end of democracy in society by limiting the roles of the several branches of government and protecting the citizen, and the various parts of the state itself, against encroachments from any source. The root idea of the Constitution is that man can be free because the state is not.

The power of constitutional review, to be exercised by some part of the government, is implicit in the conception of a written constitution delegating limited powers. A written constitution would promote discord rather than order in society if there were no accepted authority to construe it, at the least in cases of conflicting action by different branches of government or of constitutionally unauthorized governmental action against individuals. The limitation and separation of powers, if they are to survive, require a procedure for independent mediation and construction to reconcile the inevitable disputes over the boundaries of constitutional power which arise in the process of government. . . .

So far as the American Constitution is concerned, there can be little real doubt that the courts were intended from the beginning to have the power they have exercised. The Federalist Papers are unequivocal; the Debates as clear as debates normally are. The power of judicial review was commonly exercised by the courts of the states, and the people were accustomed to judicial construction of the authority derived from colonial charters. Constitutional interpretation by the courts, Hamilton said, does not by any means suppose a superiority of the judicial to the legislative power. It only supposes that the power of the people is superior to both; and that where the will of the legislature, declared in its statutes, stands in opposition to that of the people, declared in the Constitution, the judges ought to be governed by the latter rather than the former. They ought to regulate their decisions by the fundamental laws, rather than by those which are not fundamental.

Hamilton's statement is sometimes criticized as a verbal legalism. But it has an advantage too. For much of the discussion has complicated the problem without clarifying it. Both judges and their critics have wrapped themselves so successfully in the difficulties of particular cases that they have been able to evade the ultimate issue posed in the Federalist Papers.

Whether another method of enforcing the Constitution could have been devised, the short answer is that no such method has developed. The argument over the constitutionality of judicial review has long since been settled by history. The power and duty of the Supreme Court to declare statutes or executive action unconstitutional in appropriate cases is part of the living Constitution. "The course of constitutional history," Mr. Justice Frankfurter recently remarked, has cast responsibilities upon the Supreme Court which it would be "stultification" for it to evade. The Court's power has been exercised differently at different times: sometimes with reckless and doctrinaire enthusiasm; sometimes with great deference to the status and responsibilities of other branches of the government; sometimes with a degree of weakness and timidity that comes close to the betrayal of trust. But the power exists, as an integral part of the process of American government. The Court has the duty of interpreting the Constitution in many of its most important aspects, and especially in those which concern the relations of the individual and the state. The political proposition underlying the survival of the power is that there are some phases of American life which should be beyond the reach of any majority, save by constitutional amendment. In Mr. Justice Jackson's phrase, "One's right to life, liberty, and property, to free speech, a free press, freedom of worship and assembly, and other fundamental rights may not be submitted to vote; they depend on the outcome of no elections." Whether or not this was the intention of the Founding Fathers, the unwritten Constitution is unmistakable.

If one may use a personal definition of the crucial word, this way of policing the Constitution is not undemocratic. True, it employs appointed officials, to whom large powers are irrevocably delegated. But democracies need not elect all the officers who exercise crucial authority in the name of the voters. Admirals and generals can win or lose wars in the exercise of their discretion. The independence of judges in the administration of justice has been the pride of communities which aspire to be free. Members of the Federal Reserve Board have the lawful power to plunge the country into depression or inflation. The list could readily be extended. Government by referendum or town meeting is not the only possible form of democracy. The task of democracy is not to have the people vote directly on every issue, but to assure their ultimate responsibility for the acts of their representatives, elected or appointed. For judges deciding ordinary litigation, the ultimate responsibility of the electorate has a special meaning. It is a responsibility for the quality of the judges and for the substance of their instructions, never a responsibility for their decisions in particular cases. It is hardly characteristic of law in democratic society to encourage bills of attainder, or to allow appeals from the courts in particular cases to legislatures or to mobs. Where the judges are carrying out the function of constitutional review, the final responsibility of the people is appropriately guaranteed by the provisions for amending the Constitution itself, and by the benign influence of time, which changes the personnel of courts. Given the possibility of constitutional amendment, there is nothing undemocratic in having responsible and independent judges act as important constitutional mediators. Within the narrow limits of their capacity to act, their great task is to help maintain a pluralist equilibrium in society. They can do much to keep it from being dominated by the states or the Federal Government, by Congress or the President, by the purse or the sword.

In the execution of this crucial but delicate function, constitutional review by the judiciary has an advantage thoroughly recognized in both theory and practice. The power of the courts, however final, can only be asserted in the course of litigation. Advisory opinions are forbidden, and reefs of self-limitation have grown up around the doctrine that the courts will determine constitutional questions only in cases of actual controversy, when no lesser ground of decision is available, and when the complaining party would be directly and personally injured by the assertion of the power deemed unconstitutional. Thus the check of judicial review upon the elected branches of government must be a mild one, limited not only by the detachment, integrity, and good sense of the Justices, but by the structural boundaries implicit in the fact that the power is entrusted to the courts. Judicial review is inherently adapted to preserving broad and flexible lines of constitutional growth, not to operating as a continuously active factor in legislative or executive decisions. . . .

Democracy is a slippery term. I shall make no effort at a formal definition here. . . . But it would be scholastic pedantry to define democracy in such a way as to deny the title of "democrat" to Jefferson, Madison,

Lincoln, Brandeis, and others who have found the American constitutional system, including its tradition of judicial review, well adapted to the needs of a free society. As Mr. Justice Brandeis said,

the doctrine of the separation of powers was adopted by the Convention of 1787, not to promote efficiency but to preclude the exercise of arbitrary power. The purpose was, not to avoid friction, but, by means of the inevitable friction incident to the distribution of governmental powers among three departments, to save the people from autocracy.

It is error to insist that no society is democratic unless it has a government of unlimited powers, and that no government is democratic unless its legislature had unlimited powers. Constitutional review by an independent judiciary is a tool of proven use in the American quest for an open society of widely dispersed powers. In a vast country, of mixed population, with widely different regional problems, such an organization of society is the surest base for the hopes of democracy.

45

DAVID O'BRIEN

From *Storm Center*

Professor David O'Brien's fine book on the Supreme Court touches on many landmark cases in constitutional law. Few are more important than Brown v. Board of Education of Topeka, Kansas. *Today's students of American government often take* Brown *for granted, since they've lived with the Court's ruling their whole lives; thus they may forget the dramatic events surrounding the 1954 decision. In this excerpt O'Brien revisits the first* Brown *case, as well as* Brown II, *exploring the delicate relationship between the Court and public opinion. He then goes back to President Franklin Roosevelt's infamous 1937 "court-packing" scheme to illustrate another aspect of the impact of public opinion on the judiciary. Unlike the citizenry's direct and immediate reaction to Congress and the president, the communication of views between the public and the judiciary is less easy to measure, O'Brien acknowledges. Yet the Supreme Court lies, as it should, at the heart of the process that resolves the nation's monumental political issues.*

"WHY DOES the Supreme Court pass the school desegregation case?" asked one of Chief Justice Vinson's law clerks in 1952. *Brown v.*

Board of Education of Topeka, Kansas had arrived on the Court's docket in 1951, but it was carried over for oral argument the next term and then consolidated with four other cases and reargued in December 1953. The landmark ruling did not come down until May 17, 1954. "Well," Justice Frankfurter explained, "we're holding it for the election"—1952 was a presidential election year. "You're holding it for the election?" The clerk persisted in disbelief. "I thought the Supreme Court was supposed to decide cases without regard to elections." "When you have a major social political issue of this magnitude," timing and public reactions are important considerations, and, Frankfurter continued, "we do not think this is the time to decide it." Similarly, Tom Clark has recalled that the Court awaited, over Douglas's dissent, additional cases from the District of Columbia and other regions, so as "to get a national coverage, rather than a sectional one." Such political considerations are by no means unique. "We often delay adjudication. It's not a question of evading at all," Clark concluded. "It's just the practicalities of life—common sense."

Denied the power of the sword or the purse, the Court must cultivate its institutional prestige. The power of the Court lies in the pervasiveness of its rulings and ultimately rests with other political institutions and public opinion. As an independent force, the Court has no chance to resolve great issues of public policy. *Dred Scott v. Sandford* (1857) and *Brown v. Board of Education* (1954) illustrate the limitations of Supreme Court policy-making. The "great folly," as Senator Henry Cabot Lodge characterized *Dred Scott*, was not the Court's interpretation of the Constitution or the unpersuasive moral position that blacks were not persons under the Constitution. Rather, "the attempt of the Court to settle the slavery question by judicial decision was simple madness." . . . A hundred years later, political struggles within the country and, notably, presidential and congressional leadership in enforcing the Court's school desegregation ruling saved the moral appeal of *Brown* from becoming another "great folly."

Because the Court's decisions are not self-executing, public reactions inevitably weigh on the minds of the justices. . . .

. . . Opposition to the school desegregation ruling in *Brown* led to bitter, sometimes violent confrontations. In Little Rock, Arkansas, Governor Orval Faubus encouraged disobedience by southern segregationists. The federal National Guard had to be called out to maintain order. The school board in Little Rock unsuccessfully pleaded, in *Cooper v. Aaron* (1958), for the Court's postponement of the implementation of *Brown's* mandate. In the midst of the controversy, Frankfurter worried that Chief Justice Warren's attitude had become "more like that of a fighting politician than that of a judicial statesman." In such confrontations between the Court and the country, "the transcending issue," Frankfurter reminded the brethren, remains that of preserving "the Supreme Court as the authoritative organ of what the Constitution requires." When the justices move too far or too fast in their interpretation of the Constitution, they threaten public acceptance of the Court's legitimacy.

The political struggles of the Court (and among the justices) continue after the writing of opinions and final votes. Announcements of decisions trigger diverse reactions from the media, interest groups, lower courts, Congress, the President, and the general public. Their reactions may enhance or thwart compliance and reinforce or undermine the Court's prestige. Opinion days thus may reveal something of the political struggles that might otherwise remain hidden within the marble temple. They may also mark the beginning of larger political struggles for influence in the country. . . .

When deciding major issues of public law and policy, justices must consider strategies for getting public acceptance of their rulings. When striking down the doctrine of "separate but equal" facilities in 1954 in *Brown v. Board of Education (Brown I)*, for instance, the Warren Court waited a year before issuing, in *Brown II*, its mandate for "all deliberate speed" in ending racial segregation in public education.

Resistance to the social policy announced in *Brown I* was expected. A rigid timetable for desegregation would only intensify opposition. During oral arguments on *Brown II*, devoted to the question of what kind of decree the Court should issue to enforce *Brown*, Warren confronted the hard fact of southern resistance. The attorney for South Carolina, S. Emory Rogers, pressed for an open-ended decree—one that would not specify when and how desegregation should take place. He boldly proclaimed

> Mr. Chief Justice, to say we will conform depends on the decree handed down. I am frank to tell you, right now [in] our district I do not think that we will send—[that] the white people of the district will send their children to the Negro schools. It would be unfair to tell the Court that we are going to do that. I do not think it is. But I do think that something can be worked out. We hope so.

"It is not a question of attitude," Warren shot back, "it is a question of conforming to the decree." Their heated exchange continued as follows:

CHIEF JUSTICE WARREN: But you are not willing to say here that there would be an honest attempt to conform to this decree, if we did leave it to the district court [to implement]?

MR. ROGERS: No, I am not. Let us get the word "honest" out of there.
CHIEF JUSTICE WARREN: No, leave it in.
MR. ROGERS: No, because I would have to tell you that right now we
    would not conform—we would not send our white children to the
    negro schools. . . .

Agreement emerged that the Court should issue a short opinion-
decree. In a memorandum, Warren summarized the main points of
agreement. The opinion should simply state that *Brown I* held radically
segregated public schools to be unconstitutional. *Brown II* should acknowledge that the ruling creates various administrative problems, but emphasize
that "local school authorities have the primary responsibility for assessing
and solving these problems; [and] the courts will have to consider these
problems in determining whether the efforts of local school authorities"
are in good-faith compliance. . . .

Enforcement and implementation required the cooperation and coordination of all three branches. Little progress could be made, as Assistant
Attorney General Pollack has explained, "where historically there had
been slavery and a long tradition of discrimination [until] all three branches
of the federal government [could] be lined up in support of a movement
forward or a requirement for change." The election of Nixon in 1968
then brought changes both in the policies of the executive branch and
in the composition of the Court. The simplicity and flexibility of *Brown*,
moreover, invited evasion. It produced a continuing struggle over measures, such as gerrymandering school district lines and busing in the 1970s
and 1980s, because the mandate itself had evolved from one of ending
segregation to one of securing integration in public schools. . . .

"By itself," the political scientist Robert Dahl observed, "the Court is
almost powerless to affect the course of national policy." *Brown* dramatically
altered the course of American life, but it also reflected the justices'
awareness that their decisions are not self-executing. The rulings [in] *Brown*
. . . were unanimous but ambiguous. The ambiguity in the desegregation
rulings . . . was the price of achieving unanimity. Unanimity appeared
necessary if the Court was to preserve its institutional prestige while
pursuing revolutionary change in social policy. Justices sacrificed their
own policy preferences for more precise guidelines, while the Court
tolerated lengthy delays in recognition of the costs of open defiance and
the pressures of public opinion. . . .

Public opinion serves to curb the Court when it threatens to go too
far or too fast in its rulings. The Court has usually been in step with
major political movements, except during transitional periods or critical

elections. It would nevertheless be wrong to conclude, along with Peter Finley Dunne's fictional Mr. Dooley, that "th' supreme court follows th' iliction returns." To be sure, the battle over FDR's "Court-packing" plan and the Court's "switch-in-time-that-saved-nine" in 1937 gives that impression. Public opinion supported the New Deal, but turned against FDR after his landslide reelection in 1936 when he proposed to "pack the Court" by increasing its size from nine to fifteen. In a series of five-to-four and six-to-three decisions in 1935–1936, the Court had struck down virtually every important measure of FDR's New Deal program. But in the spring of 1937, while the Senate Judiciary Committee considered FDR's proposal, the Court abruptly handed down three five-to-four rulings upholding major pieces of New Deal legislation. Shortly afterward, FDR's close personal friend and soon-to-be nominee for the Court, Felix Frankfurter, wrote Justice Stone confessing that he was "not wholly happy in thinking that Mr. Dooley should, in the course of history turn out to have been one of the most distinguished legal philosophers." Frankfurter, of course, knew that justices do not simply follow the election returns. The influence of public opinion is more subtle and complex.

Life in the marble temple is not immune from shifts in public opinion. . . . The justices, however, deny being directly influenced by public opinion. The Court's prestige rests on preserving the public's view that justices base their decisions on interpretations of the law, rather than on their personal policy preferences. Yet, complete indifference to public opinion would be the height of judicial arrogance. . . .

"The powers exercised by this Court are inherently oligarchic," Frankfurter once observed when pointing out that "[t]he Court is not saved from being oligarchic because it professes to act in the service of humane ends." Judicial review is antidemocratic. But the Court's power stems from its duty to give authoritative meaning to the Constitution, and rests with the persuasive forces of reason, institutional prestige, the cooperation of other political institutions, and, ultimately, public opinion. The country, in a sense, saves the justices from being an oligarchy by curbing the Court when it goes too far or too fast with its policy-making. Violent opposition and resistance, however, threaten not merely the Court's prestige but the very idea of a government under law.

Some Court watchers, and occasionally even the justices, warn of "an imperial judiciary" and a "government by the judiciary." For much of the Court's history, though, the work of the justices has not involved major issues of public policy. In most areas of public law and policy, the fact that the Court decides an issue is more important than what it decides. Relatively few of the many issues of domestic and foreign policy that

arise in government reach the Court. When the Court does decide major
questions of public policy, it does so by bringing political controversies
within the language, structure, and spirit of the Constitution. By deciding
only immediate cases, the Court infuses constitutional meaning into the
resolution of the larger surrounding political controversies. But by itself
the Court cannot lay those controversies to rest.

The Court can profoundly influence American life. As a guardian of
the Constitution, the Court sometimes invites controversy by challenging
majoritarian sentiments to respect the rights of minorities and the principles of a representative democracy. The Court's influence is usually more
subtle and indirect, varying over time and from one policy issue to another.
In the end, the Court's influence on American life cannot be measured
precisely, because its policy-making is inextricably bound up with that of
other political institutions. Major confrontations in constitutional politics,
like those over school desegregation, school prayer, and abortion, are
determined as much by what is possible in a system of free government
and in a pluralistic society as by what the Court says about the meaning
of the Constitution. At its best, the Court appeals to the country to
respect the substantive value choices of human dignity and self-governance
embedded in our written Constitution.

46

PETER IRONS

From *Brennan vs. Rehnquist*

*The U.S. Supreme Court today is different than it was when President
Franklin Roosevelt called the justices "Nine Old Men." The Court's
membership now includes justices who are black, female, and young, and
they come from different regions, religions, and socioeconomic backgrounds.
Yet the fundamental issues faced by the Court have not changed. Legal
scholar Peter Irons examines a primary philosophical battle on the Supreme
Court: individual and minority rights protected by an active judicial branch
versus majority power, expressed by strong legislative and executive branches,
with the Court exercising judicial restraint. The battle is never better illustrated, Irons feels, than in the contrast between former Justice William J.
Brennan and Chief Justice William H. Rehnquist.*

WILLIAM J. BRENNAN, JR., and William H. Rehnquist served together on the United States Supreme Court between 1972 and 1990. During these eighteen years, they headed the Court's liberal and conservative wings, and lobbied for the votes of moderate justices. They provided intellectual and political leadership to contending sides in a battle over the Constitution that affected the lives of every American. The two justices brought divergent judicial philosophies to the Court, rooted in different values and views about the relations of individuals and the state. Each won major victories, but neither won a final triumph. . . . Setting aside unanimous decisions, Brennan and Rehnquist agreed in only 273 of 1,815 case in which one or more justices dissented, just 15 percent of the Court's divided decisions over a span of almost two decades. This was the lowest rate of agreement of any pair of justices over those years. And they disagreed in virtually every case that raised important constitutional issues.

Brennan and Rehnquist are almost totally opposite in background, philosophy, and judicial voting. During their years together, they battled over the Constitution, each trying to rally the Court's moderates to his side. The stakes were high—questions of abortion, affirmative action, capital punishment, and other controversial issues hung in the balance. . . .

This book perceives the Supreme Court as a political institution, and constitutional litigation as a form of politics. These are hardly radical— or recent—notions. "Scarcely any political question arises in the United States," Alexis de Tocqueville observed in 1835, "that is not resolved, sooner or later, into a judicial question." The Court's first major decision, *Marbury v. Madison* in 1803, drew the justices into an intensely political conflict among all three branches of the federal government. Chief Justice John Marshall did not shrink from this dispute. "It is emphatically the province and duty of the judicial department," he wrote, "to say what the law is." His opinion established the Court as the ultimate arbiter of political disputes the other branches could not resolve.

The Supreme Court remains embroiled in political disputes. . . .

There is little question that William Brennan brought with him to the Supreme Court bench a well-formed constitutional philosophy. Shaped in childhood and sharpened by law practice and judicial experience, it can be capsulized in one word: dignity. . . .

The Due Process clauses of the Constitution, added by the Fifth and Fourteenth amendments, were designed to limit governmental authority by protecting the "life, liberty, or property" of Americans from arbitrary official action. As Brennan put it, "Due process required fidelity to a more basic and more subtle principle: the essential dignity and worth of each individual." The Constitution required officials "to treat citizens not as subjects but as fellow human beings." Brennan added that "due process asks whether government has treated someone fairly, whether individual dignity has been honored, whether the worth of an individual has been acknowledged." Officials cannot answer these questions "solely by pointing to rational action taken according to standard rules. They must plumb their conduct more deeply, seeking answers in the more complex equations of human nature and experience." . . .

Another central theme of Brennan's judicial philosophy is that "due process" is a concept whose meaning is not static, frozen by the Framers in 1787, but one that changes over time, as society changes. The Framers did not intend, he argued, to impose on judges an inflexible definition of "a clause that reflects a principle as elusive as human dignity." . . .

The notion that the meaning of "due process" shifts over time imposes a burden on judges who share this approach to the Constitution. Placed by history within a "given age," Brennan said, judges "must draw on our own experience as inhabitants of that age, and our own sense of the uneven fabric of social life. We cannot delude ourselves that the Constitution takes the form of a theorem whose axioms need mere logical deduction." . . .

. . . [There is] another important theme of Brennan's jurisprudence. "The view that all matters of substantive policy should be resolved through the majoritarian process," he says, "has appeal under some circumstances, but I think ultimately it will not do." What the principle of majority rule cannot do, Brennan argues, is "to rectify claims of minority right that arise as a response to the outcomes of that very majoritarian process." When those outcomes—in voting booths and legislative chambers—display prejudice against the "outsiders" in American society, the Constitution requires judicial intervention. In Brennan's view, judges have the power and, in appropriate cases, the duty to displace majority rule when it violates the rights of minorities. "Faith in democracy is one thing," he says, "blind faith quite another." The Constitution was designed to place fundamental rights "beyond the reach of temporary political majorities."

This defense of minority rights does not lead Justice Brennan to advocate replacing what he calls legislative "imperialism" with an equivalent judicial imperialism. The Constitution does not empower judges to impose their own personal values on its provisions. But it does require them to speak, individually and collectively, for American society as a whole. "When Justices interpret the Constitution," Brennan says, "they speak for their community, not for themselves alone." This statement, of course, begs the question of how any justice can determine which "community" is relevant to the decision of a case. Some communities are delimited by geography as local, state, or national; others are defined as ethnic, religious, or racial. And the nation can be considered a "community" as a whole. Beyond these questions are those of public opinion and personal sentiment. No justice has ever proposed that the Court rely on public opinion polls in deciding controversial cases. And no justice has suggested that personal views are superior to the Constitution's demand for impersonal judging.

Justice Brennan does not evade these hard questions. He acknowledges that judges must make "substantive value choices" when they interpret constitutional provisions and that they "must accept the ambiguity inherent in the effort to apply them to modern circumstances." Justices, he says, "read the Constitution in the only way that we can: as twentieth-century Americans." He adds these words: "We look to the history of the time of framing and to the intervening history of interpretation. But the ultimate question must be: What do the words of the text mean in our time? For the genius of the Constitution rests not in any static meaning it might have had in a world that is dead and gone, but in the adaptability of its great principles to cope with current problems and current needs."

Brennan agrees that allowing unelected judges to reverse the decisions of elected lawmakers goes against the grain of democratic government. "These are important, recurrent worries," he admits. But he does not shrink from advocating "an active judiciary" as a counterweight to "legislative irresponsibility." He cites as examples of "panic" by majorities the prosecution of those who criticized American involvement in both world wars. Judges failed in each case to protect the victims of wartime hysteria, and the results "are among the least proud moments in the Court's history."

In summary, Justice Brennan's judicial philosophy begins with his deep religious faith in the "dignity" of every person, moves to the principle that government exists to serve the needs of individuals and to protect their dignity, and ends with the notion that the meaning of the Constitution must change as society changes. Judges speak for a community that is diverse and disputatious, and they must step in to prevent majorities, permanent or temporary, from trampling on the rights of minorities. The foundation of Brennan's jurisprudence is his view of the Constitution as "a living, evolving document that must be read anew" by each generation. . . .

William Rehnquist came to the bench with a clear, consistent political and legal philosophy, but without a judicial record that would show his philosophy in action. It took only a few years of votes and opinions to provide evidence that his judicial philosophy followed the path of his earlier positions. Speaking at the University of Texas Law School in 1976, he outlined his views in a speech entitled "The Notion of a Living Constitution." Of all his speeches, articles, and opinions, this address presents Rehnquist's jurisprudence in its most developed form.

In many ways, his Texas speech was simply an expanded version of the views expressed in Rehnquist's 1948 letter to the *Stanford Daily*, in which he argued that "one personal conviction is no better than another" and rejected "the implication that humanitarianism is desirable" as a moral value. His speech explicitly adopted the position of legal positivism, the notion that the legislative will is supreme and that the content of laws is not a proper concern of judges. If legislators follow the rules, they are constrained only by the explicit commands of the Constitution. The most extreme form of legal positivism—approached in the civil law system of continental Europe—does not allow for judicial review of legislation. The American form of positivism—articulated most forcefully by Robert Bork—gives judges an independent but limited role in reviewing laws, constrained by precedent and the constitutional text. In both systems, judges are expected to show deference to the legislative will. . . .

Rehnquist admitted that "in exercising the very delicate responsibility of judicial review," judges had authority to strike down laws they "find to violate some provision of the Constitution." But he took a narrow view of this authority. The concept of judicial review, he said, "has basically antidemocratic and antimajoritarian facets that require some justification" in a system based on majority rule. The idea of a "living Constitution" struck Rehnquist as a negation of "the nature of political value judgments in a democratic society." He agreed that constitutional safeguards for individual liberty "take on a generalized moral rightness or goodness." But this goodness has no source outside the premise of majority rule, no basis in any "morality" that relies on personal conscience. Constitutional protections "assume a general social acceptance," Rehnquist asserted, "neither because of any intrinsic worth nor because of any unique origins in someone's idea of natural justice but instead simply because they have been incorporated in a constitution by the people."

The major theme of Rehnquist's speech was that political majorities are entitled to enact "positive law" and to impose their moral views on minorities. Laws "take on a form of moral goodness because they have been enacted into positive law," he argued. One complement of legal positivism is moral relativism, the notion that no moral value is inherently superior to another. Rehnquist took this position as a college student and stuck by it as a justice. "There is no conceivable way," he told his

Texas audience, "in which I can logically demonstrate to you that the judgments of my conscience are superior to the judgments of your conscience, and vice versa." The "goodness" of any value is decided in the voting booth. . . .

This record shows that Rehnquist is a principled political conservative. But is he also, as he describes himself, a judicial conservative? His philosophy of deference to legislative acts is not, by itself, either liberal or conservative. Laws can be "liberal" by granting rights to minorities, or "conservative" by placing burdens on them. For example, a legislature can pass laws that protect homosexuals from discrimination, or laws that make homosexual behavior a crime. However, in consistently voting to uphold criminal convictions, to deny First Amendment claims, and to reject the claims of racial minorities and women, Rehnquist has taken a "conservative" position on the political issues raised in these cases. He is equally *not* a conservative in the sense of displaying the respect for precedent shown by those who profess "judicial restraint" as a principle. . . .

The jurisprudence of Justice Rehnquist does, in fact, distinguish him from *all* of his colleagues since he joined the Court. None has voted more consistently to uphold governmental actions, legislative and executive. And none has voted more consistently against the claims of dissenters and minorities. His "deference" principle stands in stark contrast to the "dignity" value of Justice Brennan. Their competing visions of the Constitution are rooted in historic struggles over American law and politics. . . .

Supreme Court justices are placed on the bench by elected officials who owe their positions to the electorate. How we vote in elections for senators and presidents will affect the outcome of the Court's decisions in years and decades to come. This is an awesome power, one that every American should ponder before entering the voting booth. Justices Brennan and Rehnquist have offered persuasive arguments on either side of a continuing constitutional debate. But in the end, the decision is ours.

47

DAVID YALOF

From *Pursuit of Justices*

In selecting nominees to the Supreme Court, the president faces a daunting task. Legal scholar David Yalof takes readers inside the process, pointing out the many factions in the nation, in the branches of government, and even within the president's own circle that must be considered when making a nomination. The president today has access to large amounts of information about a potential justice, but so does everyone else in the political process. Yalof gives an account of the 1993 selection of Ruth Bader Ginsburg for a seat on the Supreme Court. Lest the maneuverings and machinations surrounding the choice seem mind-boggling, remember that a Supreme Court justice is often the most significant and long lasting legacy that a president leaves behind.

———

ON JUNE 27, 1992, the Supreme Court inserted itself once again into the national debate over abortion with its surprising decision in *Planned Parenthood v. Casey*. Specifically, five of the nine justices refused to cast aside *Roe v. Wade*, the Court's controversial 1973 opinion establishing a constitutional right to abortion. Included among *Roe's* saviors that day were Sandra Day O'Connor and Anthony Kennedy, both appointees of former President Ronald Reagan. As a candidate for the presidency in 1980 and 1984, Reagan had supported a constitutional amendment to overturn *Roe*, a ruling considered to be among the most vilified of public targets for social conservatives in his party. As president, Reagan had publicly promised to appoint justices to the Supreme Court willing to reverse *Roe v. Wade*. Yet just the opposite occurred in *Casey*: a majority of the Court reaffirmed the core right to privacy first discovered in *Roe*. And in a touch of irony, two of President Reagan's own nominees had played significant roles in safeguarding the decision from the Court's conservatives.

Obviously the selection of Supreme Court nominees is among the president's most significant duties. Yet as the outcome in *Casey* demonstrates, it is a task beset with difficulties and potential frustrations. On one hand, a president ordinarily tries to choose a nominee whose influence will reach beyond the current political environment. As a beneficiary of life tenure, a justice may well extend that president's legacy on judicial matters long into the future. Yet in selecting a nominee the president must also successfully maneuver through that immediate environment, lest he suffer politically or (as in some cases) see his nominee rejected by the Senate outright. In recent years internal strife and factionalism within the executive branch have only further complicated what was already a delicate undertaking. . . .

A central question remains: why were these particular candidates chosen over others possessing similar—and in some cases superior—qualifications? The classic "textbook" portrayal of the Supreme Court nomination process depicts presidents as choosing Supreme Court justices more for their judicial politics than for their judicial talents. By this version of events, presidents, by nominating justices whose political views appear compatible with their own, try to gain increased influence over the Supreme Court. Once on the Court, a justice may then satisfy or disappoint the appointing president by his decisions. Such an oversimplified view of nomination politics usually ignores the more complex political environment in which modern presidents must act, including the various intricacies and nuances of executive branch politics.

. . . I contend that modern presidents are often forced to arbitrate among factions within their own administrations, each pursuing its own interests and agendas in the selection process. At first glance, presidential reliance on numerous high-level officials equipped with a variety of perspectives might seem a logical response to the often hostile and unpredictable political environment that surrounds modern appointments to the Court. Yet conflicts within the administration itself may have a debilitating effect on that president's overall interests. High-level advisors may be sincerely pursuing their own conceptions of what makes up the administration's best interests; but to achieve their own maximum preferred outcomes, they may feel compelled to skew the presentation of critical information, if not leave it out altogether. In recent administrations the final choice of a nominee has usually reflected one advisor's hard-won victory over his rivals, without necessarily accounting for the president's other political interests. . . .

The New Deal marked the beginning of a fundamental transformation in American politics. A national economic crisis demanded national solutions, and the government in Washington grew exponentially to meet these new demands. Beginning in the 1930s, the federal government entered one policy area after another that had previously been the exclusive province of state governments. Emergency conditions required quick institutional responses, and the executive branch in particular was drawn into critical aspects of national policymaking. Just as the character of national politics changed dramatically, the Supreme Court was undergoing a transformation of its own. Fundamental changes in the political landscape affecting Supreme Court appointments were a by-product of these changes. At least ten critical developments in American politics substantially altered the character of the modern selection process for justices:

1. The *growth and bureaucratization of the Justice Department* facilitated the investment of considerable manpower and other resources towards the consideration of prospective Supreme Court candidates. As the size of the national government grew dramatically during the early twentieth century, the government's overall legal responsibilities quickly expanded. Congress reacted by increasing the size of the Justice Department and transferring to it most litigating functions from other federal agencies. Armed with a full staff of attorneys and more extensive bureaucratic support, attorneys general in modern times have enjoyed more regular input into the selection of Supreme Court nominees, often consulting with the president well before a vacancy on the Court even arises.

The Justice Department under Franklin Roosevelt underwent a minor reorganization that affected the politics of the nomination process. Attorney General Homer Cummings merged the Division of Admiralty into the Civil Division and established the Office of Legal Counsel ("OLC"). In its infancy, the OLC served primarily as a means of supporting the attorney general in his role as legal advisor to the president. Yet like most other executive branch offices, the OLC grew steadily over time, and eventually its mission changed to meet new administration demands. Headed today by an assistant attorney general with a staff of nearly twenty lawyers, the OLC has become responsible for developing legal positions to support the administration's policy initiatives and for resolving disputes over legal policy within the executive branch. Since 1964, the OLC has been considered one of the most politicized units in the department. And in the late 1980s the Reagan administration opted to rely principally on OLC lawyers for comprehensive research and analysis of prospective Supreme Court candidates.

2. The *growth and bureaucratization of the White House* has also had an impact on the nomination process. The White House staff, once limited to a handful of personal assistants, was barely a factor in political decision-making for most of the nineteenth and early twentieth centuries. Starting with Franklin Roosevelt's administration, however, the White House staff experienced prodigious growth, expanding from just thirty-seven employees in the early 1930s to more than nine hundred by the late 1980s. As the modern presidency has brought more policymaking activities

within the White House, the White House staff has increasingly figured in matters of high presidential priority.

Modern presidents often rely on the White House Counsel's Office to assist them in screening and selecting prospective Supreme Court nominees. Thus, increasingly, the attorney general's most constant and genuine competitor for influence has been the White House Counsel. Theodore Sorenson, John Kennedy's special counsel, asserted that his duties did not overlap with the attorney general's; rather he was involved "as a policy advisor to the president with respect to legislation, with respect to his programs and messages, with respect to executive orders, and with respect to those few formally legal problems, which come to the White House." But those supposed lines of demarcation have blurred considerably during the past thirty years. Today, a president has at his disposal two distinct organizations, each with its own bureaucratic resources; the president may rely on either or both offices for counsel concerning the selection of Supreme Court nominees.

3. Paralleling the increased role for national political institutions in American life has been the *growth in size and influence of federal courts*. Congress's willingness in the past to meet increased caseloads with new judgeships has steadily multiplied the president's opportunities to place his imprint on lower court policymaking. The total number of district and circuit judgeships rose from under two hundred in 1930 to well over seven hundred by the late 1980s. Thus between thirty and forty vacancies may occur annually on the federal bench. These federal judges must be counted on to interpret, enforce, and in some cases limit the expansion of federal governmental authority. At times federal courts have even fashioned national law and policy, serving as key facilitators of social, economic, and political growth.

Senatorial courtesy, to be sure, remains the dominant factor in lower court selections, but the steady increase in the number of judgeships has provided presidents with more than an occasional opportunity to nominate candidates of their own choosing after the preferences of individual senators have been satisfied. The growing size and prestige of the D.C. Circuit have given presidents additional opportunities to hand out plum assignments: because senatorial courtesy does not apply to those seats, presidents may freely nominate ideologically compatible law professors, former administration officials, and others to positions of considerable prestige in the federal judicial system. Thus more than ever before, the federal courts today provide an especially useful "proving ground" for candidates who might one day be considered for a seat on the high court.

4. *Divided party government* has become a recurring theme in American

government since World War II. Between 1896 and 1946, opposing parties controlled the White House and the Senate during just two sessions of Congress. By contrast, split party conditions now seem almost routine. In all, the president has confronted a hostile U.S. Senate in fourteen separate Congresses since World War II. When a Democratic-led Senate considered Eisenhower's nomination of John Harlan in March 1955, it represented the first time in sixty years that a president's nominee had to undergo review in an upper chamber controlled by the opposition. Since then, fifteen of twenty-six nominees to the Court have faced an opposition-led Senate, a condition that has severely constrained presidential discretion in this context.

5. The *confirmation process has become increasingly public.* For much of our nation's history the confirmation process unfolded largely behind closed doors. Though the Senate Judiciary Committee often met and offered recommendations on nominees during the nineteenth century, closed investigative hearings were not conducted until 1873 when President Ulysses Grant unsuccessfully nominated George Williams to be chief justice. Open hearings were held for the first time only in 1916, when the Senate considered Louis Brandeis's candidacy. Nine years later Harlan Fiske Stone became the first nominee in history to appear before the committee personally. Full-fledged public hearings were finally instituted on a regular basis beginning in 1930 with President Hoover's nomination of John J. Parker.

Since 1955, virtually all Supreme Court nominees have formally testified before the Senate Judiciary committee. Hearings have been televised live since 1981, insuring heightened public access to the process. The increasingly public nature of confirmation-stage politics has placed added strain on senators, many of whom may be reluctant to spend their time and political capital on an arduous process that will only create enemies back home. Meanwhile, the president must now find nominees who, aside from meeting ideological or professional criteria, will fare well in front of television cameras when facing a barrage of senators' questions.

6. The *rise in power of the organized bar* has figured significantly in recent Supreme Court selections. The American Bar Association's Special Committee on the (federal) Judiciary (later renamed the "Standing Committee on Federal Judiciary") was founded in 1947 to "promote the nomination of competent persons and to oppose the nomination of unfit persons" to the federal courts. During the past half-century that committee has played a significant if uneven role in the appointment of lower federal court judges. Not surprisingly, the ABA has taken an especially strong interest in the nomination of Supreme Court justices as well. Beginning

with Eisenhower's nomination of Harlan in 1954, the ABA has formally reviewed all Supreme Court nominees for the Senate Judiciary Committee. Thus in selecting nominees, presidents must incorporate into their calculations the possibility that a less-than-exceptional rating from the ABA could serve as a rallying point for opposition during the subsequent confirmation process. Still, the bar's actual influence over the choice of nominees has varied largely depending upon the administration in power.

In 1956, the Eisenhower administration began to submit names of potential Supreme Court nominees to the ABA at the same time that the FBI began its background check. During this period the ABA exerted little direct influence during initial deliberations over prospective candidates. By contrast, subsequent administrations have often enlisted the committee's services during much earlier stages of the process. High-ranking officials in the Justice Department have consulted with committee members to gauge potential support for and opposition to a prospective candidate. In 1962, for instance, committee chairman Bernard G. Segal informed Kennedy administration officials that the ABA would react favorably to Byron White's nomination if it came before the Senate.

In 1971, the Nixon administration formalized this advisory relationship for a limited period, agreeing to submit a slate of candidates to the ABA for consideration prior to its public designation of that nominee. Although the arrangement soon broke down amid allegations that the ABA had leaked the names of prospective candidates to the press, the Ford administration reinstituted the procedure in 1975. Thus, immediately following Justice Douglas's retirement in November 1975, Attorney General Edward Levi furnished the ABA with a list of prospective nominees for its review. Apparently, the ABA's positive evaluation of Judge John Paul Stevens figured heavily in the final outcome. Yet Ford remains the last president to have afforded the ABA such a degree of influence during initial selection deliberations; during the past twenty years the ABA's role has again been reduced to rating nominees only *after* the president has formally submitted their names to the Senate. Conservative disenchantment with the ABA in the years following Bork's defeat* may diminish the group's role even further, especially if a Republican-controlled Senate Judiciary Committee gets an opportunity to review the qualifications of a Supreme Court nominee (an event that has not occurred since 1986).

---

*President Reagan nominated distinguished U.S. Court of Appeals Judge Robert Bork for a seat on the Supreme Court in 1987. Bork was a strict conservative who believed that judges should restrain themselves from interpreting more rights into the Constitution than the framers had actually intended. After divisive, emotional Senate hearings, Bork's nomination was defeated by the Senate. — EDS.

7. *Increased participation by interest groups* has also altered the character of the Supreme Court nomination process. This is not an entirely new phenomenon. Organized interests (including the National Grange and the Anti-Monopoly League) figured significantly in defeating Stanley Matthews's nomination to the Court in 1881. Almost fifty years later, an unlikely coalition of labor interests and civil rights groups joined together to defeat the nomination of John Parker. Since World War II, interest groups have extended their influence into the early stages of nominee selection by virtue of their increased numbers and political power. Groups such as the Alliance for Justice, People for the American Way, and the Leadership Conference on Civil Rights have made Supreme Court appointments a high priority in their respective organizations. Many interest groups now conduct their own research into the backgrounds of prospective nominees and inundate the administration with information and analysis about various individual candidates.

8. *Increased media attention* has further transformed nominee selection politics. Presidents in the nineteenth and early twentieth centuries, working outside the media's glare, could often delay the selection of a nominee for many months while suffering few political repercussions. By contrast, contemporary presidents must contend with daily coverage of their aides' ruminations concerning a Supreme Court vacancy. Reporters assigned to the "Supreme Court beat" often provide their readership with the most recent "shortlists" of candidates under consideration by the president. A long delay in naming a replacement may be viewed by the press as a sign of indecision and uncertainty on the part of the president. Delay may also work to an administration's benefit, especially if media outlets expend their own resources investigating prospective candidates and airing potential political liabilities prior to any formal commitment by the administration.

9. *Advances in legal research technology* have had a pronounced effect on the selection process. All modern participants in the appointment process, including officials within the White House and the Justice Department, enjoy access to sophisticated tools for researching the backgrounds of prospective Supreme Court candidates. Legal software programs such as LEXIS/NEXIS and WESTLAW allow officials to quickly gather all of a prospective candidate's past judicial opinions, scholarship, and other public commentary as part of an increasingly elaborate screening process. Computer searches may be either tailored around narrow subject issues or they may be comprehensive in scope. The prevalence of C-SPAN and other cable and video outlets has made it possible to analyze prospective candidates' speeches and activities that would have otherwise gone unnoticed.

Of course, advanced research technology is a double-edged sword: media outlets and interest groups may just as effectively publicize negative information about prospective candidates, undermining the president's carefully laid plans for a particular vacancy.

10. Finally, the *more visible role the Supreme Court has assumed in American political life* has increased the perceived stakes of the nomination process for everyone involved. Several of the critical developments listed above, including increased media attention and interest group influence in the nominee selection process, stem from a larger political development involving the Court itself: during this century the Supreme Court has entrenched itself at the forefront of American politics. Prior to the New Deal, the Court only occasionally tried to compete with other governmental institutions for national influence. For example, the Taney Court inserted itself into the debate over slavery with its decision in *Dred Scott v. Sanford* (1857). The Court's aggressive protection of property rights in the late nineteenth century pitted it first against state governments, and then later against Congress and the president during the early part of the twentieth century. In each instance the judiciary usually represented a political ideology in decline; after a period of time the Court eventually returned to its role as an essentially reaffirming institution.

Since the early 1940s, however, the Supreme Court has positioned itself at the center of major political controversies on a nearly continuous basis. Driven by a primarily rights-based agenda, the Court has found itself wrestling with matters embedded in the American psyche: desegregation, privacy rights, affirmative action, and law enforcement. With the Court's continuously high visibility in the American political system, each appointment of a new justice now draws the attention of nearly all segments of society. The stakes of Supreme Court appointments may only seem higher than before, but that perception alone has caused a veritable sea change in the way presidents in the late twentieth century must treat the selection of Supreme Court nominees.

These changes in the political landscape have had a profound impact on the process by which Supreme Court nominees are chosen, including the determination of who will participate in the early stages of the decisionmaking process and what type of candidates will be favored. The growth and bureaucratization of both the White House and the Justice Department have provided the president with considerable administrative resources to conduct an elaborate and comprehensive search for candidates. Still, the president's interests have not always been served by the above-described developments. The increased role the judiciary now plays in national policymaking has encouraged interest groups to increasingly assert their own distinct (and often competing) interests in the nominee selection process. Forces within the administration itself may also take a special interest in the process and its outcome. The Justice Department's preference for federal appeals judges, for example, may undermine the president's more immediate political interests by unnecessarily restricting the pool of candidates under consideration.

Certainly presidential objectives may be sacrificed whenever an ill-equipped associate or subordinate is charged with carrying out significant responsibilities in the selection process. At the same time, too many cooks may also spoil the broth, as internal strife carries its own set of negative consequences. The president's interests have often been compromised by the shift to a more bureaucratic selection process featuring multiple advisors with overlapping responsibilities. These advisors have often become advocates, striving to enlarge their own "turf" or influence over the selection process. As these competing advocates engage in conflict within the confines of the administration itself, information may be distorted; the "advice" a president receives will be based on erroneously optimistic projections about a particular outcome. Ultimately it is the president who suffers most when the full impact of negative information about candidates is not realized until after the fact, such as during a confirmation process that turns unexpectedly hostile, or later, after that individual has become a sitting justice. . . .

In contrast to his two Republican predecessors in office, ideology played little or no role at all in the selection of Supreme Court nominees during Bill Clinton's first term as president. Certainly his administration planned to draw from a pool of mostly liberal and Democratic candidates. Yet as early as fall of 1992, then-Governor Clinton was already giving public hints about his preferences for future Supreme Court nominees, and his declared emphasis was on backgrounds and political experience rather than beliefs and ideological viewpoints. For example, Clinton talked of putting a seasoned politician on the Court, someone who might be able to build judicial coalitions just as Earl Warren had done. In fact, on two separate occasions during his presidential campaign Bill Clinton the candidate glowingly spoke of New York Governor Mario Cuomo as a possible Supreme Court nominee. Of course those comments came before Bill Clinton the president was forced to weigh the effect a controversial nominee might have on his ambitious legislative agenda.

After Byron White announced his intention to retire from the Court on March 19, 1993, the Clinton administration initiated a long, drawn-out selection process that seemed to jut back and forth between satisfying the president's desire for an "ex-pol," on one hand, and bending to political reality on the other hand. Still quite early in his first term, Clinton had already found himself embroiled in a number of confirmation battles, first over the nomination of Zoë Baird to serve as attorney general, and then over the prospective nomination of Judge Kimba Wood to the same position. Lani Guinier's ill-fated bid to become civil rights head at the Justice Department soon followed.

On March 20, Clinton's first formal conference to discuss the nomination included an especially large contingent of advisors: White House Chief of Staff Thomas "Mack" McLarty, Policy Advisor Bruce Lindsey, Deputy White House Counsel Vince Foster, and Vice President Albert Gore. Foster's boss, White House Chief Counsel Bernard Nussbaum, had been invited but apparently was unable to attend. The president's requirements for the vacancy seemed apparent enough: Clinton hoped for a big-name politician for the position, who could assume a position of leadership with the Court right away. Clinton's advisors took a more realistic approach. Nussbaum had apparently provided the president with a list of forty-two candidates, including many state and federal judges; the list came replete with eight-to-ten-page legal and personal profiles.

Even in the wake of his problems filling the top post at Justice, Clinton remained keenly interested in Mario Cuomo and thus urged his aides to thoroughly investigate the governor's written record. Newspapers soon joined in the speculation, openly considering the impact a "Justice Cuomo" might have on the Supreme Court. The looming threat of a confirmation fight stopped Clinton from extending the nomination to Cuomo this early, however. Eventually, after a number of failed telephone connections between Cuomo and the president in late March, the frustrated New York governor put an end to the issue by publicly withdrawing his name from consideration. But the president still resisted drawing from the lists of federal and state judges compiled by his aides. One reporter claimed that Clinton asked his friend Richard Riley, the secretary of education and former governor of South Carolina, if he would be interested in the Supreme Court seat. According to the report, Riley politely declined. Any hope of an April announcement on the Supreme Court selection now dissipated in the wake of Cuomo and Riley's rejection of interest. On May 9 the *New York Times* reported that fully seven weeks into the selection process, the president and his aides had yet to even settle on a shortlist of candidates for the Court.

Finally in mid-May Clinton turned his attention once again to the longer list of judges his aides had compiled two months earlier. From a now-growing list of candidates, two jurists seemed to emerge as frontrunners capable of coasting through the confirmation process: Judge Jon O. Newman of the U.S. Court of Appeals for the Second Circuit and Chief Judge Stephen G. Breyer of the U.S. Court of Appeals for the First Circuit in Boston. Other names on the list included U.S. District Judge Jose Cabranes of Connecticut, Judge Amalya Kearse of the U.S. Court of Appeals for the Second Circuit, Judge Patricia Wald of the D.C. Circuit, and Gilbert Merritt, the chief judge of the U.S. Court of Appeals for the Sixth Circuit. Each of these names was leaked to the press during the final week of May and the first week of June. If Clinton was to be denied the big-name politician he had been looking for, he at least wanted to avoid the confirmation battles that had plagued him in the cases of Baird, Wood, and Guinier. Hence the administration's engagement in a "politics by trial balloon," with candidates effectively devoured by the media before the president had even committed to them as nominees.

From a shortlist of candidates that posed few political risks to the administration, Breyer's ties with key Senate Judiciary Committee members seemed to make him the most confirmable of all. A former law professor at Harvard, Breyer had served as chief counsel to the committee in the late 1970s and would now receive crucial support from both sides of the aisle. Senators Ted Kennedy (D-Mass.) and Orrin Hatch (R-Utah) had both been instrumental in pushing Breyer's nomination to the U.S. Court of Appeals in 1980, even as the approaching presidential election threatened to halt a number of President Carter's other appointments in their tracks. Hatch in particular knew and liked Breyer. As ranking Republican on the committee, Hatch alone possessed the power to guarantee the Democratic administration a smooth and uneventful confirmation process.

Yet just as the process seemed to be reaching a sense of closure in Breyer's favor, Clinton decided to reopen the process once again during the first week in June. No official had enough at stake in the process or in its results to resist Clinton's surprising decision. Certainly not Attorney General Janet Reno, who had up to that point played no role whatsoever in the recruitment process. Apparently, President Clinton was mounting one last effort to entice an experienced politician to join the Court. Cuomo's rejection seemed definitive, and further entreaties might cause embarrassment to both sides. The president then briefly considered naming Senate Majority Leader George Mitchell (D-Me.), but reasoned that he could not afford to lose another key Democrat from the Senate. For much the same reason, Senator Joseph Lieberman (D-Conn.) was quickly eliminated from consideration. A second offer to Riley was again declined.

Finally, Clinton became enamored with the idea of nominating Interior Secretary Bruce Babbitt to the Supreme Court. Like Riley, Babbitt was a former governor who had defied any real ideological labels. The president met with Babbitt to discuss the nomination for the first time on June 7. Clinton's sudden interest in Babbitt was not really surprising: He fit nearly every criteria Clinton had set forth when the search first began. Unfortunately for Babbitt, Clinton still remained "indecisive, too easily swayed by the last person with whom he'd spoken, too eager to please." The president thus opted to prolong the process with yet another trial balloon: His aides leaked Babbitt's name to the press on June 8 so they could gauge how the public might react to his candidacy.

Clinton's hesitation in naming Babbitt had two immediate consequences. First, it invited Babbitt's enemies to openly criticize him even before he enjoyed any official stamp of presidential approval. Senate minority leader Robert Dole publicly challenged Babbitt's merits, charging that his lack of judicial experience rendered him unqualified for the position. Hatch similarly joined the opposition. But the invitation to comment on Babbitt swept even more broadly: those who actually supported the interior secretary's favorable western land policies (including many environmental groups) declared their preference that Babbitt remain at the Department of the Interior. Second, by introducing Babbitt's name into the pool of candidates Clinton had inadvertently sent a signal to outsiders that the administration's shortlist was still in flux almost three months after White's announcement. At this late date there was apparently room for yet another candidate to emerge.

Wednesday, June 9 proved to be a pivotal day in Clinton's search for a successor to Justice White. The president, fresh off his "escape" on the Lani Guinier matter a few days earlier, opted to set aside Babbitt's candidacy for fear of engaging in another messy confirmation struggle with Republicans. On the president's orders, Vince Foster, his associates Ron Klain and Ricki Seidman, and private attorney James Hamilton went up to Boston to interview Breyer. That same day Bernard Nussbaum put the name of D.C. Circuit Judge Ruth Bader Ginsburg back on the list of candidates to be reviewed more carefully. Ginsburg had been on the longer list of candidates for some time, but until the first week of June she had never been considered seriously, ostensibly because of fears that her candidacy might cause a stir among key Democratic constituencies. A former ACLU litigator, Ginsburg had recently been targeted by some of the very groups she had once championed. Representatives from women's rights groups and pro-choice organizations had spoken out against her publicly, primarily because of Ginsburg's surprising criticism of the legal opinion issued in *Roe v. Wade*.

Nussbaum's renewed interest in Ginsburg so late in the selection process was no accident. When the president had prompted Senator Daniel Patrick Moynihan (D-N.Y.) for his opinion on the vacancy in May, Moynihan had offered Ginsburg as his "first and only recommendation for the Court." Immediately thereafter, Ginsburg's husband, Georgetown Law Professor Martin Ginsburg, had engineered a letter-writing campaign on his wife's behalf. According to Richard Davis, letters rushed in to the White House from two groups: (1) women's rights attorneys and (2) academics, including Columbia University President Michael Sovern, a former dean of the law school at Columbia where Ginsburg had once been a professor. At least one of the letters referred to a remark from Harvard Law School Dean Erwin Griswold, that Ginsburg was the "Thurgood Marshall of gender equality law." In a fortuitous move, Martin Ginsburg had encouraged the letter-writers to direct their efforts at Bernard Nussbaum in particular.

Although Nussbaum generally supported Breyer, he was realistic. Breyer's meeting with Foster and his aides had not gone well. The administration learned that Breyer and his wife had not paid Social Security taxes on a household worker. Once Zoë Baird's own "nanny problems" became public, Breyer had gone back and paid taxes for 1992. But other actions taken by the candidate seemed much less sincere. Breyer did not pay any back taxes from earlier years until after Justice White announced his retirement. Foster also discovered that penalties and interest due on those additional back taxes had not been paid until immediately after Cuomo withdrew his name from consideration. Despite some misgivings, Breyer was invited to join the president at a lunch scheduled for Friday June 11. This meeting also went poorly. Clinton told his aides that he felt "Breyer was selling himself too hard, that his interests in the law were too narrow, that he didn't have a big heart." The president gathered his advisors in the Oval Office at 11:15 that same evening for one last conference on the Supreme Court nomination. At this point the team advising Clinton had expanded drastically from three months earlier: along with Gore, McLarty, Lindsey, and Foster, Clinton was now joined by Nussbaum, Foster assistants Klain and Seidman, recently appointed Counselor to the President David Gergen, Policy Advisor George Stephanopoulos, White House Political Director Rahm Emmanuel, and Clinton's chief congressional liaison, Howard Paster. According to reporter Elizabeth Drew, the president asked each advisor to choose between Babbitt and Breyer. The lack of consensus that existed in the room soon became apparent:

Klain said that Breyer presented too many problems and that the President should be given another option, and he argued for taking a closer look at [Ruth Bader] Ginsburg. Nussbaum and Gergen were for Breyer. Stephanopoulos and Lindsey were for going back to Babbitt. . . . Foster was against Breyer. Gore was at first for Breyer but then moved away from that position.

After three months of looking, little had been resolved. Clinton then accepted Klain's advice and agreed to meet Ginsburg. Upon a second look, the president was now attracted to her record as a pioneer in woman's rights. Ginsburg met with the president on Sunday June 13. Aides said later that Clinton "fell in love" with Ginsburg and her story: a law review student unable to get a top flight job out of Columbia Law School, Ginsburg had gone on to litigate landmark cases in women's rights before the U.S. Supreme Court. Ginsburg's age—she was sixty years old—was never voiced as a concern. The fact that Ginsburg was Jewish—she would be the first Jewish justice since Abe Fortas resigned in 1969—was barely a factor in the decisionmaking calculus.

Clinton probably wanted to mull over Ginsburg's candidacy, and even float a trial balloon of her candidacy to the press if possible, just as he had done with Cuomo and Babbitt. Yet increasingly hostile media coverage of the nomination process had effectively eliminated that option. In recent weeks reporters had begun to mock the White House's earlier promises of a quick conclusion to the process; by the second week in June much of the press had bought into the storyline of an administration incapable of making a decision. In response, Clinton administration officials now promised a decision that same week. So Ruth Bader Ginsburg became the beneficiary of these increased pressures: the president would not have the opportunity to fluctuate again. On June 14, Clinton formally introduced Ginsburg to the press as his first nomination to the U.S. Supreme Court. Ginsburg certainly defied a number of criteria Clinton had outlined from the beginning. She was not a big-name politician. Unlike Cuomo, most Americans had never even heard of Ruth Bader Ginsburg before she was nominated for the Supreme Court. But Ginsburg had been a pioneer in woman's rights litigation, and her court of appeals record was decidedly moderate, a factor that would ease her confirmation considerably. The Senate Judiciary Committee approved Ginsburg's nomination by an 18–0 vote in August, and the Senate followed suit by a 96–3 margin. Ginsburg was eventually sworn in as an associate justice on August 10, 1993.

PART NINE

Civil Liberties and Civil Rights

48

ANTHONY LEWIS

From *Gideon's Trumpet*

Written in 1964, Gideon's Trumpet *is one of the most-assigned books in American government courses. The excerpt presented here touches on all the major points in the legal and personal story of Clarence Earl Gideon, the Florida prisoner whose case,* Gideon v. Wainwright *(1963), transformed American justice. As Gideon's story unfolds, notice the following elements in journalist Anthony Lewis's account of the landmark case that ensured all defendants legal counsel in state criminal cases:* in forma pauperis; writ of certiorari; Betts v. Brady; *stare decisis; Attorney Abe Fortas; Fourteenth Amendment; selective incorporation of the Bill of Rights; "a great marble temple"; "Oyez, oyez, oyez"; Justice Black; 9–0; court-appointed attorney Fred Turner; public defenders; not guilty; the Bay Harbor Poolroom.*

IN THE MORNING MAIL of January 8, 1962, the Supreme Court of the United States received a large envelope from Clarence Earl Gideon, prisoner No. 003826, Florida State Prison, P.O. Box 221, Raiford, Florida. Like all correspondence addressed to the Court generally rather than to any particular justice or Court employee, it went to a room at the top of the great marble steps so familiar to Washington tourists. There a secretary opened the envelope. As the return address had indicated, it was another petition by a prisoner without funds asking the Supreme Court to get him out of jail—another, in the secretary's eyes, because pleas from prisoners were so familiar a part of her work. . . .

. . . A federal statute permits persons to proceed in any federal court *in forma pauperis,* in the manner of a pauper, without following the usual forms or paying the regular costs. The only requirement in the statute is that the litigant "make affidavit that he is unable to pay such costs or give security therefor."

The Supreme Court's own rules show special concern for *in forma pauperis* cases. Rule 53 allows an impoverished person to file just one copy of a petition, instead of the forty ordinarily required, and states that the Court will make "due allowance" for technical errors so long as there is substantial compliance. In practice, the men in the Clerk's Office—a half dozen career employees, who effectively handle the Court's relations with the outside world—stretch even the rule of substantial compliance. Rule 53 also waives the general requirement that documents submitted to the Supreme Court be printed. It says that *in forma pauperis* applications should be typewritten "whenever possible," but in fact handwritten papers are accepted.

Gideon's were written in pencil. They were done in carefully formed printing, like a schoolboy's, on lined sheets evidently provided by the Florida prison. Printed at the top of each sheet, under the heading Correspondence Regulations, was a set of rules ("Only 2 letters each week . . . written on one side only . . . letters must be written in English . . . ") and the warning: MAIL WILL NOT BE DELIVERED WHICH DOES NOT CONFORM TO THESE RULES. Gideon's punctuation and spelling were full of surprises, but there was also a good deal of practiced, if archaic, legal jargon, such as "Comes now the petitioner . . . ".

Gideon was a fifty-one-year-old white man who had been in and out of prisons much of his life. He had served time for four previous felonies, and he bore the physical marks of a destitute life: a wrinkled, prematurely aged face, a voice and hands that trembled, a frail body, white hair. He had never been a professional criminal or a man of violence; he just could not seem to settle down to work, and so he had made his way by gambling and occasional thefts. Those who had known him, even the men who had arrested him and those who were now his jailers, considered Gideon a perfectly harmless human being, rather likeable, but one tossed aside by life. Anyone meeting him for the first time would be likely to regard him as the most wretched of men.

And yet a flame still burned in Clarence Earl Gideon. He had not given up caring about life or freedom; he had not lost his sense of injustice. Right now he had a passionate—some thought almost irrational—feeling of having been wronged by the State of Florida, and he had the determination to try to do something about it. Although the Clerk's Office could not be expected to remember him, this was in fact his second petition to the Supreme Court. The first had been returned for failure to include a pauper's affidavit, and the Clerk's Office had enclosed a copy of the rules and a sample affidavit to help him do better next time. Gideon persevered. . . .

Gideon's main submission was a five-page document entitled "Petition for a Writ of Certiorari Directed to the Supreme Court State of Florida." A writ of certiorari is a formal device to bring a case up to the Supreme Court from a lower court. In plain terms Gideon was asking the Supreme Court to hear his case.

What was his case? Gideon said he was serving a five-year term for "the crime of breaking and entering with the intent to commit a misdemeanor, to wit, petty larceny." He had been convicted of breaking into the Bay Harbor Poolroom in Panama City, Florida. Gideon said his conviction violated the due-process clause of the Fourteenth Amendment to the Constitution, which provides that "No state shall . . . deprive any person of life, liberty, or property, without due process of law." In what way had Gideon's trial or conviction assertedly lacked "due process of law"? For two of the petition's five pages it was impossible to tell. Then came this pregnant statement:

"When at the time of the petitioners trial he ask the lower court for the aid of counsel, the court refused this aid. Petitioner told the court that this Court made decision to the effect that all citizens tried for a felony crime should have aid of counsel. The lower court ignored this plea."

Five more times in the succeeding pages of his penciled petition Gideon spoke of the right to counsel. To try a poor man for a felony without giving him a lawyer, he said, was to deprive him of due process of law. There was only one trouble with the argument, and it was a problem Gideon did not mention. Just twenty years before, in the case of *Betts v. Brady*, the Supreme Court had rejected the contention that the due-process clause of the Fourteenth Amendment provided a flat guarantee of counsel in state criminal trials.

Betts v. Brady was a decision that surprised many persons when made and that had been a subject of dispute ever since. For a majority of six to three, Justice Owen J. Roberts said the Fourteenth Amendment provided no universal assurance of a lawyer's help in a state criminal trial. A lawyer was constitutionally required only if to be tried without one amounted to "a denial of fundamental fairness." . . .

Later cases had refined the rule of *Betts v. Brady*. To prove that he was denied "fundamental fairness" because he had no counsel, the poor man had to show that he was the victim of what the Court called "special circumstances." Those might be his own illiteracy, ignorance, youth, or mental illness, the complexity of the charge against him or the conduct of the prosecutor or judge at the trial. . . .

But Gideon did not claim any "special circumstances." His petition made not the slightest attempt to come within the sophisticated rule of *Betts v. Brady*. Indeed, there was nothing to indicate he had ever heard of the case or its principle. From the day he was tried Gideon had had one idea: That under the Constitution of the United States he, a poor man, was flatly entitled to have a lawyer provided to help in his defense. . . .

Gideon was wrong, of course. The United States Supreme Court had not said he was entitled to counsel; in *Betts v. Brady* and succeeding cases it had said quite the opposite. But that did not necessarily make Gideon's petition futile, for the Supreme Court never speaks with absolute finality when it interprets the Constitution. From time to time—with due solemnity, and after much searching of conscience—the Court has overruled its own decisions. Although he did not know it, Clarence Earl Gideon was calling for one of those great occasions in legal history. He was asking the Supreme Court to change its mind. . . .

Clarence Earl Gideon's petition for certiorari inevitably involved, for all the members of the Court, the most delicate factors of timing and strategy. The issue he presented—the right to counsel—was undeniably of first-rank importance, and it was an issue with which all of the justices were thoroughly familiar. . . .

. . . Professional comment on the Betts case, in the law reviews, had always been critical and was growing stronger, and within the Supreme Court several justices had urged its overruling. On the other hand, a majority might well draw back from so large a step. . . . At the conference of June 1, 1962, the Court had before it two jurisdictional statements asking the Court to hear appeals, twenty-six petitions for certiorari on the Appellate Docket, ten paupers' applications on the Miscellaneous Docket and three petitions for rehearing. . . .

The results of the deliberations at this conference were made known to the world shortly after ten A.M. the following Monday, June 4th, when a clerk posted on a bulletin board the mimeographed list of the Supreme Court's orders for that day. One order read:

Gideon v. Cochran 890 Misc.

The motion for leave to proceed *in forma pauperis* and the petition for writ of certiorari are granted. The case is transferred to the appellate docket. In addition to other questions presented by this case, counsel are requested to discuss the following in their briefs and oral argument:

"Should this Court's holding in *Betts v. Brady*, 316 U.S. 455, be reconsidered?" . . .

In the Circuit Court of Bay County, Florida, Clarence Earl Gideon had been unable to obtain counsel, but there was no doubt that he could have a lawyer in the Supreme Court of the United States now that it had agreed to hear his case. It is the unvarying practice of the Court to appoint a lawyer for any impoverished prisoner whose petition for review has been granted and who requests counsel.

Appointment by the Supreme Court to represent a poor man is a great honor. For the eminent practitioner who would never, otherwise, dip his fingers into the criminal law it can be an enriching experience, making him think again of the human dimensions of liberty. It may provide the first, sometimes the only, opportunity for a lawyer in some distant corner of the country to appear before the Supreme Court. It may also require great personal sacrifice. There is no monetary compensation of any kind—only the satisfaction of service. The Court pays the cost of the lawyer's transportation to Washington and home, and it prints the briefs, but there is no other provision for expenses, not even secretarial help or a hotel room. The lawyer donates that most valuable commodity, his own time. . . .

The next Monday the Court entered this order in the case of *Gideon v. Cochran:*

"The motion for appointment of counsel is granted and it is ordered that Abe Fortas, Esquire, of Washington, D.C., a member of the Bar of this Court be, and he is hereby, appointed to serve as counsel for petitioner in this case.

Abe Fortas is a high-powered example of that high-powered species, the Washington lawyer. He is the driving force in the firm of Arnold, Fortas and Porter. . . . A lawyer who has worked with him says: "Of all the men I have met he most knows why he is doing what he does. I don't like the s.o.b., but if I were in trouble I'd want him on my side. He's the most resourceful, the boldest, the most thorough lawyer I know." . . .

. . . "The real question," Fortas said, "was whether I should urge upon the Court the special-circumstances doctrine. As the record then stood, there was nothing to show that he had suffered from any special circumstances. . . .

When that transcript was read at Arnold, Fortas and Porter, there was no longer any question about the appropriateness of this case as the vehicle to challenge *Betts v. Brady.* Plainly Gideon was not mentally defective. The charge against him, and the proof, were not particularly complicated. The judge had tried to be fair; at least there was no overt bias in the courtroom. In short, Gideon had not suffered from any of the special circumstances that would have entitled him to a lawyer under the limited rule of *Betts v. Brady.* And yet it was altogether clear that a lawyer would have helped. The trial had been a rudimentary one, with a prosecution case that was fragmentary at best. Gideon had not made a single objection or pressed any of the favorable lines of defense. An Arnold, Fortas and Porter associate said later: "We knew as soon as we read that transcript that here was a perfect case to challenge the assumption of *Betts* that a man could have a fair trial without a lawyer. He did very well for a layman, he acted like a lawyer. But it was a pitiful effort really. He may have committed this crime, but it was never proved by the prosecution. A lawyer—not a great lawyer, just an ordinary, competent lawyer—could have made ashes of the case." . . .

As Abe Fortas began to think about the case in the summer of 1962, before Justice Frankfurter's retirement, it was clear to him that overruling *Betts v. Brady* would not come easily to Justice Frankfurter or others of his view. This was true not only because of their judicial philosophy in general, but because of the way they had applied it on specific matters. One of these was the question of precedent.

"In most matters it is more important that the applicable rule of law be settled than that it be settled right." Justice Brandeis thus succinctly stated the basic reason for *stare decisis*, the judicial doctrine of following precedents. . . .

Another issue . . . cut even deeper than *stare decisis*, and closer to Gideon's case. This was their attitude toward federalism—the independence of the states in our federal system of government. . . .

The Bill of Rights is the name collectively given to the first ten amendments to the Constitution, all proposed by the First Congress of the United States in 1789 and ratified in 1791. The first eight contain the guarantees of individual liberty with which we are so familiar: freedom of speech, press, religion and assembly; protection for the privacy of the home; assurance against double jeopardy and compulsory self-incrimination; the right to counsel and to trial by jury; freedom from cruel and unusual punishments. At the time of their adoption it was universally agreed that these eight amendments limited only the Federal Government and its processes. . . .

There matters stood until the Fourteenth Amendment became part of the Constitution in 1868. A product of the Civil War, it was specifically designed to prevent abuse of individuals by state governments. Section 1 provided: "No State shall make or enforce any law which shall abridge the privileges or immunities of citizens of the United States; nor shall any State deprive any person of life, liberty, or property, without due process of law; nor deny to any person within its jurisdiction the equal protection of the laws." Soon the claim was advanced that this section had been designed by its framers to *incorporate*, and apply to the states, all the provisions of the first eight amendments.

This theory of wholesale incorporation of the Bill of Rights has been adopted by one or more Supreme Court justices from time to time, but never a majority. . . .

But if wholesale incorporation has been rejected, the Supreme Court has used the Fourteenth Amendment to apply provisions of the Bill of Rights to the states *selectively*. The vehicle has been the clause assuring individuals due process of law. The Court has said that state denial of any right deemed "fundamental" by society amounts to a denial of due process and hence violates the Fourteenth Amendment. . . .

The difficult question has been which provisions of the first eight amendments to absorb. . . .

Grandiose is the word for the physical setting. The W.P.A. Guide to Washington* called the Supreme Court building a "great marble temple" which "by its august scale and mighty splendor seems to bear little relation to the functional purposes of government." Shortly before the justices moved into the building in 1935 from their old chamber across the street in the Capitol, Justice Stone wrote his sons "The place is almost bombastically pretentious, and thus it seems to me wholly inappropriate for a quiet group of old boys such as the Supreme Court." He told his friends that the justices would be "nine black beetles in the Temple of Karnak."

The visitor who climbs the marble steps and passes through the marble columns of the huge pseudo-classical facade finds himself in a cold, lofty hall, again all marble. Great bronze gates exclude him from the area of the building where the justices work in private—their offices, library and conference room. In the courtroom, which is always open to the public, the atmosphere of austere pomp is continued: there are more columns, an enormously high ceiling, red velvet hangings, friezes carved high on the walls. The ritual opening of each day's session adds to the feeling of awe. The Court Crier to the right of the bench smashes his gavel down sharply on a wooden block, everyone rises and the justices file in through the red draperies behind the bench and stand at their places as the Crier intones the traditional opening: "The honorable, the Chief Justice and the Associate Justices of the Supreme Court of the United States. Oyez, oyez, oyez. All persons having business before the honorable, the Supreme Court of the United States, are admonished to draw near and give their attention, for the Court is now sitting. God save the United States and this honorable Court."

But then, when an argument begins, all the trappings and ceremony seem to fade, and the scene takes on an extraordinary intimacy. In the most informal way, altogether without pomp, Court and counsel converse.

*The WPA, the Works Progress Administration, was started by President Franklin Roosevelt as part of the New Deal in 1935. WPA projects, designed to put people back to work during the Depression, included school and park building, theater and music performances, and map and guidebook writing.—EDS.

It is conversation—as direct, unpretentious and focused discussion as can be found anywhere in Washington. . . .

Chief Justice Warren, as is the custom, called the next case by reading aloud its full title: Number 155, Clarence Earl Gideon, petitioner, versus H. G. Cochran, Jr., director, Division of Corrections, State of Florida. . . .

The lawyer arguing a case stands at a small rostrum between the two counsel tables, facing the Chief Justice. The party that lost in the lower court goes first, and so the argument in *Gideon v. Cochran* was begun by Abe Fortas. As he stood, the Chief Justice gave him the customary greeting, "Mr. Fortas," and he made the customary opening: "Mr. Chief Justice, may it please the Court. . . . "

This case presents "a narrow question," Fortas said—the right to counsel—unencumbered by extraneous issues. . . .

"This record does not indicate that Clarence Earl Gideon was a person of low intelligence," Fortas said, "or that the judge was unfair to him. But to me this case shows the basic difficulty with Betts versus Brady. It shows that no man, however intelligent, can conduct his own defense adequately." . . .

"I believe we can confidently say that overruling Betts versus Brady at this time would be in accord with the opinion of those entitled to an opinion. That is not always true of great constitutional questions. . . . We may be comforted in this constitutional moment by the fact that what we are doing is a deliberate change after twenty years of experience—a change that has the overwhelming support of the bench, the bar and even of the states." . . .

It was only a few days later, as it happened, that *Gideon v. Wainwright* was decided. There was no prior notice; there never is. The Court gives out no advance press releases and tells no one what cases will be decided on a particular Monday, much less how they will be decided. Opinion days have a special quality. The Supreme Court is one of the last American appellate courts where decisions are announced orally. The justices, who divide on so many issues, disagree about this practice, too. Some regard it as a waste of time; others value it as an occasion for descending from the ivory tower, however briefly, and communicating with the live audience in the courtroom. . . .

Then, in the ascending order of seniority, it was Justice Black's turn. He looked at his wife, who was sitting in the box reserved for the justices' friends and families, and said: "I have for announcement the opinion and judgment of the Court in Number One fifty-five, Gideon against Wainwright."

Justice Black leaned forward and gave his words the emphasis and the drama of a great occasion. Speaking very directly to the audience in the courtroom, in an almost folksy way, he told about Clarence Earl Gideon's case and how it had reached the Supreme Court of the United States.

"It raised a fundamental question," Justice Black said, "the rightness of a case we decided twenty-one years ago, Betts against Brady. When we granted certiorari in this case, we asked the lawyers on both sides to argue to us whether we should reconsider that case. We do reconsider Betts and Brady, and we reach an opposite conclusion."

By now the page boys were passing out the opinions. There were four—by Justices Douglas, Clark and Harlan, in addition to the opinion of the Court. But none of the other three was a dissent. A quick look at the end of each showed that it concurred in the overruling of *Betts v. Brady*. On that central result, then, the Court was unanimous. . . .

That was the end of Clarence Earl Gideon's case in the Supreme Court of the United States. The opinions delivered that Monday were quickly circulated around the country by special legal services, then issued in pamphlets by the Government Printing Office. Eventually they appeared in the bound volumes of Supreme Court decisions, the United States Reports, to be cited as *Gideon v. Wainwright*, 372 U.S. 335 — meaning that the case could be found beginning on page 335 of the 372nd volume of the reports.

Justice Black, talking to a friend a few weeks after the decision, said quietly: "When *Betts v. Brady* was decided, I never thought I'd live to see it overruled." . . .

The reaction of the states to *Gideon v. Wainwright* was swift and constructive. The most dramatic response came from Florida, whose rural-dominated legislature had so long refused to relieve the problem of the unrepresented indigent such as Gideon. Shortly after the decision Governor Farris Bryant called on the legislature to enact a public-defender law. . . .

Resolution of the great constitutional question in *Gideon v. Wainwright* did not decide the fate of Clarence Earl Gideon. He was now entitled to a new trial, with a lawyer. Was he guilty of breaking into the Bay Harbor Poolroom? The verdict would not set any legal precedents, but there is significance in the human beings who make constitutional-law cases as well as in the law. And in this case there was the interesting question whether the legal assistance for which Gideon had fought so hard would make any difference to him. . . .

. . . After ascertaining that Gideon had no money to hire a lawyer of his own choice, Judge McCrary asked whether there was a local law-

yer whom Gideon would like to represent him. There was: W. Fred
Turner.

"For the record," Judge McCrary said quickly, "I am going to appoint
Mr. Fred Turner to represent this defendant, Clarence Earl Gideon." . . .

The jury went out at four-twenty P.M., after a colorless charge by the
judge including the instruction—requested by Turner—that the jury must
believe Gideon guilty "beyond a reasonable doubt" in order to convict
him. When a half-hour had passed with no verdict, the prosecutors were
less confident. At five twenty-five there was a knock on the door between
the courtroom and the jury room. The jurors filed in, and the court clerk
read their verdict, written on a form. It was *Not Guilty.*

"So say you all?" asked Judge McCrary, without a flicker of emotion.
The jurors nodded. . . .

After nearly two years in the state penitentiary Gideon was a free
man. . . . That night he would pay a last, triumphant visit to the Bay
Harbor Poolroom. Could someone let him have a few dollars? Someone
did.

"Do you feel like you accomplished something?" a newspaper reporter
asked.

"Well I did."

49

Miranda v. Arizona

*Chief Justice Earl Warren, the great liberal judge whose Court had already
handed down a number of landmark rulings—among them, Brown v.
Board of Education (1954) on desegregation in public schools, Mapp v.
Ohio (1961) on search and seizure by police, and Gideon v. Wainwright
(1963) on the right to counsel in criminal trials in state courts—wrote the
opinion in another major case, Miranda v. Arizona (1966). The case
involved Ernesto Miranda, who had been arrested for kidnapping and rape,
and who had been identified by the victim in a police lineup. Police officers
then interrogated Miranda, who subsequently signed a confession at the top
of which read that he had done so "with full knowledge of my legal rights,
understanding that any statement I make may be used against me." During
the trial, Miranda's confession was entered as evidence, and despite the
officer's testimony that Miranda had not been told of his right to have an
attorney present during interrogation, Miranda was found guilty. The Supreme Court of Arizona upheld the conviction on the grounds that Miranda*

*had not specifically requested an attorney. The case went to the U.S. Supreme
Court whose ruling resulted in what we now know as the "Miranda rights,"
a statement read to any suspect by law enforcement officers during an arrest.*

—————

Miranda v. Arizona
384 U.S. 436, 86 S.Ct. 1602 (1966)

Chief Justice WARREN delivered the opinion of the Court.

The cases before us raise questions which go to the roots of our concepts of American criminal jurisprudence: the restraints society must observe consistent with the Federal Constitution in prosecuting individuals for crime. More specifically, we deal with the admissibility of statements obtained from an individual who is subjected to custodial police interrogation and the necessity for procedures which assure that the individual is accorded his privilege under the Fifth Amendment to the Constitution not to be compelled to incriminate himself.

We dealt with certain phases of this problem recently in *Escobedo v. Illinois*, 378 U.S. 478 (1964). There, as in the four cases before us, law enforcement officials took the defendant into custody and interrogated him in a police station for the purpose of obtaining a confession. The police did not effectively advise him of his right to remain silent or of his right to consult with his attorney. Rather, they confronted him with an alleged accomplice who accused him of having perpetrated a murder. When the defendant denied the accusation and said "I didn't shoot Manuel, you did it," they handcuffed him and took him to an interrogation room. There, while handcuffed and standing, he was questioned for four hours until he confessed. During this interrogation, the police denied his request to speak to his attorney, and they prevented his retained attorney, who had come to the police station, from consulting with him. At his trial, the State, over his objection, introduced the confession against him. We held that the statements thus made were constitutionally inadmissible. . . . We adhere to the principles of *Escobedo* today.

Our holding will be spelled out with some specificity in the pages which follow but briefly stated it is this: the prosecution may not use statements, whether exculpatory or inculpatory, stemming from custodial interrogation of the defendant unless it demonstrates the use of procedural safeguards effective to secure the privilege against self-incrimination. By custodial interrogation, we mean questioning initiated by law enforcement officers after a person has been taken into custody or otherwise deprived of his freedom of action in any significant way. As for the procedural safeguards to be employed, unless other fully effective means are devised to inform accused persons of their right of silence and to assure a continuous opportunity to exercise it, the following measures are required. Prior to any questioning, the person must be warned that he has a right to remain silent, that any statement he does make may be used as evidence against him, and that he has a right to the presence of an attorney, either retained or appointed. The defendant may waive effectuation of these rights, provided the waiver is made voluntarily, knowingly and intelligently. If, however, he indicates in any manner and at any stage of the process that he wishes to consult with an attorney before speaking there can be no questioning. Likewise, if the individual is alone and indicates in any manner that he does not wish to be interrogated, the police may not question him. The mere fact that he may have answered some questions or volunteered some statements on his own does not deprive him of the right to refrain from answering any further inquiries until he has consulted with an attorney and thereafter consents to be questioned. . . .

The constitutional issue we decide in each of these cases [being decided today] is the admissibility of statements obtained from a defendant questioned while in custody or otherwise deprived of his freedom of action in any significant way. In each, the defendant was questioned by police officers, detectives, or a prosecuting attorney in a room in which he was cut off from the outside world. In none of these cases was the defendant given a full and effective warning of his rights at the outset of the interrogation process. In all the cases, the questioning elicited oral admissions, and in three of them, signed statements as well which were admitted at their trials. They all thus share salient features—incommunicado interrogation of individuals in a police-dominated atmosphere, resulting in self-incriminating statements without full warnings of constitutional rights. . . . We stress that the modern practice of in-custody interrogation is psychologically rather than physically oriented. . . . Interrogation still takes place in privacy. Privacy results in secrecy and this in turn results in a gap in our knowledge as to what in fact goes on in the interrogation rooms. A valuable source of information about present police practices, however, may be found in various police manuals and texts which document procedures employed with success in the past, and which recommend various other effective tactics. . . .

The officers are told by the manuals that the "principal psychological factor contributing to a successful interrogation is *privacy*—being alone with the person under interrogation." The efficacy of this tactic has been explained as follows:

"If at all practicable, the interrogation should take place in the investigator's office or at least in a room of his own choice. The subject should be deprived of every psychological advantage." . . .

After this psychological conditioning, however, the officer is told to point out the incriminating significance of the suspect's refusal to talk:

"Joe, you have a right to remain silent. That's your privilege and I'm the last person in the world who'll try to take it away from you. If that's the way you want to leave this, O.K. But let me ask you this. Suppose you were in my shoes and I were in yours and you called me in to ask me about this and I told you, 'I don't want to answer any of your questions.' You'd think I had something to hide, and you'd probably be right in thinking that. That's exactly what I'll have to think about you, and so will everybody else. So let's sit here and talk this whole thing over."

Few will persist in their initial refusal to talk, it is said, if this monologue is employed correctly.

In the event that the subject wishes to speak to a relative or an attorney, the following advice is tendered:

"[T]he interrogator should respond by suggesting that the subject first tell the truth to the interrogator himself rather than get anyone else involved in the matter. If the request is for an attorney, the interrogator may suggest that the subject save himself or his family the expense of any such professional service, particularly if he is innocent of the offense under investigation. The interrogator may also add, 'Joe, I'm only looking for the truth, and if you're telling the truth, that's it. You can handle this by yourself.'" . . .

Even without employing brutality, the "third degree" or the specific stratagems described above, the very fact of custodial interrogation exacts a heavy toll on individual liberty and trades on the weakness of individuals. . . .

. . . In each of the cases [heard by the court], the defendant was thrust into an unfamiliar atmosphere and run through menacing police interrogation procedures. The potentiality for compulsion is forcefully apparent, for example, in *Miranda*, where the indigent Mexican defendant was a seriously disturbed individual with pronounced sexual fantasies, and in *Stewart*, in which the defendant was an indigent Los Angeles Negro who had dropped out of school in the sixth grade. To be sure, the records do not evince overt physical coercion or patent psychological ploys. The fact remains that in none of these cases did the officers undertake to afford appropriate safeguards at the outset of the interrogation to insure that the statements were truly the product of free choice.

It is obvious that such an interrogation environment is created for no purpose other than to subjugate the individual to the will of his examiner. This atmosphere carries its own badge of intimidation. To be sure, this is not physical intimidation, but it is equally destructive of human dignity. The current practice of incommunicado interrogation is at odds with one of our Nation's most cherished principles—that the individual may not be compelled to incriminate himself. Unless adequate protective devices are employed to dispel the compulsion inherent in custodial surroundings, no statement obtained from the defendant can truly be the product of his free choice. . . .

To summarize, we hold that when an individual is taken into custody or otherwise deprived of his freedom by the authorities in any significant way and is subjected to questioning, the privilege against self-incrimination is jeopardized. Procedural safeguards must be employed to protect the privilege, and unless other fully effective means are adopted to notify the person of his right of silence and to assure that the exercise of the right will be scrupulously honored, the following measures are required. He must be warned prior to any questioning that he has the right to remain silent, that anything he says can be used against him in a court of law, that he has the right to the presence of an attorney, and that if he cannot afford an attorney one will be appointed for him prior to any questioning if he so desires. Opportunity to exercise these rights must be afforded to him throughout the interrogation. After such warnings have been given, and such opportunity afforded him, the individual may knowingly and intelligently waive these rights and agree to answer questions or make a statement. But unless and until such warnings and waiver are demonstrated by the prosecution at trial, no evidence obtained as a result of interrogation can be used against him. . . . We turn now to these facts to consider the application to these cases of the constitutional principles discussed above. . . .

On March 13, 1963, petitioner, Ernesto Miranda, was arrested at his home and taken in custody to a Phoenix police station. He was there identified by the complaining witness. The police then took him to "Interrogation Room No. 2" of the detective bureau. There he was questioned by two police officers. The officers admitted at trial that Miranda was not advised that he had a right to have an attorney present. Two hours later, the officers emerged from the interrogation room with a written confession signed by Miranda. At the top of the statement was a typed paragraph stating that the confession was made voluntarily, without threats or promises of immunity and "with full knowledge of my legal rights, understanding any statement I make may be used against me."

At his trial before a jury, the written confession was admitted into evidence over the objection of defense counsel, and the officers testified to the prior oral confession made by Miranda during the interrogation. Miranda was found guilty of kidnapping and rape. He was sentenced to 20 to 30 years' imprisonment on each count, the sentences to run concurrently. On appeal, the Supreme Court of Arizona held that Miranda's constitutional rights were not violated in obtaining the confession and affirmed the conviction. 98 Ariz. 18, 401 P. 2d 721. In reaching its decision, the court emphasized heavily the fact that Miranda did not specifically request counsel.

We reverse. From the testimony of the officers and by the admission of respondent, it is clear that Miranda was not in any way apprised of his right to consult with an attorney and to have one present during the interrogation, nor was his right not to be compelled to incriminate himself effectively protected in any other manner. Without these warnings the statements were inadmissible.

50

RICHARD POSNER

Security versus Civil Liberties

Living both in safety and in freedom have been values that the American people have always treasured. Contrary to the concerns of those who see security and civil liberties as an either/or proposition after the September 11, 2001 terrorist attacks in New York City and at the Pentagon, Richard Posner asks Americans to understand the importance of both values. Posner is a U.S. Court of Appeals judge as well as a law school lecturer. He knows all sides of this complex equation that will be weighed over and over in the coming years. Americans cannot view historical abridgements of civil liberties out of the context of their eras, he feels. Nor is the choice between security and civil liberties a fixed, clear cut one. Posner ends his piece with a suggestion that law enforcement take the opportunity created by September 11 to set new priorities for the best use of its time and effort.

———

IN THE WAKE OF THE September 11 terrorist attacks have come many proposals for tightening security; some measures to that end have already been taken. Civil libertarians are troubled. They fear that concerns about national security will lead to an erosion of civil liberties.

They offer historical examples of supposed overreactions to threats to national security. They treat our existing civil liberties—freedom of the press, protections of privacy and of the rights of criminal suspects, and the rest—as sacrosanct, insisting that the battle against international terrorism accommodate itself to them.

I consider this a profoundly mistaken approach to the question of balancing liberty and security. The basic mistake is the prioritizing of liberty. It is a mistake about law and a mistake about history. Let me begin with law. What we take to be our civil liberties—for example, immunity from arrest except upon probable cause to believe we've committed a crime, and from prosecution for violating a criminal statute enacted after we committed the act that violates it—were made legal rights by the Constitution and other enactments. The other enactments can be changed relatively easily, by amendatory legislation. Amending the Constitution is much more difficult. In recognition of this the Framers left most of the constitutional provisions that confer rights pretty vague. The courts have made them definite.

Concretely, the scope of these rights has been determined, through an interaction of constitutional text and subsequent judicial interpretation, by a weighing of competing interests. I'll call them the public-safety interest and the liberty interest. Neither, in my view, has priority. They are both important, and their relative importance changes from time to time and from situation to situation. The safer the nation feels, the more weight judges will be willing to give to the liberty interest. The greater the threat that an activity poses to the nation's safety, the stronger will the grounds seem for seeking to repress that activity, even at some cost to liberty. This fluid approach is only common sense.

Supreme Court Justice Robert Jackson gave it vivid expression many years ago when he said, in dissenting from a free-speech decision he thought doctrinaire, that the Bill of Rights should not be made into a suicide pact. It was not intended to be such, and the present contours of the rights that it confers, having been shaped far more by judicial interpretation than by the literal text (which doesn't define such critical terms as "due process of law" and "unreasonable" arrests and searches), are alterable in response to changing threats to national security.

If it is true, therefore, as it appears to be at this writing, that the events of September 11 have revealed the United States to be in much greater jeopardy from international terrorism than had previously been believed—have revealed it to be threatened by a diffuse, shadowy enemy that must be fought with police measures as well as military force—it stands to reason that our civil liberties will be curtailed. They *should* be curtailed, to the extent that the benefits in greater security outweigh the costs in reduced liberty. All that can reasonably be asked of the responsible legislative and judicial officials is that they weigh the costs as carefully as the benefits.

It will be argued that the lesson of history is that officials habitually exaggerate dangers to the nation's security. But the lesson of history is the opposite. It is because officials have repeatedly and disastrously underestimated these dangers that our history is as violent as it is. Consider such underestimated dangers as that of secession, which led to the Civil War, of a Japanese attack on the United States, which led to the disaster at Pearl Harbor; of Soviet espionage in the 1940s, which accelerated the Soviet Union's acquisition of nuclear weapons and emboldened Stalin to encourage North Korea's invasion of South Korea; of the installation of Soviet missiles in Cuba, which precipitated the Cuban missile crisis; of political assassinations and outbreaks of urban violence in the 1960s; of the Tet Offensive of 1968; of the Iranian revolution of 1979 and the subsequent taking of American diplomats as hostages; and, for that matter, of the events of September 11.

It is true that when we are surprised and hurt, we tend to overreact — but only with the benefit of hindsight can a reaction be separated into its proper and excess layers. In hindsight we know that interning Japanese-Americans did not shorten World War II. But was this known at the time? If not, shouldn't the Army have erred on the side of caution, as it did? Even today we cannot say with any assurance that Abraham Lincoln was wrong to suspend *habeas corpus* during the Civil War, as he did on several occasions, even though the Constitution is clear that only Congress can suspend this right. (Another of Lincoln's wartime measures, the Emancipation Proclamation, may also have been unconstitutional.) But Lincoln would have been wrong to cancel the 1864 presidential election, as some urged: by November of 1864 the North was close to victory, and canceling the election would have created a more dangerous precedent than the wartime suspension of *habeas corpus*. This last example shows that civil liberties remain part of the balance even in the most dangerous of times, and even though their relative weight must then be less.

Lincoln's unconstitutional acts during the Civil War show that even legality must sometimes be sacrificed for other values. We are a nation under law, but first we are a nation. I want to emphasize something else, however: the malleability of law, its pragmatic rather than dogmatic character. The law is not absolute, and the slogan "*Fiat iustitia ruat caelum*" ("Let justice be done though the heavens fall") is dangerous nonsense. The law is a human creation rather than a divine gift, a tool of government rather than a mandarin mystery. It is an instrument for promoting social welfare, and as the conditions essential to that welfare change, so must it change.

Civil libertarians today are missing something else—the opportunity to challenge other public-safety concerns that impair civil liberties. I have particularly in mind the war on drugs. The sale of illegal drugs is a "victimless" crime in the special but important sense that it is a consensual activity. Usually there is no complaining witness, so in order to bring the criminals to justice the police have to rely heavily on paid informants (often highly paid and often highly unsavory), undercover agents, wiretaps and other forms of electronic surveillance, elaborate sting operations, the infiltration of suspect organizations, random searches, the monitoring of airports and highways, the "profiling" of likely suspects on the basis of ethnic or racial identity or national origin, compulsory drug tests, and other intrusive methods that put pressure on civil liberties. The war on drugs has been a big flop; moreover, in light of what September 11 has taught us about the gravity of the terrorist threat to the United States, it becomes hard to take entirely seriously the threat to the nation that drug use is said to pose. Perhaps it is time to redirect law-enforcement resources from the investigation and apprehension of drug dealers to the investigation and apprehension of international terrorists. By doing so we may be able to minimize the net decrease in our civil liberties that the events of September 11 have made inevitable.

51

RICHARD KLUGER

From *Simple Justice*

No Supreme Court case has so changed the United States as did Brown v. Board of Education of Topeka, Kansas (1954). Volumes have been written on Brown and the aftermath of Brown, but the best place to start is with Richard Kluger's classic work. The selection here focuses on Earl Warren, the chief justice who wrote the landmark decision. The case that would reverse Plessy v. Ferguson (1896) and the "separate but equal" doctrine that the Court had upheld for half a century, was waiting to be heard when the death of Chief Justice Fred Vinson put Warren on the Court. Kluger quotes Justice Frankfurter as saying on hearing of Vinson's death, "This is the first indication I have ever had that there is a God."

Kluger explores the intricate process Warren faced in forging a majority, and eventually unanimity, for overturning "separate but equal." While those Americans who were born after Brown cannot remember a time when it was not the law of the land, Kluger takes us back to that thrilling moment of change.

IN THE TWO AND A HALF YEARS since they had last sat down to decide a major racial case, the Justices of the Supreme Court had not grown closer. Indeed, the philosophical and personal fissures in their ranks had widened since they had agreed—unanimously—to side with the Negro appellants in *Sweatt, McLaurin,* and *Henderson* in the spring of 1950. That had been a rare show of unanimity. By the 1952 Term, the Court was failing to reach a unanimous decision 81 percent of the time, nearly twice as high a percentage of disagreement as it had recorded a decade earlier. . . .

It was perhaps the most severely fractured Court in history—testament, on the face of it, to Vinson's failure as Chief Justice. Selected to lead the Court because of his skills as a conciliator, the low-key, mournful-visaged Kentuckian found that the issues before him were far different from, and far less readily negotiable than, the hard-edged problems he had faced as Franklin Roosevelt's ace economic troubleshooter and Harry Truman's Secretary of the Treasury and back-room confederate.

Fred Vinson's lot as Chief Justice . . . had not proven a happy one. . . .

What, then, could be expected of the deeply divided Vinson Court as it convened on the morning of December 13, 1952, to deliberate on the transcendent case of *Brown v. Board of Education*? The earlier racial cases—*Sweatt* and *McLaurin*—they had managed to cope with by chipping away at the edges of Jim Crow but avoiding the real question of *Plessy's* continued validity.* The Court could no longer dodge that question, though it might continue to stall in resolving it. Hovering over the Justices were all the repressive bugaboos of the Cold War era. The civil rights of Negroes and the civil liberties of political dissenters and criminal defendants were prone to be scrambled together in the public mind, and every

*The Supreme Court in *Plessy v. Ferguson* (1896) interpreted the equal protection clause of the Fourteenth Amendment to mean that the states could require separation of the races in public institutions if these institutions were equal (the "separate but equal doctrine"). From 1937 until 1954 the Court subjected "separate but equal" to increasingly rigorous scrutiny. In *Sweatt v. Painter* (1950) and *McLaurin v. Oklahoma State Regents* (1950), for example, the Court invalidated specific state racial segregationist practices in higher education on grounds that they did not permit truly equal access to black students. Yet, the Court had not overturned *Plessy.*—EDS.

malcontent was a sitting target for the red tar of anti-Americanism. No sector of the nation was less hospitable to both civil-liberties and civil-rights claimants than the segregating states of the South, and it was the South with which the Justices had primarily to deal in confronting *Brown*. . . .

And so they were divided. But given the gravity of the issue, they were willing to take their time to try to reconcile their differences. They clamped a precautionary lid on all their discussions of *Brown* as the year turned and Fred Vinson swore in Dwight David Eisenhower as the thirty-fourth President of the United States. The Justices seemed to make little headway toward resolving the problem, but they all knew that a close vote would likely be a disaster for Court and country alike. The problem of welding the disparate views into a single one was obviously complicated by the ambivalence afflicting the Court's presiding Justice. As spring came and the end of the Court's 1952 Term neared, Fred Vinson seemed to be in increasingly disagreeable and edgy spirits. Says one of the people at the Court closest to him then: "I got the distinct impression that he was distressed over the Court's inability to find a strong, unified position on such an important case."

What evidence there is suggests that those on or close to the Court thought it was about as severely divided as it could be at this stage of its deliberations. . . .

During the last week of the term in June, the law clerks of all the Justices met in an informal luncheon session and took a two-part poll. Each clerk was asked how he would vote in the school-segregation cases and how he thought his Justice would vote. According to one of their number, a man who later became a professor of law: "The clerks were almost unanimous for overruling *Plessy* and ordering desegregation, but, according to their impressions, the Court would have been closely divided if it had announced its decision at that time. Many of the clerks were only guessing at the positions of their respective Justices, but it appeared that a majority of the Justices would not have overruled *Plessy* but would have given some relief in some of the cases on the ground that the separate facilities were not in fact equal." . . .

All such bets on the alignment of the Court ended abruptly a few days later when the single most fateful judicial event of that long summer occurred. In his Washington hotel apartment, Fred M. Vinson died of a heart attack at 3:15 in the morning of September 8 [1953]. He was sixty-three.

All the members of the Court attended Vinson's burial in Louisa, Kentucky, his ancestral home. But not all the members of the Court grieved equally at his passing. And one at least did not grieve at all. Felix Frankfurter had not much admired Fred Vinson as judge or man. And he was certain that the Chief Justice had been the chief obstacle to the Court's prospects of reaching a humanitarian and judicially defensible settlement of the monumental segregation cases. In view of Vinson's passing just before the *Brown* reargument, Frankfurter remarked to a former clerk, "This is the first indication I have ever had that there is a God." . . . Fred Vinson was not yet cold in his grave when speculation rose well above a whisper as to whom President Eisenhower would pick to heal and lead the Supreme Court as it faced one of its most momentous decisions in the segregation cases. . . .

Dwight Eisenhower's principal contribution to the civil rights of Americans would prove to be his selection of Earl Warren as Chief Justice—a decision Eisenhower would later say had been a mistake. The President was on hand, at any rate, on Monday, October 5, when just after noon the clerk of the Supreme Court read aloud the commission of the President that began, "Know ye: That reposing special trust and confidence in the wisdom, uprightness and learning of Earl Warren of California, I do appoint him Chief Justice of the United States. . . ." Warren stood up at the clerk's desk to the side of the bench and read aloud his oath of office. At the end, Clerk Harold Willey said to him, "So help you God." Warren said, "So help me God." Then he stepped quickly behind the velour curtains and re-emerged a moment later through the opening in the center to take the presiding seat. His entire worthy career to that moment would be dwarfed by what followed. . . . At the reargument, Earl Warren had said very little. The Chief Justice had put no substantive questions to any of the attorneys. Nor is it likely that he had given any indication of his views to the other Justices before they convened at the Saturday-morning conference on December 12. But then, speaking first, he made his views unmistakable.

Nearly twenty years later, he would recall, "I don't remember having any great doubts about which way it should go. It seemed to me a comparatively simple case. Just look at the various decisions that had been eroding *Plessy* for so many years. They kept chipping away at it rather than ever really facing it head-on. If you looked back—to *Gaines*, to *Sweatt*, to some of the interstate-commerce cases—you saw that the doctrine of separate-but-equal had been so eroded that only the *fact* of segregation itself remained unconsidered. On the merits, the natural, the logical, and practically the only way the case could be decided was clear. The question was *how* the decision was to be reached."

At least two sets of notes survive from the Justices' 1953 conference discussion of the segregation cases—extensive ones by Justice Burton and exceedingly scratchy and cryptic ones by Justice Frankfurter. They agree on the Chief Justice's remarks. The cases had been well argued, in his judgment, Earl Warren told the conference, and the government had been very frank in both its written and its oral presentations. He said he had of course been giving much thought to the entire question since coming to the Court, and after studying the briefs and relevant history and hearing the arguments, he could not escape the feeling that the Court had "finally arrived" at the moment when it now had to determine whether segregation was allowable in the public schools. Without saying it in so many words, the new Chief Justice was declaring that the Court's policy of delay, favored by his predecessor, could no longer be permitted.

The more he had pondered the question, Warren said, the more he had come to the conclusion that the doctrine of separate-but-equal rested upon the concept of the inferiority of the colored race. He did not see how *Plessy* and its progeny could be sustained on any other theory—and if the Court were to choose to sustain them, "we must do it on that basis," he was recorded by Burton as saying. He was concerned, to be sure, about the necessity of overruling earlier decisions and lines of reasoning, but he had concluded that segregation of Negro schoolchildren had to be ended. The law, he said in words noted by Frankfurter, "cannot in 'this day and age' set them apart." The law could not say, Burton recorded the Chief as asserting, that Negroes were "not entitled to *exactly same* treatment of all others." To do so would go against the intentions of the three Civil War amendments.

Unless any of the other four Justices who had indicated a year earlier their readiness to overturn segregation—Black, Douglas, Burton, and Minton—had since changed his mind, Warren's opening remarks meant that a majority of the Court now stood ready to strike down the practice.

But to gain a narrow majority was no cause for exultation. A sharply divided Court, no matter which way it leaned, was an indecisive one, and for Warren to force a split decision out of it would have amounted to hardly more constructive leadership on this transcendent question than Fred Vinson had managed. The new Chief Justice wanted to unite the Court in *Brown.* . . .

He recognized that a number of Court precedents of long standing would be shattered in the process of overturning *Plessy,* and he regretted that necessity. It was the sort of reassuring medicine most welcomed by Burton and Minton, the least judicially and intellectually adventurous members of the Court.

He recognized that the Court's decision would have wide repercussions, varying in intensity from state to state, and that they would all therefore have to approach the matter in as tolerant and understanding a way as possible. Implicit in this was a call for flexibility in how the Court might frame its decree.

But overarching all these cushioning comments and a tribute to both his compassion as a man and his persuasive skills as a politician was the moral stance Earl Warren took at the outset of his remarks. Segregation, he had told his new colleagues, could be justified only by belief in the inferiority of the Negro; any of them who wished to perpetuate the practice, he implied, ought in candor to be willing to acknowledge as much. These were plain words, and they did not have to be hollered. They cut across all the legal theories that had been so endlessly aired and went straight to the human tissue at the core of the controversy. . . .

The Warren opinion was "finally approved" at the May 15 conference, Burton noted in his diary. The man from California had won the support of every member of the Court.

. . . Not long before the Court's decision in *Brown* was announced, Warren told *Ebony* magazine twenty years later, he had decided to spend a few days visiting Civil War monuments in Virginia. He went by automobile with a black chauffeur.

At the end of the first day, the Chief Justice's car pulled up at a hotel, where he had made arrangements to spend the night. Warren simply assumed that his chauffeur would stay somewhere else, presumably at a less expensive place. When the Chief Justice came out of his hotel the next morning to resume his tour, he soon figured out that the chauffeur had spent the night in the car. He asked the black man why.

"Well, Mr. Chief Justice," the chauffeur began, "I just couldn't find a place—couldn't find a place to . . . "

Warren was stricken by his own thoughtlessness in bringing an employee of his to a town where lodgings were not available to the man solely because of his color. "I was embarrassed, I was ashamed," Warren recalled. "We turned back immediately. . . . "

. . . In the press room on the ground floor, reporters filing in at the tail end of the morning were advised that May 17, 1954, looked like a quiet day at the Supreme Court of the United States.

All of the opinions of the Court were announced on Mondays in that era. The ritual was simple and unvarying. The Justices convened at noon. Lawyers seeking admission to the Supreme Court bar were presented to the Court by their sponsors, greeted briefly by the Chief Justice, and sworn in by the clerk of the Court. Then, in ascending order of seniority, the Justices with opinions to deliver read them aloud, every word usually, without much effort at dramaturgy. Concurrences and dissents were read after the majority opinion. And then the next case, and then the next. There was no applause; there were no catcalls. There were no television or newsreel cameras. There were no questions from the newsmen in the audience. There was no briefing session in the press room or the Justices' chambers after Court adjourned. There were no weekly press conferences. There were no appearances on *Meet the Press* the following Sunday. There were no press releases elaborating on what the Court had said or meant or done. The opinions themselves were all there was. . . .

Down in the press room, as the first three routine opinions were distributed, it looked, as predicted, like a very quiet day at the Court. But then, as Douglas finished up, Clerk of the Court Harold Willey dispatched a pneumatic message to Banning E. Whittington, the Court's dour press officer. Whittington slipped on his suit jacket, advised the press-room contingent, "Reading of the segregation decisions is about to begin in the courtroom," added as he headed out the door that the text of the opinion would be distributed in the press room afterward, and then led the scrambling reporters in a dash up the marble stairs.

"I have for announcement," said Earl Warren, "the judgment and opinion of the Court in No. 1 — *Oliver Brown et al. v. Board of Education of Topeka.*" It was 12:52 P.M. In the press room, the Associated Press wire carried the first word to the country: "Chief Justice Warren today began reading the Supreme Court's decision in the public school segregation cases. The court's ruling could not be determined immediately." The bells went off in every news room in America. The nation was listening.

It was Warren's first major opinion as Chief Justice. He read it, by all accounts, in a firm, clear, unemotional voice. If he had delivered no other opinion but this one, he would have won his place in American history.

Considering its magnitude, it was a short opinion. During its first part, no one hearing it could tell where it would come out. . . .

Without in any way becoming technical and rhetorical, Warren then proceeded to demonstrate the dynamic nature and adaptive genius of American constitutional law. . . . Having declared its essential value to the nation's civic health and vitality, he then argued for the central importance of education in the private life and aspirations of every individual. . . . That led finally to the critical question: "Does segregation of children in public schools solely on the basis of race . . . deprive the children of the minority group of equal educational opportunities?"

To this point, nearly two-thirds through the opinion, Warren had not tipped his hand. Now, in the next sentence, he showed it by answering that critical question: "We believe that it does." . . .

This finding flew directly in the face of *Plessy*. And here, finally, Warren collided with the 1896 decision. . . .

The balance of the Chief Justice's opinion consisted of just two paragraphs. The first began: "We conclude"—and here Warren departed from the printed text before him to insert the word "unanimously," which sent a sound of muffled astonishment eddying around the courtroom—"that in the field of public education the doctrine of 'separate but equal' has no place. Separate educational facilities are inherently unequal." The plaintiffs and others similarly situated—technically meaning Negro children within the segregated school districts under challenge—were therefore being deprived of the equal protection of the laws guaranteed by the Fourteenth Amendment.

The concluding paragraph of the opinion revealed Earl Warren's political adroitness both at compromise and at the ready use of the power of his office for ends he thought worthy. "Because these are class actions, because of the wide applicability of this decision, and because of the great variety of local conditions," he declared, "these cases present problems of considerable complexity. . . . In order that we may have the full assistance of the parties in formulating decrees," the Court was scheduling further argument for the term beginning the following fall. The attorneys general of the United States and all the states requiring or permitting segregation in public education were invited to participate. In a few strokes, Warren thus managed to (1) proclaim "the wide applicability" of the decision and make it plain that the Court had no intention of limiting its benefits to a handful of plaintiffs in a few outlying districts; (2) reassure the South that the Court understood the emotional wrench desegregation would cause and was therefore granting the region some time to get accustomed to the idea; and (3) invite the South to participate in the entombing of Jim Crow by joining the Court's efforts to fashion a temperate implementation decree—or to forfeit that chance by petulantly abstaining from the Court's further deliberations and thereby run the risk of having a harsh decree imposed upon it. It was such dexterous use of the power available to him and of the circumstances in which to exploit it that had established John Marshall as a judicial statesman and political tactician of the most formidable sort. The Court had not seen his like since. Earl Warren, in his first major opinion, moved now with that same sure purposefulness. . . .

It was 1:20 P.M. The wire services proclaimed the news to the nation.

Within the hour, the Voice of America would begin beaming word to the world in thirty-four languages: In the United States, schoolchildren could no longer be segregated by race. The law of the land no longer recognized a separate equality. No Americans were more equal than any other Americans.

52

ELLIS COSE

From *The Rage of a Privileged Class*

"Black rage" is a term that many Americans identify with radical groups and radical acts: the Black Panthers of the 1960s perhaps, or the 1992 Los Angeles riots. Author Ellis Cose believes that black rage is just as correctly applied to the feelings of many successful upper-middle-class African Americans today. He discusses the difficulties that highly accomplished black professionals encounter in their careers. Cose exposes the negative stereotypes that adversely affect all black youngsters. African Americans who have achieved success in a white-dominated society wonder why so many obstacles still stand in their way. Cose puts their feelings bluntly: "We are tired of waiting."

JOEL DREYFUSS IS editor of *PC Magazine*, the nation's number-one publication for owners of personal computers. He is a man with a reputation for speaking his mind—a reputation that has not always served him well, in his view. His journalistic talent has landed him a host of impressive positions: reporter for the *Washington Post*, managing editor for *Black Enterprise*, New York bureau chief for *USA Today*, Tokyo bureau chief for *Fortune*. But an unfair perception of him as a racial rabble-rouser, he believes, has limited his success.

Dreyfuss, whose parents are Haitian, grew up shuttling among Haiti, Africa, and the United States, in the tow of a father attached to the United Nations. He settled in New York, more or less for good, at the age of fifteen. When he enrolled in school, he found that despite his elite prior education, he was immediately "put in a class of basketball players." Shortly thereafter, he took an exam, and a counselor told him in apparent astonishment that he had done extremely well. He found the counselor's attitude bewildering, since until then he had always been expected to do well.

The reassessment of his abilities gained him entry to an honors program whose ethnic composition left him puzzled. In a school that was roughly 90 percent black and Hispanic, the honors program was 90 percent white. To all appearances, they had "created a school for white kids within the school." He entered City College of New York in the mid-1960s, before the open admissions policy, at a time when CCNY was considered one of the best schools in the city. The white students often asked him how he had managed to get in.

With the country caught up in the throes of rebellion, his interest in journalism blossomed. In addition to seeing journalism as force for social reform, he saw it as something of a family tradition; his father, years previously, had been publisher of an English-language paper in Haiti. Dreyfuss got a job at the Associated Press, where one evening, while helping to edit copy, he saw an AP story about three black men who had been accused of a crime. He questioned whether the racial identification was appropriate, citing AP policy prohibiting the use of racial designations unless they were somehow relevant to the story. The editor, in explaining why race was in fact relevant, asked, "Aren't blacks arming themselves?"

For Dreyfuss, the incident was a turning point. "I became outraged and I remained outraged for about twenty years." At that moment he realized that when faced with issues involving race, normally intelligent whites could become "irrational" and "would violate their own rules." He found support for that view a short while later when he went to work for the New York *Post*, where an editor involved in his hiring remarked, "Your people are trying to destroy us."

Such foolishness from editors fueled Dreyfuss's desire to seek change. He pushed his bosses to hire more blacks and criticized coverage he considered particularly witless. Not surprisingly, some found his outspokenness annoying, but his journalistic gifts nonetheless made him a standout. At the *Washington Post*, where Dreyfuss worked after leaving New York, an editor was so impressed that she took him aside to tell him that he was doing a terrific job. "How do we get more blacks as good as Joel Dreyfuss?"she asked. Dreyfuss found the remark offensive, and told her as much.

As a result of his propensity for rubbing editors the wrong way with his racial consciousness-raising, Dreyfuss was denied a coveted transfer to the California bureau. Ben Bradlee, then executive editor, acknowledged his abilities but told him that he was "a pain in the ass." The Bradlee kiss-off became a footnote in the Bradlee legend and cemented Dreyfuss's reputation as a troublemaker. For years after he left the *Post*, recalls Drey-fuss, the widely reported Bradlee remark "made it difficult for me to get a job in the mainstream media."

He tried, often at great emotional price, to live his reputation down, and learned to keep his mouth shut even when events outraged him. Yet nearly two decades after that episode, "there are still a lot of people who view me as a dangerous subversive. . . . I've been told that."

For all the pain the 1960s and '70s evoke, Dreyfuss believes they allowed certain black journalists to thrive. In those days, race was major story, and blacks were essential to covering that story. As a result, a fair number of black journalists became stars. Now he believes the best report-ing jobs are largely going to whites, a reflection not only of the changing nature of the news, but of the fact that most news organizations still have "a limited imagination when it comes to black people." . . .

The perceptual gulf, the contradictory findings, the flowering of re-sentments, the frequency of racial incidents—all lead toward an inescapable conclusion: racial discord will be with us for a long, long time. This "next generation," for all its idealism, openmindedness, and willingness to embrace equality and racial integration, is not even close to mastering the art of how to get along.

Once upon a time, of course, many thought that racial division would soon be a thing of the past, that the next generation, or perhaps the one after that, would achieve harmony where their parents could not. Martin Luther King's may have been the most famous 1960s dream, but he was not dreaming alone. Yet as today's young people come of age, many one time idealists are beginning to think that such dreams are rooted in little more than fantasy. . . .

. . . For even if racial peace is maintained, the web of stereotypes is left untouched, and those stereotypes, as already noted, are particularly destructive to blacks. They not only encourage whites to treat blacks as inferiors but also encourage blacks to see themselves as many whites would have them be.

These stereotypes spew forth from every segment of popular culture and constantly find new life in black and nonblack communities across America. Rap music, for instance, routinely portrays black men as "niggaz" and "gangstas" and black women as "bitches" and "hoes." A host of black comedians follow suit, depicting a jive-talking, foul-mouthed, illiterate stud who defines the essence of "black" for many young people. Attach-ment to this stereotype is so powerful that African Americans who choose not to personify it are often accused by other blacks of trying not to be black. Yet those with a sense of history know that the stud image did not spring from the black community but originated with whites searching for signs that blacks were intellectually inferior and morally degenerate—and therefore suitable for use as slaves. Today, through television, movies, and the innumerable interracial encounters that occur in an increasingly integrated society, blacks and whites in effect conspire to determine whether, and to what extent, the stereotypes can change—in short, what the place of African Americans will be.

Unlike recent immigrants, who are relatively free to define their own place in U.S. society, African Americans are more constrained. John Ogbu, an anthropologist at the University of California, Berkeley, who has studied immigrant and indigenous minorities, writes: "Immigrants generally regard themselves as foreigners, 'strangers' who come to America with expectation of certain economic, political, and social benefits. While anticipating that such benefits might come at some cost . . . the immigrants did not measure their success or failure primarily by the standards of white Americans, but by the standards of their homelands. Such minorities, at least during the first generation, did not internalize the effects of such discrimination, of cultural and intellectual denigration. . . . Even when they were restricted to manual labor, they did not consider themselves to be occupying the lowest rung of the American status system, and partly because they did not fully understand that system, and partly because they did not consider themselves as belonging to it, they saw their situation as temporary."

In contrast, Ogbu says, he has observed black and Mexican-American parents encouraging their children to do well in school while unconsciously passing on another, more demoralizing message: "Unavoidably, such minority parents discuss their problems with 'the system,' with their relatives, friends, and neighbors in the presence of their children. The result . . . is that such children become increasingly disillusioned about their ability to succeed in adult life through the mainstream strategy of schooling." The only way some of these kids feel they can succeed, he concludes, is to "repudiate their black peers, black identity, and black cultural frames of reference."

Few people of any race, of course, have the strength, desire, imagination, or appetite to abandon ideas they have been taught all their lives. Thus, Americans of all races continue to see each other through a prism of distorting colors, and to struggle with the problem of prejudice.

Joe Feagin, a University of Florida sociologist who has extensively studied the black middle class . . . believes that even the subtle displays of prejudice blacks today are more likely to encounter can be devastating. "Today white discrimination less often involves blatant door-slamming exclusion, for many blacks have been allowed in the corporate door. Modern discrimination more often takes the form of tracking, limiting or blocking promotions, harassment, and other differential treatment signalling disrespect." The result, writes Feagin, is the "restriction, isolation, and ostracism of middle-class blacks who have penetrated the traditionally white workplace" but who find that they are not part of the same networks that "link together not only white co-workers but also white supervisors and, in some situations, clients." And this more subtle form of exclusion produces repressed rage, inner conflict, and a deep sense of dissatisfaction: "Most middle-class blacks are caught between the desire for the American dream imbedded deeply in their consciousness and a recognition that the dream is white at its heart."

Derrick Bell, civil rights activist and legal scholar, has a perspective that is even more dispiriting than Feagin's. In *Faces at the Bottom of the Well,* Bell argues that America's brand of racism is permanent and that we must set aside the hopelessly idealistic notion that time and generosity will cure it. Since whites will never recognize blacks as equals, blacks must steel themselves for never-ending struggle: "African Americans must confront and conquer the otherwise deadening reality of our permanent subordinate status. Only in this way can we prevent ourselves from being dragged down by society's racial hostility."

In an epilogue titled "Beyond Despair," Bell invokes inspirational images from the time of slavery, when black people, "knowing there was no escape, no way out, . . . nonetheless continued to engage themselves. To carve out a humanity. To defy the murder of selfhood. Their lives were brutally shackled, certainly—but *not without meaning despite being imprisoned.*" He argues that blacks today, in accepting their tragic fate, should take a cue from the slaves who managed to beat the odds "with absolutely nothing to help—save imagination, will, and unbelievable strength and courage."

In outlining his controversial thesis Bell throws out a challenge, declaring that the proposition of permanent inequality "will be easier to reject than refute." That is certainly true, for it is a prediction about the future, which by definition has not yet arrived and hence is impossible to describe with certainty. But that does not make Bell's gloomy prognosis correct. . . .

As Mary Curtis, the *New York Times* editor, observed, "You always want to think things are going to be better." Moreover, there is plenty of time to reach the conclusion that America is beyond redemption, and there is little harm in proceeding as if it were not. As [former New Jersey senator] Bill Bradley says, "I respect Derrick Bell a lot, but I'm not at that point yet where I think this is a permanent destructive aspect of American culture that can never be overcome. . . . This is not something that you're going to give up on because it's difficult."

Bradley, of course, is white, and as he quickly acknowledges, he has not walked in Bell's shoes or fought at the same barricades as Bell: "He's battled . . . a lot longer and in a much different way than I." Yet the argument for rejecting Bell's dismal prognosis is not dependent on color, or even on experience, but on a simple and hard-nosed approach to reality: if people are destined to spend their lives in struggle, they might as well struggle against a real evil instead of fighting merely to maintain their humanity in the face of continued disrespect. Moreover, maintaining one's humanity—indeed, even drawing strength from being battered by prejudice and rejection—need not be dependent on giving up hope that America can be better. As associate Judge Ricardo Urbina of the Superior Court of the District of Columbia observes, "The very things that made me vulnerable made me strong." . . .

At Cambridge University, in an address published in the *New York Times Magazine* in 1965, James Baldwin said, "I remember when the ex-Attorney General Mr. Robert Kennedy said it was conceivable that in forty years in America we might have a Negro President. That sounded like a very emancipated statement to white people. They were not in Harlem when this statement was first heard. They did not hear the laughter and the bitterness and scorn with which this statement was greeted. From the point of view of the man in the Harlem barber shop, Bobby Kennedy only got here yesterday and now he is already on his way to the Presidency. We were here for four hundred years and now he tells us that maybe in forty years, if you are good, we may let you become President."

If there was one sentiment that consistently came through in interview after interview with very successful black people in all walks of life, it can be summed up in one phrase: *We are tired of waiting.*

53

BRON TAYLOR

From *Affirmative Action at Work*

*Former California lifeguard-turned-social science researcher Bron Taylor
studied the controversial and timely issue of affirmative action by interviewing
employees of the California State Department of Parks and Recreation.
His case study reveals the diversity of views on affirmative action in the
nation today, from hostility and fear to acceptance and advocacy. Taylor
opens with a look at the classical liberal philosophy that underlies the nation's
political system. The American values of individualism, the common good,
equal opportunity, and distributive justice all figure in the debate over
affirmative action. Using quotes and data from the parks department workers,
Taylor offers readers a perspective on affirmative action from the people who
are affected by the program on a daily basis.*

DURING A BREAK in a training session on affirmative action,
a frustrated middle-management woman asked, "What can I do to deal
with this good-old-boy network? I just can't seem to break into the
group." Moments later, a crusty, middle-aged, white, male manager, in a
parody of the woman's statement, joked to several other white men,
"What are we going to do about the good-old-boy system? Nothing,
that's what we are going to do about it. We like it just the way it is!"
Appreciative chuckles greeted his candid affirmation of the good-old-boy
network.

A young, white, male employee, who believes he almost did not get
into the California State Parks Department because of affirmative action
and who has seen friends excluded because of such programs, said emphatically, "If I ever get to a place where I have any power over hiring, I will
do everything I can to thwart this affirmative action bullshit."

A black male rank-and-file employee argued that if it were not for
affirmative action the department would still be "lily white."

A middle-aged, white, woman manager said that at one time she was
a clerical worker, without self-esteem or hopes of advancement, but
affirmative action opened up possibilities for her. Some years ago, her
supervisor, a white man supportive of affirmative action efforts to promote
women and nonwhite men, told her that she had potential and encouraged

her to go back to school to get management training. Now, although she has some negative feelings about affirmative action, she sees it as a lesser evil to the loss of talent and dignity that occurs when women and nonwhite men are not encouraged to develop their potential.

The above stories are about employees of the California State Department of Parks and Recreation, which provided the setting for this research into attitudes toward affirmative action. The stories illustrate how deeply held are the feelings that surround this issue. Affirmative action has become a critical locus of the tensions between racial groups and between men and women. From the workplace to legal, political, and philosophical literature, impassioned debates rage about the prudence and morality of affirmative action law and policy. Some politicians defend affirmative action, while others attempt to dismantle it. Given the origins of affirmative action in the civil rights movement, the rallying cry of opponents to affirmative action is a cry heavy with irony: affirmative action betrays civil rights; instead of producing new freedoms and opportunities, it has produced the tyranny of "quotas" and "reverse discrimination."

What is this phenomenon that has produced such intensity of feeling? To what extent has there been a backlash against affirmative action? Why has this backlash been so vehement in some quarters? What are the stakes involved in the affirmative action issue that contribute to the intensity of reaction, especially among those who feel directly affected by it? . . .

Given its grounding in the premises of philosophical Liberalism, affirmative action provides analysts a window through which to examine many of the critical moral dimensions of contemporary Liberal culture. Affirmative action is controversial largely because it represents and reflects several of the most critical unresolved moral conflicts within the Liberal culture. Some of these conflicts are grounded in the unresolved problems of nineteenth-century Liberalism. When I speak of Liberalism, I include conservatives, liberals, and libertarians of contemporary parlance. Despite real differences, all share the key tenets of Liberalism: rights naturally inhere in the individual, people are self-interested, acquisitive consumers (usually unchangeably so); these people compete in political and economic markets; and this competition produces at best a good society, or at least the best society people are capable of producing, and this society generally is characterized by economic growth and political freedom.

Affirmative action proponents and opponents often rest their arguments on one of Liberalism's central principles, namely, its version of distributive justice: the idea that preferred jobs and rewards ought to be distributed according to talents and qualifications (or *merit*) in a social context characterized by equality of opportunity. (This conception of distributive justice is often referred to by the terms *equal opportunity* or the *merit principle*.) It is possible, however, if the social context were to be characterized by increasing social scarcity, declining overall opportunities, and increasing conflicts over affirmative action policies, that the equal opportunity principle itself could be called into question. Since the equal opportunity version of the distributive justice principle is itself a fundamental premise of the Liberal culture, such a reevaluation could raise questions about the legitimacy of that culture. . . .

Whether or not the struggle over the principle of equal opportunity causes a reevaluation of the premises and legitimacy of Liberal market society, the affirmative action conflict remains important. It remains important because it presents the various options from contending Liberal perspectives concerning which principles of distribution—principles at issue since the beginning of Enlightenment thought—are morally warranted.

Since the Enlightenment, the type of individualism the equal opportunity principle represents has been a critical issue. Some libertarians and conservatives argue that this principle does not do enough to protect individuals, while some left-leaning liberals and leftists believe this principle is excessively individualistic and erodes the basis for social solidarity and cooperation.

Underlying this debate is the perpetual tension between concern for the general interest and concern for individual rights. Liberal thought has asserted both that individual, acquisitive, self-interested behavior is justified by its efficiency in producing collective benefits (promoting the commonweal) and that individuals have some inviolable rights against the group. But Liberalism has had problems in resolving tensions and conflicts between social welfare goals and individual rights.

Related to the basic issue here of how individual rights ought to be balanced against the commonweal are a variety of additional problems, the resolution (or nonresolution) of which will be important to the future of liberal culture. Some of these problems include: How to define terms such as *rights* and *justice, liberty* and *equality* and how these concepts are related to each other. Are individual rights absolute? Can criteria of economic efficiency be squared with principles of freedom and justice? Which of the premises from the variant forms of Liberal theory (for example, premises about human nature, market dynamics, and economic growth) hold up under analysis?

To summarize, the controversy over affirmative action is a battleground for conflicting values. The outcome of this battle may be decisive in determining which principles of distributive justice will guide public policy in America. The affirmative action controversy asks the perennial question regarding the proper relationship between individual rights and social justice, on the one hand, and the various principles of distributive justice that provide competing perspectives on rights and justice, on the other. The affirmative action issue, grounded as it is in the currently dominant equal opportunity principle, provides an appropriate window through which to examine moral meaning in our culture. . . .

My employment with the California State Department of Parks and Recreation provided the opportunity for participant observation. For fifteen years, I was a state park ocean lifeguard—a position with duties similar to that of a park ranger, with the additional responsibility for ocean rescue. I was involved in curriculum development and training for the department's affirmative action programs and with the Equal Opportunity Employment Committee (a statewide advisory committee responsible for advising and assisting the department in the creation, implementation, and evaluation of its affirmative action policies) between 1984 and 1988. The observations made while participating in these activities provided the first source of data on the views held by individuals from the various social groups.

My employment with the department gave me access to the chief of the Human Rights Office and to the director of the department, both of whom consented to the research. I entered into a research agreement with the department, which granted access for the interviews and the survey, in return for a report interpreting the results. . . .

There is an ongoing struggle within the Parks Department over the nature of its affirmative action program. The struggle is over whether or not the program should attempt to ensure "pure equal opportunity" and the hiring of the "best qualified" or to give preference to target groups. Evidence of this struggle is found throughout the department, beginning with the various ways people define the nature and purpose of affirmative action. Some say affirmative action means equal opportunity, others emphasize that affirmative action is a remedial process that temporarily gives preference to women and nonwhite men in an attempt to increase their numbers in the work force.

Periodically, there are discussions within the department's affirmative action bureaucracy (the Human Rights Office, the Equal Opportunity Employment Committee, recruiters, counselors, and so on) over whether personnel procedures should aim for equal opportunity or practice preferential treatment. For example, drafts of revised hiring procedures have been circulated that suggest adding preference points to the scores of underrepresented candidates based on the extent to which the individual's ethnic group is underrepresented. This idea was rejected, not because the pure equal opportunity version of affirmative action prevailed, but because preference could be extended without explicitly adding preference points. Many felt that preference points would engender too much controversy and hostility; some felt that preferences in general detract from the true purpose of the department's affirmative action efforts, namely, promoting pure equal opportunity. But extending preference remains the idea behind the efforts to improve the representation of women and nonwhite men in the department's work force.

Other evidence illustrating the ongoing struggle over the soul of the department's affirmative action program can be seen in the resistance by some in the department's affirmative action bureaucracy to using any language in training and in documents that characterizes affirmative action as preferential treatment. Even though certain aspects of the department's affirmative action program are clearly preferential to women and nonwhite men, some within the affirmative action bureaucracy constantly maintain that the department's program is designed to ensure that in each case the best qualified are hired and promoted. Many in the department, however, view such assertions as disingenuous. Even some employees who originally supported the department's affirmative action programs now resent them. They were told the programs were meant to ensure equal opportunity, but they became disillusioned when they saw that the programs really promoted preferential treatment.

The lack of clarity about the nature of the department's program produces tensions all the way down the line. In one recent example, a hiring panel (made up of a white man, a Hispanic woman, and a Hispanic man) scored all three white male candidates above a Hispanic candidate (the scores ranged from 79 to 93 out of 100 possible points). The Hispanic male panel member wanted to hire the Hispanic candidate, but the Hispanic female was adamantly opposed and demanded that she be shown where it is written in department policy that one minimally qualified may be hired over the best qualified. Her perspective prevailed in the discussion, and the panel recommended hiring the white male candidate. The white male district superintendent, however, although conceding that the three white male candidates were better qualified, said that meeting the minimum qualifications was sufficient. He overruled the panel's recommendation and selected the Hispanic candidate because this would help meet the department's hiring goals for Hispanics. The point to note here is that even among members of this panel, which was formed to include nonwhites sympathetic to affirmative action, there was controversy and uncertainty over what affirmative action is really supposed to be.

The overruling of the panel's recommendation was greeted by great anger among white male staff members. These men complained that such policies destroy one's incentive to improve one's skills, and also erodes the incentive of affirmative action candidates, because skill is not the criterion for hiring or advancement. Such sentiments are common in the department.

There is much hostility toward affirmative action in the Parks Department. Some of the anger toward the department's affirmative action program is related to the struggle over the nature of the program. Some employees are angered by what they think is dishonesty in how the program is presented. They say they have been told that the program promotes equal opportunity and hiring the best qualified person regardless of gender or ethnicity; however, the more they experience it, the more they realize that the program provides very strong preferences, and they feel they have little if any chance for jobs and promotions. Some are angry because they oppose preferences on principle.

Others are angry and disillusioned by the dishonesty itself. For example, one white male employee endorsed goals and hiring the "just qualified" over the "best qualified" as a way to extend a "helping hand" to people who need it, but he complained that sometimes the department is not honest. He said the department tells its people to hire the "best qualified," but they really mean hire the "adequately" qualified in order to meet the department's affirmative action hiring goals. I know of several disillusioned individuals who stopped actively supporting the program when they concluded that the department was misrepresenting its program. . . .

Some of the most outspoken critics of affirmative action believe their careers have been significantly, even irreparably, harmed by affirmative action. These people are sometimes so emotional in discussing affirmative action that their analysis of the situation becomes irrational and prone to exaggeration. For example, I heard more than once that affirmative action "quotas" preclude white men from being hired or promoted. I even heard this kind of sentiment in an entry-level ranger trainee class, where over half of the trainees were white men. In another example, a young white man came nervously into the interview carrying several sheets of notes on all the reasons affirmative action was wrong. His hands shook slightly as he explained that he did not want to forget anything. Obviously, the issue was of intense personal concern for him.

At one training session, a manager expressed a common management complaint, that the effort to meet affirmative action goals detracts from the more central mission of the department: maintaining park facilities, serving visitors, and protecting resources. A maintenance manager stated that it seemed to him that his mission (maintaining parks) and the trainer's mission (promoting affirmative action) were incompatible. When the trainer did not immediately respond to this statement, another maintenance manager, visibly agitated and with his arms folded across his chest, said loudly: "You better answer that, Buster." The intensity of this response was especially out of place given the sedate context of the training session. This manager deeply resented affirmative action. . . .

Closely related to hostility is fear about the negative consequences of affirmative action on one's career. More specifically, some interviewees feared that if their attitudes about affirmative action were to become known by certain people in the department, their careers could be ruined.

For example, one black employee, while declining to be interviewed, complained that people were always challenging him about affirmative action. He thought that a great deal of the hostility in his workplace toward affirmative action was also directed against him. He said he just tried to do his job, to do his best, but his co-workers were watching him, waiting for him to make a mistake. He was very suspicious and worried about "paybacks" if he were to state his views: "I really don't want to deal with it, it's not worth the risk, there are always repercussions. They [management] might call me in later and say 'Well, you said this. . . .'" When I explained the procedures I was using to insure confidentiality, he said he would talk to his attorney and get back to me. He never did. Another black employee, a woman, expressed fear that, with all the pressure on supervisors to meet affirmative action goals, the program had become too much of a "numbers game." She said that she was afraid of a "backlash" in response to this pressure, and she wished the pressure would be eased. . . .

In another example, I learned after conducting interviews in one location that a group of white men thought my research was not really for academic purposes but was part of a sting operation to discover who in the department was prejudiced. Some of these workers did not believe that the sampling was, in fact, random. One white man needed assurances that no personal characteristics would be mentioned in the research write-up that might make it possible for someone to identify him. He was afraid that if his views were to become known he would lose his chance for promotion. . . .

. . . [B]y far the most commonly heard complaint about how affirmative action harms the department is that it reduces the quality of employees. Many complained that affirmative action has become a "numbers game," where qualifications are less important than meeting "quotas." Even some supporters of affirmative action thought there is too much pressure to meet hiring goals; they feared that this has led (or may lead) to the hiring of unqualified workers. Some added that affirmative action hinders individual initiative and creates a work environment where excellence is not rewarded. Still others complained that affirmative action has a negative impact on the morale of white and nonwhite employees alike, by limiting the opportunities of white men, on the one hand, while calling into question the competence of women and nonwhite men, on the other hand. Concern about the quality of employees seemed to be expressed most often by white men but was shared by many women and nonwhite men. . . .

Probably the rationale most commonly offered by those promoting affirmative action within the Parks Department is that affirmative action promotes equal opportunity. This is seen in the language used by supporters. For example, although most supporters do not think that the best qualified are being hired because of the pressure on supervisors to meet numerical hiring goals, they still use language expressing the idea that—after carefully recruiting women and nonwhites and after carefully scrutinizing the personnel procedures for bias—hiring panels should hire the best qualified.

Others argued that while the ultimate ideal is pure equal opportunity and merit hiring, affirmative action is a remedial process in response to the lack of equal opportunity. The implication, seldom stated explicitly, is that sometimes the ideal has to be temporarily set aside in order to promote long-term the ideal of equal opportunity. But nevertheless, in spite of the compromising of the ideal, the rationale for affirmative action remains, ultimately, the ideal of pure equal opportunity.

Some respondents argued that affirmative action is true to equal opportunity by asserting that it is needed for women and nonwhite men to "get their foot in the door," or to be given a "fair chance" or "equal consideration" for jobs and promotions. Several respondents pointed out that, before affirmative action, many job classifications in the department were not open to women and nonwhites, and they argued that without affirmative action such persons would never have been considered seriously. Several women asserted that white men still controlled the department and that without the pressure from affirmative action, these men would not give up their monopoly of power. Thus, those expressing sentiments in favor of affirmative action justified their views in terms of the principle of equal opportunity and believed that, at least in the long term, affirmative action promotes this principle. . . .

The strongest advocates of affirmative action were those who most self-consciously rejected the individualism of the equal opportunity principle. These strong advocates were also the most likely to endorse compensatory rationales for affirmative action. But others who expressed strong individualistic sentiments (such as individual initiative, competitiveness, and merit hiring) qualified these sentiments with strong expressions of concern for their group or for the society as a whole. Greater proportions of each ethnic and gender group were more concerned about the good of the group or the whole society than endorsed compensatory rationales for affirmative action: Of those interviewed, 15–33 percent of white men, 70 percent of blacks, 60 percent of Hispanics, 67 percent of native Americans, and 75 percent of white women gave at least qualified support for affirmative action—support grounded, at least in part, in group-sensitive sentiments.

This analysis, combined with the earlier analysis of arguments against affirmative action, suggests that there is a relationship between relative individualism in one's overall moral outlook and one's view about affirmative action: the more individualistic one's moral predisposition, the more likely one is to oppose affirmative action; the more concern one expresses for the group or the social whole, the more likely one is to approve of affirmative action. . . .

Several respondents (three white men, one white woman, one black man) pointed out that social stability has been threatened by the exclusion of nonwhites from the mainstream of society and argued that affirmative action benefits society by promoting social stability and preventing revolution. Others suggested that affirmative action benefits society by promoting harmony among ethnic and gender groups or by developing the talents of individuals from groups whose talents were usually previously denied to society. Sometimes this argument was put in the form of affirmative action success stories—how a woman or nonwhite was doing a terrific job after getting a position she or he probably would not have received in the absence of affirmative action.

Another argument asserts that affirmative action integrates the work force and thereby provides better public service. For example, an ex–inner city black employee suggested that a black ranger would have greater success in dealing with black visitors than a white ranger, whom some black visitors may distrust.

Another argument, especially among managers, concerns demographic changes that are increasing the proportion of nonwhites in California.

The concern is that since groups such as Hispanics and blacks traditionally have not been exposed to or employed in nonurban parks, they may not fully appreciate their value. This argument continues that if the mission of the Parks Department is to succeed, the growing nonwhite constituency must be integrated into the department and visit the parks so that members of these groups will appreciate and support the department's mission. The overall moral argument is that affirmative action benefits both the department and society as a whole (assuming that preservation of parklands is important to society), by insuring continued public support for parks in times of great demographic change. . . .

54

PGA Tour, Inc. v. Casey Martin

The passage of the Americans with Disabilities Act in 1990 brought about vast changes in the U.S., in ways large and small, from handicapped ramps to hiring practices. In some cases, the ADA has led to court cases in which the disabled person and the organization asked to accommodate that person's needs have sought legal clarification on what the act really requires. One of the most interesting cases to come out of the ADA is the request by handicapped golfer Casey Martin that he be allowed to ride in a golf cart at professional golf tournaments. The excerpt from the 2001 Supreme Court decision begins with an instructive lesson on qualifying for the PGA tour and adhering to the Rules of Golf. Next, Martin's disability is explained. The case had earlier moved through the federal District Court and the U.S. Court of Appeals where issues such as PGA golf courses as private clubs and the playing areas as public accommodations were decided. The Supreme Court then addresses the issue of whether a professional golfer is protected by the ADA. Would allowing Martin to use a cart "fundamentally alter the nature" of a PGA tournament?

PGA Tour, Inc. v. Casey Martin
532 U.S.____(2001)

Justice STEVENS delivered the opinion of the Court.

This case raises two questions concerning the application of the Americans with Disabilities Act of 1990 to a gifted athlete: first, whether the Act protects access to professional golf tournaments by a qualified entrant with a disability; and second, whether a disabled contestant may be denied the use of a golf cart because it would "fundamentally alter the nature" of the tournaments to allow him to ride when all other contestants must walk. . . .

Petitioner PGA TOUR, Inc., a non-profit entity formed in 1968, sponsors and cosponsors professional golf tournaments conducted on three annual tours. About 200 golfers participate in the PGA TOUR; about 170 in the NIKE TOUR; and about 100 in the SENIOR PGA TOUR. PGA TOUR and NIKE TOUR tournaments typically are 4-day events, played on courses leased and operated by petitioner. The entire field usually competes in two 18-hole rounds played on Thursday and Friday; those who survive the "cut" play on Saturday and Sunday and receive prize money in amounts determined by their aggregate scores for all four rounds. The revenues generated by television, admissions, concessions, and contributions from cosponsors amount to about $300 million a year, much of which is distributed in prize money.

There are various ways of gaining entry into particular tours. For example, a player who wins three NIKE TOUR events in the same year, or is among the top-15 money winners on that tour, earns the right to play in the PGA TOUR. Additionally, a golfer may obtain a spot in an official tournament through successfully competing in "open" qualifying rounds, which are conducted the week before each tournament. Most participants, however, earn playing privileges in the PGA TOUR or NIKE TOUR by way of a three-stage qualifying tournament known as the "Q-School."

Any member of the public may enter the Q-School by paying a $3,000 entry fee and submitting two letters of reference from, among others, PGA TOUR or NIKE TOUR members. The $3,000 entry fee covers the players' greens fees and the cost of golf carts, which are permitted during the first two stages, but which have been prohibited during the third stage since 1997. Each year, over a thousand contestants compete in the first stage, which consists of four 18-hole rounds at different locations. Approximately half of them make it to the second stage, which also includes 72 holes. Around 168 players survive the second stage and advance to the final one, where they compete over 108 holes. Of those finalists, about a fourth qualify for membership in the PGA TOUR, and the rest gain membership in the NIKE TOUR. The significance of making it into either tour is illuminated by the fact that there are about 25 million golfers in the country.

Three sets of rules govern competition in tour events. First, the "Rules of Golf," jointly written by the United States Golf Association (USGA) and the Royal and Ancient Golf Club of Scotland, apply to the game as it is played, not only by millions of amateurs on public courses and in private country clubs throughout the United States and worldwide, but also by the professionals in the tournaments conducted by petitioner, the USGA, the Ladies' Professional Golf Association, and the Senior Women's Golf Association. Those rules do not prohibit the use of golf carts at any time.

Second, the "Conditions of Competition and Local Rules," often described as the "hard card," apply specifically to petitioner's professional tours. The hard cards for the PGA TOUR and NIKE TOUR require players to walk the golf course during tournaments, but not during open qualifying rounds. On the SENIOR PGA TOUR, which is limited to golfers age 50 and older, the contestants may use golf carts. Most seniors, however, prefer to walk.

Third, "Notices to Competitors" are issued for particular tournaments and cover conditions for that specific event. Such a notice may, for example, explain how the Rules of Golf should be applied to a particular water hazard or man-made obstruction. It might also authorize the use of carts to speed up play when there is an unusual distance between one green and the next tee.

The basic Rules of Golf, the hard cards, and the weekly notices apply equally to all players in tour competitions. As one of petitioner's witnesses explained with reference to "the Masters Tournament, which is golf at its very highest level . . . the key is to have everyone tee off on the first hole under exactly the same conditions and all of them be tested over that 72-hole event under the conditions that exist during those four days of the event."

Casey Martin is a talented golfer. As an amateur, he won 17 Oregon Golf Association junior events before he was 15, and won the state championship as a high school senior. He played on the Stanford University golf team that won the 1994 National Collegiate Athletic Association (NCAA) championship. As a professional, Martin qualified for the NIKE TOUR in 1998 and 1999, and based on his 1999 performance, qualified for the PGA TOUR in 2000. In the 1999 season, he entered 24 events, made the cut 13 times, and had 6 top-10 finishes, coming in second twice and third once.

Martin is also an individual with a disability as defined in the Americans with Disabilities Act of 1990 (ADA or Act). Since birth he has been afflicted with Klippel-Trenaunay-Weber Syndrome, a degenerative circulatory disorder that obstructs the flow of blood from his right leg back to his heart. The disease is progressive; it causes severe pain and has atrophied his right leg. During the latter part of his college career, because of the progress of the disease, Martin could no longer walk an 18-hole golf course. Walking not only caused him pain, fatigue, and anxiety, but also created a significant risk of hemorrhaging, developing blood clots, and fracturing his tibia so badly that an amputation might be required. For these reasons, Stanford made written requests to the Pacific 10 Conference and the NCAA to waive for Martin their rules requiring players to walk and carry their own clubs. The requests were granted.

When Martin turned pro and entered petitioner's Q-School, the hard card permitted him to use a cart during his successful progress through the first two stages. He made a request, supported by detailed medical records, for permission to use a golf cart during the third stage. Petitioner refused to review those records or to waive its walking rule for the third stage. Martin therefore filed this action. A preliminary injunction entered by the District Court made it possible for him to use a cart in the final stage of the Q-School and as a competitor in the NIKE TOUR and PGA TOUR. . . .

Congress enacted the ADA in 1990 to remedy widespread discrimination against disabled individuals. In studying the need for such legislation, Congress found that "historically, society has tended to isolate and segregate individuals with disabilities, and, despite some improvements, such forms of discrimination against individuals with disabilities continue to be a serious and pervasive social problem." ("[D]iscrimination against individuals with disabilities persists in such critical areas as employment, housing, public accommodations, education, transportation, communication, recreation, institutionalization, health services, voting, and access to public services"). Congress noted that the many forms such discrimination takes include "outright intentional exclusion" as well as the "failure to make modifications to existing facilities and practices." After thoroughly investigating the problem, Congress concluded that there was a "compelling need" for a "clear and comprehensive national mandate" to eliminate discrimination against disabled individuals, and to integrate them "into the economic and social mainstream of American life." . . .

. . . To effectuate its sweeping purpose, the ADA forbids discrimination against disabled individuals in major areas of public life, among them employment (Title I of the Act), public services (Title II), and public accommodations (Title III). At issue now, as a threshold matter, is the applicability of Title III to petitioner's golf tours and qualifying rounds, in particular to petitioner's treatment of a qualified disabled golfer wishing to compete in those events.

Title III of the ADA prescribes, as a "[g]eneral rule":

"No individual shall be discriminated against on the basis of disability in the full and equal enjoyment of the goods, services, facilities, privileges, advantages, or accommodations of any place of public accommodation by any person who owns, leases (or leases to), or operates a place of public accommodation."

The phrase "public accommodation" is defined in terms of 12 extensive categories, which the legislative history indicates "should be construed liberally" to afford people with disabilities "equal access" to the wide variety of establishments available to the nondisabled.

It seems apparent, from both the general rule and the comprehensive definition of "public accommodation," that petitioner's golf tours and their qualifying rounds fit comfortably within the coverage of Title III, and Martin within its protection. The events occur on "golf course[s]," a type of place specifically identified by the Act as a public accommodation. In addition, at all relevant times, petitioner "leases" and "operates" golf courses to conduct its Q-School and tours. As a lessor and operator of golf courses, then, petitioner must not discriminate against any "individual" in the "full and equal enjoyment of the goods, services, facilities, privileges, advantages, or accommodations" of those courses. Certainly, among the "privileges" offered by petitioner on the courses are those of competing in the Q-School and playing in the tours; indeed, the former is a privilege for which thousands of individuals from the general public pay, and the latter is one for which they vie. Martin, of course, is one of those individuals. It would therefore appear that Title III of the ADA, by its plain terms, prohibits petitioner from denying Martin equal access to its tours on the basis of his disability. . . .

Petitioner argues otherwise. To be clear about its position, it does not assert (as it did in the District Court) that it is a private club altogether exempt from Title III's coverage. In fact, petitioner admits that its tournaments are conducted at places of public accommodation. Nor does petitioner contend (as it did in both the District Court and the Court of Appeals) that the competitors' area "behind the ropes" is not a public accommodation, notwithstanding the status of the rest of the golf course. Rather, petitioner reframes the coverage issue by arguing that the competing golfers are not members of the class protected by Title III of the ADA. . . .

As we have noted, 42 USC § 12182(a) sets forth Title III's general rule prohibiting public accommodations from discriminating against individuals because of their disabilities. The question whether petitioner has violated that rule depends on a proper construction of the term "discrimination," which is defined by Title III to include: "a failure to make reasonable modifications in policies, practices, or procedures, when such modifications are necessary to afford such goods, services, facilities, privileges, advantages, or accommodations to individuals with disabilities, *unless the entity can demonstrate that making such modifications would fundamentally alter the nature* of such goods, services, facilities, privileges, advantages, or accommodations."

Petitioner does not contest that a golf cart is a reasonable modification that is necessary if Martin is to play in its tournaments. Martin's claim thus differs from one that might be asserted by players with less serious afflictions that make walking the course uncomfortable or difficult, but not beyond their capacity. In such cases, an accommodation might be reasonable but not necessary. In this case, however, the narrow dispute is whether allowing Martin to use a golf cart, despite the walking requirement that applies to the PGA TOUR, the NIKE TOUR, and the third stage of the Q-School, is a modification that would "fundamentally alter the nature" of those events. . . .

As an initial matter, we observe that the use of carts is not itself inconsistent with the fundamental character of the game of golf. From early on, the essence of the game has been shot-making—using clubs to cause a ball to progress from the teeing ground to a hole some distance away with as few strokes as possible. That essential aspect of the game is still reflected in the very first of the Rules of Golf, which declares: "The Game of Golf consists in playing a ball from the *teeing ground* into the hole by a *stroke* or successive strokes in accordance with the rules." Over the years, there have been many changes in the players' equipment, in golf course design, in the Rules of Golf, and in the method of transporting clubs from hole to hole. Originally, so few clubs were used that each player could carry them without a bag. Then came golf bags, caddies, carts that were pulled by hand, and eventually motorized carts that carried players as well as clubs. "Golf carts started appearing with increasing regularity on American golf courses in the 1950s. Today they are everywhere. And they are encouraged. For one thing, they often speed up play, and for another, they are great revenue producers." There is nothing in the Rules of Golf that either forbids the use of carts, or penalizes a player for using a cart. That set of rules, as we have observed, is widely accepted in both the amateur and professional golf world as the rules of the game. The walking rule that is contained in petitioner's hard cards, based on an optional condition buried in an appendix to the Rules of Golf, is not an essential attribute of the game itself. . . .

The force of petitioner's argument is, first of all, mitigated by the fact that golf is a game in which it is impossible to guarantee that all competitors will play under exactly the same conditions or that an individual's ability will be the sole determinant of the outcome. For example, changes in the weather may produce harder greens and more head winds for the tournament leader than for his closest pursuers. A lucky bounce may save a shot or two. Whether such happenstance events are more or less probable than the likelihood that a golfer afflicted with Klippel-Trenaunay-Weber Syndrome would one day qualify for the NIKE TOUR and PGA TOUR, they at least demonstrate that pure chance may have a greater impact on the outcome of elite golf tournaments than the fatigue resulting from the enforcement of the walking rule.

Further, the factual basis of petitioner's argument is undermined by the District Court's finding that the fatigue from walking during one of petitioner's 4-day tournaments cannot be deemed significant. The District Court credited the testimony of a professor in physiology and expert on fatigue, who calculated the calories expended in walking a golf course (about five miles) to be approximately 500 calories—"nutritionally . . . less than a Big Mac." What is more, that energy is expended over a 5-hour period, during which golfers have numerous intervals for rest and refreshment. In fact, the expert concluded, because golf is a low intensity activity, fatigue from the game is primarily a psychological phenomenon in which stress and motivation are the key ingredients. And even under conditions of severe heat and humidity, the critical factor in fatigue is fluid loss rather than exercise from walking.

Moreover, when given the option of using a cart, the majority of golfers in petitioner's tournaments have chosen to walk, often to relieve stress or for other strategic reasons. As NIKE TOUR member Eric Johnson testified, walking allows him to keep in rhythm, stay warmer when it is chilly, and develop a better sense of the elements and the course than riding a cart.

Even if we accept the factual predicate for petitioner's argument—that the walking rule is "outcome affecting" because fatigue may adversely affect performance—its legal position is fatally flawed. Petitioner's refusal to consider Martin's personal circumstances in deciding whether to accommodate his disability runs counter to the clear language and purpose of the ADA. As previously stated, the ADA was enacted to eliminate discrimination against "individuals" with disabilities, and to that end Title III of the Act requires without exception that any "policies, practices, or procedures" of a public accommodation be reasonably modified for disabled "individuals" as necessary to afford access unless doing so would fundamentally alter what is offered. To comply with this command, an individualized inquiry must be made to determine whether a specific modification for a particular person's disability would be reasonable under the circumstances as well as necessary for that person, and yet at the same time not work a fundamental alteration. ("[W]hether a person has a disability under the ADA is an individualized inquiry").

To be sure, the waiver of an essential rule of competition for anyone would fundamentally alter the nature of petitioner's tournaments. As we have demonstrated, however, the walking rule is at best peripheral to the nature of petitioner's athletic events, and thus it might be waived in individual cases without working a fundamental alteration. Therefore, petitioner's claim that all the substantive rules for its "highest-level" competitions are sacrosanct and cannot be modified under any circumstances is effectively a contention that it is exempt from Title III's reasonable modification requirement. But that provision carves out no exemption for elite athletics, and given Title III's coverage not only of places of "exhibition or entertainment" but also of "golf course[s]," its application to petitioner's tournaments cannot be said to be unintended or unexpected. Even if it were, "the fact that a statute can be applied in situations not expressly anticipated by Congress does not demonstrate ambiguity. It demonstrates breadth."

Under the ADA's basic requirement that the need of a disabled person be evaluated on an individual basis, we have no doubt that allowing Martin to use a golf cart would not fundamentally alter the nature of petitioner's tournaments. As we have discussed, the purpose of the walking rule is to subject players to fatigue, which in turn may influence the outcome of tournaments. Even if the rule does serve that purpose, it is an uncontested finding of the District Court that Martin "easily endures greater fatigue even with a cart than his able-bodied competitors do by walking." The purpose of the walking rule is therefore not compromised in the slightest by allowing Martin to use a cart. A modification that provides an exception to a peripheral tournament rule without impairing its purpose cannot be said to "fundamentally alter" the tournament. What it can be said to do, on the other hand, is to allow Martin the chance to qualify for and compete in the athletic events petitioner offers to those members of the public who have the skill and desire to enter. That is exactly what the ADA requires. As a result, Martin's request for a waiver of the walking rule should have been granted.

The ADA admittedly imposes some administrative burdens on the operators of places of public accommodation that could be avoided by strictly adhering to general rules and policies that are entirely fair with respect to the able-bodied but that may indiscriminately preclude access by qualified persons with disabilities. But surely, in a case of this kind, Congress intended that an entity like the PGA not only give individualized attention to the handful of requests that it might receive from talented but disabled athletes for a modification or waiver of a rule to allow them access to the competition, but also carefully weigh the purpose, as well as the letter, of the rule before determining that no accommodation would be tolerable.

The judgment of the Court of Appeals is
Affirmed.

55

COLTON CAMPBELL
ROGER DAVIDSON

Gay and Lesbian Issues in the Congressional Arena

Scholars Colton Campbell and Roger Davidson trace the recent history of gay rights proposals before the Congress, from the issue's invisibility to hostility as well as acceptance—and all shades of opinion in between. The authors cite particular problems that Congress has considered, including employment discrimination, same-sex marriages, and AIDS funding. Central to the gay community's efforts to win congressional support for its proposals has been its ability to organize effectively; activist groups have worked tirelessly to be heard and to win legislators' support. Lobbying for small changes, Campbell and Davidson point out, may be the only realistic course of action.

SINCE THE 1969 Stonewall riots in Greenwich Village,* gay and lesbian rights have moved from the margins of the political agenda to a more central place in the congressional arena. Gays and lesbians have the potential resources to wield influence, if not necessarily to prevail, on Capitol Hill. These resources include a substantial popular base spread throughout the country but with concentrations in major coastal cities and other urban areas. In recent years "lavender" voters have begun to

---

*The Stonewall riot occurred on July 28, 1969 in New York City's Greenwich Village. When police began a raid on the Stonewall Inn gay bar that night, as they had done before, the guests decided to resist arrest and fights erupted. Trouble continued for many nights. Stonewall is considered by many as the start of the modern gay rights movement.—EDS.

acquire electoral clout both through votes and through financial contributions, which are key ingredients in gaining access to lawmakers and key congressional staffers.

Lesbian and gay political organizations, like the Human Rights Campaign and the Log Cabin Republicans, have become increasingly professional in both organization and political strategy. They are engaging in more "inside" lobbying, channeling their efforts through formal decision-making processes within Congress. This includes testifying before committees or subcommittees to place their groups' positions on the record and communicating directly with legislators or their personal staff to promote points of view. Additionally, these groups have adopted newer forms of persuasion such as mounting computer-based campaigns to mobilize grassroots support or bundling campaign contributions for gay candidates. In many instances, lesbian and gay political organizations have begun to employ major public relations efforts in the press to shape public and congressional opinion on gay rights. Yet for every victory these groups attain, subsequent defeats follow, and lesbian and gay groups spend much of their time attempting to block antigay legislation.

Early Politics: The Congressional Closet

For many years sexual politics were limited to those very few lawmakers (and staff members) who were themselves "out of the closet" or who signed on to the issue because of concentrated populations within their electoral districts. Before 1998, no openly gay candidate had ever been elected to Congress. The first openly gay members to serve in the House—Representatives Barney Frank (D-Mass.) and Jim Kolbe (R-Ariz.), and former Representatives Robert Baumann (R-Md.), Steve Gunderson (R-Wis.), and Gerry E. Studds (D-Mass.)—either revealed their sexual orientation or were outed after they were in office. In 1998, Tammy Baldwin (D-Wis.), a lesbian, became the first person whose sexuality was well known before her initial election. Her campaign slogan: "A Different Kind of Candidate."

During the 1950s gays and lesbians were victimized by concerns over national security and moral purity. In committee hearings legislators routinely questioned federal officials about the employment of homosexuals, characterizing them as moral perverts who endangered national security. The Senate Subcommittee on Investigations recommended that all homosexual civil servants be dismissed as security risks. Many senators denounced "the false premise that what a Government employee did outside of the office on his own time, particularly if his actions did not involve his fellow employees or his work, was his own business."

The Senate offered two closely linked arguments to support its conclusion that homosexuals should be excluded from government service. The first pertained to the "character" of homosexuals, who allegedly lacked "emotional stability" and whose "moral fiber" had been weakened by sexual indulgence. The second rationale for exclusion concerned the danger of blackmail which, legislators contended, made homosexuals likely candidates for treasonable activity.

As for gay rights, which entered the agenda in the 1970s Congress traditionally turned aside these issues, under whatever rubric. Measures addressing such issues tended to be introduced toward the end of a legislative session to enable Congress to adjourn without passing or even debating them, or in nonelection years to minimize expected voter backlash. At most, Congress engaged in symbolic acts—that is, expressing an attitude of toleration but endorsing no proactive policies, or prescribing policy goals but neglecting to follow through on them. Throughout the 1980s, for example, lawmakers funded AIDS research, education, and prevention activities before they addressed the policy questions involved in trying to slow the spread of the epidemic. This afforded members an opportunity to "do something" about AIDS while avoiding the politically profound policy issues surrounding the disease. Such congressional ambivalence toward gay activism reflected the general public's attitudes on the subject; as gay rights became more widely and openly discussed, the issue moved toward a more conspicuous place in the legislative agenda.

Contemporary lawmakers appear more sympathetic to gay rights than were their predecessors. At least anecdotally, this more benign environment provides more access points and potential influence for gay and lesbian organizations. Whereas in the past such groups would achieve influence on Capitol Hill by discreetly lobbying lawmakers with whom they enjoyed proven working relationships and the strongest constituency support, today they can "find an audience or get a meeting almost when or wherever," according to the political director of the Human Rights Campaign, the nation's largest gay rights group. And yet the measurable level of progay support in Congress has declined over the past ten years, partly the result of a backlash created by opposition groups such as the Christian Coalition.

As gay rights issues and family-oriented lobbies began to be subsumed within the agenda of the civil rights movement, Congress started to address and frame various types of law reform initiatives, entailing a variety of strategies. Stated differently, as the gay movement matured, a branch of the movement increasingly created formal organizations, centered its attention on national institutions, and sought legal policy reform rather than cultural transformation. Among these issues have been AIDS research; amending existing antidiscriminatory legislation to include "sexual orientation" grounds to protect jobs and housing or to demand various social benefits currently restricted to heterosexual couples or families; and reforming legislative definitions of "spouse" to embrace gay and lesbian identity within state welfare and tax statutes.

Of the ten thousand or so bills introduced in each Congress, a preliminary search of the workload for the years 1975 through 1999 (94th through 105th Congresses) suggests that in each Congress only a very small proportion of bills—ten to twenty—dealt overtly with gay rights. Hardly any were reported out of committee, much less debated on the floor. These measures were generally worded for or against gay rights: prohibiting employment or housing discrimination on the basis of affectional or sexual orientation; providing civil claims for homosexuals; guaranteeing confidential AIDS testing; setting policy toward gays in the military; prohibiting the use of funds to promote or encourage homosexuality; and allowing organizations to exclude homosexuals from certain programs and activities involving juveniles.

The preponderance of these bills appear to have been antigay in intent. Haider-Markel's 1997 examination of congressional votes on gay-related issues from the 95th to 104th Congresses reveals similar findings. Other bills would have had an impact, even though they did not overtly deal with gay concerns. These included: proposals for amending the Legal Services Corporation Act to prohibit expenditure of funds to defend or protect homosexuality and gay rights; repealing sections of the Immigration and Nationality Act that restrict homosexuals; and substituting the terms "homosexuality or heterosexuality" for "sexual orientation" as a category for which data are collected on crimes based on prejudice. In some cases, concurrent resolutions have been introduced expressing the sense of Congress that homosexual acts and the individuals who advocate such "conduct" should be denied special consideration or protected status under law.

The first federal legislation to protect homosexuals from discrimination was not introduced until 1974. Comparable measures have been introduced in every subsequent legislative session, but only one has been reported out of committee. A limited version of the bill, applying only to employment discrimination, finally reached the Senate floor for a vote in 1996.

After the Republican takeover of the House and Senate, a conservative-led movement fueled by antipathy toward gay rights twice in 1996 set back the legislative gains of gay rights supporters. By a lopsided margin, Congress overwhelmingly approved the Defense of Marriage Act, which defines the institution of marriage, authorizes states to disregard same-sex marriages licensed in other states, and denies spousal benefits to same-sex couples. Within a whisper of victory the Senate also narrowly defeated a bill to prohibit antidiscrimination in the workplace, the Employment NonDiscrimination Act (ENDA), which would have prevented employers from firing people based on their sexual orientation. Yet the bill was crafted to appeal to moderates: it intended to exempt the military, small businesses, and nonprofit religious organizations. . . .

In the waning days of the 104th Congress, the House of Representatives was filled with heated exchanges over an unusual foray into an area of domestic law typically left to the states. The issue of same-sex marriages came to Capitol Hill following a legal challenge in Hawaii brought by three gay couples suing for the right to marry. Fearing that the actions of one state ruling could effectively force all states to recognize same-sex marriages—if, for example, gay couples from Hawaii later moved to another jurisdiction—Republicans crafted the DOMA legislation to thwart that possibility.

Sponsors said Congress needed to act because gay activists were mounting a legal campaign to force recognition of same-sex marriages against the popular will. Representative James F. Sensenbrenner Jr. (R-Wis.) charged that the issue was less about gay rights than about gay rights groups' "scheming to manipulate the full faith and credit clause to achieve through the judicial system what they cannot obtain through the democratic process." "I do not think that Congress should be forced by Hawaii's state court to recognize a marriage between two males or between two females. Congress did not pick that fight."

After a contentious two-day markup, the Subcommittee on the Constitution voted 8–4 along party lines to send the measure to the full Judiciary Committee. Mirroring partisan divisions, the full committee by a 20–10 vote approved the bill for floor consideration. All Republicans voted for the measure, joined by two Democrats (Representatives Rick Boucher of Virginia and Jack Reed of Rhode Island); all other committee Democrats opposed the act.

Democrats charged that the bill was premature and calculated to drive a wedge between moderate and liberal Democrats as well as to try to inflame the public within weeks of the presidential election. "Why are we targeting gays and lesbians, blacks and immigrants this year, now, today?" questioned Representative Cynthia McKinney (D-Ga.) "The answer, pure and simple, is politics—election year politics. The Republicans will stop at nothing to win the White House and the Congress. They will fan the flames of intolerance and bigotry right up to November. And if the result is an election won—at the expense of national unity—their attitude is, so be it."

Debate centered around two main provisions. The first declared that states were not obligated to recognize any same-sex marriages legally sanctioned in other states. Democrats quarreled over the necessity and constitutionality of this proviso. Congressional action, they argued, was unnecessary and an unconstitutional intrusion on state autonomy; Congress would be exceeding its power to regulate aspects of legal reciprocity among states. "The Defense of Marriage Act compels this Congress to exceed its boundaries of its constitutional authority," explained Representative Jesse Jackson Jr. (D-Ill.). "This bill offends the Constitution, by violating both the full faith and credit and equal protection clauses of this sacred document." Opponents argued further that the measure was premature, given that no state (not even Hawaii) had yet legalized gay marriage.

Underneath the constitutional concerns about states rights lay a fundamental disagreement about the proper definition of marriage that involved an emotional clash over religious conviction and public morality. Representative John Lewis (D-Ga.), a veteran of the civil rights movement, countered that the bill was a mean-spirited repudiation of the Declaration of Independence's guarantee of the pursuit of happiness. "You cannot tell people they cannot fall in love," he said. "As I walk past the Republican side of the aisle," Representative Anna Eshoo (D-Calif.) declared, "I expect to hear something similar to an old joke from the civil rights era: 'Some of my good friends are gay, I just wouldn't want my son or daughter to marry one.'" "The fact is, it is morally wrong," Representative Tom Coburn (R-Okla.) said of gay unions.

This second provision to DOMA that sparked much debate defined marriage in federal law as a "legal union between one man and one woman as husband and wife" and a spouse as "a person of the opposite sex who is a husband or a wife," thereby precluding homosexual couples from filing joint tax returns or making use of any spousal benefits under Social Security or other federal programs. Sponsors said they wanted to preserve heterosexual values and traditional families and not "succumb to the homosexual extremist agenda" (H7275). Representative Charles Canady (R-Fla.) spoke for many traditionalists when he declared:

We as legislators and leaders for the country are in the midst of a chaos, an attack upon God's principles. God laid down that one man and one woman is a legal union. That is marriage, known for thousands of years. That God-given principle is under attack. It is under attack. There are those in our society that try to shift us away from a society based on religious principles to humanistic principles; that the human being can do whatever they want, as long as it feels good and does not hurt others.

Proponents also argued that legalizing gay marriage would send children a message that homosexuality was appropriate, pushing them away from heterosexual relationships. They invoked concern for Judeo-Christian tenets and other traditional values. Representative Canady asked whether loosening the definition of marriage might send mixed signals:

Should this Congress tell the children of America that it is a matter of indifference whether they establish families with a partner of the opposite sex or cohabit with someone of the same sex? Should this Congress tell the children of America that we as a society believe there is no moral difference between homosexual relationships and heterosexual relationships? Should this Congress tell the children of America that in the eyes of the law the parties to a homosexual union are entitled to all the rights and privileges that have always been reserved for a man and woman united in marriage?

Opponents argued that the measure was a pernicious form of gay-bashing and that Congress should not write its own definition of marriage. "Scapegoating gay men and lesbians for the failure of marriages in this society is very good politics but very terrible social analysis," contended Representative Frank. Representative Neil Abercrombie (D-Haw.) stated: "I have heard a continuous drumbeat from some Members here about this union of a man and a women. . . . If that is the case, I presume, then, Members are going to forbid divorce and most certainly impose penalties with adultery. But I do not see it in here [legislation]" (H7485). "This bill denies a group of Americans a basic right because they lead a different lifestyle," added Representative Marty Meehan (D-Mass.). "We must be careful when we make legislative determinations on who is different. If gay people are considered 'different' today, who is to say your lifestyle or my lifestyle will not be considered different tomorrow" (H7486)?

The House passed the bill, 342 to 67. Only one Republican voted against the bill: Steve Gunderson (R-Wis.), then the only GOP lawmaker who had publicly acknowledged his homosexuality. Initially willing to affirm marriage as a heterosexual union, Gunderson broke party ranks because he saw the bill as an exercise in political intolerance. This came after Republicans refused to add language calling for a study to examine questions concerning whether same-sex couples should be able to qualify for certain legal rights such as hospital visitation and health insurance. More quietly, the Senate passed the bill by a vote of 85 to 14, Democrats casting all the votes against the measure. . . .

Extending Civil Rights Protection to Homosexuals in the Workplace

During the debate on the defense of marriage, a second measure— the Employment Non-Discrimination Act (ENDA)—was working its way through the Senate. Antidiscrimination legislation for homosexuals first appeared in the 94th Congress (1975–1977), when it was introduced by Representative Bella S. Abzug (D-N.Y.). ENDA was aimed at banning most bias against homosexuals on the job. Proponents saw the bill in the context of other civil rights legislation—proposed to prohibit job bias against homosexuals by extending federal employment discrimination protections under the 1964 Civil Rights Act to sexual orientation.

Lawmakers did not openly discuss homosexuality in the workplace until the 103d Congress (1993–1995), when the Senate Labor and Human Resources Committee, chaired by Senator Kennedy, gave the issue some attention. Speaking on the measure before the Committee, Kennedy compared removing sexual orientation as a basis for job discrimination to the way that race, gender, religion, national origin, age, and disabilities had been dealt with by previous legislation. "In the past 40 years, the nation has made significant progress in removing the burden of bigotry from our land. We now seek to take the next step on this journey of justice by banning discrimination based on sexual orientation." In the 104th Congress, however, following a declaration by three Oklahoma members—Republicans James Inhofe and Ernest Istook and Democrat Bill Brewster—that they would refuse to hire openly gay staffers, legislation was proposed to further expand prohibitions against workplace discrimination.

Senators opposed to the measure framed their arguments either on moral grounds—the definition of sexual orientation—or as a debate on legal issues. Several senators said that the bill would provide homosexuals with special treatment and cause a proliferation of litigation. "We are not speaking of extending rights that every citizen of the United States is guaranteed," argued Senator Dan Coats (R-Ind.). "Rather we are considering special rights for persons based on their lifestyle choice, as evidenced by their behavior." Senate Majority Leader Trent Lott (R-Miss.) echoed this sentiment: "This is part of a larger campaign to validate or to approve conduct that remains illegal in many States." . . .

Debate on the two gay rights initiatives was "historic." For the first time lawmakers had openly discussed sexual orientation and proposed legislation designed to enhance the rights of homosexuals. What was once unthinkable had now briefly taken center stage in Congress, in committee deliberations and on the floor. But the bottom line was that lawmakers were not ready to render a positive judgement on this previously shunned topic. . . .

Did New Leadership Force New Strategies?

Passage of the Defense of Marriage Act and defeat of the Employment Non-Discrimination Act constituted a major rejection of gay rights. The debate over gay issues on Capitol Hill has frequently divided Republicans and Democrats, with Republicans more apt to view homosexuality as a threat to traditional values and Democrats more likely to define the subject as a civil rights issue. And while gays have received greater support from Democrats, Haider-Markel suggests that increasing the number of Democrats in Congress would not immediately translate into more progay support. Progay constituencies are already represented overwhelmingly by liberal Democrats; any additions to the party's ranks would necessarily take place in states or districts that are less supportive of gay interests.

The new Republican majority in the House, needless to say, restructured power relationships. Many grassroots groups and their constituents were subject to these partisan shifts. Groups closely aligned with the Democrats were at least temporarily marginalized, while groups allied with the new majority Republicans enjoyed unprecedented access.

The new institutional arrangements on Capitol Hill forced gay rights organizations to bargain more centrally with the party leadership and to build new relationships. . . .

To become active in the legislative process, political groups must build a foundation from which a successful effort at mobilization can be launched. Organizations must be formed, and advocates must be trained, to adapt to what T. V. Smith called the "legislative way of life"; resources must be amassed to capture the attention of lawmakers. Elected officials may advance legislation intended to benefit disadvantaged groups without prompting from outside forces. But as Walker writes, "legislators know that once conflict begins over their proposals, there will be few organizations in place that can mobilize expressions of support, supply information and ideas, or raise financial resources needed to combat the program's critics."

In the years before Stonewall, organizations of gays were nearly invisible on Capitol Hill. Early efforts to organize homosexuals in promoting gay rights proved unsuccessful because of fear of the consequences. The absence of cohesiveness within the community, combined with substantial structural and moral impediments, inhibited a sense of identity, cohesion, and group consciousness among homosexuals. Group activism encompassed a collection of diverse political, social, and service organizations across Capitol Hill. Moderate groups such as the Log Cabin Republicans engaged in quiet politics rooted in personal relationships with limited roles of government over campaigns for equality, while organizations like the National Gay and Lesbian Task Force, the Gay and Lesbian Victory Fund, the Human Rights Campaign, and the Lambda Legal Defense Fund pushed broader rights-based agendas.

The identification and threat of AIDS galvanized diverse political initiatives in the gay community, prompting mobilization, fund-raising, and effective political lobbying for legislative remedies as well as efforts to educate lawmakers. Skeptical of Congress's commitment to their well-being, many gay activists began to shift their emphasis from backstairs lobbying for civil rights to more publicly visible and vigorous AIDS activism. This entry of AIDS activists into the health care scene added a new dimension to what was previously a genteel dialogue between patient advocates and clinicians, researchers, and policymakers. Increased group activism and the expansion of homosexual issues to include AIDS provided gay rights leaders an entrée to many members of Congress, helping to establish themselves as players with a social stake in the issue.

Gay activists have recently explored new ways of making themselves heard on Capitol Hill. A critical part of this political clout is campaign support. Enlarged memberships and budgets have enabled gay political organizations, through their political action committees and independent expenditures, to channel sizeable contributions to congressional campaigns throughout the nation and to even influence legislative voting behavior. Controlling for party affiliation, ideology, religious affiliation, constituency opinion, and past progay support, Haider-Markel's model of congressional decision-making suggests that, under sub-optimal conditions, gay interest groups can exert some influence over congressional voting behavior through campaign contributions and the mobilization of grassroots supporters. However, although gay and lesbian groups can sway voting behavior at the individual level, this does not necessarily aggregate into legislative victories.

56

ELLEN ALDERMAN
CAROLINE KENNEDY

From *In Our Defense*

*Two young attorneys have chosen to examine the Bill of Rights not from
the perspective of landmark Supreme Court cases, but from a grassroots
perspective. Ellen Alderman and Caroline Kennedy present the story behind
an obscure federal case involving the First Amendment and freedom of
religion. The U.S. Forest Service had decided to build a logging road through
public lands in northern California. The land is sacred to the Yurok tribe,
and the tribe hoped that the Constitution's First Amendment would protect
them in their free exercise of religion. However, in 1987 the Supreme
Court, in a close vote, decided otherwise. Alderman and Kennedy note,
however, that Congress intervened, and the land was named protected
wilderness in 1990. For now, the Yurok's sacred land is undisturbed, but
without the Supreme Court's help.*

——

"Congress shall make no law respecting an establishment of religion,
or prohibiting the free exercise thereof . . . "

WHEN THE DOGWOOD TREE blossomed twice and a whale
swam into the mouth of the Klamath River, the Yurok medicine man
knew it was time for the tribe to perform the White Deer Skin Dance.
He knew that these natural signs were messengers sent by the Great Spirit
to tell the people things were out of balance in the world. The White Deer
Skin Dance and Jump Dance are part of the World Renewal Ceremonies of
the Yurok, Karok, Tolowa, and Hoopa Indian tribes of northern California. The World Renewal Ceremonies are performed to protect the earth
from catastrophe and humanity from disease and to bring the physical
and spiritual world back in balance. Preparations for the ceremonies begin
far up in the mountains, in the wilderness known to the Indians as the
sacred "high country."

According to Indian mythology, the World Renewal Ceremonies were
initiated by the *woge*, spirits that inhabited the earth before the coming
of man. The *woge* gave culture and all living things to humanity, and the
ceremonies are held at sites along the river where these gifts were given.

The *woge* then became afraid of human contamination and retreated to the mountains before ascending into a hole in the sky. Because the mountains were the *woge's* last refuge on earth, they are the source of great spiritual power.

In recent years, there has been a quiet resurgence of traditional Indian religion in the high country. Young Indians who left to find jobs on the "other side of the mountain" are returning to their ancestral grounds. Lawrence "Tiger" O'Rourke, a thirty-two-year-old member of the Yurok tribe, worked for eight years around the state as a building contractor before returning to raise fish in the traditional Indian way.

"In the white man's world . . . you just spend all of your lifetime making money and gathering up things around you and it doesn't really have any value," Tiger says. "Here, the Spirit is still in everything—the trees, the rocks, the river . . . the different kinds of people. It's got a life spirit, so we're all connected. . . . The concrete world, it's kind of dead. It feels like something's missing and the people are afraid. . . . So this place is just right for me, I guess."

There are about five thousand others who, like Tiger, are happy to live in isolation from the "white man's world"; indeed the spiritual life of the high country depends on it. But when the U.S. Forest Service announced plans to build a logging road through the heart of the high country, many of the Yurok tribe decided they could not remain quiet any longer.

They went to court, claiming that the logging road would violate their First Amendment right to freely exercise their religion. They said it was like building a "highway through the Vatican." What the Indians wanted the courts to understand was that the salmon-filled creeks, singing pines, and mountain trails of the high country were their Vatican.

To prepare for the World Renewal Ceremony, the medicine man first notifies the dance givers that it is time. According to Indian law, only certain families are allowed to give dances and to own dance regalia. The privilege and the responsibility are passed down from generation to generation.

"In the beginning," says Tiger, a member of such a family, "the Spirit came up the river and he stayed at different people's houses. He only knocked and went in where he knew the people would take care of him. They would have a responsibility to the people, and the world, and the universe to make the ceremony, and they would always do it. It's a lot of work. You have to live a good life, you have to live with truth. Not everybody could do it."

The dance giver is also responsible for paying up all debts before the dance. Indian law puts a price on everything, and by paying the price the social balance is restored. If you insult someone, you owe that person a certain amount; if you kill a person, you must pay that person's family. Payment prevents hatred and anger from spreading to infect the community and brings the world back into harmony. . . .

The most sacred area of the high country is known as Medicine Mountain, a ridge dominated by the peaks of Doctor Rock, Peak 8, and Chimney Rock. Chimney Rock, a majestic outcropping of pinkish basalt, rises sixty-seven hundred feet above sea level. From its summit, views of receding blue waves of mountain ridges fade into the horizon in all directions. On a clear day, the shimmer of the Pacific Ocean gleams at the end of the winding silver ribbon of the Smith River below. . . .

Although only a few medicine men and Indian doctors actively use the sacred sites of the high country, the spiritual well-being of the entire tribe depends on performance of the ancient rituals. Despite more than a half century during which the government removed Indians from their villages and prohibited them from speaking their own language or practicing their religion, a few elderly Indians never left or gave up the old ways. Some young Indians, like Tiger, are returning to their homeland. And others, like Walter "Black Snake" Lara, are trying to balance the old world with the new.

Black Snake works felling trees. He says it is an honorable job in many parts of the lush California forests, but not in the high country. Of the sacred grounds he says, "The Creator fixed it that way for us. We're responsible for it."

Tiger, Black Snake, and others are struggling to maintain their fragile way of life. They are succeeding in part because the steep mountains, dense forests, and nonnavigable streams have protected their cemeteries, villages, and high country from encroachment by the "concrete" world. To them, the proposed highway was more than just a symbol of that concrete world. By the Forest Service's own estimates, each day it would bring about seventy-two diesel logging trucks and ninety other vehicles within a half mile of Chimney Rock.

Actually, the Forest Service started constructing a logging road through the Six Rivers National Forest in the 1930s. It began at either end, in the lumber-mill towns of Gasquet to the north and Orleans to the south, thus becoming known as the G-O Road. Under the Forest Service's management plan, once the road was completed, the towns would be connected and timber could be hauled to mills at either end of the forest.

In the meantime, as construction inched toward Chimney Rock, new areas of timber were opened up to logging. "They snuck that road in from both sides," says Black Snake.

By the 1970s, the two segments of the seventy-five-mile road dead-ended in the forest. Black pavement simply gave way to gravel and dirt, and then the side of a mountain. The final six-mile section needed to complete the road was known as the Chimney Rock section of the G-O Road.

The Indians feared that if the road was built it would destroy the sanctity of the high country forever. As Sam Jones, a full-blooded Yurok dance giver put it. "When the medicine lady goes out there to pray, she stands on these rocks and meditates. The forest is there looking out. [She] talks to the trees and rocks, whatever is out there. After they get through praying, their answer comes from the mountain. Our people talk in their language to them and if it's all logged off and all bald there, they can't meditate at all. They have nothing to talk to."

An influx of tree fellers, logging trucks, tourists, and campers would also destroy the ability to make medicine in the high country. The consequences were grave; if the medicine man could not bring back the power for the World Renewal Ceremonies, the people's religious existence would be threatened. And because the land itself is considered holy by the Indians, they could not move their "church" to another location. "People don't understand about our place," Black Snake says, "because they can build a church and worship wherever they want."

The Indians filed a lawsuit in federal district court in San Francisco: *Northwest Indian Cemetery Protective Association v. Peterson*. (R. Max Peterson was named as defendant in his capacity as chief of the U.S. Forest Service.) They claimed that construction of the G-O Road would destroy the solitude, privacy, and undisturbed natural setting necessary to Indian religious practices, thereby violating their First Amendment right to freely exercise their religion.

By invoking the First Amendment, the Indians joined those before them who had sought religious freedom in America. After all, many colonists came to the New World to escape religious persecution in the Old, establishing colonies that reflected the varied beliefs of their inhabitants. The Puritans of Massachusetts sought to build their "City on a Hill," Lord Baltimore founded Maryland as a colony where Catholics and Protestants would live together and prosper, William Penn led the Quakers to Philadelphia, and the Virginia planters were strong supporters of the Church of England. . . .

[Thomas] Jefferson's [1785 Virginia] statute served as one of [James]

Madison's models for the First Amendment, which, as adopted and ratified, has two components: the establishment clause and the free exercise clause. In general terms, according to the Supreme Court, the "establishment of religion clause of the First Amendment means at least this: Neither a state nor the Federal Government can set up a church. Neither can pass laws which aid one religion, aid all religions, or prefer one religion over another. . . . In the words of Jefferson, the clause against establishment of religion by law was intended to erect 'a wall of separation between church and State.'" Courts have relied on the establishment clause to strike down state support for parochial schools, statutes mandating school prayer, and the erection of religious displays (for example, nativity scenes or menorahs) on public property.

In contrast, the free exercise clause forbids the government from outlawing religious belief. It also forbids the government from unduly burdening the exercise of a religious belief. However, some regulation of conduct expressing belief is permitted. If a person claims that a government action violates his right to freely exercise his religion, courts must first determine if the asserted religious belief is "sincerely held." If so, then the burden on individual worship must be balanced against the state's interest in proceeding with the challenged action. Only if the state's interest is "compelling" will it outweigh the individual's right to the free exercise of religion.

In the two hundred years since the First Amendment was ratified, the free exercise clause has protected many whose religious beliefs have differed from those of the majority. For example, the Supreme Court has held that unemployment benefits could not be denied to a Seventh-Day Adventist fired for refusing to work on Saturday, her sabbath; nor to a Jehovah's Witness who quit his job in a weapons production factory for religious reasons. Forcing these individuals to choose between receiving benefits and following their respective religious practices violated their right to the free exercise of religion.

In 1983, the Federal District Court for the Northern District of California held that completion of the G-O Road would violate the Northwest Indians' right to freely exercise their religion. The court concluded that the G-O Road would unconstitutionally burden their exercise of sincerely held religious beliefs, and the government's interest in building the road was not compelling enough to override the Indians' interest. Therefore, the court enjoined, or blocked, the Forest Service from completing the road. When the decision was announced, the group of fifty to a hundred Indians who had traveled south to attend the trial were convinced that their medicine had been successful.

The government appealed the decision to the Ninth Circuit Court of Appeals. While the case was pending, Congress passed the California Wilderness Act, which designated much of the sacred high country as a wilderness area. Thus all commercial activity, including mining or timber harvesting, was forever banned. But as part of a compromise worked out to secure passage of the act, Congress exempted a twelve-hundred-foot-wide corridor from the wilderness, just enough to complete the G-O Road. So although the surrounding area could not be destroyed, the road could still be built. That decision was left to the Forest Service. The medicine was still working, however; in July 1986, the Ninth Circuit affirmed the district court's decision and barred completion of the road.

The government then appealed the case to the U.S. Supreme Court. It filed a "petition for certiorari," a request that the Court hear the case. The Supreme Court receives thousands of these "cert" petitions each year, but accepts only about 150 for argument and decision. In order to take the case, four justices must vote to grant "cert." If they do not, the lower-court ruling stands. Because freedom of religion is so important in the constitutional scheme, and because the case involved principles affecting the management of vast tracts of federal land, *Northwest Indian Cemetery Protective Association* was one of the 150 cases accepted.

The Indians based their Supreme Court arguments on their victories in the lower courts and on a landmark 1972 Supreme Court case, *Wisconsin v. Yoder*. In *Yoder*, three Amish parents claimed that sending their children to public high school, as required by law, violated their right to free exercise of religion. They explained that the Old Order Amish religion was devoted to a simple life in harmony with nature and the soil, untainted by influence from the contemporary world. The Amish said that public schools emphasized intellectual accomplishment, individual distinction, competition, and social life. In contrast, "Amish society emphasize[d] informal learning-through-doing; a life of 'goodness,' rather than a life of intellect; wisdom, rather than technical knowledge; community welfare, rather than competition; and separation from, rather than integration with, contemporary worldly society." The Amish said that forcing their children out of the Amish community into a world undeniably at odds with their fundamental beliefs threatened their eternal salvation. Therefore, they claimed, state compulsory education laws violated their right to freely exercise their religion. The Supreme Court agreed.

If the Supreme Court could find that freedom of religion outweighed the state's interest in compulsory education, the Indians believed that the Constitution would make room for them too. After all, Chief Justice Warren Burger had written in *Yoder*, "A way of life that is odd or even erratic but interferes with no rights or interests of others is not to be condemned because it is different." The Indians argued that, like the Amish, they wanted only to be left alone to worship, as they had for thousands of years.

But the Forest Service argued that the Indians were seeking something fundamentally different from what the Amish had won. Whereas the exemption from a government program in *Yoder* affected only the Amish, and "interfere[d] with no rights or interests of others," the Indians were trying to stop the government from managing its own resources. From the government's point of view, if the courts allowed these Indians to block the G-O Road, it would open the door for other religious groups to interfere with government action on government lands everywhere. (It did not matter to the government that the Indians considered the high country to be *their* land.) The Forest Service produced a map marked to indicate sacred religious sites in California; the red markers nearly covered the state. Giving the Indians veto power over federal land management decisions was not, in the government's view, what the free exercise clause was intended to protect. As Justice William O. Douglas once wrote, "The Free Exercise Clause is written in terms of what the government cannot do to the individual, not in terms of what the individual can exact from the government."

The singing pines, soaring eagles, and endless mountain vistas of northern California are about as far from the white marble Supreme Court on Capitol Hill as it is possible to get in the United States. Yet like thousands of Americans before them, a small group of Indians came in November 1987 to watch their case argued before the highest court in the land. Though the Indians had never put much faith in any branch of the government, they had come to believe that if the justices could see the case through "brown eyes," they would finally make room in the Bill of Rights for the "first Americans."

Some did not realize that by the time a case reaches the Supreme Court, it no longer involves only those individuals whose struggle initiated it, but has enduring repercussions throughout the country. Unlike a legal code or statute that is written with specificity, "a constitution," wrote Chief Justice John Marshall, "is framed for ages to come, and is designed to approach immortality, as nearly as human institutions can approach it." When the Supreme Court decides a case based on the Bill of Rights, it enunciates principles that become the Supreme Law of the Land, and are used by lower courts across the United States to guide their decisions.

The Indians lost by one vote. "The Constitution simply does not provide a principle that could justify upholding [the Indians'] legal claims," Justice Sandra Day O'Connor wrote for the majority. "However much we wish that it were otherwise, government simply could not operate if it were required to satisfy every citizen's religious needs and desires."

The Court accepted that the G–O Road could have "devastating effects on traditional Indian religious practices." Nonetheless, it held that the G–O Road case differed from *Yoder* because here, the government was not *coercing* the Indians to act contrary to their religious beliefs. In what may prove to be an important development in the law, the Court concluded that unless the government *coerces* individuals to act in a manner that violates their religious beliefs, the free exercise clause is not implicated, and the government does not have to provide a compelling reason for its actions.

The Court also noted the broad ramifications of upholding the Indians' free exercise claim. While the Indians did not "at present" object to others using the high country, their claim was based on a need for privacy in the area. According to the Court, under the Indians' reasoning there was nothing to prevent them, or others like them, from seeking to exclude all human activity but their own from land they held sacred. "No disrespect for the [Indian] practices is implied when one notes that such beliefs could easily require *de facto* beneficial ownership of some rather spacious tracts of public property," the Court wrote.

Justice William Brennan's emotional dissent rejected the Court's reasoning and result. The religious freedom remaining to the Indians after the Supreme Court's decision, according to Justice Brennan, "amounts to nothing more than the right to believe that their religion will be destroyed . . . the safeguarding of such a hollow freedom . . . fails utterly to accord with the dictates of the First Amendment." Justice Brennan and the two justices who joined him, Thurgood Marshall and Harry Blackmun, rejected the Court's new "coercion test."

"The Court . . . concludes that even where the government uses federal land in a manner that threatens the very existence of a Native American religion, the Government is simply not 'doing' anything to the practitioners of that faith," Justice Brennan wrote. "Ultimately the Court's coercion test turns on a distinction between government actions that compel affirmative conduct inconsistent with religious belief, and those governmental actions that prevent conduct consistent with religious belief. In my view, such a distinction is without constitutional significance." The dissenters believed instead that the Indians' religion would be severely burdened, indeed made "impossible," by the government's actions, and that the government had not shown a compelling interest in completing the road.

"They might as well rewrite the Constitution. They teach us we have freedom of religion and freedom of speech, but it's not true," says Tiger O'Rourke. "This was our place first time, our home. It's still our home, but we don't have the same rights as other Americans."

Currently, the G-O Road is stalled. The Indians are challenging the Forest Service on environmental grounds and attempting to get Congress to add the G-O Road corridor to the existing, protected wilderness area.

Like many Americans, Tiger and Black Snake say they never thought much about the Constitution until it touched their lives directly. Among the tribes of northern California, defeat has fired a new fight for their way of life, spurred intertribal outreach and educational efforts, and brought a new awareness of the legal system. "We *have* to understand the Constitution now," says Tiger O'Rourke. "We still need our line of warriors, but now they've got to be legal warriors. That's the war now, and it's the only way we're going to survive."

N.B. On October 28, 1990, the last day of its session, the 101st Congress passed legislation adding the G-O Road corridor to the Siskiyou Wilderness. This legislation ensures that the logging road will not be completed; its two spurs will remain dead-ended in the forest beneath Chimney Rock. Because the area was protected to preserve the environment rather than the Indians' religion, the Indians found their victory bittersweet. "It's all right for us. We'll use the area as we always have," says Black Snake. "But we didn't accomplish what we set out to accomplish for other tribes. [We] can't win one on beliefs." But, he adds, "maybe it's the Creator's way of seeing just how sincere we are."

57

EDWARD DE GRAZIA

From *Girls Lean Back Everywhere*

In 1990 popular music provided the courts with a classic censorship dilemma when the Miami rap group 2 Live Crew sang about subjects that some Florida public officials believed were obscene. Edward de Grazia's long and detailed study of obscenity and the First Amendment includes the story of the 2 Live Crew controversy. In this excerpt he quotes various people about their personal reactions to the group's lyrics and its freedom to sing them. Journalists, Crew members, fans, jurors, scholars, and other performers each saw the issue from different points of view. Opinions vary on whether 2 Live Crew was spreading dangerous filth about women, or whether the white power structure was trying to silence the legitimate voices of American black men. In this case, the First Amendment let 2 Live Crew be "As Nasty As They Wanna Be."

———

IN 1957, FOR THE first time, the Supreme Court spoke to the question of whether literature dealing with sex was meant to be protected by the First Amendment; the Court said that literature was protected, but that "obscenity" was *not*. The justices defined "obscenity" much as [Federal] Judge [John M.] Woolsey had [in 1933], subjectively, in terms of its ability to arouse the "average person's" prurient interest in sex. Then, in a 1964 case involving Henry Miller's erotic novel *Tropic of Cancer*, the wise and courageous Justice William J. Brennan, Jr., produced a more objective and much more liberal rule by which the freedom of literature and other arts might be measured.

In fact, the rule that Brennan announced (referred to in this book as "the Brennan doctrine") was so generously fashioned to protect literature and art that it led to the freeing of hard-core pornography. In order to ensure freedom for valued cultural expression the Supreme Court had found it necessary to free what was "obscene" as well. It did this by effectively (although not formally) abandoning the effort to define what in a literary or artistic context was undefinable—"the obscene"—and providing an efficient, because nearly absolute, defense for expression "not utterly without" literary, artistic, scientific, or other social value. Thus the Court made it close to impossible for prosecutors to prove that targeted literary or artistic works were obscene but easy for defense lawyers to demonstrate that the works of literature or art created or disseminated by their clients were entitled to First Amendment protection.

Soon the Court's critics found in the Brennan doctrine grounds to blame the Court for the "tides of pornography" that were now "seeping into the sanctity of the home." The spread of pornography was cited as evidence not that entrepreneurial capitalism had made sex a multibillion-dollar industry, but that the Supreme Court had mocked the founding fathers' intentions with regard to freedom of the press.

In 1973, the Court's new chief justice, Warren E. Burger, redefined obscenity in a way he hoped would be more palatable to conservative opinion, and this led Brennan and three others who had served on the Warren Court (Stewart, Marshall, and Douglas) to disassociate themselves from Burger's position and move into deep dissent. At that point Brennan, disdaining Burger's effort to fashion an improved definition of "the obscene," called for the abandonment of attempts to define and suppress obscenity through law. It was plain to Brennan that people who express themselves through literature and art could not be fully safe from government control unless the Court constrained government to forgo any attempt to punish purveyors of pornography and obscenity to adults.

The wisdom of Brennan's 1973 position (which he reiterated frequently in dissent) recently was confirmed when the director of a Cincinnati art gallery, the leader of a Miami rap music group, and the owner of a Fort Lauderdale record store all found themselves arrested under the Burger Court's revised definition for showing, singing, and selling what police officials and prosecutors claimed was obscene because in their judgment it did not qualify as "serious" art, or even art. Splendid as Brennan's achievements of the sixties were, they have not dispelled fears that literature and art can subvert and even destroy deeply entrenched political and religious values. And they have by no means discouraged ambitious public officials and zealous religious leaders from invoking the law to suppress artistic expression they find repellent. . . .

In Miami, in June 1990, Luther Campbell, the leader of 2 Live Crew, was arrested for singing and playing "obscene" songs; thereafter he was acquitted by jurors who, aided by experts, felt they knew artistic expression when they heard it. But in Fort Lauderdale, record-store owner Charles Freeman, who was arrested around the same time for selling a recording of the same music—the 2 Live Crew album *As Nasty As They Wanna Be*—to an undercover sheriff, was convicted by a jury that failed to see the serious artistic and political value that many other people saw in the songs. Yet the First Amendment has for the past twenty-five years been put forward by the Supreme Court as a barrier to this sort of censorship. One had hoped the issue was settled. . . .

LIZ SMITH [Columnist]: In my time I've had a lot to say about how sticks and stones can break one's bones; but words can never hurt. . . . And this column has been an active defender of First Amendment rights and also the right of others to say anything they like about those in the public eye. I've always felt if we in the press offend, at least it is better than suffering suppression, censorship, etc.

But a July 2 column by John Leo in *U.S. News & World Report*, which I clipped and put aside before I went on vacation, has me on the ropes. . . .

JOHN LEO: The issue at the heart of the controversy over the rap group 2 Live Crew is not censorship, artistic freedom, sex or even obscene language. The real problem, I think, is this: Because of the cultural influence of one not very distinguished rap group, 10- and 12-year-old boys now walk down the street chanting about the joys of damaging a girl's vagina during sex. . . .

The popular culture is worth paying attention to. It is the air we breathe, and 2 Live Crew is a pesky new pollutant. The opinion industry's advice is generally to buy a gas mask or stop breathing. ("If you don't like their album, don't buy it," one such genius wrote.) But by monitoring, complaining, boycotting, we might actually get the 2 Live Crew Pollutants out of our air. Why should our daughters have to grow up in a culture in which musical advice on the domination and abuse of women is accepted as entertainment?

LIZ SMITH: So, is censorship the answer? The performance of 2 Live Crew—so violent, so anti-female—forces an almost involuntary yes! But once you censor, or forbid or arrest the real culprits, how do you deal with other artists who "offend"? Where do you draw the line? This is a tough one. But the average child isn't likely to encounter the kind of "art" that the National Endowment is trying to ban. Kids are not all over art galleries and theaters. But pop music assails them at every level and at every moment of their lives.

What I WOULD like to see is every responsible, influential and distinguished black activist, actor and role model—Jesse Jackson, Spike Lee, Whoopi Goldberg, Arsenio Hall, Eddie Murphy, Diana Ross, et al.—raising his or her voice to decry the horrible "message" of 2 Live Crew.

I would advise famous and caring whites to do the same, though they may be accused of racism. However, the issue goes far beyond race. Clips of 2 Live Crew in concert show that the audiences are not exclusively black by any means. What they are is young and unformed and dangerously impressionable.

DEBBIE BENNETT [2 Live Crew publicist]: It's nice to see that Liz Smith is keeping racism in America alive and kicking. She's so stupid it's unbelievable. She wrote that since kids don't go to art galleries or see shows with people like Karen Finley, obscene art is okay. But since they listen to music, 2 Live Crew should be banned. Way to pass judgment on every teenager in America.

In an account of the 2 Live Crew members' trial that appeared in The Village Voice, Lisa Jones reported what two teenaged black women, courthouse fans of Luther Campbell, had to say about the prosecution and the music:

ANTOINETTE JONES (18): They're just giving Luke a hard time because he's black. He's trying to make a living like everyone else. If someone wants to listen to his music that's their business. What do they think music is? They're acting like music is a gun.

LATONIA BROOKS (17): [Their lyrics] do have to do with sex and body parts, but when they rap, they put it all together. It's not like a man on the street saying dirty words to you. Their music makes sense. What they're saying is the truth. That's what most people do in bed. I don't, but that's what most other people do in bed.

Unlike the jury that convicted the record-store owner Charles Freeman for selling the "obscene" album, 2 Live Crew's jury was not all white; it found all three Crew members not guilty. Two of the (white) jurors told reporters why they had voted to acquit.

SUSAN VAN HEMERT (JUROR): I basically took it as comedy.

BEVERLY RESNICK (JUROR): This was their way of expressing their inner feelings; we felt it had some art in it.

The verdict came after four days of testimony during which the jurors "spent hours" listening to, and occasionally laughing at, two garbled tape recordings of a performance by the group that had been made by undercover deputies from the Broward County sheriff's office. The tapes, one of which had been enhanced by the police to eliminate background noise, were the prosecution's only evidence.

Defense lawyers Bruce Rogow and Allen Jacobi won the case by producing expert witnesses to testify about the artistic and political values in the group's songs, a strategy like the one that defense lawyers in the Cincinnati Mapplethorpe case had successfully used. One of the 2 Live Crew witnesses, *Newsday* music critic John Leland, gave an annotated history of hip-hop music. Another, Duke University professor and literary critic Henry Louis Gates, Jr, placed the music in its African-American oral and literary tradition. Gates explained the "signifying," and the use of "hyperbole" and "parody"; he described why it was the artistic works like *As Nasty As They Wanna Be* were not to be taken literally. This probably was the evidence which persuaded the jury that there was at least a reasonable doubt that the music was obscene.

Gates said that the Crew's lyrics took one of the worst stereotypes about black men—that they are oversexed animals—and blew it up until it exploded. He also suggested that the "clear and present danger" doctrine that judges still sometimes used to justify the suppression of speech was not applicable to the Crew's music.

PROFESSOR HENRY LOUIS GATES, JR.: There is no cult of violence [in this music]. There is no danger at all [from] these words . . . being sung.

The Crew's chief lyricist defended the group's music, and its success, on essentially political grounds.

MARK ROSS (AKA BROTHER MARQUIS): The bottom line is getting dollars and having your own. It's really a black thing with us. Even though people might say we're not positive role models to the black community, that if you ask us about our culture, we talk about sex, it's not really like that. I'm well aware of where I come from, I know myself as a black man. I think I'm with the program, very much so. You feel I'm doing nothing to enhance my culture, but I could be destroying my culture, I could be out there selling kids drugs.

Performers and purveyors of rap music, like curators of art galleries, are engaged in the communication of images and ideas through artistic means. Because of this, interference with their work by policemen, prose-cutors, or judges violates the freedoms guaranteed under the First Amend-ment. No one can intelligently suggest that the country's musicians and distributors of music are not as entitled to be free in their professional activities as its writers and booksellers and museum curators are. The only constitutional limitations permissible with respect to songs are also applicable to books, paintings, photographs, films, and the other arts, as to all speech and press—which is to say, the restraints ought to be limited in their application to persons who use music intentionally to incite others to crime or violence, or who force nonconsenting or captive audiences to listen to it.

Purposeful disseminations to children of music that may be deemed "obscene" *for them* (in the constitutional sense mentioned in *Miller v. California*) would raise different questions. When 2 Live Crew played Fort Lauderdale, they were not arrested and charged with inviting or alluring minors to hear their sexually explicit songs, playing to "captive audiences" of persons who did not wish to hear what was played and could not escape it, or intentionally inciting the men in the room to rape or sexually abuse women. They were charged with singing lyrics that policemen, prosecutors, and lower court judges had heard about, decoded, and decided were not art, but were obscene. . . .

58

MARY ANN GLENDON

From *Rights Talk*

Individual rights lie at the heart of America's political system. Unfortunately, in the view of legal scholar Mary Ann Glendon, today's "rights talk" makes a mockery of the real meaning of rights. Legitimate, deeply-rooted rights have given way to what are nothing more than demands. Little thought is given to whether a right is basic or merely a convenience; to the effect of one person's claim of a right on others; to the weighing of rights versus responsibilities. Glendon, as a strong supporter of individual rights, asks people to return to a more common-sense, less artificial, definition of rights. Daily, in their private lives, Americans embrace a genuine and true concept of rights, not the "rights talk" of the public arena.

IN THE SPRING of 1990, men and women in East Germany and Hungary participated in the first fully free elections that had taken place in any of the East European countries since they came under Soviet control in 1945. Excitement ran high. The last people to have voted in that part of the world were now in their seventies. Some young parents, casting a ballot for the first time, brought their children with them to see the sight. Many, no doubt, will long remember the day as one marked with both festivity and solemnity. Meanwhile, in the United States, public interest in politics appears to be at an all-time low. Two months before the 1988 presidential election, polls revealed that half the voting-age public did not know the identity of the Democratic vice-presidential candidate and could not say which party had a majority in Congress. In that election, only half the eligible voters cast ballots, thirteen percent less than in 1960. Americans not only vote less than citizens of other liberal democracies, they display a remarkable degree of apathy concerning public affairs. Over a period of twenty years, daily newspaper readership has fallen from seventy-three percent of adults to a mere fifty-one percent. Nor have the readers simply become viewers, for ratings of network evening news programs have dropped by about twenty-five percent in the past ten years, and the slack has not been taken up by cable television news. Cynicism, indifference, and ignorance concerning government appear to be pervasive. By all outward indicators, the right and obligation to vote—a subject of wonder to East Europeans, and the central concern of many of us who worked in the civil rights movement in the 1960s—is now held here in rather low esteem.

Poor voter turnouts in the United States are, of course, mere symptoms of deeper problems, not least of which are the decline of broadly representative political parties, and the effect of the "sound-bite" on serious and sustained political discussion. On this deeper level lies the phenomenon with which this book is concerned: the impoverishment of our political discourse. Across the political spectrum there is a growing realization that it has become increasingly difficult even to define critical questions, let alone debate and resolve them.

Though sound-bites do not permit much airing of issues, they seem tailor-made for our strident language of rights. Rights talk itself is relatively impervious to the other more complex languages we still speak in less public contexts, but it seeps into them, carrying the rights mentality into spheres of American society where a sense of personal responsibility and of civic obligation traditionally have been nourished. An intemperate rhetoric of personal liberty in this way corrodes the social foundations on which individual freedom and security ultimately rest. While the nations of Eastern Europe are taking their first risk-laden and faltering steps toward democracy, the historic American experiment in ordered liberty is thus undergoing a less dramatic, but equally fateful, crisis of its own. It is a crisis at the very heart of the American experiment in self-government, for it concerns the state of public deliberation about the right ordering of our lives together. In the home of free speech, genuine exchange of ideas about matters of high public importance has come to a virtual standstill.

This book argues that the prominence of a certain kind of rights talk in our political discussions is both a symptom of, and a contributing factor to, this disorder in the body politic. Discourse about rights has become the principal language that we use in public settings to discuss weighty questions of right and wrong, but time and again it proves inadequate, or leads to a standoff of one right against another. The problem is not, however, as some contend, with the very notion of rights, or with our strong rights tradition. It is with a new version of rights discourse that has achieved dominance over the past thirty years.

Our current American rights talk is but one dialect in a universal language that has developed during the extraordinary era of attention to civil and human rights in the wake of World War II. It is set apart from rights discourse in other liberal democracies by its starkness and simplicity, its prodigality in bestowing the rights label, its legalistic character, its exaggerated absoluteness, its hyper-individualism, its insularity, and its silence with respect to personal, civic, and collective responsibilities.

This unique brand of rights talk often operates at cross-purposes with our venerable rights tradition. It fits perfectly within the ten-second formats currently preferred by the news media, but severely constricts opportunities for the sort of ongoing dialogue upon which a regime of ordered liberty ultimately depends. A rapidly expanding catalog of rights— extending to trees, animals, smokers, nonsmokers, consumers, and so on—not only multiplies the occasions for collisions, but it risks trivializing core democratic values. A tendency to frame nearly every social controversy in terms of a clash of rights (a woman's right to her own body vs. a fetus's right to life) impedes compromise, mutual understanding, and the discovery of common ground. A penchant for absolute formulations ("I have the right to do whatever I want with my property") promotes unrealistic expectations and ignores both social costs and the rights of others. A near-aphasia concerning responsibilities makes it seem legitimate to accept the benefits of living in a democratic social welfare republic without assuming the corresponding personal and civic obligations.

As various new rights are proclaimed or proposed, the catalog of individual liberties expands without much consideration of the ends to which they are oriented, their relationship to one another, to corresponding responsibilities, or to the general welfare. Converging with the language of psychotherapy, rights talk encourages our all-too-human tendency to place the self at the center of our moral universe. In tandem with consumerism and a normal dislike of inconvenience, it regularly promotes the short-run over the long-term, crisis intervention over preventive measures, and particular interests over the common good. Saturated with rights, political language can no longer perform the important function of facilitating public discussion of the right ordering of our lives together. Just as rights exist for us only through being articulated, other goods are not even available to be considered if they can be brought to expression only with great difficulty, or not at all.

My principal aim . . . has been to trace the evolution of our distinctive current rights dialect, and to show how it frequently works against the conditions required for the pursuit of dignified living by free women and men. With stories and examples drawn from disputes over flag-burning, Indian lands, plant closings, criminal penalties for homosexual acts, eminent domain, social welfare, child support, and other areas, I have endeavored to demonstrate how our simplistic rights talk simultaneously reflects and distorts American culture. It captures our devotion to individualism and liberty, but omits our traditions of hospitality and care for the community. In the images of America and Americans that it projects, as well as in the ideals to which it implicitly pays homage, our current rights talk is a verbal caricature of our culture—recognizably ours, but with certain traits wildly out of proportion and with some of our best features omitted.

Our rights-laden political discourse does provide a solution of sorts to the communications problems that beset a heterogeneous nation whose citizens decreasingly share a common history, literature, religion, or customs. But the "solution" has become part of the problem. The legal components of political discourse, like sorcerers' apprentices, have taken on new and mischief-making connotations when liberated from their contexts in the speech community of lawyers. (A person has no duty to come to the aid of a "stranger.") With its nonlegal tributaries rapidly dwindling, political rhetoric has grown increasingly out of touch with the more complex ways of speaking that Americans employ around the kitchen table, in their schools, workplaces, and in their various communities of memory and mutual aid.

Under these circumstances, what is needed is not the abandonment, but the renewal, of our strong rights tradition. But it is not easy to see how we might develop a public language that would be better suited in complexity and moral seriousness to the bewildering array of difficulties that presently face us as a mature democracy in an increasingly interdependent world. Nor is it readily apparent how the public forum, dominated as it is by images rather than ideas, could be reclaimed for genuine political discourse.

We cannot, nor would most of us wish to, import some other country's language of rights. Nor can we invent a new rhetoric of rights out of whole cloth. A political Esperanto* without roots in a living cultural tradition would die on the vine. . . . In many settings, employing a grammar of cooperative living, American women and men sound better and smarter than our current political discourse makes them out to be. The best resource for renewing our political discourse, therefore, may be the very heterogeneity that drives us to seek a simple, abstract, common language. The ongoing dialogue between freedom and responsibility, individualism and community, present needs and future plans, that takes place daily in a wide variety of American speech communities could help to revitalize our rights tradition as well as our political life.

*Esperanto was a language created in the late 1880s using simplified grammar and vocabulary borrowed from many languages in an attempt to create a common, universal method of communication. Esperanto was not accepted by people, however, and never achieved wide popularity. — EDS.

PART TEN

Public Opinion

59

JAMES BRYCE

From *The American Commonwealth*

In James Bryce's massive study of the United States, no topic is treated in more adulatory a way than public opinion. It is a little more than one hundred years after the distinguished British visitor's unabashed praise of the American people, whom he saw "freely and constantly reading, talking, and judging of public affairs with a view to voting thereon." Was Bryce writing about the United States when he described a nation that is "patient, tolerant, reasonable, and . . . more likely to be unembittered and unvexed by class divisions"? Perhaps America has not yet quite reached the point Bryce anticipated; maybe Bryce was right, and the United States today is too critical of itself; or, maybe Bryce was wrong.

———

OF ALL the experiments which America has made, this is that which best deserves study, for her solution of the problem differs from all previous solutions, and she has shown more boldness in trusting public opinion, in recognizing and giving effect to it, than has yet been shown elsewhere. Towering over Presidents and State governors, over Congress and State legislatures, over conventions and the vast machinery of party, public opinion stands out, in the United States, as the great source of power, the master of servants who tremble before it. . . .

In the United States public opinion is the opinion of the whole nation, with little distinction of social classes. The politicians, including the members of Congress and of State legislatures, are, perhaps not (as Americans sometimes insinuate) below, yet certainly not above the average level of their constituents. They find no difficulty in keeping touch with outside opinion. Washington or Albany may corrupt them, but not in the way of modifying their political ideas. They do not aspire to the function of forming opinion. They are like the Eastern slave who says "I hear and obey." Nor is there any one class or set of men, or any one "social layer," which more than another originates ideas and builds up political doctrine for the mass. The opinion of the nation is the resultant of the views, not of a number of classes, but of a multitude of individuals, diverse, no doubt, from one another, but, for the purposes of politics far less diverse than if they were members of groups defined by social rank or by property.

The consequences are noteworthy. One is, that statesmen cannot, as in Europe, declare any sentiment which they find telling on their friends or their opponents in politics to be confined to the rich, or to those occupied with government, and to be opposed to the general sentiment of the people. In America you cannot appeal from the classes to the masses. What the employer thinks, his workmen think. What the wholesale merchant feels, the retail storekeeper feels, and the poorer customers feel. Divisions of opinion are vertical and not horizontal. Obviously this makes opinion more easily ascertained, while increasing its force as a governing power, and gives the people, that is to say, all classes in the community, a clearer and stronger consciousness of being the rulers of their country than European peoples have. Every man knows that he is himself a part of the government, bound by duty as well as by self-interest to devote part of his time and thoughts to it. He may neglect this duty, but he admits it to be a duty. . . .

. . . The government is his own, and he individually responsible for its conduct. . . . The Americans are an educated people. . . . They know the constitution of their own country, they follow public affairs, they join in local government and learn from it how government must be carried on, and in particular how discussion must be conducted in meetings, and its results tested at elections. . . .

That the education of the masses is nevertheless a superficial education goes without saying. It is sufficient to enable them to think they know something about the great problems of politics: insufficient to show them how little they know. The public elementary school gives everybody the key to knowledge in making reading and writing familiar, but it has not time to teach him how to use the key. . . . This observation, however, is not so much a reproach to the schools, . . . as a tribute to the height of the ideal which the American conception of popular rule sets up. . . . For the functions of the citizen are not . . . confined to the choosing of legislators, who are then left to settle issues of policy and select executive rulers. The American citizen is virtually one of the governors of the republic. Issues are decided and rulers selected by the direct popular vote. Elections are so frequent that to do his duty at them a citizen ought to be constantly watching public affairs with a full comprehension of the principles involved in them, and a judgment of the candidates derived from a criticism of their arguments as well as a recollection of their past careers. As has been said, the instruction received in the common schools and from the newspapers, and supposed to be developed by the practice of primaries and conventions, while it makes the voter deem himself capable of governing, does not completely fit him to weigh the real merits of statesmen, to discern the true grounds on which questions ought to be decided, to note the drift of events and discover the direction in which parties are being carried. He is like a sailor who knows the spars and ropes of the ship and is expert in working her, but is ignorant of geography and navigation; who can perceive that some of the officers are smart and others dull, but cannot judge which of them is qualified to use the sextant or will best keep his head during a hurricane. . . .

The frame of the American government has assumed and trusted to the activity of public opinion, not only as the power which must correct and remove the difficulties due to the restrictions imposed on each department, and to possible collisions between them, but as the influence which must supply the defects incidental to a system which works entirely by the machinery of popular elections. Under a system of elections one man's vote is as good as another, the vicious and ignorant have as much weight as the wise and good. A system of elections might be imagined which would provide no security for due deliberation or full discussion, a system which, while democratic in name, recognizing no privilege, and referring everything to the vote of the majority, would in practice be hasty, violent, tyrannical. It is with such a possible democracy that one has to contrast the rule of public opinion as it exists in the United States. Opinion declares itself legally through elections. But opinion is at work at other times also, and has other methods of declaring itself. It secures full discussion of issues of policy and of the characters of men. It suffers nothing to be concealed. It listens patiently to all the arguments that are addressed to it. Eloquence, education, wisdom, the authority derived from experience and high character, tell upon it in the long run, and have, perhaps not always their due influence, but yet a great and growing influence. Thus a democracy governing itself through a constantly active public opinion, and not solely by its intermittent mechanism of elections, tends to become patient, tolerant, reasonable, and is more likely to be unembittered and unvexed by class divisions.

It is the existence of such a public opinion as this, the practice of freely and constantly reading, talking, and judging of public affairs with a view to voting thereon, rather than the mere possession of political rights, that gives to popular government that educative and stimulative power which is so frequently claimed as its highest merit.

60

WALTER LIPPMANN

From *The Phantom Public*

Walter Lippmann was a prominent American journalist who wrote during the first half of the twentieth century. In his much-read book on public opinion, The Phantom Public, *Lippmann took a hard and realistic look at the role played by the American people in government decision-making. His conclusions were startlingly critical. He portrayed citizens as relatively uninformed, often disinterested, and usually haphazard in their views. Opinions emerge only in time of crisis, and then fade quickly. Many people do not participate at all. Lippmann extended his harsh judgment to political leaders who skillfully manipulate public opinion. To soften his criticisms, Lippmann pointed to what he believed to be the fallacy behind public opinion: "It is bad for a fat man to try to be a ballet dancer." To expect more of the public, Lippmann felt, was an unrealistic and self-defeating illusion.*

———

THE PRIVATE CITIZEN today has come to feel rather like a deaf spectator in the back row, who ought to keep his mind on the mystery off there, but cannot quite manage to keep awake. He knows he is somehow affected by what is going on. Rules and regulations continually, taxes annually and wars occasionally remind him that he is being swept along by great drifts of circumstance.

Yet these public affairs are in no convincing way his affairs. They are for the most part invisible. They are managed, if they are managed at all, at distant centers, from behind the scenes, by unnamed powers. As a private person he does not know for certain what is going on, or who is doing it, or where he is being carried. No newspaper reports his environment so that he can grasp it; no school has taught him how to imagine it; his ideals, often, do not fit with it; listening to speeches, uttering opinions and voting do not, he finds, enable him to govern it. He lives in a world which he cannot see, does not understand and is unable to direct.

In the cold light of experience he knows that his sovereignty is a fiction. He reigns in theory, but in fact he does not govern. . . .

There is then nothing particularly new in the disenchantment which the private citizen expresses by not voting at all, by voting only for the head of the ticket, by staying away from the primaries, by not reading speeches and documents, by the whole list of sins of omission for which he is denounced. I shall not denounce him further. My sympathies are with him, for I believe that he has been saddled with an impossible task and that he is asked to practice an unattainable ideal. I find it so myself for, although public business is my main interest and I give most of my time to watching it, I cannot find time to do what is expected of me in the theory of democracy; that is, to know what is going on and to have an opinion worth expressing on every question which confronts a self-governing community. And I have not happened to meet anybody, from a President of the United States to a professor of political science, who came anywhere near to embodying the accepted ideal of the sovereign and omnicompetent citizen. . . .

[Today's theories] assume that either the voters are inherently competent to direct the course of affairs or that they are making progress toward such an ideal. I think it is a false ideal. I do not mean an undesirable ideal. I mean an unattainable ideal, bad only in the sense that it is bad for a fat man to try to be a ballet dancer. An ideal should express the true possibilities of its subject. When it does not it perverts the true possibilities. The ideal of the omnicompetent, sovereign citizen is, in my opinion, such a false ideal. It is unattainable. The pursuit of it is misleading. The failure to achieve it has produced the current disenchantment.

The individual man does not have opinions on all public affairs. He does not know how to direct public affairs. He does not know what is happening, why it is happening, what ought to happen. I cannot imagine how he could know, and there is not the least reason for thinking, as mystical democrats have thought, that the compounding of individual ignorances in masses of people can produce a continuous directing force in public affairs. . . .

The need in the Great Society not only for publicity but for uninterrupted publicity is indisputable. But we shall misunderstand the need seriously if we imagine that the purpose of the publication can possibly be the informing of every voter. We live at the mere beginnings of public accounting. Yet the facts far exceed our curiosity. . . . A few executives here and there . . . read them. The rest of us ignore them for the good and sufficient reason that we have other things to do. . . .

Specific opinions give rise to immediate executive acts; to take a job, to do a particular piece of work, to hire or fire, to buy or sell, to stay here or go there, to accept or refuse, to command or obey. General opinions give rise to delegated, indirect, symbolic, intangible results: to a vote, to a resolution, to applause, to criticism, to praise or dispraise, to audiences, circulations, followings, contentment or discontent. The specific opinion may lead to a decision to act within the area where a man has personal jurisdiction, that is, within the limits set by law and custom, his personal power and his personal desire. But general opinions lead only to some sort of expression, such as voting, and do not result in executive acts except in coöperation with the general opinions of large numbers of other persons.

Since the general opinions of large numbers of persons are almost certain to be a vague and confusing medley, action cannot be taken until these opinions have been factored down, canalized, compressed and made uniform. . . . The making of one general will out of a multitude of general wishes . . . consists essentially in the use of symbols which assemble emotions after they have been detached from their ideas. Because feelings are much less specific than ideas, and yet more poignant, the leader is able to make a homogeneous will out of a heterogeneous mass of desires. The process, therefore, by which general opinions are brought to cooperation consists of an intensification of feeling and a degradation of significance. Before a mass of general opinions can eventuate in executive action, the choice is narrowed down to a few alternatives. The victorious alternative is executed not by the mass but by individuals in control of its energy. . . .

. . . We must assume, then, that the members of a public will not possess an insider's knowledge of events or share his point of view. They cannot, therefore, construe intent, or appraise the exact circumstances, enter intimately into the minds of the actors or into the details of the argument. They can watch only for coarse signs indicating where their sympathies ought to turn.

We must assume that the members of a public will not anticipate a problem much before its crisis has become obvious, nor stay with the problem long after its crisis is past. They will not know the antecedent events, will not have seen the issue as it developed, will not have thought out or willed a program, and will not be able to predict the consequences of acting on that program. We must assume as a theoretically fixed premise of popular government that normally men as members of a public will not be well informed, continuously interested, nonpartisan, creative or executive. We must assume that a public is inexpert in its curiosity, intermittent, that it discerns only gross distinctions, is slow to be aroused and quickly diverted; that, since it acts by aligning itself, it personalizes whatever it considers, and is interested only when events have been melodramatized as a conflict.

The public will arrive in the middle of the third act and will leave before the last curtain, having stayed just long enough perhaps to decide who is the hero and who the villain of the piece. Yet usually that judgment will necessarily be made apart from the intrinsic merits, on the basis of a sample of behavior, an aspect of a situation, by very rough external evidence. . . .

. . . The ideal of public opinion is to align men during the crisis of a problem in such a way as to favor the action of those individuals who may be able to compose the crisis. The power to discern those individuals is the end of the effort to educate public opinion. . . .

Public opinion, in this theory, is a reserve of force brought into action during a crisis in public affairs. Though it is itself an irrational force, under favorable institutions, sound leadership and decent training the power of public opinion might be placed at the disposal of those who stood for workable law as against brute assertion. In this theory, public opinion does not make the law. But by canceling lawless power it may establish the condition under which law can be made. It does not reason, investigate, invent, persuade, bargain or settle. But, by holding the aggressive party in check, it may liberate intelligence. Public opinion in its highest ideal will defend those who are prepared to act on their reason against the interrupting force of those who merely assert their will.

That, I think, is the utmost that public opinion can effectively do. With the substance of the problem it can do nothing usually but meddle ignorantly or tyrannically. . . .

For when public opinion attempts to govern directly it is either a failure or a tyranny. It is not able to master the problem intellectually, nor to deal with it except by wholesale impact. The theory of democracy has not recognized this truth because it has identified the functioning of government with the will of the people. This is a fiction. The intricate business of framing laws and of administering them through several hundred thousand public officials is in no sense the act of the voters nor a translation of their will. . . .

Therefore, instead of describing government as an expression of the people's will, it would seem better to say that government consists of a body of officials, some elected, some appointed, who handle professionally, and in the first instance, problems which come to public opinion spasmodically and on appeal. Where the parties directly responsible do not work out an adjustment, public officials intervene. When the officials fail, public opinion is brought to bear on the issue. . . .

This, then, is the ideal of public action which our inquiry suggests. Those who happen in any question to constitute the public should attempt only to create an equilibrium in which settlements can be reached directly and by consent. The burden of carrying on the work of the world, of inventing, creating, executing, of attempting justice, formulating laws and moral codes, of dealing with the technic and the substance, lies not upon public opinion and not upon government but on those who are responsibly concerned as agents in the affair. Where problems arise, the ideal is a settlement by the particular interests involved. They alone know what the trouble really is. No decision by public officials or by commuters reading headlines in the train can usually and in the long run be so good as settlement by consent among the parties at interest. No moral code, no political theory can usually and in the long run be imposed from the heights of public opinion, which will fit a case so well as direct agreement reached where arbitrary power has been disarmed.

It is the function of public opinion to check the use of force in a crisis, so that men, driven to make terms, may live and let live.

61

V. O. KEY

From *Public Opinion and American Democracy*

Professor V. O. Key was a pioneer in the study of many facets of modern American politics, including elections, political parties, and public opinion. His detailed study of public opinion attempted to explain the relationship between the people's opinions and the political leadership's opinions. Key's analysis is complicated but clear in its recognition of both elite and mass influence. A particularly useful concept is Key's "opinion dike." He believed that the public's opinion keeps leaders from straying too far outside the parameters acceptable to the people in the making of policy. Most important, Key lifted the blame for "indecision, decay, and disaster" from the shoulders of the public onto the leadership stratum where, he alleged, it really belongs.

THE EXPLORATION of public attitudes is a pursuit of endless fascination—and frustration. Depiction of the distribution of opinions within the public, identification of the qualities of opinion, isolation of the odd and of the obvious correlates of opinion, and ascertainment of the modes of opinion formation are pursuits that excite human curiosity. Yet these endeavors are bootless unless the findings about the preferences, aspirations, and prejudices of the public can be connected with the workings of the governmental system. The nature of that connection has been suggested by the examination of the channels by which governments become aware of public sentiment and the institutions through which opinion finds more or less formal expression.

When all these linkages are treated, the place of public opinion in government has still not been adequately portrayed. The problem of opinion and government needs to be viewed in an even broader context. Consideration of the role of public opinion drives the observer to the more fundamental question of how it is that democratic governments manage to operate at all. Despite endless speculation on that problem, perplexities still exist about what critical circumstances, beliefs, outlooks, faiths, and conditions are conducive to the maintenance of regimes under which public opinion is controlling, at least in principle, and is, in fact, highly influential. . . . Though the preceding analyses did not uncover the secret of the conditions precedent to the practice of democratic politics, they pointed to a major piece of the puzzle that was missing as we sought to assemble the elements that go into the construction of a democratic regime. The significance of that missing piece may be made apparent in an indirect manner. In an earlier day public opinion seemed to be pictured as a mysterious vapor that emanated from the undifferentiated citizenry and in some way or another enveloped the apparatus of government to bring it into conformity with the public will. These weird conceptions, some of which were mentioned in our introductory chapter, passed out of style as the technique of the sample survey permitted the determination, with some accuracy, of the distribution of opinions within the population. Vast areas of ignorance remain in our information about people's opinions and aspirations; nevertheless, a far more revealing map of the gross topography of public opinion can now be drawn than could have been a quarter of a century ago.

Despite their power as instruments for the observation of mass opinion, sampling procedures do not bring within their range elements of the political system basic for the understanding of the role of mass opinion within the system. Repeatedly, as we have sought to explain particular distributions, movements, and qualities of mass opinion, we have had to go beyond the survey data and make assumptions and estimates about the role and behavior of that thin stratum of persons referred to variously as the political elite, the political activists, the leadership echelons, or the influentials. In the normal operation of surveys designed to obtain tests of mass sentiment, so few persons from this activist stratum fall into the sample that they cannot well be differentiated, even in a static description, from those persons less involved politically. The data tell us almost nothing about the dynamic relations between the upper layer of activists and mass opinion. The missing piece of our puzzle is this elite element of the opinion system. . . .

While the ruling classes of a democratic order are in a way invisible because of the vagueness of the lines defining the influentials and the relative ease of entry to their ranks, it is plain that the modal norms and standards of a democratic elite have their peculiarities. Not all persons in leadership echelons have precisely the same basic beliefs; some may even regard the people as a beast. Yet a fairly high concentration prevails around the modal beliefs, even though the definition of those beliefs must be imprecise. Fundamental is a regard for public opinion, a belief that in some way or another it should prevail. Even those who cynically humbug the people make a great show of deference to the populace. The basic doctrine goes further to include a sense of trusteeship for the people generally and an adherence to the basic doctrine that collective efforts should be dedicated to the promotion of mass gains rather than of narrow class advantage; elite elements tethered to narrow group interest have no slack for maneuver to accommodate themselves to mass aspirations. Ultimate expression of these faiths comes in the willingness to abide by the outcome of popular elections. The growth of leadership structures with beliefs including these broad articles of faith is probably accomplished only over a considerable period of time, and then only under auspicious circumstances.

If an elite is not to monopolize power and thereby to bring an end to democratic practices, its rules of the game must include restraints in the exploitation of public opinion. Dimly perceptible are rules of etiquette that limit the kinds of appeals to public opinion that may be properly made. If it is assumed that the public is manipulable at the hands of unscrupulous leadership (as it is under some conditions), the maintenance of a democratic order requires the inculcation in leadership elements of a taboo against appeals that would endanger the existence of democratic practices. Inflammation of the sentiments of a sector of the public disposed to exert the tyranny of an intolerant majority (or minority) would be a means of destruction of a democratic order. Or by the exploitation of latent differences and conflicts within the citizenry it may at times be possible to paralyze a regime as intense hatreds among classes of people come to dominate public affairs. Or by encouraging unrealistic expectations among the people a clique of politicians may rise to power, a position to be kept by repression as disillusionment sets in. In an experienced democracy such tactics may be "unfair" competition among members of the politically active class. In short, certain restraints on political competition help keep competition within tolerable limits. The observation of a few American political campaigns might lead one to the conclusion that there are no restraints on politicians as they attempt to humbug the people. Even so, admonitions ever recur against arousing class against class, against stirring the animosities of religious groups, and against demagoguery in its more extreme forms. American politicians manifest considerable restraint in this regard when they are tested against the standards of behavior of politicians of most of those regimes that have failed in the attempt to establish or maintain democratic practices. . . .

. . . Certain broad structural or organizational characteristics may need to be maintained among the activists of a democratic order if they are to perform their functions in the system. Fundamental is the absence of sufficient cohesion among the activists to unite them into a single group dedicated to the management of public affairs and public opinion. Solidification of the elite by definition forecloses opportunity for public choice among alternative governing groups and also destroys the mechanism for the unfettered expression of public opinion or of the opinions of the many subpublics. . . .

. . . Competitive segments of the leadership echelons normally have their roots in interests or opinion blocs within society. A degree of social diversity thus may be, if not a prerequisite, at least helpful in the construction of a leadership appropriate for a democratic regime. A series of independent social bases provide the foundations for a political elite difficult to bring to the state of unification that either prevents the rise of democratic processes or converts them into sham rituals. . . .

Another characteristic may be mentioned as one that, if not a prerequisite to government by public opinion, may profoundly affect the nature of a democratic order. This is the distribution through the social structure of those persons highly active in politics. By various analyses, none founded on completely satisfactory data, we have shown that in the United States the political activists—if we define the term broadly—are scattered through the socio-economic hierarchy. The upper-income and occupational groups, to be sure, contribute disproportionately; nevertheless, individuals of high political participation are sprinkled throughout the lesser occupational strata. Contrast the circumstances when the highly active political stratum coincides with the high socioeconomic stratum. Conceivably the winning of consent and the creation of a sense of political participation and of sharing in public affairs may be far simpler when political activists of some degree are spread through all social strata. . . .

Allied with these questions is the matter of access to the wider circles of political leadership and of the recruitment and indoctrination of these political activists. Relative ease of access to the arena of active politics may be a preventive of the rise of intransigent blocs of opinion managed by those denied participation in the regularized processes of politics. In a sense, ease of access is a necessary consequence of the existence of a somewhat fragmented stratum of political activists. . . .

This discussion in terms of leadership echelons, political activists, or elites falls painfully on the ears of democratic romantics. The mystique of democracy has in it no place for ruling classes. As perhaps with all powerful systems of faith, it is vague on the operating details. Yet by their nature governing systems, be they democratic or not, involve a division of social labor. Once that axiom is accepted, the comprehension of democratic practices requires a search for the peculiar characteristics of the political influentials in such an order, for the special conditions under which they work, and for the means by which the people keep them in check. The vagueness of the mystique of democracy is matched by the intricacy of its operating practices. If it is true that those who rule tend sooner or later to prove themselves enemies of the rights of man—and there is something to be said for the validity of this proposition—then any system that restrains that tendency however slightly can excite only awe. . . .

Analytically it is useful to conceive of the structure of a democratic order as consisting of the political activists and the mass of people. Yet this differentiation becomes deceptive unless it is kept in mind that the democratic activists consist of people arranged along a spectrum of political participation and involvement, ranging from those in the highest posts of official leadership to the amateurs who become sufficiently interested to try to round up a few votes for their favorite in the presidential campaign. . . . It is in the dynamics of the system, the interactions between these strata, that the import of public opinion in democratic orders becomes manifest. Between the activists and the mass there exists a system of communication and interplay so complex as to defy simple description; yet identification of a few major features of that system may aid in our construction of a general conception of democratic processes.

Opinion Dikes

In the interactions between democratic leadership echelons and the mass of people some insight comes from the conception of public opinion as a system of dikes which channel public action or which fix a range of discretion within which government may act or within which debate at official levels may proceed. This conception avoids the error of personifying "public opinion" as an entity that exercises initiative and in some way functions as an operating organism to translate its purposes into governmental action.

In one of their aspects the dikes of opinion have a substantive nature in that they define areas within which day-to-day debate about the course of specific action may occur. Some types of legislative proposals, given the content of general opinion, can scarcely expect to attract serious attention. They depart too far from the general understandings of what is proper. A scheme for public ownership of the automobile industry, for example, would probably be regarded as so far outside the area of legitimate public action that not even the industry would become greatly concerned. On the other hand, other types of questions arise within areas of what we have called permissive consensus. A widespread, if not a unanimous, sentiment prevails that supports action toward some general objective, such as the care of the ill or the mitigation of the economic hazards of the individual. Probably quite commonly mass opinion of a permissive character tends to develop in advance of governmental action in many areas of domestic policy. That opinion grows out of public discussion against the background of the modal aspirations and values of people generally. As it takes shape, the time becomes ripe for action that will be generally acceptable or may even arouse popular acclaim for its authors. . . .

The idea of public opinion as forming a system of dikes which channel action yields a different conception of the place of public opinion than does the notion of a government by public opinion as one in which by some mysterious means a referendum occurs on very major issue. In the former conception the articulation between government and opinion is relatively loose. Parallelism between action and opinion tends not to be precise in matters of detail; it prevails rather with respect to broad purpose. And in the correlation of purpose and action time lags may occur between the crystallization of a sense of mass purpose and its fulfillment in public action. Yet in the long run majority purpose and public action tend to be brought into harmony. . . .

The argument amounts essentially to the position that the masses do not corrupt themselves; if they are corrupt, they have been corrupted. If this hypothesis has a substantial strain of validity, the critical element for the health of a democratic order consists in the beliefs, standards, and competence of those who constitute the influentials, the opinion-leaders, the political activists in the order. That group, as has been made plain, refuses to define itself with great clarity in the American system; yet analysis after analysis points to its existence. If a democracy tends toward indecision, decay, and disaster, the responsibility rests here, not in the mass of the people.

62

LAWRENCE JACOBS
ROBERT SHAPIRO

From *Politicians Don't Pander*

Lawrence Jacobs and Robert Shapiro challenge the premise popular in the 1990s that politicians cater to what the public wants: a finger in the wind of public opinion makes policy. No, they find, politicians don't pander. In fact, the authors suggest that the opposite is true. More often, politicians ignore what the mainstream of the public wants, attempting instead to create a version of public opinion that accords with the politicians' views. Media coverage aids in this upside down relationship between the people and their representatives. The end result is that the American people do not believe that the government reflects their views; they do not trust their leaders. To Jacobs and Shapiro, the question of how much public opinion truly shapes policy lies at the heart of American democracy.

THE WAY CONGRESS HANDLED the impeachment of President Bill Clinton revealed a lot about American politics. Commentators and the American public were visibly struck by the unyielding drive of congressional Republicans to remove Clinton from office in the face of clear public opposition. The Republicans' disregard for the preferences of the great majority of Americans contradicted perhaps the most widely accepted presumption about politics—that politicians slavishly follow public opinion.

There was little ambiguity about where Americans stood on Clinton's personal behavior and impeachment. The avalanche of opinion polls during 1998 and early 1999 showed that super-majorities of nearly two-thirds of Americans condemned the president's personal misdeeds, but about the same number approved his job performance, opposed his impeachment and removal from office, and favored a legislative censure as an appropriate alternative punishment.

Despite Americans' strong and unchanging opinions, congressional

Republicans defied the public at almost every turn. Beginning in the fall of 1998, the Republican-led House of Representatives initiated impeachment proceedings; its Judiciary Committee reported impeachment articles; and it passed two articles of impeachment on the House floor. Neither the House nor the Senate allowed a vote on the option supported by the public—censure. For all the civility in the Senate trial of the president on the House-passed articles of impeachment, the Republicans' pursuit of Clinton was checked not by a sudden attentiveness to public opinion but rather by the constitutional requirement of a two-thirds vote and the bipartisan support that this demanded.

The impeachment spectacle reveals one of the most important developments in contemporary American politics—the widening gulf between politicians' policy decisions and the preferences of the American people toward specific issues. The impeachment of Clinton can be added to the long list of policies that failed to mirror public opinion: campaign finance reform, tobacco legislation, Clinton's proposals in his first budget for an energy levy and a high tax on Social Security benefits (despite his campaign promises to cut middle-class taxes), the North American Free Trade Agreement (at its outset), U.S. intervention in Bosnia, as well as House Republican proposals after the 1994 elections for a "revolution" in policies toward the environment, education, Medicare, and other issues.

Recent research . . . provides evidence that this list is not a quirk of recent political developments but part of a trend of declining responsiveness to the public's policy preferences. The conventional wisdom that politicians habitually respond to public opinion when making major policy decisions is wrong. . . .

The Republicans' handling of impeachment fits into a larger pattern in contemporary American politics. . . .

. . . First, Republicans disregarded public opinion on impeachment because their political goals of attracting a majority of voters was offset by their policy goals of enacting legislation that politicians and their supporters favored. The ideological polarization of congressional Republicans and Democrats since the mid-1970s, the greater institutional independence of individual lawmakers, and other factors have raised the political benefits of pursuing policy goals that they and their party's activists desire. Responding to public opinion at the expense of policy goals entailed compromising their own philosophical convictions and risked alienating ideologically extreme party activists and other supporters who volunteer and contribute money to their primary and general election campaigns. Only the heat of an imminent presidential election and the elevated attention that average voters devote to it motivate contemporary politicians to respond to public opinion and absorb the costs of compromising their policy goals.

Indeed, the Republicans' relentless pursuit of impeachment was largely driven by the priority that the domineering conservative wing of the party attached to their policy goal (removing Clinton) over their political goals (appealing to a majority of Americans). Moderate Republicans could not ignore the risk of opposing impeachment—it could lead to a challenge in the next primary election and diminished campaign contributions.

Our second point is that politicians pursue a strategy of *crafted talk* to change public opinion in order to offset the potential political costs of not following the preferences of average voters. Politicians track public opinion not to make policy but rather to determine how to craft their public presentations and win public support for the policies they and their supporters favor. Politicians want the best of both worlds: to enact their preferred policies and to be reelected.

While politicians devote their resources to changing public opinion, their actual influence is a more complex story. Politicians themselves attempt to change public opinion not by directly persuading the public on the merits of their policy choices but by "priming" public opinion: they "stay on message" to highlight standards or considerations for the public to use in evaluating policy proposals. Republicans, for example, emphasized "big government" to prompt the public to think about its uneasiness about government. Politicians' efforts to sway the public are most likely to influence the perceptions, understandings, and evaluations of specific policy proposals such as Republican proposals in 1995 to significantly reduce spending on Medicare to fund a tax cut. But even here, politicians' messages promoting their policy proposals often provoke new or competing messages from their political opponents and the press that complicate or stymie their efforts to move public opinion. In addition, efforts to influence the public's evaluations of specific proposals are unlikely to affect people's values and fundamental preferences (such as those underlying support for Medicare, Social Security, and other well-established programs). We distinguish, then, between political leaders' attempts to alter the public's perceptions, evaluations, and choices concerning very specific proposals (which are susceptible but not certain to change) and Americans' values and long-term preferences (which tend to be stable and particularly resistant to short-term manipulation). In short, politicians' confidence in their ability to move public opinion by crafting their statements and actions boosts their willingness to discount majority opinion; but the reality is that efforts to change public opinion are difficult and are often most successful when deployed against major new policy proposals by the opposition, which has the more modest task of increasing the public's uncertainty and anxiety to avoid risk.

Politicians respond to public opinion, then, but in two quite different ways. In one, politicians assemble information on public opinion to design government policy. This is usually equated with "pandering," and this is most evident during the relatively short period when presidential elections are imminent. The use of public opinion research here, however, raises a troubling question: why has the derogatory term "pander" been pinned on politicians who respond to public opinion? The answer is revealing: the term is deliberately deployed by politicians, pundits, and other elites to belittle government responsiveness to public opinion and reflects a long-standing fear, uneasiness, and hostility among elites toward popular consent and influence over the affairs of government. It is surely odd in a democracy to consider responsiveness to public opinion as disreputable. We challenge the stigmatizing use of the term "pandering" and adopt the neutral concept of "political responsiveness." We suggest that the public's preferences offer both broad directions to policymakers (e.g., establish universal health insurance) and some specific instructions (e.g., rely on an employer mandate for financing reform). In general, policymakers should follow these preferences.

Politicians respond to public opinion in a second manner—they use research on public opinion to pinpoint the most alluring words, symbols, and arguments in an attempt to move public opinion to support their desired policies. Public opinion research is used by politicians to manipulate public opinion, that is, to move Americans to "hold opinions that they would not hold if aware of the best available information and analysis. . . . " Their objective is to *simulate responsiveness.* Their words and presentations are crafted to change public opinion and create the *appearance* of responsiveness as they pursue their desired policy goals. Intent on lowering the potential electoral costs of subordinating voters' preferences to their policy goals, politicians use polls and focus groups not to move their positions closer to the public's but just the opposite: to find the most effective means *to move public opinion closer to their own desired policies.*

Political consultants as diverse as Republican pollster Frank Luntz and Clinton pollster Dick Morris readily confess that legislators and the White House "don't use a poll to reshape a program, but to reshape your argumentation for the program so that the public supports it." Indeed, Republicans' dogged pursuit of impeachment was premised on the assumption that poll-honed presentations would ultimately win public support for their actions. We suggest that this kind of overconfidence in the power of crafted talk to move public opinion explains the political overreaching and failure that was vividly displayed by Clinton's health reform effort during the 1993–94 period and the Republicans' campaign for their policy objectives beginning with their "Contract with America" during 1995–96. Crafted talk has been more effective in opposing rather than promoting policy initiatives partly because the news media represent and magnify disagreement but also because politicians' overconfidence in crafted talk has prompted them to promote policy goals that do not enjoy the support of most Americans or moderate legislators.

Our argument flips the widespread image of politicians as "pandering" to public opinion on its head. Public opinion is not propelling policy decisions as it did in the past. Instead, politicians' own policy goals are increasingly driving major policy decisions and public opinion research, which is used to identify the language, symbols, and arguments to "win" public support for their policy objectives. Responsiveness to public opinion and manipulation of public opinion are not mutually exclusive: politicians manipulate public opinion by tracking public thinking to select the actions and words that resonate with the public.

Our third point is that politicians' muted responsiveness to public opinion and crafting of their words and actions has a profound impact on the mass media and on public opinion itself. In contrast to others who emphasize the nearly unlimited independence and power of the mass media, we argue that press coverage of national politics has been driven by the polarization of politicians and their reliance on crafting their words and deeds. The press focuses on political conflict and strategy because these are visible and genuine features of contemporary American politics. The combination of politicians' staged displays and the media's scrutiny of the motives behind them produced public distrust and fear of major government reform efforts. We do not treat policymaking, media coverage, and public opinion as parts that can be studied one at a time; rather, we study their dynamic configurations and processes of interdependence. Democratic governance and the process of public communications are inseparably linked. . . .

We argue that politicians' pursuits of policy goals have created a reinforcing spiral or cycle that encompasses media coverage and public opinion. It is characterized by three features. First, the polarization of Washington political elites and their strategies to manipulate the media and gain public support have prompted the press to increasingly emphasize or frame its coverage in terms of political conflict and strategy at the expense of the substance of policy issues and problems. Although news reports largely represent the genuine contours of American politics, the media's organizational, financial, and professional incentives prompt them to exaggerate the degree of conflict in order to produce simple, captivating stories for their audiences.

Second, the increased political polarization and politicians' strategy of crafting what they say and do (as conveyed through press coverage) raise the probability of both changes in public understandings and evaluations of specific policy proposals, and public perceptions that proposals for policy change make uncertain or threaten the personal well-being of individual Americans. The presence of a vocal political opposition, combined with the media's attentiveness to the ensuing conflict and the public's skittishness about change, often prevents reformers from changing public opinion as they intended.

Third, the cycle closes as the media's coverage and the public's reaction that was initially sparked by politicians' actions feed back into the political arena. How politicians appraise the media's coverage of their initial actions affects their future strategy and behavior. Politicians latch on to any evidence of changes in public opinion that are favorable to their positions in order to justify their policies and to increase the electoral risk of their rivals for opposing them. . . .

The public's perception that government officials do not listen to or care much about their views accelerated in the 1970s and peaked in the 1990s. Paralleling this trend, polls by Gallup, the Pew Center, and the Center on Policy Attitudes during the second half of the 1990s consistently found that large majorities doubted the founding premise of American government—popular sovereignty and consent of the governed. Over 60 percent of the public (according to responses to a diverse set of survey questions) believed that elected officials in Washington and members of Congress "lose touch" or are "out of touch with average Americans" and do not understand what "most Americans" or "people like you" think. . . .

Increasing political responsiveness to centrist opinion would not produce neutral changes in government policy but ones that can have profound political implications. Politicians who respond to public opinion would enact policies that defied today's calcified political categories of liberal and conservative. The public, on balance, is more conservative on social issues than Democrats; it is less liberal, for instance, toward homosexuality and criminal behavior. On the other hand, the public is supportive of proposals for political reforms and progressive economic, health, and environmental programs, which Republicans reject. More responsive government might well pursue more conservative social policies and more progressive economic and political ones.

The most important implication of raising responsiveness is to reaffirm the spirit and content of democracy in America. The continued slippage in government responsiveness threatens the foundation of our democratic order and the meaning of rule by and for the people. Whether *democratic* government survives is not foreordained or guaranteed; it is the challenge of each generation to be vigilant and reassert its importance. Insisting that politicians follow the popular will and allow citizens to engage in unfettered public debate is central to that struggle.

63

THOMAS CRONIN

From *Direct Democracy*

Although the United States is a representative—republican—system of government, elements of direct democracy have been introduced on the state and local levels over time, especially in the early twentieth century during the Progressive era. Initiative, referendum, and recall give citizens an immediate and direct voice in their government, beyond just electing officials. Professor Thomas Cronin explains these instruments of direct democracy and cites California's 1978 tax-cutting Proposition 13 as a leading example of an important statewide ballot question. Controversy swirls over the wisdom of such exercises in direct democracy. Cronin weighs the advantages against the potential problems of allowing voters to have a direct say in policy-making. His conclusion is that initiative, referendum, and recall will neither destroy American government nor save it. Yet in the twenty-first century, with voters' openly-expressed distrust of public officials, direct democracy will surely become more and more a part of the state and local political scene.

FOR ABOUT A hundred years Americans have been saying that voting occasionally for public officials is not enough. Political reformers contend that more democracy is needed and that the American people are mature enough and deserve the right to vote on critical issues facing their states and the nation. During the twentieth century, American voters in many parts of the country have indeed won the right to write new laws and repeal old ones through the initiative and referendum. They have also thrown hundreds of state and local officials out of office in recall elections.

Although the framers of the Constitution deliberately designed a republic, or indirect democracy, the practice of direct democracy and the debate over its desirability are as old as English settlements in America. Public debate and popular voting on issues go back to early seventeenth-century town assemblies and persist today in New England town meetings.

Populist democracy in America has produced conspicuous assets and conspicuous liabilities. It has won the support and admiration of many enthusiasts, yet it is also fraught with disturbing implications. Its most important contributions came early in this century in the form of the initiative, referendum, and recall, as a reaction to corrupt and unresponsive state legislatures throughout the country. Most of us would not recognize what then passed for representative government. "Bills that the machine and its backers do not desire are smothered in committee; measures which they do desire are brought out and hurried through their passage," said Governor Woodrow Wilson at the time. "It happens again and again that great groups of such bills are rushed through in the hurried hours that mark the close of the legislative sessions, when everyone is withheld from vigilance by fatigue and when it is possible to do secret things." The threat, if not the reality, of the initiative, referendum, and recall helped to encourage a more responsible, civic-minded breed of state legislator. These measures were not intended to subvert or alter the basic character of American government. "Their intention," as Wilson saw it, was "to restore, not to destroy, representative government."

The *initiative* allows voters to propose a legislative measure (statutory initiative) or a constitutional amendment (constitutional initiative) by filing a petition bearing a required number of valid citizen signatures.

The *referendum* refers a proposed or existing law or statute to voters for their approval or rejection. Some state constitutions require referenda; in other states, the legislature may decide to refer a measure to the voters. Measures referred by legislatures (statutes, constitutional amendments, bonds, or advisory questions) are the most common ballot propositions. A *popular* or *petition referendum* (a less frequently used device) refers an already enacted measure to the voters before it can go into effect. States allowing the petition referendum require a minimum number of valid citizen signatures within a specified time. There is confusion about the difference between the initiative and referendum because *referendum* is frequently used in a casual or generic way to describe all ballot measures.

The *recall* allows voters to remove or discharge a public official from office by filing a petition bearing a specified number of valid signatures demanding a vote on the official's continued tenure in office. Recall procedures typically require that the petition be signed by 25 percent of those who voted in the last election, after which a special election is almost always required. The recall differs from impeachment in that the people, not the legislature, initiate the election and determine the outcome with their votes. It is a purely political and not even a semijudicial process.

American voters today admire and respect the virtues of representative government, yet most of them also yearn for an even greater voice in how their laws are made. They understand the defects of both representative and direct democracy and prefer, on balance, to have a mixture of the two. Sensible or sound democracy is their aspiration.

Although Americans cannot cast votes on critical national issues, voters in twenty-six states, the District of Columbia, and hundreds of localities do have the right to put measures on their ballots. Legislatures can also refer measures to the public for a general vote. And constitutional changes in every state except Delaware must be approved by voters before becoming law. Voters in fifteen states and the District of Columbia can also recall elected state officials, and thirty-six states permit the recall of various local officials.

When Americans think of their right to vote, they think primarily of their right to nominate and elect legislators, members of school boards and of city councils, and the American president. Yet California's famous Proposition 13 in June 1978 focused nationwide attention on the public's right to participate in controversial tax decision making, as Californians voted to cut their property taxes by at least half. More voters participated in this issue contest than in the same day's gubernatorial primaries.

California's Proposition 13 had two additional effects. It triggered similar tax-slashing measures (both as bills and as direct legislation by the people) in numerous other states, and it encouraged conservative interest groups to use the initiative and referendum processes to achieve some of their goals. In the past decade conservative interests have placed on state and local ballots scores of measures favoring the death penalty, victims' rights, English-only regulations, and prayer in schools, and opposing taxation or spending, pornography, abortion, and homosexuality. Several states have regularly conducted referenda on issues ranging from a nuclear freeze to seat-belt laws. Citizens are now voting on hundreds of initiatives and referenda at state and local levels. . . .

Skeptics, however, worry about tyranny by the majority and fear voters are seldom well enough informed to cast votes on complicated, technical national laws. People also worry, and justifiably, about the way well-financed special interest groups might use these procedures. Corruption at the state level is much less common today than it was early in the century, but special interests are surely just as involved as ever. The power of campaign contributions is clear. The advantages to those who can afford campaign and political consultants, direct mail firms, and widespread television and media appeals are very real. Although in theory Americans are politically equal, in practice there remain enormous disparities in individuals' and groups' capacities to influence the direction of government. And although the direct democracy devices of the initiative, referendum, and recall type are widely available, the evidence suggests it is generally the organized interests that can afford to put them to use. The idealistic notion that populist democracy devices can make every citizen a citizen-legislator and move us closer to political and egalitarian democracy is plainly an unrealized aspiration.

The initiative, referendum, and recall were born in an era of real grievances. They made for a different kind of democracy in those areas that permitted them. At the very least, they signaled the unacceptability of some of the most corrupt and irresponsible political practices of that earlier era. It is fashionable among political analysts today to say that although they have rarely lived up to their promises, neither have they resulted in the dire outcomes feared by critics. Yet they have had both good and questionable consequences. . . .

By examining direct democracy practices we can learn about the strengths and weaknesses of a neglected aspect of American politics, as well as the workings of representative democracy. We seek to understand it so we can improve it, and to improve it so it can better supplement rather than replace our institutions of representative government. . . .

A populist impulse, incorporating notions of "power to the people" and skepticism about the system has always existed in America. Americans seldom abide quietly the failings and deficiencies of capitalism, the welfare state, or the political decision rules by which we live. We are, as historian Richard Hofstadter wrote, "forever restlessly pitting ourselves against them, demanding changes, improvements, remedies." Demand for more democracy occurs when there is growing distrust of legislative bodies and when there is a growing suspicion that privileged interests exert far greater influences on the typical politician than does the common voter.

Direct democracy, especially as embodied in the referendum, initiative, and recall, is sometimes viewed as a typically American political response to perceived abuses of the public trust. Voters periodically become frustrated with taxes, regulations, inefficiency in government programs, the inequalities or injustices of the system, the arms race, environmental hazards, and countless other irritations. This frustration arises in part because more public policy decisions are now made in distant capitals, by remote agencies or private yet unaccountable entities—such as regulatory bodies, the Federal Reserve Board, foreign governments, multinational alliances, or foreign trading combines—instead of at the local or county level as once was the case, or as perhaps we like to remember. Champions of populist democracy claim many benefits will accrue from their reforms. Here are some:

• Citizen initiatives will promote government responsiveness and accountability. If officials ignore the voice of the people, the people will have an available means to make needed law.

• Initiatives are freer from special interest domination than the legislative branches of most states, and so provide a desirable safeguard that can be called into use when legislators are corrupt, irresponsible, or dominated by privileged special interests.

• The initiative and referendum will produce open, educational debate on critical issues that otherwise might be inadequately discussed.

• Referendum, initiative, and recall are nonviolent means of political participation that fulfill a citizen's right to petition the government for redress of grievances.

• Direct democracy increases voter interest and election-day turnout. Perhaps, too, giving the citizen more of a role in governmental processes might lessen alienation and apathy.

• Finally (although this hardly exhausts the claims), citizen initiatives are needed because legislators often evade the tough issues. Fearing to be ahead of their time, they frequently adopt a zero-risk mentality. Concern with staying in office often makes them timid and perhaps too wedded to the status quo. One result is that controversial social issues frequently have to be resolved in the judicial branch. But who elected the judges?

For every claim put forward on behalf of direct democracy, however, there is an almost equally compelling criticism. Many opponents believe the ordinary citizen usually is not well enough informed about complicated matters to arrive at sound public policy judgments. They also fear the influence of slick television advertisements or bumper sticker messages.

Some critics of direct democracy contend the best way to restore faith in representative institutions is to find better people to run for office. They prefer the deliberations and the collective judgment of elected representatives who have the time to study complicated public policy matters, matters that should be decided within the give-and-take process of politics. That process, they say, takes better account of civil liberties.

Critics also contend that in normal times initiative and referendum voter turnout is often a small proportion of the general population and so the results are unduly influenced by special interests: big money will win eight out of ten times.

A paradox runs throughout this debate. As the United States has aged, we have extended the suffrage in an impressive way. The older the country, the more we have preached the gospel of civic participation. Yet we also have experienced centralization of power in the national government and the development of the professional politician. The citizen-politician has become an endangered species.

Representative government is always in the process of development and decay. Its fortunes rise and fall depending upon various factors, not least the quality of people involved and the resources devoted to making it work effectively. When the slumps come, proposals that would reform and change the character of representative government soon follow. Direct democracy notions have never been entirely foreign to our country— countless proponents from Benjamin Franklin to Jesse Jackson, Jack Kemp, and Richard Gephardt have urged us to listen more to the common citizen. . . .

The American experience with direct democracy has fulfilled neither the dreams and expectations of its proponents nor the fears of its opponents.

The initiative and referendum have not undermined or weakened representative government. The initiative, referendum, and recall have been no more of a threat to the representative principle than has judicial review or the executive veto. Tools of neither the "lunatic fringe" nor the rich, direct democracy devices have become a permanent feature of American politics, especially in the West.

The initiative, referendum, and recall have not been used as often as their advocates would have wished, in part because state legislatures have steadily improved. Better-educated members, more-professional staff, better media coverage of legislative proceedings, and longer sessions have transformed the legislative process at the state level, mostly for the better. Interest groups once denied access to secret sessions now regularly attend, testify, and participate in a variety of ways in the legislative process. Although individuals and some groups remain frustrated, the level and intensity of that frustration appear to be lower than the discontent that prompted the popular democracy movements around the turn of the century.

Still, hundreds of measures have found their way onto ballots in states across the country, and 35 to 40 percent of the more than 1,500 citizen-initiated ballot measures considered since 1904 have won voter approval. About half of these have been on our ballots since World War II. A few thousand legislatively referred measures have also been placed on the ballot, and at least 60 percent of these regularly win voter approval.

Popular, or petition, referenda, placed on the ballot by citizens seeking a voter veto of laws already passed by state legislatures, have been used infrequently. . . . Recall, used mainly at the local and county level, is seldom used against state officials. The marvel is that all these devices of popular democracy, so vulnerable to apathy, ignorance, and prejudice, not only have worked but also have generally been used in a reasonable and constructive manner. Voters have been cautious and have almost always rejected extreme proposals. Most studies suggest that voters, despite the complexity of measures and the deceptions of some campaigns, exercise shrewd judgment, and most students of direct democracy believe most American voters take this responsibility seriously. Just as in candidate campaigns, when they give the benefit of the doubt to the incumbent and the burden of proof is on the challenger to give reasons why he or she should be voted into office, so in issue elections the voter needs to be persuaded that change is needed. In the absence of a convincing case that change is better, the electorate traditionally sticks with the status quo.

Few radical measures pass. Few measures that are discriminatory or would have diminished the rights of minorities win voter approval, and most of the exceptions are ruled unconstitutional by the courts. On balance, the voters at large are no more prone to be small-minded, racist, or sexist than are legislators or courts.

A case can be made that elected officials are more tolerant, more educated, and more sophisticated than the average voter. "Learning the arguments for freedom and tolerance formulated by notables such as Jefferson, Madison, Mill, or the more libertarian justices of the Supreme Court is no simple task," one study concludes. "Many of those arguments are subtle, esoteric, and difficult to grasp. Intelligence, awareness, and education are required to appreciate them fully." Yet on the occasional issues affecting civil liberties and civil rights that have come to the ballot, voters have generally acted in an enlightened way. This is in part the case because enlightened elites help shape public opinion on such occasions through endorsements, news editorials, talk-show discussions, public debates, and legislative and executive commentary. Further, those voting on state and local ballot measures are usually among the top 30 or 40 percent in educational and information levels.

The civic and educational value of direct democracy upon the electorate has been significant, but this aspect of the promise of direct democracy was plainly overstated from the start. Most voters make up their minds on ballot issues or recall elections in the last few days, or even hours, before they vote. The technical and ambiguous language of many of these measures is still an invitation to confusion, and about a quarter of those voting in these elections tell pollsters they could have used more information in making their decisions on these types of election choices.

Like any other democratic institution, the initiative, referendum, and recall have their shortcomings. Voters are sometimes confused. On occasion an ill-considered or undesirable measure wins approval. Large, organized groups and those who can raise vast sums of money are in a better position either to win, or especially to block, approval of ballot measures. Sometimes a recall campaign is mounted for unfair reasons, and recall campaigns can stir up unnecessary and undesirable conflict in a community. Most of these criticisms can also be leveled at our more traditional institutions. Courts sometimes err, as in the *Dred Scott* decision and in *Plessy v. Ferguson* or *Korematsu*. Presidents surely make mistakes (FDR's attempt to pack the Supreme Court, 1937; Kennedy's Bay of Pigs fiasco, 1961; Nixon's involvement in the Watergate break-in and subsequent coverup, 1972–1974; Reagan's involvement in the Iran-contra arms deal, 1986). And legislatures not only make mistakes about policy from time to time but wind up spending nearly a third of their time amending, changing, and correcting past legislation that proved inadequate or wrong. In short, we pay a price for believing in and practicing democracy — whatever the form.

Whatever the shortcomings of direct democracy, and there are several, they do not justify the elimination of the populist devices from those state constitutions permitting them. Moreover, any suggestion to repeal the initiative, referendum, and recall would be defeated by the voters. Public opinion strongly supports retaining these devices where they are allowed. . . .

In sum, direct democracy devices have not been a cure-all for most political, social, or economic ills, yet they have been an occasional remedy, and generally a moderate remedy, for legislative lethargy and the misuse and nonuse of legislative power. It was long feared that these devices would dull legislators' sense of responsibility without in fact quickening the people to the exercise of any real control in public affairs. Little evidence exists for those fears today. When popular demands for reasonable change are repeatedly ignored by elected officials and when legislators or other officials ignore valid interests and criticism, the initiative, referendum, and recall can be a means by which the people may protect themselves in the grand tradition of self-government.

PART ELEVEN

Interest Groups

64

ALEXIS DE TOCQUEVILLE

From *Democracy in America*

Interest-group politics remains a big part of U.S. government today—for good and bad. But it is not as new a part as it may seem. Young French aristocrat Alexis de Tocqueville, visiting in 1831, observed how naturally Americans formed "associations." Just like today, groups were formed "to promote the public safety, commerce, industry, morality, and religion." In a country that emphasized individuality, Tocqueville felt, group allegiances gave people the power to work together to reach shared goals. American interest groups were out in the open, meeting freely to advance their view- points. Tocqueville, whose earlier selection from Democracy in America *opened this book, placed great faith in interest groups as a way that minorities could protect themselves from "tyranny of the majority." Today, one wonders how he would suggest that the nation protect itself from the tyranny of interest groups.*

———

IN NO COUNTRY IN the world has the principle of association been more successfully used, or more unsparingly applied to a multitude of different objects, than in America. Besides the permanent associations, which are established by law under the names of townships, cities, and counties, a vast number of others are formed and maintained by the agency of private individuals.

The citizen of the United States is taught from his earliest infancy to rely upon his own exertions, in order to resist the evils and the difficulties of life; he looks upon the social authority with an eye of mistrust and anxiety, and he only claims its assistance when he is quite unable to shift without it. This habit may even be traced in the schools of the rising generation, where the children in their games are wont to submit to rules which they have themselves established, and to punish misdemeanors which they have themselves defined. The same spirit pervades every act of social life. If a stoppage occurs in a thoroughfare, and the circulation of the public is hindered, the neighbors immediately constitute a deliberative body; and this extemporaneous assembly gives rise to an executive power, which remedies the inconvenience, before anybody has thought of recur- ring to an authority superior to that of the persons immediately concerned. If the public pleasures are concerned, an association is formed to provide for the splendor and the regularity of the entertainment. Societies are formed to resist enemies which are exclusively of a moral nature, and to diminish the vice of intemperance: in the United States associations are established to promote public order, commerce, industry, morality, and religion, for there is no end which the human will seconded by the collective exertions of individuals, despairs of attaining. . . .

An association consists simply in the public assent which a number of individuals give to certain doctrines; and in the engagement which they contract to promote the spread of those doctrines by their exertions. The right of associating with such views is very analogous to the liberty of unlicensed writing; but societies thus formed possess more authority than the press. When an opinion is represented by a society, it necessarily assumes a more exact and explicit form. It numbers its partisans, and compromises their welfare in its cause: they, on the other hand, become acquainted with each other, and their zeal is increased by their number. An association unites the efforts of minds which have a tendency to diverge in one single channel, and urges them vigorously towards the one single end which it points out.

The second degree in the right of association is the power of meeting. When an association is allowed to establish centres of action at certain important points in the country, its activity is increased, and its influence extended. Men have the opportunity of seeing each other; means of execution are more readily combined; and opinions are maintained with a warmth and energy which written language cannot approach.

Lastly, in the exercise of the right of political association, there is a third degree: the partisans of an opinion may unite in electoral bodies, and choose delegates to represent them in a central assembly. This is, properly speaking, the application of the representative system to a party.

Thus, in the first instance, a society is formed between individuals professing the same opinion, and the tie which keeps it together is of a purely intellectual nature: in the second case, small assemblies are formed which only represent a faction of the party. Lastly, in the third case, they constitute a separate nation in the midst of the nation, a government within the Government. . . .

It cannot be denied that the unrestrained liberty of association for political purposes is the privilege which a people is longest in learning how to exercise. If it does not throw the nation into anarchy, it perpetually augments the chances of that calamity. On one point, however, this perilous liberty offers a security against dangers of another kind; in countries where associations are free, secret societies are unknown. In America, there are numerous factions, but no conspiracies. . . .

The most natural privilege of man, next to the right of acting for himself, is that of combining his exertions with those of his fellow-creatures, and of acting in common with them. I am therefore led to conclude that the right of association is almost as inalienable as the right of personal liberty. . . .

65

E. E. SCHATTSCHNEIDER

From *The Semisovereign People*

The late 1950s and early 1960s was a time when political scientists placed their focus on the interest group theory of American politics. Although hardly a new idea, interest group politics was studied intensely, sometimes to be idealized as the perfect model of government and other times critiqued as the downfall of democracy. Scholar E. E. Schattschneider's much-cited book explored the "pressure system" in American politics, dominated by "organized" (as opposed to informal), "special-interest" (not public-interest) groups. Schattschneider's conclusion was that "the pressure system has an upper-class bias." Decades later, political scientists might not use the exact same language as Schattschneider, who relied on the concept of class in his analysis. Today, vastly different degrees of organization, financial resources, and intensity separate interest group claimants in the competition for getting their issues heard by the government.

MORE THAN any other system American politics provides the raw materials for testing the organizational assumptions of two contrasting kinds of politics, *pressure politics* and *party politics*. The concepts that underlie these forms of politics constitute the raw stuff of a general theory of political action. The basic issue between the two patterns of organization is one of size and scope of conflict; pressure groups are small-scale organizations while political parties are very large-scale organizations. One need not be surprised, therefore, that the partisans of large-scale and small-scale organizations differ passionately, because the outcome of the political game depends on the scale on which it is played.

To understand the controversy about the scale of political organization it is necessary first to take a look at some theories about interest-group politics. Pressure groups have played a remarkable role in American politics, but they have played an even more remarkable role in American political theory. Considering the political condition of the country in the first third of the twentieth century, it was probably inevitable that the discussion of special interest pressure groups should lead to development of "group" theories of politics in which an attempt is made to explain everything in terms of group activity, i.e., an attempt to formulate a universal group theory. Since one of the best ways to test an idea is to ride it into the ground, political theory has unquestionably been improved by the heroic attempt to create a political universe revolving about the group. Now that we have a number of drastic statements of the group theory of politics pushed to a great extreme, we ought to be able to see what the limitations of the idea are. . . .

One difficulty running through the literature of the subject results from the attempt to explain *everything* in terms of the group theory. On general grounds it would be remarkable indeed if a single hypothesis explained everything about so complex a subject as American politics. Other difficulties have grown out of the fact that group concepts have been stated in terms so universal that the subject seems to have no shape or form.

The question is: Are pressure groups the universal basic ingredient of all political situations, and do they explain everything? To answer this question it is necessary to review a bit of rudimentary political theory.

Two modest reservations might be made merely to test the group dogma. We might clarify our ideas if (1) we explore more fully the possibility of making a distinction between public interest groups and special-interest groups and (2) if we distinguished between organized and unorganized groups. . . .

As a matter of fact, the distinction between *public* and *private* interests is a thoroughly respectable one; it is one of the oldest known to political theory. In the literature of the subject the public interest refers to general or common interests shared by all or by substantially all members of the community. Presumably no community exists unless there is some kind of community of interests, just as there is no nation without some notion of national interests. If it is really impossible to distinguish between private and public interests the group theorists have produced a revolution in political thought so great that it is impossible to foresee its consequences. For this reason the distinction ought to be explored with great care.

At a time when nationalism is described as one of the most dynamic forces in the world, it should not be difficult to understand that national interests actually do exist. It is necessary only to consider the proportion of the American budget devoted to national defense to realize that the common interest in national survival is a great one. Measured in dollars this interest is one of the biggest things in the world. Moreover, it is difficult to describe this interest as special. The diet on which the American leviathan feeds is something more than a jungle of disparate special interests. In the literature of democratic theory the body of common agreement found in the community is known as the "consensus" without which it is believed that no democratic system can survive.

The reality of the common interest is suggested by demonstrated capacity of the community to survive. There must be something that holds people together.

In contrast with the common interests are the special interests. The implication of this term is that these are interests shared by only a few people or a fraction of the community; they *exclude* others and may be *adverse* to them. A special interest is exclusive in about the same way as private property is exclusive. In a complex society it is not surprising that there are some interests that are shared by all or substantially all members of the community and some interests that are not shared so widely. The distinction is useful precisely because conflicting claims are made by people about the nature of their interests in controversial matters. . . .

Is it possible to distinguish between the "interests" of the members of the National Association of Manufacturers and the members of the American League to Abolish Capital Punishment? The facts in the two cases are not identical. First, *the members of the A.L.A.C.P. obviously do not expect to be hanged.* The membership of the A.L.A.C.P. is not restricted to persons under indictment for murder or in jeopardy of the extreme penalty. *Anybody* can join A.L.A.C.P. Its members oppose capital punishment although they are not personally likely to benefit by the policy they advocate. The inference is therefore that the interest of the A.L.A.C.P. is not adverse, exclusive or special. It is not like the interest of the Petroleum Institute in depletion allowances. . . .

We can now examine the second distinction, the distinction between organized and unorganized groups. The question here is not whether the distinction can be made but whether or not it is worth making. Organization has been described as "merely a stage or degree of interaction" in the development of a group.

The proposition is a good one, but what conclusions do we draw from it? We do not dispose of the matter by calling the distinction between organized and unorganized groups a "mere" difference of degree because some of the greatest differences in the world are differences of degree. As far as special-interest politics is concerned the implication to be avoided is that a few workmen who habitually stop at a corner saloon for a glass of beer are essentially the same as the United States Army because the difference between them is merely one of degree. At this point we have a distinction that makes a difference. . . .

If we are able, therefore, to distinguish between public and private interests and between organized and unorganized groups we have marked out the major boundaries of the subject; *we have given the subject shape and scope.* We are now in a position to attempt to define the area we want to explore. Having cut the pie into four pieces, we can now appropriate the piece we want and leave the rest to someone else. For a multitude of reasons *the most likely field of study is that of the organized, special-interest groups.* The advantage of concentrating on organized groups is that they are known, identifiable and recognizable. The advantage of concentrating on special-interest groups is that they have one important characteristic in common: they are all exclusive. This piece of the pie (the organized special-interest groups) we shall call the *pressure system.* The pressure system has boundaries we can define; we can fix its scope and make an attempt to estimate its bias. . . .

The organized groups listed in the various directories (such as *National Associations of the United States,* published at intervals by the United States Department of Commerce) and specialty yearbooks, registers, etc., and the *Lobby Index,* published by the United States House of Representatives, probably include the bulk of the organizations in the pressure system. All compilations are incomplete, but these are extensive enough to provide us with some basis for estimating the scope of the system. . . .

When lists of these organizations are examined, the fact that strikes the student most forcibly is that *the system is very small.* The range of organized, identifiable, known groups is amazingly narrow; there is nothing remotely universal about it. There is a tendency on the part of the publishers of directories of associations to place an undue emphasis on business organizations, an emphasis that is almost inevitable because the business community is by a wide margin the most highly organized segment of society. Publishers doubtless tend also to reflect public demand for information. Nevertheless, the dominance of business groups in the pressure system is so marked that it probably cannot be explained away as an accident of the publishing industry. . . .

The business or upper-class bias of the pressure system shows up everywhere. Businessmen are four or five times as likely to write to their congressmen as manual laborers are. College graduates are far more apt to write to their congressmen than people in the lowest educational category are. . . .

Broadly, the pressure system has an upper-class bias. There is over-

whelming evidence that participation in voluntary organizations is related
to upper social and economic status; the rate of participation is much
higher in the upper strata than it is elsewhere. . . .

The bias of the system is shown by the fact that *even nonbusiness
organizations reflect an upper-class tendency*. . . .

The class bias of associational activity gives meaning to the limited
scope of the pressure system, because *scope and bias are aspects of the same
tendency*. The data raise a serious question about the validity of the proposition that special-interest groups are a universal form of political organization reflecting *all* interests. As a matter of fact, to suppose that everyone
participates in pressure-group activity and that all interests get themselves
organized in the pressure system is to destroy the meaning of this form
of politics. The pressure system makes sense only as the political instrument
of a segment of the community. It gets results by being selective and
biased; *if everybody got into the act the unique advantages of this form of
organization would be destroyed, for it is possible that if all interests could be
mobilized the result would be a stalemate*.

Special-interest organizations are most easily formed when they deal
with small numbers of individuals who are acutely aware of their exclusive
interests. To describe the conditions of pressure-group organization in
this way is, however, to say that it is primarily a business phenomenon.
Aside from a few very large organizations (the churches, organized labor,
farm organizations, and veterans' organizations) the residue is a small
segment of the population. *Pressure politics is essentially the politics of small
groups*.

The vice of the groupist theory is that it conceals the most significant
aspects of the system. The flaw in the pluralist heaven is that the heavenly
chorus sings with a strong upper-class accent. Probably about 90 percent
of the people cannot get into the pressure system.

The notion that the pressure system is automatically representative of
the whole community is a myth fostered by the universalizing tendency
of modern group theories. *Pressure politics is a selective process* ill designed
to serve diffuse interests. The system is skewed, loaded and unbalanced
in favor of a fraction of a minority. . . .

The competing claims of pressure groups and political parties for the
loyalty of the American public revolve about the difference between
the results likely to be achieved by small-scale and large-scale political
organization. Inevitably, the outcome of pressure politics and party politics
will be vastly different.

66

THEODORE LOWI

From *The End of Liberalism*

No assessment of the importance of interest groups in American politics would be complete without this classic work by Theodore Lowi. Lowi presents a ground-breaking criticism of interest-group politics, which he calls "interest-group liberalism" and "pluralism." Look for his arguments about the supposed-balance among groups. Note Lowi's view about government's role in perpetuating interest-group politics. His questioning of the actual definition of an interest group is important. Lowi then considers how interest-group politics treats the American people as a whole: "The public is shut out." His final argument is stunning: interest groups resist change; they become institutionalized, with government approval, and in the end are really conservative.

————

THE MOST clinically accurate term to capture the American variant . . . is *interest-group liberalism*. It is liberalism because it is optimistic about government, expects to use government in a positive and expansive role, is motivated by the highest sentiments, and possesses a strong faith that what is good for government is good for the society. It is interest-group liberalism because it sees as both necessary and good a policy agenda that is accessible to all organized interests and makes no independent judgment of their claims. It is interest-group liberalism because it defines the public interest as a result of the amalgamation of various claims. A brief sketch of the working model of interest-group liberalism turns out to be a vulgarized version of the pluralist model of modern political science: (1) Organized interests are homogeneous and easy to define. Any duly elected representative of any interest is taken as an accurate representative of each and every member. (2) Organized interests emerge in every sector of our lives and adequately represent most of those sectors, so that one organized group can be found effectively answering and checking some other organized group as it seeks to prosecute its claims against society. And (3) the role of government is one of insuring access to the most effectively organized, and of ratifying the agreements and adjustments worked out among the competing leaders.

This last assumption is supposed to be a statement of how a democracy works and how it ought to work. Taken together, these assumptions amount to little more than the appropriation of the Adam Smith "hidden hand" model for politics, where the group is the entrepreneur and the equilibrium is not lowest price but the public interest. . . .

. . . Interest-group liberalism . . . had the approval of political scientists because it could deal with so many of the realities of power. It was further appealing because large interest groups and large memberships could be taken virtually as popular rule in modern dress. . . . And it fit the needs of corporate leaders, union leaders, and government officials desperately searching for support as they were losing communal attachments to their constituencies. . . .

A[n] . . . increasingly important positive appeal of interest-group liberalism is that it helps create the sense that power need not be power at all, control need not be control, and government need not be coercive. If sovereignty is parceled out among groups, then who is out anything? As a major *Fortune* editor enthusiastically put it, government power, group power, and individual power may go up simultaneously. If the groups to be controlled control the controls, then "to administer does not always mean to rule." The inequality of power and the awesome coerciveness of government are always gnawing problems in a democratic culture. . . .

In sum, leaders in modern, consensual democracies are ambivalent about government. Government is obviously the most efficacious way of achieving good purposes, but alas, it is efficacious because it is coercive. To live with that ambivalence, modern policy-makers have fallen prey to the belief that public policy involves merely the identification of the problems toward which government ought to be aimed. It pretends that through "pluralism," "countervailing power," "creative federalism," "partnership," and "participatory democracy" the unsentimental business of coercion need not be involved and that unsentimental decisions about how to employ coercion need not really be made at all. Stated in the extreme, the policies of interest-group liberalism are end-oriented but ultimately self-defeating. Few standards of implementation, if any, accompany delegations of power. The requirement of standards has been replaced by the requirement of participation. The requirement of law has been replaced by the requirement of contingency. As a result, the ends of interest-group liberalism are nothing more than sentiments and therefore not really ends at all. . . .

. . . Interest-group liberals have the pluralist paradigm in common and its influence on the policies of the modern state has been very large and very consistent. Practices of government are likely to change only if there is a serious reexamination of the theoretical components of the public philosophy and if that reexamination reveals basic flaws in the theory. Because they guide so much of the analysis of succeeding chapters, contentions about the fundamental flaws in the theory underlying interest-group liberals ought to be made explicit here at the outset. Among the many charges to be made against pluralism, the following three probably best anticipate the analysis to come.

1. The pluralist component has badly served liberalism by propagating the faith that a system built primarily upon groups and bargaining is self-corrective. Some parts of this faith are false, some have never been tested one way or the other, and others can be confirmed only under very special conditions. For example, there is the faulty assumption that groups have other groups to confront in some kind of competition. Another very weak assumption is that people have more than one salient group, that their multiple or overlapping memberships will insure competition, and at the same time will keep competition from becoming too intense. This concept of overlapping membership is also supposed to prove the voluntary character of groups, since it reassures us that even though one group may be highly undemocratic, people can vote with their feet by moving over to some other group to represent their interests. Another assumption that has become an important liberal myth is that when competition between or among groups takes place the results yield a public interest or some other ideal result. As has already been observed, this assumption was borrowed from laissez-faire economists and has even less probability of being borne out in the political system. One of the major Keynesian* criticisms of market theory is that even if pure competition among factors of supply and demand did yield an equilibrium, the equilibrium could be at something far less than the ideal of full employment at reasonable prices. Pure pluralist competition, similarly, might produce political equilibrium, but the experience of recent years shows that it occurs at something far below an acceptable level of legitimacy, or access, or equality, or innovation, or any other valued political commodity.

2. Pluralist theory is also comparable to laissez-faire economics in the extent to which it is unable to come to terms with the problem of imperfect competition. When a program is set up in a specialized agency, the number of organized interest groups surrounding it tends to be re-

*Keynesians are economists who subscribe to the ideas of Englishman John Maynard Keynes. Keynes provided the economic basis for President Franklin Roosevelt's New Deal in the 1930s by advocating government intervention in the economy to "prime the pump" during the Depression. Keynesians opposed pure market theory in which the economy would balance itself by competition. Instead, they believed that government must create jobs by spending money it borrowed, in order to stimulate employment and consumption, thereby eventually building the economy back to prosperity. — EDS.

duced, reduced precisely to those groups and factions to whom the special-
ization is most salient. That almost immediately transforms the situation
from one of potential competition to one of potential oligopoly. As
in the economic marketplace, political groups surrounding an agency
ultimately learn that direct confrontation leads to net loss for all the
competitors. Rather than countervailing power there is more likely to be
accommodating power. Most observers and practitioners continue to hold
on to the notion of group competition despite their own recognition that
it is far from a natural state. [Economist John Kenneth] Galbraith was
early to recognize this but is by no means alone is his position that "the
support of countervailing power has become in modern times perhaps
the major peace-time function of the Federal government." Group competition in Congress and around agencies is not much of a theory if it
requires constant central government support.

3. The pluralist paradigm depends upon an idealized conception of
the group. Laissez-faire economics may have idealized the enterprise and
the entrepreneur but never more than the degree to which the pluralist
sentimentalizes the group, the group member, and the interests. We have
already noted the contrast between the traditional American or Madisonian definition of the group as adverse to the aggregate interests of the
community with the modern view that groups are basically good things
unless they break the law or the rules of the game. To the Madisonian,
groups were a necessary evil much in need of regulation. To the modern
pluralist, groups are good, requiring only accommodation. Madison went
beyond his definition of the group to a position that "the regulation of
these various interfering interests forms the principal task of modern
legislation." This is a far cry from the sentimentality behind such notions
as "supportive countervailing power," "group representation in the interior
processes of . . . ," and "maximum feasible participation." . . .

The problems of pluralist theory are of more than academic interest.
They are directly and indirectly responsible for some of the most costly
attributes of modern government: (1) the atrophy of institutions of popular
control; (2) the maintenance of old and the creation of new structures of
privilege; and (3) conservatism in several senses of the word. These three
hypotheses do not exhaust the possibilities but are best suited to introduce
the analysis of policies and programs in the next six chapters.

1. In *The Public Philosophy*, Walter Lippmann was rightfully concerned
over the "derangement of power" whereby modern democracies tend
first toward unchecked elective leadership and then toward drainage of
public authority from elective leaders down into the constituencies. However, Lippmann erred if he thought of constituents as only voting constitu-

encies. Drainage has tended toward "support-group constituencies," and with special consequences. Parceling out policy-making power to the most interested parties tends strongly to destroy political responsibility. A program split off with a special imperium to govern itself is not merely an administrative unit. It is a structure of power with impressive capacities to resist central political control.

When conflict of interest is made a principle of government rather than a criminal act, programs based upon such a principle cut out all of that part of the mass of people who are not specifically organized around values salient to the goals of that program. The people are shut out at the most creative phase of policy-making—where the problem is first defined. The public is shut out also at the phase of accountability because in theory there is enough accountability to the immediate surrounding interests. In fact, presidents and congressional committees are most likely to investigate an agency when a complaint is brought to them by one of the most interested organizations. As a further consequence, the accountability we do get is functional rather than substantive; and this involves questions of equity, balance, and equilibrium, to the exclusion of questions of the overall social policy and whether or not the program should be maintained at all. It also means accountability to experts first and amateurs last; and an expert is a person trained and skilled in the mysteries and technologies of that particular program.

Finally, in addition to the natural tendencies, there tends also to be a self-conscious conspiracy to shut out the public. One meaningful illustration, precisely because it is such an absurd extreme, is found in the French system of interest representation in the Fourth Republic. As the Communist-controlled union, the Confédération Générale du Travail (CGT), intensified its participation in postwar French government, it was able to influence representatives of interests other than employees. In a desperate effort to insure that the interests represented on the various boards were separated and competitive, the government issued a decree that "each member of the board must be *independent of the interests he is not representing.*"

2. Programs following the principles of interest-group liberalism tend to create and maintain privilege; and it is a type of privilege particularly hard to bear or combat because it is touched with a symbolism of the state. Interest-group liberalism is not merely pluralism but is *sponsored* pluralism. Pluralists ease our consciences about the privileges of organized groups by characterizing them as representative and by responding to their "iron law of oligarchy" by arguing that oligarchy is simply a negative name for organization. Our consciences were already supposed to be

partly reassured by the notion of "overlapping memberships." But however true it may be that overlapping memberships exist and that oligarchy is simply a way of leading people efficiently toward their interests, the value of these characteristics changes entirely when they are taken from the context of politics and put into the context of pluralistic government. The American Farm Bureau Federation is no "voluntary association" if it is a legitimate functionary within the extension system. Such tightly knit corporate groups as the National Association of Home Builders (NAHB), the National Association of Real Estate Boards (NAREB), the National Association for the Advancement of Colored People (NAACP), or the National Association of Manufacturers (NAM) or American Federation of Labor-Congress of Industrial Organizations (AFL-CIO) are no ordinary lobbies after they become part of the "interior processes" of policy formation. Even in the War on Poverty, one can only appreciate the effort to organize the poor by going back and pondering the story and characters in *The Three Penny Opera*. The "Peachum factor" in public affairs may be best personified in Sargent Shriver and his strenuous efforts to get the poor housed in some kind of group before their representation was to begin. . . .

The more clear and legitimized the representation of a group or its leaders in policy formation, the less voluntary its membership in that group and the more necessary is loyalty to its leadership for people who share the interests in question. And, the more widespread the policies of recognizing and sponsoring organized interest, the more hierarchy is introduced into our society. It is a well-recognized and widely appreciated function of formal groups in modern society to provide much of the necessary everyday social control. However, when the very thought processes behind public policy are geared toward these groups they are bound to take on the involuntary character of *public* control.

3. The conservative tendencies of interest-group liberalism can already be seen in the two foregoing objections: weakening of popular control and support of privilege. A third dimension of conservatism, stressed here separately, is the simple conservatism of resistance to change. David Truman, who has certainly not been a strong critic of self-government by interest groups, has, all the the same, provided about the best statement of the general tendency of established agency-group relationships to be "highly resistant to disturbance":

New and expanded functions are easily accommodated, provided they develop and operate through existing channels of influence and do not tend to alter the relative importance of those influences. Disturbing changes are those that modify either the content or the relative strength of the component forces operating through an administrative agency. In the face of such changes, or the threat of them, the "old line" agency is highly inflexible.

If this already is a tendency in a pluralistic system, then agency-group relationships must be all the more inflexible to the extent that the relationship is official and legitimate.
Innumerable illustrations will crop up throughout the book. They will be found in new areas of so-called social policy, such as the practice early in the War on Poverty to co-opt neighborhood leaders, thereby creating more privilege than alleviating poverty. . . . Old and established groups doing good works naturally look fearfully upon the emergence of competing, perhaps hostile, new groups. That is an acceptable and healthy part of the political game—until the competition between them is a question of "who shall be the government?" At that point conservatism becomes a matter of survival for each group, and a direct threat to the public interest. Ultimately this threat will be recognized.

67

JEFFREY BIRNBAUM

From *The Lobbyists*

Journalist Jeffrey Birnbaum takes readers back to 1990, when Republican President Bush and the Democratic Congress took on the budget bill. From the start, the complex negotiations were fertile territory for Washington's corporate lobbyists. Lobbying is not a much-loved or well-respected activity. It epitomizes life "inside the Beltway." This excerpt from Birnbaum's fascinating account focuses on Wayne Thevenot, one of the many lobbyists who got involved in 1990's behind-the-scenes budget maneuverings. Thevenot, of Concord Associates (whose most important client was the National Realty Committee) was a Washington veteran who began as a congressional aide decades ago. Interest groups and lobbying, as James Madison anticipated, are inevitable in a large, diverse nation. Still, K Street, where many lobbying firms have their offices, might not have been exactly what Madison had in mind.

"Okay," the President says. "Let's talk."

IT IS THE BRIGHT, clear morning of Tuesday, June 26, 1990, and President George Bush is meeting in the White House with his economic advisers and the congressional leaders of both parties. Together, over steaming coffee in the private quarters, they face a crisis. The federal budget deficit is careening out of control, and efforts to negotiate a solution are getting nowhere. At around 8:30 A.M., after an hour of fruitless talk, the Democrats finally assert that the President has run out of choices. He must renounce his "no new taxes" pledge—the oath that was instrumental in getting him elected. He must make a public statement, they say, about the need to raise taxes.

The room grows silent.

Then the President utters those fateful words.

Not long thereafter, a short statement is quietly tacked on to a bulletin in the White House press room. "It is clear to me that both the size of the deficit problem and the need for a package that can be enacted require all of the following," it reads, including the real shocker: "tax revenue increases."

The announcement hits Washington like an explosion. . .

Later that morning in another part of town, the phones start ringing at Concord Associates, a small lobbyists-for-hire company that overlooks the Treasury Department in the Willard Office Building. Wayne Thevenot, a balding former staffer in the Senate, gets a call from his wife, Laura, who is also a lobbyist. And James Rock, a bearded former aide in the House, hears from his wife, Sue, who works inside the government on the staff of the Senate's budget committee. Both women bring the same news about the President's announcement, and both men confess embarrassment. "How could I not have known?" they each wonder. As lobbyists, they are no longer part of the government, but they know enough high officials in Washington to hear about most significant things before they are announced.

This time, as usual, they had plenty of opportunity to know in advance. Four days earlier, Rock had attended a lobbyists' breakfast where Robert C. Byrd, the powerful chairman of the Senate Appropriations Committee, was the featured speaker. And just the day before, Thevenot had been among a small group of lobbyists who paid Senate Minority Leader Robert Dole to have lunch with them at the 116 Club, an exclusive haunt for lobbyists on Capitol Hill. If anyone in Washington had known what the President was going to do, these two would have. But apparently they knew nothing; neither had breathed a word about the momentous change.

Thevenot and Rock are surprised about the turn of events, but they are not disappointed. Far from it. This is just the kind of news lobbyists love; it gives them something to act on. As a result, their expensively decorated offices now hum with excitement. Unlike [American Trucking

Association lobbyist Thomas] Donohue and [his aide, Kenneth] Simonson, who work only for the truckers, Thevenot and Rock are freelance lobbyists. They sell their services to almost anyone who is willing to pay their fees. That means that bad news for corporate America is good news for them. Crisis is their stock-in-trade, and that is precisely what the President's statement has created. His words have greatly enhanced the prospect for a big tax increase and that probably will mean more clients for Thevenot and Rock—if they are able to act quickly. So Rock parks himself in a chair across from Thevenot, who sits behind his oversized partner's desk, and they begin to plot and plan. They decide to contact the liquor distributors with whom they had once met; surely they will fear a tax increase now and will want to hire more lobbyists. Maybe there is reason to talk to securities firms too, they speculate; and some extra retainers from the real estate industry ought to be easy to find. "It's time to go to work," Rock concludes. "Now!" . . .

Washington has become a club in which the line between those inside and those outside the government is not clearly drawn. Corporate lobbyists have so suffused the culture of the city that at times they seem to be part of the government itself. One result is that corporate America, once a perennial sacrificial lamb when it came to government crackdowns, has become something of a sacred cow. Not only are lawmakers and policymakers reluctant to make changes that would hurt businesses, they even have a tendency to try to help them, as long as budgetary pressures do not interfere. In 1990, Congress passed, and President Bush signed, the biggest deficit-reduction bill ever. But of its approximately $140 billion in tax increases over five years, only 11 percent came from corporations. The rest came from individual, taxpaying families.

Most people outside of Washington see the world of corporate lobbyists in caricature: fat, cigar-smoking men who wine and dine the nation's lawmakers while shoving dollar bills into their pockets. If lobbyists were always so crass, surely they would be easier to understand. If they were so blatant, they would not be nearly as effective as they often are. And they are effective, at least on the margins. But it is there, in relatively small changes to larger pieces of legislation, that big money is made and lost. Careful investment in a Washington lobbyist can yield enormous returns in the form of taxes avoided or regulations curbed—an odd, negative sort of calculation, but one that forms the basis of the economics of lobbying.

The lobbyists' trade bears close similarity to the ancient board game Go, the object of which is to surround the enemy completely, cut him off from any avenue of escape, and thus defeat him. Blocking the decisionmaker at every turn is the object of any successful lobbying campaign. Equally important is not to allow the decision-maker to know that he or she is being entrapped. That makes lobbying both high-powered and discreet, a dangerous combination.

Over time, the sheer pervasiveness of corporate lobbyists has had a major impact on government policy, beyond just the lucrative margin of legislation. The fact that lobbyists are everywhere, all the time, has led official Washington to become increasingly sympathetic to the corporate cause. This is true among Democrats as well as among Republicans.

Lawmakers' workdays are filled with meetings with lobbyists, many of whom represent giant corporations. And their weekends are stocked with similar encounters. When lawmakers travel to give speeches, they rarely address groups of poor people. The big-money lobbies often pick up the tab, and their representative fill the audiences, ask the questions, and occupy the luncheon tables and throng the cocktail parties that accompany such events. "That's the bigger issue," contends one congressional aide. "Who do these guys hang out with? Rich people. If you spend your time with millionaires, you begin to think like them." Lobbyists provide the prism through which government officials often make their decisions. . . .

Every lawmaker's chief interest is getting reelected. So lobbyists see it as their job to persuade lawmakers that voters are on the lobbyists' side. To that end, Washington has become a major marketing center, in which issues are created by interest groups and then sold like toothpaste to voters from Portland, Maine, to Portland, Oregon. Thanks to Washington-based direct-mail and telemarketing wizardry, corporations can solicit letters and phone calls from voters in any district in the nation. And clever Washington-based lobbyists know that the best way to guarantee that their point of view will be heard is to take constituents with them when they go to speak to members of Congress.

Lobbyists also function as unpaid staff to the decision-makers, who often don't have enough people on their own payrolls. Lobbyists contribute the money that lawmakers need to get reelected. And, more important, lobbyists provide information about both policy and process that government officials often cannot get from their own, often underfunded government agencies. Lobbyists are the foot soldiers and the friends of the people who run the government.

Sometimes corporate lobbyists are adversaries of the men and women who wield the federal government's enormous power. In every battle, there are winners and losers. And, sometimes, the lobbyists are the losers. Lobbyists also fight among themselves, because the corporate world is far from monolithic. As in any industry, there are also plenty of bad lobbyists. Money is wasted; campaigns can be sloppy and ham-handed. Sometimes corporate lobbyists seem to succeed despite themselves. They are the gang that couldn't shoot straight, but they manage to hit their target often enough to make a difference.

Despite their key role in the world of government, lobbyists are almost always the junior players, because, ultimately, they do not make the decisions. Taken as a group, they are a kind of underclass in the nation's capital, a lower caste that is highly compensated, in part, to make up for their relatively low stature in the city's severely stratified culture. At the top of the hierarchy are members of Congress and Cabinet secretaries. Next come congressional and Cabinet staffs. And then, at the bottom, come lobbyists. Lobbyists chafe at this. But their status is readily apparent. Frequently they suffer the indignity of standing in hallways or reception areas for hours at a time. Theirs are the first appointments canceled or postponed when other business calls. They do not even like to be called "lobbyists." They prefer "consultants" or "lawyers." They also use euphemisms like "When I left the Hill . . . " to describe the moment they left the congressional payroll to take a lobbying job.

One lobbyist put his predicament succinctly: "My mother has never introduced me to her friends as 'my son, the lobbyist.' My son, the Washington representative, maybe. Or the legislative consultant. Or the government-relations counsel. But never as the lobbyist. I can't say I blame her. Being a lobbyist has long been synonymous in the minds of many Americans with being a glorified pimp." . . .

The Main Street of lobbying is K Street, a short stretch through the heart of the sleek downtown. Spanking-new office buildings, filled with law firms, lobbying firms, and the allied services of the influence industry, sprang up everywhere in the city, eventually forming an almost unbroken corridor that stretched from Georgetown at one end of the city to Capitol Hill at the other. When even more office space was needed, metal and stone edifices were built on the Virginia side of the Potomac River. By the 1990s, Washington was home to about eighty thousand lobbyists of one kind or another, and the number was still growing. . . .

Thevenot could ingratiate himself with the best of them, and often did. He once declared at a lobbyists' Christmas party that he wished one day to be the "kissee rather than the kisser." But he was not cloying in his demeanor. He could be full of country charm and bawdy wit, with a hail-fellow manner to match. Yet he carried himself with the broad-shouldered confidence of the weight lifter he once was. He drove big cars and worked for big money. But more than that, he was a big man in Washington, a member in good standing of the political fraternity there. He might have been just a lobbyist, but in some circles he was a near equal of the lawmakers whose votes he worked to influence. He had been around for so long, he said, that to many lawmakers he was "as familiar as an old shoe." And he liked it that way.

At age fifty-four, Thevenot was sometimes bored by the repetitiveness of the legislative process. Other times he was frustrated by his inability to get things done. And having come of age in the Washington of the 1960s and early 1970s, he was forever bemoaning the "bullshitters and hurrah merchants" who were calling themselves politicians in the 1980s. But he still had not lost his touch or enthusiasm. He said he was "barnacle-encrusted," and deep down, still found fun—and, more important, profit—in playing the insider's game.

Thevenot was an access man. He survived on his ability to be accepted and trusted by the people with clout in Congress; his reputation rose and fell on having his telephone calls returned. He was not a technician. When he lobbied for changes in the tax code, for instance, he usually was versed only in the basic facts of the matter. For answers to deeper questions, he brought along an expert. But almost no one considered his need for backup a deficiency. Thevenot's job was more about strategy than details. He had to know whom to ask, when to ask, and how to ask for help, none of which was a simple question in the Byzantine world of Washington.

The secret of Thevenot's entrée was buried deep in the bayous and cotton fields of rural Louisiana. The third-oldest of eight children, Thevenot was the son of a failed farmer. "We built a house, started a farm, and proceeded to get poor," Thevenot recalled. "We also were the only ones who spoke clear English" in a region where Cajun patois was more the norm. His skill with language and his interest in government had brought him to where he was.

In the early 1960s, Thevenot worked as a television reporter for the NBC affiliate in Baton Rouge, and was part of the gang that covered the antics of the colorful governor, Earl Long. In 1963, Thevenot went over to the other side and became campaign manager for Gillis Long, a cousin of Russell's, who was waging an uphill fight for the U.S. House of Representatives against a two-term incumbent. Thevenot did a tremendous volume of work: everything from hiring hillbilly bands to trying to keep the candidate's driver out of jail. And when Gillis Long won, Thevenot's ticket to Washington had been punched.

The only problem was that the headstrong Thevenot was not interested in working for the even more headstrong Gillis Long. Thevenot told

Long that he would be his friend forever, but never again his employee. So Gillis Long telephoned Russell Long, then a U.S. senator, and asked him to find Thevenot a job. The one he found turned out to be as an elevator operator, but, in the hands of the resourceful Thevenot, it became a job with possibilities.

Between trips, Thevenot wrote speeches for his Senate patron. Soon, he moved out of the elevator and into more responsible positions on the staffs of committees that were run by Russell Long. These included panels with jurisdiction over small-business and post-office legislation. No matter what his title was officially, Thevenot always functioned as a top aide to Russell Long, who went on to become one of the most powerful men in Washington as chairman of the Senate Finance Committee.

When Russell Long had been drinking and was bruising for a brawl, Thevenot was there to spirit him away. He was also confidant to the mighty and friend to those who would become that way. He knew "Johnny" Breaux when he was a fellow staffer on Capitol Hill; Breaux went on to become a U.S. senator—in the seat vacated by Russell Long. Thevenot knew "Tommy" Boggs when he was the chubby teenage son of House Majority Leader Hale Boggs of Louisiana; in 1989 Boggs was running one of the biggest lobbying law firms in Washington. In short, Thevenot belonged to Washington's tight-knit Louisiana mafia, which like the Tabasco sauce from back home, wielded a fiery punch even in small quantities. "Thevenot's a piece of work," Senator Breaux explained. "He adds color to an otherwise bland city."

When Thevenot first left the Hill in 1975, he worked briefly for an investment-banking firm. But he soon realized that his life was too closely tied to Congress to abandon the Hill completely. Besides, he thought, becoming a lobbyist would get him faster to what was then his goal: making lots of money. "I decided that there was a point of diminished returns to being a staffer. I got to a point where I just sort of ran out of good ideas," he said. "I also had a family and financial obligations. I was making thirty-five thousand dollars a year, with four kids who had to go to college eventually. It was just not enough. So after nearly thirteen years it was just time to get out and cash in.

"I gave up the idea of changing the world. I set about to get rich."

With two friends, Thevenot set up the lobbying firm of Thevenot, Murray and Scheer. They represented a variety of business interests, but Thevenot was most drawn to real estate. After a few years, he left the partnership to become president and chief lobbyist for the National Realty Committee, one of the burgeoning new trade associations that represented specialized industry factions. The business world had grown too complex and too fragmented for huge umbrella organizations, such as the U.S. Chamber of Commerce and the National Association of Manufacturers, to represent adequately. So in 1969 the biggest real estate developers banded together to form an elite group. In the early 1980s, Thevenot became its most successful and best-known mouthpiece, and helped lead it to many victories on Capitol Hill.

The National Realty Committee's most sweeping win came in 1981, when real estate was lavished with new tax breaks at the prodding of President Reagan. That caused a spurt in development around the country, which redefined the skylines of the nation's cities and filled the pockets of Thevenot's clients with gold. Projects were planned not so much for the rent that they would bring in as for the tax benefits. The boom, however, was so excessive that it was not long before the tax goodies were taken away. "See-through skyscrapers" with no occupants to speak of were becoming a national embarrassment, and there was nothing that Thevenot could do about it. The Tax Reform Act of 1986 made real estate one of its biggest victims. Not only were the 1981 benefits excised, but some tax breaks of older vintage were trimmed away as well. It was a bloodbath for the industry. But, in typical form, Thevenot expressed his chagrin with a smile. "At least our people have nice big buildings of their own to jump from," he said.

Thevenot was not blamed for the disaster. Lobbyists rarely are when the industries they represent lose a legislative fight. He could have stayed with the National Realty Committee forever; indeed, he was on retainer to the group through 1989, at $7,500 a month plus expenses, and continued to function as its top lobbyist. But he wanted a change, and a chance to make more money. So he decided to leave the full-time employ of the real estate industry and go out on his own. He affiliated with William Boardman, a tax lawyer and lobbyist for the engineering and construction industries, who had rented some fancy new office space (at about $45 a square foot) in the Willard Office Building, which had been renovated with the help of Thevenot's early 1980s tax breaks. The two men called themselves Concord Associates, a reference to Boardman's Boston-area roots; on the elegantly papered walls they hung drawings of Revolutionary War scenes from battles around Concord.

In appearance, Thevenot was an odd mixture that mirrored the competing demands of his vocation—one part soft, another part hard as nails. He had the cherubic face of a Kewpie doll, and only slightly more hair. But he also had the beefy hands and swagger of the roughneck he was during the hardworking summers of his youth in sweltering Morgan City, Louisiana. Thevenot had come a long way since then. When Congress reconvened in January 1989, he had been an invited guest at some of the fanciest gatherings in the nation's capital, and he spent most of his time hopping from one private party to another. Senator Charles Robb of Virginia had held a bash for three thousand people at Union Station to celebrate his election. But thanks to the National Realty Committee checks that Thevenot had delivered to Robb's campaigns in the past, Thevenot had been invited to a far smaller, more intimate party in the new senator's office.

What Thevenot did there was collect information, which for him was no insignificant task. He explained, "We're talking to everybody we can about what the general mood of the Congress is. What issues are they going to deem important? How are the members lining up? How strongly they feel, for example, about new taxes to deal with the deficit problem. That is what we do, it's a network, it's a game. All the people that we know, and we've done favors for, gotten jobs for, sent them business, are part of it. What you know and your ability to interpret it—your ability to understand what's important and what's not—is what it's all about."

68

WILLIAM GREIDER

From *Who Will Tell the People*

Almost every excerpt in this section is a criticism of interest groups. Students of American government need to know the problems inherent in group-based politics. Journalist William Greider, whose approach to writing about government is undeniably counter-culture, provides a story both tragic and uplifting. He details the politicization of Washington, D.C. janitors from powerless working-poor laborers, into the "Justice for Janitors" organization. Greider's account of the janitors' "rude and crude" tactics is both sad and shocking. The lesson to be drawn from the janitors' strategy, however, is depressing. Think about Greider's janitors as you sit in college classrooms or the professional offices college graduates occupy. How do they get cleaned and neatened for us each morning?

———

THE QUALITY OF democracy is not measured in the contentment of the affluent, but in how the political system regards those who lack personal advantages. Such people have never stood in the front ranks of politics, of course, but a generation ago, they had a real presence, at least more than they have now. The challenging conditions they face in their daily lives were once part of the general equation that the political system took into account when it decided the largest economic questions. Now these citizens are absent from politics—both as participants and as the subjects of consideration.

These citizens are not the idle poor, though many hover on the edge of official poverty and virtually all exist in a perpetual condition of economic insecurity. These are working people—the many millions of Americans who fill the society's least glamorous yet essential jobs and rank at the bottom of the ladder in terms of compensation. A large segment of working-class Americans has effectively become invisible to the political debate among governing elites. They are neither seen nor heard nor talked about.

Their absence is a crucial element in the general democratic failure of modern politics. . . .

Like other citizens who have lost power, the humblest working folk have figured out how politics works in the modern age. They know that their only hope is "rude and crude" confrontation. To illustrate this reality, we turn to a group of citizens in Washington, D.C., who are utterly remote from power—the janitors who clean the handsome office buildings in the nation's capital. In a sense, they clean up each night after the very people and organizations that have displaced people like themselves from the political debate. While they work for wages that keep them on the edge of poverty, their political grievances are not heard through the regular channels of politics.

Like other frustrated citizens, the janitors have taken their politics, quite literally, into the streets of the nation's capital.

In late afternoon on a warm June day, while the people in suits and ties were streaming out of downtown office buildings and heading home, a group of fourteen black and Hispanic citizens gathered on the sidewalk in front of 1150 Seventeenth Street Northwest and formed a loose picket line. They were the janitors who cleaned this building every night and, though hardly anyone noticed or cared, they were declaring themselves "on strike" against poverty wages.

"Fire me? Don't bother me one bit. Can't do worse than this," Lucille Morris, a middle-aged black woman with two daughters, said. She was passing out picket signs to hesitant coworkers, most of them women. "Hold 'em up!" she exhorted the others. "Let 'em know you're tired of this mess."

Others grinned nervously at her bravado. An older Hispanic woman dressed in work clothes started into the building and was intercepted by one of the strikers. "She says she's just going in to use the bathroom," Leila Williams reported, "but she's coming back out." Williams, a sweet-faced grandmother who lives with her sixteen-year-old grandson in one of the poorest wards of southeast Washington, was wearing a bright red union tee-shirt that proclaimed: "Squeeze Me Real Hard—I'm Good Under Pressure."

"No one is working—this building isn't going to get cleaned tonight," the organizer from the Services Employees International Union announced with satisfaction. "And nobody's going to get fired," Jay Hessey reassured. "The company can't find enough people to do these jobs at this pay."

"I've been here eleven years and I still get the same pay the newcomers get—$4.75 an hour," Lucille Morris said. "We be doing like two people's work for four hours a night. We don't get nothing in the way of benefits. You get sick, you sick. You stay out too long, they fire you."

"One lady been here for fourteen years and she still get five dollars an hour for doing the bathrooms," Leila Williams added. "They give you another quarter an hour for doing the toilets. When we pass inspections, you know, they always treat us. They give us pizza or doughnuts, like that. We don't want no treats. We want the money."

The SEIU, a union that mainly represents people who do society's elementary chores, launched its "Justice for Janitors" strategy nationwide in 1987 and has staged scores of similar strikes in downtown Washington as well as other major cities. Because of the way federal government now regulates the workers' right to organize for collective action, regular union-organizing tactics have been rendered impotent. So the workers mostly stage symbolic one-night walkouts to grab attention.

The real organizing tactic is public shame—theatrical confrontations intended to harass and embarrass the owners and tenants of the buildings. The janitors will crash the owner's dinner parties and leaflet his neighborhood with accusatory handbills. They will confront the building's tenants at social events and demand help in pressuring the owners.

They, for instance, targeted Mortimer Zuckerman, the real-estate developer who owns *The Atlantic* magazine and *U.S. News & World Report*, with a nasty flier that declared: "Mort Zuckerman might like to be seen as a public citizen, responsible editor, intellectual and all-around good guy. To the janitors who clean his buildings, he is just another greedy real-estate operator." They hounded Zuckerman at important banquets and even in the Long Island Hamptons at celebrity softball games, in which he is a pitcher.

The owners and managers of some five hundred office buildings in Washington have developed an efficient system that insulates them from both unions and higher wages. Each owner hires an independent contractor to service the building and the competitive bidding for contracts is naturally won by the firm that pays the least to the janitors. About six thousand workers—most of them black or Hispanic—are left without any practical leverage over the arrangement. When the union signs up workers and demands its legal right to bargain for a contract in their behalf, the building owner promptly fires the unionized cleaning contractor and hires a new one who is nonunion. Old janitors are fired, new ones are recruited and the treadmill continues.

This management device keeps janitors like Lucille Morris stuck permanently at the same wage level year after year, hovering just above the legal minimum required by law, a wage level that provides less than $10,000 a year at full-time hours.

But these janitors do not even get full-time work from their employers. By doubling the size of the crews, the contractors can hold the workers to a four-hour shift each night and, thus, legally exclude the janitors from all of the employee benefits the firms provide to full-time employees— health insurance, pensions, paid vacations, paid sick leave. The law protects this practice too.

In order to survive, these women and men typically shuttle each day between two or three similar low-wage jobs, all of which lack basic benefits and other protections. Some of the janitors, those who are supporting families, qualify as officially poor and are eligible for food stamps, public housing or other forms of government aid. In effect, the general taxpayers are subsidizing these low-wage employers—the gleaming office buildings of Washington and their tenants—by providing welfare benefits to people who do work that is necessary to the daily functioning of the capital's commerce.

In another era, this arrangement might have been called by its right name—exploitation of the weak by the strong—but in the contemporary political landscape that sort of language is considered passé. Exploitative labor practices are subsumed under the general principle of economic efficiency and the consequences are never mentioned in the political debates on the great social problems afflicting American cities. The government may authorize welfare for the indigent, but it will not address the wages and working conditions that impoverish these people. . . .

For the city of Washington, the political neglect constitutes a social irony, for many of these janitors live in the same troubled neighborhoods where the vicious street combat over drugs occurs. The community is naturally horrified by the violence among the young drug merchants and, without much success, has deployed both police and National Guard to suppress it. Yet the city is oblivious to the plight of the janitors—the people who are working for a living, trying to be self-supporting citizens and must live in the midst of the dangerous social deterioration.

Economists might not see any connection between these two social problems, but any teenager who lives in one of the blighted neighborhoods can grasp it. One group of poor people, mostly young and daring, chooses a life of risk and enterprise with the promise of quick and luxurious returns. Another group of poor people, mostly older men and women, patiently rides the bus downtown each night, and in exchange for poverty wages, they clean the handsome office buildings where the lawyers and lobbyists work. When the janitors stage their occasional strikes, they are harassing the very people who have helped block them out of governing issues—the policy thinkers, the lawyers and lobbyists and other high-priced talent who have surrounded the government in order to influence its decisions.

By coincidence, one of the tenants at 1150 Seventeenth Street, where they were picketing, was the American Enterprise Institute, the conservative think tank that produces policy prescriptions for the political debates of Washington. When the service-employees union organizers approached AEI for support, their request was brushed off, but AEI has had quite a lot to say about minimum-wage laws and their supposedly deleterious effects. In recent years, AEI has published at least nine different scholarly reports arguing against the minimum wage. This position faithfully represents the interests of AEI's sponsoring patrons—the largest banks and corporations in America.

But the SEIU organizers insisted they were not trying to make an ideological point by picking on AEI. The real target was the building owner, which operated a dozen downtown buildings in a similar manner. Besides, they explained, most of the ostensibly liberal policy groups in Washington are no different, from the janitors' point of view.

Indeed, the next strike was planned against another building, also owned by the Charles E. Smith Management Company, which served as the home of the Urban Institute, a liberal think tank that specializes in studying the afflictions of the urban poor. The Urban Institute, though presumably more sympathetic to the working poor, has also published scholarly pamphlets questioning the wisdom of laws to improve their wages.

The Urban Institute scholars are regarded as a liberal counterpoise to such conservative institutions as AEI but, in fact, the liberals are financed, albeit less generously, by the same business and financial interests that pay for the conservative thinkers—Aetna Insurance, $75,000; Chase Manhattan Bank, $15,000; Exxon, $75,000; General Electric, $35,000; Southwestern Bell, $50,000 and so on. The commonly held illusion in Washington politics is that supposedly disinterested experts contend with each other over defining the "public good" from different viewpoints. Yet many of them get their money from the same sources—business and financial interests.

Like other tenants, officials at the Urban Institute insisted the janitors' pay was not their problem. It was a dispute for the cleaning contractor or the building owner to resolve. The SEIU organizers were twice turned down in their efforts to meet with the Urban Institute's officers, so they went out to picket their private homes and tried to crash the institute's banquet for its board of directors.

"Isn't it the same kind of issue any time you pass someone on the street who's homeless?" asked Isabel V. Sawhill, a senior fellow at the institute who is an authority on the "underclass" and related social questions. "It's hard to get involved as an individual in all these microdecisions to change the system. It can't be done at that level. Laws and policies have to be changed."

But these weren't exactly distant strangers one passed on the street. They were the very people who cleaned the office each night, carried out the trash, vacuumed the carpet and scrubbed the sinks and toilets.

"Actually, we never see them," Sawhill allowed. "I do sometimes see them, I admit, because I hang around late, but most people don't."

The janitors, it is true, were mostly invisible. Despite several years of flamboyant efforts, the janitors' campaign had gained very little presence in the civic consciousness of Washington. Public shame is not a terribly reliable lever of political power. For one thing, it only works if widely communicated, and the major media, including *The Washington Post*, had largely ignored the fractious little dramas staged by the janitors.

"People are yawning at them," said Richard Thompson, president of General Maintenance Service, Inc., the largest employer of low-wage janitors. "If there were really a justice question, people in this city would react. There are a lot of government and city government folks who wouldn't stand for it."

The janitors thought they would embarrass both local politicians and congressional Democrats when they targeted a strike at the new shopping complex in Union Station, which is owned by the federal government. Instead, the janitors were fired and commerce continued without interference from the government. Though the Democratic party is ostensibly sympathetic to people like the janitors, Democrats also rely on the real-estate industry as a major source of campaign money.

After an hour or so of picketing on Seventeenth Street, the janitors got into vans and drove over to a museum at New York Avenue and Thirteenth Street where a local charity was holding its annual fund-raising gala. The strikers had no quarrel with the charity, but they did wish to embarrass David Bruce Smith, a young man who is an officer in his grandfather's real-estate company and was serving as chairman of the benefit dinner.

The women in red tee-shirts and the union organizers spread out along the sidewalk and began giving handbills to any who would take them. "Talk with David Bruce Smith," the leaflet asked. "The Janitors Deserve Some Benefits Too!"

The encounter resembled a sidewalk parody of class conflict. As people began arriving for the event, an awkward game of dodging and ducking ensued between the black janitors and the white dinner guests in evening dress. Women from the charity dinner stationed themselves at curbside and, as cars pulled up for the valet parking, they warned the arriving guests about what awaited them. The black women came forward offering their leaflets, but were mostly spurned, as people proceeded swiftly to the door.

"Look, we are a charitable organization and this is political," a man complained bitterly to the union organizers. "People are going to see this and say, what? Are you trying to embarrass me? They're coming here to enjoy themselves."

Jay Hessey reminded him of the constitutional right to petition for redress of grievances. Three D.C. police cars were on hand in the event the janitors violated the law by blocking the doorway or waving placards. It's unfair, the official sputtered, to target an organization that is devoted to charitable activities. It was unfair, the janitors agreed, but then so is life itself. Some people get valet parking. Some people get an extra quarter for cleaning the toilets.

As tempers rose, Hessey stood toe-to-toe with the angry officials and rebuffed them with an expression of utter indifference to their distress. Hessey's colloquial term for the janitor's rude theater—"In your face"— was the essence of their politics. Cut off from the legitimate avenues of political remedy, the janitors had settled on what was left. Like it or not, fair or unfair, people were going to consider, at least for a few uncomfortable moments, the reality known to these janitors.

Most of the guests followed instructions and darted past the demonstrators to the door, but this greatly amused Lucille Morris and Leila Williams and their companions. It had taken considerable courage for these black and Hispanic cleaning women to stand on a sidewalk in downtown Washington and confront well-to-do white people from the other side of town. Once they were there, the women found themselves enjoying the encounter.

It was the white people who turned grim and anxious. Without much success, the black women followed couples to the doorway, urging them to read the handbills. An elegantly dressed woman in silk turned on them and snapped: "You know what? For three hundred dollars, you should be able to enjoy your evening!"

When a mother and daughter streaked past Leila Williams, refusing her handbill, she called after them: "All right, ladies. But you might be standing out here yourself sometime."

"That's right," another janitor exclaimed. "The Lord gave it all, the Lord can take it away."

Their exercise in public shame was perhaps not entirely futile. The elegant woman in silk evidently thought better of her harsh words to the black women because, a few minutes later, she returned outside and discreetly asked them for a copy of their leaflet. She mumbled an expression of sympathy and promised to help, then returned to the banquet.

The janitors may lack formal educations and sophisticated experience with finance but they understand the economic situation well enough.

They know, for instance, that unionized janitors in New York City or Philadelphia will earn two or three times more for doing the very same work. They know that in Washington the federal government and some major private employers, like *The Washington Post* and George Washington University, pay nearly twice as much to janitors and also provide full employee benefits. They know, because the union has explained it for them, that janitorial services represent a very small fraction of a building's overall costs and that even dramatic pay increases would not wreck the balance sheets of either the owners or the tenants.

The problem, as they see it, is not economics. Their problem is power and no one has to tell the janitors that they don't have any. Collective action is the only plausible means by which they can hope to change things. But even the opportunity for collective action has been gravely weakened for people such as these.

The janitors' predicament provides a melodramatic metaphor for a much larger group of Americans—perhaps 20 million or more—who have also lost whatever meager political presence they once had. These are not idlers on welfare or drug addicts, though they often live among them. These are working people, doing necessary jobs and trying to live on inadequate incomes.

These Americans have been orphaned by the political system. They work in the less exalted occupations, especially in the service sector, making more than the minimum wage but less than a comfortable middle-class income. Most have better jobs and higher wages than the Washington janitors—office clerks, hospital attendants, retail salespeople—but are trapped by similar circumstances. Among health-care workers, for instance, one third earn less than $13,000 a year. Some occupations that used to be much higher on the wage scale—airline stewardesses or supermarket clerks—have been pushed closer to the low end by the brutal giveback contracts that labor unions were compelled to accept during the 1980s.

The incomes of the group I'm describing range roughly upward from the poverty line (around $10,000 for a family of three) to somewhere just short of the median household income of around $35,000. "Working poor" does not accurately describe most of them but then neither does "middle class." The poor still suffer more in their daily lives, of course, but even the poor are represented in politics by an elaborate network of civic organizations.

If one asks—Who are the biggest losers in the contemporary alignment of governing power?—it is these people who are economically insecure but not officially poor. During the last generation and especially the last decade, they have been effectively stripped of political protections against exploitation in the workplace. Neither party talks about them or has a serious plan to address their grievances. In the power coordinates that govern large national questions, these people literally do not exist. . . .

After many weeks of pressure and rude confrontations, the D.C. janitors found that some people do respond to the tactics of public embarrassment. After twice rebuffing them, officials at the Urban Institute agreed to support the janitors' plea for better wages. Mortimer Zuckerman also evidently had a change of heart, for his real-estate company abruptly agreed to bargain with the union for contracts at three buildings. The Charles E. Smith Company retreated too after the expressions of community concern generated by the janitors' appearance at the charity dinner.

These breakthroughs for "Justice for Janitors" might be taken as heart-warming evidence that "the system works," as Washington political columnists like to say. But the real meaning was the contrary. The janitors' union, like others, has figured out that the way politics gets done nowadays is not by electing people to office or passing bills in Congress. Politics gets done by confronting power directly, as persistently and rudely as seems necessary.

For all its weaknesses, the irregular methodology exemplified by "Justice for Janitors" has become the "new politics" of the democratic breakdown. Other labor unions, large and small, have adopted similar strategies designed to "shame" corporations into accepting decent labor relations. They confront prominent shareholders at public gatherings or testify against the companies at zoning hearings and before government agencies. They assemble critical dossiers on a corporation's environmental record that will shock the public and drive off consumers. These and other corporate-campaign strategies are sometimes effective in forcing a company to respond to its workers. Like the "Justice for Janitors" campaign, however, the tactics are driven by the worker's essential weakness, not the potential power that lies in their collective strength. In the present circumstances, what else works?

69

ROBERTO SURO

From *Strangers Among Us*

This selection offers insights on how one Hispanic activist group developed. Author Roberto Suro first takes readers into the Los Angeles Flats to watch las madres, *the unofficial protectors of this Hispanic immigrant neighborhood. From their role in stopping street gang violence,* las madres *has grown into a grassroots political organization with broader goals. This group represents an important part of a large and growing new political constituency. Among its concerns are immigration, citizenship, and California's Proposition 187 that removed many benefits from illegal immigrants. The process of absorbing new citizens remains a real challenge for America, Suro notes, but one that cannot and should not be ignored.*

━━━━━

DOWN IN THE FLATS [east of the Los Angeles River] in the evenings, a third group roams the street, moving through the shadows between the day people and the night people. They are *las madres* (the mothers). Dressed in blue jeans or simple cotton dresses, they make sandwiches for the laborers, and then many nights, especially on weekends, they set out to street corners where there might be trouble among the thirteen street gangs that inhabit the Flats. The mothers are immigrants and natives, Spanish speakers, English speakers, and bilinguals. Most have big families in poor households, and most of them work—sewing in sweatshops, cleaning other people's homes and offices. *"Caminadas de amor"* (strolls for love) are what they call their forays. Carrying snacks and soft drinks, they go to the corners, sometimes as many as twenty of them at a time, and encircle their heavily armed progeny.

"They wait for us. They know we are coming and they wait for us because they like it," said Paula Hernández, one of the stalwarts of the group. "All we ever ask of them is to show respect for others. That, and we pray for them and listen to them. They are always having problems with other gangs and the police, and if we listen to them and treat them in a serious way, we can tell them they cannot solve their problems without showing respect for others."

The mothers deal with the police through a neighborhood watch organization, run clothing drives, operate a day-care center, and help support an alternative school for dropouts. With the Jesuits at the Dolores Mission, they also help run a shelter for battered women and a bakery to provide jobs for neighborhood boys. Considering how bad things are, *las madres* are not going to redeem the Flats anytime soon. But, amid the bougainvillea and the bungalows, beneath the freeway overpasses, they try to maintain order. At the heart of a sophisticated metropolis and within sight of office towers housing international banks, the mothers are the most coherent civilizing force in their community, more potent than the police, more consistent than any government agency, more respected than the schools. They represent yet another form of identity that is growing in the barrios. The mothers are a voice of resistance against life at the bottom of a stratified society. They echo the protests of the civil rights era, but in immigrant tones. They use Spanish words to master the downtown bureaucracies of public housing and Medicaid. *Las madres* represent a form of Latino identity that is as pragmatic as it is cultural and that remains proudly ethnic even as it seeks to engage America.

"Of course we are scared, and we get tired because we work all day and then come back to this," said Mrs. Hernández, gesturing down a dark alley where young male voices could be heard cackling.

Sheltered in the orange glare of a streetlight, the mothers formed a tight circle. They are bound together by more than civic spirit. Like most Latinos, *las madres* emerge from a culture that places little stock in institutions. They are at most a generation or two removed from countries where governments are more feared than trusted.

They've grown up believing that *compadrazgo* is the strongest bond outside the family. When the parents of a newborn child ask another couple to serve as the baby's godparents, the four become *compadres*, and it is understood that thenceforth their friendship is a bond for life that can be relied on for practical and emotional support even when relatives fail to heed the call. The baptism ceremony celebrates the ties among the adults as much as the arrival of an infant. And *compadrazgo* is just a formal expression of the kind of networking that begins with kinship and that usually goes much further in Latino cultures, especially in small towns and rural areas.

So there is something very Mexican about six women standing under a streetlight, looking out for their families and for one another, just as there was something very Mayan about how Juan Chanax and his *compadres* helped one another find work. But in places like the Flats, those linkages are finding new expressions and are being put to new purposes as these communities contend with the twin challenges of urban decay and steady immigration.

The mothers of the Dolores Mission are allied with an umbrella group called Las Madres de East L.A. It became one of the best-known community organizations in the city after it won a long battle to keep a prison out of the barrio, and then it won national fame by enlisting middle-class Anglo environmental groups to help it defeat plans to build a toxic-waste incinerator nearby. These battles in the 1980s helped promote a new civil rights cause, environmental racism, which alleges that environmental hazards have been inordinately, even intentionally, concentrated in poor and minority communities.

With little coordination or hierarchy, the mothers in the Flats and all across East L.A. also form a powerful grassroots political force. They helped elect Gloria Molina as the first Hispanic on the Los Angeles County Commission, and they have given important backing to several other insurgent political campaigns. When Proposition 187, the anti–illegal immigration initiative, held a huge lead in the polls, they went door-to-door to make sure that at least barrio voters would reject it.*

And this is not just a Los Angeles phenomenon. In the late 1980s and during the 1990s, barrio community organizations helped elect candidates, most of them women, to top offices in El Paso, Houston, Miami, and

*Proposition 187 would prohibit illegal immigrants from receiving social or welfare services, ban them from public schools and universities, and prevent them from receiving publicly funded health care except in emergencies.—EDs.

New York. In defiance of well-established Latino political bosses, many of these *madres* became the fresh faces and surprise winners when the ballots were counted.

"Sometimes someone says they wish things could be like they are in Mexico," Paula Hernández said. "They think women don't have to worry about their families so much there. Well, it is true women have to do more here. We are away from the children more because we work more, and that makes problems. But it is here that we have learned to get over our fear of saying what we think. It is here we have learned to work together as mothers. That happened because we were here."

Whether they are in Congress or out in the streets pacifying gang bangers, all this activism by Hispanic women reflects two political developments that are fundamentally American: the increasing prominence of women in electoral politics and the growing dynamism of community-action groups that coalesce on specific issues at the neighborhood level. These are national trends that cut across regions, economic classes, and racial or ethnic groups, and there is nothing distinctly Latino or immigrant about them. Indeed, outside the United States, Latino political culture remains male-dominated despite significant changes in the status of women over the past thirty years.

Using minority-group status to get leverage on institutions, electing female politicians, creating community-based organizations to funnel government funds into their neighborhoods—on all these many fronts Latino immigrants are adapting to the United States and learning to use American tools to fix their problems. But at the end of the day as they walk in the dark, traveling between the day people and the night people, making a community out of both, they are *comadres*, creating a sisterhood just as their mothers and grandmothers and generations of Latinas did before them in places far away. The *madres* are neither American nor Mexican. They are creating something new in the barrios out of the old ways they brought from the south and the tools they discovered on American terrain.

Down in the Flats when it started getting late, the mothers had gone home, and the night people dispersed to make their rounds. Cars screeched away. As one big black-and-red sedan pulled out, four or five firecrackers flew from the windows in a kind of mock drive-by. Some of the remaining lads flinched, their hands reaching to their pockets.

At the mission door, the day people started filing in, giving their number to a man with a clipboard. They rolled themselves in olive drab blankets, propped bundled clothes under their heads, and read *fotonovelas*, which are comic books with photos of actors instead of drawings and with soap-opera plots instead of superhero fantasies.

"*Los Angeles ya es Latino,*" Los Angeles is already Latino. The sentence was spoken by a man in white painter pants and a faded work shirt as he smoked a last cigarette before going in to stretch out on his pew. Earlier, he had entertained me and several other of the laborers with stories of how he had crossed the border so many times that he no longer used a *coyote,* a guide. He told tales of escaping from police who pursued him unjustly in Mexico and of eluding immigration agents in the United States. It was a migrant's *corrido* sung by a nicotine campfire. The mission door was about to close, and now the man was talking about California's [then] governor, Pete Wilson, who had been much in the news those days with his plans to balance the state government's budget by shutting down the border.

"Los Angeles is already Latino. It is too late for Wilson. What is he going to do? Deport us and all the Chicanos, too? If he wants to send two million people to Mexico, okay, let him do it; Mexico will send six million back. Then all of California will be Latino."

Two young laborers, teenagers by their looks, were terribly amused by this and so the older man indulged them. He was a natural-born ham, and before he had finished his cigarette, he had them in stitches.

"If he tries to send all the Latinos out of Los Angeles, all the *blancos* will go crazy in their dirty houses and all the *koreanos* with no one to work for them will go crazy, too. And so they will invite us—yes, *invite* us—to build a subway from Tijuana to Los Angeles that goes right under the border and under the noses of *la migra* [the immigration authorities]."

One of the boys tried to put icing on the joke as they walked into the church. "Yeah, we will get on the subway in Tijuana and they will serve us steaks at tables with napkins, and by the time we are finished eating, we will be here at Union Station."

"*Los Angeles ya es Latino.*" . . .

In old downtown Los Angeles on land not far from where the Spanish monks built their mission, an odd sight developed during the winter of 1994–1995. Crowds of Latinos began forming on the sidewalks in the chilly predawn hours. They lined up and waited for the offices of the Immigration and Naturalization Services to open so that they could apply for citizenship. In Los Angeles and then in every major city across the country, immigrants suddenly rushed to seek naturalized status in such numbers that they quickly overwhelmed the bureaucracy. It started shortly after the election that produced Proposition 187 and the Republican majority in Congress, and it occurred spontaneously, with little direction or encouragement from political leaders or advocacy groups. As months and then years passed and the number of Latinos seeking citizenship remained at flood stage, it became apparent that something fundamental had changed in the mentality of the barrio.

Prior to this boom in naturalization, conventional wisdom held that immigrants in the United States acquired citizenship in proportion to the distance they had traveled to get here. So, Asians and Europeans routinely naturalized almost as soon as they became eligible, usually after five years as permanent legal immigrants. By contrast, Canadians and Mexicans rarely would become citizens even after living in the United States for decades. Along with immigrants from the Caribbean and Central America, they retained intense ties to their homelands and often lived with the dream of returning.

As a result, every barrio had a huge supply of potential citizens. That reservoir had swelled when the immigrants who came in the surge of the 1980s reached eligibility, and then it grew even larger as the nearly 3 million beneficiaries of the 1986 amnesty became eligible. In 1995, applications for citizenship topped a million nationwide, nearly twice as many as the year before. By 1997, the INS was expecting close to 2 million citizenship applications.

The long lines of Latinos seeking U.S. citizenship marked a turning point. Like the Dominicans in Washington Heights after the 1992 riots, Latino newcomers all around the country were shocked out of their sojourner mentality by the anti-immigrant backlash. Legal immigrants realized that even though they paid taxes like everyone else, they could still lose access to a social safety net that citizens took for granted. The backlash, however, did not generate the kind of counterreaction typical of minority-group politics. Latinos did not protest or march to demand recognition of their rights. They did not mobilize as a group, nor did they generate a telegenic leader who spoke for their interests. The rush to naturalization was a simple act of self-defense, in part because citizenship offered some protection from the loss of benefits. More important, however, it was a declaration by people who had long lived between two lands that they had begun to consider the United States their permanent home.

Latino immigrants will become citizens with the same quiet relentlessness they showed in entering the country, creating communities, and getting jobs. They are also becoming voters. Together with native-born Latinos, they already make up a significant slice of the electorate in New

York, Chicago, Los Angeles, and a number of smaller cities. As with the Irish and the Jews early in this century, the Latinos' political importance will be magnified because they are concentrated in a few highly visible places and because they may be able to swing key states in very close races. Southern California has the potential to become a Latino political bastion in the next twenty years even with no further immigration. More than half of all the youths in Los Angeles County are Latinos, and by the year 2010 Latinos will considerably outnumber Anglos in the entire L.A. metropolitan area. All those kids who carried Mexican flags to protest Proposition 187 have only to grow up and the politics of California and the nation will change for a generation or more. Despite the mathematical inexorability of this change, its direction is not clear. There is always the chance Latinos might fail to translate their numbers into real clout. With the exception of the Miami Cubans, Latino voters have gone Democratic so predictably and by such large margins in the past that the new citizens might suffer the fate of African-Americans, who are often taken for granted because Democrats know they have nowhere else to go. Or if the new Latinos fail to articulate a distinct political identity for themselves, they might eventually resemble the Puerto Ricans and become secondary players who are constantly struggling to make themselves heard.

Initially the leaders and candidates will emerge from the ranks of Mexican-American and Puerto Rican activists who are steeped in minority-group politics, but over time, as immigrants and the children of immigrants enter the arena, it seems likely that Latinos will develop a broader political identity. Their attitudes and agendas will necessarily evolve as a reaction to their experiences with American public institutions, everything from the neighborhood school to Congress. This is perhaps the greatest source of uncertainty about the future, because Latinos are becoming American citizens at a time when America is at best ambivalent about their presence. After the backlash embodied in Proposition 187 and the restrictionist proposals in Washington, many politicians reversed field. The 1996 election produced intimations of how fast the Latino vote was growing, and leaders of both parties grew apprehensive about seeming blatantly anti-immigrant. So, elderly immigrants were not kicked out of nursing homes, and in 1997 a few provisions of immigration law were modified to soften punitive actions against Central Americans who had overstayed temporary permits and illegals in the process of fixing their status. But all that amounted to mollification at a time when a continued economic expansion generated demand for new workers and temporarily relieved some of the nation's anti-immigrant anxiety. Even with sinking welfare rolls and a shrinking budget deficit, new immigrants are still denied access to America's social safety net. Immigration is widely regarded as convenient, even desirable in good economic times, but that is not a commitment to ensuring the successful integration of a large number of newcomers, especially those who most need help from their hosts. The potential for a renewed backlash remains very real, and so it is likely that today's Latino immigrants will establish their political identity in a nation that oscillates between uneasy acceptance and fearful rejection of them.

For the first time since the Voting Rights Act of 1965 opened polling places in the Deep South to blacks, the United States is enfranchising a large new group of people who have been marked as outsiders. This is not primarily a political process or a matter that can be settled with legislation and policy directives. Latino immigrants are on the brink of taking important steps that will define their place in American society for generations to come. Latino newcomers are well along in this process, but much of what they have accomplished thus far has been done quietly. Most Americans hardly noticed the barrios until they grew large. Now the key tasks ahead can only be accomplished loudly and in the public arena. Immigrants must establish links with the United States as vibrant as those they have maintained with their home countries. The barrios must be converted from self-enclosed enclaves into organic American communities intimately connected with the cities around them. Businesses and neighborhood organizations created primarily to facilitate migration and settlement must now turn to long-term goals. And the United States must stop looking at recently arrived immigrants as appendages that can be disposed of when they are unwanted. That means reaching a new understanding of how American society cares for and absorbs people who come from abroad, work hard, remain poor, and fill their homes with children. In the early part of the next century, the new Latino immigrants will become part of the American nation. They are here already. They are not going to leave. It will happen, but the process of integration is never easy or peaceful. There is conflict on the horizon, but beyond the conflict, there may be signs of hope.

70

DAN BALZ
RONALD BROWNSTEIN

From *Storming the Gates*

Dan Balz and Ronald Brownstein bring readers into a National Rifle Association leadership meeting. The NRA is one of the most powerful interest groups in the United States. While gun ownership is the group's main focus, its broader mission is to resist what members see as the ever-increasing power of the national government. Other groups, based on their own particular issues, share the NRA's basic distrust of Washington.

WHAT BOTHERS JOHN COLLINS is not so much the new gun-control laws—he expected as much from Bill Clinton and the Democrats in Congress—as the video cameras on the highways in his hometown of Las Vegas. The progression worries him, the small steps, the imperceptible advances. Remember, at first, they were supposed to keep an eye on traffic? Now the cameras are being used to give out traffic tickets. What's next? Monitoring where people drive? Cataloguing license plates? "Little by little," he said ominously, letting the thought trail off in a haze of cigarette smoke.

Tanned and leathery, Collins delivered this warning while standing outside a ballroom in a downtown Phoenix hotel one sizzling afternoon in May 1995. Inside, leaders of the National Rifle Association (NRA), at once perhaps the most powerful and embattled lobby in the country, were handing out awards at a gala luncheon. Collins was one of some twenty thousand gun enthusiasts who had gathered for the NRA's annual convention. A few blocks away, in the Phoenix Convention Center, dozens of manufacturers had set up booths, displaying the latest in shotguns and handguns and telescopic sights. There were hunting bows, crafted as carefully as sculptures, and camouflage outfits and leather jackets with the names of gun manufacturers emblazoned across the back like baseball teams.

Browsing through the stacks of merchandise (down to infant-sized NRA T-shirts that read "Protecting your right to keep and bear arms, for now and for the future") was one of the two principal activities at the convention. The other was talking politics. Stephen Donnell, an NRA board member who has been with the organization for fifty years, waited until Collins had finished his disquisition on highway cameras before offering his own opinion on the state of the nation. "The real issue isn't gun control," he said. "The question is whether we are going to be subjects of the government or whether we are going to be citizens and the government is going to be subject to us." Donnell suggested digging up old newsreels of Hitler and Mussolini to gain an understanding of where Clinton was trying to take the country. What was the connection? "The similarity," John Collins jumped in, "is in the direction they are going."

Not far from Collins and Donnell, David Dutton, a slim, bearded psychologist from the small town of Coarsegold, California, was sitting on a bench, wearing a T-shirt with pictures of Bill and Hillary Clinton above the inscription "Dual Airbags." Friendly but passionate, Dutton picked up where Collins and Donnell left off. "The federal government has become a hydra-headed monster," Dutton said. "Almost any federal agency they want to cut, I would be in favor of. It's grown out of hand. It's a malignant cancer." People used to be free in America, he said almost wistfully. "Now if you pump leaded gas in your car, it's a federal offense."

Not everyone who gathered at the NRA convention was so angry at government. But most were. Like Collins, they had grievances that extended well beyond guns and gun control. Indeed, few of them said they had suffered any personal inconvenience from either the ban on semi-automatic assault weapons or the waiting period for handgun purchases Congress had approved over the previous two years. To most of them, gun control had ascended from the practical to the symbolic. Gun control was just the means to the end of enlarging government and giving Washington more power to control the lives of its citizens. Washington was taking away guns to clear the path for taking away other rights: This was the article of faith. One man from Colorado raged at being required to give his fingerprints to obtain a driver's license. Another complained about federal environmental regulations that favored turtles over farmers and snails over ranchers. Another said government welfare programs were undermining traditional moral values. Speed limits, restraints on the use of public lands, all the infringements on liberty that society demands to uphold order seemed to them an intolerable web of rules and regulations too thick to evade or even comprehend.

What made these sentiments all the more remarkable was their source. The NRA convention had a small-town, blue-collar flavor, and the men who pored over shotguns and swapped hunting stories seemed like the sort who might have broken up antiwar demonstrations with their fists twenty-five years ago. Now they sounded like the Weathermen themselves, branding the government as corrupt, voracious, malevolent. "We're going into a situation where there is a police state mentality," one man said. Another man added: "I'm not saying there is any definite, immediate conspiracy to turn America into a tyranny. But as a matter of principle, people should be afraid of their government."

At their most extreme, these beliefs bordered on the antigovernment paranoia expressed by the two men accused of blowing up a federal office building in Oklahoma City just a month before the NRA meeting. Yet they usually stopped short. Everyone in Phoenix condemned the violence, and if there was any sympathy for the bombers it was kept well hidden. Still, the intensity of the alienation from government was palpable. When these men talked about Washington, many of them conjured up images of revolution—peaceful or political, but revolution nonetheless. In the same way they once might have spoken of Moscow as a threat to their freedom, now they pointed at their own capital. "I consider the federal government to be the greatest threat to our liberty today," Dutton said. "We've defeated communism. We've defeated Nazism. The last threat is inside the Beltway."

These angry white men are one legion in a grassroots movement that has rewritten the political equation of the 1990s, and in the process helped to transform the Republican Party. With social movements on the left like labor unions and civil rights organizations diminished in power, an army of conservative grassroots groups has mobilized middle-class discontent with government into a militant political force, reaching for an idealized past with the tools of the onrushing future: fax machines, computer bulletin boards, and the shrill buzz of talk radio. They have forged alliances with the Gingrich generation of conservatives and strengthened their hand as the dominant voice within the GOP family. Like a boulder in a highway, the conservative populist movement has become an enormous, often impassable obstacle in the path of President Clinton. No single factor in the Republican revival after Bush's defeat has been more important than the party's success at reconnecting with and invigorating the profusion of anti-Washington and antigovernment movements sprouting in every state.

These movements exist in concentric circles of alienation from government. At the farthest edge are extremist tax protesters, survivalists, and elements of the militia movement so alienated from society that they can imagine taking up arms against it. But most of the energy has been contained within the boundaries of mainstream politics. Probably not in this century have so many distinct groups, with such a broad range of grievances, simultaneously targeted the government in Washington as their enemy. The conservative, or antigovernment, populist coalition operates on at least half a dozen fronts: gun owners led by the 3.5-million-member NRA; Christian conservatives organized primarily through televangelist Marion G. (Pat) Robertson's Christian Coalition, which now counts 1.7 million members in seventeen hundred local chapters; the movement to impose term limits on members of Congress; the network of more than eight hundred state and local antitax organizations; small-business owners spearheaded by the six-hundred-thousand-member National Federation of Independent Business (NFIB), which has surpassed more conciliatory big business organizations as a legislative force in Washington; the Perot movement; and the "wise use" and property rights movements that have amalgamated ranchers, farmers, off-road enthusiasts, loggers, and miners—as well as multinational mining and timber companies—into a coalition demanding the rollback of environmental regulations, increased access to public lands, and government compensation for environmental rules that prevent landowners from developing their property.

Even this list doesn't encompass the entire range of populist right-of-center uprisings through the early 1990s, from the movements that opposed the North American Free Trade Agreement (NAFTA) and the world trade treaty known as GATT to the anti-immigration and anti-affirmative action movements that began in California and have spread elsewhere over time. "There is a synergy," said conservative political consultant Craig Shirley. "It is feeding on itself. It is keeping itself in motion."

These movements sort largely into two camps. In one are the Christian Coalition and other groups drawn to politics primarily by fears of cultural decline and the breakdown of the family. In the other are the secular organizations—like the National Federation of Independent Business, the followers of Ross Perot, the term limits and property rights movements, and the NRA—motivated mostly by opposition to the expansion of government spending and regulation. There are significant differences between and even within these camps, but the conservative populist coalition is more demographically and ideologically coherent than many on the left assume. To a striking degree, Americans in these groups express common attitudes and exhibit similar lifestyles. Gun ownership is considerably more common among groups within the antigovernment coalition than among the population as a whole. Nearly half of small-business owners consider themselves born-again Christians. Gun owners, Christian conservatives, and small-business owners are all heavy listeners to talk radio. In many states, small-business owners, antitax advocates, and Perot activists provided the foundation of support for the term limits movement. The 1995 term limits ballot initiative in Mississippi, for example, was directed by Mike Crook, a field organizer for the Christian Coalition who was also a member of the NRA. "The links are all there," Crook says. "They are all interrelated. All of these grassroots organizations . . . amount to taking back our country for the people."

PART TWELVE

Voting and Elections

71

FRANCES FOX PIVEN
RICHARD CLOWARD

From *Why Americans Still Don't Vote*

This is not the first book that Frances Fox Piven and Richard Cloward have written on voting—or more precisely, nonvoting—among the American public. More than a decade after writing Why Americans Don't Vote, *the authors observe that many Americans still don't vote, despite reforms such as the 1993 National Voter Registration Act—"motor voter." The reasons behind nonvoting go deeper than ease of registration, Piven and Cloward believe. Many potential voters, especially people with low incomes and from minority groups, don't participate because they are alienated from the entire political process. As activists in the Human Service Employees Registration and Voter Education program, Piven and Cloward place blame on politicians who have failed to capture the attention and allegiance of America's unrepresented millions.*

⎯⎯

THIS BOOK IS ABOUT AN electoral reform project called Human SERVE (Human Service Employees Registration and Voter Education), which we initiated in 1983. Our purpose was to make voter registration available in welfare and unemployment offices, and in private sector agencies such as day care and family planning. The book discusses the ideas that informed the project, the complex dynamics of the reform effort itself, and the outcome.

We undertook the project because it was clear by 1980 that a Republican/business/Christian Right coalition was coming to power and that the New Deal and Great Society programs—which have always been of central interest to us—were seriously threatened. At the same time, registration and voting levels among the recipient constituencies of these programs were low and falling. We thought it might be possible to raise voting levels through registration reform and thus strengthen resistance to the attack on entitlements.

In the late 1980s, a national voting rights coalition of civil rights, good government, labor, and religious groups took up this strategy of registration reform, and persuaded Democrats in Congress (joined by several Republicans) to pass the National Voter Registration Act of 1993, which a Democratic president signed in May of that year. The Act required that, beginning in 1995, voter registration be made available in AFDC, Food Stamps, Medicaid, and WIC agencies and in agencies serving disabled Americans. It also required that people be allowed to register when they get or renew driver's licenses. It was this last provision that gave the Act its tag name "motor voter." The states were also required to permit people to register by mail, and the Federal Election Commission was ordered to design a mail form that the states were required to use if they failed to design their own. With this reform, historic barriers to voter registration that had kept voting down among blacks and many poor whites in the South and among many in the northern industrial working class were largely abolished. . . .

The right to vote is the core symbol of democratic politics. Of course, the vote itself is meaningless unless citizens have other rights, such as the right to speak, write, and assemble; unless opposition parties can compete for power by offering alternative programs, cultural appeals, and leaders; and unless diverse popular groupings can gain some recognition by the parties. And democratic arrangements that guarantee formal equality through the universal franchise are inevitably compromised by sharp social and economic inequalities. Nevertheless, the right to vote is the feature of the democratic polity that makes all other political rights significant. "The electorate occupies, at least in the mystique of [democratic] orders, the position of the principal organ of governance."

Americans generally take for granted that ours is the very model of a democracy. Our leaders regularly proclaim the United States to be the world's leading democracy and assert that other nations should measure their progress by the extent to which they develop electoral arrangements that match our own. At the core of this self congratulation is the belief that the right to vote is firmly established here. But in fact the United States is the only major democratic nation in which the less-well-off, as well as the young and minorities, are substantially underrepresented in the electorate. Only about half of the eligible population votes in presidential elections, and far fewer vote in off-year elections. As a result, the United States ranks at the bottom in turnout compared with other major democracies. Moreover, those who vote are different in politically important respects from those who do not. Voters are better off and better educated, and nonvoters are poorer and less well educated. Modest shifts from time to time notwithstanding, this has been true for most of the twentieth century and has actually worsened in the last three decades. In sum, the active American electorate overrepresents those who have more and underrepresents those who have less. . . .

Three conditions made the National Voter Registration Act of 1993 possible. One was the growth of an influential national voting rights coalition committed to making government agency registration the law of the land.

A second condition was the rapid spread of motor voter programs in the states. When the NVRA was enacted in 1993, twenty-nine states had motor voter programs. Most were just starting up and had registered few people. Still, it mattered in the congressional debates that more than half the states had opted for this reform. John L. Sousa, chief counsel of the Senate committee that had jurisdiction over voter registration, would later say, "We wanted this voter registration reform bill to reflect what's already happening in the states." When the National Voter Registration Act came up for consideration in the early 1990s, *Washington Post* political columnist David Broder remarked that "by building on the State experience, its sponsors have done something that is all too rare in Washington: They allowed the design to be field-tested before taking it national."

The third condition explaining why reform succeeded is ironic. Neither party thought that voter registration reform would change electoral outcomes. One report after another appeared in the 1980s concluding that nonvoters were "carbon copies" of voters. It was not self-evident that the Democrats would benefit more; greater voting for the Democrats by the poor and minorities could potentially be offset by higher voting for the Republicans by young people.

This political situation was altogether different from the circumstances preceding the enactment of the Voting Rights Act of 1965. Then, the endangered southern Democratic political leadership fought tooth and nail to prevent the enfranchising of blacks, since new black voters would undermine the apartheid basis of the "Southern Democracy." It took massive turbulence—civil disobedience campaigns in the South and civil disorder in the northern cities—to force national Democratic leaders to override southern opposition. But nothing like that was necessary to win voter registration reform three decades later. . . .

The NVRA reforms produced an unprecedented increase in voter registration. Turnout, however, did not rise. . . .

. . . Four years into the NVRA system, turnout had fallen another 2.8 percentage points, from 38.8 percent in 1994 to 36 percent in 1998. Moreover, "Southern turnout dropped 3.6 points to 30.5 percent, a larger drop than the rest of the nation." Florida and Kentucky reported that as few as 20 percent of those registered in public assistance agencies went to the polls. In sum, more accessible registration procedures did not increase voting rates.

Why? A formidable body of evidence and opinion predicted that what Arend Lijphart calls "voter-friendly" registration rules lead to higher turnout levels. In fact, we think the procedures of the National Voter Registration Act (NVRA) should over time bring us close to the automatic voter registration procedures that characterize European polities, which Powell concluded could boost turnout by 14 percentage points. More recently, in 1992, Ruy Teixiera conducted an exhaustive review of the American data and reported that, while voter registration barriers could not explain the recent declines in turnout, they nevertheless remained the most costly feature of the voting act in the United States. He concluded that the reduction of these costs was the single most credible reform that would increase turnout, by 8 to 15 percentage points. Comparisons of turnout in states with the least restrictive registration arrangements and in other states yield similar estimates of a potential increase of from 9 to 15 percentage points. So why have the expectations implicit in these arguments so far been disappointed? Why the continuing fall in turnout, rising registration rates notwithstanding?

Most studies of voter turnout attempt to disaggregate the effects of registration barriers and an array of other influences. If registration barriers are less significant in depressing turnout, then other factors must be more significant. Consistent with the traditional emphasis on social-psychological explanations, the usual approach has been to scrutinize changes in the capacities and attitudes of individual voters in the search for the factors contributing to the demobilization of the electorate. All else being equal, some changes in the characteristics of voters are expected to raise turnout while other factors depress turnout. Thus the growing numbers of young people in the electorate, who have traditionally voted less, at least in the United States, should depress turnout. But rising educational levels should increase turnout, at least in the United States. All this is familiar. The new variable proposed by recent analyses is that lower turnout seems to be associated with the fact that Americans are less embedded in social networks that encourage participation. Teixiera, for example, emphasizes "a substantial decline in social connectedness" through family and church.

The perspective on the causes of low turnout . . . reveals the limits of attempts to disaggregate the impact of particular variables on voter turnout. The effects of legal and procedural barriers are closely intertwined with the political factors that draw people to the ballot box, and especially with the strategies the political parties employ to attract or pull voters to the polls. Moreover, the barriers and political appeals and strategies together go far to determine which individual-level variables are related to turnout.

When issue and cultural appeals resonate with the electorate, contests are tight, and the parties work to get the vote out, then legal and procedural barriers matter much less—as in the big cities in the years immediately after the introduction of voter registration barriers at the beginning of the century. And under these conditions, the relationship between turnout and education and income evaporates. To put the matter clearly, hotly contested elections about intensely felt issues still draw voters, and when they do, the impact of barriers dwindles, and so do differentials in turnout that can be ascribed to individual-level social and psychological traits. Rosenstone and Hansen point to the mayoral election in Chicago in 1983 when the nomination of Harold Washington raised black turnout by 17 percentage points, despite a restrictive voter registration system, because the keenly felt issue in the election was racial ascendance in the city's political regime.

But when political appeals lose their salience and party efforts to bring people to the polls slacken, as they did in the wake of progressive-era party reforms, voter registration barriers loom much larger, class-related disparities in voting widen, and so should the impact of such individual traits as education, income, or social connectedness. Moreover, the pattern of nonparticipation that is initially constructed by the interplay of barriers and party indifference tends to reproduce itself over time. Party operatives assume, even naturalize, low participation rates, and hence tend to take the absence of the marginalized for granted in fashioning appeals and mobilizing strategies. In time the attitudes of the marginalized come to reflect their disaffection with a party system that pays them little heed.

Thus, the most provocative data reported in recent studies purporting to account for declining turnout describe dramatic changes in attitudes toward politics over the past three decades. "Americans," say Rosenstone and Hansen, "have lost their confidence in the effectiveness of their actions." They have also lost their attachment to electoral politics: Americans are less satisfied with the electoral choices offered them and, indeed, had less good to say even about the parties and candidates they favored than they had in the 1960s. Abramson, Aldrich, and Rohde also emphasize the erosion of party loyalties and a declining belief in the responsiveness of politicians to voter influence. And Teixiera reports consistent findings.

Changes in political attitudes are of course changes in individual-level traits, but since the traits at issue are attitudes toward politics, and since they have changed so rapidly, it seems reasonable to suspect that the broader political system is implicated. If turnout is falling because of declining party loyalties or lowered feelings of political efficacy, something is probably going on in the larger environment of American politics.

. . . [W]e argued that the correlation of such individual-level attributes as education with turnout was misleading, that it did not reflect the direct impact of education on participation but the tilt of party appeals and strategies away from the less educated and worse-off, and toward the more educated and better-off. The decline in political efficacy and increase in political alienation, and the impact of these attitudes on turnout, suggests a further elaboration of the relationship between individual-level attributes and politics. The political system not only selectively mobilizes people according to their class-related attributes, but it also creates the attributes that depress turnout. On both these counts, the statistical evidence on the bearing of individual attributes on turnout points the finger of blame at the performance of the American political parties.

This . . . is not the place to begin an examination of the features of recent American electoral politics that are increasing various measures of political alienation. The much discussed and debated decline of party organization (at least in the Democratic party), the flood of special interest money pouring into the campaigns, the growing presence of the K Street lobbyists, the gap between the issues Americans say are important and the national legislative agenda, the increasing complexity of policy initiatives riddled with pork barrel giveaways—all of these probably contribute to growing public cynicism. Perhaps the rise of neoliberalism as the current ideological orthodoxy also turns people away from electoral politics, if only because it argues the futility of government intervention in a world dominated by markets, especially international markets. In short, the political parties and their interest-group allies are constructing a political environment that is demobilizing the American electorate, lowered barriers notwithstanding.

The very success of this development may even help to explain why the business opposition to government agency registration we initially anticipated never materialized. In the late nineteenth century, at least some business interests treated the shape and scale of electoral participation as a potential threat to their influence and worked to reduce participation by the lower strata. But on the eve of the twenty-first century, the big automobile companies readily conceded Election Day as a paid holiday to unionized auto workers. Predictably, Republican party leaders railed at the contract concession, as they had railed at the NVRA. But General Motors, Ford, and Daimler Chrysler, the world's three largest auto companies, were unfazed. Perhaps electoral politics has evolved to the stage where money, advertising, and special-interest lobbies, together with the dampening effect on democratic aspirations of neoliberal ideology, have combined to neutralize the age-old class threat posed by an enfranchised population.

It followed from our perspective on the closely interbraided causes of low turnout that we did not think voter registration would have its most important effects on turnout directly. True, accessible voter registration procedures would lower the costs, in rational-choice terms, of the voting act, and Human SERVE's public relations material emphasized that if registration barriers were eliminated, millions of new voters could flock to the polls. But we personally did not believe that the mere fact of lower costs was likely to draw people to the polls in large numbers. Rather, . . . our hope was that once rates of registration rose among low income and minority citizens, this pool of newly available voters would attract at least some entrepreneurial politicians who would then begin to raise the issues and organize the get-out-the-vote efforts that would bring new voters to the polls.

That has yet to happen. In fact, however logical such recruitment efforts might seem from a narrow focus on electoral incentives, the century-long reliance of the American parties on electoral demobilization . . . suggests that it may never happen. So does our own very limited success in trying to make allies, even of politicians who were likely to benefit at the polls. Some Democratic governors issued executive orders to be sure, but then declined to implement them. Even when state legislatures controlled by Democrats mandated motor voter, they refused to include social agencies as registration sites. Our successes at initiating registration in some municipal agencies were typically short-lived; when we stopped prodding, registration flagged or ceased. . . .

The moral seems to us clear. The scale and shape of the active electorate can determine electoral outcomes. But left to themselves, the parties are unlikely to work to expand participation. Perhaps part of the reason is simply that politicians have come to absorb the conventional wisdom that ascribes nonparticipation to the individual traits of voters. More likely, they mouth such explanations for comfort. Indeed, party competition is more likely to take the form of strategies to demobilize sectors of the electorate, than of strategies to expand it. . . .

In sum, we think it possible that the NVRA and the pool of potential voters it is creating might yet matter in American politics. If it does, it is not likely to be because the dynamic of electoral competition itself prods the major parties to reach out to new voters. It is more likely to be because a new surge of protest, perhaps accompanied by the rise of minor parties and the electoral cleavages that both movements and minor parties threaten, forces political leaders to make the programmatic and cultural appeals, and undertake the voter recruitment, that will reach out to the tens of millions of Americans who now remain beyond the pale of electoral politics.

72

POLITICAL STAFF OF THE
WASHINGTON POST

From *Deadlock*

If this excerpt seems long, consider the topic: the 2000 presidential election. This is a very short version of the 36 days that followed a memorable election night, Nov. 7, 2000. The writers for the Washington Post *covered the story moment by moment, through the intricate and unexpected twists and turns that occurred as Florida's electoral votes were attempted to be assigned to either George W. Bush or to Al Gore. From the Voter News Service (VNS) exit polls on Nov. 7 that began the networks' embarrassing projection errors until the 5 to 4 U.S. Supreme Court decision over a month later to halt the Florida recount and thereby end the dispute in Bush's favor, the* Post *writers give a reprise of some of the highlights. Hanging chads from punch-out ballots, precise time deadlines, county canvassing boards, and the Florida state courts all figured in the drama. The 2000 election is one that Americans will not soon forget.*

————

IN THE YEAR 2000, George W. Bush and Albert Gore Jr. fought the longest and most expensive presidential campaign in the history of the country. In the end, after a 36-day post-election battle in Florida that eclipsed the campaign itself for drama and raw partisanship, the 43rd president of the United States was determined by a bitterly divided U.S. Supreme Court late on a cold December night.

The Florida deadlock capped a decade of neck-and-neck political competition. If the 1990s had proved anything, it was that Democrats and Republicans were at parity in national politics. In 1992, Democrats recaptured the White House after a 12-year absence. Two years later, Republicans took control of the House and Senate, pushing Democrats into the minority in the House for the first time in 40 years. But in 1996 President Clinton easily won reelection, the first Democrat since

Franklin D. Roosevelt to win consecutive terms. Then in 1998 came Monica Lewinsky and the partisan upheaval of the first impeachment proceedings in more than a century.

The 2000 campaign offered the possibility of an election that finally would resolve the impasse, an election that might signal clearly which party the voters trusted more and why. It didn't turn out that way.

If not the most charismatic candidates ever to run for president, George W. Bush and Al Gore nonetheless battled over big issues—how to educate America's children, how to ensure retirement security for current and future generations, how to sustain economic prosperity, how to define America's role as the world's lone superpower. They were as well matched politically as they were different personally, and from the beginning of the general election campaign in the spring of 2000 to the campaign's final weeks, neither could gain a significant advantage. Their race sprawled from one coast to the other, and as Election Day neared, states that had not been competitive in recent elections suddenly became crucial to the outcome. What happened in Florida is the focus of this book. . . .

The deadlock in Florida was an almost unimaginable fluke, like tossing a quarter and having it come to rest on its edge. The virtual tie in Florida was a once-every-few-centuries proposition, and so was a presidential election that hinged on a single deadlocked state. It was a longshot wrapped in a longer shot. And so it happened that laws and institutions built for the press of the commonplace were called on to face the extraordinary.

The election dispute in Florida went on for 36 days—a whirlwind of more than 50 lawsuits, and appeals to every possible court, news conferences, protests, speeches, public hearings, private strategies and televised ballot-counting sessions. It was an all-out war involving America's canniest political soldiers and some of its best legal minds.

Now, in the aftermath, it's possible to start sorting out the threads and peering behind the scenes. It's possible to see more clearly how the candidates reacted and endured. To see George W. Bush, steeled for a long fight, hunkering down at his ranch with friends, furious when they tuned in *Saturday Night Live* and its savage satires. To see Al Gore, intimately managing his recount effort while seething to friends about the enemies he believed were betraying him. He spent part of one fateful afternoon on the phone trying to find out if the mayor of Miami-Dade County had sold him down the river.

And while Gore remained doggedly optimistic, many of his most experienced advisers, including those with the greatest knowledge of recounts, were clear-eyed realists, knowing just how hard it is for any candidate to reverse the results after Election Day. Nearly four days before Gore decided to surrender, his campaign chairman told him: "Forget it."

It's possible to see the key role Gore played in shaping the perception that he had lost a race that was, in fact, a virtual tie. On election night, after the networks declared Bush the winner, Gore cemented that impression by congratulating his opponent—without ever speaking to his own grassroots operatives, who could have warned him that the race was actually too close to call.

It's possible to trace the long arc of the Bush strategy, which was based on the assumption that Gore's chief weapon was the Florida Supreme Court. From the first days, the Bush forces began moving to bring the state legislature and the federal courts—especially the U.S. Supreme Court—into position to thwart that advantage. The role of Katherine Harris, Florida's Republican secretary of state—and her key adviser, placed at her side by the Bush team—comes into focus. While Harris brooded over the parallels of her ordeal to that of the biblical Queen Esther, she stalled the ballot-counting so critical to Gore's hopes.

The key contribution of Bush's brother, Florida Gov. Jeb Bush, can also be seen: His legal staff, in the first hours after Election Day, moved to keep the state's biggest law firms off Gore's team.

It's possible to understand the pivotal decisions, on both sides, not to pursue an unprecedented—and legally unfounded—statewide hand count of all ballots. And to realize the importance of the Gore team's mishandling of the issue of overseas absentee ballots—a mistake that was exacerbated when Sen. Joseph I. Lieberman abandoned his ground forces on this issue, without warning, on national television. The resulting disarray allowed the Bush team to demand hurried recounts, thus padding their lead. They called this the "Thanksgiving Stuffing."

And even as Gore protested on television that his team had nothing to do with lawsuits challenging thousands of ballots in two Florida counties, his forces arranged behind the scenes for organized labor to push the cases. Meanwhile, a major Gore donor—a Silicon Valley billionaire—backed the effort with huge cash donations and a chartered jet.

These are the sort of decisions, alliances, power plays, snap judgments and personality flaws revealed when a flukishly close election is played out for staggeringly high stakes. Both sides were nimble and brilliant and occasionally shady; both sides were also capable of miscalculations, divisions and blame. The best and worst of politics were on display in those 36 days, and both sides trafficked in each. This is how it happened. . . .

Murray Edelman looks like a college professor, balding and bespectacled, and he has the credentials to match, starting with a doctorate from the University of Chicago. But his business is television news. He runs a small yet intensely influential information factory in a dingy suite of offices near New York's Penn Station: Voter News Service. VNS spends countless months producing absolutely nothing, just getting ready. Then, when a national election comes around, for a few thrilling hours the service produces the most valuable commodity in the world—inside skinny.

That's the day VNS sends thousands of very temporary employees into precincts across the country. These survey takers wait with clipboards in hot sun or driving rain or swirling snow outside the schools and churches and community centers where the business of democracy gets done. They ask voters as they leave: Which candidate did you choose? What's your age, race, gender, religion, income, past voting habits? Thousands and thousands of surveys are completed in a matter of hours, and then tabulated and tallied and transmitted to New York where, in a mad scramble of data crunching, the numbers are aggregated and stratified and broken into batches, then poured into the waiting computers of news organizations around the country. Moments after these batches land, the switchboards of America's political system light up like Vegas. Reporters and editors begin calling their best sources to share the numbers, and these sources in turn pass the word to their own best sources. Between about 1 p.m. and late afternoon on Election Day, any self-respecting pol in America would dump a call from the pope for some fresh exit poll numbers.

Later, after the polls close, the VNS surveyors wait at scientifically selected precincts for actual results, which they relay as soon as possible to headquarters—which swells temporarily into a vast brokerage of data, with hundreds of operators answering hundreds of phones. Then the data flow into the VNS computers. When enough data reach Edelman's computer, he predicts the winner of the Senate seat or presidential electoral votes in question.

Edelman learned his craft from the dean of exit polls, Warren Mitofsky. Together, they ran the polls for CBS, back when that was the richest and best TV news operation ever. They were in the forefront as the networks gradually consolidated their Election Day numbers harvesting. Exit polling remained a separate enterprise for a long time, however, as the cash-rich networks jealously guarded their claims to be first and best with predictions. It was 1990 before they threw in together on this effort, and formed what would become VNS.

On November 7, Election Day, Edelman's temporary offices were a fifth of a mile above Wall Street, on the 93rd floor of the World Trade

Center. More than 200 operators were taking calls and collecting surveys; twice that number, in New York and Cincinnati, tap-tapped at keyboards entering actual results as they came in. There was a data manager for each state, a trouble desk, a legal desk, lots of temporary walls and low dividers and glowing screens—"like something out of *Blade Runner*," one witness reported. Murray Edelman sat surrounded by screens at a long table in the restricted-access Decision Room. Only a close look at his computer displays spoiled the high-tech atmosphere—they looked like something out of the Atari years, ridiculously antique and kludgy, multicolored numbers on dark backgrounds written in the all-but-lost language of Mitofsky's sacred computational texts. The basic models for predicting elections from exit polls have not changed in a generation, and neither have the computers, nor even many of the analysts.

Next to the Decision Room was a row of little offices with killer views northward to the heart of Manhattan and the Empire State Building. In these rooms toiled the network representatives, in constant touch with data analysts at each VNS member outfit. For a few years after the founding of the consortium, the members all deferred to Edelman's decisions about when to call races. In 1994, however, ABC broke ranks and formed its own decision desk, using the VNS data to scoop the others. The next time around every network had its own team of experts to rip through the numbers. This year, the competition was fiercer than ever, with VNS calling races, and also the VNS members—CBS, ABC, NBC, Fox, CNN and the Associated Press—doing the same. Six teams (CBS and CNN shared a team) all racing to make the quickest sense of the same riddles.

Midafternoon—2:09 p.m. Eastern time, to be exact—the first slice of exit poll data was dumped by VNS into the computers of subscribers around the country. (*The Washington Post* was one, paying $15,000 for national exit poll numbers and smaller amounts—ranging from $3,500 to $5,600—for results from selected states.) The election was extremely tight, VNS reported: Bush had 49 percent of the sketchy early survey, Gore 48 percent. In Florida, the numbers said Gore 50, Bush 47.

At the Fox News decision desk on Manhattan's Sixth Avenue, John Ellis, a veteran political analyst who had been hired to run the upstart network's operation, was combing through the survey results. The phone rang on his desk.

"Ellis, Bush here."

It was the Republican nominee for president, who happened to be John Ellis's cousin. Bush was done with his workout and now he wanted to chew over the numbers. "Here we go again," Bush said. "Looks tight, huh?"

"I wouldn't worry about early numbers," Ellis answered reassuringly. Your dad had bad early numbers in '88 and he wound up winning by seven. So who knows?"

But in fact the data contained some very disturbing news for the Bush team. The campaign's internal polls in the final days of the race showed them leading by five points in Florida—now these numbers suggested they were behind by three. Blacks and Jews, two constituencies energized by Gore's voter turnout effort, were hitting the polls in big numbers. The national data were unsettling, too. Gore was gaining ground. In state after state, the exit polls showed a closer contest than Bush had been led to believe—the projections of a fairly comfortable Republican win were falling to pieces. At one point that day, campaign chairman Don Evans looked up from the poll numbers and said, "Every piece of paper we've had here has turned to crap."

At 5:30, after another wave of exit poll results, Ellis walked outside for a cigarette and called his cousin at Bush's private number in the mansion. "Is it really this close?" Bush asked him.

"Yeah," Ellis answered. "It's really close." . . .

The decision desks were squirreled away in buildings all across Manhattan, cramped, grim, slapdash—and packed with talent. "Election night is probably the most exciting night to come around every two years. And a good presidential election night—one that's close—that's what I dream of," says the blustery guru, Warren Mitofsky. That's why he was running the CBS desk, as he has done, off and on, for decades. Excitement was the juice that attracted number jockeys from polling companies and consulting combines across the country. Joe Lenski, for example. Normally, he's vice president of Edison Media Research, crafting polls that require weeks of analysis. But when Americans vote, he sits for a day at Mitofsky's right hand. "It's like a video game," he says of calling elections. "You get the same thrill an Air Force pilot must get flying a jet plane."

Early on Election Day, after glancing at the first exit polls, the networks polished off about two-thirds of the races, the easy calls. Incumbency is a staggering advantage in American politics. Very few ins become outs. That left the close Senate contests—and a presidential cliffhanger. But when 7 p.m. reached the East Coast and polls began closing in a large number of states, the race for the White House suddenly appeared quite simple on the ancient screens of the VNS computers. The early numbers were all Al Gore.

As the experts watched the real numbers arrive, they sensed they might be seeing the decisive story of 2000. The screens displayed, to the trained eye, nine different models for analyzing votes—tracking pre-election polls, exit polling, party turnout, geographical influences and so on. One display simply reported the slowly gathering actual results. At 7:50 p.m. the model at the top of the screen—the one marked "composite"—showed Florida at 51.4 percent for Gore and 46.2 percent for Bush. Next to the keyword STATUS on the right hand side of the screen appeared the word CALL.

If anything, the initial reports from key precincts suggested to some analysts that Gore was actually doing even better than the VNS screens projected. John Moody, the Fox vice president in charge of election night coverage, began badgering John Ellis to make the call. NBC, CBS and CNN had all given Florida to Gore, he said. Ellis's team wanted to wait for a few more precincts, but the pressure was piling up furiously.

"Okay, Florida goes Gore," Ellis shouted to Moody. It was 7:52 p.m.

Within minutes, Ellis's phone was ringing. It was cousin Jeb. "Are you sure?" the Florida governor asked.

"Jeb, I'm sorry," Ellis said. "I'm looking at a screenful of Gore."

"But the polls haven't closed in the Panhandle."

"It's not going to help," Ellis answered. "I'm sorry."

The networks' decision made no sense to Bush strategist Karl Rove. As he compared notes with Jeb Bush by phone, each man reinforced the other's skepticism. Rove's office was adjacent to polling director Dowd's at campaign headquarters, and each had a huge glass window on the corridor. A crowd of campaign staffers milled about, peering in at the two strategists as they and other senior staff members groped for hope in the Florida vote counts. Months earlier, the campaign had put together a detailed model of Florida, showing what it would take from each county to carry the state. Comparing the real results to their model, the Bush team quickly concluded that the state was still far too close to call.

But Florida was in the Gore column, and with it came the confident pronouncements from the television pundits that W. was finished. Only one dissenting voice was immediately heard. Mary Matalin, CNN's conservative pundit, was well-versed in grassroots politics, having run the get-out-the-vote effort for three Republican presidential candidates. When she heard Florida called for Gore, she sat down in an empty cubicle at CNN's Washington bureau, and started calling the Republican field commanders in Florida. They assured her there was no way Gore had carried the state.

"I'm going to go out on a limb here," she said when she returned to the air. "We have early data. The spread is 2 percent. The raw total is just 4,000 votes at this point. If it continues at this pace, there are half a million absentee ballots out there."

CNN's veteran election analyst, Bill Schneider, scoffed. "When we call the state," he intoned, "we're pretty sure that state is going to go for the winner."

Weeks later, the VNS experts would conclude that they were victims of a weird confluence: The exit polls overestimated the Gore vote, falling just barely within the margin of error. And they underestimated the Bush vote, by miscalculating the number of absentee ballots. This was the beginning of the worst night ever for the decision desks, and in the aftermath some pollsters would ask if the data crunchers allowed themselves to be swayed by the sexy story glimmering, mirage-like, on their computers. Gore had been the laggard all along in this race—for him to win in the end would make great melodrama. Did Gore's genuinely strong showings in Pennsylvania and Michigan cast a halo over the interpretation of the Florida results?

Not so, Mitofsky said afterward. "It's only the second time in 33 years I've seen a sample on election night give us a wrong winner without serious data errors. The chances are 1 in 200." . . .

An internal investigation eventually determined that VNS significantly miscalculated the absentee turnout. Early voting is one of the hottest trends in politics, and the election forecasters have not kept up. Nothing in the exit polling models developed by Mitofsky and Edelman took absentee voting of a significant magnitude into account—a simple, devastating, mistake.

That wasn't the only problem. The choice of sample precincts in the Tampa area turned out to be too Democratic. Then the first round of actual vote totals from selected Florida precincts, used to check the exit poll results, didn't include any from Tampa—so the network decision teams couldn't discover the Democratic oversample. In other words, each little mistake compounded the next. One of the unspoken assumptions of a complex model, like the VNS projections, is that an error in one candidate's favor in one factor will probably be shaved down by a skew in the other candidate's favor somewhere else. In Florida, in the first hour, every little botch skewed in Gore's direction.

Perhaps if an astute analyst had only one race to study that night, the huge early advantage projected for Gore in the decisive Tampa precincts would have set off alarm bells. But in the reality of election night—with 51 distinct presidential races to watch, plus Senate and gubernatorial contests—the ambiguities of the Florida data were lost in a sea of flashing numbers, until it was too late. . . .

As the deadlock wore on, Gore's team grew more and more frustrated.

Twelve days after the election, nothing was going the way Gore thought it should. He and his friends worked the phones constantly, soliciting information, decoding motives, seeking the pressure points that might influence the South Florida boards. They finally made a breakthrough in Broward County.

For many years, the Broward elections office got its legal advice from assistant county attorney Norman Ostrau. He was a particular authority on voting law, having served as a legislator on the Florida House elections committee. Assistant county attorney Andrew Meyers, on the other hand, had never advised the canvassing board. He was an appellate lawyer for the county. When Gore requested a recount, Meyers was out of town working on a case concerning citrus canker, a disease menacing Florida's orange groves. Meyers did have access to a lot of information about the election dispute, though. His wife was a lawyer with Mitchell Berger's firm, which had become a key part of the Gore effort in Florida. She was a strong Gore supporter even before the deadlock.

Ostrau had advised the canvassing board to follow a narrow standard for counting ballots. "Hanging chads"—that is, partly perforated rectangles hanging by no more than two corners—should be counted as votes, but nothing else. Ostrau said this standard was based on the law in Texas. Meyers felt his colleague had it wrong, that the Texas statute was much broader, allowing for pierced chads, even dimpled chads, to be counted— if the board felt that was the voter's intention. So, without consulting Ostrau, Meyers drafted a brief for the Florida Supreme Court urging the justices to order the South Florida counties to adopt that more liberal approach.

Then, on Sunday, November 19, Meyers showed up at the counting session and told the board what it ought to do. The two-corner rule, he said, "is impermissibly narrow." He also met privately with each board member. Meyers recalled Judge Lee complaining that perfectly clear votes were being cast aside because of the hanging-chad rule. Meyers had the answer: "Why don't you change the standard?"

They did.

The Broward canvassers went back through the ballots they already had counted, and suddenly the votes poured in for Gore. Six days later, when the Broward effort finally wheezed to a stop, the canvassing board and its deputized counters had examined more than 500,000 ballots. Result: a net gain of 567 votes for Gore. Broward was the only county that delivered on Gore's expectations. Indeed, Broward exceeded Gore's hopes.

The abrupt change in the counting standard convinced Republicans that the fix was in. They came to view the Broward recount room as nothing less than a crime scene. The GOP even got permission to supply fresh tapes for the surveillance cameras so that the existing tapes could be extracted and used, potentially, as inculpatory evidence. Ed McNally, a local lawyer and Bush volunteer, carried with him snapshots of a Broward sheriff's deputy counting chads, in clusters of five, on a tabletop. They'd become detached during the handling of the ballots—a sign, McNally insisted, of "extraordinary irregularities."

Nothing was more irregular than the Case of the Immaculate Chad. A punch card turned up with a chad lodged snugly in the hole for Gore—but it was backward. The rectangle was plainly on the wrong side of the card. This chad wasn't dangling, or hanging, wasn't one-corner or two-corner—it simply appeared to have left one card and found its way back into a hole on another card. When it went through the machine, the card had registered as a Gore vote, so the board gave it to the vice president once again. The board members figured the speck of paper must have migrated.

Meanwhile, Jane Carroll, the elections supervisor, never did quite figure out where Andrew Meyers had come from, "but I know he didn't fall out of heaven," she said later. "Someone sent him."

As for Meyers, he agreed that perhaps he should have alerted the board that he had family ties to the Gore campaign. "In a legal sense, there was no conflict," he said afterward. "But in hindsight, I probably should have mentioned it earlier."

Miami had a lot of ballots to recount, roughly 650,000. They were locked in blue metal file boxes along one wall of the spacious, soul-less, climate-controlled Tabulation Room on the 19th floor of the county building. They started on Monday, November 20. Elections supervisor David Leahy brought in a fairly small corps of counters, just 25 teams, but there was little need for more, he felt. There always would be a bottleneck in the process. Florida law required all disputed ballots to be judged by the three-member canvassing board. It was impossible to move faster than those three people could go. In Miami, the canvassing board members started with a mountain of undervotes, more than 10,000 of them, examining each card, one by one by one.

Leahy would look at each ballot and announce his verdict. The other board members would examine it, as would the partisan observers. Objections would be made. Some ballots were clear, some were hard to decipher. A number would be scrawled on the back of each challenged ballot, and a court reporter had to record the number. Using this process the board managed to count roughly one ballot per minute—60 per hour. Twelve hours a day was about the limit of their endurance: "It's just eyestrain,"

Leahy later explained. "You look at ballots for so long and comes a point where you just get bleary-eyed."

By the end of work on Tuesday, 139 precincts had been manually counted, resulting in a net gain of 157 votes for Gore. It was slow going, but Leahy believed they could achieve their goal of finishing by December 1.

That night, the Florida Supreme Court ordered all hand counts completed by November 26. . . .

Looking back, after the war was over, both Republicans and Democrats point to the decision of the Miami canvassing board to stop counting— a severe blow to Gore's hopes of gaining the lead—as one of the critical moments. . . .

The November 26 deadline set by the Florida Supreme Court was fast approaching. Only Palm Beach was still counting. The Gore team had pretty much given up on the recounts. It carefully tracked the "yield rate" in each county—namely, the percentage of unread ballots that the canvassing boards converted into votes. The enthusiastic recounters of Broward managed a yield rate of 20 to 25 percent. In Palm Beach, it was a modest 5 percent. "There are hundreds of votes that are not being counted," local Gore attorney Ben Kuehne said brusquely.

As the deadline approached, the Palm Beach board members realized they might not be able to finish at all. On the afternoon of Sunday, November 26, hours before the Florida Supreme Court's deadline, Judge Burton faxed a letter to Secretary of State Harris seeking an extension until 9 a.m. Monday. This was the backup deadline allowed by the court in case the secretary of state's office was not open on Sunday. But Harris's office most definitely was open.

At 3:15 p.m., having received no answer, Burton stood up from the counting table and walked to a back office in the Emergency Operations Center, where he made a call to Clay Roberts, the state's elections director. A short while later, the canvassing board received a letter from Harris holding firm to the deadline. Burton was miffed: "I don't know what the difference is between sending it at 5 p.m. or at 7:30 p.m."

After all they had been through, for all the board's ambivalence about the count, the Palm Beach canvassers were now deeply committed to having their work validated. They'd plowed through half a million ballots—the idea that their new tally might be ignored was hard to take.

The board picked up the pace. But at 4:25 p.m., Burton announced that the count could not possibly be completed by 5 p.m. Soon afterward, county officials began feeding a hieroglyph of partial results into a fax machine to Tallahassee. Just before 5 p.m., the machine jammed. But it was quickly fixed, and word came back that the papers had been received one minute before the deadline: 4:59 p.m.

And they kept counting, just in case—faster and faster. The party observers now seemed more cooperative. Then, at 6:05 p.m., a wave of gloom came over Burton's face. Katherine Harris, he had learned, would not even accept the partial results they had sent. (Harris's lawyers would later laugh at the idea. They couldn't even read the partial results, they insisted.)

Finally, at 7:06 p.m., almost exactly 19 days after the polls closed, the Palm Beach board finished counting its votes. Gore wound up netting 174 votes—far fewer than the Gore team believed he was entitled to. There were 5,924 ballots left in dispute, according to Gore strategist Dennis Newman. Of those, 4,987 were "dimpled" ballots, he said—2,971 for Gore and 2,016 for Bush. If these had all been counted as votes, Gore would have gained another 955—more than enough to win Florida and the election.

"I believe they did a real good job to be evenhanded and fair, to be consistent," Newman said of the Palm Beach board. "They were just consistently wrong."

Judge Burton was more philosophical:

"This has been an amazing experience," he said afterward. "This is democracy. . . . This was the best and worst of politics." . . .

Nearly five weeks after the election had ended in a virtual tie, an elections supervisor in Leon County named Ion Sancho stood up in the community room of the county public library and said simply: "The process may begin."

With scarcely a murmur, eight judges and their assistants hunkered down to tally the roughly 9,000 undervotes left unstudied when the Miami-Dade canvassing board halted its recount on Thanksgiving eve. In Duval County—greater Jacksonville—elections officials met a computer programmer from Miami bearing the software to instruct their counting machines to separate nearly 5,000 undervotes from the mountain of 292,000 ballots cast on Election Day. In Sarasota, a county judge corralled an official van and headed to a satellite office at the other end of the county to collect 65 boxes of ballots.

In Collier County, on the Gulf Coast, the canvassing board needed five hours that Saturday just to decide how to count 40 absentee ballots.

"We've set up a system that has a built-in margin of error of 3 percent, one way or another," the board's chairman lamented. "To tell us on Friday to count them by Monday is ridiculous."

In Pinellas County, on Tampa Bay, Commissioner Robert Stewart pondered the recount effort and mused: "Damn, we need a better process."

And so it went all over Florida. As it was from the beginning, the reliability of hand counting was in the eye, or party affiliation, of the beholder. Democrats extolled a heroic effort moving along quickly with noble intentions. Republicans saw chaos. In Austin, Hughes felt her stomach sink as she watched on television. "Well," she thought, "once again, we're counting votes."

But no one had much chance to contemplate the matter. At 2:40 p.m., CNN reported that the U.S. Supreme Court had ordered an immediate halt to the effort. Gore was on the phone with Ron Klain when the news broke. It was the vice president's lowest moment.

In Tallahassee, the chief local judge, George S. Reynolds III, confirmed the news and issued his order 12 minutes later. At 3 p.m., court spokesman Terre Cass was once more at the microphones. "We have stayed the recount," she said.

The simmering divisions in the U.S. Supreme Court had boiled over. The stay order—and the related decision to hear oral arguments on Bush's appeal on Monday, December 11—was issued by a bare 5 to 4 majority, perfectly splitting the court's most conservative members from its most liberal ones. . . .

The election of 2000 will be scrutinized and debated for generations. Did the right candidate win? Was the election stolen? Many Democrats believe it was. Republicans angrily reject that claim, but many of them were hurling charges of larceny themselves when it seemed possible that the Democrats would prevail in Florida's recount.

The vote was so close in Florida—well within any statistical margin of error, given that more than 6 million votes were cast—that whoever lost could have mustered some convincing evidence that in some measure the result was unfair.

"No matter who won Florida, the loser would have been able to say, 'Yes, but was that a real win or not?'" said Andrew Kohut of the Pew Research Center. "And people accepted that real early. By the second week or so, polls were showing that people thought it would be a flawed outcome no matter who wins." But Kohut said that while the public early on judged that Florida would produce a questionable winner, "They said whoever comes out the winner we will accept as the next president."

Some Democrats see the combination of problems that appeared to hamper African American voters in Florida's polling booths as—at least in part—a deliberate effort to suppress their impact on the election. Some Republicans see the hasty decision by the television networks to call Florida for Gore while polling booths in the state's heavily Republican Panhandle were still open as an act influenced by liberal media bias that had the effect of suppressing Bush votes.

Many of these broad allegations can be difficult to evaluate because there is little hard evidence to definitively support or refute them.

There are still serious questions to be examined about the allegations of disenfranchisement of African American voters in Florida. Computer analysis of the voting suggests that the percentage of spoiled ballots was higher in predominantly African American precincts. The U.S. Commission on Civil Rights held hearings in Florida in January and will issue a report about the state's presidential vote.

Various news organizations, including *The Washington Post*, have also launched projects to examine many of the ballots in Florida—those with more than one vote for president or those with no apparent vote for president. Eventually these investigations will provide more detailed information about what those ballots showed: how many had dimpled chads or hanging chads or obvious votes for Bush or Gore, whatever other markings were included on the ballots.

The descriptions of each ballot, which will be released publicly when completed, will enable news organizations, political scientists, elections officials and the parties to understand in detail what mistakes voters made and how votes slipped through the cracks. It will also attempt to assess the reliability of hand recounts. The findings may provide a much more detailed inventory of Florida's disputed ballots, but this inventory is not intended to "call" the election after the fact.

The role the television networks played on election night remains controversial. Not once but twice the major networks incorrectly called Florida. The networks and Voter News Service, which conducted the exit polls and provided precinct data to the networks, have acknowledged the disaster of election night. The networks face congressional scrutiny over their policies for calling state-by-state results and will undertake internal reviews that likely will affect their decision making in future elections.

Just as some Republicans blame the networks for distorting Florida's outcome, so do Democrats. What if the networks had never projected George W. Bush the winner in Florida and flashed up their graphics naming him the 43rd president of the United States? Some advisers to Al Gore believe the whole dynamic of the battle for Florida would have been different. Their argument is that, from the moment Bush was declared the president-elect, Gore was cast in the position of trying to change the outcome of the election, of trying to take something away from Bush. Had the networks simply shown the state too close to call, with Gore leading in the popular vote nationally and with neither candidate holding an electoral college majority, their task would have been more straightforward and their actions less subject to criticism.

"Had it not been called and it was just 'Dead Heat' headlines and the networks had said, 'We can't call this,' I think our fight in Florida would have been viewed a lot more legitimately," said William Daley, who was Gore's campaign chairman.

A more technical issue concerns the design of the ballots in Florida. The evidence is clear that the infamous butterfly ballot in Palm Beach County confused many voters, at least some of whom believe they voted for Patrick J. Buchanan when they intended to vote for Gore. The former vice president's advisers seriously considered whether to challenge the ballot in court but concluded there was no remedy even if they proved the ballot was illegal. Neither party had objected to the ballot.

Nearly every tactical decision made by the candidates during the last two weeks of the election comes into play as the participants replay the election. For instance, what if Gore had worked harder in his home state of Tennessee, whose 10 electoral votes would have made him president? What if Gore had poured more money into New Hampshire or West Virginia, two small states that nonetheless could have given him enough extra electoral votes to win? In fact, many Gore advisers wrote off Tennessee before the final days. They believed they had a better chance of winning other states of similar size—Wisconsin, for example—but only if they steered extra effort there. In West Virginia, they knew Gore was slipping and debated what to do about it. But to some Gore advisers, the state wasn't large enough to worry about. Florida and Michigan and Pennsylvania and other big states were more important.

Every day the participants were forced to make potentially huge decisions, with little time to think. Gore had to decide in the first days the counties in which to ask for a recount. Bush had to decide at the same time whether to go into federal court, a step that would make him the first candidate in the courts despite public warnings from his lawyers about the dangers of spiraling legal battles. . . .

Both sides can look back at the 36 days and ask about this decision or that ruling, this legal call or that political judgment. But it is clear, in retrospect, that there were two significant turning points in the final weeks of the battle.

The first came one day after the Florida Supreme Court extended the deadline for certification to November 26 and ordered the counties to keep the recounts going. That decision came late on a Tuesday night, two days before Thanksgiving. The next day, the Miami–Dade canvassing board resumed counting, then at midday abruptly called off the count, declaring there was no way to meet even the extended deadline. The decision represented a huge setback to Gore, whose entire strategy was based on putting points on the board, as his advisers so often put it. If Miami–Dade never represented the numerical linchpin of Gore's recount strategy, the county offered the prospect of providing enough extra votes to put Gore ahead of Bush at some point before the November 26 deadline.

Democrats remain bitter over the Republican protests in Miami–Dade that day, led by a group of congressional staffers. Some of these Democrats also believe the news media underplayed the role of those staffers, arguing that had Clinton administration officials been caught doing the same thing, the coverage—and condemnation—would have been enormous. The decision to stop counting in Miami–Dade forced the Gore team to expend precious energy and resources trying to undo the action. In retrospect, they believe, they might have done better to make sure the Palm Beach canvassing board continued working on Thanksgiving and completed its work before the 5 p.m. deadline on November 26.

Even more significant, Gore advisers believe, was the December 9 decision by the U.S. Supreme Court to stop the statewide recount that had been ordered the previous day by the Florida Supreme Court. That final weekend marked a moment of maximum jeopardy for Bush, and many of his advisers knew it. They feared that at some point that weekend that Gore might pull ahead in the count, largely because they believed there were no rigorous or uniform standards for examining the ballots.

Bush campaign chairman Don Evans told Bush after the recount had been halted that day that he was convinced Bush would win if the counting were later resumed, but he was in the minority in the Bush camp. Gore strategists believe they would have pulled ahead if the counting had proceeded to its conclusion.

"They were always ahead," said Gore strategist Michael Whouley. "If we had once pulled ahead it would have changed the whole dynamic."

"I think we would have stayed ahead," Ginsberg said. "But the more arguing there was over ballots that were standardless, the messier it was and the more chaotic it was. That's really not how you want the presidency of the United States decided."

The Supreme Court's decision to stay the counting prevented that possibility from developing.

Florida exposed how fragile democracy can be—and underscored how much it depends on the faith of ordinary people that the system is fair and equitable. Many will argue that the country survived the battle just fine. There was no constitutional crisis, there were no riots in the streets. Perhaps no state could withstand the scrutiny Florida's voting system has and will continue to receive. But politicians in both major parties believe there is now a clear need to address the problems Florida exposed.

The challenges include what to do about faulty voting machines, how to improve voter education and whether oversight of elections should be lodged in the hands of partisan Republicans and partisan Democrats. And there remains unresolved what once seemed like a simple question: What constitutes a vote? Florida is hardly the only state in the country without a clear answer.

73

KATHLEEN SULLIVAN
DEREK CRESSMAN

The Constitution and Campaign Reform:
Hearings Before the Senate Committee on Rules and Administration

In 2000, Congress continued an ongoing process of considering reforms to campaign finance laws. The 1974 Federal Election Campaign Act, the initial reform that limited contributions, had also created unintended consequences; political action committee (PAC) money from influential interest groups began to dominate elections, especially for Congress. The 2000 congressional hearings were a result of pressure from some citizen organizations, certain candidates, and particular interest groups that wanted changes made in the existing law. Two years later, a campaign finance reform bill did become law, although its final outcome remains unclear, both because of court challenges and, of course, "unintended consequences." In this reading, two contrasting voices on campaign reform face off. Kathleen Sullivan, Dean of the Stanford Law School, takes the position that it is impossible to close loopholes allowing money into politics. And it is undesirable, she feels, to try to limit political speech in any way before an election. Only disclosure will work. On the other hand, Derek Cressman, the campaign finance analyst for the United States Public Interest Research Group, advocates lower contribution limits to allow average Americans more influence over candidates for office. Notice also the format of a congressional hearing, with comments from the chairman, the Hon. Mitch McConnell of Kentucky.

THE CHAIRMAN [Hon. Mitch McConnell (R-KY)]. We have a scheduling dilemma here that I hope that this panel can accommodate.

Dean Sullivan who is on the next panel is going to have to leave shortly. I wonder if there is any chance the three of you could stay around. Could you do that? Let us bring up the other panel and get Dean Sullivan in here.

MR. GLASSER. I always enjoy hearing Dean Sullivan.

THE CHAIRMAN. Good. Thank you very much. . . .

Dean Sullivan [Dean, Stanford Law School], if you would lead off, we would appreciate that. . . .

MS. SULLIVAN. Thank you, Mr. Chairman, Senator Dodd, Senator Feinstein, and Members of the committee for the privilege of allowing me to testify before you on this very important matter.

A great deal of what I have to say has already been eloquently expressed by Mr. Glasser and Professor Gora. So let me try to highlight a few points and just add a little bit more to what they have said.

The first point to make is that it is really false to talk about American Government today as being a hotbed of corruption. This is quite arguably the cleanest government in the world and the cleanest government in the history of the country. If we talk about corruption, I think we have to understand that what is being described by that term is not the lining of anybody's pockets in this Government. That is something that is checked vigorously by our criminal laws and by the vigilance of our wonderfully free press. It is really a matter of inequality of influence. That is what is really being described by the term "corruption."

The second point to make is that the problem here is that the efforts of campaign finance reform in the past coupled with *Buckley*'s noble, but flawed attempt at compromise, have left us in the worst of all possible worlds, both from the perspective of democracy and from the perspective of the First Amendment freedom of speech.

*Buckley** said that the Government may limit the supply of political money through contribution limits which it upheld, but it did not say anything about limiting the demand, and, of course, the demand has escalated because, in this country, we have private ownership of the media. There are alternate systems, but they have not worked very well, and in

---

Buckley v. Valeo (1976) is an important Supreme Court decision on campaign finance law. The Court said that a candidate cannot be prevented from spending as much of his own money as he wishes on his campaign, based on the First Amendment's freedom of speech guarantee. Campaign finance laws limiting other contribution amounts, however, are allowable. — EDS.

a system with private ownership of the media, a need to reach large electorates, relatively weak parties compared to other parts of the world, candidates need a lot of money to run for office.

When you limit the supply of political money through contribution limits, but you do not limit the demand, of course, the money will go elsewhere. The money will go to the substitutes that you are focusing on today and that current reformers are focusing on. It will go to secondary organizations such as the parties, in tertiary organizations such as PACs and independent issue groups.

Now, if that is the case, what have we done with three decades of campaign finance reform? We have driven the money away from the candidates who are accountable to the American people, who can be checked at the polls if they are thought to be beholden to special interests, and toward other organizations which are harder for the people to control, to the parties and to independent organizations. Especially hard to control are those independent organizations that are driven by campaign finance laws themselves to be indirect and obscure and coy about whom they are representing because they have to avoid triggering regulation for express advocacy.

That is a role I do not think the Framers would be able to recognize. The Framers who talked about robust political speech being at the core of the First Amendment would not recognize a regime that says you have got to be careful about hiding the fact that you are supporting a candidate, try to at all costs avoid inciting anyone to vote. That is, what political speech is all about is trying to persuade people to vote, and it should be able to be expressed and unashamed and open instead of covert or, as Justice Kennedy said in his eloquent dissent in the *Shrink Missouri Government* case, it should not have to be driven underground. Political speech should not have to be driven underground.

I appreciate very much Senator Feinstein's efforts in her description of her bill to say she would like the speech above the table, rather than under the table. I think that is exactly right. The First Amendment is about political speech that should be open, robust, and unashamed.

If we have driven the money away from the candidate to these other places, the reformers say, "Oh, well, it is time to shut all those loopholes down," but I would submit to you that you cannot shut all those loopholes down in a system of freedom of speech. You cannot shut all those loopholes down because money can always have somewhere else to go.

You heard in the earlier panel about the ability of some wealthy persons in this society to buy and control media outlets, and, of course, the very same editorial boards who advocate campaign finance reform for others would be loathe to impose that kind of campaign finance reform on themselves. We do not hear the editorial boards of the major papers saying they will abstain from electoral endorsements in the 60 days before an election, and we would not expect to hear that from them. Or, the money can go elsewhere because individuals have an absolutely protected constitutional right even after *Buckley* to engage in independent expenditures to advocate issues, and individuals have their right even to engage in independent expenditures to make express advocacy for and against candidates.

So I would agree very much with Professor Gora and Mr. Glasser that the appropriate regulatory response by Congress now ought not to be to try to add more limits. They have failed. They are antidemocratic, and they raise profound constitutional problems.

It is rather to do the three things that have been earlier described, to liberalize the contribution limits, because obviously it is not any benefit to a candidate's time to have to chase many more people to raise the same amount of money. If we hold to the contribution limits that the court upheld in *Buckley*, the $1,000 contribution that was upheld then is worth about $380 today. Nobody can possibly think that you are a fat cat if you give $380 in year 2000 dollars to a candidate.

Second, to enforce a robust system of disclosure. One thing that has changed in the 25 years since *Buckley* is that there has been a revolution in communications technology led in large part by the scientists and engineers in Northern California that both Senator Feinstein and I are lucky enough to live in. That communications revolution makes the possibility of genuine, effective disclosure of who contributes what to candidates, possible in the way it was not possible 25 years ago. Instantaneous disclosure of contributions to candidates over the Internet is the best disinfectant. That is a situation that the court upheld in *Buckley*, and if there is disclosure, then the press can follow the money and the people can follow the money. If there is any concern about the money, it can be checked by those who are authorized by our system of Government to check it, namely the voters.

Just in closing, a couple of comments on some of the constitutional issues that have been raised about bans on soft money and further restrictions on issue ads.

First, the idea that you would close down loopholes by banning soft money, that is, subjecting all contributions to parties, even if they are not used for express candidate advocacy, to the limits on individual contributions and PAC contributions and to the ban on union and corporation contributions, I do think that a ban on soft money does raise very serious

First Amendment issues, even under our existing law and in fact would take a constitutional amendment to change.

It also raises a serious policy question. You might say in a time when parties are weakened through various forces in our development over the last few years, what is wrong with having stronger parties. Parties are good for democracy, but the constitutional question is raised by the fact that this interferes with the ability to associate with parties for purposes that parties serve other than simply advocating candidate election or defeat in a particular election, and it does so without the one justification the court has ever upheld for restricting this kind of political speech.

Remember, *Buckley's* blessing of contribution limits is an exception to our general First Amendment principles. We do not normally allow political speech to be limited, and we do not normally allow it to be limited based on speculation about appearances of corruption. You can limit speech to stop somebody from shouting "fire" in a crowded theater, but we do not normally limit speech because we think some arsonist might some day say "fire" in a crowded theater. We usually require evidence.

Buckley is a narrow exception to the rule that we usually require very strong justifications for limiting political speech, and it said that one exception is where there is a danger that money will go to a candidate and exact a quid pro quo. I give you money for your campaign; you give me a favor in legislation.

That danger is not posed when people give money to a party. A party is not a candidate. A party represents a diverse set of candidates. It is just like you are not buying one stock. You are buying into a mutual fund, and a party cannot be corrupted in the same way as a candidate, and that is why the one justification the Court has ever accepted really does not apply to soft-money contributions, and I think it is a huge over-reading of prior Supreme Court cases to say that they have ever authorized bans on soft money. . . .

The last point, and I am sure that other panelists will expand on this, I think there are also serious constitutional First Amendment questions posed by any attempt to expand the definition of contributions to a candidate to cover any form of issue ads other than express advocacy.

There is a really serious question whether bureaucrats should ever be able to draw a line between that ad that permissibly speaks about issues and that ad which advocates the election or defeat of a candidate.

In fact, you could hardly think of a more pure example of the kind of license or regime that the authors of the First Amendment were against, the idea of Government bureaucrats deciding whether or not political speech critical of Government may or may not go forward because it is too close to an election.

I think the Framers would also be appalled at the idea that political speech has to be shut up just when it could be most effective; that is, in the 60 days before an election. Doesn't that turn the First Amendment on its head to say just when political speech should be at its most robust, it ought to be shut down, if there is a danger it might influence anyone to vote?

The Supreme Court made it clear that that kind of protection for speech applies even to corporations and to unions because the principle of freedom of speech is not just about who gets to say things. It is about what gets said, and unions do have the freedom of speech to speak on issues if they do not contribute directly to candidates.

In conclusion, disclosure is better than limits. Public financing, notwithstanding the great administrative problems it raises, is a better solution. Floors are better than ceilings, and raising the contribution limits rather than trying to shut down loopholes is the way to go. A constitutional amendment would be a very bad idea. . . .

Mr. Cressman?

MR. CRESSMAN [Campaign Finance Analyst, U.S. Public Interest Research Group]. Thank you. The PIRGs are non-profit, non-partisan citizen organizations that conduct research, educate the public, and advocate for public policy that we feel benefits the public interest. I am here today to address the question of whether the current Federal contribution limits on hard money are too low, too high, or just right. It is the PIRGs' contention that current limits are too high and that they should certainly not be increased as called for in legislation pending before the committee.

First, let me address the problem with our current campaign finance system and how that relates to the hard money limits. My first point is that money is a significant factor in determining who runs for office and who wins elections. Fund-raising potential not only influences a prospective candidate's decision to run for office, and it is also an indicator of their political viability, as other folks have testified today.

In the last election, the candidates who spent the most won 94 percent of general election Senate races and 95 percent of House races. I suspect that most members of Congress would agree that money heavily influences elections as well. After all, why else would candidates bother raising money? However, I would welcome any member of Congress to disprove this conclusion by vowing to raise less funds than your challenger in the next election.

But there is less agreement as to whether or not it is a bad thing that money plays such a heavy role in election outcomes. If contributions were coming from a representative cross-section of America, money raised would then be a good barometer of candidate's public support and we would find that the candidates who raised the most money had the most public support and would win the election. We might then conclude that there is not a serious problem with money in politics.

But campaign contributions do not come from a broad cross-section of America. Most candidates for Federal office depend upon the support of a few individuals who can afford to give substantially. In this year's presidential primary, Al Gore and George W. Bush raised three-quarters of their total campaign funds in 1999 from maximum $1,000 donors. Contributions under $200 accounted for less than 10 percent of the total funds raised. And fewer than one out of every 1,000 citizens gave a contribution of more than $200 to a presidential candidate last year.

This number would be somewhat less troubling if large donors were representative of the population. But instead, most large donors are older, white males with vast financial resources. According to a recent national survey, 95 percent of large donors were white, 80 percent were male, 50 percent were over 60 years of age, and 81 percent had annual incomes greater than $100,000. These numbers are dramatically different from the population of the United States and the donors are not at all representative of the American public politically.

The solution would be to set contribution limits that are within striking distance of what most Americans can afford to donate. Candidates would then raise their funds from ordinary citizens, and the candidates who raised the most money truly would be the candidates with the most public support.

Low contribution limits are favored by the public, they are accepted by the courts, and they are sound public policy. A 1994 poll found that 77 percent of the public supported reducing individual contribution limits. The public has demonstrated their support for contribution limits much lower than the current Federal limits at polling booths on election day as well. In the past six years, at least 11 States have moved to lower their contribution limits with all but three of these States coming by a direct vote of the people, not incumbent politicians. These initiatives passed by overwhelming margins, and many of them called for contribution limits as low as $100 for most races.

These citizen efforts to lower contribution limits initially met resistance from the lower Federal courts, but recently the U.S. Supreme Court issued a ruling that clears the way for the States and Congress to continue lowering contribution limits. This January, the U.S. Supreme Court issued the ruling *Nixon v. Shrink Missouri Government PAC*, and in that ruling the Court specifically upheld contribution limits of $275 for State legislative races in Missouri and $1,075 for statewide.

More generally, the Court said that the States and Congress could set contribution limits as low as they saw fit. The Court also explicitly rejected the argument that inflation had eroded the meaning of the original $1,000 limit and held that the $1,000 limit upheld in *Buckley v. Valeo* was not a constitutional minimum.

Federal candidates are clearly able to raise sufficient funds to campaign under the current Federal hard money limits, and in fact congressional candidate fund-raising has gone up at a rate 50 percent greater than the rate of inflation since 1974, and 2.3 times the rate of increase in the wages of ordinary Americans. On average, candidates have never raised more money than they are raising today.

So if the public supports low contribution limits and the courts allow them, it then remains for the U.S. Congress to debate contribution limits on their merit as public policy. This policy question should be about what is appropriate today, not about how to adjust a figure that was not by itself adequate in 1974.

When Congress enacted the $1,000 individual limit in 1974 the limits only affected about 6 percent of donors at the time. The real impact of the 1974 FECA amendments was to come from the mandatory spending limits that were struck down by the Supreme Court. Were those spending limits in place today and indexed for inflation, House candidates could have spent no more than $203,000 in the last election. But instead, the average winning candidate spent $650,000.

So to look only at the $1,000 limit in isolation and conclude that a limit that was designed to have little impact in 1974 should now be raised so that it again has little impact, grossly ignores the intent of Congress in 1974 and misconstrues the real question about contribution limits.

The correct question to be asking is whether or not contribution limits are set at levels that are affordable to average Americans. If they are not, then a small group of wealthy donors capable of giving more than ordinary Americans will inevitably have much more influence on the elections process; a wholesale corruption that distorts the process of democracy. A $1,000 contribution is no more affordable to an average American today than it was in 1974, and hence the limit should be lowered and not increased.

The examples from States that have lowered contribution limits found that candidates could continue to campaign and that a greater number of citizens contributed after limits had been lowered. Candidates altered their fund-raising tactics, spending less time calling wealthy donors and more time at grass roots events. In short, the process works and I would invite you to read the written part of my testimony that details that.

But Senators, raising contribution limits in the name of reform is like throwing gasoline on a fire. Rather than helping put it out, it will make the situation dangerously worse. Candidates will raise more money from fewer citizens and further reduce the role of average Americans in the political process.

Now recently there has been support for higher contribution limits because some candidates feel they could spend less time raising funds. But I would suggest that just the opposite is true. The larger amount that an individual can contribute, the more special attention a donor will expect to receive for their contribution. If I am going to give $50 to a candidate for the U.S. Senate, I do not expect them to call me on the phone. But if I am going to give $1,000, I expect a personal call.

If the contribution were lowered, more Senate and House candidates would be able to raise funds in the way that Governor Bush and Senator McCain did in the last presidential race, by using pioneers as surrogates and raising small funds over the Internet. There would be a lot less pressure for candidates to spend time calling donors one on one. Rather, they could spend time at $25-a-plate spaghetti dinners or hot dog cookouts and talk to many donors at once since each donor would have lower expectations for personal attention.

If the limit is raised, candidates will be able to raise the same total amount that they do now through making fewer phone calls. But the fact that their opponent will also be raising greater sums means that the amount that must be raised for a typical Senate campaign will simply escalate dramatically and candidates will be back on the phone scraping for every large contribution they can get.

Now no campaign finance system is neutral, and we all know that. Any system will tend to advantage certain kinds of candidates, both challengers and incumbents, and comparatively disadvantage others. The best policy would be to create a system that lets the marketplace of ideas determine elections, not the financial marketplace. Setting limits that are above the level that ordinary Americans can afford will advantage candidates backed by big donors and disadvantage those who rely on small contributions.

Our current system grossly distorts the marketplace of ideas, to the point where Congress is no longer representative of the American public. A recent study by two political scientists documented the growing gap between what the public wants Congress to do and what Congress really does. Twenty years ago Congress did what the majority of Americans wanted about two-thirds of the time. But today Congress follows the wishes of the majority only about 40 percent of the time. The professors concluded that lawmakers answer to the extreme ideological elements of their party, to their contributors, and to special interests.

The result of this gap is a shocking lack of respect in the trust of the institution of Congress. In 1999, only 29 percent of Americans trusted the Government in Washington to do the right thing. That survey also found that 63 percent of respondents feel the Government serves the special interests while only 25 percent said it serves the public interest, and a majority of 54 percent said that we do not have a Government, of, by and for the people.

Now because no campaign finance system is neutral, there understandably tends to be a certain amount of concern about whether changes in our campaign finance system would benefit one party over another, or incumbents as a group over challengers.

Now U.S. PIRG is not in the business of giving advice to any political party but let me suggest to both parties that from a public policy viewpoint these concerns are minimal, and even from a partisan viewpoint they are overblown. Candidates of all stripes will simply adapt to whatever system is put in place, and both Republican and Democratic parties will quickly adjust to be competitive under the new rules.

And since we are in the final days of March Madness and we have been using a lot of sports analogies this morning, let me illustrate my point with a basketball analogy. The NCAA, the current rules reward players who have incredible athletic ability, smarts, and height. If the NCAA were to change the height of the basketball hoop it would certainly alter which type of players would be advantaged relative to others. But games would remain competitive as all players would adapt under the new rules. All teams would seek players who excelled under those rules, and any temporary advantages that one team might have over the other would quickly be erased.

Likewise, with Federal election campaigns, the current rules do favor a certain type of candidate. Candidates who are millionaires and can spend their own money to win election clearly have an advantage, as we have heard from other panelists, as do those candidates who are capable of raising large sums of money from a small group of wealthy donors. Candidates who are able—

THE CHAIRMAN. Mr. Cressman, as I mentioned to the other two witnesses as well, if you could get toward the conclusion we would appreciate it.

MR. CRESSMAN. Sure. I would be happy to wrap it right up. If Congress were to raise contribution limits, both the Republican and Democratic parties would recruit candidates who took positions that were favorable to the fewer than 1 percent of Americans who can give contributions of more than $1,000. I have no doubt that there are talented politicians in both parties who would find ways to be competitive with this constituency, through making compromises on some issues and pushing the envelope on others in order to hold their party's coalition of donors together and fracture support of the other party. That is what politics is about.

But likewise, I have no doubt that both the Republican and Democratic parties would be able to aggressively compete under different rules that required candidates to seek small contributions from ordinary Americans.

Now I realize that I am testifying today before the equivalent of the Olympic Dream Team in basketball. The members of the Senate Rules Committee are here in part because you have mastered the rules of the current game and you are to be commended for that. But I would encourage you to think about the game that you would rather play. Would you rather spend time seeking support from your constituents or raising money from a small group of wealthy donors? Would you rather compete in the marketplace of ideas or the financial marketplace?

Think also about the game that the American people want to see played. It may well be that the current members of the Senate could all be reelected under the current rules of the game, but there is a danger that the American people will tire of a game that is no longer being played for their benefit. If Congress' ratings continue to slip you risk not only damaging the standings of both major teams, but of the institution of Congress itself. . . .

So with that I am happy to wrap and happy to take any questions.

74

DENNIS JOHNSON

From *No Place for Amateurs*

Behind the scenes of every political campaign today is a political consultant. Political consulting is a thriving business whose skills are employed not just by candidates for national office, but those running for state and local positions too. Referendum questions placed on state ballots are managed by consultants. No race is too small or too obscure to be aided by consulting firms, whether big time ones led by the famous (James Carville, Dick Morris) or the anonymous one or two person basement operation. Dennis Johnson reveals the multitude of tasks that consultants perform for a campaign. He also gives some good tips on movies to rent on the topic: The War Room *and* Wag the Dog *are particularly good choices for those who enjoy the blend of fact and fiction.*

I don't want to read about you in the press. I'm sick and tired
of consultants getting famous at my expense. Any story that
comes out during the campaign undermines my candidacy.

—BILL CLINTON to his new 1996 reelection consultants
Dick Morris and Doug Schoen

JUST DAYS BEFORE THE 1996 Democratic National Convention, a smiling, confident Bill Clinton was featured on the cover of *Time* magazine. Pasted on Clinton's right shoulder was a cut-out photo of political consultant Dick Morris, "the most influential private citizen in America," according to *Time*. On the eve of Clinton's renomination, *Time* was sending its readers a backhanded pictorial message: here is the most powerful man in the world, who fought his way back from political oblivion, and perched on his shoulder is the reason why. Suddenly the once-secretive, behind-the-scenes consultant was a household name. In the early months of the reelection campaign, Morris worked hard at being the unseen political mastermind and strategist. "Being a man of mystery helps me work better," he confided to George Stephanopoulos. While Bill Clinton's 1992 consultants were talk-show regulars, wrote best-sellers, and traveled the big-dollars lecture circuit, Morris was the backroom schemer. Many media outlets had trouble even finding a file photo of the elusive Dick Morris, adding to the mystery and illusion of power.

Morris had been Clinton's earliest political adviser back in Arkansas during the first run for governor. They had a rocky relationship over the years, but following the Republican takeover of Congress in November 1994, Bill Clinton began meeting secretly with Morris. Working out of the Jefferson Hotel in Washington, using the code name "Charlie," Morris plotted the president's comeback. He was the anonymous, behind-the-scenes consultant who would retool Clinton's image, reposition his policies, and help revive his faltering presidency.

Throughout his career, Bill Clinton had a reputation for discarding political consultants. Those who helped him capture the White House in 1992—Mandy Grunwald, Stanley Greenberg, Paul Begala, and James Carville—were nowhere to be seen following the 1994 election upheaval. By the spring of 1995, Morris had assembled his own team, including veteran media consultants Bob Squier, Bill Knapp, and Hank Sheinkopf, and pollsters Mark Penn and Doug Schoen. They met regularly with several White House insiders to plan the remarkable political comeback of Bill Clinton.

Morris's anonymity was shattered when he was caught with his long-time prostitute companion by the supermarket tabloid the *Star*. The tabloid deliberately timed its bombshell story for maximum effect on the Democratic convention, with the scandal erupting on the day that Bill Clinton accepted his party's renomination for the presidency. Morris and his wife immediately left the Chicago convention and the Clinton campaign, retreating to their Connecticut home, besieged by reporters and photographers. Morris, the political consultant turned nefarious celebrity, had become a late-night dirty joke, damaged goods, and certainly a political liability. There were rumors that he was sharing sensitive White House information with his prostitute girlfriend, and Morris shocked many by announcing that months earlier he had signed a secret book deal to write the inside story of Clinton's reelection comeback. Morris now had plenty of free time to write his version of the 1996 campaign, work the talk-show circuit, join a twelve-step sex addiction program, retool his tarnished image, and pocket his $2.5 million book advance. Though the Morris scandal scarcely damaged the Clinton campaign, it ended up being everything President Clinton objected to: Dick Morris was getting famous—and rich—at his expense. For the moment, Morris joined a short list of celebrity political consultants who became as famous and often far more handsomely paid than their clients.

For years Americans had been unwittingly exposed to campaign posturing and manipulation engineered by political consultants. In the 1990s they grew curious about the manipulators. Suddenly, political consultants were hot properties. Movies, documentaries, and books gave us a glimpse of consultants at work. A film documentary, *The War Room*, made media stars of James Carville and George Stephanopoulos in Bill Clinton's 1992 presidential campaign headquarters. Reporter Joe Klein's best-selling roman à clef, *Primary Colors*, detailed with unnerving accuracy the seamy side of the presidential quest by an ambitious young Southern governor and his avaricious campaign team. Later John Travolta starred as the silver-haired young presidential candidate in the inevitable movie version. *Vote for Me*, a PBS documentary, showed hard-charging New York media consultant Hank Sheinkopf patiently coaching his candidate, an Alabama Supreme Court judge, on the fine points of camera angles and voice projection. Another film documentary, *The Perfect Candidate*, chronicled the highly charged campaign of conservative lightning rod Oliver North and his consultant Mark Goodin as they battled and lost to the uninspiring, wooden Charles Robb in the 1994 Virginia Senate race.

In the movie *Wag the Dog*, the president's spin doctor (Robert De Niro) and a high-powered Hollywood myth-maker (Dustin Hoffman) conjure up a wartime incident in Albania to cover up the president's sexual indiscretions with a twelve-year-old girl. Michael J. Fox portrayed the energetic, earnest young White House aide, a George Stephanopoulos clone, in the film *An American President* (1995), and later reprised the role in a television series, *Spin City*, with Fox serving as an aide to an unprincipled, vacuous mayor of New York City.

The bookshelf was suddenly filling up with insider accounts by political consultants. Well-traveled, controversial Republican consultant Ed Rollins skewered many of his campaign rivals and former clients in a book entitled *Bare Knuckles and Back Rooms*. On the dust jacket was the middle-aged, balding Rollins, poised with his boxing gloves, ready to take on the rough and tumble of politics. Carville and his Republican-operative wife, Mary Matalin, teamed up on the lecture circuit, hawked credit cards and aspirin in television commercials, and wrote a best-selling memoir, *All's Fair: Love, War, and Running for President*.

Carville, Stephanopoulos, and Paul Begala reappeared during the Lewinsky scandal* and the impeachment hearings. Begala returned as the loyal defender inside the White House bunker, while Carville attacked

---

*The Lewinsky scandal led to President Bill Clinton's 1998–99 impeachment by the House of Representatives and subsequent acquittal in a Senate trial. Clinton was charged with being untruthful, in legal proceedings, about revealing his sexual relationship with Monica Lewinsky, a White House intern. —EDS.

special prosecutor Kenneth Starr on television talk shows and through an angry book. . . . *And the Horse He Rode in On: The People v. Kenneth Starr.* Stephanopoulos, meanwhile, singed by the president's betrayal, distanced himself from the White House and publicly criticized Clinton's behavior in his 1999 book, *All Too Human.* Morris, too, resurfaced on talk shows, wrote political columns, advised Clinton on how to deflect criticism during the Lewinsky scandal, and penned another book, immodestly titled *The New Prince: Machiavelli Updated for the Twenty-first Century.*

Despite the notoriety and self-promotion of Morris, Carville, and others, the celebrity consultant is the exception, not the rule. Most political consultants toil in the background, content to ply their craft in anonymity. Even at the presidential campaign level, consultants generally labor in obscurity. Few Americans had ever heard of Don Sipple or Bill McInturff, consultants in Bob Dole's dysfunctional 1996 presidential race, or Bill Clinton's 1996 consultants Bill Knapp, Doug Schoen, and Marius Penczner. Very few have ever heard of George W. Bush's chief strategist Karl Rove, Al Gore's media consultant Carter Eskew, or John McCain's consultant Mike Murphy.

Political consultants, both controversial and anonymous, have become essential players in the increasingly technological, fast-paced, often brutal world of modern elections. Through it all, they have changed the face of modern American politics.

Political Consultants at Work

In earlier decades, campaigns were financed and run by local or state political parties. They were fueled by local party activists and volunteers, by family, friends, and close political supporters. By the early 1960s presidential campaigns and statewide campaigns for governor and senator began seeking out media and polling firms to help deliver their messages to voters. During the next two decades, there emerged both a new industry, political management, and a new professional, the campaign consultant. By the 1980s every serious presidential candidate, nearly every statewide candidate, and a large number of congressional candidates were using the services of professional political consultants.

The 1990s witnessed yet another transformation. Candidates for office below the statewide level were beginning to seek the advice of professional political consultants. For many candidates, the dividing line was the $50,000 campaign: those who could not raise that kind of money had to rely solely on volunteer services, and those above this threshold usually sought professional assistance. In some local political jurisdictions, record amounts of campaign funds were being raised to pay for campaign services, and races for medium-city mayor, county sheriff, or local judge took on the techniques and tactics once seen only in statewide, professionally managed contests. Professional consulting services, such as phone banks, telemarketing, and direct mail, were supplanting the efforts once provided by volunteers and party loyalists. This multibillion-dollar industry is now directed by professional consultants who make the key decisions, determine strategy, develop campaign communications, and carry out campaign tactics for their clients.

The influence of political consultants goes well beyond getting candidates elected to office. They play an increased role in ballot measures by helping clients determine ballot strategy, framing issues, and even providing the campaign foot soldiers who gather signatures for ballot petitions. Consultants use marketing and mobilization skills to orchestrate pressure on legislators. Political telemarketers link angered constituents directly with the telephones of members of Congress. Overnight, they can guarantee five thousand constituent telephone calls patched directly to a legislator's office. Political consultants are also finding lucrative markets internationally, serving presidential and other candidates throughout the world.

In the commercial world, a business that generates less than $50 million is considered a small enterprise. By that measure, every political consulting firm, except for some of the vendors, is a small business. Most of the estimated three thousand firms that specialize in campaigns and elections have ten or fewer staffers and generate just several hundred thousand dollars in revenue annually. Only a few firms, such as media consultant Squier, Knapp, and Dunn, generate millions of dollars in revenue; most of this money, however, passes through the consultants' hands to pay television advertising costs.

Leading polling firms, such as the Tarrance Group or Public Opinion Strategies, may have forty to eighty employees; most are support staff working the telephones and part of the back office operations. Quite a few firms are cottage enterprises—one- or two-person boutiques, often in speciality markets such as event planning, opposition research, fundraising, or media buying. Many political consulting firms operate out of the basement of the principal's home with no more than telephone lines, computers, fax machines, and online access. For example, even after he became famous as Clinton's principal political adviser, James Carville and his assistants worked out of the "bat cave," a basement studio apartment on Capitol Hill that served as Carville's home and nerve center for his far-flung political operations.

Firms that rely solely on campaign cycles are exposed to the rollercoaster of cash flow: many lean months, with very little money coming in from clients, countered by a few fat months, when the bulk of the revenue pours in. In addition to the on-off flow of cash, the firms must deal with the logistical difficulties of juggling many candidates during the crucial last weeks of the campaign cycle and the enormous time pressures of a busy campaign season. Some consulting firms have around-the-clock operations during critical weeks of the campaign. These political emergency rooms are geared to handle any last-minute crisis. During long stretches when there are few campaign opportunities, professionals and support staff may have to be let go until the cycle picks up again.

One of the most difficult but necessary tasks is to even out the steep curves in the election cycle so that money and resources flow more regularly. Consultants have developed several strategies for this: convincing candidates to hire consultants earlier in the cycle, stretching out the amount of time they stay with campaigns, and seeking out off-year races, especially down the electoral ladder, such as mayoral races, general assembly, and other local contests, many of which in past years would not have sought professional assistance. Consultants are becoming more involved in the growing business of initiatives, referenda, and issues management. Many of these campaigns are tied to the same election cycle as candidate campaigns, but others are tied to local, state, or congressional issue cycles. Political consulting firms also pursue clients from the corporate and trade association world and international clients. By spreading out business, consulting firms are able to stay competitive, smooth out the peaks and valleys of the election cycle, and keep their heads above water.

In the 1980s firms began to shift away from heavy reliance on candidate campaigns. For example, the late Matt Reese, one of the founders of the political consulting business, who had worked for more than four hundred Democratic candidates, changed direction after the 1982 elections to concentrate on corporate and trade association clients. Republican consultant Eddie Mahe shifted his business from 100 percent candidate-based in 1980 to about fifteen percent candidate-based in the early 1990s, picking up corporate and other clients. In the mid-1970s Wally Clinton's pioneering political telemarketing firm, the Clinton Group, gained 90 percent of its work from candidates, but has since moved away from reliance on candidates to issues and corporate work. Many successful consulting firms have followed this pattern and now have much of their business coming from noncandidate campaigns.

As corporations have discovered the value of grassroots lobbying and issues management, consultants who specialize in direct mail and political telemarketing have shifted focus to legislative and issues work. Corporate and trade association organizations took special notice of the successful political consultant-orchestrated grassroots campaign run against President Clinton's 1993–94 health care proposal. For political consultants, such work is often far more lucrative, more reliable, and less stress-inducing than working for candidates in competitive election cycles. Some of the most successful political consulting firms have less than half of their revenue coming from candidate campaigns. . . .

What Consultants Bring to Campaigns

Candidates, not consultants, win or lose elections. In 1996 voters chose Bill Clinton, not media consultant Bob Squier; they rejected Bob Dole, not pollster Bill McInturff. Candidates alone face the voters and ultimately bear the responsibility for the tone and expression of their campaign. Sometimes reputations are diminished and images tarnished by the campaign itself. For example, George Bush will be remembered for permitting a down-and-dirty campaign that included the infamous "Revolving Door" and Willie Horton* commercials in his 1988 presidential campaign. In that same year, Michael Dukakis will be remembered for his ride in a military vehicle, hunkered down in an oversized battle helmet, looking goofy. Alphonse D'Amato and Charles Schumer will be remembered for the abusive, in-your-face campaigns they waged in the 1998 New York Senate race.

While candidates are ultimately responsible for their campaigns, there is no way they can compete, let alone win, without professional help. Professional consultants bring direction and discipline to the campaign. Few enterprises are as unpredictable, vulnerable, and chaotic as a modern campaign. So much can go wrong: the candidate might go "off message," in which case the campaign loses focus; internal party feuds might threaten the success of the entire campaign; fund-raising might fall short of expectations, choking the life out of the entire enterprise. All the while, the opponent's campaign is raising more money, attacking with a sharp, clear message, redefining the race in its own terms, grabbing media attention, and efficiently mobilizing its resources. Campaign professionals are needed

---

*The Willie Horton ad is a famous—or infamous—negative ad from the 1988 Bush-Dukakis presidential campaign. An independent PAC created the initial ad that accused Democratic candidate, Gov. Michael Dukakis of Massachusetts, of allowing convicted murderer William Horton out of prison on a weekend furlough; Horton committed several violent crimes while on furlough. Because Horton was black and his victims were white, the ad stirred up racial tensions that lurked not too far beneath the surface of the 1988 Bush-Dukakis campaign.—EDS.

to bring order out of chaos, maintain message and strategy discipline, and keep the campaign focused.

The best consultants are able to define the race on their own terms — not the terms set by the opposition, the media, or outside third parties. In the end, the campaign boils down to letting voters know the answers to some very simple questions: who the candidate is, what the issues are, and why this race is important. Following are some examples of defining issues and messages.

From the 1996 Clinton-Gore reelection campaign:

DEFINING ISSUE: Who is better prepared to lead this country into the next century?
MESSAGE: "Building a bridge to the twenty-first century."

From the 1980 Reagan-Bush campaign:

DEFINING ISSUE: The shortcomings of the Carter administration's policies.
MESSAGE: "Are you better off today than you were four years ago?"

Republican consultant Lee Atwater was fond of saying that he knew that the message of his campaign was hitting home when he would go to a local Kmart and ask shoppers what they thought of the contest, and they'd simply parrot the message he had developed.

Professionals also take campaign burdens off the candidate. Campaigns are exhausting, placing extraordinary physical and emotional demands upon the candidate. The campaign staff, and especially the campaign manager, absorb as much of the stress of the campaign as possible. A campaign manager may serve as official campaign optimist, psychologist, and hand-holder for the candidate or, often, the candidate's spouse. The manager will make the tough personnel and tactical choices when the campaign starts going bad, and be the unofficial heavy (or whipping boy) when needed.

Consultants, particularly those in niche or vendor industries, provide legal, tax, and accounting services for the increasingly complex financial disclosure reporting requirements. They provide expertise in buying television time and placing radio and television commercials. Consulting firms capture and analyze television commercials aired by opponents and other races, and offer both quantitative and qualitative analysis from survey research, focus-group, and dial-group findings. Increasingly campaigns depend on specialists who also can provide a technological edge. Consul-

tants provide online retrieval systems and websites, computer-assisted telephone technology, voter and demographic databases, and geo-mapping
and sophisticated targeting techniques so that a campaign can know, block
by block and house by house, who is likely to vote and for whom they
would cast a ballot. Strategists are able to use predictive technologies,
traditional statistical techniques such as regression analysis, and new artificial intelligence technologies such as neural nets and genetic algorithms
to target potential voters.

Above all, consultants bring experience from other campaigns. Every
campaign has its unique circumstances, events, and dynamics. But campaigns are also great recycling bins. When a consultant has worked for
fifteen or twenty-five races, campaigns begin to fall into predictable patterns: messages and themes, issues, and tactics reappear, taking on slight
variations—new twists to old challenges. Veteran consultants can save a
candidate from making mistakes, spot opportunities quickly, and take
advantage of changing circumstances. As veteran consultant Joseph R.
Cerrell put it, tongue in cheek, we need consultants—"to have someone
handy who has forgotten more about media, mail, fund-raising and strategy than most candidates will ever know."

Growing reliance on professional consultants is costly: the price of
admission to elections has risen substantially. The campaign, for many
candidates, becomes a perverse full-time game of chasing dollars. Consultants have seen business grow because of the superheated fund-raising
activities of the national Democratic and Republican parties, the explosion
of soft money, and issues advocacy.

The best consultants aren't afraid of a fight. They know that in many
cases an election can be won only if they drop the pretense of reasoned,
civilized campaigning and take the gloves off. Campaigns engage in rough
tactics because they work. Opposition researchers dig deep into personal
lives, seeking out misdeeds and character flaws. Pollsters test-market negative material before focus and electronic dial meter groups. Then the
media team cuts slash-and-burn thirty-second clips, using all the tricks of
the trade: unflattering black-and-white photos of the opponent, ominous
music and sound effects, and distorted features, salted with authentic-
sounding textual material, often taken out of context. The direct mail
pieces may get even uglier. The goal is to drive up the opponent's negatives,
to paint the opponent in such unflattering ways that enough voters have
only a negative view of that candidate.

Certainly not all campaigns use negative tactics. Candidates are often
very reluctant to engage in mudslinging or demagoguery. Voters are turned
off by negative campaigns and feel alienated from the democratic process.

But campaign consultants see negative campaigning as a tool, not so much a question of political ethics or morality. If the only way to win is to go negative, then negative it is.

Professional consultants bring many weapons to a campaign. The campaign's theme and message are communicated through television and radio commercials, through direct mail pieces, and increasingly through campaign websites. Those communications are developed and honed through the use of sophisticated research analyses, especially survey research, focus groups, and dial meter sessions. Even more fundamental is the campaign's deadliest weapon, candidate and opposition research. . . .

Professional campaigns and the political consulting industry will flourish in the decades to come. Candidates for public office—both incumbents and challengers—will not hesitate to raise increasingly larger sums of campaign funds to pay for professional consultants and their services. Despite the occasional outburst from elected officials or the public, candidates need, want, and for the most part appreciate the assistance they receive from professional consultants. We may see profound changes in campaign financing, communications, and technology. Through it all, professional consulting will endure, adapt, and prosper. Professionals have become indispensable players in modern campaigns.

75

KATHLEEN HALL JAMIESON

From *Dirty Politics*

One of the most memorable campaign ads from a presidential election is the famous—or infamous—1988 Willie Horton ad. The original ad came from a political action committee (PAC) independent of President Bush's campaign. Political scientist Kathleen Hall Jamieson describes the content of the anti-Dukakis message. It showed William Horton, whom the ad referred to as "Willie," a convicted murderer, who had been given a weekend furlough while Michael Dukakis was governor of Massachusetts. The ad tells viewers that during this furlough, Horton kidnapped a couple and stabbed the man and raped the woman. Jamieson examines the Bush campaign's follow-up spot and reveals how the Willie Horton story became like a drama, filled with dangerous misinterpretations and untrue implications about the crime. William Horton was black. The couple was white.

The Republicans had successfully played the "race card," with fear being a winning issue in the 1988 presidential election.

ALMOST THREE YEARS after George Bush decisively defeated Democrat Michael Dukakis to become the president of the United States, a group of voters in Pineville, Louisiana, was asked, "Can you tell me what you remember as being important in the 1988 presidential campaign?" The individuals in the group responded.

Hmm.
I'm trying to think.
1988?
LEADER: '88.
That's the last one.
Dukakis.
That was Dukakis.
It's about time for another one isn't it?
That time again. It was Dukakis wasn't it?
I just knew I couldn't vote for him.
Seems like the Democratic man that ran, he had a lot of problems. His wife and so forth.
A lot of that didn't come out 'til after the election, though.
That's right.
A lot of us didn't know of her personal problems. They hid . . . that was pretty well hid. She admitted that was . . . I don't know that was a . . .
I think the big thing against him was that, wasn't his criminal . . . I mean not his criminal record, but his . . . the handling of, um . . .
The handling of his state programs.
His state programs. I think that influenced a lot of people, how they voted.
And again, it was still a social aspect of dealing with social issues. And, uh, Bush was more international and people developing things for themselves. Giving them an opportunity to do their own thing and that will support our country. By that I mean build up business and the taxes then, and the income from growth and everything will take care of our country. I saw those as two distinct things.
FOCUS GROUP LEADER: You had just mentioned how he handled state issues. Can you think of any specific issues?
Well, I think right off the . . . the one I'm thinking about was his . . . his handling of a criminal, um, and I can't right now . . .
What do you mean, a pardon of someone who has . . .
Willie Horton.
Yeah. A pardon.
Pardon.
Yeah. He pardoned that guy that went out and killed someone.

Afterwards. You know, he released this known . . . I guess he was a murderer wasn't he? Originally. And they released him anyway and he went out and killed . . .

Immediately and killed people again.

Right after getting out.

And this was brought out that he was releasing people really without seemingly too much thought. I think that had a lot to do with it.

William Horton and Michael Dukakis are now twinned in our memory. The fact that the memories are factually inaccurate does not diminish their power. Dukakis did not pardon Horton nor did the furloughed convict kill.

Although it does recount the facts of the Horton case, this chapter is not one more rehash of who did what to whom in the 1988 campaign. Instead, it sets a context for the book by examining how voters and reporters came to know what they know of politics. It argues that, in politics as in life, what is known is not necessarily what is believed, what is shown is not necessarily what is seen, and what is said is not necessarily what is heard. It then examines how in the Horton case consultants exploited the psychological quirks that characterize humans.

These quirks include a pack-ratlike tendency to gather up and interrelate information from various places, a disposition to weigh accessible, dramatic data more heavily than abstract statistical information, and a predilection for letting fears shape perception of what constitutes "fact."

At the same time, we have conventionalized journalistic norms that reward messages that are dramatic, personal, concise, visual, and take the form of narrative. In 1988, the psychological dispositions of the public coupled with the news norms to produce an environment in which an atypical but dramatic personification of deep-seated fears would displace other issues and dominate the discourse of the campaign. That dramatic, visual, personalized narrative told the "story" of William Horton.

The role that ads, Bush rhetoric, news, and audience psychology played in transforming William Horton's name for some into a symbol of the terrors of crime and for others of the exploitation of racist fears shows the powerful ways in which messages interact and the varying responses they evoke in individuals. Like pack rats, voters gather bits and pieces of political information and store them in a single place. Lost in the storage is a clear recall of where this or that "fact" came from. Information obtained from news mixes with that from ads, for example.

Although Bush had been telling the tale on the stump since June, in the second week in September 1988, the Horton story broke into prime time in the form of a National Security Political Action Committee (NSPAC) ad. The ad tied Michael Dukakis to a convicted murderer who had jumped furlough and gone on to rape a Maryland woman and assault her fiancé. The convict was black, the couple white.* The ad opens with side-by-side pictures of Dukakis and Bush. Dukakis's hair is unkempt, the photo dark. Bush, by contrast, is smiling and bathed in light. As the pictures appear, an announcer says "Bush and Dukakis on crime." A picture of Bush flashes on the screen. "Bush supports the death penalty for first-degree murderers." A picture of Dukakis. "Dukakis not only opposes the death penalty, he allowed first degree murderers to have weekend passes from prison." A close-up mug shot of Horton flashes onto the screen. "One was Willie Horton, who murdered a boy in a robbery, stabbing him nineteen times." A blurry black-and-white photo of Horton apparently being arrested appears. "Despite a life sentence, Horton received ten weekend passes from prison." The words "kidnapping," "stabbing," and "raping" appear on the screen with Horton's picture as the announcer adds, "Horton fled, kidnapping a young couple, stabbing the man and repeatedly raping his girlfriend." The final photo again shows Michael Dukakis. The announcer notes "Weekend prison passes. Dukakis on crime."

When the Bush campaign's "revolving door" ad began to air on October 5, viewers read Horton from the PAC ad into the furlough ad. This stark black-and-white Bush ad opened with bleak prison scenes. It then cut to a procession of convicts circling through a revolving gate and marching toward the nation's living rooms. By carefully juxtaposing words and pictures, the ad invited the false inference that 268 first-degree murderers were furloughed by Dukakis to rape and kidnap. As the bleak visuals appeared, the announcer said that Dukakis had vetoed the death penalty and given furloughs to "first-degree murderers not eligible for parole. While out, many committed other crimes like kidnapping and rape."

The furlough ad contains three false statements and invites one illegitimate inference. The structure of the ad prompts listeners to hear "first-degree murderers not eligible for parole" as the antecedent referent for

---

*In his article "The Road to Here," included in Larry Sabato's *Toward the Millennium: The Elections of 1996*, journalist Tom Rosenstiel points out that much negative campaigning ironically originates in the primaries among fellow party members. It was fellow Democrat Al Gore who first unearthed the Willie Horton incident regarding Democrat Michael Dukakis during the presidential primaries in 1988. —EDS.

"many." Many of whom committed crimes? First-degree murderers not eligible for parole. Many of whom went on to commit crimes like kidnapping and rape? First-degree murderers not eligible for parole.

But many unparoleable first-degree murderers did not escape. Of the 268 furloughed convicts who jumped furlough during Dukakis's first two terms, only four had ever been convicted first-degree murderers not eligible for parole. Of those four not "many" but one went on to kidnap and rape. That one was William Horton. By flashing "268 escaped" on the screen as the announcer speaks of "many first-degree murderers," the ad invites the false inference that 268 murderers jumped furlough to rape and kidnap. Again, the single individual who fits this description is Horton. Finally, the actual number who were more than four hours late in returning from furlough during Dukakis's two and a half terms was not 268 but 275. In Dukakis's first two terms, 268 escapes were made by the 11,497 individuals who were given a total of 67,378 furloughs. In the ten-year period encompassing his two completed terms and the first two years of his third term (1987–88), 275 of 76,455 furloughs resulted in escape.

This figure of 275 in ten years compares with 269 who escaped in the three years in which the program was run by Dukakis's Republican predecessor, who created the furlough program.

Still the battle of drama against data continued. After the Bush campaign's furlough ad had been on the air for two and a half weeks, in the third week of October, PAC ads featuring the victims of Horton began airing. One showed the man whose fiancée had been raped by the furloughed Horton. "Mike Dukakis and Willie Horton changed our lives forever," said Cliff Barnes, speaking in tight close-up. "He was serving a life term, without the possibility of a parole, when Governor Dukakis gave him a few days off. Horton broke into our home. For twelve hours, I was beaten, slashed, and terrorized. My wife, Angie, was brutally raped. When his liberal experiment failed, Dukakis simply looked away. He also vetoed the death penalty bill. Regardless of the election, we are worried people don't know enough about Mike Dukakis."

The second ad was narrated by the sister of the teenager killed by Horton. "Governor Dukakis's liberal furlough experiments failed. We are all victims. First, Dukakis let killers out of prison. He also vetoed the death penalty. Willie Horton stabbed my teenage brother nineteen times. Joey died. Horton was sentenced to life without parole, but Dukakis gave him a furlough. He never returned. Horton went on to rape and torture others. I worry that people here don't know enough about Dukakis's record." The words that recur in the two ads are: "liberal," "experiment," "rape," worry that "people don't know enough about Dukakis," "vetoed the death penalty."

Taken together the ads created a coherent narrative. Dukakis furloughed Horton (PAC ads), just as he had furloughed 267 other escapees (Bush revolving door ad). Horton raped a woman and stabbed her fiancé (crime-quiz and victim PAC ads). Viewers could infer what must have happened to the victims of the other 267 escapees. . . .

The Horton narrative fit the requirements of news. Unlike the "soft" news found in feature stories of the sort pioneered by Charles Kuralt on television, hard news is about an event that treats an issue of ongoing concern. Because violent crime is dramatic, conflict ridden, evokes intense emotions, disrupts the social order, threatens the community, and can be verified by such official sources as police, it is "newsworthy." If one believed Bush's version of the facts, a convicted murderer who should have been executed had been furloughed to rape, torture, and murder again. In newscasts, the villain Horton appeared incarnated in a menacing mug shot. To personalize and dramatize, the news camera showed him in close-up; the less inflammatory visuals in the controversial PAC ad were shot mid-screen. Appearing in tight close-ups both in news and in the ads, the sister of the teenager Horton allegedly killed and the fiancé and now husband of the woman he raped told of their torment and urged a vote against the second villain in the story, Michael Dukakis. . . .

Helping propel the false generalizations from the isolated case of Horton to hordes of others who presumably did what he had done were complex and unspoken references to race. " 'Crime' became a shorthand signal," note Thomas and Mary Edsall, "to a crucial group of white voters, for broader issues of social disorder, evoking powerful ideas about authority, status, morality, self-control, and race." "Any reference to capital punishment," argues political scientist Murray Edelman, "is also a reference to the need to restrain blacks and the poor from violence. The liberal argument that poor people and blacks are disproportionately targeted by capital punishment laws doubtless fuels this fear in a part of the public. That the association is subtle makes it all the more potent, for 'capital punishment,' like all condensation symbols, draws its intensity from the associations it represses." Without actually voicing the repressed associations, the image of Horton on the screen as the announcer notes that Dukakis opposes the death penalty serves to raise them. " 'Weekend Passes' [which I have called the Horton ad] is not about Willie Horton," says NSPAC's Floyd Brown. "It's about the death penalty. George Bush stood on the side of the majority. Michael Dukakis stood on the side of the minority. The death penalty is where we win our audience."

The 1990 General Social Survey of Racial Stereotyping among White Americans demonstrates that racial prejudice correlates with support for capital punishment. According to Kinder and Mendelberg, "white Americans who regard blacks as inferior are quite a bit more likely to favor the death penalty for convicted murderers."

In the last week of October 1988, ninety-three members of ten focus groups demonstrated the power of the Horton narrative to elicit racially based fear. "If you saw an ad on prison furloughs with scenes in a prison," these voters were asked, "remember as best you can" the "race or ethnic identity" of the "people you saw in the ad. . . . " Of those who did recall the ad, nearly 60 percent (59.9 percent, 43 individuals) reported that most of the men were black. In fact, only two of the "prisoners" are identifiably black. One of them is the only one in the ad to ever look directly into the camera.

When asked to write out everything "you know about William Horton," all but five of the focus group respondents included the fact that Horton is black in their description. All but twelve wrote that the woman raped was white. One-third of the respondents indicated Horton's race twice in their descriptions. And one focus group respondent referred to Horton throughout his description as "this Black Man." Twenty-eight percent of those in the focus groups indicated that he had committed murder while on furlough. . . .

All narrative capitalizes on the human capacity and disposition to construct stories. A compelling narrative such as the Horton saga controls our interpretation of data by offering a plausible, internally coherent story that resonates with the audience while accounting causally for otherwise discordant or fragmentary information.

When news and ads trace the trauma and drama of a kidnapping and rape by a convicted murderer on furlough, the repetition and the story structure give it added power in memory. Visceral, visual identifications and appositions are better able to be retrieved than statistical abstractions.

Repeatedly aired oppositional material carries an additional power. Material aired again and again is more likely to stay fresh in our minds. The same is true for attacks.

Cognitive accessibility is upped by those message traits that characterize the Republicans' use of Horton: the dramatic, the personally relevant, the frequently repeated topic or claim—the menacing mug shot, circling convicts, empathic victims—and seemingly uncaring perpetrator—the Massachusetts governor.

When it came to William Horton, our quirks as consumers of political information worked for the Republicans and against the Democrats. In our psychic equations, something nasty has greater power and influence than something nice. When evaluating "social stimuli," negative information carries more weight than positive information. Additionally, negative information seems better able than positive to alter existing impressions and is easier to recall. Televised images that elicit negative emotion result in better recall than those that evoke positive ones. As a result, attacks are better remembered than positive reasons for voting for a candidate. And dissatisfied, disapproving voters are more likely to appear at their polling place than their more satisfied neighbors.

Messages that induce fear dampen our disposition to scrutinize them for gaps in logic. When the message is fear arousing, personal involvement and interest in it minimize systematic evaluation. In the language of cognitive psychology, "[L]arge levels of negative affect such as fear may override cognitive processing."

The Horton story magnifies fear of crime, identifies that fear with Dukakis, and offers a surefire way of alleviating the anxiety—vote for Bush. . . .

The power of the Horton mini-series was magnified as it unfolded soap-opera-like in news and ads; broadcasts that focused on the tale's strategic intent and effect couldn't effectively challenge its typicality. And since statistics don't displace stories nor data, drama, the native language of Dukakis didn't summon persuasive visions of the cops he had put on the street or the murders and rapes that hadn't been committed in a state whose crime rate was down. Abetted by news reports, amplified by Republican ads, assimilated through the cognitive quirks of audiences, William Horton came to incarnate liberalism's failures and voters' fears.

76

STEPHEN ANSOLABEHERE
SHANTO IYENGAR

From *Going Negative*

The weakening of political parties, growing voter cynicism, and negative campaign advertising: Political scientists Stephen Ansolabehere and Shanto Iyengar interrelate these complex developments in American politics. Illustrating their thesis with some memorable election campaign attack ads, the authors contend that a vicious cycle has developed. Middle-of-the-road, independent-minded voters are increasingly alienated by negative campaigns, with the result that politics becomes more and more the province of those on the ideological extremes.

———

ONCE UPON A TIME, this country divided itself neatly along party lines. Most people voted; those who did not tended to be poorer, less well-educated, and more apathetic, but still party loyal. The line between participants and nonparticipants was a fault line of sorts, but it was not terribly worrisome. Civic duty ideally would involve everyone, but, even falling short of the ideal, we were at least expressing our national will in our elections. Television has changed all that. Now, we are split by a new division: between loyalists and apathetics. On the one hand, media propaganda can often shore up loyalists to vote for their traditional party; on the other hand, that same propaganda is increasingly peeling off a band of citizens who turn from independence to apathy, even antipathy, toward our political institutions.

Pollsters and political scientists first noticed this new fault line in 1964. The number of people who proclaimed themselves independent of traditional party labels rose sharply in the mid-1960s. At the same time, candidates embraced television as a new means of independent communication with the voters. Politicians no longer needed the legions of party workers to get their messages across; they could effectively establish personal connections with their constituents using television advertising. In addition, there arose a new class of campaign manager—the media consultant, who typically had worked on Madison Avenue and viewed selling politics much like selling any other product. By the end of the 1960s, media consultants had filled the shoes left vacant by the then-extinct ward healers and precinct captains. Within the political parties, chaos reigned. The old-style politicos in both the Democratic and Republican parties battled and lost to a new regime of populists and progressives, who opened up the parties' nominating process to all comers. By most accounts, these reforms did even greater harm to the parties, shamelessly opening schisms that in earlier years were smoothed over behind closed doors.

At the time many observers mistakenly saw in the combination of televised political advertising and the nonpartisan voter the advent of a new age in America. Television advertising was to have produced a new kind of independent politician, not beholden to special interests and not part of the problems that voters increasingly associated with Washington.

That day has not dawned. To be sure, the ranks of Independent voters have swollen since 1964, and television advertising is now the mainstay of contemporary political campaigns. The political parties, however, remain ascendent in elections and in government. Despite an occasional Independent candidacy and the rise of the personal electoral followings of many candidates, electoral competition is still between Republicans and Democrats. What is more, government, especially Congress, has become even more polarized and partisan than ever. The parties in Congress represent two increasingly cohesive and extreme positions.

The electorate has reacted with frustration and anger. In recent years, the political pulsetakers have registered record lows in political participation, record highs in public cynicism and alienation, and record rates of disapproval of the House of Representatives, the institution designed to represent the public will.

The single biggest cause of the new, ugly regime is the proliferation of negative political advertising on TV. Our argument is that a new synthesis in American politics has failed to emerge precisely because of the ways that partisans and nonpartisans react to televised political messages. Like product advertising, successful political advertising reflects people's beliefs, experiences, and preferences. One consequence of this simple axiom is that political campaigns reinforce the loyalties of partisans. Nonpartisans, by contrast, usually tune out political advertising. They find politicians, politics, and government distasteful; political advertising simply sounds like more of the same. Only negative messages resonate with such attitudes. As political campaigns have become more hostile over the last two decades, nonpartisans have heard plenty to reinforce their low opinions of politics. Unfortunately, negative campaigning only reinforces the nonpartisans' disillusionment and convinces them not to participate in a tainted process. As a result, nonpartisans have not become the electoral force that they might have. Instead, political advertising has produced a party renaissance, even though partisans are an increasingly unrepresentative segment of the public. . . .

The electorate has grown weary of the nastiness and negativity of campaigns. They are mad at the candidates, mad at the parties, mad at the media, and mad at anyone else who steps into the electoral arena. Many people now choose to stay home on election day; others openly express their dissatisfaction with the candidates and the parties among which they must choose. People no longer feel that they vote *for*, only against. If venom isn't really what the public is after, why do candidates insist on going negative?

Politicians and campaign consultants are, by and large, not mean-spirited people who conspire to scare voters away from the polls. The reality is more complex. The negative tenor of campaigns can be traced to the competitive nature of political advertising, to the activities of organized interests, and, last but not least, to the ways in which reporters cover the campaign. Politicians, interest groups, and journalists all act in ways that serve their own best interests. Few of these players really want to produce highly negative campaigns, but the interplay among them produces the kind of campaigns that voters have come to loathe.

"Politics," Lloyd Bentsen reflected after the 1988 election, "is a contact sport." The main event is the head-to-head competition between the candidates. This, above all else, drives candidates to assail one another with thirty-second spot ads. Put bluntly, candidates attack out of fear: fear that the opposition will throw the first punch, fear that they will appear weak if they don't respond in kind. In politics, the best defense is a strong offense, and negative advertising is the most expedient way to fend off the opposition's attacks.

In addition, candidates attack to expand the scope of the political conflict, to drag organized interests and the media into the fray. Political campaigns have about them the same excitement as a prize fight. The more intense the conflict, the more people are drawn to it. Political campaigns, however, are not nearly as orderly as professional boxing matches. No ropes keep the audience from joining in. The more a candidate attacks, the more she makes news; the more conflict there is, and stories about the conflict, the more likely the candidate's proponents are to join the fray. Corporations, professional associations, unions, and other organizations have large stakes in the outcomes of elections, and they don't remain on the sidelines long. These organizations put up millions of dollars to underwrite the candidate's campaign activities; they also aggressively publicize their support of and opposition to politicians independent of the candidate's own campaigning. Through unrestrained independent advertising, interest groups can and do influence the tone, the issues, and even the outcome of elections.

The media are less partisan, but have an equally important effect on the tenor of campaigns. Journalists report the campaign with the verve of sportswriters covering a title fight. Their job, after all, is to sell papers and attract viewers, and elections are full of great material—the mistakes and weaknesses of the candidates, the twists and turns of public opinion, and the jabs and hooks of political debate. Campaign commercials, especially the negative ones, are ideally suited to the dictates of a good news story. They pack a sensational story with good visuals and good sound into thirty brief seconds. Nothing grabs the public's attention like the smell of a scandal or the prospect of a political upset. Such stories make for entertaining reading, but they don't instill confidence in the political system. . . .

. . . [M]ost consultants subscribe to Roger Ailes's first dictum of politics: "If you get punched, punch back." The best way to defuse an attack is typically to counterattack. Here are examples of three common tactics.

---

1. Defend Against the Charges

Attack by Representative Wayne Dowdy against Senator Trent Lott, Mississippi U.S. Senate race, 1988.

SCENE: A stretch limousine barrels through a small town.

ANNOUNCER: Trent Lott says he needs to keep his taxpayer-paid, $50,000-a-year chauffeur in Washington. You can vote for a party politician who looks at life through tinted windows. Or you can vote for a Senator who sees Mississippi through the eyes of its people.

Response by Trent Lott.

GEORGE AWKWARD [Lott's African-American bodyguard, speaking directly into the camera, with the American flag in the background]: I've been a detective in a security police force in Washington, D.C., for 27 years. Wayne Dowdy calls me a chauffeur. He offends every law enforcement officer who puts his life on the line every day. Mr. Dowdy, I'm nobody's chauffeur. [pause] Got it?

---

2. Counterattack on the Same Question or on Issues that are of Greater Concern to Voters

Attack by Bruce Herschensohn on Barbara Boxer, California Senate race, 1992.

HERSCHENSOHN [speaking directly into the camera]: Ya know. A hundred and forty-three bounced checks. Wow, that's . . . that's . . . a lot. That's really a lot. That's what my opponent did. It added up to more than what most Californians make in well over a year. Forty-one thousand dollars in bounced checks. Boy. I Mean, do you want her trying to balance your budget? Our government's budget? Gee.

ANNOUNCER: Fight back with Herschensohn.

Boxer's response.

HERSCHENSOHN [newsclips]: "What I want is the repeal of *Roe v. Wade*" . . . "We need more offshore oil drilling and nuclear power plants" . . . "Demolish the Department of Energy and Education" . . . "I oppose any cuts in defense."

ANNOUNCER: That's what Bruce Herschensohn wants. Is that what you want?

3. ASSAIL THE OPPOSITION'S CREDIBILITY

Attack by Russell Feingold on Senator Robert Kasten, Wisconsin U.S. Senate race, 1992.

FEINGOLD [holding newspaper with headline about Senator Robert Kasten's negative campaign tactics]: If things are going to change around here, this man must be defeated in November. Not much has been written about Russ Feingold to attack. So the only option is to make something up.

FEINGOLD [holding up mock tabloid endorsement by Elvis Presley]: You voters know better than to believe everything you read.

Senator Robert Kasten's counterattack.

ELVIS IMPERSONATOR [sitting in pink Cadillac with 1950s music blaring, looking at cardboard cutout of Feingold holding mock tabloid]: I don't make many appearances. But when I heard that he was telling tales how I endorsed him, I had to come forward. You know that Russ has been in politics for more than a decade. Feingold plans to raise our taxes over $300 billion. Well, the King would never support that. Take it from the King, this Russ Feingold record has got me all shook up.

Feingold's parting shot.

FEINGOLD [close up]: A while ago, I warned you about my opponent's history of making things up. I figured when he started distorting the truth about me, you'd take it with a grain of salt.

[Feingold picks up a jar of salt and starts pouring it on the ground. The camera zooms in on the growing pile.]

FEINGOLD: Well, get ready, because now he's telling you I have a plan to raise thousands of dollars of taxes on the middle class. Not true. Senator Kasten knows I haven't proposed any such tax increases. Period. The truth is the Senator has made up something so big that a few grains of salt won't be enough. A shovelful would be more like it.

[Camera pulls back to show Feingold holding a shovel.]

Tit-for-tat. And so it goes with many campaigns today. A negative advertisement triggers a negative response and, in turn, a negative reply. Increasingly, even positive commercials provoke attacks. Candidates who promote a particular ideology or program seem especially susceptible to criticism. Stick your neck out and get your head chopped off. . . .

Whatever its causes, negative politics generates disillusionment and distrust among the public. Attack advertisements resonate with the popular beliefs that government fails, that elected officials are out of touch and quite corrupt, and that voting is a hollow act. The end result: lower turnout and lower trust in government, regardless of which party rules.

The marginal voter—the Independent—feels the pinch of negative advertisements most sharply. Attack ads produce the highest drop in political efficacy and in intentions to participate among nonpartisans. Most of these people have shed their traditional party attachments not because they feel ambivalent about which of the two parties they should support, but because they dislike politics in general. The hostile tenor of campaign advertising further reinforces their contempt for candidates, parties, and government. As a result, negative campaigning divides the American electorate into a voting public of party loyalists and a nonvoting public of apathetics.

With each election this schism widens. Though their growth has been glacial, Independents are now the single largest of the "partisan" groups in the electorate—36 percent, according to the Gallup poll. They tend not to vote, and regardless of which party is in the majority, they do not feel that the government represents their ideas and interests. Each succeeding election raises their frustration higher yet. Our evidence is that the political campaigns deserve much of the blame for the Independents' retreat from the polls. Positive campaign advertising generally fails to reach Independents. Nonpartisans do not find the typical political commercial compelling or persuasive, and they are only further angered, frustrated, and alienated by negative campaigning. The current climate of attack politics strengthens their resolve to remain Independents, but weakens their electoral voice.

As a consequence, electoral politics [is] becoming less representative. Elected officials respond mainly to the opinions of those who vote, which is increasingly a partisan and ideologically extreme crowd. Contemporary campaigning discourages nonpartisans from expressing their interests and frustrations at the polls; it thus obstructs politicians from hearing their anger.

77

MARK MONMONIER

From *Bushmanders and Bullwinkles*

Why is a geography professor's book included in a reader on American government? First, learn the vocabulary of professor Mark Monmonier: remapping, redistricting, reapportionment, gerrymandering. Every decade a census is taken of the U.S. population. While many citizens are aware of the importance of the census's demographic statistics in determining how many people live where and how well in the U.S., few realize the political consequences of the census. It decides how the 435 House of Representatives districts will be reapportioned so that they are equal in population, ensuring "one person, one vote" in the House. The electoral college is affected too, as are state legislative districts. Monmonier looks at the case study of New York City's so-called Bullwinkle District, drawn in 1992 to encompass a majority of one minority group—Hispanics. He explains why various disparate groups favor such gerrymanders. Monmonier gives political scientists a special reason to study with care the results of the recent 2000 and forthcoming 2010 censuses.

—————

"REMAP" IS NOT IN THE dictionary, but it should be, as both verb and noun. Every ten years America counts heads, reallocates seats in the House of Representatives, and raises the blood pressure of elected officials and wannabe lawmakers by remapping election districts for Congress and state legislatures. And many jurisdictions also reconfigure city councils, town boards, or school districts. Because the way political cartographers relocate district boundaries affects who runs as well as who wins, a remap can strongly influence, if not determine, what a government does or doesn't do, what activities it bans or encourages, and which citizens absorb the costs or reap the benefits. Although "redistricting" refers to the process of drawing lines while "reapportionment" more narrowly connotes the reallocation of House seats among the states, neither term adequately alludes to the map itself as an object of debate and manipulation, if not litigation and ridicule.

Equally important is "gerrymander," a dictionary term with two shades of meaning. For many political scientists, gerrymandering is nothing more than deliberately increasing the number of districts in which a particular party or group is in the majority. They see this kind of manipulation as neither unfair nor illegal: if a state's constitution lets the party in power enhance its control, so be it. But for the media, the general public, and some judges, the term suggests sinister shapes that signify unfair if not illegal manipulation and undermine confidence in our electoral system. Although legal scholars differ on whether irregularly shaped districts are "expressive harms" that warrant judicial intervention, the post-1990 remap made unprecedented use of electronic cartography to craft cleverly contorted, racially motivated gerrymanders.

I wrote *Bushmanders and Bullwinkles* to promote an informed appreciation of redistricting, including the variety of plausible remaps and their diverse effects. In showing how boundaries can serve or disadvantage political parties, incumbents, and racial or ethnic groups, I want to make readers aware of how legislators, judges, and other elected officials use the decennial remap to promote personal or ideological agendas. Although the discussion frequently raises questions of fairness, my goal is not a cynical deconstruction of a fundamental political process but a skeptical, and I hope insightful, look at the complex relationships among geography, demography, and power. . . .

George Herbert Walker Bush, forty-first president of the United States, shares a unique political legacy with Elbridge Gerry, our fifth vice president, under James Madison. In 1812, while Gerry was governor of Massachusetts, his party, Thomas Jefferson's Democratic-Republicans, controlled the state legislature. In redrawing senatorial district boundaries after the census of 1810, the Jeffersonians hoped to win more seats by packing Federalist voters into a few strongholds while carving out a long, thin Republican district along the northern, western, and southwestern edges of Essex County. Gerry disliked the plan but signed the remap into law anyway—a veto, he thought, would be improper. The Federalist press was not amused. When a reporter pointed out the new district's lizardlike appearance, his editor exclaimed, "Salamander! Call it a Gerrymander!" Artist-cartoonist Elkanah Tisdale added the wings, teeth, and claws (FIG.

1.1) that enshrined Gerry's name in the language as a political pejorative, with its hard *g* mispronounced like the *j* in Jerry. Ironically, the sinuous district crafted by the governor's cronies is far less troublesome in form, if not intent, than the cartographic manipulations encouraged by the Department of Justice under the Bush administration. I call them "bush-manders."

This new species is also more ragged around the edge than its nineteenth-century ancestors. In figure 1.2, for instance, New York State's Twelfth Congressional District, crafted as a Hispanic-majority district in 1992, looks more intricate and fragile than the famed Essex County senatorial district of 1812. Although the unadorned Massachusetts prototype provoked cynical slurs, Tisdale's sinister enhancements probably account for its longevity as a political icon: widely reproduced in books and articles on electoral manipulation, the classic gerrymander is rarely rendered as an unembellished contour. By contrast, New York's Twelfth District needs no adornments to explain journalists' delight in labeling it the "Bullwinkle District," after the loquacious moose who shared a Saturday morning spotlight with his cartoon-show sidekick Rocky the flying

FIGURE 1.1. The newly configured Essex County, Massachusetts, senatorial district, as embellished by Elkanah Tisdale. Originally published in the Boston *Gazette* for March 26, 1812. From James Parton, *Caricature and Other Comic Art* (New York: Harper and Brothers, 1877), 316.

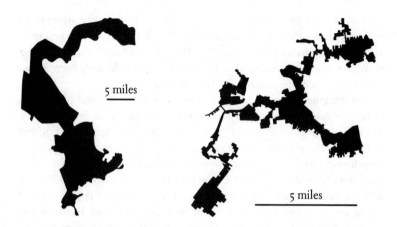

FIGURE 1.2. Silhouettes of the classic 1812 gerrymander of Essex County (left) and New York's Twelfth Congressional District as configured in 1992 (right). Left-hand map redrawn from map in the Boston *Weekly Messenger*, March 6, 1812, as reproduced in Elmer C. Griffith, *The Rise and Development of the Gerrymander* (Chicago: Scott, Foresman, 1907), 69. Right-hand map compiled from U.S. Bureau of the Census, *Congressional District Atlas: 103rd Congress of the United States* (Washington, D.C., 1993).

squirrel. Although the narrow rows of comblike prongs and wider blobs awkwardly connected by thin corridors only faintly resemble antlers, once some clever wag linked the district's contour to the beloved talking moose, the name stuck. Nicknames are rare, though: most bushmanders inspire descriptions like "the 'Z' with drips" (Louisiana's Fourth District), a "spitting amoeba" (Maryland's Third District), and "a pair of earmuffs" (Illinois's Fourth District).

The emergence of these new political critters in the early 1990s is partly a consequence of the Voting Rights Act, passed in 1965 and modified several times. In addition to banning racial discrimination in voter registration, the law defends the right of minority voters to elect candidates of their choice and demands federal scrutiny where past abuse has been especially flagrant. Among other provisions, the Department of Justice must approve the postcensus remap in several states, mostly in the South, as well as the three New York City boroughs containing parts of the Bullwinkle District. Interpreted broadly, the Voting Rights Act also prohibits political cartographers from splitting a district in which members of a minority group constitute a majority. This stricture raises a thorny question: Can the Justice Department deny preclearance when a state chooses not to form a thinly stretched minority-majority district? In rejecting plans submitted by Georgia and North Carolina, George Bush's map editors answered with an assertive "Yes!" Intimidated by earlier rulings as well as eager to accommodate black and Hispanic leaders, New York's mapmakers won preclearance on their first try.

Bushmanders would be difficult, if not impossible, without computers. In Gerry's day, and for more than a century thereafter, the basic building block for congressional districts was the county. Although New England mapmakers eagerly split counties along town lines, political cartographers elsewhere preferred to combine whole counties wherever possible and to split cities, if needed, only along existing precinct boundaries. To explore different configurations, they spread out their maps on a large floor and tallied district populations by hand or by adding machine. Redistricting became more troublesome after the mid-1960s, when the Supreme Court insisted that states not only reconfigure congressional and legislative districts every ten years, as the Constitution intends, but minimize variation among districts in population size. In the early 1990s, with the Civil Rights Division of the Justice Department poised to reject plans that ignored possible minority-majority districts, states turned to interactive computers, electronic maps, and detailed census data, which made it easy to accumulate blocks inhabited by African Americans or Spanish-speaking Americans and link dispersed minority neighborhoods with thin corridors inhabited by few, if any, nonminority "filler people." To ignore this technology was to invite federal judges to draw the lines themselves. After all, Justice officials in Washington had similar tools, as did African American and Hispanic interest groups eager to sue for apparent violations of the Voting Rights Act.

The result typically was a district difficult to describe with maps or words. New York City's Bullwinkle District, for instance, is a polygon with no fewer than 813 sides. In a bill approved by the state legislature and signed into law by the governor in June 1992, District 12's perimeter requires 217 lines of verbal description, which read like the itinerary of a taxi driver trying desperately to run up the meter. Figure 1.3 shows how part of the boundary twisting across Brooklyn helped elect a Hispanic to the House of Representatives by capturing blocks rich in Spanish surnames while avoiding blocks where Hispanics are a minority. The line became law as

to Linwood street, to Glenmore avenue, to Cleveland street, to Pitkin avenue, to Warwick street, to Glenmore avenue, to Jerome street, to Pitkin avenue, to Warwick street, to Glenmore avenue, to Jerome street, to Pitkin avenue, to Barbey street, to Glenmore avenue, to Schenck avenue, to Liberty avenue, to Barbey street,

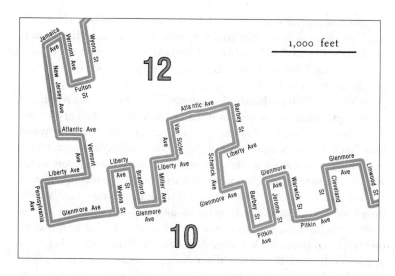

FIGURE 1.3. Excerpt from U.S. Bureau of the Census, *Congressional District Atlas: 103rd Congress of the United States* (Washington, D.C., 1993), NEW YORK-16.

to Atlantic avenue, to Van Siclen avenue, to Liberty avenue, to Miller avenue, to Glenmore avenue, to Bradford street, to Liberty avenue, to Wyona street, to Glenmore avenue, to Pennsylvania avenue, to Liberty avenue, to Vermont avenue, to Atlantic avenue, to New Jersey avenue, to Jamaica avenue, to Vermont avenue, to Fulton street, to Wyona street. . . .

Lawmakers are word people, and before they vote on a redistricting bill, boundaries composed on a computer screen are converted to verbose lists of street segments, watercourses, and other fixed features.

Because politicians and election officials need to see where voters live, redistricting officials convert the lists back into maps. To supplement the electoral maps of individual states, the Bureau of the Census publishes the *Congressional District Atlas*, a standardized cartographic reference for the fifty states. Because the *Atlas*'s letter-size pages are too small to show on one map the intricate details of computer-crafted gerrymanders, a single district can extend across a dozen pages or more. In the edition for the 103rd Congress, published in 1993, fragments of New York City's Bullwinkle District appear on twenty-two pages. Identified vaguely on the separate, single-page county maps for Brooklyn, Manhattan, and Queens, District 12 crops up in greater detail on eighteen partial-county inset maps, mostly printed one to a page, at various scales. Figure 1.3, extracted from one of the Brooklyn (Kings County) insets, illustrates the symbols and level of detail. Especially complex portions of the boundary in parts of Queens required eight additional subinset maps—insets of insets—focused on small areas at even larger scales. The cartography of bushmanders is, to coin a word, insetuous. . . .

Why would a Republican administration favor African American and Latino candidates, almost certain to be Democrats? For the same reason that Elbridge Gerry's Jeffersonian Republicans packed Federalist voters into Essex County's inner district: by creating safe districts in which minority candidates were likely to win, the Bush Republicans added white voters to formerly Democratic districts, which responded, as hoped, by electing Republicans. There was another advantage, though. A widely shared resentment of minority-majority districts, often perceived as yet another affirmative action strike at the prerogatives and values of the white middle-class majority, fueled white dislike for the Democrats' policies and politicians. Because the GOP did not openly advocate minority districts, Republican candidates were free to rail against the bushmanders' flagrantly contorted shapes. Reinforcing the perception of an antiwhite conspiracy were lawsuits filed by aggrieved "filler people" and promptly challenged by pro-civil rights Democrats. Adding to the irony, federal judges appointed by Presidents Reagan and Bush won the public approval of white Republicans by condemning the racial gerrymanders that helped their party take over the House in 1994. . . .

Our examination of the American way of redistricting raises three issues: Should race matter, should shape matter, and should geography matter. The post-2000 remap and the prospect of ever more outrageous congressional districts—but with less overt concern for ethnicity—raises a fourth, perhaps more fundamental question: What next?

The answer to the race question is so obviously affirmative (Who can deny the salient divisiveness of race in American society?) that the query needs rephrasing, with emphasis on *how* rather than *whether*. Indeed, since the early 1950s Congress and the courts have repeatedly wrestled with *how* race should matter. In the process we buried Jim Crow,* as a century earlier we dismantled slavery, and during the 1990s we demonstrated that

---

*Jim Crow laws were common throughout the South, beginning in the 1890s, as a way of enforcing legal segregation of the races in the post–Civil War period. Such laws mandated racial segregation in all public facilities, such as schools, trains, playgrounds, and even drinking fountains. Along with Jim Crow laws, black Americans were often prevented from registering to vote by poll taxes, literacy tests, and "grandfather" clauses. These forms of legal discrimination in the United States lasted until the 1950s and 1960s.—EDS.

a remap designed to encourage minority candidates need not injure white voters. Given most incumbents' irresistible urge to curry favor with all constituents, regardless of color, was anyone truly surprised when political scientist David Canon found that black-majority districts work quite well in representing whites? But in increasing the electability of minority candidates we have produced weird silhouettes that invoke public ridicule and judicial reprimand—shapes like the North Carolina district that white plaintiffs denounced as "harmful" and Justice Sandra Day O'Connor labeled "bizarre."

If minority-majority districts are at all harmful, the more likely victims are African Americans and Hispanics. That's the verdict of social scientists who question the effects of minority-majority districts on the "substantive representation" of minority groups, which refers to the groups' clout in getting laws passed and funding approved. Using the remap to increase "descriptive representation"—getting more people of color into House seats—concentrates minority voters into comparatively few black-majority or Hispanic-majority districts, thereby undermining minority support for white Democrats, their traditional allies. And a Congress with an increased number of minority representatives might well be a Congress dominated by Republicans, who are less likely to promote policies favored by minority-group leaders. At least that's the apparent result of the Republican takeover of the House in the 1994 elections and Congress's subsequent retreat from affirmative action into welfare reform and other tenets of the GOP's Contract with America. With time, though, stronger black and Hispanic caucuses and more experienced minority incumbents might prove a worthwhile investment.

Should shape matter? Not really, argue legal scholars like Pamela Karlan, who defends bizarre districts by noting the courts' inability "to identify a concrete harm to any identifiable individual." In a similar vein, political scientist Micah Altman, who examined the effects of geometrically irregular minority-majority districts on public confidence, found "no support for the hypothesis that 'ugly' districts send pernicious messages to voters that affect their attitudes toward government or Congress." Quoting a phrase rampant in recent redistricting lawsuits, Altman notes, "The only detectable effect of shape was on turnout. Moreover, I could find no evidence that bizarre districts cause 'expressive harms.'" And who can argue that the weirdly shaped or questionably contiguous districts drawn to promote minority representation are more difficult to represent than the far larger districts stretched across sparsely populated reaches of the American West? After all, dispersed minorities in parts of Chicago,

New York City, or the rural South share common concerns much like the coastal issues that unite island residents with their mainland neighbors. Both kinds of districts constitute communities of interest in which compactness and contiguity have little relevance.

Shape will continue to matter, though, because highly irregular districts, at odds with how most Americans think elections districts should look, are a form of cartographic mischief. For this reason, tiny silhouette maps, with little relevance to how well a district can be represented, are enormously effective as propaganda against graphically flagrant gerrymanders of any sort, partisan as well as racial. And when the judiciary targets only racial gerrymanders, as in the 1990s, Rorschach-like silhouettes even provided a clever Why me? defense of deposed bushmanders: one of the most effective arguments supporting the Texas minority-majority districts struck down in *Bush v. Vera** was a poster that juxtaposed four anonymous silhouettes and dared the viewer to separate two districts overturned by the Court from two equally irregular white-majority districts allowed to stand. Most viewers, I suspect, wondered why the Supreme Court didn't reject them all. . . .

If the Constitution mandates neither compactness nor contiguity, should geography matter? Absolutely, as long as we understand that geography means more than a simplistic sense of shape and distance. Because of vastly improved transport and communication, the geography that's relevant for the twenty-first century is very different from the geography of 1790, 1920, or even 1960. And though the slogan "all politics is local" remains valid, proximity plays a very different role today than in the heyday of ward politics and strong party loyalty. Demographic affinity—nothing new, really—is more germane to most concerns than neighborhoods are, and even neighborhood issues like crime and zoning frequently precipitate local alliances among geographically dispersed groups like elderly residents and upper-middle-class homeowners. Although African Americans, Hispanics, born-again Christians, young urban professionals, and other demographic clusters might have much in common with their neighbors, communities of interest are almost always larger and more fragmented than one's immediate neighborhood. As a result, traditional

---

Bush v. Vera (1996) was a Supreme Court case challenging the constitutionality of three Texas congressional districts that had been deliberately drawn up—gerrymandered—to create a majority of minority group voters; two districts were comprised of a majority of black Texans, one of Hispanic Texans. The unusual shape of the districts and their lack of a compact design led the Court to declare them invalid. Texas had to redraw the district lines.—EDS

district boundaries, whether for congressional, state legislative, or city council districts, do not work as well as they once did.

Can the contorted boundaries drafted in the early 1990s to equalize district populations and protect coherent minority voting rights really work better than more traditional borders? Maybe, maybe not. But they're clearly less dysfunctional than silhouette maps and caustic critics suggest. North Carolina's I-85 District, for instance, strongly reflects in both its name and its shape the radical reduction of functional distance between its seemingly dispersed nodes. And intricate inner city districts like New York's Bullwinkle District or Chicago's "pair of earmuffs" are comparatively compact in a social-geographic space based on personal interaction rather than surveyor's instruments. . . .

What's certain is a shift of approximately eleven House seats after the 2000 census. Although "equal proportions" reapportionment might well produce a few cliff-hangers, as it did in 1990, demographers expect Arizona, Georgia, and Texas to gain two seats each, while redistricting officials in New York and Pennsylvania face a remap with two fewer districts. Completing the exchange, Colorado, Florida, Montana, Nevada, Utah, and perhaps California should each pick up a seat, while Connecticut, Illinois, Michigan, Mississippi, Ohio, Oklahoma, and Wisconsin will each redistrict with one representative fewer.

What's not clear is whether redistricting committees will push partisan gerrymandering well beyond the public's begrudging tolerance of 1990s-style bushmanders and Bullwinkles.

78

LANI GUINIER

From *The Tyranny of the Majority*

Law professor Lani Guinier was withdrawn from consideration for the position of assistant attorney general for civil rights in the Justice Department, early in the Clinton administration, because of the storm of controversy over her views on representation in American elections. Critics called her the "quota queen." Professor Guinier explains here that she never advocated quotas, but rather, along with James Madison, she is resisting "the tyranny of the majority." In a diverse society, Guinier believes, winner-take-all elections shut the minority out from having any input at all. Through ideas such as cumulative voting, minorities could elect representatives without damaging the majority's voice. Guinier never received the Senate Judiciary Committee hearing she wished for in order to defend her views, but her ideas remain interesting ones.

———————

I HAVE ALWAYS wanted to be a civil rights lawyer. This lifelong ambition is based on a deep-seated commitment to democratic fair play—to playing by the rules as long as the rules are fair. When the rules seem unfair, I have worked to change them, not subvert them. When I was eight years old, I was a Brownie. I was especially proud of my uniform, which represented a commitment to good citizenship and good deeds. But one day, when my Brownie group staged a hatmaking contest, I realized that uniforms are only as honorable as the people who wear them. The contest was rigged. The winner was assisted by her milliner mother, who actually made the winning entry in full view of all the participants. At the time, I was too young to be able to change the rules, but I was old enough to resign, which I promptly did.

To me, fair play means that the rules encourage everyone to play. They should reward those who win, but they must be acceptable to those who lose. The central theme of my academic writing is that not all rules lead to elemental fair play. Some even commonplace rules work against it.

The professional milliner competing with amateur Brownies stands as an example of rules that are patently rigged or patently subverted. Yet, sometimes, even when rules are perfectly fair in form, they serve in practice to exclude particular groups from meaningful participation. When they do not encourage everyone to play, or when, over the long haul, they do not make the losers feel as good about the outcomes as the winners, they can seem as unfair as the milliner who makes the winning hat for her daughter.

Sometimes, too, we construct rules that force us to be divided into winners and losers when we might have otherwise joined together. This idea was cogently expressed by my son, Nikolas, when he was four years old, far exceeding the thoughtfulness of his mother when she was an eight-year-old Brownie. While I was writing one of my law journal articles, Nikolas and I had a conversation about voting prompted by a *Sesame Street Magazine* exercise. The magazine pictured six children: four children had raised their hands because they wanted to play tag; two had their hands down because they wanted to play hide-and-seek. The magazine asked its readers to count the number of children whose hands were raised and then decide what game the children would play.

Nikolas quite realistically replied, "They will play both. First they will play tag. Then they will play hide-and-seek." Despite the magazine's "rules," he was right. To children, it is natural to take turns. The winner may get to play first or more often, but even the "loser" gets something. His was a positive-sum solution that many adult rule-makers ignore.

The traditional answer to the magazine's problem would have been a zero-sum solution: "The children—all the children—will play tag, and only tag." As a zero-sum solution, everything is seen in terms of "I win; you lose." The conventional answer relies on winner-take-all majority rule, in which the tag players, as the majority, win the right to decide for all the children what game to play. The hide-and-seek preference becomes irrelevant. The numerically more powerful majority choice simply subsumes minority preferences.

In the conventional case, the majority that rules gains all the power and the minority that loses gets none. For example, two years ago Brother Rice High School in Chicago held two senior proms. It was not planned that way. The prom committee at Brother Rice, a boys' Catholic high school, expected just one prom when it hired a disc jockey, picked a rock band, and selected music for the prom by consulting student preferences. Each senior was asked to list his three favorite songs, and the band would play the songs that appeared most frequently on the lists.

Seems attractively democratic. But Brother Rice is predominantly white, and the prom committee was all white. That's how they got two proms. The black seniors at Brother Rice felt so shut out by the "democratic process" that they organized their own prom. As one black student put it: "For every vote we had, there were eight votes for what they wanted. . . . [W]ith us being in the minority we're always outvoted. It's as if we don't count."

Some embittered white seniors saw things differently. They complained that the black students should have gone along with the majority: "The majority makes a decision. That's the way it works."

In a way, both groups were right. From the white students' perspective, this was ordinary decisionmaking. To the black students, majority rule sent the message: "we don't count" is the "way it works" for minorities. In a racially divided society, majority rule may be perceived as majority tyranny.

That is a large claim, and I do not rest my case for it solely on the actions of the prom committee in one Chicago high school. To expand the range of the argument, I first consider the ideal of majority rule itself, particularly as reflected in the writings of James Madison and other founding members of our Republic. These early democrats explored the relationship between majority rule and democracy. James Madison warned, "If a majority be united by a common interest, the rights of the minority will be insecure." The tyranny of the majority, according to Madison, requires safeguards to protect "one part of the society against the injustice of the other part."

For Madison, majority tyranny represented the great danger to our early constitutional democracy. Although the American revolution was fought against the tyranny of the British monarch, it soon became clear that there was another tyranny to be avoided. The accumulations of all powers in the same hands, Madison warned, "whether of one, a few, or many, and whether hereditary, self-appointed, or elective, may justly be pronounced the very definition of tyranny."

As another colonist suggested in papers published in Philadelphia, "We have been so long habituated to a jealousy of tyranny from monarchy and aristocracy, that we have yet to learn the dangers of it from democracy." Despotism had to be opposed "whether it came from Kings, Lords or the people."

The debate about majority tyranny reflected Madison's concern that the majority may not represent the whole. In a homogeneous society, the interest of the majority would likely be that of the minority also. But in a heterogeneous community, the majority may not represent all competing interests. The majority is likely to be self-interested and ignorant or indifferent to the concerns of the minority. In such case, Madison observed, the assumption that the majority represents the minority is "altogether fictitious."

Yet even a self-interested majority can govern fairly if it cooperates with the minority. One reason for such cooperation is that the self-interested majority values the principle of reciprocity. The self-interested majority worries that the minority may attract defectors from the majority and become the next governing majority. The Golden Rule principle of reciprocity functions to check the tendency of a self-interested majority to act tyrannically.

So the argument for the majority principle connects it with the value of reciprocity: You cooperate when you lose in part because members of the current majority will cooperate when they lose. The conventional case for the fairness of majority rule is that it is not really the rule of a fixed group — The Majority — on all issues; instead it is the rule of shifting majorities, as the losers at one time or on one issue join with others and become part of the governing coalition at another time or on another issue. The result will be a fair system of mutually beneficial cooperation. I call a majority that rules but does not dominate a Madisonian Majority.

The problem of majority tyranny arises, however, when the self-interested majority does not need to worry about defectors. When the majority is fixed and permanent, there are no checks on its ability to be overbearing. A majority that does not worry about defectors is a majority with total power. . . .

But if a group is unfairly treated, for example, when it forms a racial minority, *and* if the problems of unfairness are not cured by conventional assumptions about majority rule, then what is to be done? The answer is that we may need an *alternative* to winner-take-all majoritarianism. In this book, a collection of my law review articles, I describe the alternative, which, with Nikolas's help, I now call the "principle of taking turns." In a racially divided society, this principle does better than simple majority rule if it accommodates the values of self-government, fairness, deliberation, compromise, and consensus that lie at the heart of the democratic ideal.

In my legal writing, I follow the caveat of James Madison and other early American democrats. I explore decisionmaking rules that might work in a multi-racial society to ensure that majority rule does not become majority tyranny. I pursue voting systems that might disaggregate The Majority so that it does not exercise power unfairly or tyrannically. I aspire to a more cooperative political style of decisionmaking to enable all of the students at Brother Rice to feel comfortable attending the same prom. In looking to create Madisonian Majorities, I pursue a positive-sum, taking-turns solution.

Structuring decisionmaking to allow the minority "a turn" may be necessary to restore the reciprocity ideal when a fixed majority refuses to cooperate with the minority. If the fixed majority loses its incentive to follow the Golden Rule principle of shifting majorities, the minority never gets to take a turn. Giving the minority a turn does not mean the minority gets to rule; what it does mean is that the minority gets to influence decisionmaking and the majority rules more legitimately.

Instead of automatically rewarding the preferences of the monolithic majority, a taking-turns approach anticipates that the majority rules, but is not overbearing. Because those with 51 percent of the votes are not assured 100 percent of the power, the majority cooperates with, or at least does not tyrannize, the minority. . . .

In the end, I do not believe that democracy should encourage rule by the powerful—even a powerful majority. Instead, the ideal of democracy promises a fair discussion among self-defined equals about how to achieve our common aspirations. To redeem that promise, we need to put the idea of taking turns and disaggregating the majority at the center of our conception of representation. Particularly as we move into the twenty-first century as a more highly diversified citizenry, it is essential that we consider the ways in which voting and representational systems succeed or fail at encouraging Madisonian Majorities.

To use Nikolas's terminology, "it is no fair" if a fixed, tyrannical majority excludes or alienates the minority. It is no fair if a fixed, tyrannical majority monopolizes all the power all the time. It is no fair if we engage in the periodic ritual of elections, but only the permanent majority gets to choose who is elected. Where we have tyranny by The Majority, we do not have genuine democracy.

My life's work, with the essential assistance of people like Nikolas, has been to try to find the rules that can best bring us together as a democratic society. Some of my ideas about democratic fair play were grossly mischaracterized in the controversy over my nomination to be Assistant Attorney General for Civil Rights. Trying to find rules to encourage fundamental fairness inevitably raises the question posed by Harvard Professor Randall Kennedy in a summary of this controversy: "What is required to create political institutions that address the needs and aspirations of all Americans, not simply whites, who have long enjoyed racial privilege, but people of color who have long suffered racial exclusion from policy-making forums?" My answer, as Professor Kennedy suggests, varies by situation. But I have a predisposition, reflected in my son's yearning for a positive-sum solution, to seek an integrated body politic in which all perspectives are represented and in which all people work together to find common ground. I advocate empowering voters and their representatives in ways that give even minority voters a chance to influence legislative outcomes. . . .

Concern over majority tyranny has typically focused on the need to monitor and constrain the substantive policy outputs of the decisionmaking process. In my articles, however, I look at the *procedural* rules by which preferences are identified and counted. Procedural rules govern the process by which outcomes are decided. They are the rules by which the game is played.

I have been roundly, and falsely, criticized for focusing on outcomes. Outcomes are indeed relevant, but *not* because I seek to advance particular ends, such as whether the children play tag or hide-and-seek, or whether the band at Brother Rice plays rock music or rap. Rather, I look to outcomes as *evidence* of whether all the children—or all the high school seniors—feel that their choice is represented and considered. The purpose is not to guarantee "equal legislative outcomes"; equal opportunity to *influence* legisative outcomes regardless of race is more like it.

For these reasons, I sometimes explore alternatives to simple, winner-take-all majority rule. I do not advocate any one procedural rule as a universal panacea for unfairness. Nor do I propose these remedies primarily as judicial solutions. They can be adopted only in the context of litigation after the court first finds a legal violation.

Outside of litigation, I propose these approaches as political solutions if, depending on the local context, they better approximate the goals of democratic fair play. One such decisionmaking alternative is called cumulative voting, which could give all the students at Brother Rice multiple votes and allow them to distribute their votes in any combination of their choice. If each student could vote for ten songs, the students could plump or aggregate their votes to reflect the intensity of their preferences. They could put ten votes on one song; they could put five votes on two songs. If a tenth of the students opted to "cumulate" or plump all their votes for one song, they would be able to select one of every ten or so songs played at the prom. The black seniors could have done this if they chose to, but so could any other cohesive group of sufficient size. In this way, the songs preferred by a majority would be played most often, but the songs the minority enjoyed would also show up on the play list.

Under cumulative voting, voters get the same number of votes as there are seats or options to vote for, and they can then distribute their votes in any combination to reflect their preferences. Like-minded voters can vote as a solid bloc or, instead, form strategic, cross-racial coalitions to gain mutual benefits. This system is emphatically not racially based; it allows voters to organize themselves on whatever basis they wish.

Corporations use this system to ensure representation of minority shareholders on corporate boards of directors. Similarly, some local municipal and county governments have adopted cumulative voting to ensure representation of minority voters. Instead of awarding political power to geographic units called districts, cumulative voting allows voters to cast ballots based on what they think rather than where they live.

Cumulative voting is based on the principle of one person–one vote because each voter gets the same total number of votes. Everyone's preferences are counted equally. It is not a particularly radical idea; thirty states either require or permit corporations to use this election system. Cumulative voting is certainly not antidemocratic because it emphasizes the importance of voter choice in selecting public or social policy. And it is neither liberal nor conservative. Both the Reagan and Bush administrations approved cumulative voting schemes pursuant to the Voting Rights Act to protect the rights of racial- and language-minority voters.

But, as in Chilton County, Alabama, which now uses cumulative voting to elect both the school board and the county commission, any politically cohesive group can vote strategically to win representation. Groups of voters win representation depending on the exclusion threshold, meaning the percentage of votes needed to win one seat or have the band play one song. That threshold can be set case by case, jurisdiction by jurisdiction, based on the size of minority groups that make compelling claims for representation.

Normally the exclusion threshold in a head-to-head contest is 50 percent, which means that only groups that can organize a majority can get elected. But if multiple seats (or multiple songs) are considered simultaneously, the exclusion threshold is considerably reduced. For example, in Chilton County, with seven seats elected simultaneously on each governing body, the threshold of exclusion is now one-eighth. Any group with the solid support of one-eighth the voting population cannot be denied representation. This is because any self-identified minority can plump or cumulate all its votes for one candidate. Again, minorities are not defined solely in racial terms.

As it turned out in Chilton County, both blacks and Republicans benefited from this new system. The school board and commission now each have three white Democrats, three white Republicans, and one black Democrat. Previously, when each seat was decided in a head-to-head contest, the majority not only ruled but monopolized. Only white Democrats were elected at every prior election during this century.

Similarly, if the black and white students at Brother Rice have very different musical taste, cumulative voting permits a positive-sum solution to enable both groups to enjoy one prom. The majority's preferences would be respected in that their songs would be played most often, but the black students could express the intensity of their preferences too. If the black students chose to plump all their votes on a few songs, their minority preferences would be recognized and played. Essentially, cumulative voting structures the band's repertoire to enable the students to take turns.

As a solution that permits voters to self-select their identities, cumulative voting also encourages cross-racial coalition building. No one is locked into a minority identity. Nor is anyone necessarily isolated by the identity they choose. Voters can strengthen their influence by forming coalitions to elect more than one representative or to select a range of music more compatible with the entire student body's preferences.

Women too can use cumulative voting to gain greater representation. Indeed, in other countries with similar, alternative voting systems, women are more likely to be represented in the national legislature. For example, in some Western European democracies, the national legislatures have as many as 37 percent female members compared to a little more than 5 percent in our Congress.

There is a final benefit from cumulative voting. It eliminates gerrymandering. By denying protected incumbents safe seats in gerrymandered districts, cumulative voting might encourage more voter participation. With greater interest-based electoral competition, cumulative voting could promote the political turnover sought by advocates of term limits. In this way, cumulative voting serves many of the same ends as periodic elections or rotation in office, a solution that Madison and others advocated as a means of protecting against permanent majority factions. . . .

My nomination became an unfortunate metaphor for the state of race relations in America. My nomination suggested that as a country, we are in a state of denial about issues of race and racism. The censorship imposed against me points to a denial of serious public debate or discussion about racial fairness and justice in a true democracy. For many politicians and policymakers, the remedy for racism is simply to stop talking about race.

Sentences, words, even phrases separated by paragraphs in my law review articles were served up to demonstrate that I was violating the rules. Because I talked openly about existing racial divisions, I was branded "race obsessed." Because I explored innovative ways to remedy racism, I was branded "antidemocratic." It did not matter that I had suggested race-neutral election rules, such as cumulative voting, as an alternative to remedy racial discrimination. It did not matter that I never advocated quotas. I became the Quota Queen.

The vision behind my by-now-notorious law review articles and my less-well-known professional commitments has always been that of a fair and just society, a society in which even adversely affected parties believe in the system because they believe the process is fair and the process is inclusive. My vision of fairness and justice imagines a full and effective voice for all citizens. I may have failed to locate some of my ideas in the specific factual contexts from which they are derived. But always I have tried to show that democracy in a heterogeneous society is incompatible with rule by a racial monopoly of any color.

By publishing these law journal articles as a collection, I hope to spark the debate that was denied in the context of my nomination. We will have lost more than any one individual's opportunity for public service if we fail to pursue the public thirst for information about, and positive-sum solutions to, the issues at the heart of this controversy. The twentieth-century problem—the problem of the color line, according to W. E. B.

Du Bois—will soon become a twenty-first-century problem if we allow opposing viewpoints to be silenced on issues of race and racism.

I hope that we can learn three positive lessons from my experience. The first lesson is that those who stand for principles may lose in the short run, but they cannot be suppressed in the long run. The second lesson is that public dialogue is critical to represent all perspectives; no one viewpoint should be permitted to monopolize, distort, caricature, or shape public debate. The tyranny of The Majority is just as much a problem of silencing minority viewpoints as it is of excluding minority representatives or preferences. We cannot all talk at once, but that does not mean only one group should get to speak. We can take turns. Third, we need consensus and positive-sum solutions. We need a broad public conversation about issues of racial justice in which we seek win-win solutions to real-life problems. If we include blacks and whites, and women and men, and Republicans and Democrats, and even people with new ideas, we will all be better off.

Political Parties

PART THIRTEEN

Political Parties

79

WALTER DEAN BURNHAM

From *Critical Elections and the Mainsprings of American Politics*

Political science can offer few clear-cut theories of how politics works. Because of the variable of human nature as well as the impossibility of measuring and predicting political events with exactness, political science is often less a "science" and more an "art." A few attempts at developing major theories to explain and predict politics have been made, however. One is the theory of "critical realignments." Professor Walter Dean Burnham was one of the first to try to explain why certain presidential elections throughout American history mark significant long-term changes in the social and economic direction of the nation. Citing 1800, 1828, 1860, 1896, and 1932, Burnham describes the characteristics of a critical or realigning election, the most dramatic being its supposed "uniform periodicity." They occur at roughly equal intervals apart in time.

FOR MANY DECADES it has been generally recognized that American electoral politics is not quite "all of a piece" despite its apparent diverse uniformity. Some elections have more important long-range consequences for the political system as a whole than others, and seem to "decide" substantive issues in a more clear-cut way. There has long been agreement among historians that the elections of those of 1800, 1828, 1860, 1896, and 1932, for example, were fundamental turning points in the course of American electoral politics.

Since the appearance in 1955 of V. O. Key's seminal article, "A Theory of Critical Elections," political scientists have moved to give this concept quantitative depth and meaning. . . .

It now seems time to attempt at least an interim assessment of the structure, function, and implications of critical realignments for the American political process. Such an effort is motivated in particular by the author's view that critical realignments are of fundamental importance not only to the system of political action called "the American political process" but also to the clarifications of some aspects of its operation. It seems particularly important in a period of obvious political upheaval not only to identify these phenomena and place them in time, but to integrate them into a larger (if still very modest) theory of movement in American politics.

Such a theory must inevitably emphasize the elements of stress and abrupt transformation in our political life at the expense of the consensual, gradualist perspectives which have until recently dominated the scholar's vision of American political processes and behavior. For the realignment phenomenon focuses our attention on "the dark side of the moon." It reminds us that politics as usual in the United States is not politics as always; that there are discrete types of voting behavior and quite different levels of voter response to political stimuli, depending on what those stimuli are and at what point in time they occur; and that American political institutions and leadership, once defined (or redefined) in a "normal phase" of our politics, seem to become part of the very conditions that threaten to overthrow them. . . .

In its "ideal-typical" form, the critical realignment differs from stable alignments eras, secular [gradual] realignments, and deviating elections in the following basic ways.

1. The critical realignment is characteristically associated with short-lived but very intense disruptions of traditional patterns of voting behavior. Majority parties become minorities; politics which was once competitive becomes noncompetitive or, alternatively, hitherto one-party areas now become arenas of intense partisan competition; and large blocks of the active electorate—minorities, to be sure, but perhaps involving as much as a fifth to a third of the voters—shift their partisan allegiance.

2. Critical elections are characterized by abnormally high intensity as well.

a. This intensity typically spills over into the party nominating and platform-writing machinery during the upheaval and results in major shifts in convention behavior from the integrative "norm" as well as in transformations in the internal loci of power in the major party most heavily affected by the pressures of realignment. Ordinarily accepted "rules of the game" are flouted; the party's processes, instead of performing their usual integrative functions, themselves contribute to polarization.

b. The rise in intensity is associated with a considerable increase in ideological polarizations, at first within one or more of the major parties and then between them. Issue distances between the parties are markedly increased, and elections tend to involve highly salient issue-clusters, often with strongly emotional and symbolic overtones, far more than is customary in American electoral politics. One curious property of established leadership as it drifts into the stress of realignment seems to be a tendency to become more rigid and dogmatic, which itself contributes greatly to the explosive "bursting stress" of realignment. . . .

c. The rise in intensity is also normally to be found in abnormally heavy voter participation for the time. . . .

3. Historically speaking, at least, national critical realignments have not occurred at random. Instead, there has been a remarkably uniform periodicity in their appearance. . . .

4. It has been argued, with much truth, that American political parties are essentially constituent parties. That is to say, the political-party subsystem is sited in a socioeconomic system of very great heterogeneity and diversity. . . .

Critical realignments emerge directly from the dynamics of this constituent-function supremacy in American politics. . . . In other words, realignments are themselves constituent acts: they arise from emergent tensions in society which, not adequately controlled by the organization or outputs of party politics as usual, escalate to a flash point; they are issue-oriented phenomena, centrally associated with these tensions and more or less leading to resolution adjustments; they result in significant transformations in the general shape of policy; and they have relatively profound aftereffects on the roles played by institutional elites. They are involved with redefinitions of the universe of voters, political parties, and the broad boundaries of the politically possible.

To recapitulate, then, eras of critical realignment are marked by short, sharp reorganizations of the mass coalitional bases of the major parties which occur at periodic intervals on the national level; are often preceded by major third-party revolts which reveal the incapacity of "politics as usual" to integrate, much less aggregate, emergent political demand; are closely associated with abnormal stress in the socioeconomic system; are marked by ideological polarizations and issue-distances between the major parties which are exceptionally large by normal standards; and have durable consequences as constituent acts which determine the outer boundaries of policy in general, though not necessarily of policies in detail. . . . There is much evidence . . . that realignments do recur with rather remarkable regularity approximately once a generation, or every thirty to thirty-eight years.

The precise timing of the conditions which conduce to realignment is conditioned heavily by circumstance, of course: the intrusion of major crises in society and economy with which "politics as usual" in the United States cannot adequately cope, and the precise quality and bias of leadership decisions in a period of high political tension, cannot be predicted in specific time with any accuracy. Yet a broadly repetitive pattern of oscillation between the normal inertia of mass electoral politics and the ruptures of the normal which realignments bring about is clearly evident from the data. So evident is this pattern that one is led to suspect that the truly "normal" structure of American electoral politics at the mass base is precisely this dynamic, even dialectic polarization between long-term inertia and concentrated bursts of change in this open system of action. It may well be that American political institutions, including the major political parties, are so organized that they have a chronic, cumulative tendency toward underproduction of other than currently "normal" policy outputs. They may tend persistently to ignore, and hence not to aggregate, emergent political demand of a mass character until a boiling point of some kind is reached.

In this context, the rise of third-party protests as what might be called protorealignment phenomena would be associated with the repeated emergence of a rising gap between perceived expectations of the political process and its perceived realities over time, diffused among a constantly increasing portion of the active electorate and perhaps mobilizing many hitherto inactive voters. . . .

The periodic rhythm of American electoral politics, the cycle of oscillation between the normal and the disruptive, corresponds precisely to the existence of largely unfettered developmental change in the socioeconomic system and its absence in the country's political institutions. Indeed, it is a prime quantitative measure of the interaction between the two. The socioeconomic system develops but the institutions of electoral politics and policy formation remain essentially unchanged. Moreover, they do not have much capacity to adjust incrementally to demand arising from socioeconomic dislocations. Dysfunctions centrally related to this process become more and more visible, until finally entire classes, regions, or other major sectors of the population are directly injured or come to see themselves as threatened by imminent danger. Then the triggering event occurs, critical realignments follow, and the universe of policy and of electoral coalitions is broadly redefined. It is at such moments that the constitution–making role of the American voter becomes most visible, and his behavior, one suspects, least resembles the normal pattern. . . .

In this context, then, critical realignment emerges as decisively important in the study of the dynamics of American politics. It is as symptomatic of political nonevolution in this country as are the archaic and increasingly rudimentary structures of the political parties themselves. But even more importantly, critical realignment may well be defined as the chief tension-management device available to so peculiar a political system. Historically it has been the chief means through which an underdeveloped political system can be recurrently brought once again into some balanced relationship with the changing socioeconomic system, permitting a restabilization of our politics. . . . Granted the relative inability of our political institutions to make gradual adjustments along vectors of *emergent* political demand, critical realignments have been as inevitable as they have been necessary to the normal workings of American politics. Thus once again there is a paradox: the conditions which decree that coalitional negotiation, bargaining, and incremental, unplanned, and gradual policy change become the dominant characteristic of American politics in its normal state also decree that it give way to abrupt, disruptive change with considerable potential for violence. . . .

Such a dynamically oriented frame of reference presupposes a holistic view of American politics which is radically different from that which until very recently has tended to dominate the professional literature. The models of American political life and political processes with which we are most familiar emphasize the well-known attributes of pluralist democracy. There are not stable policy majorities. Intense and focused minorities with well-defined interests exert influence on legislation and administrative rule making out of all proportion to their size. The process involves gradual, incremental change secured after bargaining has been completed among a wide array of interested groups who are prepared to accept the conditions of bargaining. It is true that such descriptions apply to a "politics as usual" which is an important fragment of political reality in the United States, but to describe this fragment as the whole of that reality is to assume an essentially ideological posture whose credibility can be maintained only by ignoring the complementary dynamics of American politics as a whole. . . .

The reality of this process taken as a whole seems quite different from the pluralist vision. It is one shot through with escalating tensions, periodic electoral upheavals, and repeated redefinitions of the rules and outcomes-in-general of the political game, as well as redefinitions—by no means always broadening ones—of those who are in fact permitted to play it. One very basic characteristic of American party politics which emerges from a contemplation of critical realignments is a profound incapacity of established political leadership to adapt itself sequentially—or even incrementally?—to emergent political demand generated by the losers in our stormy socioeconomic transformations. American political parties are not action instrumentalities of definable and broad social collectivities; as organizations they are, consequently, interested in control of offices but not of government in the broader sense of which we have been speaking.

It follows from this that once successful routines are established or reestablished for winning office, there is no motivation among party leaders to disturb the routines of the game. These routines are disturbed not by adaptive change within the party-policy system, but by the application of overwhelming external force.

80

DAVID BRODER

From *The Party's Over*

As his book title cleverly implies, journalist David Broder acknowledges the decline of American political parties. Writing in the early 1970s, he mourns their weakening and holds out hope for a reinvigorated party system. Broder attributes many of America's governmental problems to the parties' problems, and he pleads for stronger party unity in Congress and an expanded role for parties in the campaign process. Turning to voters, Broder asks for less ticket-splitting and more partisan allegiance. As the decades have passed, Broder's observations about the decline of the parties—dealignment, as scholars term it—have been borne out. His hopes for the rejuvenation of American political parties have proved less promising. Among most voters and even many office-holders, the Democratic and Republican parties are no longer the heart of the American political process.

MY VIEW IS that American politics is at an impasse, that we have been spinning our wheels for a long, long time; and that we are going to dig ourselves ever deeper into trouble, unless we find a way to develop some political traction and move again. I believe we can get that traction, we can make government responsible and responsive again, only when we begin to use the political parties as they are meant to be used. And that is the thesis of this book.

It is called *The Party's Over*, not in prophecy, but in alarm. I am not predicting the demise of the Republicans or the Democrats. Party loyalties have been seriously eroded, the Democratic and Republican organizations weakened by years of neglect. But our parties are not yet dead. What happens to them is up to us to decide. If we allow them to wither, we will pay a high price in the continued frustration of government. But, even if we seek their renewal, the cost of repairing the effects of decades of governmental inaction will be heavy. The process will be painful and expensive. Whatever the fate of our political parties, for America the party *is* over. . . .

. . . The reason we have suffered governmental stalemate is that we have not used the one instrument available to us for disciplining government to meet our needs. That instrument is the political party.

Political parties in America have a peculiar status and history. They are not part of our written Constitution. The Founding Fathers, in fact, were determined to do all they could to see they did not arise. Washington devoted much of his Farewell Address to warning his countrymen against "the dangers of party in the state." And yet parties arose in the first generation of the nation, and have persisted ever since. Their very durability argues that they fill a need. That need is for some institution that will sort out, weigh, and, to the extent possible, reconcile the myriad conflicting needs and demands of individuals, groups, interests, communities and regions in this diverse continental Republic, organize them for the contest for public office; and then serve as a link between the constituencies and the men chosen to govern. When the parties fill their mission well, they tend to serve both a unifying and a clarifying function for the country. Competitive forces draw them to the center, and force them to seek agreement on issues too intense to be settled satisfactorily by simple majority referendum. On the other hand, as grand coalitions, they are capable of taking a need felt strongly by some minority of the population and making it part of a program endorsed by a majority.

When they do not function well, things go badly for America. The coming of the Civil War was marked by a failure of the reconciling function of the existing parties. Long periods of stagnation, too, can be caused by the failure of the parties to bring emerging public questions to the point of electoral decision. When the parties fail, individual citizens feel they have lost control of what is happening in politics and in government. They find themselves powerless to influence the course of events. Voting seems futile and politics a pointless charade. . . .

The governmental system is not working because the political parties are not working. The parties have been weakened by their failure to adapt to some of the social and technological changes taking place in America. But, even more, they are suffering from simple neglect: neglect by Presidents and public officials, but, particularly, neglect by the voters. It is to remind us that the parties can be used for positive purposes that this book is written.

Some students of government who share this view of the importance of political parties in American government nonetheless think it futile to exhort readers on their behalf. Such political scientists as James L. Sund-quist and Walter Dean Burnham, whose knowledge of American political history is far deeper than my own, believe we are simply in the wrong stage of the political cycle to expect anything but confused signals and weak responses from the parties.

The last major party realignment, it is generally agreed, took place in 1932, and set the stage for the New Deal policies of government intervention in the economy and the development of the welfare state. We are, these scholars argue, perhaps overdue for another realignment, but until an issue emerges which will produce one, an issue as powerful as the Great Depression, it is futile to complain that party lines are muddled and governmental action is all but paralyzed. Their judgment may be correct, but I do not find it comforting. The cyclical theory of party realignment is an easy rationalization for throwing up our hands and doing nothing. But we do not know when the realignment will take place. Some scholars have thought there was a thirty-six-year cycle, with 1896 and 1932 as the last "critical elections." But 1968, the scheduled date, on this theory, for another "critical election," has come and gone, and our drift continues. . . .

. . . Basically, I believe that our guarantee of self-government is no stronger than our exercise of self-government; and today the central in-struments of self-government, the political parties, are being neglect-ed or abused. We must somehow rescue them if we are to rescue our-selves. . . .

. . . Popular dissatisfaction with the two-party system is manifested in many ways: by the decline in voting; by the rise in the number of voters who refuse to identify themselves with either party; by the increase in ticket splitting, a device for denying either party responsibility for govern-ment; and by the increased use of third parties or ad hoc political coalitions to pressure for change. . . . Is there not a better way to resolve our differ-ences, to move ahead on our common problems? I believe there is. . . . The instrument that is available to us . . . is the instrument of responsible party government. The alternative to making policy in the streets is to make it in the voting booth. . . .

But, if that is to be more than a cliché answer, there must be real choices presented at election time—choices involving more than a selec-tion between two sincere-sounding, photogenic graduates of some cam-paign consultant's academy of political and dramatic arts. The candidates must come to the voters with programs that are comprehensible and relevant to our problems; and they must have the kind of backing that makes it possible for them to act on their pledges once in office.

The instrument, the only instrument I know of, that can nominate such candidates, commit them to a program and give them the leverage and alliances in government that can enable them to keep their promises, is the political party. . . .

. . . Where do we turn? To ourselves. Obviously, that must be the answer. There is no solution for America except what we Americans devise. I believe that we have the instrument at hand, in the party system, that can break the long and costly impasse in our government. But it is up to us to decide whether to use it.

What would it entail on our part if we determined to attempt responsible party government? First, it would mean giving strong public support to those reform efforts which in the recent past have been carried on entirely by a small group of concerned political insiders, aimed at strengthening the machinery of political parties and government.

We should seek to strengthen the liaison between the presidency and Congress, on a mutual basis, and between the presidency and the heads of state and local government. We should elect the President in the same way we elect all other officials, by direct vote of his constituents, with high man winning.

We should expand the role and responsibilities of the party caucuses and the party leaders in Congress. The caucus should choose the floor leaders and policy committee members, the legislative committee chairmen and committee members, not on the basis of seniority but on the basis of ability and commitment to the party program. That leadership ought to be held accountable for bringing legislation to which the party is committed to a floor vote in orderly and timely fashion, with adequate opportunity for debate and particularly for consideration of opposition party alternatives. But procedures for due consideration should not justify devices like the filibuster, which prevent the majority party from bringing its measures to a final vote. . . .

We need to take every possible measure to strengthen the presidential nominating convention as the key device for making the parties responsible. The current effort to open the Democratic delegate-selection process to wider public participation is a promising start, and its emphasis on the congressional-district nominating convention offers corollary benefits for integrating congressional and presidential constituencies. Both parties should experiment with devices for putting heavier emphasis on the platform-writing phase of the convention's work, including the possibility of a separate convention, following the nomination, where the party's officeholders and candidates debate the program on which they pledge themselves to run and to act if elected.

Most important of all the structural reforms, we need to follow through the effort to discipline the use of money in politics, not only by setting realistic limits on campaign spending and by publicizing individual and organizational gifts, but also by channeling much more of the money (including, in my view, all general election spending) through the respective party committees, rather than through individual candidates' treasuries.

We need to strengthen the party organizations and their staffs, and recapture for them the campaign management functions that have been parceled out to independent firms which tend to operate with a fine disdain for the role of party and policy in government. We need to devise ways to make television—the prime medium of political communication—somewhat more sensitive to the claims of the parties to be a regular part of the political dialogue, and to protect the vital institution of the nominating convention from being distorted by the demands of the television cameras.

All these reforms would help, I believe, but they would not accomplish the invigoration of responsible party government unless they were accompanied by a genuine increase in the participation by the public in party affairs. The cure for the ills of democracy truly is more democracy; our parties are weak principally because we do not use them. To be strong and responsible, our parties must be representative; and they can be no more representative than our participation allows. Millions more of us need to get into partisan political activity.

We need also to become somewhat more reflective about what we do with our votes. We need to ask ourselves what it is that we want government to accomplish, and which candidate, which party comes closest to espousing that set of goals. That may sound so rationalistic as to be unrealistic. But this nation has more education, more communication, more leisure available to it than ever before. In the nineteenth century, James Bryce wrote of us, "The ordinary citizens are interested in politics, and watch them with intelligence, the same kind of intelligence (though a smaller quantity of it) as they apply to their own business. . . . They think their own competence equal to that of their representatives and office-bearers; and they are not far wrong." Are we to think less of ourselves today?

Finally, we need to examine some of our habits. It seems to me we should ask, before splitting a ticket, what it is we hope to accomplish by dividing between the parties the responsibility for government of our country, our state or our community. Do we think there is no difference between the parties? Do we distrust them both so thoroughly that we wish to set them against each other? Do we think one man so superior in virtue and wisdom that he must be put in office, no matter who accompanies him there? Why are we splitting our tickets? My guess is that, if we asked those questions, we would more often be inclined to give a temporary grant of power to one party at a time, rather than dividing responsibility so skillfully between the parties that neither can govern. If we were willing to risk this strategy, knowing that we would be able to throw the rascals out if they failed, we might even discover to our amazement that they are not always rascals.

81

KENNETH BAER

From *Reinventing Democrats*

Electoral politics in the U.S. is not merely a contest between opposing candidates running under the competing party labels of Democrats and Republicans. Underneath the surface, there are struggles within each political party for dominance and control over the principles that will guide that party. In this selection, Kenneth Baer takes us inside the Democratic Party to look at a faction that developed in the mid 1980s, as a response to the electoral victories of Republican president Ronald Reagan in 1980 and 1984. The heart of the Democratic Party, some party members felt, did not recognize that the Democratic Party had to undergo major changes in its outlook if it hoped to win elections; old style Democratic liberalism was obsolete. Thus was born the Democratic Leadership Council, a group of moderates within the party who de-emphasized "big government" solutions. Baer traces the DLC's attempts to rebuild the party in its image, from the success of DLC leader Bill Clinton's 1992 election to the presidency, through the failure of the 1994 congressional elections when Republicans triumphed. Changes to the parties and the party system are not visible only at major realigning elections, Baer notes; change can also come from within the parties, subtly and incrementally.

EVER SINCE WOODROW WILSON REVIVED the tradition of reporting in person on the state of the Union to Congress, the yearly address has become a celebrated political ritual. Each year, a president makes the trip down Pennsylvania Avenue to deliver a speech on the nation's progress and on the coming year's agenda. Heavy with policy, these speeches are usually unmemorable. Yet at times the words match the ceremony of the event. Who can forget the "four freedoms" outlined by Franklin Roosevelt in 1941? Perhaps it is this potential for history, or perhaps the excitement of the coming policymaking year, that has made this address so eagerly anticipated. During an election year, the stakes are higher, and the anticipation is understandably greater.

On one such occasion, the president of the United States took his position at the rostrum in the House of Representatives chamber. Behind him sat the Republican Speaker of the House, and in one of the first rows in front of him was the Republican Senate majority leader. The president began his speech by, unsurprisingly, affirming that the state of the Union was strong. He celebrated the growth of the economy; the creation of new businesses and new jobs; the decline in the welfare rolls and in the crime, poverty, and teen pregnancy rates; and the prevailing peace. Then, in laying out his thoughts on how the country could best confront its future problems, the president slowly and clearly proclaimed: "The era of big government is over."

One would imagine that at this point, the members of the Republican congressional majority would leap to their feet with applause, relishing the accomplishments of this president, and especially his clear exposition of a belief that, in one form or another, has been central to their party's thinking for at least a century. Yet the Republicans sat sourly in their seats, for there was one problem with this scenario. The president speaking these words in 1996 was a Democrat: Bill Clinton. He was the man who had led the Democratic Party in capturing the White House for the first time in twelve years. And ten months after this speech, he became the first Democratic president to win reelection to a second full term since Franklin Roosevelt in 1936.

Indeed, this statement, which has received wide attention and analysis, was not simply a rhetorical flourish. It was not some odd historical side note. Nor was it a craven attempt to mimic the GOP. Rather, this sentence, and the entire speech in which it was spoken, marked a profound change in the Democratic Party. A party that for the past thirty years had been seen as profligate "tax-and-spenders," reflexive defenders of federal governmental programs, pacifist isolationists, and advocates of an active social liberalism now had a president who championed the reinvention of government, welfare reform, fiscal restraint, economic growth, free trade, mainstream values, and an internationalist foreign policy. A party that had seen only one of its nominees elected to the presidency during this time now had a leader who had won the White House once and was poised to do it again.

This transformation did not happen overnight. Nor was it the result of a radical change in the condition of the country or in the electorate. Rather, this new public philosophy, and the electoral success apparently tied to it, was the product of a conscious and sustained effort by a group of "New Democrats" and their most important organizational form, the Democratic Leadership Council (DLC). Formed in the aftermath of the 1984 election by a group of elected officials who believed that the Democratic Party was in danger of marginalization and even extinction, the DLC argued that the party had to craft a mainstream public philosophy that had wide electoral appeal.

With the election of Clinton, the DLC's former chairman, to the presidency, the New Democrats have seen many of their ideas become national policy and some of their most prominent members enter the presidential cabinet and staff. As a result, the DLC and New Democrats in and around the organization have become the principal rival to the national party's dominant liberal faction. The appeal of New Democratic policymaking and politics to key parts of the electorate has strengthened the Democratic Party nationally at the expense of the Republicans. In short, over the past decade, the DLC and the New Democrats have become one of the most influential forces in the Democratic Party and in American politics.

Indeed, some pundits and scholars view Clinton's use of the New Democratic public philosophy to reposition the Democratic Party in the eyes of the electorate as his most substantive legacy. "Clinton, I think, will . . . be remembered for reforming the Federal Government and for reshaping his party," judged Jacob Weisberg. The 2000 elections will speak to the accuracy of this statement, but already we know that any Republican standard-bearer will have to challenge the Democratic nominee on an altered political terrain where the Democrats can claim to have balanced the budget, grown the economy, reformed welfare, and reduced crime. No matter what happens in the year 2000, it is safe to assume that the DLC and the New Democrats will be at the center of any debate, or battle, to chart the future of the Democratic Party for the next century. . . .

On a more abstract level, I intend to offer a framework for understanding how modern parties and their public philosophies change. In both scholarly and popular analysis, the dominant paradigm of electoral and ideological change within the party system is realignment theory. In its basic form, this theory holds that only a national crisis, such as a war or an economic depression, can prompt a new line of partisan cleavage in the electorate. This split, in turn, comes to the fore in a "realigning" or "critical" election in which "the basic party attachments" of voters are significantly altered to produce a change in the party in control of the government. If this party effectively handles the crisis and these new partisan loyalties hold and are proved durable, then a realignment is said to have occurred. Most political scientists who subscribe to realignment theory agree that this process occurred, for example, after 1860 (prompted by the Civil War) and after 1932 (prompted by the Great Depression).

Yet as the story of the DLC shows, it is possible for a party faction consciously to change the public philosophy of a party and attract new voters during "normal" political times, without a major national crisis and a precipitating critical election. That is, a group of policy entrepreneurs can facilitate change within a party so that it can adapt to long-term, deeper socioeconomic and political trends. . . .

The DLC story begins in the aftermath of the election of Ronald Reagan in 1980 with a group of congressmen organized in the House Democratic Caucus. Under the leadership of Caucus Chairman Gillis Long of Louisiana and his top aide, Al From, these young, proto-New Democrats began the task of developing and promoting an alternative public philosophy to rejuvenate the defeated Democrats. When their failure to affect the platform, strategy, makeup, and success of the 1984 Democratic presidential ticket became clear, this group—plus like-minded governors such as Chuck Robb of Virginia and senators such as Sam Nunn of Georgia—formed the DLC in February 1985.

Almost immediately, their plans to use the DLC as a vehicle to develop a new public philosophy and to change the party itself were in jeopardy. Liberals within the party demonized the DLC as "Democrats for the Leisure Class" and even charged that the New Democrats were right-wing and racist. At the same time, wanting to preserve party unity, the Democratic National Committee tried to co-opt the DLC by moving in the rogue organization's direction. Taken together, these reactions threatened the DLC's very existence, prompting the organization to shift its tactics and embrace a "big-tent" strategy of moderating its rhetoric and stances in order to attract a broad array of members and blunt these attacks.

The big tent may have ensured the DLC's short-term survival, but it also undermined the New Democrats' effectiveness. During the 1988 nominating campaign, the DLC hoped that the southern regional primary, "Super Tuesday," would propel a New Democratic candidate, such as Senator Al Gore of Tennessee, to the nomination. Yet once again, the

DLC failed to shape the party platform or ticket. Indeed, Super Tuesday did more to increase the influence of the New Democrats' main nemesis, the Reverend Jesse Jackson, than to help the New Democratic cause. Its effort to work within the party, specifically, tinkering with the nominating process, made the DLC appear ineffective and marginal. Questions of why it should exist at all intensified.

Yet in 1988, another presidential defeat erased these doubts and breathed new life into the DLC. Realizing the failure of its big-tent format, the DLC began to take a more adversarial stance. It presented a lucid and biting critique of the political strategy of the national Democratic Party; established the Progressive Policy Institute (PPI), a think tank to develop fully a New Democratic public philosophy; and embarked on an aggressive presidential strategy. Said differently, the DLC wanted to take over the party by battling for its head.

This plan brought Al From—now executive director of the DLC—to Little Rock, Arkansas, in the spring of 1989 to personally persuade Governor Bill Clinton to take over the DLC, which From promised would be retooled as a springboard for his presidential run. Clinton accepted, and throughout 1990 and 1991, the DLC plied the governor with critical aid during this important "invisible primary" phase of the campaign. The organization unveiled a developed and distinct public philosophy that took controversial stands on a variety of issues, and it established state chapters to give its putative candidate a reason to travel the country and a chance to construct a network of supporters in key states. This work culminated in the DLC's first convention held in Cleveland in May 1991. There, the organization ratified a New Democratic policy platform, highlighted its nationwide strength, and provided a showcase for its chairman, Clinton. Throughout this process, the DLC faced liberal attacks, from broadsides launched by Jackson to picketing by union workers. But this criticism did not derail the DLC, and by October 1991, the New Democrats had their candidate. . . .

Yet during the first two years of the Clinton presidency, it seemed that Clinton had abandoned the New Democrats and that the DLC's presidential strategy had failed. Due to a combination of the nature of his victory in both the nominating contest and the general election plus the makeup of Congress, Clinton either proposed "Old" (liberal) Democratic policies or offered New Democratic policies but by way of Old Democratic politics. By 1994, the DLC was demoralized. Its man was in the White House, but nothing seemed to have changed.

In the elections of 1994, everything seemed to change. The Republicans took over Congress, significantly altered the political landscape, and, in the process, reinvigorated the DLC and the New Democratic effort. This outcome convinced Clinton to reembrace the New Democratic public philosophy and created a political situation that practically compelled him to do so. By the time he ran for reelection in 1996, Clinton could point to his balanced budget plan, his signature on a welfare reform bill, and a number of initiatives targeted to the middle class to burnish his New Democratic credentials. With his return to the New Democratic issue agenda and electoral strategy, he handily won reelection.

In claiming victory in 1996, Bill Clinton proclaimed that "the vital American center is alive and well." But as the Clinton era comes to a close and the contest to replace him commences, how vital are the New Democrats? Has the DLC really changed the public philosophy of the Democratic Party? And if so, what does this tell us about how a change in the public philosophy of an American political party can—and cannot— occur? The answer to these questions is in many ways premature, as the New Democratic experiment is still a young one. . . .

Although of a personal nature, the scandal that engulfed Clinton in 1998 especially affected the DLC and the New Democrats. On one level, it directly threatened the viability of their most powerful supporter and of the DLC's presidential strategy. On another level, it indirectly risked overshadowing Clinton's efforts to remake the Democratic Party in his image. DLC Chairman Lieberman was the first prominent Democrat to chastise Clinton publicly for his behavior, yet his and the DLC's position on the scandal never really wavered from that of the White House. The organization condemned the sin but loved the sinner; it would oppose his impeachment.

With Clinton unable to champion his policy agenda and unwilling to antagonize congressional liberals who would judge him, policy innovation, especially of a New Democratic kind, ground to a halt. Yet the DLC began to look beyond the scandal—and even the Clinton presidency— focusing on ensuring that the New Democratic public policy and the politics and policies implicit in it outlasted Clinton's second term. . . .

In "Five Realities that Will Shape 21st Century Politics," [William] Galston and [Elaine] Kamarck outlined what they believed to be the five dynamics shaping American politics at the end of the century. The first was that increasing returns on education have propelled more and more Americans out of the middle class, forming a "new learning class" of better-educated, wealthier, more mobile, and more self-reliant Americans. To Galston and Kamarck, this phenomenon explained the decreasing size of the middle class and the increasing gap between rich and poor, two developments bemoaned by liberals. This "new reality" meant that, from a policy perspective, it was crucial to provide a higher quality of education to more people, and from a political perspective, it was a "mistake to believe that Democrats can construct majorities based on a swelling pool of poor and near-poor Americans waiting to be mobilized by an old-fashioned politics of redistribution."

The other realities that Galston and Kamarck outlined included the rise of "wired workers"—those who use computers on the job, work in self-directed groups, and do not need to rely on large mediating institutions (such as labor unions) for information; the passing of the New Deal generation, with its fondness for centralized government, from the electorate; the dominance of suburbia in political life; an increase in the number of children concentrated in fewer households, a situation demanding policies to help them based not on self-interest but on community; and the increasing diversity of the country, which demanded "unifying appeals to shared national values" in place of identity politics. These realities, naturally, pointed to the need to embrace the New Democratic public philosophy. In addition, they became the central arguments for policy prescriptions and political strategies detailed in speeches and articles written by DLC leaders. . . .

The challenge in interpreting the progress of the DLC is that all this evidence is preliminary. Because the New Democrats are trying to remake the public philosophy of the party without the help of a national crisis to polarize the electorate and without a critical election to realign voters into new partisan attachments, it is too soon—even after six years of a Clinton presidency—to know what eventually will become of the New Democratic public philosophy. But what is clear is that contrary to what critics on both the left and the right have contended, the DLC's positions amount to a coherent New Democratic public philosophy, one whose main components are already recognizable. Moreover, parsing it into the four main components of a public philosophy—a theory of governance, views about the ends of society, the role of government and different levels of government in society, and the role of the country in the world— we see too that the New Democratic public philosophy is distinct from the liberal public philosophy.

In their clearest break from the liberal faction's thinking, the New Democrats believe that the federal government should not be the primary focus for reform efforts. Answers to societal problems and provision of social goods should be sought first in the private sector, then among local and state governments, and only then at the federal level. Underlying this belief, in turn, is a greater reliance on the community and faith in the free market, a faith born out of the belief that the Information Age, with its global, information-based economy, has made centralized bureaucratic structures obsolete. Unlike Republicans, many of whom also want to devolve many governmental functions to the state and local levels, New Democrats want to change the federal relationship to make government more effective, not to destroy it. Furthermore, these tenets do not mean that New Democrats see no role for governmental action, as many on the right do. Rather, if a situation warrants federal involvement, the New Democrats prefer to use market mechanisms, not centralized bureaucracies, to implement policy.

The New Democratic public philosophy also breaks with the liberal interpretation of equality. Hearkening back to pre-1968 liberalism, the New Democrats endorse an equality of opportunity, not of results. They believe that the role of government is to provide equal access to opportunity, not to ensure that resources are distributed more equally. This belief dovetails with the New Democrats' view that the relationship between citizen and state should be one of reciprocal obligation. Simply put, they argue that citizens do not have unconditional rights to certain government benefits. Rather, the provision of many government services is contingent on a reciprocal responsibility on the part of the citizen, either to take the initiative to capitalize on them or to use them to serve society. In this, it can be said that the New Democrats are almost communitarian, placing social responsibilities ahead of individual rights, an inverse of the priorities of New Politics liberalism. To these values—which the DLC and Clinton summarize as "opportunity, responsibility, and community"—the New Democrats add internationalism. Like their neoconservative and southern Democrat forefathers, they ardently support free trade, oppose deep cuts in the military, and believe that the United States should actively promote democracy and market economics throughout the world.

Finally, from the New Democratic public philosophy comes an implicit political strategy. The New Democrats reject the interest-group foundation of postwar liberalism. They do not want to cobble together the demands of particular interests in order to "reach down" to secure the further allegiance of its current base, a base that appears insufficient for electoral victory. Instead, they want to use their public philosophy as a platform from which to "reach out" to constituencies that were once reliably Democratic, as well as to groups—such as the middle class, suburbanites, and "wired workers"—that they believe are key to future electoral victories.

Presently, we cannot know whether the New Democrats will ultimately succeed in replacing the liberal public philosophy as the dominant set of beliefs of the Democratic Party. Putting this uncertainty aside, what has and has not worked for the DLC? Although the ending of the story remains to be written, the rise of the New Democrats and of the DLC already provides us with tentative answers. A group of reformers first needs an institutional base, preferably outside the aegis of the national party. Unlike other groups that opposed the dominant liberal faction, notably the neoliberals and southern Democrats, the New Democrats were organized into a distinct institution. Initially, they were based in the Committee on Party Effectiveness within the House Democratic Caucus, and then briefly in the National House Democratic Caucus, again based in Congress. Yet being part of the House Democratic Caucus and tied to the political standing of its chairman, Gillis Long, these groups were neither sufficiently focused nor independent enough to garner wide attention from other political elites, much less to effect broad changes in the party. As part of the caucus, the CPE had to include and attend to a wide array of concerns and political outlooks, thus muting the distinctiveness and development of its positions.

Consequently, the New Democrats established the DLC outside the party organization. Interestingly, the reaction of the national party leadership to this move underscores the necessity not only of having an institutional base but also of having one outside of party control. A chairman of an American political party has an overriding need to keep the various factions in his coalition unified. His dominant instinct, then, is to co-opt, not to confront, dissenting elements. So although the DLC was formed outside of the party structure, it did not mean that the organization was free of its constraints. The DNC deliberately tried to placate the DLC in order to defuse its challenge.

At the same time, the dominant liberal faction aided in this effort by aggressively condemning the New Democrats as conservative, racist, and sexist. To this group, the New Democratic alternative was not fit even to enter the debate about the future of the party, much less win it. Faced with this potentially fatal criticism, the DLC embarked on a "big-tent" strategy to blunt these criticisms, a tack that also blunted its own efficacy. Thus, contrary to those who bemoan the weakness of American political parties, it appears that they are fairly resilient. Even extraparty organizations can be constrained and coopted by the party itself. However, if the crisis that warranted the formation of the extraparty organization in the first place should deepen, it can serve as a powerful force of rejuvenation. . . .

. . . After decades in which the parties have been unrepresentative of the views of their rank and file and of the general electorate and in which more and more Americans have ceased to identify with either party, the resurgence of factions eager to place their parties within the mainstream represents a step toward more responsible parties and a healthier democracy. It is an encouraging development in the ongoing American struggle to cure "the mischiefs of faction." . . .

82

EARL BLACK
MERLE BLACK

From *The Rise of Southern Republicans*

What was once the Solid Democratic South is no longer solid nor Democratic. Sibling political scientists Earl and Merle Black, experts on southern politics, dissect an important change that has been occurring since the 1980s. First with support for Republican President Ronald Reagan in 1980 and 1984 and then for Republican congressional candidates in subsequent elections, southern white voters now back Republican candidates more than Democratic ones. Professors Black find that the source of this "Great White Switch" was due initially to the issue of race and civil rights. Nowadays, the appeal of the Republican party for white southerners lies in its conservative party positions on issues like the scope of the federal government's power, taxes, and family values. African American Democrats and moderate independent southerners still count, of course, and that's why the South today is a competitive, up-for-grabs region at election time—just like the rest of the nation.

REPUBLICANS FROM THE SOUTH have transformed American politics. The collapse of the solid Democratic South and the emergence of southern Republicanism, first in presidential politics and later in elections for Congress, have established a new reality for America: two permanently competitive national political parties. Not since Democrats battled Whigs before the Civil War has there been such a thoroughly nationalized two-party system. The Democratic party has always been a national enterprise, commanding durable strength in both the South and the North. Traditionally, the Republican party's geographic reach was quite different. A broadly based *northern* party, Republicans maintained active wings in the Northeast, Midwest, West, and Border states but secured only a nominal presence in the South. Apart from the short-lived Reconstruction era, for many generations southern Republicanism "scarcely deserve[d] the name of party. It waver[ed] somewhat between an esoteric cult on the order of a lodge and a conspiracy for plunder in accord with the accepted customs of our politics."

When the Republicans recaptured both houses of Congress in 1994 for the first time since 1952, they did not construct their Senate and House majorities in the old-fashioned way. Republican control of Congress traditionally involved a purely sectional strategy in which enormous Republican surpluses in the North trumped huge Republican deficits in the South. The novel feature of the Republicans' 1994 breakthrough was its national character. Republicans won majorities of House and Senate seats in both the North *and* the South, a feat they had not achieved since 1872, and their new southern majorities were vital to the Republicans' national victories. Across the nation Republicans as well as Democrats now realistically believe they have fighting chances to win both the White House and Congress in any particular election. Focusing on elections to both the Senate and the House of Representatives, this book examines the regional causes and national consequences of rising southern Republicanism.

It is easy to forget just how thoroughly the Democratic party once dominated southern congressional elections. In 1950 there were no Republican senators from the South and only 2 Republican representatives out of 105 in the southern House delegation. Nowhere else in the United States had a major political party been so feeble for so many decades. A half-century later Republicans constituted *majorities* of the South's congressional delegations—13 of 22 southern senators and 71 of 125 representatives. This immense partisan conversion is our subject. Just as the emergence of southern Republicanism restored competition to America's presidential politics, so has the rise of Republican senators and representatives from the South revitalized congressional politics.

The old southern politics was transparently undemocratic and thoroughly racist. "Southern political institutions," as V. O. Key Jr. demonstrated, were deliberately constructed to subordinate "the Negro population and, externally, to block threatened interferences from the outside with these local arrangements." By protecting white supremacy, southern Democrats in Congress institutionalized massive racial injustice for generations. Eventually the civil rights movement challenged the South's racial status quo and inspired a national political climate in which southern Democratic senators could no longer kill civil rights legislation. Led by President Lyndon B. Johnson of Texas, overwhelming majorities of northern Democrats and northern Republicans united to enact the Civil Rights Act of 1964 and the Voting Rights Act of 1965. Landmark federal intervention reformed southern race relations and helped destabilize the traditional one-party system. In the fullness of time the Democratic party's supremacy gave way to genuinely competitive two-party politics.

But if the old solid Democratic South has vanished, a comparably solid Republican South has not developed. Nor is one likely to emerge. Republican politicians hold majorities of the region's House and Senate seats, but their majorities are much smaller than those traditionally maintained by southern Democrats. Even more important, neither Republicans nor Democrats enjoy majority status among the southern electorate. In the old southern politics, whites overwhelmingly considered themselves Democrats and voted accordingly. Political battles in the contemporary South feature two competitive minority parties rather than the unmistakable domination of a single party. . . .

Modern competitive two-party politics is grounded in the region's rapidly growing and immensely diverse population. The central political cleavage, as ancient as the South itself, involves race. When the Republican party nominated Arizona Senator Barry Goldwater—one of the few northern senators who had opposed the Civil Rights Act—as their presidential candidate in 1964, the party attracted many racist southern whites but permanently alienated African-American voters. Beginning with the Goldwater-versus-Johnson campaign more southern whites voted Republican than Democratic, a pattern that has recurred in every subsequent presidential election. Two decades later, in the middle of Ronald Reagan's presidency, more southern whites began to call themselves Republicans than Democrats, a development that has also persisted. These two Great White Switches, first in presidential voting and then almost a generation later in partisan identification, laid the foundations for highly competitive two-party politics in the South. Gradually a new southern politics emerged in which blacks and liberal to moderate whites anchored the Democratic party while many conservative and some moderate whites formed a growing Republican party that owed little to Abraham Lincoln but much to Goldwater and even more to Reagan. Elections in the contemporary South ordinarily separate extraordinarily large Democratic majorities of blacks from smaller Republican majorities of whites.

Yet modern southern politics involves more than its obvious racial divisions. The South, an increasingly complex society, is the largest region in the United States. More than 84 million people, three of every ten Americans according to the 2000 Census, now reside in the eleven states of the old Confederacy. During the 1990s the region's population grew by 19 percent, much faster than the increase (11 percent) that occurred in the rest of the nation, and its congressional delegation expanded from 125 to 131 seats in the 2002 apportionment. The South's population growth was rooted in the liberating effects of civil rights legislation and the tremendous expansion of the economy. As Dan Balz and Ronald Brownstein have concluded, "The decline of the agrarian South and the rise of a modern economy grounded in manufacturing, defense, tourism, services, and technology has been, by anyone's measure, one of the great success stories of the late twentieth century—but in creating a more diversified society, the South's transformation made it difficult for Democrats to speak for the interests of all, as they once claimed to do." Whites and blacks born and raised in the region no longer had to leave in search of better opportunities in the North. Many individuals reared elsewhere in the nation and world—whites, blacks, Hispanics, Asians, and others—now found the South an acceptable, even desirable, place in which to work and retire.

The rise of a middle and upper-middle class has produced millions of voters with substantial incomes subject to substantial federal and state taxation. Many of these upwardly mobile individuals, wanting to keep the lion's share of their earnings, view the Republicans as far more sympathetic than the Democrats to their economic interests and aspirations. Another major fault line divides white southerners who are part of the religious right political movement (strongly pro-Republican) from the much larger group who are not (slightly pro-Republican). And among whites who are not attracted to conservative religious groups, men are strongly pro-Republican while women are more evenly divided in their partisanship. Thus economic class, religion, and gender also structure the social foundations of southern two-party politics. . . .

The unique characteristics of the South's modern House delegation can best be appreciated when set against historical patterns of representation. . . .

White supremacy was the undisguised political theory and standard practice of the racist white Democrats who ended Reconstruction. Violence, intimidation, and extensive ballot-box fraud converted a congressional delegation that was nine-tenths white Republican in 1866 into one that was almost four-fifths white Democratic by 1874. An artificially Democratic electorate replaced an artificially Republican electorate. There was nothing remotely "normal" or "constitutional" about the relentlessly undemocratic and morally corrosive mechanisms that restored white Democrats to their preeminence in the southern House delegation.

Although white Republicans (unlike black Republicans) could never be stamped out completely, the term "Solid South" accurately described the white Democrats' prominence in Congress. As the protracted agrarian upheavals of the late nineteenth century subsided and the remaining black voters were driven out of the political system, the southern delegation settled down to almost perfect white Democratic domination. Having eliminated their racial and partisan opponents from the electorate, racially conservative white Democrats chosen by racially conservative white voters easily monopolized the region's congressional delegation.

The Great Depression and New Deal maintained the lopsided partisan division of the southern House delegation. Outside the South the greatest economic catastrophe of the twentieth century revived the Democratic party and discredited the Republican party in many congressional districts. Because southern Republicans already hovered close to zero, in the South the Great Depression simply gave most whites additional reasons to hate Republicans and powerfully reinforced Democratic supremacy. Before federal intervention into southern race relations, congressional representation in the region amounted to a simple story of sustained white Democratic power.

Most of the white Democrats who served through the mid-1960s defended racial segregation and worked hard to prevent civil rights legislation. Gradually, however, as the older Democratic segregationists departed, they were replaced by younger white Democratic politicians who understood that cultivating biracial coalitions was essential to their survival. Many of the white Republicans who began to win congressional elections positioned themselves as far more conservative on racial issues than their Democratic opponents. Yet with widespread acceptance of the finality of racial change, little remains of the overt racial rhetoric that often characterized the first generation of southern Republican congressmen. By and large, Republican House members from the South emphasize their economic and social conservatism. After federal intervention the gap between white Democrats and white Republicans began to narrow, but as late as 1990 white Democrats still outnumbered white Republicans by better than three to two.

Striking partisan changes in southern representation occurred during the 1990s. In 1991, following the last election based on districts established after the 1980 Census, the South's delegation consisted of 72 white Democrats, 39 white Republicans, and 5 black Democrats. Ten years later, after the creation of many new majority black districts, it included 71 white Republicans, 1 white independent . . . who caucused with the Republicans, 37 white Democrats, and 16 black Democrats. . . .

In the South the Reagan realignment of the 1980s was a momentous achievement. By transforming the region's white electorate, Ronald Reagan's presidency made possible the Republicans' congressional break-through in the 1990s. The secular realignment of southern white voters, chiefly involving conservative men and women, occurred in two distinct stages. Greater white support for Republican *presidential candidates* commenced in 1964, but the more fundamental Republican advantage in *partisan identification* emerged two decades later. The extended lag between the presidential and partisan realignments allowed Democrats to dominate southern elections to Congress long after federal intervention had ended racial segregation and started to destabilize the one-party system.

The Great White Switch in presidential voting appeared immediately after Congress passed and Democratic president Lyndon Johnson signed the 1964 Civil Rights Act. Republican Barry Goldwater easily defeated Johnson among white southerners. Since 1964 more whites have voted Republican than Democratic in every single presidential election. Similar changes in southern party affiliation, however, did not immediately accompany the white switch in presidential voting. Partisan realignments require political leaders whose performance in office expands the party's base of reliable supporters. Not until Reagan's presidency did more southern whites begin to think of themselves as Republicans than as Democrats. Reagan was the first Republican presidential candidate to poll back-to-back landslide majorities from white southerners; and his vice president, George Bush, captured the presidency in 1988 by running on the strategy that Reagan had mastered: attracting substantial majorities from conservative and moderate whites, while implicitly conceding the votes of blacks and liberal whites.

Important as his electoral victories were, Reagan's presidency had a far more crucial impact upon many southern whites. His optimistic conservatism and successful performance in office made the Republican party respectable and useful for millions of southern whites. Many of them, for the first time in their lives, began to think of themselves as Republicans. The Great White Switch in partisan identification created a much more competitive playing field for two-party politics, one that ultimately encouraged, expanded, and intensified Republican campaign activity for Senate and House seats.

The Republican approach to top-down party building in the South was modeled upon its successful strategy in presidential elections: realign white conservatives as a reliable source of Republican support and neutralize white moderates as a consistent foundation of Democratic strength. Reagan attracted a majority of white conservatives into the Republican party and persuaded many other conservatives to think of themselves as "independents" rather than as Democrats. The Republican president had a different impact on southern white moderates. He eroded their traditional attachment to the Democratic party and increased their Republican ties, thereby neutralizing a huge, longstanding Democratic advantage among this critically important segment of the southern electorate.

By *realigning* white conservatives and *dealigning* white moderates, Reagan produced a *partial* realignment of the southern white electorate. . . .

"The situation was ripe for the culmination of the Republican southern strategy," emphasized [Numan] Bartley. The California Republican turned out to be the most popular president among southern whites since Franklin Roosevelt. Utilizing "anecdote over analysis," acting from "ideological principles when possible" but willing to "compromise when necessary," as Charles W. Dunn and J. David Woodward characterized his style, Reagan appealed to the emotions, aspirations, and interests of the region's conservative and moderate white voters. According to journalist Lou Cannon, who had covered Reagan's entire political career, "the ideological core of Reaganism" encompassed three priorities: "lower tax rates, a stronger military force and reduced government spending." These objectives resonated powerfully among conservative and moderate whites in the South. Deliberately avoiding any explanation of how his priorities might be simultaneously achieved, Reagan instead promoted "values that have a base in the collective subconscious of every American," according to Dunn and Woodward. Reagan "promised a new era of national renewal emphasizing traditional values—the dignity of work, love for family and neighborhood, faith in God, belief in peace through strength and a commitment to protect freedom as a legacy unique to America."

In 1980 the Democratic and Republican parties also differed in many important respects over the proper role of the federal government. "The Democratic party platform favored affirmative action, federally funded abortions, and busing, and it endorsed the Equal Rights Amendment to the point of denying party support to candidates who opposed the amendment and encouraging boycotts of states that refused to ratify it," Bartley noted, whereas "Reagan's Republican platform disavowed busing and abortion, ignored the Equal Rights Amendment, demanded prayer be allowed in the schools, and advocated family values." Throughout the campaign he emphasized "a visceral hatred of burgeoning federalism," of the ever-growing presence of federal laws, rules, and regulations in domestic affairs. "I would take the lead in getting the government off the *backs* of the people of the United States and turning you loose," promised Reagan. As a former Democrat who had switched to the Republican party late in his life, Reagan knew how to appeal to a southern white electorate that contained many born-and-bred Democrats. "Now I know what it's like to pull that Republican lever for the first time because I used to be a Democrat myself," Reagan would say. "But I can tell you—it only hurts for a minute." . . .

Rising congressional Republicanism in the oldest regional stronghold of the Democratic party has reshaped the Republicans into a truly national party for the first time since Reconstruction. Not since Whigs fought Democrats in the 1830s and 1840s has American politics been based on a thoroughly nationalized two-party system. Because leaders in both parties can easily see ways to win or lose their House and Senate majorities, the national stakes of each election cycle are permanently high. A retirement here, an unexpected death there, to say nothing about short-term political trends helping one party or the other—all these factors contribute to the seesaw nature of the modern party battle. In its unmitigated ferocity contemporary congressional partisanship reflects the new reality that the results of national elections are no longer foregone Democratic victories or assured Republican triumphs.

Thus the South's political transformation holds extraordinary consequences for America. Old-fashioned sectional conflict has dissipated, but sectional considerations continue to pervade national politics through the conservative agenda pursued by Republican congressional leaders from the South. As it has been in presidential politics for some time, the South is now at the epicenter of Republican and Democratic strategies to control Congress. In order to comprehend national political dynamics, it is therefore more important than ever to understand the changing South.

83

JESSE VENTURA

From *I Ain't Got Time to Bleed*

One of the biggest upsets of the 1998 elections was Reform Party candidate Jesse Ventura's victory over two accomplished politicians for the governorship of Minnesota. As he is fond of saying to his wrestling fans, radio listeners, film watchers, and anyone else who will listen, "I didn't need this job." Ventura, clearly no career politician, was able to beat his Democratic and Republican opponents by appealing particularly to two subsets of voters: first, those who were fed up with the usual brand of politics, and second, those who were new voters and who had not yet been activated. Ventura promised to give all citizens a voice and to do so honestly and forthrightly. Apparently, Ventura did not need the governor's job, since he announced his decision not to run again.

———————

I DIDN'T NEED THIS JOB. I ran for governor to find out if the American dream still exists in anyone's heart other than mine. I'm happy to say that it does. I'm living proof that the myths aren't true. The candidate with the most money isn't always the one who wins. You don't have to be a career politician to serve in public office. You don't have to be well connected or propped up by special-interest groups. You don't even have to be a Democrat or a Republican. You can stand on your own two feet and speak your mind, because if people like where you're coming from, they will vote you in. The will of the people is still the most powerful force in our government. We can put whomever we choose into office, simply by exercising that will.

We're a nation of bootstrappers. We're visionaries. And we're not afraid to turn our visions into reality. That's the great thing about Americans—the word *can't* isn't part of our vocabulary. We've always been a can-do people. And we still are, despite all the negative things we hear about how corrupt our government has become, and despite the fact that we've become too reliant on that same government for things it has no business providing. We might have lost sight of it a little bit, but we are still the keepers of the American dream.

How else could a guy like me have become the governor of Minnesota? Look at me: I'm no career politician—I'm a six-foot-four, 250-pound ex–Navy SEAL, pro wrestler, radio personality, and film actor. I only got into politics in the first place because I have a pretty noticeable habit of speaking my mind. But I guess a good bit of what I had to say must have made sense to people, because they elected me twice.

This book is mostly about me, about where I stand, and about where I came from. But what's happening in Minnesota right now is far bigger than me. History is being made. Like many other people across the nation, Minnesotans are fed up with the good-old-boy network that cares more about keeping itself well ensconced than it does about carrying out the voters' wishes. In 1998's gubernatorial race, I gave them an alternative.

I'm a Minneapolis native with working-class roots. My collar's indelibly blue. I belong to the private sector, and that's where I'm returning the minute my term as governor is over. I stand for the common man because I am him. That's one reason the people of Minnesota elected me: I know where they're coming from because I came from the same place.

They also voted for me, I think, because I'm not easy to ignore. I'm big, I'm loud, and I'm not afraid to say what I think. But I also got a powerful set of ethics from my parents, some serious hard-core discipline from the Navy SEALs, and some decent people skills from my careers as a professional wrestler, film actor, and radio personality. And I can talk to people without talking down to them.

But if I had to pick one reason Minnesotans voted for me, I would have to say that it is because I tell the truth. I stand tall and speak freely, even when it isn't politically expedient to do so. That, above all, is what I think Minnesotans voted for: honesty.

This book has two purposes: first, to tell you where I stand—and why—on the issues that affect us all. Anybody who offers themselves for public office owes you that; and second, to tell you the story of what made me who I am. I'm an ordinary guy who went for his dreams and made them happen. The only things I've ever been handed are extraordinary guidance and lifelong friendship, without which I could never have achieved all that I have. But I'm no golden child. I've had basically the same opportunities as most of you. And if a guy like me can become the governor, so could you. That's the way American government is supposed to work.

Unfortunately, there's an idea out there that's very destructive to the American electoral system. It's the idea that you have to cast your vote for whoever's most likely to win, because otherwise you're wasting your vote. That is simply not true. There is no such thing as a wasted vote.

Voting is not supposed to be just a popularity contest. It's not like betting on a horse race. It's our responsibility when we vote to vote for the ideas we would like to see become public policy. We have to choose our candidates by the things they stand for, not by their ratings in the polls. When we bow to the pressure of the polls, we get exactly the phenomenon we're complaining about now: career politicians who will say anything to get your vote and who don't stand for anything except what the latest poll tells them to support. Yet somehow, that's become the standard. But it doesn't have to be that way.

I understand why so many people don't vote anymore, and I sympathize with them. It can seem like a waste of time when the only candidates you see in the news are cookie-cutter copies of the ones you saw in the last election and the election before that. But these days you have to look beyond what the media tells you to think and make up your own mind about the issues. Your choices aren't limited to the party favorites who have the money and the influence to get themselves into the limelight. You can vote for anybody you want. My stand on voting is that if you don't cast your vote, you forfeit your right to whine about the government.

When I announced that I was running for governor, everybody said I couldn't win. They said my campaign was an exercise in futility. The media thought I was a joke. My opponents pretended I didn't exist. But on November 3, 1998, the people of Minnesota came out in droves and made it happen. This election had the largest voter turnout (in years without a presidential election) in Minnesota's history and almost the largest in the country's history. We shocked the world. We wasted the system with "wasted" votes.

My Democratic opponent, Attorney General Hubert H. "Skip" Humphrey III, called our victory a "wake-up call of the first order." Even my Republican opponent, Saint Paul Mayor Norm Coleman, said that we ignited a spark, even though he said he didn't have any idea what that spark was. They knew I was popular, but neither of them had any idea how I won.

How did I do it? With a secret weapon that the other two candidates didn't have: The people who put me in office were overwhelmingly people who had never participated in the system before, and a huge number of these new voters were college-age people.

The bottom line is that my opponents were boring. They were the same old brand of career politicians, the kind that comes out of the woodwork every four years, spouts the same old rhetoric about the same issues, and then disappears. People don't bother to come to the polls anymore because they don't see the point. The candidates are virtually indistinguishable from each other. Minnesotans might not have been quite sure what they were getting when they voted for me, but one thing they knew for sure: It wouldn't be business as usual!

There's a brand-new generation in Minnesota that has just come into the electoral system. They saw this election as an opportunity to be heard. They've infused Minnesota politics with new blood. And as long as we do what we have to do to keep this new generation involved, we're going to turn this system around.

My victory is important for another reason. I'm the first member of the Reform Party to win a statewide office. There's been talk recently that the Reform Party has had it. People have been saying that we're going to go the way of most other third parties: We'll show up and bark just loud enough to get the two traditional parties back in line a little, then we'll quietly disappear. But our government needs more than just a face-lift—it needs a major overhaul. The Reform Party's work is far from over. In fact, it's barely begun.

We have to build this party from the bottom up. It must be a grassroots organization, or else it's meaningless. And if you look at it that way, then no election is insignificant. No win for the party is too small. A government that is truly by the people has to be grassroots at its foundation. It has to come from the bottom up.

Think of the alternative. If the party's controlled from the top, then whose hands is it in? Career politicians. The comfortably ensconced people who are many levels removed from the working people of this country. The fact that our nation's government is controlled by people like that is at the heart of every complaint I hear about our government today.

Standard operating procedure in our political system today is that everyone's owned, either by one of the two parties or by special-interest groups. Career politicians are bought and sold. And that's how I'm different: No one owns me. I come with no strings attached. All the lobbyists in Minnesota are running scared right now because suddenly the rules of the game have changed. They have no leverage with me. They have no in.

One of the first things I did during the transition period between the election and the inauguration was to bring in thirteen citizens from across the state. These were people who were either first-time voters or who hadn't voted in five consecutive elections. I asked each of them a question: Now that you've come into the system, how do we keep you involved?

Their answers were very clear, very honest. They said, It's the same story every four years. Whenever an election's coming up, all the politicians come out and give you the same song and dance about the same issues, all the way up until they get elected. Then you don't hear any more from them until it's time for them to get elected again. We're tired of it. If you want to keep us involved, don't tell us what you think we want to hear, tell us the truth. . . .

I decided to run for governor because I got mad. In 1997, the State of Minnesota had a budget surplus of more than four billion dollars. The voters wanted that surplus returned to them because, in their opinion, they'd been overcharged. But Minnesota legislators chose to ignore the wishes of the people and instead dreamed up all kinds of pork-barrel projects to make themselves look good when reelection time came. Some of that surplus money was bonded to pay for high-profile projects that the people didn't want. As a result, our children are going to have to assume the payments on the out-of-date convention centers and sports facilities these politicians built to help themselves get reelected. Is that how we show our children we care for them? Is that the kind of public servants the voters really want?

I also saw that a lot of people had no voice in decisions affecting their taxes. For example, there's a group called the Metropolitan Council that can levy taxes in a seven-county area that makes up the Twin Cities, even though the council seats aren't filled by elections. Nowhere else in the state is there this extra layer of government. Another example is people who own lakeshore property. They are also highly taxed but receive very few municipal services and have no say in policy matters. In my book, these are both cases of taxation without representation.

I want to make government more directly accountable to the people. If I'd run for governor and lost because no one was interested in or cared about what I want to do, that would have been fine with me. It's their choice. But I wasn't going to be weeded out because the system said I couldn't win.

My campaign was anything but run-of-the-mill. My opponents were in suits. I was wearing jeans and a Minnesota Timberwolves jacket, and my campaign slogan was "Retaliate in '98." Since so many people were convinced I didn't have a chance, early on in the race the thought of voting for me was considered pointless but fun. Garrison Keillor even said voting for me was like throwing toilet paper in the trees to piss off Dad. I became the candidate of choice for the rebellious. But I went out and made myself available to people. I listened. And I learned.

Unlike my opponents, not a penny of my campaign money came from special-interest groups. Instead, my supporters relied on Minnesota's Political Campaign Refund program, which allowed them to donate fifty dollars each to my campaign, and then get a fifty-dollar refund from the state after the election. I spent $600,000 on my campaign; my opponents together spent close to $13 million.

I knew that in order for the campaign to work, everyone in the state needed to know that Jesse Ventura was a candidate for governor. Many people are not on the Internet. Many people don't read newspapers. But nearly everyone watches TV, so that's where I focused my campaign. I got on TV and promised the people that there would be no big-money power brokers behind the scenes, yanking their governor's chain. I promised I'd be there to serve the people, not the special interests. And I promised to be honest with them.

A lot of people laughed at the idea of this big, beefy feather-boa-wearing ex–pro wrestler and film actor as the head of state. OK, so maybe it's funny. But there are precedents. Other entertainers have successfully gone into politics: Ronald Reagan. Senator Fred Thompson. Clint Eastwood. Sonny Bono. Even Gopher from *The Love Boat*, Fred Grandy. I'll let you in on a secret about being an entertainer: It's all about communicating, about being able to see things from a bunch of different perspectives. There's a lot about entertainment that translates directly to the kind of public relations that you have to do in politics. When you're serving in a public office, you have to be able to communicate extremely well. It didn't bother me all that much that people laughed. To tell the truth, it bothered me more when they stopped laughing after the election.

It's strange how before this victory, nobody took me seriously. Now, suddenly, everyone's lost their sense of humor. Yes, I now have a heavy responsibility, which I take very seriously. But I'm still the same person I always was. It reminds me of Voltaire's quote about God being "a comedian playing before an audience that can't laugh." That applies to me, too—not to put myself on God's level, but people take me as far more serious than I am. I don't know where our sense of humor has gone in this country. I'm finding out that when I talk to the media, a lot of the time I have to throw up my hands and say, "That's a JOKE!"

Politics is not my life. I have a career in radio and another career in film. I have a wife who is the sweetest person in the world and two kids who are growing up into terrific, well-rounded people. I don't need or want to spend the rest of my life in politics. When I'm finished with my term as governor, I'm going back to the life that's waiting for me in the private sector. For one thing, it pays better. And for another, none of the other careers I've had in my life has kept me trapped in my own home and under surveillance twenty-four hours a day. I'm accustomed to answering only to myself and my family. Now I have to answer to the entire state of Minnesota. But I'm taking on this responsibility, willingly and voluntarily, because I have a vision for how to make things better. And as a citizen of the greatest democracy in the world, I have a duty to do my small part.

This is all new to me, and I feel a little like the Rodney Dangerfield character in *Back to School*. But I'll adapt. I'll do what needs to be done. The responsibility doesn't scare me. I've been through SEAL training. I've faced death and lived to tell about it. Nothing that happens in the next four years can possibly be as tough as that.

You can rest assured that I have plans for the next four years. I'm here to affect policy as much as I can. But no matter how the next four years go, I've challenged the status quo and won. I've restored people's confidence in our political system. I've awakened their hope. My victory is part of a much bigger picture. It's a wake-up call. It's the beginning of a political revolution.

PART FOURTEEN

The Media

84

HARRISON SALISBURY

From *A Time of Change*

Veteran reporter Harrison Salisbury looks back on several pivotal events in American politics, as he remembers his years as a New York Times *correspondent. First, we read about the assassination of President Kennedy through the eyes of the paper's national editor. Then, Salisbury recalls the violence and turmoil of the 1968 Democratic Convention in Chicago, as Mayor Daley's police attacked anti-war protesters in the streets. Salisbury's long tenure with the* Times *qualifies him to critique that great paper's coverage of those events: "The gap between hot reality in Chicago and the cool of the air-conditioned offices in New York was wide as an ocean."*

I HAVE SPENT most of my life on the front lines of reporting, and it has often been a stormy passage. I was thrown out of the University of Minnesota as editor of the college daily for my uppity campaigns against the administration. I nearly lost my first journeyman's job for my reports on the Great Depression in my hometown of Minneapolis. Stalin and Molotov threatened to expel me from Russia in World War II. Some editors of the *New York Times* wanted to fire me for my reports from Moscow; Moscow banned me from Russia for the same reports. Birmingham entered millions of dollars in libel suits because I warned that the city was going to blow up in race violence—which it did. Lyndon Johnson and the Pentagon exploded when I went behind the enemy lines to Hanoi during Vietnam.

So it has been, and that is the way it should be. If a reporter is not a "disturber of the peace," he should go into cost accounting. I said at the time of Hanoi that, if I was getting nothing but bouquets, I must be missing part of the story—the vital part. . . .

I got to know Jack Kennedy in the Presidential campaign of 1960. I covered both Kennedy and Nixon in that year, and I was not wild about either. I often spoke of Kennedy as a "lace curtain Nixon," by which I meant I did not think there was much difference, if any, in their ideology. That was not true, but there was, I think, a nubbin of truth in my remark. Nixon was shabby in character but had a better grasp of the world. He had seen more of it and thought more. Kennedy had style; there were not many reporters he didn't charm, but he was lazy. I think that had he not been martyred, his Presidential rating would be much lower. Most newsmen thought Kennedy loved them. That was not true. I have observed every President since Calvin Coolidge. None of them loved the press. FDR, Kennedy, and Reagan were the best at conning the reporters, Hoover and Carter the worst. One of Harry Truman's most amiable traits was his honest dislike of reporters. He put up with the marriage of his beloved Margaret to Clifton Daniel, but it was a bitter pill that Clifton was a newspaperman.

Jack Kennedy gave me a lift one evening from West Virginia, where he was campaigning against Hubert Humphrey. He was on his way to Washington. The plane was a puddle-jumper, and only the two of us were aboard. He spent the brief ride cursing "those sons-a-bitches," the newspaper men. He had a big envelope of clips which he pawed through and tossed away. Most of them seemed to be pieces about his father Joseph, and most of them, Jack felt, went out of their way to dig up the old Joe Kennedy scandals—his borderline bank manipulations, his speculative deals in Wall Street, the maneuvers that got him the Scotch whiskey franchises and the great Chicago Merchandise Mart (where in prohibition days, the building almost empty, a huge speakeasy with a 100-foot bar was the liveliest activity under its roof—I often ate my lunch there), and his role as spokesman for America First* and appeasement before FDR yanked him out of London as the U.S. ambassador. "Bastards," gritted Kennedy as he leafed through the reports. "Just a bunch of lies. They never tell the truth. Bunch of bastards." I didn't talk up the case for newspapering. It was his father, and he was a true member of the clan—the Kennedys against the world and, in this case, against the newsmen. But I had been given an insight into the true Kennedy feeling about the press. One thing was certain about the Kennedys. You were with them or against them. Totally. The press was on the other side.

I don't want to suggest that Nixon had any more love for the press. I think the feeling of the two men was mutual in this regard. But Kennedy could put on a bravado act, make a half dozen important Washington correspondents believe they were real friends (inside the clan). Nixon was a poor actor. His lies stuck out like cold sores. He was forever wrapping his anger at the press in a sleazy tangle of "I know what your problems are," or "Of course you have your job to do," "I don't mean to include you personally," and then out would come the hurt and anger. I guess

---

*America First was a prominent "isolationist" organization in the 1930s. The group opposed American involvement in European affairs, especially our taking sides against Hitler's Germany and its expansionist policies.—EDS.

you could say that, in his way, Nixon was the more honest man. Jack rarely let his distaste show in public. . . .

By the time Jack Kennedy was shot to death in Dallas at 12:30 P.M. of November 22, 1963, a lot had changed for me. Reluctantly I had bowed to Turner Catledge's insistence and taken on the post of national editor of the *New York Times*. (Catledge coined the title "Director of National Correspondence" so as not to hurt the feelings of Ray O'Neill, who held the title "National Editor.")

Catledge's proposal had reached me in Kabul, Afghanistan, where I was trying to persuade the authorities to let me go through the Khyber Pass. A small war was in progress. I never did get to the Khyber, going to Tashkent, Bokhara, and Mongolia instead. I had to accept Catledge's proposal—much as I preferred reporting. He had twice tried to make me an editor, and I knew I couldn't say no a third time. But I did get his pledge that once or twice a year I could abandon my desk and go off on a reporting trip. The promise was meticulously kept by Catledge and Punch Sulzberger, even after I set up the Op-Ed page and became an associate editor of the *Times*.

I had concluded before going to work for the *Times* in 1949 that the essence of journalism was reporting and writing. I wanted to find things out—particularly things which no one else had managed to dig out—and let people have the best possible evidence on which to make up their minds about policy. It was essentially a gloss on the old Scripps slogan: "Give Light and the People Will Find Their Way." I have never ceased to believe in it.

One day in November 1963 I was sitting at the long table in the third floor dining room of the Century Club, waiting for my lunch.

At that moment, just on one o'clock, the waiter having brought my purée mongole, Alfred De Liagre, the theatrical producer, elegant as always in English tweeds, rounded into the room, raised his voice over the cheerful hum of Century conversation, and said, a bit theatrically: "Gentlemen, I am sorry to interrupt, but the President has just been shot in the head . . . in Dallas." I dropped my napkin, leaped down the stairs, and ran the two and a half blocks west on 43rd Street to 229, up on the elevator, and to my national news desk just south of my old spot, the Hagerty desk which I had occupied for nine years. There I would remain almost continuously for the next several days.

I was used to violence in the South, violence in the country as a whole. It seemed to me that I had inhabited a violent world since I had come back from the deceptive quiet of the Moscow streets—violence in the slums of Brooklyn and Manhattan, a nationwide uprooting of populations, technological revolution in the farm belt, the bondage of the great cities in straitjackets of steel and concrete freeways, and now rising terror in the South.

Dallas . . . Kennedy . . . violence . . . it seemed an almost inevitable pattern, and my mind leaped instantly to the passion in Dallas that had raged since before Kennedy's election. Dallas had seemed like another country, ranting against *everything*. I knew of the threats and the hate ads that spewed out before the Kennedy visit. I had hardly gotten on the telephone to order staff to Dallas—everyone I could reach who could fly in by nightfall—than my mind spun with thoughts of a conspiracy by the radical right or even—I hardly dared formulate the thought—by some in the die-hard LBJ camp who so hated the Kennedys. What it might be I did not know. But plots, conspiracy, coups raced through my head. From the vicious anti-Kennedy propaganda, there seemed to me but one short step to a conspiracy to assassinate the President. . . .

. . . On November 27, 1963, five days after Kennedy was killed, the first moment I had time and strength to put down what I felt, I wrote a memorandum to myself. I said that in the year 2000 the Kennedy assassination would still be a matter of debate, new theories being evolved how and why it happened. The lone, crazed killer would not then—or ever—be accepted. It offended nature. For the Sun King to be struck down by a vagrant with bulging eyes—no, the concept was repugnant to our very being. For a man so noble the cause of death must lie in high conspiracy, the most powerful courtiers, the great barons, the captains of the earth. . . .

It was no surprise to me that the Warren Commission report did not halt the "revelations," the rumors, the legend making of the conspiracy theorists, now grown to a kind of carrion industry.

I did not think the Warren Commission had dug out any essential fact that the *Times* had not found in its intense coverage in the days and weeks after the assassination. The coverage had begun with classic reportage—Tom Wicker's on-the-scenes eyewitness. It could not be beat. Tom was the only *Times* man in Dallas that day. I made one contribution to Tom's beautiful story. At 5 P.M. I ordered him—no, *command* is the word—to halt reporting and start writing. No interruptions. Any new details we could put into the piece, if necessary, after it went into type about 8:30 P.M. that night. Just write every single thing you have seen and heard. Period. He did. No more magnificent piece of journalistic writing has been published in the *Times*. Through Tom's eye we lived through each minute of that fatal Friday, the terror, the pain, the horror, the mindless tragedy, elegant, blood-chilling prose.

To this day not one material fact has been added to the *New York Times* account of the assassination and the events that followed it. . . .

Ever since I arrived at the Union Station from Minneapolis on a frozen January 13, 1931, I have thought of Chicago as *my* city. . . .

Nothing that happens in Chicago really surprises me. But the 1968 Democratic National Convention was an exception. I expected trouble. I expected violence. I expected the nomination of Lyndon Baines Johnson. I was right about trouble and violence. I was wrong—but perhaps not that wrong—about Lyndon.

On the night of August 28, 1968, a Wednesday, I was sitting at my command post in the press section of the convention hall at the Chicago Stockyards. I *knew* there would be violence. It had been building up.

Robert Kennedy had been assassinated in June in Los Angeles. Martin Luther King had been killed in Memphis in [April]. The country was going up in smoke. One afternoon I was running to board an airplane in Newark when I heard a young woman ask the man she was with: "What's all that smoke?" He (and I) looked back. "Oh," he said, "It's just Newark burning down. Let's hurry." From the takeoff I could see Newark's black ghetto burning in the rage of King's murder.

That was my America in the summer of 1968. No way that Chicago, Hog Butcher Chicago, Daley's Chicago, wouldn't explode.

I had arrived on the watch for a Draft Johnson movement. I hadn't believed LBJ was sincere in his March 31 speech.

Mayor Daley didn't seem to take LBJ's "withdrawal" any more seriously than I did. Daley had backed Robert Kennedy until Robert was killed, then switched to LBJ. He prepared a monster birthday party for Lyndon at Soldier Field. It sounded like a campaign kickoff to me. By this time the White House was leaking to every visitor nasty stories about Humphrey. He was a loser. "He cries too much." There was no doubt what the White House was up to. I was not amazed when on an inspection of the Chicago Amphitheater, I stumbled into a storeroom where LBJ placards, banners, and posters were stacked to the ceiling. Everything was set for the convention to rise and sweep LBJ into the nomination.

But nothing in Chicago went according to plan. The antiwar forces— David Dellinger, Tom Hayden, and the Yippies led by Abbie Hoffman— had mustered their supporters by the thousand. Daley mobilized his forces—8,000 police, 5,000 Illinois guardsmen (some 5,000 U.S. regulars were alerted and held in reserve). The convention hall looked like Hitler's last bunker, barbed wire coils everywhere, barricades, checkpoints outside and inside the hall. American politics had never seen such security.

Confrontation quickly became the order of the day. The decibel count went up and up. The higher it rose, the faster prospects for a Johnson coup de theatre faded. The Secret Service would not guarantee his safety. He was confined to his Texas ranch, on the telephone to Daley, but the Blue Helmets washed LBJ out with their street brawls. Daley had to cancel the Soldier Field birthday party. Those tons of LBJ banners never left the stadium bins. . . .

Behind cordons of police and barbed wire the convention hall was an island of quiet. Not so the central convention hotel, the Conrad Hilton, which spanned a long block on Michigan Avenue. The police beat and hounded young people from Lincoln Park down to Grant Park opposite the Hilton.

Tony Lukas, just back from the Congo wars, was handling the street story. He knew the protesters, the gentle pacifists, the wild radicals, the eccentric Yippies. He knew them all.

On Tuesday evening Wallace Turner, the best of the *Times's* investigative reporters, was walking back to his hotel. He spotted three or four squad cars blocking a street. In a courtyard he saw a huddle of police and heard a patrolman say: "Sergeant, can I have me a hippie to beat the shit out of?"

The next evening it started.

Tom Wicker was standing at the big window of the *Times* news room on the twenty-first story of the Conrad Hilton, looking down on Michigan Avenue, when he saw the police charge past the National Guardsmen into Grant Park. Several hundred youngsters sat there singing; "God Bless America." The Daley men burst among them, beating, kicking, and dragging them by the feet to paddy wagons. "These are our children!" Wicker exclaimed. Next day he wrote a column headed: "These were our children, and the police were beating them." His colleague Ned Kenworthy rushed for the elevator, down to the street, two blocks up Michigan and over into the park. "Get out! Get Out!" he shouted to the young people. "The police are coming. You're doing no good to your cause." (They were mostly Gene McCarthy supporters.)

Times reporter John Kifner was with the young people marching down Michigan. He watched police charge, clubs and blackjacks swinging. He watched them drive young and old back against the Hilton and through the plate-glass window, shards splintering, police tumbling into the dark, air-conditioned, panel-lined bar, beating and slugging everyone in their path.

Kifner raced to a telephone. He got Charlotte Curtis on the line. She was filling in for Sylvan Fox, a deskman who had suffered a heart attack and been sent to the hospital by ambulance. Charlotte Curtis listened a moment to Kif and then handed the telephone to Lukas. "You better take this yourself."

At the stockyards I was going crazy. A *Times* photographer had been beaten and dragged off—no one knew where—by the police. I was on the phone to the hospital, to the police, to Lukas' post at Tribune Tower, to our main news room in the Hilton and, most of all, to New York, trying to convey to the editors that the story had shifted away from the convention hall, where the slow nominating process was underway, onto the Chicago streets. It wasn't politics this night; it was a riot. The editors found it hard to grasp.

Kifner was trying to get Lukas to understand. "I've just witnessed something unbelievable," Kifner told him. "The police have charged on a lot of innocent people and driven them through the glass window in the Hilton cocktail lounge, following them in and are beating them."

"Come on, John," said Tony. "Don't get carried away. Don't give me that stuff. I don't believe it."

"I saw it with my own eyes," Kifner insisted.

"You saw them inside, beating people up?"

"I did."

So Lukas wrote it. He knew Kifner was an experienced reporter. If Kifner saw it, it happened.

Kenworthy was writing what he saw, too, the young people singing, police charges, bystanders' reactions, 1,500 or 2,000 words. But trouble arose in New York. I got on the phone again and again, telling the responsible editors, Abe Rosenthal and night editor Ted Bernstein, that Chicago had gone into orbit. They didn't believe me. They thought the reporters had gone out of control. I told the editors to look at TV. The TV cameras were beginning to focus on the streets. Finally most of Lukas' story was published, but only a couple of paragraphs of Kenworthy. "We don't want to influence the convention balloting" was the excuse.

I knew it was hard for anyone to get the feel of Chicago that night, anyone who did not smell the teargas and vomit in the Hilton halls, who did not hear the crack of walnut sticks on skulls, who did not see the blood-stained carpets, who did not witness the police frog-walking people out of the hotel and into patrol wagons, flailing unfortunate youngsters, male or female, who appeared on the scene; you had to see the face of Mayor Daley, sitting in the front row of the Convention, mouthing "you son of a bitch" as Senator Abraham Ribicoff of Connecticut tried to remonstrate from the podium against the hatred loosed on Chicago that night by Daley and his men.

The gap between hot reality in Chicago and the cool of the air conditioned offices in New York was wide as an ocean. A news analysis that Lukas wrote of the "blundering" of Daley and the "brutality of his blue-helmeted police" said Daley and his police had turned certain defeat for the young radicals into a startling victory. This language was too blunt for New York. "Blundering" became "miscalculation" and "Brutality" became "over-reaction."

Nowhere in the *Times* the next morning was the true tragedy of Chicago delineated, the hideous blow to American democracy inflicted by Daley's truculence and the abandon of the young; the tawdry tainting of the nomination so grudgingly released by LBJ to hapless Hubert Horatio Humphrey. Nor did we catch the melodrama of LBJ's last hurrah, setting the stage for the triumph of Richard Nixon. I left Chicago convinced that LBJ was a "mean man." And I felt that I and my *New York Times* had fallen far short of our capability to present to the country a sharp-edge, unshadowed picture of Chicago. . . .

The *New York Times* electrified the nation in 1871 when it exposed the financial crimes of Tammany and the Tweed ring. It dozed through the Koch* years, even sending its outraged and brutally honest columnist, Sydney Schanberg, to the showers. The press drowsed along with the government and its opulent contractors until *Challenger* blew up. Nearly twenty years ago Emma Rothschild in *The New Yorker* forecast the demise of Detroit. It took David Halberstam's book to detail the sordid story not of Japanese skill but of American sloth. The press slept.

I could go on and on. The world of electronic journalism, once sparkling with men like Edward R. Murrow and Walter Cronkite, slipped into the gray wasteland, with bottom-line barons taking it over, men whose testicles seemed to have been replaced by puffballs. . . . The press yawns. Candidate after candidate rolls out of the electronic image processors. Nobody hires Sy Hersh to see what skeletons lurk behind their gussified hairdos. I mean real scandals, not Gary Hart trifles.

And no one complains of all this. Not the public, not Congress, not the White House—heavens, no, not the White House. Not opposition parties. Not the princes of the press—with a few honorable exceptions:

---

*Edward Koch was the mayor of New York City from 1979 through 1989.—Eds.

the *New York Times*, the *Washington Post*, the *Boston Globe*, the *Los Angeles Times*. The others are too busy with their accountants and tax lawyers. We sleep. Oh, a few eccentrics raise a paranoid cry of Conspiracy. But nothing breaks the somnolence. We are, it seems, as Lincoln Steffens found Philadelphia, corrupt and content. . . .

There is no story—literally none—which the great electronic news media and the billion-dollar press aggregates cannot extract, be it from the Kremlin or the Pentagon, and bring to the public of America. Instead, they tinker with sitcoms and fourcolor ad pages. Priorities? Forget it.

85

KATHARINE GRAHAM

From *Personal History*

The Watergate story has been told from many sides: the Watergate burglars, President Nixon's aides, reporters Bob Woodward and Carl Bernstein, to name only a few who have added to the scandal's record. In this excerpt from her acclaimed book recounting a life filled with both joy and tragedy, Katharine Graham adds an indispensable account to the Watergate legacy. Graham was the owner and publisher of the Washington Post, *and thereby gave Woodward and Bernstein the backing they needed to pursue the Watergate story. She describes the requirement that "two sources" be used to confirm each facet of the story as it unfolded. She relates the pressure put on the* Post *as Watergate-related issues moved into the court system. The revelation of White House tapes, Graham feels, was the key to the whole story coming to light. Interestingly, Graham was never let in on nor ever requested to be let in on the hidden identity of Deep Throat, Woodward's and Bernstein's inside source. Graham died just a few years after her memoir was published.*

ON SATURDAY MORNING, June 17, 1972, Howard Simons called to say, "You won't believe what happened last night." He was right. I barely believed him, and listened with equal amounts of amusement and interest as he told me of a car that crashed into a house where two people had been making love on a sofa and went right out the other side.

To top that, he related the fantastic story that five men wearing surgical gloves had been caught breaking into the headquarters of the Democratic National Committee.

President Nixon was in Key Biscayne, Florida, at the time. His press secretary, Ron Ziegler, dismissed the incident as "a third-rate burglary attempt," adding, "Certain elements may try to stretch this beyond what it is." None of us, of course, had any idea how far the story would stretch; the beginning—once the laughter died down—all seemed so farcical. . . .

The story of the break-in appeared on the front page of Sunday's paper, "5 Held in Plot to Bug Democrats' Office Here," with [veteran *Post* police reporter Al] Lewis's byline. Contributing to the story were several staff writers, including Bob Woodward and Carl Bernstein, who also did a separate report with background information on the suspects, four of whom, Carl discovered, were from Miami, where they had been involved in anti-Castro activities. Phil Geyelin's editorial appearing the next day in the *Post* was titled "Mission Incredible," and began with a quote from the CBS television show "Mission Impossible": "As always, should you or any of your force be caught or killed, the Secretary will disavow any knowledge of your actions. . . . "

What we were seeing, of course, was the legendary tip of the iceberg. And we might never have known the size of the iceberg had it not been for the extraordinary investigative and reporting efforts of Woodward and Bernstein, famous names now but then two young men who had never worked together, one of whom (Woodward) had not even been long at the paper. In some ways it was a natural pairing, since their qualities and skills complemented each other. Both are bright, but Woodward was conscientious, hardworking, and driven, and Bernstein messy and undisciplined. He was, however, the better writer, more imaginative and creative. In other ways the relationship was oil and water, but the end product came out right, despite—or perhaps because of—the strange mix. . . .

From the beginning, Bob distinguished himself, and there was no question in the editors' minds whom they were going to send to court to cover the break-in. Carl Bernstein, on the other hand, had been at the *Post* since the fall of 1966 but had *not* distinguished himself. He was a good writer, but his poor work-habits were well known throughout the city room even then, as was his famous roving eye. In fact, one thing that stood in the way of Carl's being put on the story was that Ben Bradlee was about to fire him. Carl was notorious for an irresponsible expense account and numerous other delinquencies—including having rented a car and abandoned it in a parking lot, presenting the company with an enormous bill. But Carl, looking over Bob's shoulder while he reworked Al Lewis's notes, immediately got hooked on this strange story and was off and running. It was Harry who saved him when both Ben and Howard wanted to fire him, saying that he was pursuing the Watergate story with verve, working hard, and contributing a great deal. And it was Carl who made the first connection of the crisp new $100 bills in the pockets of the burglars to money raised for the Nixon campaign.

Woodward and Bernstein clearly were the key reporters on the story—so much so that we began to refer to them collectively as Woodstein—but the cast of characters at the *Post* who contributed to the story from its inception was considerable. As executive editor, Ben was the classic leader at whose desk the buck of responsibility stopped. He set the ground rules—pushing, pushing, pushing, not so subtly asking everyone to take one more step, relentlessly pursuing the story in the face of persistent accusations against us and a concerted campaign of intimidation.

Howard Simons, with his semi-independent pocket of authority on the paper, helped move the story along enormously, particularly with his attitude, as Woodward later described it, of "inquisitiveness and 'Let's find out what's going on.'" Harry Rosenfeld said of Howard, "When the kids were running one way or the other, he would—if it was called for—stand up and screw the tide." It was Howard who carried the story in its early days. . . .

From the start, Woodward and Bernstein followed the trail of the Watergate burglars with alacrity and skill, and a lot of elbow grease. From the time Bob went to court and heard James McCord say "CIA," he was hooked on the story. When Carl came up with Howard Hunt's address book, and the two found in it the name "Colson" and the phrase "W. House," they, like Herblock, decided there was a connection to the White House. When it was discovered that numerous calls had been made from the phone of Bernard Barker, one of the burglars, to an office shared by Gordon Liddy and another lawyer at the Committee to Re-elect the President, whose acronym, CRP, quickly turned into the unfortunate CREEP, Woodward and Bernstein were off and running.

On August 1, over a month after the break-in, the first big story appeared under the joint byline of Bernstein and Woodward, reporting on the connection of the burglars to CRP. Three weeks later, on August 22, President Nixon was renominated with great fanfare at the Republican National Convention in Miami. The next week, apparently trying to declare the Watergate affair finished, Nixon announced that John Dean, counsel to the president, had thoroughly investigated the break-in and said, "I can state categorically that his investigation indicates that no one in the White House staff, no one in this administration, presently employed, was involved in this very bizarre incident. What really hurts is if you try to cover it up." Again, we learned only later, from John Dean's testimony, that he had never heard of "his" investigation until the president made that statement. Strange, indeed.

On September 15, a federal grand jury indicted the original five burglars as well as two former White House aides, E. Howard Hunt and G. Gordon Liddy. It was on that same day—but this came to light only two years later—that Nixon spoke to two of his aides, the White House chief of staff, Bob Haldeman, and John Dean, making threats of economic retaliation against the *Post*: "[I]t's going to have its problems. . . . The main thing is the *Post* is going to have damnable, damnable problems out of this one. They have a television station . . . and they're going to have to get it renewed. . . . And it's going to be God damn active here. . . . [T]he game has to be played awfully rough." Of our lawyer, Nixon said, "I wouldn't want to be in Edward Bennett Williams's position after this election. We are going to fix the son of a bitch, believe me. We are going to. We've got to, because he is a bad man."

Two weeks later, a seminal Bernstein and Woodward article appeared on page one of the *Post*. They had dug up information that there was a secret fund in the safe of Maurice Stans—former secretary of commerce, but finance chairman for CRP at the time—which was controlled by five people, one of whom was [Attorney General] John Mitchell, and which was to be used to gather intelligence on the Democrats. Thus the story reached a new level, involving Mitchell himself, not only in his new role in the campaign, but when he was still attorney general, since Woodward and Bernstein had unearthed Mitchell-authorized expenditures from the fund from the previous year.

CRP denied the story artfully—and graphically. In an effort to check it out, Bernstein, having been told by a press aide at CRP that there was "absolutely no truth to the charges," called Mitchell directly, reaching him at a hotel in New York, where Mitchell answered the phone himself. When Carl told him about the story, Mitchell exploded with exclamations of "JEEEEEEESUS," so violent that Carl felt it was "some sort of primal scream" and thought Mitchell might die on the telephone. After he'd read him the first two paragraphs, Mitchell interrupted, still screaming, "All that crap, you're putting it in the paper? It's all been denied. Katie Graham's gonna get her tit caught in a big fat wringer if that's published. Good Christ! That's the most sickening thing I ever heard."

Bernstein was stunned and called Ben at home to read him Mitchell's quotes and discuss adding them to the already prepared article. Ben told

Carl to use it all except the specific reference to my "tit." The quote was changed to read that I was "gonna get caught in a big fat wringer." Ben decided he didn't have to forewarn me. (Later he told me, "That was too good to check with you, Katharine." I would have agreed with Ben's decision.) As it was, I was shocked to read what I did in the paper, but even more so to hear what Mitchell had actually said, so personal and offensive were the threat and the message. I ran into Carl by accident the next day and asked him if he had any other messages for me.

It was quite a temper tantrum on Mitchell's part—and especially strange of him to call me Katie, which no one has ever called me. Bob later observed that the interesting thing for him was that Mitchell's remark was an example of the misperception on the part of the Nixon people that I was calling all the shots and that I was the one who was printing everything on Watergate. In any case, the remark lived on in the annals of Watergate and was one of the principal public links of me with the affair. Later, though before Watergate had ended, I received a wonderful present from a California dentist who, using the kind of gold normally used to fill teeth, had crafted a little wringer complete with a tiny handle and gears that turned just like a regular old washing-machine wringer. And some time after that, Art Buchwald presented me with a tiny gold breast, which he had had made to go with the wringer. I occasionally wore the two of them together on a chain around my neck, and stopped only when a reporter threatened to tell Maxine Cheshire. . . .

. . . We always did our best to be careful and responsible, especially when we were carrying the burden of the Watergate reporting. From the outset, the editors had resolved to handle the story with more than the usual scrupulous attention to fairness and detail. They laid down certain rules, which were followed by everyone. First, every bit of information attributed to an unnamed source had to be supported by at least one other, independent source. Particularly at the start of Watergate, we had to rely heavily on confidential sources, but at every step we double-checked every bit of material before printing it; where possible, we had three or even more sources for each story. Second, we ran nothing that was reported by any other newspaper, television, radio station, or other media outlet unless it was independently verified and confirmed by our own reporters. Third, every word of every story was read by at least one of the senior editors before it went into print, with a top editor vetting each story before it ran. As any journalist knows, these are rigorous tests.

Yet, despite the care I knew everyone was taking, I was still worried. No matter how careful we were, there was always the nagging possibility that we were wrong, being set up, being misled. Ben would repeatedly

reassure me—possibly to a greater extent than he may have actually felt—
by saying that some of our sources were Republicans, Sloan especially,
and that having the story almost exclusively gave us the luxury of not
having to rush into print, so that we could be obsessive about checking
everything. There were many times when we delayed publishing something until the "tests" had been met. There were times when something
just didn't seem to hold up and, accordingly, was not published, and there
were a number of instances where we withheld something not sufficiently
confirmable that turned out later to be true.

At the time, I took comfort in our "two-sources" policy. Ben further
assured me that Woodward had a secret source he would go to when he
wasn't sure about something—a source that had never misled us. That
was the first I heard of Deep Throat, even before he was so named by
Howard Simons, after the pornographic movie that was popular in certain
circles at the time. It's why I remain convinced that there was such a
person and that he—and it had to be a he—was neither made up nor
an amalgam or a composite of a number of people, as has often been
hypothesized. The identity of Deep Throat is the only secret I'm aware
of that Ben has kept, and, of course, Bob and Carl have, too. I never
asked to be let in on the secret, except once, facetiously, and I still don't
know who he is.

This attention to detail and playing by our own strict rules allowed us
to produce, as Harry Rosenfeld later said, "the longest-running newspaper
stories with the least amount of errors that I have ever experienced or
will ever experience." . . .

The Washington Post Company had been in the public eye for several
months—certainly more than I was comfortable with, and in ways we
might not have wished. We didn't seek out the celebrity; it was thrust
on us. During a *Newsweek* sales meeting at the time, I said it reminded
me somewhat of the old story about the man who'd been tarred and
feathered and ridden out of town on a rail. When asked how he felt, he
said, "Except for the honor of the thing, I would rather have walked."

By early 1973, I was growing increasingly anxious and thought I
ought to meet with Woodward and Bernstein in addition to the editors.
Surprisingly, to this point—seven months into the story—I had had hardly
any contact with the reporters. So, on January 15, Bob and Howard and
I sat down to lunch together (Carl was out of town). Characteristically,
Bob went right downstairs to the newsroom afterwards and made extensive
notes about what we'd said—even going so far as to write down what
we ate, the main course being eggs Benedict, which led to our future
reference to this gathering as the "eggs-Benedict lunch."

My apprehensions about the whole Watergate affair were evident. "Is it all going to come out?" Woodward reported that I asked anxiously. "I mean, are we ever going to know about all of this?" As Bob later wrote, he thought it was the nicest way possible of asking, "What have you boys been doing with my newspaper?" He told me then that they weren't sure all of it ever *would* come out: "Depression seemed to register on her face. 'Never?' she asked. 'Don't tell me never.'"

It was also at this lunch that Woodward told me he had told no one the name of Deep Throat. "Tell me," I said quickly, and then, as he froze, I laughed, touched his arm, and said that I was only kidding—I didn't want to carry that burden around. He admitted that he was prepared to give me the name if I really wanted it, but he was praying I wouldn't press him. This luncheon was reassuring for me—or at least I gave the appearance of being reassured—but I remained nervous. Looking back, I'm surprised I wasn't even more frightened.

The period leading up to the trial of the "Watergate Seven," which began on January 8, 1973, had been extremely tense. Colson was talking around Washington about going to our national advertisers or our investors. A Wall Street friend of mine, André Meyer, a man with administration contacts, called me and asked me to come to see him. When I did, he advised me to be very careful of everything I did or said and—just like in the movies—he warned me "not to be alone." "Oh, André," I said, "that's really absurdly melodramatic. Nothing will happen to me."

"I'm serious," he said. "I've talked to them, and I'm telling you not to be alone." André never explained what his fears were based on, and I still have no idea what he had heard or even meant, but I certainly got the point about how serious he was. I lay awake many nights worrying, though not about my personal safety. Beyond its reputation, the very existence of the *Post* was at stake. I'd lived with White House anger before, but I had never seen anything remotely like the kind of fury and heat I was feeling targeted at us now. It seemed at times that we should really be worrying about some bizarre Kafkaesque plot—that maybe we were being led down a road to discredit the paper.

The moments of anxiety increased in quantity and intensity. Naturally, we were worried when our stories were denied repeatedly and vehemently. Even we, it seems, underestimated for a long time the capacity of government to hide and distort the truth. Finally, a series of events began to unfold in our favor. Three days after the beginning of the trial, Howard Hunt pleaded guilty to six of the charges against him. Four days later, the other burglars followed suit. On January 30, Liddy and McCord were convicted, continuing to claim that no higher-ups were involved and that they had not received any money. In fact, Hunt had urged the burglars to plead guilty and go to jail, assuring them he would take care of them.

Toward the end of February, a civil subpoena was served on five of us from the *Post*, and we were ordered to appear in the U.S. District Court to testify on our sources in the Democratic Party's civil suit against the Committee to Re-elect the President. The subpoena required that we produce a whole host of material, including documents, papers, letters, photographs, tapes, manuscripts, notes, copies, and final drafts of stories about Watergate. As Ben Bradlee put it, they asked us to bring "everything except the lint in our pockets." My name was misspelled, but I was subpoenaed, along with Woodward and Bernstein, Howard Simons, and another reporter, Jim Mann, who had worked on a few of the early Watergate stories. Our lawyers decided to give me some of the reporters' notes. Bradlee had reassured Bernstein and Woodward that we would fight this case for as long as it took, adding:

. . . and if the Judge wants to send anyone to jail, he's going to have to send Mrs. Graham. And, my God, the lady says she'll go! Then the Judge can have that on his conscience. Can't you see the pictures of her limousine pulling up to the Women's Detention Center and out gets our gal, going to jail to uphold the First Amendment? That's a picture that would run in every newspaper in the world. There might be a revolution.

At some point, Woodward had met with Deep Throat, who told him that the subpoenas were part of a response induced by Nixon's rampage against the *Post*, and that he, Nixon, would use the $5 million left over from his campaign "to take the *Post* down a notch." "It will be wearing on you but the end is in sight," Deep Throat told Woodward.

In the end, the subpoenas were quashed, but not before we had spent a great deal of energy and money. The intervening drama was intense. I wrote a friend, "The outrage of it is lost in the absurdity," also noting that one of the editors on the *Post*, who was not served, was said to be suffering from a case of "subpoena envy." . . .

The continuing efforts of the *Post*, and, *finally*, other newspapers and other media as well, and the Congress and the courts helped expose the size of the iceberg. There began a steady stream of revelations, with more and more evidence of scheming and political chicanery coming to light. Wiretaps of several journalists were revealed. We were told by many people that the *Post*'s building was bugged and even that I was being followed. Some of this was clearly an overreaction in an environment rife with paranoia. We did a sweep of our phones throughout the building and in my office and the offices of key editors, but turned up nothing. I'm fairly sure that my phones were never tapped, nor do I believe I was ever followed, but the atmosphere was so infected that this kind of suspicion didn't seem irrational at all.

In June 1973, Woodward and Bernstein wrote that the White House had maintained a list of "political enemies" in 1971 and 1972, and the disclosure surprised few of us. By that time, many people—several of my friends among them—regarded it as an honor to be on it. The list was yet another sign of the peculiar mentality of the small group of men running the country. I can't remember whether my name actually appeared on it, but it was clear to me that I was on it whether my name was written down or not.

A month later, a seismic Watergate event occurred—the turning point, the pivotal moment. In the course of his testimony before the Senate investigating committee, Alexander Butterfield, another Haldeman aide, revealed that there was a voice-activated recording system in the White House. Consequently, the vast majority of conversations the president had had in the Oval Office were on tape, a fact the president himself had clearly lost sight of; or perhaps he assumed that no one knew and that therefore the existence of the system would never become public knowledge. However, someone had to have installed this thing as well as run it, and that someone was Alexander Butterfield. As Woodward later said, it was yet another "incredible sequence of events, and luck for us and bad luck for Nixon. Wrong decisions, wrong turns. But full disclosure of it hung by that fragile thread that could have been cut hundreds of times."

Without the tapes, the true story would never have emerged. In fact, I believe that we at the *Post* were really saved in the end by the tapes and the lucky chance that they weren't destroyed. After the discovery of the tapes, people actually began waiting in the alley outside our building for the first edition of the paper, giving additional meaning to the phrase "hot off the presses." Everyone was now following the story.

Who knows why Nixon didn't destroy the tapes? He seemed to think that they were valuable and that he could defend their privacy, which for a long time he tried to do. . . .

. . . On March 1, 1974, indictments were handed down by a grand jury for seven former Nixon-administration and campaign officials for allegedly conspiring to cover up the Watergate burglary.

What next? On May 9, the House Judiciary Committee began formal hearings on the possible impeachment of Nixon. Though some of my friends, including André Meyer, suggested that the *Post* was trying to "extract every last drop of blood" from the president, I believed that we were following and reporting the impeachment process in a reasoned and dispassionate way, and replied to André, "I hardly see how anyone, no matter how ill-intentioned, could pervert this . . . to 'extracting every last drop of blood.' . . . It really has more to do with what is best for the country now and in the future, than it has to do with this president— who no longer matters, whereas the country does." Privately, I felt that impeachment was right, but my personal opinion didn't get mixed up in the paper's ongoing reporting. . . .

Watergate continued on its way toward an ending none of us could have imagined two years earlier. Even as late as the summer of 1974, amazing as it may seem after all that had been revealed and all the constitutional processes that had taken place—the grand juries, the courts, the congressional committees—Nixon was still blaming the press for his predicament, saying at one point that, if he had been a liberal and "bugged out of Vietnam," the press would never have played up Watergate. Despite Nixon's protestations to his supporter Rabbi Baruch Korff that Watergate would be remembered as "the broadest but thinnest scandal in American history," it went on being revealed as anything but.

On July 8, the United States Supreme Court heard arguments in a historic special session in the case of the *United States* v. *Richard M. Nixon.* What was at stake was whether the Court would order the release of the White House tapes. The next day, House Judiciary Committee Chairman Peter Rodino divulged many of the differences between what the White House had released and what the committee had found on certain tapes, indicating that Nixon had played an active role in the cover-up, which was still going on.

On July 24, 1974, events moved inexorably forward as the Supreme Court ruled unanimously that Nixon had no right to withhold evidence in criminal proceedings and ordered him to turn over the additional White House tapes that had been subpoenaed by Jaworski. On July 27, 29, and 30, respectively, the House Judiciary Committee adopted three articles of impeachment, charging President Nixon with obstruction of justice, failure to uphold laws, and refusal to produce material subpoenaed by the committee.

Editorially, the *Post* did not come out for resignation, as many other papers did. We believed, as an independent paper, that people would behave wisely and judiciously if given the information necessary to make their decisions, and that the process should be allowed to work.

Finally, on August 5, the long-anticipated "smoking gun" turned up. Three new transcripts were released by the White House, recounting conversations between Nixon and Haldeman on June 23, 1972, six days after the original break-in. The tapes showed that the president had personally ordered a cover-up and that he had directed efforts to hide the involvement of his aides in the break-in through a series of orders to conceal details about it known to himself but not to the FBI. This was such a dramatic and obviously final development that I left Martha's Vineyard, where I had gone for my August vacation, and flew immediately to Washington.

Nixon initially said that he would not resign, that he believed the constitutional process should be allowed to run its course. All ten Republicans on the House Judiciary Committee who had voted against impeachment then announced they would vote in favor of at least the obstruction-of-justice article. We led the paper with the possibility of Nixon's resignation, but made no predictions, despite speculation on every side.

On August 8, President Nixon announced that he would resign the next day. I stayed at the paper all that day. Together, many of us watched Nixon's television appearance about his decision to resign. . . .

As a story, Watergate was in many ways a journalist's dream—although it didn't seem that way in those first months when we were so alone. But the story had all the ingredients for major drama: suspense, embattled people on both sides, right and wrong, law and order, good and bad.

Watergate—that is, all of the many illegal and improper acts that were included under that rubric—was a political scandal unlike any other. Its sheer magnitude and reach put it on a scale altogether different from past political scandals, in part because of the unparalleled involvement of so many men so close to the president and because of the large amounts of money raised, stashed, and spent in covert and illegal ways. This was indeed a new kind of corruption in government.

Even today, some people think the whole thing was a minor peccadillo, the sort of thing engaged in by lots of politicians. I believe Watergate was an unprecedented effort to subvert the political process. It was a pervasive, indiscriminate use of power and authority from an administration with a passion for secrecy and deception and an astounding lack of regard for the normal constraints of democratic politics. To my mind, the whole thing was a very real perversion of the democratic system—from firing people who were good Republicans but who might have disagreed with Nixon in the slightest, to the wiretappings, to the breaking and entering of Ellsberg's psychiatrist's office, to the myriad dirty tricks, to the attempts to discredit and curb the media. As I said in a speech at the time, "It was

a conspiracy not of greed but of arrogance and fear by men who came
to equate their own political well-being with the nation's very survival
and security."

The role of the *Post* in all of this was simply to report the news. We
set out to pursue a story that unfolded before our eyes in ways that made
us as incredulous as the rest of the public. The *Post* was never out to "get"
Nixon, or, as was often alleged, to "bring down the president." It always
seemed to me outrageous to accuse the *Post* of pursuing the Watergate
story because of the Democratic bias of the paper. A highly unusual
burglary at the headquarters of a national political party is an important
story, and we would have given it the same treatment regardless of which
party was in power or who was running for election. I was often asked
why we didn't cover Ted Kennedy's debacle at Chappaquiddick* as fully
as we were covering Watergate. The point is, we did, and the further
point is that the Kennedys were probably as angry at us then as the Nixon
administration was. Throughout Watergate, I was amazed at the regular
allegations that somehow we had created the agony of Watergate by
recklessly pursuing certain stories and thereby causing the turmoil that
the president was in. How could anyone make this argument in light of
the fact that the stories we reported turned out to be true?

In the end, Nixon was his own worst enemy. The *Post* had no enemies
list; the president did. Nixon seemed to regard the *Post* as incurably liberal
and ceaselessly anti-administration. In fact, the *Post* supported a great
many of his policies and programs, but his paranoia, his hatred of the
press, his scheming, all contributed to bringing him down—helped along
by the appropriate constitutional processes, including the grand juries,
courts, and Congress. Woodward and Bernstein were critical figures in
seeing that the truth was eventually told, but others were at least as
important: Judge Sirica; Senator Sam Ervin and the Senate Watergate
Committee; Special Prosecutors Cox and Jaworski; the House Impeachment Committee under Representative Peter Rodino. The *Post* was an
important part—but only a part—of the Watergate story.

My own role throughout Watergate is both easy and hard to define.
Watergate no doubt was the most important occurrence in my working
life, but my involvement was basically peripheral, rarely direct. For the

*In 1969, Senator Ted Kennedy was involved in a car accident on the summer resort island
of Martha's Vineyard. A young woman, Mary Jo Kopechne, was in the car with the senator;
she drowned when the car plunged off a bridge into the water. Kennedy swam away from
the scene and did not tell authorities about the accident for many hours, but he was never
officially charged with wrong-doing in the incident.—Eds.

most part I was behind-the-scenes. I was a kind of devil's advocate, asking questions all along the way—questions about whether we were being fair, factual, and accurate. I had a constant conversation with Ben and Howard, as I did with the top two editorial writers, Phil and Meg, so I was informed in general. As was my habit before Watergate, I often attended the daily morning editorial meetings, where the issues were regularly discussed and where editorial policy was formed.

What I did primarily was stand behind the editors and reporters, in whom I believed. As time went on, I did this more publicly, defending us in speeches and remarks to groups around the country—indeed, internationally as well. My larger responsibility was to the company as a whole—beyond the paper—and to our shareholders.

I have often been credited with courage for backing our editors in Watergate. The truth is that I never felt there was much choice. Courage applies when one has a choice. With Watergate, there was never *one* major decisive moment when I, or anyone, could have suggested that we stop reporting the story. Watergate unfolded gradually. By the time the story had grown to the point where the size of it dawned on us, we had already waded deeply into its stream. Once I found myself in the deepest water in the middle of the current, there was no going back.

It was an unbelievable two years of pressured existence, which diminished only a little as other publications joined us and as the separate investigations and the court cases spawned by Watergate began to confirm and amplify our reporting. When it was perfectly obvious that our existence as a company was at stake, we of course became embattled. Watergate threatened to ruin the paper. The *Post* and The Washington Post Company survived partly because of the great skill and tenacity that our reporters and editors and executives brought to bear throughout the crisis, and partly because of luck.

In fact, the role of luck was essential in Watergate—and luck was on our side. One has to recognize it and use it, but without luck the end result for us could have been very different. From the first incident of the guard finding the taped door at the Watergate building, to the police sending to the scene of the crime a beat-up-looking undercover car that was cruising in the area rather than a squad car that might have tipped off the burglars, to the sources willing—some even eager—to talk and help, we were lucky. We were lucky that the original burglary took place in Washington and was a local story. We were lucky that those under investigation compounded their own situation by further mistakes and misassessments. We were lucky we had the resources to pursue the story. We were lucky that both Woodward and Bernstein were young and single and therefore willing and able to work sixteen- and eighteen-hour days, seven days a week for months on end, at least with fewer repercussions than married men might have had. We were lucky Nixon was eccentric enough to set up a taping system in the White House, without which he might have completed his term. . . .

As astounding as Watergate was to the country and the government, it underscored the crucial role of a free, able, and energetic press. We saw how much power the government has to reveal what it wants when it wants, to give the people only the authorized version of events. We relearned the lessons of the importance of the right of a newspaper to keep its sources confidential.

The credibility of the press stood the test of time against the credibility of those who spent so much time self-righteously denying their own wrong-doing and assaulting us by assailing our performance and our motives. In a speech I made in 1970—before the Pentagon Papers and before Water-gate—I said: "[T]he cheap solutions being sought by the administration will, in the long run, turn out to be very costly." Indeed, they did.

86

LARRY SABATO

From *Feeding Frenzy*

When political scientist Larry Sabato published his 1991 book on the media's role in campaigning, he gave a term to a phenomenon others had already seen: a feeding frenzy. The press en masse attacks a wounded politician whose record—or more accurately, his or her character—has been questioned. Every network and cable station participates, often without any real evidence to back up the rumor. Sabato's list of thirty-six examples ends in 1990; knowledgeable readers will be able to update the list. Paradoxically, the spectacular success of the Washington Post's *Bob Woodward and Carl Bernstein in investigating Watergate set the stage for recent feeding frenzies. Today, just the fear of being a media target may deter many qualified people from entering public service, Sabato notes.*

———————

IT HAS BECOME a spectacle without equal in modern American politics: the news media, print and broadcast, go after a wounded politician like sharks in a feeding frenzy. The wounds may have been self-inflicted, and the politician may richly deserve his or her fate, but the journalists now take center stage in the process, creating the news as much as reporting it, changing both the shape of election-year politics and the contours of government. Having replaced the political parties as the screening committee for candidates and officeholders, the media propel some politicians toward power and unceremoniously eliminate others. Unavoidably, this enormously influential role—and the news practices employed in exercising it—has provided rich fodder for a multitude of press critics.

These critics' charges against the press cascade down with the fury of rain in a summer squall. Public officials and many other observers see journalists as rude, arrogant, and cynical, given to exaggeration, harassment, sensationalism, and gross insensitivity. . . .

Press invasion of privacy is leading to the gradual erasure of the line protecting a public person's purely private life. This makes the price of public life enormously higher, serving as an even greater deterrent for those not absolutely obsessed with holding power—the kind of people we ought least to want in office. Rather than recognizing this unfortunate consequence, many in journalism prefer to relish their newly assumed role of "gatekeeper," which, as mentioned earlier, enables them to substitute for party leaders in deciding which characters are virtuous enough to merit consideration for high office. As ABC News correspondent Brit Hume self-critically suggests:

We don't see ourselves institutionally, collectively anymore as a bunch of journalists out there faithfully reporting what's happening day by day. . . . We have a much grander view of ourselves: we are the Horatio at the national bridge. We are the people who want to prevent the bad characters from crossing over into public office.

Hume's veteran ABC colleague Sander Vanocur agrees, detecting "among some young reporters a quality of the avenging angel: they are going to sanitize American politics." More and more, the news media seem determined to show that would-be emperors have no clothes, and if necessary to prove the point, they personally will strip the candidates naked on the campaign trail. The sheer number of journalists participating in these public denudings guarantees riotous behavior, and the "full-court press" almost always presents itself as a snarling, unruly mob more bent on killing kings than making them. Not surprisingly potential candidates deeply fear the power of an inquisitorial press, and in deciding whether to seek office, they often consult journalists as much as party leaders, even sharing private vulnerabilities with newsmen to gauge reaction. The *Los Angeles Times's* Washington bureau chief, Jack Nelson, had such an encounter before the 1988 campaign season, when a prospective presidential candidate "literally asked me how long I thought the statute of limitations was" for marital infidelity. "I told him I didn't know, but I didn't think [the limit] had been reached in his case!" For whatever reasons, the individual chose not to run.

As the reader will see later in this volume, able members of the news corps offer impressive defenses for all the practices mentioned thus far, not the least of which is that the press has become more aggressive to combat the legions of image makers, political consultants, spin doctors, and handlers who surround modern candidates like a nearly impenetrable shield. Yet upon reflection, most news veterans recognize that press excesses are not an acceptable antidote for consultant or candidate evils. In fact, not one of the interviewed journalists even attempted to justify an increasingly frequent occurrence in news organizations: the publication of gossip and rumor *without convincing proof*. Gossip has always been the drug of choice for journalists as well as the rest of the political community, but as the threshold for publication of information about private lives has been lowered, journalists sometimes cover politics as "Entertainment Tonight" reporters cover Hollywood. A bitter Gary Hart* observed: "Rumor and gossip have become the coins of the political realm," and the *New York Times's* Michael Oreskes seemed to agree: "1988 was a pretty sorry year when the *National Enquirer* was the most important publication in American journalism." With all the stories and innuendo about personal vice, campaigns appear to be little more than a stream of talegates (or in the case of sexual misadventures, tailgates).

The sorry standard set on the campaign trail is spilling over into coverage of governmental battles. Ever since Watergate,† government scandals have paraded across the television set in a roll call so lengthy and numbing that they are inseparable in the public consciousness, all joined at the Achilles' heel. Some recent lynchings such as John Tower's failure to be confirmed as secretary of defense,‡ rival any spectacle produced by

---

*Former Senator (D-Col.) Gary Hart's 1988 presidential candidacy ended after media revelations about his extramarital relations with Donna Rice.—EDS.

†Watergate began with the 1972 break-in at the Democratic National headquarters by several men associated with President Nixon's re-election committee. Watergate ended two years later with the resignation of President Nixon. Nixon and his closest aides were implicated in the coverup of the Watergate burglary. Tapes made by President Nixon of his Oval Office conversations revealed lying and obstruction of justice at the highest levels of government.—EDS.

‡In 1989, the Senate rejected President Bush's nominee for secretary of defense, former Texas Senator John Tower. Senate hearings produced allegations that Tower was an excessive drinker and a womanizer.—EDS.

colonial Salem. At the same time more vital and revealing information is ignored or crowded off the agenda. *Real* scandals, such as the savings-and-loan heist or the influence peddling at the Department of Housing and Urban Development in the 1980s, go undetected for years. The sad conclusion is inescapable: The press has become obsessed with gossip rather than governance; it prefers to employ titillation rather than scrutiny; as a result, its political coverage produces trivialization rather than enlightenment. And the dynamic mechanism propelling and demonstrating this decline in news standards is the "feeding frenzy." . . .

The term *frenzy* suggests some kind of disorderly, compulsive, or agitated activity that is muscular and instinctive, not cerebral and thoughtful. In the animal world, no activity is more classically frenzied than the feeding of sharks, piranhas, or bluefish when they encounter a wounded prey. These attack-fish with extraordinarily acute senses first search out weak, ill, or injured targets. On locating them, each hunter moves in quickly to gain a share of the kill, feeding not just off the victim but also off its fellow hunters' agitation. The excitement and drama of the violent encounter builds to a crescendo, sometimes overwhelming the creatures' usual inhibitions. The frenzy can spread, with the delirious attackers wildly striking any object that moves in the water, even each other. Veteran reporters will recognize more press behavior in this passage than they might wish to acknowledge. This reverse anthropomorphism can be carried too far, but the similarity of piranha in the water and press on the campaign trail can be summed up in a shared goal: If it bleeds, try to kill it.

The kingdom of politics and not of nature is the subject of this volume, so for our purposes, a feeding frenzy is defined as the press coverage attending any political event or circumstance where a critical mass of journalists leap to cover the same embarrassing or scandalous subject and pursue it intensely, often excessively, and sometimes uncontrollably. No precise number of journalists can be attached to the term *critical mass*, but in the video age, we truly know it when we see it; the forest of cameras, lights, microphones, and adrenaline-choked reporters surrounding a Gary Hart, Dan Quayle, or Geraldine Ferraro is unmistakable. [The following table] contains a list of thirty-six events that surely qualify as frenzies. They are occasions of sin for the press as well as the politicians, and thus ideal research sites that will serve as case studies for this book. A majority (twenty-one) are drawn from presidential politics, while seven examples come from the state and local levels, with the remaining eight focused on government scandals or personal peccadilloes of nationally recognized political figures. . . .

Conditions are always ripe for the spawning of a frenzy in the brave

FEEDING FRENZIES: CASE STUDIES USED FOR THIS BOOK

From Presidential Politics
1952   Richard Nixon's "secret fund"
1968   George Romney's "brainwashing" about Vietnam
1968   Spiro Agnew's "fat Jap" flap
1969   Ted Kennedy's Chappaquiddick
1972   Edmund Muskie's New Hampshire cry
1972   Thomas Eagleton's mental health
1976   Jimmy Carter's "lust in the heart" *Playboy* interview
1976   Gerald Ford's "free Poland" gaffe
1979   Jimmy Carter's "killer rabbit"
1980   Billygate (Billy Carter and Libya)
1983   Debategate (Reagan's use of Carter's debate briefing books)
1984   Gary Hart's age, name, and signature changes
1984   Jesse Jackson's "Hymietown" remark
1984   Geraldine Ferraro's family finances
1985/86   Jack Kemp's purported homosexuality
1987   Gary Hart and Donna Rice
1987   Joseph Biden's plagiarism and Michael Dukakis's "attack video"
1987   Pat Robertson's exaggerated résumé and shotgun marriage
1988   Dukakis's mental health
1988   Dan Quayle (National Guard service, Paula Parkinson, academic
            record, rumors such as plagiarism and drugs)
1988   George Bush's alleged mistress

From the State and Local Levels
1987/88   Governor Evan Mecham on the impeachment trail (Arizona)
1987/88   Chuck Robb and the cocaine parties (Virginia)
1983/90   Mayor Marion Barry's escapades (District of Columbia)
1987   Governor Dick Celeste's womanizing (Ohio)
1988   Mayor Henry Cisneros's extramarital affair (San Antonio, Texas)
1989/90   Governor Gaston Caperton's "soap opera" divorce (West Virginia)
1990   Texas governor's election: drugs, rape, and "honey hunts"

Noncampaign Examples
1973/74   The Watergate scandals
1974   Congressman Wilbur Mills and stripper Fanne Foxe
1986/87   The Iran-Contra affair
1987   Supreme Court nominee Douglas Ginsburg's marijuana use (and
            campaign repercussions)
1989   John Tower's losing fight to become secretary of defense
1989   Speaker Jim Wright's fall from power
1989   Tom Foley's rocky rise to the Speakership
1989/90   Barney Frank and the male prostitute

new world of omnipresent journalism. Advances in media technology have revolutionized campaign coverage. Handheld miniature cameras (minicams) and satellite broadcasting have enabled television to go live anywhere, anytime with ease. Instantaneous transmission (by broadcast and fax) to all corners of the country has dramatically increased the velocity of campaign developments today, accelerating events to their conclusion at breakneck speed. Gary Hart, for example, went from front-runner to ex-candidate in less than a week in May 1987. Continuous public-affairs programming, such as C-SPAN and CNN, helps put more of a politician's utterances on the record, as Senator Joseph Biden discovered to his chagrin when C-SPAN unobtrusively taped Biden's exaggeration of his résumé at a New Hampshire kaffeeklatsch in 1987. (This became a contributing piece of the frenzy that brought Biden down.) C-SPAN, CNN, and satellite broadcasting capability also contribute to the phenomenon called "the news cycle without end," which creates a voracious news appetite demanding to be fed constantly, increasing the pressure to include marginal bits of information and gossip and producing novel if distorting "angles" on the same news to differentiate one report from another. The extraordinary number of local stations covering national politics today—up to several hundred at major political events—creates an echo chamber producing seemingly endless repetitions of essentially the same news stories. This local contingent also swells the corps traveling the campaign trail. In 1988 an estimated two thousand journalists of all stripes flooded the Iowa caucuses, for instance. Reporters not infrequently outnumber participants at meetings and whistlestops. . . .

Whether on the rise or not, the unfortunate effects of pack journalism are apparent to both news reporters and news consumers: conformity, homogeneity, and formulaic reporting. Innovation is discouraged, and the checks and balances supposedly provided by competition evaporate. Press energies are devoted to finding mere variations on a theme (new angles and wiggle disclosures), while a mob psychology catches hold that allows little mercy for the frenzy victim. CNN's Frank Sesno captures the pack mood perfectly:

I've been in that group psychology; I know what it's like. You think you're on to something, you've got somebody on the run. How dare they not come clean? How dare they not tell the full story? What are they trying to hide? Why are they hiding it? And you become a crusader for the truth. Goddammit, you're going to get the truth! . . .

Sesno's crusader spirit can be traced directly to the lingering effects of the Watergate scandal, which had the most profound impact of any modern event on the manner and substance of the press's conduct. In many respects Watergate began the press's open season on politicians in a chain reaction that today allows for scrutiny of even the most private sanctums of public officials' lives. Moreover, coupled with Vietnam and the civil rights movement, Watergate shifted the orientation of journalism away from mere description—providing an accurate account of happenings—and toward prescription—helping to set the campaign's (and society's) agendas by focusing attention on the candidates' shortcomings as well as certain social problems.

A new breed and a new generation of reporters were attracted to journalism, and particularly its investigative arm. As a group they were idealistic, though aggressively mistrustful of all authority, and they shared a contempt for "politics as usual." Critics called them do-gooders and purists who wanted the world to stand at moral attention for them. Twenty years later the Vietnam and Watergate generation dominates journalism: They and their younger cohorts hold sway over most newsrooms, with two-thirds of all reporters now under the age of thirty-six and an ever-increasing share of editors and executives drawn from the Watergate-era class. Of course, many of those who found journalism newly attractive in the wake of Watergate were not completely altruistic. The ambitious saw the happy fate of the *Washington Post's* young Watergate sleuths Bob Woodward and Carl Bernstein, who gained fame and fortune, not to mention big-screen portrayals by Robert Redford and Dustin Hoffman in the movie *All the President's Men*. As *U.S. News & World Report's* Steven Roberts sees it:

A lot of reporters run around this town dreaming of the day that Dustin Hoffman and Robert Redford are going to play them in the movies. That movie had more effect on the self-image of young journalists than anything else. Christ! Robert Redford playing a journalist? It lends an air of glamour and excitement that acts as a magnet drawing young reporters to investigative reporting.

The young were attracted not just to journalism but to a particular *kind* of journalism. The role models were not respected, established reporters but two unknowns who refused to play by the rules their seniors had accepted. "Youngsters learned that deductive techniques, all guesswork, and lots of unattributed information [were] the royal road to fame, even if it wasn't being terribly responsible," says Robert Novak. After all, adds columnist Mark Shields, "Robert Redford didn't play Walter Lippmann and Dustin Hoffman didn't play Joseph Kraft." (Kraft, like Lippmann, had a long and distinguished career in journalism.) . . .

A clear consequence of Watergate and other recent historical events was the increasing emphasis placed by the press on the character of candidates. As journalists reviewed the three tragic but exceptionally capable figures who had held the presidency since 1960, they saw that the failures of Kennedy, Johnson, and Nixon were not those of intellect but of ethos. Chappaquiddick, Spiro Agnew, and the Eagleton affair reinforced that view. The party affiliations and ideology of these disappointing leaders varied, but in common they possessed defects of personality, constitution, and disposition. In the world of journalism (or academe), as few as two data points can constitute a trend; these six together constituted an irrefutable mother lode of proof. "We in the press learned from experience that character flaws could have very large costs," says David Broder, "and we couldn't afford to ignore them if we were going to meet our responsibility." . . .

[A] troubling consequence of modern media coverage for the political system has to do with the recruitment of candidates and public servants. Simply put, the price of power has been raised dramatically, far too high for many outstanding potential officeholders. An individual contemplating a run for office must now accept the possibility of almost unlimited intrusion into his or her financial and personal life. Every investment made, every affair conducted, every private sin committed from college years to the present may one day wind up in a headline or on television. For a reasonably sane and moderately sensitive person, this is a daunting realization, with potentially hurtful results not just for the candidate but for his or her immediate family and friends. To have achieved a nongovernmental position of respect and honor in one's community is a source of pride and security, and the risk that it could all be destroyed by an unremitting and distorted assault on one's faults and foibles cannot be taken lightly. American society today is losing the services of many exceptionally talented individuals who could make outstanding contributions to the commonweal, but who understandably will not subject themselves and their loved ones to abusive, intrusive press coverage. Of course, this problem stems as much from the attitudes of the public as from those of the press; the strain of moral absolutism in portions of the American people merely finds expression in the relentless press frenzies and ethicsgate hunts. . . . *New York Times* columnist Anthony Lewis is surely correct when he suggests, "If we tell people there's to be absolutely nothing private left to them, then we will tend to attract to public office only those most brazen, least sensitive personalities. Is that what we want to do?"

87

HOWARD KURTZ

From *Spin Cycle*

During much of Bill Clinton's second term, rumor and scandal dogged the president. Some Americans believed the accusations and some did not. Some thought them relevant to the running of the executive branch; others did not. The White House responded to the media barrage by trying to influence the press's coverage. That's called spin, and journalist Howard Kurtz portrays the Clinton administration as masters of spin. He introduces us to several of President Clinton's then-spinmeisters and the techniques they used. But spin has its costs and as time went on, Kurtz feels, "the damage to his presidency would never be repaired."

———◆———

. . . THE PRESIDENT'S APPROVAL RATING was hovering at around 60 percent in the polls, and for all the scandalous headlines and political bumps in the road, the country finally seemed to have grown comfortable with him. [Press Secretary Mike] McCurry and his colleagues had mastered the art of manipulating the press and were reaping the dividends.

And now, just when they thought they had survived the worst of the investigations and the harshest media scrutiny, the latest sex scandal had hit them like a punch in the stomach. They were reeling, depressed, uncertain of the facts but all too certain that Clinton's days might be numbered. The irony was inescapable: The president who worried so openly about his historical legacy, who staunchly insisted that Whitewater was nothing next to Watergate, might make history by following Richard Nixon into oblivion because he could not resist a lowly intern. For now, at least, McCurry and his colleagues could not spin their way out of this one. They did not know whether Bill Clinton was telling the truth about Monica Lewinsky, and some of them suspected he was not.

The White House spin operation had plenty of experience in crisis management. A yearlong investigation into campaign fundraising abuses and influence-peddling charges had built to a dramatic crescendo in the fall of 1997. On the morning of October 3, the Clintonites were once again on the defensive. The Justice Department had just decided to expand its investigation into questionable fundraising calls by Vice President Al Gore and was moving toward a stepped-up probe as well of Bill Clinton's frenetic efforts to raise campaign cash in the 1996 election. The relentless charges that the administration had improperly vacuumed up millions of dollars by crassly selling access to the president was now reaching critical mass. *The New York Times*, not surprisingly, trumpeted the new developments as its lead story.

But there was another article vying for attention that day at the top of the *Times*'s venerable front page, one that probably resonated with many more readers than were following the twists and turns of the latest Washington scandal. Four days earlier, one of the administration's least favorite investigative reporters, Jeff Gerth, who had long been tormenting Clinton and his wife, Hillary, over the Whitewater affair, had weighed in with a lengthy *Times* report on how federal inspections of imported food had plummeted just as scientists were finding more outbreaks of food-borne diseases. In fact, Gerth had learned that David Kessler, the former head of the Food and Drug Administration, had failed to persuade Clinton to give his agency the power to bar imported food that did not meet American standards. The story was a major embarrassment, but Clinton had a genius for stealing good ideas from his enemies, even those he most despised in the press. And so the White House promptly staged a ceremony in the picturesque Rose Garden as Clinton proposed giving the FDA new power to ban imported fruit and vegetables, the very power he had refused to grant years earlier. Mike McCurry even credited the *Times* for its role in spotlighting the problem.

"I've never seen anything like it," Kessler told Gerth. "They're terrified of you." Still, the White House had managed to neutralize the dogged Jeff Gerth, who called McCurry to thank him for the acknowledgment.

The day's dueling headlines revealed a larger truth about the Clinton White House and its turn-on-a-dime ability to reposition its battered leader. The central mystery of Bill Clinton's fifth year in office was how a president so aggressively investigated on so many fronts could remain so popular with the American people. Indeed, his approval rating was nearly as lofty as that of Ronald Reagan at the peak of his powers, and with the economy humming along at an impressive clip, bad news was failing to make much of a dent in those numbers.

To be sure, Clinton's performance had helped create the sense that the country was doing just fine on his watch. But it was a carefully honed media strategy—alternately seducing, misleading, and sometimes intimidating the press—that maintained this aura of success. No day went by without the president and his coterie laboring mightily to generate favorable headlines and deflect damaging ones, to project their preferred image on the vast screen of the media establishment.

For much of Clinton's first term, these efforts to control the message were clumsy at best. . . .

The second-term lineup was more seasoned but less adventurous. Senior adviser Rahm Emanuel assumed Stephanopoulos's role of behind-the-scenes press handler. Special counsel Lanny Davis became the chief spinmeister on the burgeoning fundraising scandal, an effort crisply supervised by deputy chief of staff John Podesta. Communications director Ann Lewis handled the substantive planning. Chief of staff Erskine Bowles presided over the entire operation like the corporate executive he was. Counselor Doug Sosnik served up political advice, joined over the summer by colorful strategist Paul Begala and former journalist Sidney Blumenthal. McCurry stayed on for a final mission, determined to broker a cease-fire between the president and a hostile press corps. He and his colleagues were engaged in a daily struggle to control the agenda, to seize the public's attention, however fleetingly, for Clinton's wide-ranging initiatives. They had to manage the news, to package the presidency in a way that people would buy the product.

The small group of journalists who shouted questions at the press secretary each day in the White House Briefing Room had a very different agenda. They were focused, almost fixated, on scandal, on the malfeasance and misfeasance and plain old embarrassments that had seemed to envelop this administration from the very start. They were interested in conflict, in drama, in behind-the-scenes maneuvering, in pulling back the curtain and exposing the Oz-like manipulations of the Clinton crowd. It was their job to report what the president said, but increasingly they saw it as their mission to explain why he said it and what seedy political purpose he was trying to accomplish along the way.

When the reporters had the upper hand, the headlines were filled with scandal news, a cascade of Watergate-style charges that drowned out nearly everything else. Indeed, they had plenty of material to work with. The Whitewater investigation, which had dragged on throughout the first term, involved the Clintons' role in a complicated Arkansas land deal, their partnership with a crooked couple, and allegations of a subsequent cover-up. The Travelgate probe involved charges that the first lady had orchestrated the ouster of seven employees of the White House travel office so the work could be given to friends of the Clintons. The Filegate inquiry involved charges that White House aides had deliberately obtained the sensitive FBI files of prominent Republicans. The Paula Jones lawsuit turned on allegations by a former Arkansas state employee that Clinton, while governor, had asked for sex in a Little Rock hotel room. And the campaign finance scandal, in its broadest form, involved an alleged conspiracy by Clinton and Gore to use the perks of high office to solicit cash from foreign operatives, Asian American donors, and garden-variety fat cats, perhaps in exchange for political favors.

Against this dark backdrop, what the White House press operatives did was to launder the news—to scrub it of dark scandal stains, remove unsightly splotches of controversy, erase greasy dabs of contradictions, and present it to the country crisp and sparkling white. The underlying garment was the same, but it was often unrecognizable.

A larger challenge loomed as well—simply put, to change the subject, and to do so without the benefit of dramatic presidential action like fighting a war or battling a recession or tackling some grave national crisis. When the White House team broke through, they secured precious column inches and airtime for Clinton's proposals on national education standards or seat-belt enforcement or funding for mammograms, efforts that the president's people felt resonated far more broadly than the inside-the-Beltway obsessions of the media. . . .

The reporters' frustrations began to boil over in the final weeks of the 1996 campaign, when allegations first surfaced that foreign funny money had been funneled to the Clinton camp and the White House seemed unable or unwilling to provide answers. McCurry, who usually insisted on steering such questions to the White House lawyers, reluctantly assumed control of the scandal defense just days before the election. Even as Clinton and his compatriots celebrated his triumphant reelection in Little Rock, McCurry knew that they had kept the lid on a pressure cooker that was ready to blow.

As the fundraising scandal gathered steam, McCurry and his new ally, Lanny Davis, bore the brunt of the hostile media inquiries. Within the White House they battled for disclosure, for getting the bad news behind them. But there were limits to how far McCurry and Davis would go, documents they would not release, questions they would not answer. They insisted day after day that Bill Clinton and Al Gore had done nothing out of the ordinary in dialing for dollars, sipping coffee with shady Chinese operatives, or renting out the Lincoln Bedroom, even when an avalanche of embarrassing documents decimated their denials. A few mistakes, they maintained, but nothing the other side didn't do in spades.

The White House partisans were convinced that the public was tuning it all out, that most Americans viewed this as the typical Beltway follies, but the journalists were filled with moral fervor, determined that readers and viewers should care and that somehow they would make them care. The Clintonites were equally determined to rout the journalistic naysayers and prove that they could govern in this scandal-charged atmosphere. Neutralizing the media had become ground zero in the struggle for supremacy, and the spin would clearly be as important as the substance. . . .

Bill Clinton, Al Gore, and Erskine Bowles were in the Treaty Room, the president's private study in the residence, where he often watched CNN, on the evening of February 12. McCurry walked in around 10:30, having just dispatched an aide to the loading dock of *The Washington Post*, six blocks north, where you could buy the bulldog edition for a quarter. Even in an age when most newspapers were on the World Wide Web, this was still the fastest way to get the next day's *Post*, especially if your business was damage control.

There it was, the paper's lead story, an ominous-sounding Bob Woodward bombshell. McCurry knew it was coming because he had been on the phone with Woodward. The four men and a few aides, seated on chairs and sofas, sat reading the handful of copies that had just come off the presses.

It was the strangest goddamn piece: the Justice Department had uncovered evidence that representatives of the People's Republic of China tried to direct foreign contributions to the Democrats before the 1996 election. The Chinese embassy was used for the planning, according to electronic eavesdropping by federal agencies.

That was it. Who was involved? What contributions did they direct? How much money? When did it happen? The story didn't say. Just a couple of tantalizing details from Woodward's legendary sources. What the hell did it mean? The president and the vice president and the chief of staff didn't know anything about it. They chewed over the story, tried to decipher its meaning like some ancient hieroglyphics. It seemed like a work in progress.

Still, they knew all too well that any story with Woodward's byline had a certain cachet around town. The tireless reporter had helped drive Richard Nixon out of this very house two decades earlier, was one of the heroes of the movie *All the President's Men*. The assembled officials recalled the scene in which Jason Robards, playing Ben Bradlee, threw a half-baked story back at Woodward and Bernstein and barked, "You just don't have it." Perhaps, it was suggested, a *Post* editor should have delivered that line on this story.

McCurry received few press calls about the piece that night. It was almost as if the entire Washington press corps was still trying to divine its importance. Upon convening the 9:15 gaggle in his office for about thirty reporters the next morning, he said: "I'm having a hard time making heads or tails of the story." He added that Clinton was "puzzled" by it but "very concerned" about the allegation. That was about all he could say.

Helen Thomas was dissatisfied. "Every question is like pulling teeth," she said.

"I'm being very careful, and you know from recent experience I have good reason to be very careful," McCurry said. "You got a problem?"

"Yeah, the problem is trying to figure out what's going on."

"I'm not breezy on this subject," McCurry allowed.

"I forgive you," Thomas said.

Administration officials were worried that the flap would overshadow the visit later that day of Israel's prime minister, Benjamin Netanyahu. At a photo session with the Israeli leader, Clinton asked the assembled reporters not to start a "feeding frenzy." He promised to take their questions later in the day.

McCurry held the two o'clock gaggle for the cameras. The briefing room, crowded with visiting Israeli journalists, was unusually noisy. On television it looked as though he had the audience's undivided attention. In the room, journalists were whispering along the wall, stepping outside for a smoke, walking in from lunch. It took all of McCurry's concentration to focus on the seven cameras mounted along a riser at the back of the room and ignore the chatter in the aisles.

McCurry began by referring questions on the possible role of the Chinese government to Deputy Attorney General Jamie Gorelick, who, as he well knew, wasn't commenting.

Wolf Blitzer, undeterred, tried a different tack: "How concerned is the president, though, that there is a story out there that there possibly could have been some improper Chinese government activity designed to influence us—"

"The story, while puzzling to the president, was of concern to him, and he fully expects that any matters like that would be properly investigated," McCurry replied.

Helen Thomas tried to get McCurry to detail the gist of the matter. "Can you explain why it is that the president is puzzled or what in particular it is that causes him puzzlement?"

"The story."

"Yes, but what about it?"

"The story, what's reported, the news in the story."

"But what about it is puzzling?"

"It just seems puzzling, the news of the story."

McCurry wasn't about to repeat the allegations for television. Let the reporters characterize it any way they wanted. He wasn't going to serve as Woodward's press agent.

Two hours later, fielding questions with Netanyahu, Clinton tried to frame the issue in general terms. "Obviously, it would be a very serious matter for the United States if any country were to attempt to funnel funds to one of our political parties for any reason whatever," he said.

The China story was all over the networks. "In Washington tonight, there's a major buzz in the highest circles over a page-one story in today's *Washington Post* about the possible role of the Chinese government in raising funds for the Democratic National Committee," Tom Brokaw said on NBC.

Over at CBS, Rita Braver reported that "White House insiders are genuinely puzzled and concerned about this report—especially the possibility it may be another indirect result of their aggressive fundraising tactics."

McCurry barely had time to catch his breath before the press found new grist for its ever-churning mill. The next morning the administration released more than one hundred pages of National Security Council documents in an effort to bolster the nomination of outgoing White House aide Anthony Lake to head the CIA. In one document an NSC official warned that a major Democratic contributor, Johnny Chung, was a "hustler" trying to exploit the Clintons; Chung was nevertheless allowed to bring six Chinese businessmen to watch the president's Saturday radio address in March 1995. Wolf Blitzer was on the lawn within an hour, standing on a rubber mat to avoid the muddy grass. "Some of these documents do contain additional political embarrassments for the White House," he said into the camera.

The White House decided to put Lanny Davis on the talk-show circuit that weekend. The shows had been clamoring for Davis for weeks, but the White House booker, Stuart Schear, kept saying he wasn't ready, wasn't sufficiently steeped in scandal minutiae. The real reason was tactical in nature. White House officials didn't like to put Davis on the weekend shows because that would trigger another round of scandal segments. Since Davis's sole mission was to clean up after the fundraising mess, his very presence set the agenda. But a critical mass of scandal stories had been building up, and the White House needed someone to respond to the charges. Schear sent word that Davis was available.

In the space of twenty-four hours, Davis spoke to Wolf Blitzer on

Inside Politics Weekend, to Tony Snow on *Fox News Sunday*, to Tim Russert on *Meet the Press*. Davis had clearly decided to stay on defense. "I'm not here to make news," he told Fox staffers before the show. The litany of questions was remarkably similar: The alleged Chinese involvement in Democratic fundraising. The parade of thugs and favor seekers at the White House coffees. A new *Washington Post* report that the administration had changed its policy toward Guam after a visit by Hillary Clinton prompted $900,000 in contributions to the Clinton campaign and the party. Davis listened to the questions with a slightly bemused expression and then unleashed his rapid-fire answers, trying to finish each rhetorical salvo before he was interrupted.

"The president regards these allegations as very serious," he told Blitzer.

"No governmental action ever resulted from a contribution," he told Snow.

"There's no policy affected by contributions to this president," he told Russert.

Darting from studio to studio, Davis got the names confused. He called Tony Snow "Brit." He twice referred to Congressman McIntosh as McIntyre. But the only time he really stumbled was when he had to acknowledge that, for all his assurances that contributions did not change administration policy, he had never personally discussed the question with the president. Brit Hume quickly moved in, asking how often he had met with Clinton since becoming White House special counsel.

"Several times," Davis said.

"Three? Two?"

"I don't want to go into it any further than that," Davis said. . . .

The Washington Post was hours away from publishing a story that Kenneth Starr was investigating whether Clinton had had an affair with a twenty-four-year-old former White House intern, had lied about it under oath, and had urged her to lie as well. Sue Schmidt, the hard-driving Whitewater reporter so loathed by the administration, had the goods on the supposed affair involving Monica Lewinsky. Schmidt's colleague Peter Baker was calling Podesta for comment. A new crisis was about to explode. . . .

But the White House instantly paid a price for the years of aggressive spinning, for the evasive answers that had angered so many journalists through so many scandals. Most of the reporters automatically assumed that Clinton was lying, that he had in fact been carrying on with Monica Lewinsky and was pathetically trying to cover it up. They had been through too many bimbo eruptions, heard too many of Clinton's carefully hedged denials. When a shaky-looking Clinton sat down for a previously scheduled interview that afternoon with PBS's Jim Lehrer, he said that "there is no sexual relationship" with Lewinsky. Suddenly Begala's phone was ringing off the hook: Why did Clinton use the present tense? Was he leaving open the possibility of a past affair? Was he deliberately fudging once again? . . .

There were more dangers yet to come: Lewinsky's potential testimony to Ken Starr, possible accounts of sexual episodes from other women, the Paula Jones trial itself. *The Washington Post*, which had played down the Kathleen Willey tale that McCurry worked so hard to contain, now gave her account page-one prominence, noting that she maintained that Clinton had "fondled her breast and put her hand on his genitals." And in a rude reminder that the campaign finance investigation was still going strong, Charlie Trie, Clinton's old pal, was indicted for illegal fundraising. Still, there was little joy in this dizzying blur of a scandal, even for the hard-bitten reporters, for Clinton's conduct was so breathtakingly tawdry and the consequences so sad for the country.

By now, the Clintonites had retreated to what they were calling a "hunker-down strategy." They would not answer further questions about Lewinsky, and neither would Clinton. After days of insisting that the president wanted to gather the facts and tell his story, the White House made clear that he would not, perhaps for a long time. After more than a year of talking up a policy of full disclosure, they now resorted, in Nixonian fashion, to an all-out stonewall. McCurry lamely told reporters he was "out of the loop." The press secretary no longer wanted to know. This was about survival now. The administration had made the hard political calculation that the public anger was subsiding and they could ride out the storm. If many Americans thought Clinton was lying, so be it. He was far more popular than his media adversaries, the strategists reasoned, and that was what ultimately mattered. The journalists would continue to investigate, to fill the air with sexual charges, but the president would trump them simply by insisting that he was busy with the country's work.

As Bill Clinton dug in for the long haul, one could see, at long last, the limits of spin. When it worked, the coordinated strategy of peddling a single line to the press, of browbeating some reporters and courting others, was stunningly effective. Damage could be contained, scandal minimized, bad news relegated to the fringes of the media world. But each time an administration did that, each time it beat back the negative publicity with shifting explanations and document dumps and manufactured announcements designed to change the subject, it paid a price. The journalists were more skeptical the next time around, less willing to give the Clinton spin team the benefit of the doubt. At some point, even a reelected president dogged by endless scandal can no longer defy the laws of political gravity.

As Clinton remained mum about the details of what did or did not happen with Monica Lewinsky, his aides' efforts to counter the negative publicity without knowing the facts were all too transparent. They asked Mark Penn to take a poll to assess the damage. They uncorked all the techniques that had worked so well for so long—blaming the press, denouncing their accusers, assailing right-wing enemies, blitzing the talk shows. But even the best spin cannot work if it is totally untethered from substance, and, in the absence of hard information about the president and the intern, the loyalists' spin had become surreal. The press wasn't buying it, and neither was much of the public. The journalists were caught up in a frenzy of unprecedented intensity, with all sorts of uncorroborated allegations echoing through the headlines and the newscasts. But for a president who loved to fill the public space with great torrents of words, his silence was the loudest sound of all.

As the state of siege grew deeper, it remained unclear whether this would be the scandal that forced Bill Clinton from office or whether he would manage yet again to hang on. What was all too clear was that the damage to his presidency would never be repaired. Clinton's efforts to persuade the press that he had an ambitious second-term agenda, to reach a rapprochement with his media antagonists, to rise above his slippery public image, had failed. The spinmeisters could no longer save him from himself. The president would have his place in history, but it was not the one he had imagined.

88

BRADLEY PATTERSON

From *The White House Staff: The Advance Office*

Never on screen, not even allowed to snack from the "reporters' buffet," the White House advance team is charged with planning every presidential visit down to the last detail. After reading this account of the painstaking attention to detail required to make a trip successful and memorable, the two minutes of footage of a presidential visit on the nightly news will never seem the same again. In this excerpt, Bradley Patterson describes the many elements that go into presidential travel, from security to transportation to cele-

bration: "three thousand balloons are recommended," notes the author. And don't forget the president's plane. Some people, Patterson discovers, will show up at the airport only to see Air Force One. *The advance team must make sure everything goes exactly as planned, including "The Moment" that sticks forever in the minds of the crowd and, the team hopes, that appears on page one of every newspaper.*

━━━━━━

PRESIDENTS NEVER stay home. From Shawnee Mission High School to the emperor's palace, from the Kentucky State Fair to the Kremlin, the president of the United States is visitor in chief, representing now his government, now his party, now all the people of the nation. As chief of state, he has words of encouragement for the National Association of Student Councils; as chief partisan, he addresses a Senate candidate's closing rally; as national spokesman, he stands on the cliff above Normandy Beach; and as chief diplomat, he spends weary hours at the Wye Retreat Center, extracting tenuous Middle East peace agreements from skeptical antagonists. The lines between his roles are of course never quite that distinct: in each place he travels, the president is all these "chiefs" at once.

His national and political roles are public and he wants them to be so: cameras and the press are invited to witness every handshake, film each ceremony, record all the ringing words. A presidential trip is often substantive, but it is also always theater: each city an act, every stop a scene. As the Secret Service recognizes, however, in any balcony can lurk a John Wilkes Booth, at any window a Lee Harvey Oswald; a Sara Jane Moore or a John Hinckley may emerge from any crowd.* One other presidential role is quintessential but usually more concealed: as commander in chief, the American president must always—no matter where he is in the world—be able to reach his national security command centers.

A presidential trip, therefore, is not a casual sojourn: it is a massive expedition, its every mile planned ahead, its every minute preprogrammed. The surge of cheering thousands must stop just short of a moving cocoon of security; curtained behind each VIP receiving line is the military aide with the "doomsday briefcase." Except for the military aide with the "satchel," all of the first lady's travel presents similar requirements for minute care and advance attention.

These massive expeditions are the responsibility of the White House

---

*Booth assassinated President Abraham Lincoln. Oswald, at least according to official findings, was the assassin of President John Kennedy. Moore and Hinckley made assassination attempts on Presidents Gerald Ford and Ronald Reagan, respectively.—EDS.

Advance Office. How large a job is this? In seven years in office, President Clinton made some 2,500 appearances in over 800 foreign or domestic cities or destinations, plus some 450 appearances at public events in the Washington area. The pace of the work in the Advance Office was nothing short of breathtaking.

While each chief executive's travel style is different, trip preparations are similar; the art of "advancing" is common to presidency after presidency, although new technological gadgetry has made the whole trip-preparation process swifter and more efficient.

Within any White House staff, trip planning calls for intricate choreography among more than a dozen separate offices: cabinet affairs, communications, domestic policy, intergovernmental, legislative, medical, military, national security (if the trip is overseas), scheduling, political, public liaison, press, Secret Service, social, speechwriting, transportation, the vice president's office, and the first lady's staff. The Advance Office is the orchestrator of this cluster and the manager of all the forthcoming on-scene arrangements.

How does the Advance Office organize a presidential trip? . . .

A domestic presidential visit can get its start from any one of the hundreds of invitations that pour into the White House, but more likely it originates from within, as a homegrown idea. What policy themes is the president emphasizing? To which areas of American life does he wish to draw attention? Educational excellence, industrial competitiveness, athletic prowess, racial harmony, minority achievement, environmental improvement . . . ? At campaign time, of course, electoral issues are foremost: What voters are targeted, which senators need help?

Like the daily schedule . . . , a trip is not a casual event but a calculated piece of a larger theme — and, as such, is designed to convey a message. A presidential trip, in other words, is an instrument of persuasion.

Forward planning for domestic presidential trips may be done from four to eight weeks in advance but is more likely compressed into an even shorter lead time. As soon as the desired message is framed and agreed to, through discussions within the White House, the Advance Office reviews the choices for domestic travel: Where in the country can the presidential theme best be dramatized? Which groups, which sponsors, which cities or towns? What already-scheduled local event could the president join, transforming it into an illustration of his own policy initiative? Local and state calendars are scanned, the *Farmer's Almanac* is studied. Invitations are searched, private suggestions reviewed. Long lists are discussed with the Scheduling Office and vetted into short lists; tentative alternatives are identified. If the president is campaigning, all the processes mentioned here are melded together: the president may do twelve to eighteen events in a week.

For domestic trips, in previous years, "site surveys" would be undertaken perhaps six weeks ahead of time, and "pre-advance" teams would be sent out weeks beforehand. Money then became tighter and staffs smaller. The Bush Advance Office staff totaled eighteen; the Clinton White House had only twelve, four of whom were interns. Communications have speeded up as well. "Reactivity time"—that is, the period needed to respond to changes in circumstances—has dwindled, with the consequence that lead time for decisions may be greatly shortened, alterations more easily tolerated, last-minute revisions accepted. All arrangements can be more flexible; some can be consummated with only hours to spare. The final "go" decision, therefore, has sometimes been made as little as two weeks before the event—or less, as Clinton Advance Office director Paige Reffe described:

I was walking into an afternoon meeting in the deputy chief of staff's office that I thought was supposed to be about the first family's vacation . . . and the deputy turns to me and says, "By the way, we are thinking of the president going to New York at nine o'clock to meet with the TWA Flight 800 families." I said, "Nine o'clock when?" And she said, "Nine o'clock tomorrow morning," about eighteen hours from now. I said, "I didn't bring my top hat, I didn't bring my cane, and I don't have any rabbits to pull out today. . . . Let's stop *thinking* about this; there is a 5:30 P.M. flight to Kennedy; I can get people on that flight. I can actually get something set up if the decision is made in the next hour." In the end, sometimes those things are easier than normal events, because there isn't time for people to start picking them apart and making changes.

Floods, disasters, hurricane damage, funerals: a presidential presence is often required. But then the advance office looks less like a long-range-planning unit and more like a firehouse.

The White House counsel makes a key determination: Is any part of the trip for a clearly political purpose? Is the president going to be partisan in speech and act, or will he be entirely "presidential"? In scrupulous detail, all the proposed meetings, site events, rallies, and addresses are divided into rigid categories so that mathematically precise formulas can be used to allocate expenses between the political sponsors and the government: "21.7 percent of the trip is political, 78.3 percent is official," explains one illustrative memorandum. The counsel and the political affairs director sign off on the allocation. If the White House asks any federal political appointees to serve as volunteers on the advance team (which it often does), they must take annual leave if they work on any part of the trip that is political—and any expenses they incur must be paid for by the host political group or by party national headquarters.

Funding is a sensitive issue. There is a four-way division: (1) Assuming the trip is nonpolitical, the White House budget itself supports only the travel expenses of the advance teams and the presidential party (and its VIP guests), including the staff of the White House Press Office. (2) For any trip, political or not, the government covers those costs that relate to the president's security. In this category are the costs incurred by the White House Military Office (financed by the Department of Defense); this office covers the expenses of its medical personnel, military aides, and the White House Communications Agency (WHCA), which supplies lights and amplification equipment as well as its own ample communications gear. Also in this category are the costs incurred by the Secret Service (actually part of the Treasury Department), which has its own budget for travel and equipment (including the presidential limousine and other special cars). The Military Office's *Air Force One* will be supplied, but its costs must be reimbursed if the trip is political. (3) Members of the White House press corps pay for their own travel expenses (via reimbursement to the White House Travel Office). (4) All local "event" expenses must be borne by host groups: for example, the costs of renting a hall, constructing risers for the press, furnishing the stage backdrops, providing banners and hand-held signs, printing and sending out flyers, printing tickets, arranging for advertising, and providing motorcade vehicles for nonfederal dignitaries. A letter spelling out these financial obligations is sent to the host, who must send back a signed formal agreement.

The government's actual total cost for a domestic presidential trip is almost impossible to pin down, but it is high. No host group, political or otherwise, could afford all the charges, including those relating to security. Therefore, no matter what reimbursement is obtained, there is a significant publicly financed subsidy for any presidential expedition. It is simply the cost of having a president who travels.

Within the White House, an Advance Office "staff lead' is named who will head up all the advance work. In addition, a trip coordinator is designated—a stay-on-home-base "ringmaster" to whom the advance team's queries are directed and on whose desk all plans and all logistical details are centralized. "She is the lifeline for the advance people," explained Bush advance director John Keller. "Whenever the advance people call back to the office, that's the one they talk to."

Once the two lead people are designated, internal assignments are specified. It is a broad "ring": the Intergovernmental Affairs and Political Affairs Offices will recommend governors, mayors, or local officials to be asked to sit on the dais; the legislative affairs staff will identify the senators and representatives who would be affronted if they were not invited to accompany the president. If the trip is political, the political affairs director will compose a detailed list of themes that will gain a warm local reception, and of issues to avoid. The event will usually be designated as "open press"—but if not, the Press Office will organize a pool of the White House press corps, and the media relations unit will prepare credentials for the local press.

Speechwriters are at work, the medical staff makes its preparations, the Secret Service will ask its local field agents to supplement its regular presidential protective detail. WHCA will box up a mobile satellite sending and receiving station along with the president's armored "Blue Goose" podium. The Air Force will make sure that the local airport can handle the "footprint" of the huge 747 *Air Force One* and will stash two presidential limousines, the necessary Secret Service vehicles, and WHCA's "Road-runner" communications van into a C-141 transport. If it is called for, the Marine Corps will add in HMX-1, one of the presidential helicopters.

The White House advance team itself is assembled. Headed by the staff lead, the team includes representatives from many of the offices just mentioned. Unless the occasion is unusually complicated, current practice is for the advance team for a domestic trip to leave the White House only six days before the president is scheduled to arrive (seven for a RON—"remain overnight"—visit). In what is likely to be a rather frantic final five days, the advance team must complete an unbelievably complicated checklist: one such list was twenty-six pages long and included 485 items.

The team visits the airport, draws (and faxes to Washington) rough site diagrams—showing where planes, helicopters, and cars will park—and reviews the planned arrival ceremonies. Who will the greeters be? (Each hand-shaker must be approved in Washington.) Are the toe strips in place to show the greeters where to stand? Where is the rope line? The team is admonished: "Inconvenience as few commercial airline passengers as possible." Not even a wheeled set of stairs needs to be commandeered; *Air Force One* has its own mobile stairs.

The motorcade is organized with minute precision. The advance team is reminded that "all the substantive success in the world can be overshadowed if those involved cannot get where they need to be." The motorcade may be the standard minimum of twenty-four vehicles or it may be a hundred cars long. Each car is labeled and spotted on the diagram; every driver must be approved by the Secret Service. The last two cars, which are called "stragglers," will pick up staff members who may have missed the departure; the stragglers can also be used as alternates in case of breakdowns. Motorcades used to be important for generating crowds of sidewalk spectators—but no longer. Primarily for security reasons, the line of cars speeds by: the onlookers not only don't see the president, they can't even figure out which limo he is in.

Each event site must be examined in detail: What will be the backdrop, the "storyboard"—that is, the picture that television will capture? "Distill the message into a brief and catchy phrase," advises the detail-conscious Advance Manual, but "you *do not* want shiny white letters on shiny yellow vinyl." This is not some "pizza-parlor's grand opening." Walking routes are plotted: for the president, the guests, the press, the staff, and the public (more diagrams). There must be a presidential "holding room" where he meets sponsors and guests. What will be the program? What kind of audience is expected—students? senior citizens? friendly? skeptical? How long will it take for them to go through the magnetometers? If hotel overnights are planned, floor plans are needed.

No team is without its conflicts. The press advance staffers want to have an airport arrival at high noon, big crowds, remarks, greetings, bands, balloons ascending, people pressing against the ropes. The Secret Service looks through different eyes. "If they had their way," commented one advance veteran, "they would have the president arrive after dark, in an out-of-the-way corner of the airport, put him into a Sherman tank, lead him to a bank, and have him spend the night in a vault." He added: "They would say, 'You cannot choose that route,' and we would counter, 'No, he *will* drive that avenue, you go ahead and protect him.'" Since the assassination attempt on Reagan, the Secret Service wins more of these battles.

There are conflicts with the local hosts as well: Who will sit on the dais? Will spaces be saved for the local as well as the national press? One sponsoring group for a fund-raiser had sold every seat on the floor of a gymnasium: the advance team had to insist that the tables and seats be squeezed together to make room for the camera platforms. There must be two sets of such risers: one facing the speaker and one at an angle in the rear, for over-the-shoulder "cutaway" shots of the president together with the audience he is addressing. With luck, the risers can be borrowed; the advance team is instructed: "Don't go cutting down virgin forest to build press risers for one-time-only use."

The White House advance person, the instructions make clear, is a diplomat-in-temporary-residence, "the mover and the shaker, the stroker and the cajoler, the smoother of ruffled feathers and the soother of hard feelings. The staff lead is the captain of a great team." But the captain is forewarned: shun all media interviews. "*Never* be a spokesman or go on the record with the press. . . . You are invisible to the camera. Your work is done just outside the four corners of the picture frame. You do not eat up an inch of the screen that is the canvas that you and your colleagues have designed to be a 'picture of the day.' You and your advance team colleagues are not the story, the *president's visit* is. . . . And don't snack on the buffet food which the working press has paid for. . . . But get the job done."

A former advance chief slyly recalls:

To be a successful advance person . . . you have to have that minor crooked side to you, and you have to be willing to do whatever you have to do. That doesn't necessarily mean breaking the law, but it means that you can't be shy and you have to be assertive. If I tell you to go find a podium, I know you're going to come back and you're going to find a podium. You may have just happened to have gotten it from that event three doors down, and they're wondering where their podium is right now, but the fallout had there not been a podium would be a hell of a lot bigger than somebody asking where the podium came from!

The advance team may include nongovernmental companions: technical experts from the news networks, news photographers, and representatives from the White House Correspondents Association. Satellite time must be reserved, transmitting "dishes" placed, camera angles planned. What will be the dramatic scenes? Where will the sun be?

The advance team's instructions leave no doubt as to the purpose of a presidential trip: "The President has a point to make and that's the message. The message of a trip . . . is the *mission* of a trip . . . The public events of a trip are the expression of the message. It is central to advance work and deserves a lot of time and energy. Every event or site must capture or reinforce the reason the President is there. . . . The trip's message has already been through a wringer of careful deliberation at the White House."

The government team and the news planning team represent institutions that are different and often at odds. In this mini-universe, however, they have a common purpose: to get the fullest stories and the best pictures to the most people the fastest. "All of them know that, visually and technically, there are right and wrong ways to do things," explained one former participant, "and this is true whoever is president; it's a professional business." Such symbiosis disturbed newsman Martin Schram, however. He quoted a colleague: "In a funny way, the . . . advance men and I have the same thing at heart—we want the piece to look as good as it possibly can. . . . That's their job and that's my job. . . . I'm looking for the best pictures, but I can't help it if the audiences that show up, or that are grouped together by the . . . [White House] look so good. . . . I can't help it if it looks like a commercial." Schram then adds, "That is what White House video experts . . . are counting on. Offering television's professionals pictures they could not refuse was at the core of the . . . officials' efforts to shape and even control the content of the network newscasts."

A Clinton advance officer described this duality from another angle:

The most frustrating part of my job: . . . the advance team will make sure that [the press] are supplied with very nice visuals, with a great venue for the speech, and then you will see the most unbelievable choice of pictures that the producer or editor or newspaper . . . will actually decide to run. . . . We put all that blood, sweat, and tears into creating this beautiful visual backdrop and instead they will wind up with pictures of the president talking with some aide backstage. . . . The picture that we actually got out of all this hard work was completely disconnected from the story we were trying to achieve. So I think that coziness may not be as prevalent as it used to be . . . not with the people who are deciding what goes on the evening news or the front page. . . . It is also a function of volume: President Clinton travels exponentially more than President Reagan; editors probably tire of running the pictures that we "give" them.

There are still other items on the final checklist: "Effect of the motorcade on normal commuting patterns," "Lighting: 320 foot-candles on the speaker and 200 foot-candles on the crowd," "Overtime cost estimate," "Other appropriate music—can the band play it?" "Empty seats filled or draped," "List of gifts accepted for the President," "Bad weather alternative."

The advance team has a daily "countdown" meeting, where the team members make sure that they are all on the same page. "Never miss it!" warns the manual. There is also a daily conference call to home base, with the trip coordinator and all the affected White House offices. "Date-time stamp and file every piece of paper," the team is instructed, and "Keep Everybody Informed."

If the trip is political and a big rally is scheduled, the advance team will include another specialist, a "crowd-builder," who comes with the attitude that this "is a historic occasion, a great party, the biggest thing to ever happen to this town. If Joe Public misses it, Joe Public will regret it for the rest of his/her life. So, Joe Public better pack up the kids and bring Grandma and Grandpa or they will have missed one of the biggest days in their town's history!"

The local hosts must do the actual work, mobilizing hundreds of enthusiastic volunteers. A vast menu of techniques is systematically used, but all are on the advance team's checklist: not a single step is left to chance. For illustration:

—Event sites should be "expandable" or "collapsible," so that new seats can be added or empty chairs removed.
—Ten times as many handbills should be printed as there are places to be filled: enough for every shopping-center grocery bag, for door handles in parking lots, to tape to mirrors in public rest rooms, even to lay (right side up) on busy sidewalks. One last idea is suggested: "Stand on top of the highest building in town and throw the handbills into the wind." Leaflets must list the event as beginning at least one half hour before it will actually start: a president on the platform with a crowd still at the gates is chaos.
—*Air Force One* should be mentioned in leaflets for an airport rally; some folks will come just to see the plane. News stories about the history of presidential aircraft should be used to spark the interest of the crowd (but mention of their cost should be avoided).
—Bands, cheerleaders, pom-pom girls, and drill teams are to be mobilized (but the Secret Service has to check every make-believe rifle).
—Banner-painting parties are suggested, with supplies of butcher paper and tempera paint; a "hand-held sign committee" should be organized.
—Three thousand balloons are recommended, with balloon rises preferred over balloon drops. The truly experienced may try to do both simultaneously in the same auditorium: helium in the ones to go up, air in the ones to come down. The hall manager must be consulted first, however: the risen balloons will cling to the ceiling for two days afterwards.

No matter how rah-rah some aspects of a trip may be, White House advance staffers are forever conscious that it is the president of the United States who is there. They strive for a "colorful and mediagenic setting"—but never at the expense of the dignity of the person or the office. Their instructions state: "The President must never be allowed into a potentially awkward or embarrassing situation, and the advance person is sometimes the only one who can keep that from happening. . . . For example, an oversized cowboy hat, a live farm animal, an Indian headdress, or a Shriner's 'Fez' could produce a decidedly un-presidential photograph. Common sense must be used to make sure that the dignity of the office of the President is never compromised by the well-intentioned generosity of local partisans."

And no thank you to sound trucks, bands on flatbed trailers, elephants, clowns, and parachutists.

Like crowd-raising, press-advancing is a special skill of the advance team. At a major event site, a press area must be set apart. Camera platforms and radio tables must be of the required size and height, and press-only magnetometers must be installed. Each event site must be equipped with a half-dozen long-distance telephones, and each desk needs an electric outlet for plugging in a laptop. Four nearby rooms are reserved (at their cost) for the three television networks to edit their tapes. A filing center is set up with tables and chairs for a hundred people; the press secretary and his staff need a large adjoining office area with six tables to hold their equipment. "We duplicate the White House Press Office on the scene of a presidential visit," one expert explained. "The White House press staff can do their work just as if they were at 1600 Pennsylvania Avenue."

The advance team stays on site, completing its prodigious checklist, until the very moment the president is to arrive.

Back at the White House, the formal press announcement is made, with the local sponsors tipped off ahead of time and the necessary representatives, senators, governors, and mayors likewise alerted just before the White House release. The speechwriters have prepared their drafts, idea notes, or complete remarks ahead of time for arrivals, departures, and each stop in between (but word processors and copiers are aboard *Air Force One* if last-minute changes are ordered). The earlier sketches of airports, motorcade arrival and departure points, corridors, rooms, and walkways are transformed into minute diagrams, with arrows drawn in showing each presidential footstep.

When its own thousand details are done, the White House Press Office compiles a "Press Schedule Bible," which is given out to the national press representatives.

On the morning before the day of departure, the Advance Office holds a final trip briefing for the chief of staff; it will be the chief of staff who gives the final imprimatur for the *Air Force One* manifest. The advance team staff lead composes the president's and first lady's personal schedule sheets. Even when airborne, *Air Force One*'s communications desk buzzes with last-minute advice from the advance team waiting at the arrival site.

As the presidential party approaches the runway, what goes through an advance person's mind? One veteran remembers: "There are a hundred bad variables when you look at a situation and go down your list. What you try to do is to reduce those down to zero. You never get them to zero, but if you get them down to six or five or four when the event occurs, then the odds are with you, and if they do go wrong they are at least in the manageable range."

The Advance Manual emphasizes: Pictures of the president standing behind the podium are dull stuff, and could just as well be snapped in the Rose Garden. Plan to have the cameras catch the president doing something unique and special, of exciting human-interest quality:

The high point . . . is "The Moment," the one snippet of action that visually tells the story of why the trip was undertaken in the first place. Media organizations need this moment to encapsulate the event. It will be rare that a newspaper will carry the complete transcript and equally rare that a local affiliate will broadcast the event "live" on television. . . . So we strive to create a moment: that ten-second slice of uplifting video . . . or that full-color, top-of-the-fold newspaper photo. . . . As the cliche goes, a picture is worth a thousand words. . . . "The Moment" is what you make of it. Don't let a visit go by without creating one.

PART FIFTEEN

Political Economy and Public Welfare

89

JOHN KENNETH GALBRAITH

From *The Affluent Society*

Writing in the late 1950s as an associate of soon-to-be-president John Kennedy, eminent Economics Professor John Kenneth Galbraith made an eloquent case for liberal economics. He contrasted Americans' indulgence in private spending with the inadequacy of available public monies. "Social balance" was Galbraith's goal. His influential book touched on many facets of the American economy: the tax system, military spending, educational and urban problems. Although his plea for a bigger government role in allocating the use of the nation's wealth is undeniably out of vogue in the current political era, Galbraith has been unwavering in his support of these principles over the years. The question open to debate today is: Did the United States follow Galbraith's economic prescription too far, or not far enough?

———

. . . WE MUST find a way to remedy the poverty which afflicts us in public services and which is in such increasingly bizarre contrast with our affluence in private goods. This is necessary to temper and, more hopefully, to eliminate the social disorders which are the counterpart of the present imbalance. It is necessary in the long run for promoting the growth of private output itself. Such balance is a matter of elementary common sense in a country in which need is becoming so exiguous that it must be cherished where it exists and nurtured where it does not. To create the demand for new automobiles, we must contrive elaborate and functionless changes each year and then subject the consumer to ruthless psychological pressures to persuade him of their importance. Were this process to falter or break down, the consequences would be disturbing. In the meantime, there are large ready-made needs for schools, hospitals, slum clearance and urban redevelopment, sanitation, parks, playgrounds, police and a thousand other things. Of these needs, almost no one must be persuaded. They exist because, as public officials of all kinds and ranks explain each day with practiced skill, the money to provide for them is unavailable. So it has come about that we get growth and increased employment along the dimension of private goods only at the price of increasingly frantic persuasion. We exploit but poorly the opportunity along the dimension of public services. The economy is geared to the least urgent set of human values. It would be far more secure if it were based on the whole range of need. . . .

. . . For a very large part of our public activity, revenues are relatively static. Although aggregate income increases, many tax systems return a comparatively fixed dollar amount. Hence new public needs, or even the increase in the requirements for old ones incident on increasing population, require affirmative steps to transfer resources to public use. There must first be a finding of need. The burden of proof lies with those who propose the expenditure. Resources do not automatically accrue to public authority for a decision as to how they may best be distributed to schools, roads, police, public housing and other claimant ends. We are startled by the thought. It would lead to waste.

But with increasing income, resources do so accrue to the private individual. Nor when he buys a new automobile out of increased income is he required to prove need. We may assume that many fewer automobiles would be purchased than at present were it necessary to make a positive case for their purchase. [Yet] such a case must be made for schools. . . . The solution is a system of taxation which automatically makes a pro rata share of increasing income available to public authority for public purposes. The task of public authority, like that of private individuals, will be to distribute this increase in accordance with relative need. Schools and roads will then no longer be at a disadvantage as compared with automobiles and television sets in having to prove absolute justification.

The practical solution would be much eased were the revenues of the federal government available for the service of social balance. These, to the extent of about four-fifths of the total, come from personal and corporation income taxes. Subject to some variations, these taxes rise rather more than proportionately with increases in private income. Unhappily they are presently preempted in large measure by the requirements (actual or claimed) of national defense and the competition of arms. . . .

Hopefully the time will come when federal revenues and the normal annual increase will not be preempted so extensively for military purposes. Conventional attitudes hold otherwise; on all prospects of mankind, there is hope for betterment save those having to do with an eventual end, without war, to the arms race. Here the hard cold voice of realism warns there is no chance. Perhaps things are not so utterly hopeless. . . .

However, even though the higher urgency of federal expenditures for social balance is conceded, there is still the problem of providing the revenue. And since it is income taxes that must here be used, the question of social balance can easily be lost sight of in the reopened argument over equality. The truce will be broken and liberals and conservatives will join battle on this issue and forget about the poverty in the public services that awaits correction and, as we shall see presently, the poverty of people which can only be corrected at increased public cost. All this—schools, hospitals, even the scientific research on which increased production depends—must wait while we debate the ancient and unresolvable question of whether the rich are too rich.

The only hope—and in the nature of things it rests primarily with liberals—is to separate the issue of equality from that of social balance. The second is by far the more important question. The fact that a tacit truce exists on the issue of inequality is proof of its comparative lack of social urgency. In the past, the liberal politician has countered the conservative proposal for reduction in top bracket income taxes with the proposal that relief be confined to the lower brackets. And he has insisted that any necessary tax increase be carried more than proportionately by the higher income brackets. The result has been to make him a co-conspirator with the conservative in reducing taxes, whatever the cost in social balance; and his insistence on making taxes an instrument of greater equality has made it difficult or impossible to increase them. Meanwhile the individuals with whom he sympathizes and whom he seeks to favor are no longer the tax-ridden poor of Bengal or the First Empire* but people who, by all historical standards, are themselves comparatively opulent citizens. In any case, they would be among the first beneficiaries of the better education, health, housing and other services which would be the fruits of improved social balance, and they would be the long-run beneficiaries of more nearly adequate investment in people.

The rational liberal, in the future, will resist tax reduction, even that which ostensibly favors the poor, if it is at the price of social balance. And, for the same reason, he will not hesitate to accept increases that are neutral as regards the distribution of income. His classical commitment to greater equality can far better be kept by attacking as a separate issue the more egregious of the loopholes in the present tax law. These loopholes . . . are strongly in conflict with traditional liberal attitudes, for this is inequality sanctioned by the state. There is work enough here for any egalitarian crusader. . . .

. . . One final observation may be made. There will be question as to what is the test of balance—at what point may we conclude that balance

*Bengal is a poverty-stricken region on the Indian subcontinent. The First Empire is probably a reference to the time of the ancient world civilizations, including Mesopotamia, Egypt, India, China, Greece, and Rome. According to the historical interpretation of Karl Marx, these early empires resulted from the oppression of certain groups by those who dominated, with slavery as the chief economic force.—EDS.

has been achieved in the satisfaction of private and public needs. The answer is that no test can be applied, for none exists. The traditional formulation is that the satisfaction returned to the community from a marginal increment of resources devoted to public purposes should be equal to the satisfaction of the same increment in private employment. These are incommensurate, partly because different people are involved, and partly because it makes the cardinal error of comparing satisfaction of wants that are systematically synthesized as part of an organic process with those that are not.

But a precise equilibrium is not very important. For another mark of an affluent society is the existence of a considerable margin for error on such matters. The present imbalance is clear, as are the forces and ideas which give the priority to private as compared with public goods. This being so, the direction in which we move to correct matters is utterly plain. We can also assume, given the power of the forces that have operated to accord a priority to private goods, that the distance to be traversed is considerable. When we arrive, the opulence of our private consumption will no longer be in contrast with the poverty of our schools, the unloveliness and congestion of our cities, our inability to get to work without struggle and the social disorder that is associated with imbalance. But the precise point of balance will never be defined. This will be of comfort only to those who believe that any failure of definition can be made to score decisively against a larger idea.

90

MILTON FRIEDMAN

From *Free to Choose*

Conservative economists are numerous today. But none can compete for style and consistency of viewpoint with Nobel Prize–winning Economics Professor Milton Friedman. Friedman has been the voice of conservative economics over the past half-century, during times when his ideas received little public acceptance. Free to Choose, written with his wife Rose Friedman, became the basis for an informative, entertaining—and controversial—TV series. Friedman's central theme is "freedom," both in economics and in politics. He advocates that the maximum amount of economic power be left to individual citizens, to make their own choices, with the least possible control placed in the central government's province. Big government is Friedman's target. In the excerpt, Friedman mentions his heroes, classical economists Adam Smith and Friedrich Hayek. The name of Milton Friedman will join that list for future generations of conservatives.

———

THE STORY of the United States is the story of an economic miracle and a political miracle that was made possible by the translation into practice of two sets of ideas—both, by a curious coincidence, formulated in documents published in the same year, 1776.

One set of ideas was embodied in *The Wealth of Nations*, the master-piece that established the Scotsman Adam Smith as the father of modern economics. It analyzed the way in which a market system could combine the freedom of individuals to pursue their own objectives with the extensive cooperation and collaboration needed in the economic field to produce our food, our clothing, our housing. Adam Smith's key insight was that both parties to an exchange can benefit and that, *so long as cooperation is strictly voluntary,* no exchange will take place unless both parties do benefit. No external force, no coercion, no violation of freedom is necessary to produce cooperation among individuals all of whom can benefit. That is why, as Adam Smith put it, an individual who "intends only his own gain" is "led by an invisible hand to promote an end which was no part of his intention. Nor is it always the worse for the society that it was no part of it. By pursuing his own interest he frequently promotes that of the society more effectually than when he really intends to promote it. I have never known much good done by those who affected to trade for the public good."

The second set of ideas was embodied in the Declaration of Independence, drafted by Thomas Jefferson to express the general sense of his fellow countrymen. It proclaimed a new nation, the first in history established on the principle that every person is entitled to pursue his own values: "We hold these truths to be self-evident, that all men are created equal, that they are endowed by their Creator with certain unalienable Rights; that among these are Life, Liberty, and the pursuit of Happiness." . . .

Economic freedom is an essential requisite for political freedom. By enabling people to cooperate with one another without coercion or central direction, it reduces the area over which political power is exercised. In addition, by dispersing power, the free market provides an offset to whatever concentration of political power may arise. The combination of economic and political *power* in the same hands is a sure recipe for tyranny. . . .

Ironically, the very success of economic and political freedom reduced its appeal to later thinkers. The narrowly limited government of the late nineteenth century possessed little concentrated power that endangered the ordinary man. The other side of that coin was that it possessed little power that would enable good people to do good. And in an imperfect world there were still many evils. Indeed, the very progress of society made the residual evils seem all the more objectionable. As always, people took the favorable developments for granted. They forgot the danger to freedom from a strong government. Instead, they were attracted by the good that a stronger government could achieve—if only government power were in the "right" hands. . . .

These views have dominated developments in the United States during the past half-century. They have led to a growth in government at all levels, as well as to a transfer of power from local government and local control to central government and central control. The government has increasingly undertaken the task of taking from some to give to others in the name of security and equality. . . .

These developments have been produced by good intentions with a major assist from self-interest. [Yet] even the strongest supporters of the welfare and paternal state agree that the results have been disappointing. . . .

The experience of recent years—slowing growth and declining productivity—raises a doubt whether private ingenuity can continue to overcome the deadening effects of government control if we continue to grant ever more power to government, to authorize a "new class" of civil servants to spend ever larger fractions of our income supposedly on our behalf. Sooner or later—and perhaps sooner than many of us expect—an ever bigger government would destroy both the prosperity that we owe to the free market and the human freedom proclaimed so eloquently in the Declaration of Independence.

We have not yet reached the point of no return. We are still free as a people to choose whether we shall continue speeding down the "road to serfdom," as Friedrich Hayek entitled his profound and influential book, or whether we shall set tighter limits on government and rely more heavily on voluntary cooperation among free individuals to achieve our several objectives. Will our golden age come to an end in a relapse into the tyranny and misery that has always been, and remains today, the state of most of mankind? Or shall we have the wisdom, the foresight, and the courage to change our course, to learn from experience, and to benefit from a "rebirth of freedom"? . . . If the cresting of the tide . . . is to be followed by a move toward a freer society and a more limited government rather than toward a totalitarian society, the public must not only recognize the defects of the present situation but also how it has come about and what we can do about it. Why are the results of policies so often the opposite of their ostensible objectives? Why do special interests prevail over the general interest? What devices can we use to stop and reverse the process? . . .

. . . Whenever we visit Washington, D.C., we are impressed all over again with how much power is concentrated in that city. Walk the halls of Congress, and the 435 members of the House plus the 100 senators are hard to find among their 18,000 employees—about 65 for each senator and 27 for each member of the House. In addition, the more than 15,000 registered lobbyists—often accompanied by secretaries, typists, researchers, or representatives of the special interest they represent—walk the same halls seeking to exercise influence.

And this is but the tip of the iceberg. The federal government employs close to 3 million civilians (excluding the uniformed military forces). Over 350,000 are in Washington and the surrounding metropolitan area. Countless others are indirectly employed through government contracts with nominally private organizations, or are employed by labor or business organizations or other special interest groups that maintain their headquarters, or at least an office, in Washington because it is the seat of government. . . .

. . . Both the fragmentation of power and the conflicting government policies are rooted in the political realities of a democratic system that operates by enacting detailed and specific legislation. Such a system tends to give undue political power to small groups that have highly concentrated interests, to give greater weight to obvious, direct, and immediate effects of government action than to possibly more important but concealed, indirect, and delayed effects, to set in motion a process that sacrifices the general interest to serve special interests, rather than the other way around. There is, as it were, an invisible hand in politics that operates in precisely the opposite direction to Adam Smith's invisible hand. Individuals who intend only to promote the *general interest* are led by the invisible political hand to promote a *special interest* that they had no intention to promote. . . .

The benefit an individual gets from any one program that he has a special interest in may be more than canceled by the costs to him of many programs that affect him lightly. Yet it pays him to favor the one program, and not oppose the others. He can readily recognize that he and the small group with the same special interest can afford to spend enough money and time to make a difference in respect of the one program. Not promoting that program will not prevent the others, which do him harm, from being adopted. To achieve that, he would have to be willing and able to devote as much effort to opposing each of them as he does to favoring his own. That is clearly a losing proposition. . . .

Currently in the United States, anything like effective detailed control of government by the public is limited to villages, towns, smaller cities, and suburban areas—and even there only to those matters not mandated by the state or federal government. In large cities, states, Washington, we have government of the people not by the people but by a largely faceless group of bureaucrats.

No federal legislator could conceivably even read, let alone analyze and study, all the laws on which he must vote. He must depend on his numerous aides and assistants, or outside lobbyists, or fellow legislators, or some other source for most of his decisions on how to vote. The unelected congressional bureaucracy almost surely has far more influence today in shaping the detailed laws that are passed than do our elected representatives.

The situation is even more extreme in the administration of government programs. The vast federal bureaucracy spread through the many government departments and independent agencies is literally out of control of the elected representatives of the public. Elected Presidents and senators and representatives come and go but the civil service remains. Higher-level bureaucrats are past masters at the art of using red tape to delay and defeat proposals they do not favor; of issuing rules and regulations as "interpretations" of laws that in fact subtly, or sometimes crudely, alter their thrust; of dragging their feet in administering those parts of laws of which they disapprove, while pressing on with those they favor. . . .

Bureaucrats have not usurped power They have not deliberately engaged in any kind of conspiracy to subvert the democratic process. Power has been thrust on them. . . .

The growth of the bureaucracy in size and power affects every detail of the relation between a citizen and his government. . . . Needless to say, those of us who want to halt and reverse the recent trend should oppose additional specific measures to expand further the power and scope of government, urge repeal and reform of existing measures, and try to elect legislators and executives who share that view. But that is not an effective way to reverse the growth of government. It is doomed to failure. Each of us would defend our own special privileges and try to limit government at someone else's expense. We would be fighting a many-headed hydra that would grow new heads faster than we could cut old ones off.*

Our founding fathers have shown us a more promising way to proceed: by package deals, as it were. We should adopt self-denying ordinances that limit the objectives we try to pursue through political channels. We should not consider each case on its merits, but lay down broad rules limiting what government may do. . . .

We need, in our opinion, the equivalent of the First Amendment to limit government power in the economic and social area—an economic Bill of Rights to complement and reinforce the original Bill of Rights. . . .

The proposed amendments would alter the conditions under which legislators—state or federal, as the case may be—operate by limiting the total amount they are authorized to appropriate. The amendments would give the government a limited budget, specified in advance, the way each of us has a limited budget. Much special interest legislation is undesirable, but it is never clearly and unmistakably bad. On the contrary, every measure will be represented as serving a good cause. The problem is that there are an infinite number of good causes. Currently, a legislator is in a weak position to oppose a "good" cause. If he objects that it will raise taxes, he will be labeled a reactionary who is willing to sacrifice human need for base mercenary reasons—after all, this good cause will only require raising taxes by a few cents or dollars per person. The legislator is in a far better position if he can say, "Yes, yours is a good cause, but we have a fixed budget. More money for your cause means less for others. Which of these others should be cut?" The effect would be to require the special interests to compete with one another for a bigger share of a fixed pie, instead of their being able to collude with one another to make the pie bigger at the expense of the taxpayer. . . .

. . . The two ideas of human freedom and economic freedom working together came to their greatest fruition in the United States. Those ideas are still very much with us. We are all of us imbued with them. They are part of the very fabric of our being. But we have been straying from them. We have been forgetting the basic truth that the greatest threat to human freedom is the concentration of power, whether in the hands of government or anyone else. We have persuaded ourselves that it is safe to grant power, provided it is for good purposes.

*The Hydra was a mythical Greek monster that grew two heads for each one that was chopped off. It was killed by the hero Hercules.—EDS.

Fortunately, we are waking up. . . .

Fortunately, also, we are as a people still free to choose which way we should go—whether to continue along the road we have been following to ever bigger government, or to call a halt and change direction.

91

MICHAEL HARRINGTON

From *The Other America*

Poverty in the United States is not new, but it took social critic Michael Harrington's acclaimed book, published in 1962, to bring the reality of "the other America" in the midst of the "affluent society" to the nation's attention. Harrington's study of the middle class's withdrawal from the problems of poor city-dwellers marked the philosophical start of the "war on poverty," which was to begin later in the 1960s. Harrington explored the situation of people who were poor within a society of plenty. His characterization of the poor as "socially invisible" and "politically invisible" led to wide public recognition of the problem of poverty in America. In his later writings, Harrington continued his theme of poverty amidst wealth, warning of increasing class polarization, while holding out hope for a unified national effort to end economic and social inequality.

THERE IS a familiar America. It is celebrated in speeches and advertised on television and in the magazines. It has the highest mass standard of living the world has ever known.

In the 1950s this America worried about itself, yet even its anxieties were products of abundance. The title of a brilliant book was widely misinterpreted, and the familiar America began to call itself "the affluent society." There was introspection about Madison Avenue and tail fins*; there was discussion of the emotional suffering taking place in the suburbs. In all this, there was an implicit assumption that the basic grinding economic problems had been solved in the United States. In this theory the nation's problems were no longer a matter of basic human needs, of food,

---

*Madison Avenue, in New York City, is the traditional home of the advertising industry. It is there that plans have been hatched for selling Americans products that they may not yet really know they want—like, in the 1950s, cars with tail fins.—EDS.

shelter, and clothing. Now they were seen as qualitative, a question of learning to live decently amid luxury.

While this discussion was carried on, there existed another America. In it dwelt somewhere between 40,000,000 and 50,000,000 citizens of this land. They were poor. They still are.

To be sure, the other America is not impoverished in the same sense as those poor nations where millions cling to hunger as a defense against starvation. This country has escaped such extremes. That does not change the fact that tens of millions of Americans are, at this very moment, maimed in body and spirit, existing at levels beneath those necessary for human decency. If these people are not starving, they are hungry, and sometimes fat with hunger, for that is what cheap foods do. They are without adequate housing and education and medical care.

The Government has documented what this means to the bodies of the poor, and the figures will be cited throughout this book. But even more basic, this poverty twists and deforms the spirit. The American poor are pessimistic and defeated, and they are victimized by mental suffering to a degree unknown in Suburbia.

This book is a description of the world in which these people live; it is about the other America. Here are the unskilled workers, the migrant farm workers, the aged, the minorities, and all the others who live in the economic underworld of American life. . . .

The millions who are poor in the United States tend to become increasingly invisible. Here is a great mass of people, yet it takes an effort of the intellect and will even to see them. . . .

. . . The other America, the America of poverty, is hidden today in a way that it never was before. Its millions are socially invisible to the rest of us. No wonder that so many misinterpreted [economist John Kenneth] Galbraith's title and assumed that "the affluent society" meant that everyone had a decent standard of life. The misinterpretation was true as far as the actual day-to-day lives of two-thirds of the nation were concerned. Thus, one must begin a description of the other America by understanding why we do not see it.

There are perennial reasons that make the other America an invisible land.

Poverty is often off the beaten track. It always has been. . . .

. . . The American city has been transformed. The poor still inhabit the miserable housing in the central area, but they are increasingly isolated from contact with, or sight of, anybody else. Middle-class women coming in from Suburbia on a rare trip may catch the merest glimpse of the other America on the way to an evening at the theater, but their children are segregated in suburban schools. The business or professional man may drive along the fringes of slums in a car or bus, but it is not an important experience to him. The failures, the unskilled, the disabled, the aged, and the minorities are right there, across the tracks, where they have always been. But hardly anyone else is.

In short, the very development of the American city has removed poverty from the living, emotional experience of millions upon millions of middle-class Americans. Living out in the suburbs, it is easy to assume that ours is, indeed, an affluent society.

This new segregation of poverty is compounded by a well-meaning ignorance. A good many concerned and sympathetic Americans are aware that there is much discussion of urban renewal. Suddenly, driving through the city, they notice that a familiar slum has been torn down and that there are towering, modern buildings where once there had been tenements or hovels. There is a warm feeling of satisfaction, of pride in the way things are working out: the poor, it is obvious, are being taken care of. . . .

And finally, the poor are politically invisible. It is one of the cruelest ironies of social life in advanced countries that the dispossessed at the bottom of society are unable to speak for themselves. The people of the other America do not, by far and large, belong to unions, to fraternal organizations, or to political parties. They are without lobbies of their own; they put forward no legislative program. As a group, they are atomized. They have no face; they have no voice.

Thus, there is not even a cynical political motive for caring about the poor, as in the old days. Because the slums are no longer centers of powerful political organizations, the politicians need not really care about their inhabitants. The slums are no longer visible to the middle class, so much of the idealistic urge to fight for those who need help is gone. Only the social agencies have a really direct involvement with the other America, and they are without any great political power. . . .

Indeed, the paradox that the welfare state benefits those least who need help most is but a single instance of a persistent irony in the other America. Even when the money finally trickles down, even when a school is built in a poor neighborhood, for instance, the poor are still deprived. Their entire environment, their life, their values, do not prepare them to take advantage of the new opportunity. The parents are anxious for the children to go to work; the pupils are pent up, waiting for the moment when their education has complied with the law.

Today's poor, in short, missed the political and social gains of the thirties. They are, as Galbraith rightly points out, the first minority poor in history, the first poor not to be seen, the first poor whom the politicians could leave alone. . . .

What shall we tell the American poor, once we have seen them? Shall we say to them that they are better off than the Indian poor, the Italian poor, the Russian poor? That is one answer, but it is heartless. I should put it another way. I want to tell every well-fed and optimistic American that it is intolerable that so many millions should be maimed in body and in spirit when it is not necessary that they should be. My standard of comparison is not how much worse things used to be. It is how much better they could be if only we were stirred. . . .

First and foremost, any attempt to abolish poverty in the United States must seek to destroy the pessimism and fatalism that flourish in the other America. In part, this can be done by offering real opportunities to these people, by changing the social reality that gives rise to their sense of hopelessness. But beyond that (these fears of the poor have a life of their own and are not simply rooted in analyses of employment chances), there should be a spirit, an élan, that communicates itself to the entire society.

If the nation comes into the other America grudgingly, with the mentality of an administrator, and says, "All right, we'll help you people," then there will be gains, but they will be kept to the minimum; a dollar spent will return a dollar. But if there is an attitude that society is gaining by eradicating poverty, if there is a positive attempt to bring these millions of the poor to the point where they can make their contribution to the United States, that will make a huge difference. The spirit of a campaign against poverty does not cost a single cent. It is a matter of vision, of sensitivity. . . .

Second, this book is based upon the proposition that poverty forms a culture, an interdependent system. In case after case, it has been documented that one cannot deal with the various components of poverty in isolation, changing this or that condition but leaving the basic structure intact. Consequently, a campaign against the misery of the poor should be comprehensive. It should think, not in terms of this or that aspect of poverty, but along the lines of establishing new communities, of substituting a human environment for the inhuman one that now exists. . . .

There is only one institution in the society capable of acting to abolish poverty. That is the Federal Government. In saying this, I do not rejoice, for centralization can lead to an impersonal and bureaucratic program, one that will be lacking in the very human quality so essential in an approach to the poor. In saying this, I am only recording the facts of political and social life in the United States. . . .

[However] it is not necessary to advocate complete central control of such a campaign. Far from it. Washington is essential in a double sense: as a source of the considerable funds needed to mount a campaign against the other America, and as a place for coordination, for planning, and the establishment of national standards. The actual implementation of a program to abolish poverty can be carried out through myriad institutions, and the closer they are to the specific local area, the better the results. There are, as has been pointed out already, housing administrators, welfare workers, and city planners with dedication and vision. They are working on the local level, and their main frustration is the lack of funds. They could be trusted actually to carry through on a national program. What they lack now is money and the support of the American people. . . .

There is no point in attempting to blueprint or detail the mechanisms and institutions of a war on poverty in the United States. There is information enough for action. All that is lacking is political will. . . .

These, then, are the strangest poor in the history of mankind.

They exist within the most powerful and rich society the world has ever known. Their misery has continued while the majority of the nation talked of itself as being "affluent" and worried about neuroses in the suburbs. In this way tens of millions of human beings became invisible. They dropped out of sight and out of mind; they were without their own political voice.

Yet this need not be. The means are at hand to fulfill the age-old dream: poverty can now be abolished. How long shall we ignore this underdeveloped nation in our midst? How long shall we look the other way while our fellow human beings suffer? How long?

92

THOMAS SOWELL

From *Civil Rights: Rhetoric or Reality?*

During the mid-1980s, few black voices spoke from a conservative point of view. Almost all African Americans were liberals, supporting liberal Demo-cratic candidates and following the lead of civil rights activists. Scholar Thomas Sowell took a different position, which placed him radically out of the mainstream of most of his colleagues. Today, Sowell's ideas are commonly heard, although they are still controversial within the minority community. He questions the reason for the differences between black and white income levels, attributing the gap to family structure and cultural norms, not to color. Sowell uses a historical assessment of African–American progress to support his arguments. Before the 1964 Civil Rights Act, he claims, black Americans were rapidly advancing in education, employment, and quality of life. After the act, progress in some areas was reversed. Sowell blames civil rights leaders who placed their own agenda above the genuine welfare of the black community.

———

BLACKS HAVE a history in the United States that is quite different from that of other American ethnic groups. The massive fact of slavery looms over more than half of that history. The Jim Crow laws and policies*, which not only segregated but discriminated, were still going strong in that part of the country where most blacks lived, in the middle of the twentieth century. "Lynching" meant—almost invariably—the lynching of blacks by whites. Blacks were widely believed to be genetically inferior in intelligence, both in the North and the South, long before Arthur Jensen's writings on the subject appeared. James B. Conant's 1961 book, *Slums and Suburbs*, reported a common assumption among school officials around the country that black children were not capable of learning as much as white children. . . .

Given the unique—and uniquely oppressive—history of blacks, it would follow almost inevitably from the civil rights vision that blacks would today suffer far more than other groups from low income, broken homes, and the whole litany of social pathology. But like so many things that follow from the civil rights vision, it happens not to be true in fact. Blacks do not have the lowest income, the lowest educational level, or the most broken homes among American ethnic groups. The habit of comparing blacks with "the national average" conceals the fact that there are other groups with very similar—and sometimes worse—social pathology. The national average is just one point on a wide-ranging spectrum. It is not a norm showing where most individuals or most groups are. The difference in income between Japanese Americans and Puerto Ricans is even greater than the difference between blacks and whites, though most of the factors *assumed* to cause black-white differences are not present in differences between Japanese Americans and Puerto Ricans. . . .

*Jim Crow laws were common throughout the South, beginning in the 1890s, as a way of enforcing legal segregation of the races in the post–Civil War period. Such laws mandated racial segregation in all public facilities, such as schools, trains, playgrounds, and even drinking fountains. Along with Jim Crow laws, black Americans were often prevented from registering to vote by poll taxes, literacy tests, and "grandfather" clauses. These forms of legal discrimination in the United States lasted until the 1950s and 1960s. — EDS.

In short, the historical uniqueness of blacks has not translated into a contemporary uniqueness in incomes, occupations, I.Q., unemployment, female-headed households, alcoholism, or welfare dependency, however much blacks may differ from the mythical national average in these respects. All of these represent serious difficulties (sometimes calamities) for blacks, and indirectly for the larger society, but the question here is the *cause*. If that cause is either a unique history or a unique genetics, blacks would differ not only from the national average but also from other groups that share neither that history nor the same genetic background. . . .

Blacks and whites are not just people with different skin colors. Nor is a history of slavery the only difference between them. Like many other groups in contemporary America—and around the world and down through history—blacks and whites have different cultures that affect how they live individually and collectively. At the same time, there is sufficient overlap that some sets of blacks have a home life and family pattern very similar to those of most whites. Insofar as color is the over-riding factor in economic position, this will make relatively little difference in the incomes of such sets of blacks. Insofar as such cultural factors reflect traits that prove valuable and decisive in the marketplace, such sets of blacks should have incomes comparable to those of whites. . . .

A comparison of black and white male youths in 1969—again, before affirmative action—throws light on the role of color and culture. Harvard economist Richard Freeman compared blacks and whites whose homes included newspapers, magazines, and library cards, and who had also gone on to obtain the same number of years of schooling. There was no difference in the average income of these whites compared to these blacks. This had not always been true. In earlier periods, such cultural factors had little weight. But by 1969 it was true—during "equal opportunity" policies and before "affirmative action."

Home and family life differ in other ways between blacks and whites. Husband-wife families are more prevalent among whites than among blacks, though declining over time among both groups. About half of all black families with children are one-parent families, while more than four-fifths of all white families with children are two-parent families. But what of those black families that are two-parent families—more like the white families in this respect and perhaps in other respects as well? To the extent that racial discrimination is the crucial factor in depressing black income, there should be little difference between the incomes of these black families relative to their white counterparts than there is between the incomes of blacks and whites as a whole. But insofar as family structure reflects cultural values in general, those blacks whose family structure reflects more general norms of behavior should be more fortunate in the job market as well.

For more than a decade, young black husband-wife families outside the South have had incomes virtually identical to those of young white husband-wife families outside the South. In some years black families of this description have had incomes a few percentage points higher than their white counterparts. Today, where husbands and wives are both college-educated, and both working, black families of this description earn slightly *more* than white families of this description—nationwide and without regard to age.

The implication of all this is not, of course, that blacks as a group are doing as well as whites as a group—or are even close to doing as well. On the contrary. The average income of blacks as a group remains far behind the average income of whites as a group. What we are trying to find out is the extent to which this is due to cultural differences rather than color differences that call forth racism and discrimination. . . .

Anyone who has been privileged to live through the past generation of changes among blacks knows that there have been many changes that cannot be quantified. One need only listen to an interview with a Bill Russell or an O. J. Simpson, or many other articulate black athletes today, and compare that with interviews with black athletes of a generation ago, to appreciate just one symptom of a profound transformation that has affected a wide segment of the black population.

It may be understandable that black politicians and civil rights organizations would want to claim the lion's share of the credit for the economic improvements that black people have experienced. But despite their constant attempts to emphasize the role of the demand side of the equation, and particularly discrimination and anti-discrimination laws, the fact is that enormous changes were taking place on the supply side. Blacks were becoming a different people. More were acquiring not only literacy but higher levels of education, skills, and broader cultural exposure. The advancement of blacks was not simply a matter of whites letting down barriers.

Much has been made of the fact that the numbers of blacks in high-level occupations increased in the years following passage of the Civil Rights Act of 1964. But the number of blacks in professional, technical, and other high-level occupations more than doubled in the decade *preceding* the Civil Rights Act of 1964. In other occupations, gains by blacks were greater during the 1940s—when there was practically no civil rights legislation—than during the 1950s. In various skilled trades, the income of blacks relative to whites more than doubled between 1936 and 1959. The trend was already under way. It may well be that both the economic and the legal advances were products of powerful social transformations taking place in the black population and beginning to make themselves felt in the consciousness of whites, as well as in the competition of the marketplace.

Knowledge of the strengths of blacks has been ignored or repressed in a different way as well. Few people today are aware that the ghettos in many cities were far safer places two generations ago than they are today, both for blacks and for whites. Incredulity often greets stories by older blacks as to their habit of sleeping out on fire escapes or on rooftops or in public parks on hot summer nights. Many of those same people would not dare to walk through those same parks today in broad daylight. In the 1930s whites went regularly to Harlem at night, stayed until the wee hours of the morning, and then stood on the streets to hail cabs to take them home. Today, not only would very few whites dare to do this, very few cabs would dare to be cruising ghetto streets in the wee hours of the morning.

Why should discussion of positive achievements by blacks ever be a source of embarrassment, much less resentment, on the part of black leaders? Because many of these positive achievements occurred in ways that completely undermine the civil rights vision. If crime is a product of poverty and discrimination as they say endlessly, why was there so much less of it when poverty and discrimination were much worse than today? If massive programs are the only hope to reduce violence in the ghetto, why was there so much less violence long before anyone ever thought of these programs? Perhaps more to the point, have the philosophies and policies so much supported by black leaders contributed to the decline in community and personal standards, and in family responsibility, so painfully visible today? For many, it may be easier to ignore past achievements than to face their implications for current issues. . . .

The civil rights vision and the civil rights leadership continue pushing an approach which has proved counterproductive for the mass of disadvantaged blacks, beneficial primarily to those already advantaged, and which accumulates resentments against all blacks.

93

TOMMY THOMPSON

From *Power to the People*

From Franklin Roosevelt's New Deal to Lyndon Johnson's Great Society, welfare programs in the U.S. were run primarily by the national government. The 1990s marked a shift of power from the federal government to the states and local communities. Then governor of Wisconsin, Republican Tommy Thompson, remarks on this shift, as well as recounting the frustrations of the past federal setup and the challenges of the states' newfound power. As one example, Thompson discusses the politics of welfare and the practicalities of bringing about Wisconsin's new welfare reform, W2 (Wisconsin Works). Changes did happen. President Bill Clinton signed a welfare reform bill in 1996. Later, Thompson became President George W. Bush's Health and Human Resources (HHS) Secretary.

"YOU HAVE two ears and one mouth. Use them in that proportion and you'll do just fine."

It was one of my father's favorite instructions to me, my sister, and my two brothers, the sort of "Midwestern intellect" I heard often while growing up in the small farming community of Elroy, Wisconsin. It is good advice for anyone, but especially for politicians. I have been the governor of Wisconsin for ten years, and I have always tried to follow that common-sense rule. Now, I'm trying to get Washington to do the same.

Like most Americans, my experience with the federal government has not been particularly pleasant. It is very hard to get Washington to listen. The federal bureaucracy seems impervious to ordinary citizens and governors alike. And yet, it appears to be everywhere, touching more of our everyday lives. Having dealt with Washington on numerous issues over the past decade, I can easily understand why many Americans are fed up with a government they view as increasingly unresponsive, wasteful, and inefficient at solving problems. I'm convinced most government officials in Washington actually have two mouths and one ear.

Since 1986, I have trudged regularly to the nation's capital, asking for more flexibility to make specific changes in federal programs affecting my state. Usually I was met with indifference. I'd have to schedule appointments weeks in advance, only to have a congressman say no to my request for more state-level authority. Even some congressmen from Wisconsin were not that eager to return more decision-making back home. And in most other congressional offices I was treated much like any other suppliant asking for something with very little to offer in return. "Governor who?" the earnest young staffers asked. It was as though Congress couldn't quite figure out how I or forty-nine other governors were relevant to their decision-making.

Asking Washington to give up any amount of control is not a pleasant undertaking. Having dealt with three different presidential administrations, I know the procedure all too well. It essentially means getting down on bended knee and kissing the rings of appointed bureaucrats who have the power to decide whether a governor—duly elected by the citizens of an entire state—can be trusted to change federal programs that clearly are failing. And it has mattered very little whether Democrats or Republicans were in charge. A capital city that runs on the political philosophy of "I can run your life better than you can" naturally fosters a certain arrogance among its inhabitants, regardless of political party. I felt as though Washington had actual contempt for those who didn't live and work inside the Beltway.

But Washington is starting to listen. Now when I visit Capitol Hill, members of Congress actually come out of their offices to greet me. "Tommy, how are you? Good to see you. Have any new ideas?" they ask. And these are just the Democrats.

The American political landscape is beginning to change. After nearly a century of consolidating more and more power in Washington, Congress appears genuinely interested in devolving power back to states and local communities. I know this for sure because on January 12, 1995, I was testifying before the Senate Labor Committee on the need to overhaul federal job-training programs. As Senator Edward Kennedy began his opening remarks before my testimony, I was bracing for a few partisan shots to the chin.

Instead, the senior senator from Massachusetts said, "I just want to say that we have heard great things about your training program, and that Wisconsin is really one of the outstanding states in terms of these programs. I know from the people whom I respect the most in my state that they have a very high regard for what you have done in Wisconsin. So we are looking forward to hearing from you."

"Great things . . . outstanding . . . looking forward to hearing from" me. I was temporarily speechless. But for the next hour or so we had a cordial, informative discussion about the importance of giving states more flexibility in running job-training programs. . . .

It is time for Washington—its politicians and bureaucrats—to realize they are not paragons of virtue: the states have innovative ideas that work. It is time for them to acknowledge that a one-size-fits-all brand of government handed down from Washington doesn't work today and will not work to meet the challenges of the next century.

America's last major political reform, the Progressive movement, started a century ago in the Republican Party of Wisconsin. It spread first across the Midwest and then many of its ideas were adopted and adapted by Republicans and Democrats. Today, governors—some in the very same states that launched the first Progressive movement—are succeeding with a new wave of innovative reforms and asking Washington to return power and authority to the states. For good reason.

In many ways, what's happening today at the state level is strikingly similar to the grassroots Progressive movement of a century ago. In fact, those today who call for the devolution of power from Washington back to the states are voicing a prominent theme of the early Progressives. Wisconsin Progressive Robert La Follette and his contemporaries strongly believed the states were America's laboratories of democracy. Woodrow Wilson, an early Progressive, warned as governor of New Jersey, "I suspect that the people of the United States understand their own interests better than any group of men in the confines of the country understand them. I don't want a smug lot of experts to sit down behind closed doors in Washington and play providence to me."

After nearly a century of increasing federal authority, this central issue has again risen to the surface of today's political debate. Can people be trusted to govern themselves at the state and local level, or do we need Washington to impose its mandates on all of us?

As we answer that question, America's laboratories of democracy are demonstrating new successes, solving problems where Washington has failed. Successful innovations at the state level are occurring when many of us are sick and tired of the partisan squabbling and arrogance that dominates the federal government. It's no coincidence. People today are trying to work things out closer to home. . . .

In late 1993, as I approached another election, Wisconsin welfare rolls had declined more than those of any other state—down by 19 percent since we first started the reforms in 1987. During the same period, welfare rolls had shot up by 30 percent nationally. We had dropped from the eighth highest state in the nation in percentage of people on welfare to thirty-first. This was too much for Democrats in the state legislature. Although several conservative Democrats had supported many of my reforms, the official posture of the more liberal Democrat leaders had been to criticize and try to block or dismantle many of them. They were beginning to understand that they were on the wrong end of the issue. Welfare reform was working in Wisconsin, and the people supported it.

Walter Kunicki, the Democrat speaker of the assembly, was thinking about running against me in 1994. He had seen Bill Clinton take the issue away from Republicans on the national level, and he wanted to pull a fast one on me. Kunicki said we had tried a lot of pilot projects here and there, but Governor Thompson was really just tinkering around the edges. If the governor were really serious about welfare reform, Kunicki said, he would support legislation to end it completely. Kunicki proposed abolishing welfare completely in Wisconsin. He didn't propose an alternative, he just said we should abolish it by 1999. It was hollow, just like Bill Clinton's promise to "end welfare as we know it."

Even so, it was a bold political strategy. Replacing the entire AFDC [Aid to Families with Dependent Children] system and coming up with a completely new alternative to welfare would be a huge task. It was a radical idea, and he was convinced I would veto it, which would hand the Democrats bragging rights on welfare reform in the next election.

Jerry Whitburn, whose leadership had helped guide us to the next level of reform over the past three years, was skeptical. This was a blatantly political move by the Democrats, and it should be vetoed. Maybe he was right. As the secretary of the department that would have to do most of the work, he knew what he was talking about. But I couldn't stop thinking, "This is a golden opportunity. How can the Democrats be so dumb to give me this chance to completely replace welfare?"

The bill passed both houses of the legislature, with the final vote occurring late on a Tuesday night. At seven-thirty the next morning, my senior staff met for our regular breakfast meeting. Jerry remained cool to the idea. I put down my fork and said, "Jerry, I'm going to sign it." And I later raised the ante—we moved up the timetable to end welfare by 1997.

The Democrats never even scored the political points they were after. I won the election in 1994, and for the first time since I had come to office, Republicans won both houses of the state legislature.

Despite his earlier reservations, Jerry enthusiastically threw himself into the project. He immediately put together a team of experts in DHSS [Department of Housing and Social Services] to design the replacement— as we had done with Work Not Welfare. After eight years of implementing reforms, this was a group of people who knew more about changing welfare than anyone in the nation. He put together a bipartisan group of legislative leaders and a group of business and community-based leaders to work with us on the project.

We also enlisted the help of the Hudson Institute, a respected national think tank based in Indianapolis. In 1994, I met with Hudson Institute president Les Lenkowsky to discuss my goals for the alternative to welfare. I said I wanted a program built around work. I wanted to end the cash benefit premise of welfare and replace it with a real-world concept: pay for performance. Everyone would have to work, and only work would pay. I described it as a new contract in which government and low-income families have concomitant responsibilities. Government would agree to provide child care, health care, and other assistance for a limited time to help people find and keep a job. In return, people must be willing to take personal responsibility for themselves and their families. They have to get up in the morning, get the kids fed and off to school or day care, and get themselves to a job, just like ordinary hardworking Americans. . . .

In early 1995, Massachusetts Governor William Weld hired Jerry Whitburn away from me. Before he left to run Massachusetts's welfare programs, Jerry presented me with a name that Jim Malone of DHSS had come up with for the program we were developing to replace welfare. It was W2—Wisconsin Works. We were going to replace the welfare check with a paycheck—something we had talked about when I first hired him as DHSS secretary in 1991.

No other state was in a position to do this. No other state had comparable experience in the field, experimenting, discovering what works. In many ways, all we had to do was put the pieces together. Washington was fighting over whether it should give states the authority to run welfare, Clinton had vetoed the welfare reform bill passed by the new Republican Congress, but we were moving ahead without them. Really, the building blocks for W2 were what our laboratory of ideas had discovered over the past eight years. From the WEJT [Wisconsin Employment and Job Training] program I had expanded in 1987, we learned that people move faster when you require them to do something, either training or work. From the JOBS program that grew out of WEJT, we learned that the transition to work was faster still when you add an actual work requirement instead of just training. From Work First, we learned that many people don't even need the first welfare check when you help them look at other options as soon as they come in to apply. And from Work Not Welfare, we learned that people achieve self-sufficiency fastest when you combine an immediate work requirement with a time limit, which instills a sense of urgency, and encourages saving that government check for when they really need it.

We decided that W2 should focus on moving people into private sector jobs as soon as possible. That meant an immediate full-time work requirement and time limits, but it also meant community-based partnerships with private employers. So we expanded the model we had set up in Work Not Welfare to create Community Steering Committees comprising local businesses, charities, and civic groups to coordinate job placement for people. And since W2 would be a jobs program rather than a cash benefit program, we decided to eliminate our welfare department and shift responsibility for W2 to our new jobs department. Building on lessons from Work First and Work Not Welfare, we replaced "economic support" workers with financial planners and employment specialists. Welfare workers who had been spending 80 percent of their time doing paperwork would now spend 90 percent of their time working directly with people who need help.

We also knew that W2 would cost more money up front. The welfare reforms we had implemented since 1987 had reduced Wisconsin welfare rolls by 36 percent. As a result, taxpayers were saving $19 million each and every month. Our reforms have saved the state and federal government nearly $1 billion since 1987. Yet to achieve those savings, I had invested more money on the front end. To help people make the transition from welfare to work, we invested more money in child care, health care, transportation, and caseworkers who would work with people one-on-one. Child care expenditures alone increased by more than 300 percent, from $13 million in 1987 to $56 million in 1995. If W2 would require everyone to work immediately, we were going to have to expand child care funding even more substantially. And we knew from our other experiments that providing up to twelve months of child care and health insurance after people had left welfare to work helped them get off welfare and stay off. That would mean even more money. Yet I wanted to make W2 as close to the real world as possible, so we developed a provision that would require W2 participants to co-pay for these benefits as they began earning money.

As we began to develop a concrete, comprehensive replacement to welfare that reflected the lessons we had learned from welfare reform, we confronted an issue that dooms many government programs. How could we construct a program that achieves what we believe will work without making it so rigid that it cannot adjust to the realities of helping people with different needs and abilities? The last thing I wanted to do was replace one bureaucracy with another. We wanted to place people in private sector jobs, but we knew that some individuals would not be able to be placed in private sector jobs right away. There was no model in place to base this on—we had to use the experience we had gained over the previous eight years.

We decided that we needed to create different levels of jobs—levels that would reflect the "readiness levels" most people fit into when they showed up at the welfare office. At the same time, however, I didn't want to create a make-work program of government-funded jobs. It was essential to me that we build in incentives for people to move up the ladder to private employment as soon as possible. So we created three levels of subsidized employment. The lowest level paid the least, the next level paid more, and the final level paid the most, but none of them paid as much as a private sector job.

To further encourage people to move up the ladder and into unsubsidized jobs in the private sector, we limited the amount of time anyone could be in a subsidized job. Again, we put two-year time limits on each category of subsidized jobs, although an individual cannot spend two years in each of the three levels. We established an overall limit of five years on a person's eligibility for W2. Individuals can use the five years of help all at once or pieces at a time when they need it, but after using a total of five years of services, they are no longer eligible for assistance. This is a combination of the "ticking clock" and "savings account" approach we had tried with Work Not Welfare.

Our premise in establishing job levels for W2 was that everyone is capable of performing some kind of work. The highest level of subsidized employment we called trial jobs. After private sector jobs, this is the level we would require most recipients to start with, based on our experience running the statewide JOBS program and other reforms. Trial jobs are for people who have good attitudes toward work but aren't immediately employable, usually because they have very little experience holding down a job. W2 will place them in a private sector job and provide a subsidy to the employer. When they gain enough work experience, W2 will help them find an unsubsidized job, with the same employer if possible.

The middle rung of the job ladder is community service jobs. These are for a limited number of people whose poor work habits and skills make them unemployable with a private firm, even with a subsidy. They will be provided government-funded jobs in the community to gain basic work skills. The lowest level is transitional jobs, for people who have serious impediments to work. In addition to work, transitional jobs include services such as vocational rehabilitation and drug and alcohol treatment, to further prepare participants for work.

In addition to the work requirements, we incorporated elements of earlier reforms that had worked. We incorporated school attendance requirements from Learnfare, child support enforcement from Children First, and parental and family responsibility provisions—such as no additional pay for having more children—from PFR. After more than a year of work putting the program together, I introduced it to the now-Republican controlled state legislature in 1995. On April 25, 1996, I signed W2 into law . . .

People, ordinary people, have a hard time being heard over the massive machinery of Washington—the grinding bureaucracy, the din of special interests, the partisan squabbling, and the clamor of the "inspectors"— the media. Sometimes, I think it really makes people who work in Washington hard of hearing.

I've learned that it is not so hard to listen when you are campaigning for elected office. Not only are you out there constantly shaking hands, you have pollsters and political advisers who can tell you exactly what percent of the population wants this or that. You can be responsive merely by talking about things—until you are elected. Then you are accountable, or you are supposed to be accountable, for getting things done. That is one thing Bill Clinton doesn't seem to understand—the difference between campaigning and governing. It is one thing to make promises that sound good to people and quite another to actually get them done.

Making it happen, making government truly effective, boils down to commitment and leadership. It means sticking with your ideas even when you're fighting an uphill battle, or taking a battering in the press. And when you think you've changed things, it means realizing that you're only part-way there. I hope [Wisconsin's experience] will encourage people to expect more of themselves and of their states. I hope it will encourage more governors and legislators to try different things. Wisconsin's experience shows that when you have a good idea and the courage to stick with it—even if it's not politically popular at the time—you can change government for the better. . . .

94

THERESA FUNICIELLO

From *Tyranny of Kindness*

The debate in the 1990s about welfare reform got very technical: AFDC, Food Stamps, block grants, entitlements, workfare. While the details of the 1996 reforms are important, first, Theresa Funiciello pleads, consider the plight of the women and children who receive welfare. Funiciello, a former AFDC recipient, chronicles the bureaucratic maze that a needy person must navigate to get any aid at all. She exposes the vast sums of public and private money spent on the "poverty industry." Too little of it gets to the poor. Too much of it goes into the pockets of those who claim that they're helping the poor. Welfare is an emotional issue, both to hard-working taxpayers and to recipients in dire need of assistance.

————

MY FIRST EXPERIENCE with Aid to Families with Dependent Children (AFDC)—welfare—was in upstate New York, three months after the birth of my daughter, on the heels of the departure of her father. It was 1973. I was twenty-six years old, nursing an infant, and alone. Welfare was humiliating on a personal level, and administratively it was nuts. But there wasn't anything I could do about it. At least that's what I thought.

In 1975 I moved to New York City. Like so many others, I was searching for opportunity. When I couldn't find paying work, I had my second encounter with welfare. It was nuts here, too.

Fortunately, in the city there were many thousands of others in the same boat. Looking for sympathetic advice, I stumbled onto a sturdy little volunteer organization of mostly welfare mothers, the Downtown Welfare Advocate Center (DWAC). The women at DWAC thought something could be done about the welfare, and they set about doing it. They helped people with problems negotiate the chaotic system and they helped change the way welfare mothers felt about themselves in relation to it. They also tried to influence the welfare bureaucracy. They said mothering was work. They said single mothers and children made up 95 percent of the entire AFDC population. They said welfare was a women's issue. I came back for more.

My third, fourth, and hundred-and-fifth encounters with the welfare system took place on behalf of other women as I, too, learned how to sort out the mess and be an "advocate." By late 1976, I was also organizing to change the way people thought about welfare—essential to changing the entire system from bottom to top. Over the next few years, DWAC sponsored a membership organization, which peaked at about six thousand members in 1981. Almost all were welfare mothers.

It was during this period that DWAC began to interact with the mega-charities on a fairly regular basis. These were agencies with millions of dollars in their coffers and nifty salaries for employees who "helped the poor." Actually, many of the social welfare professionals seemed to do little more than refer people who needed help to us and have luncheons to discuss the problem. It took many more years and many incarnations to find out what they were really about.

I moved on from DWAC to work at a small "change-oriented" (as they liked to call themselves) foundation that purported to give money to projects that poor people worked on. That was maybe ten percent true. So, in 1983, when Mario Cuomo became governor and his newly appointed commissioner of the New York State Department of Social Services (DSS) offered me a job, I was ready to take on the beast from inside the belly. Just maybe things could be changed from the inside.

At DSS, my worst nightmares became fire-breathing realities. Millions of dollars were regularly dispensed in contracts to virtually useless "non-profit" agencies. DSS was a patronage trough. Poor people were not the beneficiaries. They weren't even in on the deal.

Nevertheless, I'd learned a couple important lessons at DSS. One was that incompetence is a heavy contender with greed as prime motivator of the bureaucracy. Second, any time there's money to be had, every manner of opportunist crawls out for a piece. Combined, these fundamentals form the basis of public policy.

It didn't take too much intelligence to figure out the idiocy of paying thousands of dollars a month to "shelter" a homeless family instead of paying for a real apartment. Various layers of government blamed one another—but *they* were setting the rules, not Martians. Taxpayers were bilked and poor people were sacrificed as hundreds of millions of dollars were poured into the sinkholes of the social welfare establishment. Shelters. Soup kitchens. Name it. Nationwide, poverty is big business—as long as you are politically connected.

The consequence to poor people of this ever-expanding poverty industry has been that over the past two decades, the purchasing power of welfare benefits has fallen in every state in the country, in spite of the fact that aggregate spending on most other social programs has soared. It was not quite by accident, nor quite by design. Boosted by the unseeing but hardly innocent eye of the media, the poverty industry has become a veritable fifth estate. Acting as stand-ins for actual poor people, they mediate the politics of poverty with government officials. The fifth estate is a large and ever-growing power bloc that routinely and by whatever means necessary trades off the interests of poor people to advance its own parochial agenda. From the charities fleecing the state and the public, to the champagne fund-raisers charged off to Uncle Sam, to the corporations developing ever more ways of getting tax deductions for having their trash hauled away free of charge, the fix is in.

Charities have been powerful since they first popped on the scene during the middle of the nineteenth century. Run exclusively by men, they were originally premised solely on the negative — stopping behaviors they believed to be inbred and causally connected to poverty. They believed the problem would continue unchecked if poor people were able to resist their services and exist outside of charity-run poorhouses. The charities fought long and hard against "outdoor relief" (cash assistance) for poor families. The struggle was temporarily checked with the passage of the Social Security Act, which established AFDC in 1935. Poor mothers could live in their own homes and raise their children. The compromise wrested by the nascent social work profession was that, unlike social security insurance, wherein a check would go directly from the federal government to the recipient, AFDC would be mediated by them. Both the public welfare bureaucracy and its private extension (charities) expanded.

Almost every president since has promised some sort of reform of the welfare system. But it wasn't until the 1960s that the welfare rolls exploded, landing the issue back onto center stage. Launching the Great Society, President Johnson declared "War on Poverty" and spewed social service dollars in every direction (except into the pockets of poor people, that is). In part, the new programs would stimulate the economy, as tens of thousands of jobs were created to "help the poor." Few poor people got any of these jobs, however. Most of the decent ones went to middle-class social welfare professionals, who were perceived to be an important cog in a deteriorating Democratic party machine.

Despite the largess of the Great Society, a chain reaction of inner-city riots spanning several years soon shocked the nation. The rioting was a total enigma to most people — in the wake of all the anti-poverty legislative gifts. But poor people were neither receiving the money directly nor truly influencing how it would be spent. In addition to the generalized anomie caused by poverty, the indignities of welfare and unemployment, and long-repressed racial bitterness, the riots were an expression of grave despair over a government agenda and monies said to be *for them* that for the most part were getting nowhere near actual poor people.

As the agencies that *did* cash in grew and reinvented themselves, it became apparent that they were in an inherent conflict of interest with poor people. Welfare mothers, for instance, wanted an adequate guaranteed income, which would have rendered many of the activities of the social welfare professionals meaningless. The agencies wanted a guaranteed income, too: for themselves. With the money and power to lobby effectively, they got it.

As the misery of poor people increased, so did the cacophony of private interests competing for government contracts, foundation grants, donations by individuals and corporations, and tax advantages for the donations to "correct" their version of the problem. The only people who did not cash in, the only ones absent from the debate in any public way, as ever, were poor. It was not for lack of trying. Many poor women, myself included, attempted to reframe the debate, but the charitable opposition was too comfortable and powerful.

Over a period of nearly two decades, I went from being a homeless welfare mother to being an organizer of welfare mothers, an establishment insider at DSS, an adviser to some members of the New York state legislature, and a consultant for various prominent social welfare agencies. I have seen it from all sides now. I remain appalled.

The view from the bottom is substantially different from that of any other vantage point. Usually, you won't learn about it in books. Certainly it can't be found in classrooms, newsrooms, boardrooms, or bedrooms of the not so poor or the rich and famous. . . .

Tyranny of Kindness takes a look at social policy in the United States from the perspective of people who live with the consequences. I do not pretend to be "objective." I don't believe anyone can be. I do try to present some barely known history and facts that are often misinterpreted or kept discreetly, esoterically buried in reams of public and private documents. Judge for yourself, but judge. Perhaps we can work together to address the issue of poverty in ways that are truly meaningful. . . .

My own rude awakening came when, in my midtwenties, I became a welfare mother. I was single and had a baby whose father was better at providing fear than the necessities of life. When my daughter was three months old, I kicked him out. It had finally dawned on me that he (1) might kill me one of these days, (2) might try to hurt her, or (3) might kill us both in one of his blind drunks.

I didn't dwell on the consequences of kicking him out. I didn't even think about having to go on welfare. Even if I had thought about it, the result would have been the same. My father was dead, and my mother lived on social security. My father had been superstitious, so he had no private life insurance. In any event, without parents or other resources to fall back on, I did what I had to do. I soon became slave to what we (welfare mothers in New York) called "the welfare." It is a crude and irrational system of income distribution, usually capricious and often downright cruel. I have spent the better part of my adult life trying to figure it out. During the first four of those years, I was on and off the rolls intermittently.

The first time I applied for welfare was in early December of 1973. I was crushed when I received no welfare check until after Christmas. I experienced a profound sadness for my three-month-old daughter on Christmas Eve; her future seemed to loom so bleak. I wasn't the crying type, but every now and then I felt these tears rolling down my cheeks, almost as if they belonged to someone else.

A year and a half later, I got a summer job miles from where we lived, so I had to move. Since the job was in a resort town, I couldn't afford to live there either. We moved from one county to another, and I worked in still a third. I had a hunch that I might be entitled to some help with child-care expenses, but I didn't have anyone besides the welfare department to ask. I did that in all three counties. I was told that I didn't qualify for "day care" because *day care* meant daytime, and I worked nights. This, as it turned out, was not true, but at the time I didn't know it. What's more, though I was also entitled to other supplemental welfare benefits (of which I was equally ignorant), I never got them either. Instead, because I took the job, I was cut off welfare entirely, lost my food stamps and my medicaid. The job paid more than minimum wage. Nonetheless, I was worse off than before. First, I worked nights, like many single mothers, so that I could spend most of my daughter's waking hours with her. This meant that she was sleeping while I was awake, and I had to be awake when she was. By Labor Day, I was, to put it mildly, overtired, overweary, overstrained, overdriven, overfatigued, overspent, and worn out.

There were countless problems associated with money. In theory I had more than when we were on welfare. In practice it wasn't quite the case. On welfare, I could wear whatever passed for clothes without giving much thought to it. On my paying job, the expectations were not so lax.

I had less energy for cooking items like dried beans half the day, baking bread, or fashioning nutritious soups out of assorted food scraps. I was living in a small city now, so I could not grow any food because I had no garden in which to sow seeds. I quickly discovered that the faster the food, the more it cost. I also had the expense of traveling back and forth to this job five nights a week. Not only did this extract gas dollars but my car had a seemingly endless capacity to languish at the mechanic's when I couldn't figure out how to fix it myself. Getting sick was out of the question. Not only would I go unpaid if I didn't show up at work but I could not afford a doctor for myself under any circumstances and I would have been reluctant to take my daughter to one had she gotten sick.

By far the most traumatic dilemma for both me and the baby, though, was child care. I could afford very little. Capitulating to the social pressure to be off welfare, I left my daughter at age one and a half with people who could not begin to match my parenting skills. And for what? For her? For me? For money? Or so people would stop watching what I bought at the grocery store? (When you pull out your food stamps at a checkout counter, all eyes within fifty feet—with the exception of those like you, who will be soon facing the music—run a quick tabulation and analysis of your purchases.)

When that job ended, I went to a state employment office in Albany, looking for better-paying work. Foolishly, I told the truth on my application. When the employment official found out I was a single mother who had recently been on welfare, he told me he was not allowed to refer me for a job. He explained that the department had to compete with private employment firms and that it was customary not to send single mothers out for job interviews since employers generally didn't want them, no matter what their skills were. At the time, there was a coding system at employment agencies to tell prospective interviewers in advance such things as your marital status (for women only) and the color of your skin (for nonwhites, of course). This ensured that certain undesirable "types" didn't get sent on interviews. Another staff person approached me and asked if I would like to file a lawsuit against them for the practice, saying he could get me a free lawyer. I gave it only brief consideration. My political consciousness at the time was, to say the least, limited. I also figured that if I went along with them I'd be stuck on welfare for years to come while I waited around for this lawsuit.

Instead, just after my daughter's second birthday in September of 1975, I moved to New York City. I was convinced we'd never escape poverty if I couldn't find better-paying work, so I went stalking "opportunity" in the city. As it turned out, I was shortly looking to get back on welfare, finding no job coupled with acceptable child care screaming out for my skills, such as they were. There didn't seem to be much of a market for brains, and I couldn't type. I could only answer one phone line at a time. I had a college degree (acquired on scholarships), but it wasn't worth much in a city teeming with hundreds of thousands of other baby-boom graduates, many of whom had connections and no babies.

I went to the welfare with all my papers and baby in tow. After waiting interminable days for an appointment, I was finally told that I didn't qualify because I didn't have a place to live. I said that I didn't have any place to live because I didn't have any money with which to rent an apartment, and, if they would just help me, I could remedy that. I was sent packing.

In no time, I obtained a letter from a friend saying I lived in her apartment and went back to the welfare, only this time at another center, to avoid being recognized. (New York City had some forty-six welfare centers at the time. One out of every eleven welfare recipients in the country lives there.) I went through the same process, filling out reams of forms and waiting anxiously for my "appointment." There was a sign on the wall in this center stating, NO MATTER WHAT TIME YOUR APPOINTMENT IS, IF YOU ARE NOT HERE BY 8:30 A.M., YOU WILL NOT BE SEEN. After examining my application, the intake worker told me we were not eligible for welfare because we had no furniture. I started to panic but refrained from strangling her. She told me to go back where I had come from. But I couldn't.

When I got enough of a grip on myself to act, I realized that I needed to know what you had to *have*, not simply what you *didn't* have, to get on welfare in New York, because, though I didn't have any of it, I was willing to say I did. Of course, what they were telling me was not true, but, once again, I was not privy to that little piece of information. Even if I had known, I wouldn't have had the slightest idea what to do about it. I converted one of the few dollars I had left into dimes, got hold of a phone book, and proceeded to call organizations listed in the yellow pages. After a series of unproductive calls, it occurred to me to call New York NOW [National Organization for Women]. I had noticed, after all, that most of the people in the centers were women with kids. I'd heard from a friend who was on welfare, but with whom I was unable to get in touch, that there was some kind of welfare mothers' group in New York, and I inquired about it. They actually knew of it and gave me the number for the Downtown Welfare Advocate Center (DWAC, which whites usually pronounced phonetically and blacks pronounced with a flair I preferred: "DEE-wac").

Some weeks later, with the help of a law student, John Morken, who volunteered at the center, I received a welfare check and got a room in an apartment share for my baby and me. John and my friend Ann Phillips kept trying to convince me to come to DWAC some Sunday for meetings of welfare mothers who talked about their problems and about the notion of "welfare rights," whatever that was. Having virtually no political interests, I was disinclined. Sometime later, I finally relented. There were only a handful of women present at the meeting that first day I went. I don't remember what I expected, but it was more or less a consciousness-raising session for welfare mothers. It was 1975, and little did I know that I would be involved with this organization for more than a decade.

One woman there, Diana Voelker, was particularly impressive. She had grown up on the streets of New York, been a gang member. She, too, was a welfare mother, with a beautiful blond child about seven years old. Diana acted tough, but I was later to find out that was all cover. Throughout the meeting she, and to some extent the others, was "organizing" me, although I didn't know it at the time. Diana said things like "They try to make you feel guilty like you've done something wrong. There's nothing wrong with you; it's the system that's all screwed up. You're a mother, and that's a job and it's an important one." There was a poster on the wall that said WOMEN HOLD UP HALF THE SKY.

PART SIXTEEN

America in a Changed World

95

BENJAMIN BARBER

From *Jihad vs. McWorld*

In this selection political scientist Benjamin Barber writes from the perspective of an advocate of democracy—the right of the people to be a voice in a genuine citizen-led society. In his important 1995 book, that takes on additional meaning after September 11, 2001, Barber contrasts two visions of the world, neither one of which is compatible with the kind of democracy he believes in. One vision is the world engaged in Jihad, "in which culture is pitted against culture, people against people, tribe against tribe"; if students had trouble understanding what Barber meant when he wrote in 1995, they have no trouble understanding it today. The contrary vision is McWorld, "onrushing economic, technological, and ecological forces that demand integration and uniformity and mesmerize peoples everywhere with fast music, fast computers, and fast food." This, too, is easily understood. Jihad and McWorld feed off one another—but in opposition. Neither one has any place for a citizen-based democracy where all participate. Barber's analysis is incisive, original, and scary.

———

HISTORY IS NOT OVER. Nor are we arrived in the wondrous land of techné promised by the futurologists. The collapse of state communism has not delivered people to a safe democratic haven, and the past, fratricide and civil discord perduring, still clouds the horizon just behind us. Those who look back see all of the horrors of the ancient slaughterbench reenacted in disintegral nations like Bosnia, Sri Lanka, Ossetia, and Rwanda and they declare that nothing has changed. Those who look forward prophesize commercial and technological interdependence—a virtual paradise made possible by spreading markets and global technology—and they proclaim that everything is or soon will be different. The rival observers seem to consult different almanacs drawn from the libraries of contrarian planets.

Yet anyone who reads the daily papers carefully, taking in the front page accounts of civil carnage as well as the business page stories on the mechanics of the information superhighway and the economics of communication mergers, anyone who turns deliberately to take in the whole 360-degree horizon, knows that our world and our lives are caught between what William Butler Yeats called the two eternities of race and soul: that of race reflecting the tribal past, that of soul anticipating the cosmopolitan future. Our secular eternities are corrupted, however, race reduced to an insignia of resentment, and soul sized down to fit the demanding body by which it now measures its needs. Neither race nor soul offers us a future that is other than bleak, neither promises a polity that is remotely democratic.

The first scenario rooted in race holds out the grim prospect of a retribalization of large swaths of humankind by war and bloodshed: a threatened balkanization of nation-states in which culture is pitted against culture, people against people, tribe against tribe, a Jihad in the name of a hundred narrowly conceived faiths against every kind of interdependence, every kind of artificial social cooperation and mutuality: against technology, against pop culture, and against integrated markets; against modernity itself as well as the future in which modernity issues. The second paints that future in shimmering pastels, a busy portrait of onrushing economic, technological, and ecological forces that demand integration and uniformity and that mesmerize peoples everywhere with fast music, fast computers, and fast food—MTV, Macintosh, and McDonald's—pressing nations into one homogenous global theme park, one McWorld tied together by communications, information, entertainment, and commerce. Caught between Babel and Disneyland, the planet is falling precipitously apart and coming reluctantly together at the very same moment.

Some stunned observers notice only Babel, complaining about the thousand newly sundered "peoples" who prefer to address their neighbors with sniper rifles and mortars; others—zealots in Disneyland—seize on futurological platitudes and the promise of virtuality, exclaiming "It's a small world after all!" Both are right, but how can that be?

We are compelled to choose between what passes as "the twilight of sovereignty" and an entropic end of all history; or a return to the past's most fractious and demoralizing discord; to "the menace of global anarchy," to Milton's capital of hell, Pandaemonium; to a world totally "out of control."

The apparent truth, which speaks to the paradox at the core of this book, is that the tendencies of both Jihad *and* McWorld are at work, both visible sometimes in the same country at the very same instant. Iranian zealots keep one ear tuned to the mullahs urging holy war and the other cocked to Rupert Murdoch's Star television beaming in *Dynasty, Donahue,* and *The Simpsons* from hovering satellites. Chinese entrepreneurs vie for the attention of party cadres in Beijing and simultaneously pursue KFC franchises in cities like Nanjing, Hangzhou, and Xian where twenty-eight outlets serve over 100,000 customers a day. The Russian Orthodox church, even as it struggles to renew the ancient faith, has entered a joint venture with California businessmen to bottle and sell natural waters under the rubric Saint Springs Water Company. Serbian assassins wear Adidas sneakers and listen to Madonna on Walkman headphones as they take aim through their gunscopes at scurrying Sarajevo civilians looking to fill family watercans. Orthodox Hasids and brooding neo-Nazis have both turned to rock music to get their traditional messages out to the new generation, while fundamentalists plot virtual conspiracies on the Internet.

Now neither Jihad nor McWorld is in itself novel. History ending in the triumph of science and reason or some monstrous perversion thereof (Mary Shelley's Doctor Frankenstein) has been the leitmotiv of every philosopher and poet who has regretted the Age of Reason since the Enlightenment. Yeats lamented "the center will not hold, mere anarchy is loosed upon the world," and observers of Jihad today have little but historical detail to add. The Christian parable of the Fall and of the possibilities of redemption that it makes possible captures the eighteenth-century ambivalence—and our own—about past and future. I want, however, to do more than dress up the central paradox of human history in modern clothes. It is not Jihad and McWorld but the relationship between them that most interests me. For, squeezed between their opposing forces, the world has been sent spinning out of control. Can it be that what Jihad and McWorld have in common is anarchy: the absence of common will and that conscious and collective human control under the guidance of law we call democracy?

Progress moves in steps that sometimes lurch backwards; in history's twisting maze, Jihad not only revolts against but abets McWorld, while McWorld not only imperils but re-creates and reinforces Jihad. They produce their contraries and need one another. My object here then is not simply to offer sequential portraits of McWorld and Jihad, but while examining McWorld, to keep Jihad in my field of vision, and while dissecting Jihad, never to forget the context of McWorld. Call it a dialectic of McWorld: a study in the cunning of reason that does honor to the radical differences that distinguish Jihad and McWorld yet that acknowledges their powerful and paradoxical interdependence.

There is a crucial difference, however, between my modest attempt at dialectic and that of the masters of the nineteenth century. Still seduced by the Enlightenment's faith in progress, both Hegel and Marx believed reason's cunning was on the side of progress. But it is harder to believe that the clash of Jihad and McWorld will issue in some overriding good. The outcome seems more likely to pervert than to nurture human liberty. The two may, in opposing each other, work to the same ends, work in apparent tension yet in covert harmony, but democracy is not their beneficiary. In East Berlin, tribal communism has yielded to capitalism. In Marx-Engelsplatz, the stolid, overbearing statues of Marx and Engels face east, as if seeking distant solace from Moscow: but now, circling them along the streets that surround the park that is their prison are chain eateries like T.G.I. Friday's, international hotels like the Radisson, and a circle of neon billboards mocking them with brand names like Panasonic, Coke, and GoldStar. New gods, yes, but more liberty?

What then does it mean in concrete terms to view Jihad and McWorld dialectically when the tendencies of the two sets of forces initially appear so intractably antithetical? After all, Jihad and McWorld operate with equal strength in opposite directions, the one driven by parochial hatreds, the other by universalizing markets, the one re-creating ancient subnational and ethnic borders from within, the other making national borders porous from without. Yet Jihad and McWorld have this in common: they both make war on the sovereign nation-state and thus undermine the nation-state's democratic institutions. Each eschews civil society and belittles democratic citizenship, neither seeks alternative democratic institutions. Their common thread is indifference to civil liberty. Jihad forges communities of blood rooted in exclusion and hatred, communities that slight democracy in favor of tyrannical paternalism or consensual tribalism. McWorld forges global markets rooted in consumption and profit, leaving to an untrustworthy, if not altogether fictitious, invisible hand issues of public interest and common good that once might have been nurtured by democratic citizenries and their watchful governments. Such governments, intimidated by market ideology, are actually pulling back at the very moment they ought to be aggressively intervening. What was once understood as protecting the public interest is now excoriated as heavy-handed regulatory browbeating. Justice yields to markets, even though, as Felix Rohatyn has bluntly confessed, "there is a brutal Darwinian logic to these markets. They are nervous and greedy. They look for stability and transparency, but what they reward is not always our preferred form of democracy." If the traditional conservators of freedom were democratic constitutions and Bills of Rights, "the new temples to liberty," George Steiner suggests, "will be McDonald's and Kentucky Fried Chicken."

In being reduced to a choice between the market's universal church and a retribalizing politics of particularist identities, peoples around the globe are threatened with an atavistic return to medieval politics where local tribes and ambitious emperors together ruled the world entire, women and men united by the universal abstraction of Christianity even as they lived out isolated lives in warring fiefdoms defined by involuntary (ascriptive) forms of identity. This was a world in which princes and kings had little real power until they conceived the ideology of nationalism. Nationalism established government on a scale greater than the tribe yet less cosmopolitan than the universal church and in time gave birth to those intermediate, gradually more democratic institutions that would come to constitute the nation-state. Today, at the far end of this history, we seem intent on re-creating a world in which our only choices are the secular universalism of the cosmopolitan market and the everyday particularism of the fractious tribe.

In the tumult of the confrontation between global commerce and parochial ethnicity, the virtues of the democratic nation are lost and the instrumentalities by which it permitted peoples to transform themselves into nations and seize sovereign power in the name of liberty and the commonweal are put at risk. Neither Jihad nor McWorld aspires to rese-cure the civic virtues undermined by its denationalizing practices; neither global markets nor blood communities service public goods or pursue equality and justice. Impartial judiciaries and deliberative assemblies play no role in the roving killer bands that speak on behalf of newly liberated "peoples," and such democratic institutions have at best only marginal influence on the roving multinational corporations that speak on behalf of newly liberated markets. Jihad pursues a bloody politics of iden-tity, McWorld a bloodless economics of profit. Belonging by default to McWorld, everyone is a consumer; seeking a repository for identity, everyone belongs to some tribe. But no one is a citizen. Without citizens, how can there be democracy? . . .

Jihad is, I recognize, a strong term. In its mildest form, it betokens religious struggle on behalf of faith, a kind of Islamic zeal. In its strongest political manifestation, it means bloody holy war on behalf of partisan identity that is metaphysically defined and fanatically defended. Thus, while for many Muslims it may signify only ardor in the name of a religion that can properly be regarded as universalizing (if not quite ecumenical), I borrow its meaning from those militants who make the slaughter of the "other" a higher duty. I use the term in its militant construction to suggest dogmatic and violent particularism of a kind known to Christians no less than Muslims, to Germans and Hindis as well as to Arabs. The phenomena to which I apply the phrase have innocent enough beginnings: identity politics and multicultural diversity can represent strategies of a free society trying to give expression to its diversity. What ends as Jihad may begin as a simple search for a local identity, some set of common personal attributes to hold out against the numbing and neutering uniformities of industrial modernization and the colonizing culture of McWorld. . . .

McWorld is a product of popular culture driven by expansionist commerce. Its template is American, its form style. Its goods are as much images as matériel, an aesthetic as well as a product line. It is about culture as commodity, apparel as ideology. Its symbols are Harley-Davidson motorcycles and Cadillac motorcars hoisted from the roadways, where they once represented a mode of transportation, to the marquees of global market cafés like Harley-Davidson's and the Hard Rock where they become icons of lifestyle. You don't drive them, you feel their vibes and rock to the images they conjure up from old movies and new celebrities, whose personal appearances are the key to the wildly popular international café chain Planet Hollywood. Music, video, theater, books, and theme parks—the new churches of a commercial civilization in which malls are the public squares and suburbs the neighborless neighborhoods— are all constructed as image exports creating a common world taste around common logos, advertising slogans, stars, songs, brand names, jingles, and trademarks. Hard power yields to soft, while ideology is transmuted into a kind of videology that works through sound bites and film clips. Videology is fuzzier and less dogmatic than traditional political ideology: it may as a consequence be far more successful in instilling the novel values required for global markets to succeed. . . .

Nowhere is the tension between democracy and Jihad more evident than in the Islamic world, where the idea of Jihad has a home of birth but certainly not an exclusive patent. For, although it is clear that Islam is a complex religion that by no means is synonymous with Jihad, it is relatively inhospitable to democracy and that inhospitality in turn nurtures conditions favorable to parochialism, antimodernism, exclusiveness, and hostility to "others"—the characteristics that constitute what I have called Jihad.

While *Jihad* is a term associated with the moral (and sometimes armed) struggle of believers against faithlessness and the faithless, I have used it here to speak to a generic form of fundamentalist opposition to modernity that can be found in most world religions. In their massive five-volume study of fundamentalisms, Martin E. Marty and R. Scott Appleby treat Sunni and Shiite Islam but pay equal attention to Protestantism and Catholicism in a variety of European, and North and South American forms, to Hinduism, to the Sikhs, to Theravada Buddhism, to Confucianist Revivalism, and to Zionism. Marty and Appleby take fundamentalist religions to be engaged in militancy, in a kind of permanent *fighting*: they are "militant, whether in the use of words and ideas or ballots or, in extreme cases, bullets." They fight back, struggling reactively against the present in the name of the past; they fight for their religious conception of the world against secularism and relativism; they fight with weapons of every kind, sometimes borrowed from the enemy, carefully chosen to secure their identity; they fight against others who are agents of corruption; and they fight under God for a cause that, because it is holy, cannot be lost even when it is not yet won. The struggle that is Jihad is not then just a feature of Islam but a characteristic of all fundamentalisms. Nevertheless, *Jihad* is an Islamic term and is given its animating power by its association not just with fundamentalism in general but with Islamic fundamentalism in particular and with the armed struggles groups like Hamas and Islamic Jihad have engaged in. There are moderate and liberal strands in Islam, but they are less prominent at present than the militant strand. . . .

If McWorld in its most elemental negative form is a kind of animal greed—one that is achieved by an aggressive and irresistible energy, Jihad in its most elemental negative form is a kind of animal fear propelled by anxiety in the face of uncertainty and relieved by self-sacrificing zealotry—an escape out of history. Because history has been a history of individuation, acquisitiveness, secularization, aggressiveness, atomization, and immoralism it becomes in the eyes of Jihad's disciples the temporal chariot of wickedness, a carrier of corruption that, along with time itself, must be rejected. Moral preservationists, whether in America, Israel, Iran, or India, have no choice but to make war on the present to secure a future more like the past: depluralized, monocultured, unskepticized, reenchanted. Homogenous values by which women and men live orderly and simple lives were once nurtured under such conditions. Today, our lives have become pulp fiction and *Pulp Fiction* as novel, as movie, or as life promises no miracles. McWorld is meager fare for hungry moralists and shows only passing interest in the spirit. However outrageous the deeds associated with Jihad, the revolt the deeds manifest is reactive to changes that are themselves outrageous.

This survey of the moral topography of Jihad suggests that McWorld—the spiritual poverty of markets—may bear a portion of the blame for the excesses of the holy war against the modern; and that Jihad as a form of negation reveals Jihad as a form of affirmation. Jihad tends the soul that McWorld abjures and strives for the moral well-being that McWorld, busy with the consumer choices it mistakes for freedom, disdains. Jihad thus goes to war with McWorld and, because each worries the other will obstruct and ultimately thwart the realization of its ends, the war between them becomes a holy war. The lines here are drawn not in sand but in stone. The language of hate is not easily subjected to compromise: the "other" as enemy cannot easily be turned into an interlocutor. But as McWorld is "other" to Jihad, so Jihad is "other" to McWorld. Reasoned communication between the two is problematic when for the partisans of Jihad both reason and communication appear as seductive instrumentalities of the devil, while for the partisans of McWorld both are seductive instrumentalities of consumerism. For all their dialectical interplay with respect to democracy, Jihad and McWorld are moral antinomies. There is no room in the mosque for Nintendo, no place on the Internet for Jesus—however rapidly "religious" channels are multiplying. Life cannot be both play and in earnest, cannot stand for the lesser gratification of a needy body and simultaneously for the greater glory of a selfless soul. Either the Qur'an speaks the Truth, or Truth is a television quiz show. History has given us Jihad as a counterpoint to McWorld and made them inextricable; but individuals cannot live in both domains at once and are compelled to choose. Sadly, it is not obvious that the choice, whatever it is, holds out much promise to democrats in search of a free civil society.

Should would-be democrats take their chances then with McWorld, with which they have shared the road to modernity but that has shown so little interest in them? Or try to reach an accommodation with Jihad, whose high moral purpose serves democracy's seriousness yet leaves but precious little space for its liberties? As it turns out, neither Jihad nor McWorld—and certainly not the quarrel between them—allows democracy much room. . . .

If my fundamental analysis of the dialectics that bind Jihad and McWorld together continues to be validated by current events, there are, nonetheless, issues raised by critics that merit some reply. . . .

My discussion of Jihad—indeed the very use of the word in the title—has drawn . . . criticism. . . . For although I made clear that I deployed Jihad as a generic term quite independently from its Islamic theological origins, and although I insisted that Islam has itself both democratic and nondemocratic manifestations and potentials, some readers felt the term singled out Islam and used it in pejorative ways to criticize non-Islamic phenomena. While extremist groups like Islamic Jihad have themselves associated the word with armed struggle against modernizing, secular infidels, I can appreciate that the great majority of devout Muslims who harbor no more sympathy for Islamic Jihad than devout Christians feel for the Ku Klux Klan or for the Montana Militia might feel unfairly burdened by my title. I owe them an apology, and hope they will find their way past the book's cover to the substantive reasoning that makes clear how little my argument has to do with Islam as a religion or with resistance to McWorld as a singular property of radical Muslims.

I have much less sympathy for those who read only one or another section of the book and concluded, lazily, that I must be writing either about McWorld alone or Jihad alone. Some critics have simply lumped *Jihad vs. McWorld* in together with Pandemonium prophets like Robert D. Kaplan (*The Ends of the Earth*) and Samuel P. Huntington ("The Clash of Civilizations"), dismissing us all as Pandoric pessimists. But as must be clear to anyone who reads the book cover to cover, it is finally about neither Jihad nor McWorld but about democracy—and the dangers democracy faces in a world where the forces of commerce and the forces reacting to commerce are locked in struggle. . . .

96

SAMUEL HUNTINGTON

From *The Clash of Civilizations*

Renowned scholar Samuel Huntington's 1996 book has received much attention since the terrorist attacks against the United States in 2001. Writing several years earlier, Huntington anticipates the vastly changed landscape of world conflict after the collapse of Soviet communism and after the end of the U.S.-Soviet Cold War. "Power is shifting from the long predominant West to non-western civilizations," Huntington writes. He explores the reasons why he believes this is happening, emphasizing the renewal of religion as central to the changes in power. Religious conflicts, especially between Islam and Christianity, are inevitable, the author feels. Not all Americans will agree with Huntington's grim thesis, but his ideas are important reading for people who have been brought up in the United States. Modernism, reason, progress, and prosperity are key American values, but not necessarily those of much of the rest of the world.

IN THE POST-COLD WAR WORLD, for the first time in history, global politics has become multipolar *and* multicivilizational. During most of human existence, contacts between civilizations were intermittent or nonexistent. Then, with the beginning of the modern era, about A.D. 1500, global politics assumed two dimensions. For over four hundred years, the nation states of the West—Britain, France, Spain, Austria, Prussia, Germany, the United States, and others—constituted a multipolar international system within Western civilization and interacted, competed, and fought wars with each other. At the same time, Western nations also expanded, conquered, colonized, or decisively influenced every other civilization. During the Cold War global politics became bipolar and the world was divided into three parts. A group of mostly wealthy and democratic societies, led by the United States, was engaged in a pervasive ideological, political, economic, and, at times, military competition with a group of somewhat poorer communist societies associated with and led by the Soviet Union. Much of this conflict occurred in the Third World outside these two camps, composed of countries which often were poor, lacked political stability, were recently independent, and claimed to be nonaligned.

In the late 1980s the communist world collapsed, and the Cold War international system became history. In the post-Cold War world, the most important distinctions among peoples are not ideological, political, or economic. They are cultural. Peoples and nations are attempting to answer the most basic question humans can face: Who are we? And they are answering that question in the traditional way human beings have answered it, by reference to the things that mean most to them. People define themselves in terms of ancestry, religion, language, history, values, customs, and institutions. They identify with cultural groups: tribes, ethnic groups, religious communities, nations, and, at the broadest level, civilizations. People use politics not just to advance their interests but also to define their identity. We know who we are only when we know who we are not and often only when we know whom we are against.

Nation states remain the principal actors in world affairs. Their behavior is shaped as in the past by the pursuit of power and wealth, but it is also shaped by cultural preferences, commonalities, and differences. The most important groupings of states are no longer the three blocs of the Cold War but rather the world's seven or eight major civilizations. Non-Western societies, particularly in East Asia, are developing their economic wealth and creating the basis for enhanced military power and political influence. As their power and self-confidence increase, non-Western societies increasingly assert their own cultural values and reject those "imposed" on them by the West. The "international system of the twenty-first century," Henry Kissinger has noted," . . . will contain at least six major powers—the United States, Europe, China, Japan, Russia, and probably India—as well as a multiplicity of medium-sized and smaller countries." Kissinger's six major powers belong to five very different civilizations, and in addition there are important Islamic states whose strategic locations, large populations, and/or oil resources make them influential in world affairs. In this new world, local politics is the politics of ethnicity; global politics is the politics of civilizations. The rivalry of the superpowers is replaced by the clash of civilizations. . . .

The philosophical assumptions, underlying values, social relations, customs, and overall outlooks on life differ significantly among civilizations. The revitalization of religion throughout much of the world is reinforcing these cultural differences. Cultures can change, and the nature of their impact on politics and economics can vary from one period to another. Yet the major differences in political and economic development among civilizations are clearly rooted in their different cultures. East Asian economic success has its source in East Asian culture, as do the difficulties East Asian societies have had in achieving stable democratic political systems. Islamic culture explains in large part the failure of democracy to emerge in much of the Muslim world. Developments in the postcommunist societies of Eastern Europe and the former Soviet Union are shaped by their civilizational identities. Those with Western Christian heritages are making progress toward economic development and democratic politics; the prospects for economic and political development in the Orthodox countries are uncertain; the prospects in the Muslim republics are bleak.

The West is and will remain for years to come the most powerful civilization. Yet its power relative to that of other civilizations is declining. As the West attempts to assert its values and to protect its interests, non-Western societies confront a choice. Some attempt to emulate the West and to join or to "bandwagon" with the West. Other Confucian and Islamic societies attempt to expand their own economic and military power to resist and to "balance" against the West. A central axis of post-Cold War world politics is thus the interaction of Western power and culture with the power and culture of non-Western civilizations.

In sum, the post-Cold War world is a world of seven or eight major civilizations. Cultural commonalities and differences shape the interests, antagonisms, and associations of states. The most important countries in the world come overwhelmingly from different civilizations. The local conflicts most likely to escalate into broader wars are those between groups and states from different civilizations. The predominant patterns of political and economic development differ from civilization to civilization. The key issues on the international agenda involve differences among civilizations. Power is shifting from the long predominant West to non-Western civilizations. Global politics has become multipolar and multicivilizational. . . .

The distribution of cultures in the world reflects the distribution of power. Trade may or may not follow the flag, but culture almost always follows power. Throughout history the expansion of the power of a civilization has usually occurred simultaneously with the flowering of its culture and has almost always involved its using that power to extend its values, practices, and institutions to other societies. A universal civilization requires universal power. Roman power created a near-universal civilization within the limited confines of the Classical world. Western power in the form of European colonialism in the nineteenth century and American hegemony in the twentieth century extended Western culture throughout much of the contemporary world. European colonialism is over; American hegemony is receding. The erosion of Western culture follows, as indigenous, historically rooted mores, languages, beliefs, and institutions reassert themselves. The growing power of non-Western societies produced by modernization is generating the revival of non-Western cultures throughout the world.

A distinction exists, Joseph Nye has argued, between "hard power," which is the power to command resting on economic and military strength, and "soft power," which is the ability of a state to get "other countries to *want* what it wants" through the appeal of its culture and ideology. As Nye recognizes, a broad diffusion of hard power is occurring in the world and the major nations "are less able to use their traditional power resources to achieve their purposes than in the past." Nye goes on to say that if a state's "culture and ideology are attractive, others will be more willing to follow" its leadership, and hence soft power is "just as important as hard command power." What, however, makes culture and ideology attractive? They become attractive when they are seen as rooted in material success and influence. Soft power is power only when it rests on a foundation of hard power. Increases in hard economic and military power produce enhanced self-confidence, arrogance, and belief in the superiority of one's own culture or soft power compared to those of other peoples and greatly increase its attractiveness to other peoples. Decreases in economic and military power lead to self-doubt, crises of identity, and efforts to find in other cultures the keys to economic, military, and political success. As non-Western societies enhance their economic, military, and political capacity, they increasingly trumpet the virtues of their own values, institutions, and culture.

Communist ideology appealed to people throughout the world in the 1950s and 1960s when it was associated with the economic success and military force of the Soviet Union. That appeal evaporated when the Soviet economy stagnated and was unable to maintain Soviet military strength. Western values and institutions have appealed to people from other cultures because they were seen as the source of Western power and wealth. This process has been going on for centuries. Between 1000 and 1300, as William McNeill points out, Christianity, Roman law, and other elements of Western culture were adopted by Hungarians, Poles, and Lithuanians, and this "acceptance of Western civilization was stimulated by mingled fear and admiration of the military prowess of Western princes." As Western power declines, the ability of the West to impose Western concepts of human rights, liberalism, and democracy on other civilizations also declines and so does the attractiveness of those values to other civilizations.

It already has. For several centuries non-Western peoples envied the economic prosperity, technological sophistication, military power, and political cohesion of Western societies. They sought the secret of this success in Western values and institutions, and when they identified what they thought might be the key they attempted to apply it in their own societies. To become rich and powerful, they would have to become like the West. Now, however, these Kemalist attitudes have disappeared in East Asia. East Asians attribute their dramatic economic development not to their import of Western culture but rather to their adherence to their own culture. They are succeeding, they argue, because they are different from the West. Similarly, when non-Western societies felt weak in relation to the West, they invoked Western values of self-determination, liberalism, democracy, and independence to justify their opposition to Western domination. Now that they are no longer weak but increasingly powerful, they do not hesitate to attack those same values which they previously used to promote their interests. The revolt against the West was originally legitimated by asserting the universality of Western values; it is now legitimated by asserting the superiority of non-Western values.

The rise of these attitudes is a manifestation of what Ronald Dore has termed the "second-generation indigenization phenomenon." In both former Western colonies and independent countries like China and Japan, "The first 'modernizer' or 'post-independence' generation has often received its training in foreign (Western) universities in a Western cosmopolitan language. Partly because they first go abroad as impressionable teenagers, their absorption of Western values and life-styles may well be profound." Most of the much larger second generation, in contrast, gets its education at home in universities created by the first generation, and the local rather than the colonial language is increasingly used for instruction. These universities "provide a much more diluted contact with metropolitan world culture" and "knowledge is indigenized by means of translations—usually of limited range and of poor quality." The graduates of these universities resent the dominance of the earlier Western-trained generation and hence often "succumb to the appeals of nativist opposition movements." As Western influence recedes, young aspiring leaders cannot look to the West to provide them with power and wealth. They have to find the means of success within their own society, and hence they have to accommodate to the values and culture of that society. . . .

In the first half of the twentieth century intellectual elites generally assumed that economic and social modernization was leading to the withering away of religion as a significant element in human existence. This assumption was shared by both those who welcomed and those who deplored this trend. Modernizing secularists hailed the extent to which science, rationalism, and pragmatism were eliminating the superstitions, myths, irrationalities, and rituals that formed the core of existing religions. The emerging society would be tolerant, rational, pragmatic, progressive, humanistic, and secular. Worried conservatives, on the other hand, warned of the dire consequences of the disappearance of religious beliefs, religious institutions, and the moral guidance religion provided for individual and collective human behavior. The end result would be anarchy, depravity, the undermining of civilized life. "If you will not have God (and He is a jealous God)," T. S. Eliot said, "you should pay your respects to Hitler or Stalin."

The second half of the twentieth century proved these hopes and fears unfounded. Economic and social modernization became global in scope, and at the same time a global revival of religion occurred. This revival, *la revanche de Dieu*, Gilles Kepel termed it, has pervaded every continent, every civilization, and virtually every country. In the mid-1970s, as Kepel observes, the trend to secularization and toward the accommodation of religion with secularism "went into reverse. A new religious approach took shape, aimed no longer at adapting to secular values but at recovering a sacred foundation for the organization of society—by changing society if necessary. Expressed in a multitude of ways, this approach advocated moving on from a modernism that had failed, attributing its setbacks and dead ends to separation from God. The theme was no longer *aggiornamento* but a 'second evangelization of Europe,' the aim was no longer to modernize Islam but to 'Islamize modernity.'"

This religious revival has in part involved expansion by some religions, which gained new recruits in societies where they had previously not had them. To a much larger extent, however, the religious resurgence involved people returning to, reinvigorating, and giving new meaning to the traditional religions of their communities. Christianity, Islam, Judaism, Hinduism, Buddhism, Orthodoxy, all experienced new surges in commitment, relevance, and practice by erstwhile casual believers. In all of them fundamentalist movements arose committed to the militant purification of religious doctrines and institutions and the reshaping of personal, social, and public behavior in accordance with religious tenets. The fundamentalist movements are dramatic and can have significant political impact. They are, however, only the surface waves of the much broader and more fundamental religious tide that is giving a different cast to human life at the end of the twentieth century. The renewal of religion throughout the world far transcends the activities of fundamentalist extremists. In society after society it manifests itself in the daily lives and work of people and the concerns and projects of governments. The cultural resurgence in the secular Confucian culture takes the form of the affirmation of Asian values but in the rest of the world manifests itself in the affirmation of religious values. The "unsecularization of the world," as George Weigel remarked "is one of the dominant social facts in the late twentieth century." . . .

How can this global religious resurgence be explained? Particular causes obviously operated in individual countries and civilizations. Yet it is too much to expect that a large number of different causes would have produced simultaneous and similar developments in most parts of the world. A global phenomenon demands a global explanation. However much events in particular countries may have been influenced by unique factors, some general causes must have been at work. What were they?

The most obvious, most salient, and most powerful cause of the global religious resurgence is precisely what was supposed to cause the death of religion: the processes of social, economic, and cultural modernization that swept across the world in the second half of the twentieth century. Long-standing sources of identity and systems of authority are disrupted. People move from the countryside into the city, become separated from their roots, and take new jobs or no job. They interact with large numbers of strangers and are exposed to new sets of relationships. They need new sources of identity, new forms of stable community, and new sets of moral precepts to provide them with a sense of meaning and purpose. Religion, both mainstream and fundamentalist, meets these needs. As Lee Kuan Yew explained for East Asia:

We are agricultural societies that have industrialized within one or two generations. What happened in the West over 200 years or more is happening here in about 50 years or less. It is all crammed and crushed into a very tight time frame, so there are bound to be dislocations and malfunctions. If you look at the fast-growing countries — Korea, Thailand, Hong Kong, and Singapore — there's been one remarkable phenomenon: the rise of religion. . . . The old customs and religions — ancestor worship, shamanism — no longer completely satisfy. There is a quest for some higher explanations about man's purpose, about why we are here. This is associated with periods of great stress in society.

People do not live by reason alone. They cannot calculate and act rationally in pursuit of their self-interest until they define their self. Interest politics presupposes identity. In times of rapid social change established identities dissolve, the self must be redefined, and new identities created. For people facing the need to determine Who am I? Where do I belong? religion provides compelling answers, and religious groups provide small social communities to replace those lost through urbanization. All religions, as Hassan al-Turabi said, furnish "people with a sense of identity and a direction in life." In this process, people rediscover or create new historical identities. Whatever universalist goals they may have, religions give people identity by positing a basic distinction between believers and nonbelievers, between a superior in-group and a different and inferior out-group.

In the Muslim world, Bernard Lewis argues, there has been "a recurring tendency, in times of emergency, for Muslims to find their basic identity and loyalty in the religious community—that is to say, in an entity defined by Islam rather than by ethnic or territorial criteria." Gilles Kepel similarly highlights the centrality of the search for identity: "Re-Islamization 'from below' is first and foremost a way of rebuilding an identity in a world that has lost its meaning and become amorphous and alienating." In India, "a new Hindu identity is under construction" as a response to tensions and alienation generated by modernization. In Russia, the religious revival is the result "of a passionate desire for identity which only the Orthodox church, the sole unbroken link with the Russians' 1000-year past, can provide," while in the Islamic republics the revival similarly stems "from the Central Asians' most powerful aspiration: to assert the identities that Moscow suppressed for decades." Fundamentalist movements, in particular, are "a way of coping with the experience of chaos, the loss of identity, meaning and secure social structures created by the rapid introduction of modern social and political patterns, secularism, scientific culture and economic development." The fundamentalist "movements that matter," agrees William H. McNeill, " . . . are those that recruit from society at large and spread because they answer, or seem to answer, newly felt human needs. . . . It is no accident that these movements are all based in countries where population pressure on the land is making continuation of old village ways impossible for a majority of the population, and where urban-based mass communications, by penetrating the villages, have begun to erode an age-old framework of peasant life."

More broadly, the religious resurgence throughout the world is a reaction against secularism, moral relativism, and self-indulgence, and a reaffirmation of the values of order, discipline, work, mutual help, and human solidarity. Religious groups meet social needs left untended by state bureaucracies. These include the provision of medical and hospital services, kindergartens and schools, care for the elderly, prompt relief after natural and other catastrophes, and welfare and social support during periods of economic deprivation. The breakdown of order and of civil society creates vacuums which are filled by religious, often fundamentalist, groups. . . .

. . . "More than anything else," William McNeill observes, "reaffirmation of Islam, whatever its specific sectarian form, means the repudiation of European and American influence upon local society, politics, and morals." In this sense, the revival of non-Western religions is the most powerful manifestation of anti-Westernism in non-Western societies. That revival is not a rejection of modernity; it is a rejection of the West and of the secular, relativistic, degenerate culture associated with the West. It is a rejection of what has been termed the "Westoxification" of non-Western societies. It is a declaration of cultural independence from the West, a proud statement that: "We will be modern but we won't be you." . . .

Some Westerners, including [former] President Bill Clinton, have argued that the West does not have problems with Islam but only with violent Islamist extremists. Fourteen hundred years of history demonstrate otherwise. The relations between Islam and Christianity, both Orthodox and Western, have often been stormy. Each has been the other's Other. The twentieth-century conflict between liberal democracy and Marxist-Leninism is only a fleeting and superficial historical phenomenon compared to the continuing and deeply conflictual relation between Islam and Christianity. At times, peaceful coexistence has prevailed; more often the relation has been one of intense rivalry and of varying degrees of hot war. Their "historical dynamics," John Esposito comments, " . . . often found the two communities in competition, and locked at times in deadly combat, for power, land, and souls." Across the centuries the fortunes of the two religions have risen and fallen in a sequence of momentous surges, pauses, and countersurges. . . .

A . . . mix of factors has increased the conflict between Islam and the West in the late twentieth century. First, Muslim population growth has generated large numbers of unemployed and disaffected young people who become recruits to Islamist causes, exert pressure on neighboring societies, and migrate to the West. Second, the Islamic Resurgence has given Muslims renewed confidence in the distinctive character and worth of their civilization and values compared to those of the West. Third, the West's simultaneous efforts to universalize its values and institutions, to maintain its military and economic superiority, and to intervene in conflicts in the Muslim world generate intense resentment among Muslims. Fourth, the collapse of communism removed a common enemy of the

West and Islam and left each the perceived major threat to the other. Fifth, the increasing contact between and intermingling of Muslims and Westerners stimulate in each a new sense of their own identity and how it differs from that of the other. Interaction and intermingling also exacerbate differences over the rights of the members of one civilization in a country dominated by members of the other civilization. Within both Muslim and Christian societies, tolerance for the other declined sharply in the 1980s and 1990s.

The causes of the renewed conflict between Islam and the West thus lie in fundamental questions of power and culture. *Kto? Kovo?* Who is to rule? Who is to be ruled? The central issue of politics defined by Lenin is the root of the contest between Islam and the West. There is, however, the additional conflict, which Lenin would have considered meaningless, between two different versions of what is right and what is wrong and, as a consequence, who is right and who is wrong. So long as Islam remains Islam (which it will) and the West remains the West (which is more dubious), this fundamental conflict between two great civilizations and ways of life will continue to define their relations in the future even as it has defined them for the past fourteen centuries. . . .

The underlying problem for the West is not Islamic fundamentalism. It is Islam, a different civilization whose people are convinced of the superiority of their culture and are obsessed with the inferiority of their power. The problem for Islam is not the CIA or the U.S. Department of Defense. It is the West, a different civilization whose people are convinced of the universality of their culture and believe that their superior, if declining, power imposes on them the obligation to extend that culture throughout the world. These are the basic ingredients that fuel conflict between Islam and the West.

In the 1950s Lester Pearson warned that humans were moving into "an age when different civilizations will have to learn to live side by side in peaceful interchange, learning from each other, studying each other's history and ideals and art and culture, mutually enriching each others' lives. The alternative, in this overcrowded little world, is misunderstanding, tension, clash, and catastrophe." The futures of both peace and Civilization depend upon understanding and cooperation among the political, spiritual, and intellectual leaders of the world's major civilizations. In the clash of civilizations, Europe and America will hang together or hang separately. In the greater clash, the global "*real* clash," between Civilization and barbarism, the world's great civilizations, with their rich accomplishments in religion, art, literature, philosophy, science, technology, morality, and compassion, will also hang together or hang separately. In the emerging era, clashes of civilizations are the greatest threat to world peace, and an international order based on civilizations is the surest safeguard against world war.

97

ERIC ALTERMAN

From *Who Speaks for America?*

Foreign policy has usually been considered the special province of high-level experts and statesmen. Average citizens may have opinions and even input into domestic issues, but when it comes to foreign policy, only people at the highest levels, with the greatest training and knowledge, can make legitimate decisions. Journalist Eric Alterman questions this thesis in his exploration of the role of everyday citizens in the making of foreign policy. In a democracy, shouldn't the people take part in such decision-making? Expertise, the author suggests, is what gives the "foreign policy establishment" its power. Yet Alterman's counter to this is simple: "Much of the American public is indeed ignorant, but it is not stupid." With many examples from the past and present in American diplomacy, Alterman makes a strong case for a foreign policy process that is more inclusive of average citizens' views.

IN THE WINTER OF 1998, the Clinton administration was preparing to launch an attack on Iraq in retaliation for Saddam Hussein's unwillingness to comply with the United Nations inspection regime. Support for the plan, however, appeared lukewarm in the extreme. Among our erstwhile allies, only England and Canada believed the military route to be the correct one. At home, the plan seemed to raise more questions than answers among the American people. Even Tom Clancy, the right-wing technothriller novelist—and about as reliable a supporter of all forms of military action as one is likely to find anywhere—complained in the *New York Times* that the president had failed to address the nation's most fundamental concerns: "Who has explained to the American people why it is necessary to send our sons and daughters into harm's way?" Clancy asked. "Who has prepared us and the world for the unpalatable consequences of even a successful attack? How likely is failure, and what would be the consequences?"

In an attempt to quell such anxieties, as it simultaneously garnered support at home and demonstrated its resolve abroad, the administration contacted top executives at CNN and arranged for a worldwide broadcast of a national "town meeting" at Ohio State University. The administration sent Secretary of State Madeleine Albright, Secretary of Defense William Cohen, and National Security Advisor Samuel "Sandy" Berger. As soon as the meeting began, the administration wished it hadn't. First came the loud protests of members of the Spartacist League, the Trotskyite splinter group. When they finally quieted down, an unending barrage of extremely tough and thoughtful questions demonstrated just how ill conceived was the plan for which the Clinton administration was seeking approval.

The problem was not, as administration officials later tried to claim, that the event was hampered by insufficient advance work or too large and unwieldy an audience. Rather, the top national security officials of the United States government were wholly unprepared to answer the kinds of questions with which Ohio citizens had armed themselves. Here are some of the questions asked by members of the audience on that cold February afternoon:

- The American administration has the might and the means to attack the Iraqi state, but does it have the moral right to attack the Iraqi nation? [Cheers, applause.]

- This administration has raised concerns about Iraq's threats to its neighbors, yet none of these neighbors seem too threatened. . . . Furthermore, the international community has been opposed to the bombings. If nobody's asking us for their help, how can you justify further U.S. aggression in the region? [Applause, shouts.]

- If push comes to shove and Saddam will not back down . . . or keep his word, are we ready and willing to send the troops in? [Cheers, applause.]

- President Carter . . . was quoted yesterday as saying that up to 100,000 innocent Iraqi civilians could be killed. Is that something, Secretary Albright, [Shouts, applause] that you think is a realistic possibility? Since we are unsure where Iraq's weapons are, how can we direct a bombing strike against them?

- Why bomb Iraq when other countries have committed similar violations? . . . For example, Turkey has bombed Kurdish citizens. Saudi Arabia has tortured political and religious dissidents. Why does the United States apply different standards of justice to these countries? [Cheers, applause.]

Good questions, every one of them. And the audience at Ohio State asked many more that were equally piercing and intelligent. Yet the gathered administration officials thought such concerns had no merit and were irrelevant to the task at hand. To the viewer at home, it appeared as if the questioners and the government officials were speaking two different languages. In response to the questioner who raised the issue of the inconsistency of the application of U.S. human rights policies, for instance, the secretary of state lectured, "I suggest, sir, that you study carefully what American foreign policy is, what we have said exactly about the cases that you have mentioned. Every one of them have been pointed out. Every one of them we have clearly stated our policy on. And if you would like, as a former professor, I would be delighted to spend fifty minutes with you describing exactly what we are doing on those subjects." But she did not offer a single sentence in response to the question that might fairly be considered an answer.

One anonymous administration official tried to blame the CNN anchors for the public relations debacle, insisting that moderators "Judy [Woodruff] and Bernie [Shaw] looked like they were deer caught in the headlights, they had no control over the management of this." But the true problem was an insurmountable clash of cultures. In the official meeting rooms and academic conferences, to say nothing of high-minded forums such as *Nightline* and *Newshour with Jim Lehrer*, foreign policy discussion is considered a matter for professionals only. When "the public" enters into the discussion, it is usually only in the context of a problem that needs to be managed or an inconvenience that must be finessed. Here was a public empowered by television cameras and a worldwide audience that would not defer and would not go away. The result was not only a genuine roadblock on the administration's road to war, but also a national demonstration of the distance between the governing and the governed when it comes to matters of foreign and military policy.

Speaking on *CBS Evening News*, Dan Rather called the meeting "unruly, disorganized and badly staged." A conservative *Time* magazine essayist complained that the event had been "worthless as a means of preparing the country for war." President Clinton tried to be more generous. He later referred to the Ohio State meeting as "a good old-fashioned American debate," but added, "I believe strongly that most Americans support our policy. They support our resolve." Clinton rushed, however, to undo the damage by throwing his support behind a last-ditch diplomatic effort to avert war by United Nations secretary-general Kofi Annan. Annan succeeded, and this time, war was avoided. The larger lessons of

Ohio State, however, remained unlearned. The administration promised better advance work next time but no institutionalized methods of consultation or even mutual education between itself and the public on foreign policy issues. The media, as is its wont, soon forgot about Ohio State and moved on to the next scandal du jour. The problem itself, went away—or so the foreign policy establishment and the media that covers it would like to believe.

The democratization of American foreign policy is a problem that worries precious few people. In the United States, frequently termed "the world's leading democracy" by pundits and politicians, foreign policy has been deliberately shielded from the effects of democratic debate, with virtually no institutionalized democratic participation. True, we have elections. But elections occur too infrequently to have much of an impact on all but the highest-profile foreign policy decision, and in any case they rarely turn on foreign policy questions. Even in 1968, with an issue as central and divisive as Vietnam, the presidential candidates failed to offer the public a clear choice. During the Cold War, it may have been possible to argue that the survival of the nation itself depended upon the ability of our leaders to make immediate decisions regarding nuclear war. These effectively precluded the untidy mechanisms of the democratic process. Excluding a tiny percentage of decisions that deal with potential terrorist threats, that argument has passed into history along with the Soviet Union. Similarly, it may once have been possible to contend that many Americans were unaffected by most foreign policy decisions. But in an era where a decision to enter into a given trade accord with one nation can literally wipe out an entire industry or geographic community, where the failure to contain environmental destruction on one part of the globe can make life all but unbearable on another, where a new strain of E. coli bacteria found in Peruvian carrots can infect conventioneers in Minneapolis, and where tens of millions of Americans have their pension plans invested in global mutual funds, it is anachronistic to the point of willful blindness to argue that "foreign" policy exists apart and distinct from "domestic" policy. How, then, can the United States claim to be a functioning democracy when one of the most crucial aspects of public policy allows for almost no democratic participation?

Yet the issue fails to engage. According to a 1997 poll, majorities ranging from 55 to 66 percent say that events in Mexico, Western Europe, Asia, and Canada had little or no impact on them. They prefer to pay attention to those issues that do. Of the thousands of foreign policy monographs published in the past decade by various academics, mandarins, and aspiring secretaries of state, an extremely small percentage focus on the role that the public plays in determining—or even reacting to—those policies. A far greater percentage of the foreign policy community in Washington and in academia is concerned with the problem of improving other nations' democratic practices than with examining the character of our own. The same is true of the specialist's publication *Journal of Democracy*, which has published just a handful of articles even remotely concerned with the United States internal policies. Within the larger populace, and even in the informed debate of the Washington punditocracy, the issue simply does not arise.

At this point the reader might ask if I am not begging an obvious question: Can foreign policy be democratic at all, particularly in a country where most people prefer to remain ignorant of the details of their own politics and culture, much less anyone else's? Indeed, the problem is hardly unique to our time and place. No democracy, it must be admitted at the outset, deals well with this problem; not France, not Germany, not England, not Japan. The conflict may be endemic to democracy itself. Alexis de Tocqueville observed long ago that in the conduct of foreign affairs, "democratic governments do appear decidedly inferior to others." Foreign policy, he lamented, requires none of the good qualities peculiar to democracy but demands the cultivation of those sorely lacking. Democracies found it "difficult to coordinate the details of a great undertaking and to fix on some plan and carry it through with determination" and had "little capacity for combining measures in secret and waiting patiently for the result." The diplomatic historian Walter LaFeber calls this phenomenon "the Tocqueville problem in American history." How, LaFeber wonders, can a "democratic republic, whose vitality rests on the pursuit of individual interests with a minimum of central governmental direction, create the necessary national consensus for the conduct of an effective, and necessarily long-term, foreign policy?"

The problem is real, but hardly insoluble. Much of the American public is indeed ignorant, but it is not stupid. Over time, Americans have demonstrated an impressive consistency of values in foreign policy, one that is easily obscured by the polling data that focuses on immediate reactions to various crises. The public's values . . . are a good deal closer to the liberal republican values of the country's original founders than are those of the establishment that professes to represent them. The problem is not that the public does not care. Rather, it has no idea how to force the government to respond to its preferences.

Even if the American people were as incompetent as the members of the foreign policy establishment believe they are, that would be an unacceptable argument for their exclusion from the policy-formation process. In a democracy, a majority of the people have a right to be wrong. "Democracy," insisted Sidney Verba, former president of the American Political Science Association, in a 1995 address to his membership, "implies responsiveness by governing elites to the needs and preferences of the citizenry. More than that, it implies equal responsiveness." The rule of political equality forms the foundational basis of the American political system. It is expressed by our belief in the principle of "one person, one vote."

When Americans complain about the quality of our democracy, their focus is almost always close to home. Crime, drugs, taxes, and schools dominate the agenda while issues of electoral reform and "money politics" floated until recently in the background, most often raised by gadflies such as Ross Perot and Ralph Nader. Yet no nationally significant politician speaks of consulting the American people directly about the conduct of a foreign policy issue, and to my knowledge, no politically significant grassroots leader has put forth a plan to do so either. Despite all the populist anger at "elitist" Washington politicians and bureaucrats that has characterized American debate in recent decades, Americans remain meekly deferential when it comes to foreign policy. In a 1989 survey for the Carnegie Council on Ethics and International Affairs, the Wirthlin Group found that nearly 50 percent of those questioned disagreed with the statement that the "general public is qualified to participate in deciding on U.S. foreign policy."

The U.S. foreign policy establishment, made up of government officials, congressional staffers, insider academics, think-tank partisans, and the lawyers and bankers who shuttle back and forth into these jobs with each change of administration, concur wholeheartedly with this portion of the public. When I first began this study, I approached the head of a prestigious liberal foreign policy think tank in Washington about housing it. "I don't really believe there should be any democracy in foreign policy," he told me. "The people don't know what the [expletive deleted] they want." When I returned to the same think tank to give a talk on [this] subject . . . to its interns, an extremely self-satisfied young man announced that he did not "see why people who don't know anything about foreign policy should have the same say in what happens as those of us who do." . . .

To the degree that the makers of U.S. foreign policy recognize a role for the public in policy formation at all, it is usually that of the quietly attentive student. The responsibility of the president, for instance, according to former national security adviser Zbigniew Brzezinski, is not to act in accordance with the wishes of his voters but to "enlighten the public about global complexities and generate support for his policies." That

Americans may not wish for their government to invade a particular country should not affect a policymaker's decision-making process, according to former Bush administration official Richard N. Haass. "Interventions tend to rise and fall on their merits. Success will create support that may not have existed beforehand—Grenada and the protection of Gulf shipping are cases in point—while failure will drain any support that might have existed." Grenada, explains Haass, referring to the tiny nutmeg-producing island invaded by U.S. forces under President Reagan, "shows that a president who has the courage to lead will win public support if he acts wisely and effectively." Some officials and former officials have gone so far as to argue that the president's powers to conduct foreign policy are akin to those of a general in the army. When Congress challenged George Bush's friendliness to the Chinese regime in the aftermath of the Tiananmen Square massacre, Secretary of State James Baker was sharply critical. "Leadership on this issue," he insisted, "should come from the president as commander-in-chief." General Maxwell Taylor gave this view added (and ominous) power when he explained to a television journalist in 1971 that "a citizen should know those things he needs to be a good citizen and to discharge his functions." Given what Taylor and his cohorts believed the American people "needed" to know about U.S. policy in Vietnam, his view would appear to contain within it the seeds of tragedy as well as deadly irony. . . .

What becomes clear to anyone who studies the problem carefully is that the American people do not accept the foreign policy establishment's definition of the nation's priorities in the world but do not know how to force a reassessment. Most Americans, unlike the members of the foreign policy establishment, do not live to conduct foreign policy; rather, they conduct foreign policy to live. They believe, by vast majorities, that "U.S. foreign policy should service the U.S. domestic agenda rather than remain focused on traditional internationalist problems." In a 1989 poll, designed explicitly to discover the "values" that underlay Americans' foreign policy attitudes, nearly 90 percent of those questioned insisted that "America has a moral responsibility to concentrate on domestic policy before concentrating on foreign policy." Seven years later, a series of focus groups undertaken by the National Issues Forum, a polling and educational organization, determined that almost all participants believed that "domestic needs have been neglected at the expense of foreign affairs." This belief is not the result of ignorance, insufficient education, stupidity, or an inability of the foreign policy establishment to reach the larger public. This is a core American value. At the National Issues Convention in Austin in January 1996, the percentage of participants who believed that

the United States would be "better off if we just stayed at home and did
not concern ourselves with problems in other parts of the world" increased
by 25 percent to nearly one out of two people after each participant had
the opportunity to consult with experts, facilitators, and one another.
Seventy percent agreed that the "U.S. should shift resources back into
helping its own economy now that the Cold War is over." When polled,
Americans consistently choose "protecting American jobs" as their most
important foreign policy priority, but the goal barely registers among
business and opinion elites. Clearly, if it knew how to do so, the public
would demand a foreign policy that served those interests, one that focused
more on protecting jobs than promoting unfettered trade, one that eschewed far-flung adventures to concentrate on strengthening the American economy and society. Finally, and most importantly, the American
people would like to see a foreign policy that ceases to operate as if foreign
policy and domestic policy were somehow separate realms. And in this
regard, it is the American people who share the viewpoint of the nation's
founders and comprehend the world of today with greater realism and
sophistication than their alleged intellectual superiors.

Foreign policy experts regard their competence as sufficient reason
that they alone should determine the overall direction of U.S. foreign
policy. (The day-to-day operation of that policy is unarguably beyond the
capacities of any large-scale democratic system.) But the makers of U.S.
foreign policy are unwilling to own up to increasing amounts of evidence
that the values they believe should underlie the nation's foreign policy
are at odds with those of the people in whose name they profess to act
and speak.

The values of the foreign policy establishment are less reflective of
the political interests of most Americans than of the transnational class of
bankers, lobbyists, lawyers, and investors from which they are drawn.
These "experts" are so shielded from the struggles of everyday American
life that they have become, as John Dewey predicted, "a class with private
interests and private knowledge." This development should hardly surprise
anyone, nor is it cause for scandal. But it is a reality, and if we are to call
ourselves a democracy, we must address it.

The disjunction between elite and mass values in foreign policy has
been growing ever since the United States began to take on the accoutre-
ments of empire. Beginning with the Cold War, however, these differences
became contradictions, frequently antidemocratic in character. The elites
demanded public sacrifice for their policies but employed deceitful means
to build support for them. The exposure of these tawdry tactics has done
much to destroy public confidence in virtually all American institutions.

For instance, according to extensive public research done over a period of decades, the American public views the Vietnam War to have been "more than a mistake" and to have been "fundamentally wrong and immoral." Most members of the elite, committed to the idea of empire and, hence, to the means of defending it, find this view not merely simplistic and wrongheaded but personally offensive. The gulf, moreover, has increased rather than receded with time. When questioned by the National Issues Forum in 1996, members of the public could not credit U.S. foreign policy with a single significant accomplishment that improved their lives, or anyone else's for that matter. Rather, "participants felt that when it comes to foreign affairs, the public has been regularly misled by leaders from both parties for many years." . . .

Historically, the elite's method of dealing with popular disapproval of foreign policy has been simply to ignore it and to cover up evidence of unpopular policies whenever necessary. This was the case for President Franklin Roosevelt, who did so for brave and farsighted reasons between 1939 and 1941, and it remains true today. Unfortunately, Roosevelt's example has led many of his successors to equate their own political interests with the Nazi threat to civilization. Presidents now routinely defy the clearly stated values of the American people and then lie about it. In doing so, they undermine the democratic foundation of our political system. Richard Nixon and Henry Kissinger were guilty of this transgression when they secretly expanded the Vietnam War into Cambodia and then covered up the evidence. Ronald Reagan and Oliver North were equally culpable when they sold missiles to the Ayatollah and used the profits to funnel guns to the Nicaraguan contras. Both of these actions resulted in celebrated scandals, but they did not dissuade future presidents from engaging in the same practices.

Today, presidential actions that defy the unmistakable foreign policy preferences of the American people and are then covered up by their perpetrators are not even considered cause for scandal. For instance while the public was unarguably unenthusiastic about NAFTA, it did cite "stopping the inflow of illegal drugs" as a top priority in the most recent CCFR poll. During the NAFTA battle, however, according to a *New York Times* report, the Bush administration "often exaggerated the Mexican government's progress in the fight against drugs, playing down corruption and glossing over failures." John P. Waters, a senior official for international drug policy in the Bush White House, explained, "People desperately wanted drugs not to become a complicating factor for NAFTA. There was a degree of illicit activity that was just accepted." Motivated by what one former official called "the bigger picture," the Bush administration went so far as to overlook the killing by corrupt Mexican Army officers of seven U.S. DEA officers who were in hot pursuit of a smuggler's aircraft in Veracruz.

The administration's actions in this incident were not reported until almost five years after it took place. Had Americans wished to vote in 1992 on the basis of the foreign policy issue about which they professed to care most deeply, they would not have had the requisite information. Unless someone happened to be a particularly careful reader of the *New York Times*, a category that excludes more than 99 percent of all U.S. voters, he would probably never have seen or heard any mention of this policy at all. In such cases, democracy is subverted and the peoples' wishes denied.

To protect NAFTA, the U.S. government's whitewash of the involvement of high-level Mexican officials in drug smuggling has continued and even expanded on a bipartisan basis under President Clinton. As an example of conflicts between elite and public goals, it is U.S. foreign policy writ large. Presidents and their advisers understand that the public's natural deference and disinclination to question the details of official policy regarding foreign adversaries gives them enormous latitude to pursue policies in conflict with Americans' professed values and beliefs. In matters of war and peace in particular, Americans' patriotic desire to support their president usually overwhelms their natural bias against involvement in foreign wars. Politicians and members of the punditocracy exploit this phenomenon by deliberately exaggerating potential physical threats to the United States and by manipulating Americans' deep-seated racial fears and insecurities. With regard to trade policy and the protection of American jobs, the elite has managed to exploit the incantatory power of the term "free trade" in order to overcome mass objections to policies that sacrifice workers' wages and job security on the altar of economic efficiency.

To begin to map the potential contours of a new, democratically based foreign policy, we need to be cognizant of a dizzying number of historical trends, issues, and characterological developments within both America and the world at large. The idea, once again, is to identify the enduring collective values of the American people and then to translate these into workable and consistent political policies. Simply reading poll numbers is insufficient, for precious little polling has been done on values as opposed to mere attitudes and opinions. Furthermore, Americans frequently hold conflicting values with varying degrees of intensity, both within themselves as individuals and among themselves as groups. Listen to Ruben Alcala, a retired steelworker in Merrillville, Indiana, explain his feelings about the efficacy of the Clinton administration's Bosnia policy in mid-1995: "I'm not really following it that closely. I can't understand why it's going on so long, or why. It's a shame so many people are suffering. Sometimes I think maybe we should [intervene]. Then I think, no, let them take care of their own. Let someone else solve it. The U.S. is the greatest country in the world. Should we be the world's policeman? No, that's what we got the U.N. for."

Mr. Alcala seems to believe that a UN military force is an alternative to an American intervention. At the moment of his comment, however, the president and his advisers were facing the question of whether to deploy American troops as part of a UN peacekeeping force. Mr. Alcala insists that the United States is the world's "greatest country" but does not begin to define the meaning of those words. Were it to imply U.S. responsibility to help enforce a peace accord in Bosnia, Mr. Alcala immediately terms this the U.S. acting as the "world's policeman" and hence inappropriate. Though he is clearly troubled by "so many people suffering," he is divided between wishing to find some way to alleviate that suffering and simply defining the problem as one outside the realm of his nation's concerns. How, then, to craft a foreign policy that accurately reflects the values that underlie Mr. Alcala's confusing concerns, that honors the genuine pride and patriotism he feels about his country without pandering to his ignorance and fear?

98

GEORGE KENNAN

From *Around the Cragged Hill*

From his 1947 authorship of the major statement of America's Cold War containment doctrine under the pseudonym "X" to his 1993 reflections on the past and future of the nation, George Kennan has been one of the country's leading statesmen and thinkers. In this excerpt, Kennan concerns himself with the future of American foreign policy, urging politicians and citizens to place national interests in the forefront of their thinking. He criticizes the once-popular idea that the United States is a nation destined for greatness, and suggests a new kind of isolationism in foreign affairs that would allow national resources to go where they are most needed within the country. Kennan includes some warnings for his beloved State Department, the hub of foreign policymaking: the many fragmented interests that converge there must be sorted out, using the nation's interest as the only criterion of their importance. "The hour may be late, but there is nothing that says it is too late," writes Kennan. As Alexis de Tocqueville knew about the fragile democracy, America, Kennan also knows: "The challenge is to see what could be done, and then to have the heart and the resolution to attempt it."

———

THE PASSING OF THE Cold War, in presenting us a world which appears to be devoid of anything that could be seen as a major great-power enemy of this country, also obviously presents us with a problem for which few of us are prepared. One has to go back to the 1920s to find anything that could be even remotely regarded as a precedent for it; and even then, conditions have changed so greatly since that time that the precedent would be of very little relevance.

What presents itself, in this situation, is a demand for nothing less than a redesigning of the entire great pattern of America's interaction with the rest of the world. To treat this whole subject in a graceful and coherent form within the limits of a single chapter in a book of this nature would surpass the capacity of this writer. He can only attempt, as a starter, to sketch out what he feels should be the main thrust and balance of American policy in the remaining years of the century, and then to give at least a partial elucidation of this concept by commenting on several significant aspects of the problem, without attempting to bring all of these individual comments into one, comprehensive statement.

Anyone who sets out to design or to conduct the foreign policy of a great country has to be clear as to the interests that policy is supposed to serve. Only if the image of these interests is clear in his mind can the policy he evolves have coherence and usefulness.

Those who conduct American foreign policy have two sets of interests to bear in mind. First, there are the parochial interests of the country itself, in the most narrow and traditional sense of that term. Second, there are the interests that engage this country as a participant in the affairs of the international community as a whole. Both of these sets of interests deserve our respect and attention. But it is those of our own country, in the narrower sense, that lie closest to our hearts; and they demand our first consideration.

There is nothing wrong about this allotment of priorities. It is not the dictate of a national selfishness or disregard for others. This particular territory and these particular people, ourselves, are all that we, as a national state, have control over. The management of our society, and this in a creditable way, is for us an unavoidable responsibility as well as a privilege.

Unless we meet this responsibility, no one else will; for there is none who could. And unless we meet it creditably, there will be very little that we can do for others—very little that we can do even to serve global interests. The first requirement for a successful participation by the United States in the confrontation with international environmental problems, for instance, will be success in coping even halfway creditably with the similar problems within its own territory.

But there is another reason, too, why the service to our own national interest is more than just selfishness. Our society serves, for better or for worse, as an example for much of the rest of the world. The life of no other people is so widely and closely observed, scrutinized, and sometimes imitated. So true is this that it is not too much to say that the American people have it in their power, given the requisite will and imagination, to set for the rest of the world a unique example of the way a modern, advanced society could be shaped in order to meet successfully the emerging tests of the modern and the future age.

The example, in any case, is going to be there, whether favorable or otherwise, and whether we like it or not. Our handling of our own problems is going to be carefully watched by others, no matter what we do. But if the example is only one of failure—of the evasion of challenge, of the inability to cope with our own major problems—this will be for others, aside from the loss of respect for us, a source of discouragement, a state of mind which can have far-reaching consequences, and for which we will bear a measure of responsibility. It is because no country can hope to be, over the long run, much more to others than it is to itself that we have a moral duty to put our own house in order, if we are to take our proper part in the affairs of the rest of the world.

But beyond the above, and as a background for all that follows in this chapter, I should make it clear that I am wholly and emphatically rejecting any and all messianic concepts of America's role in the world: rejecting, that is, the image of ourselves as teachers and redeemers to the rest of humanity, rejecting the illusions of unique and superior virtue on our part, the prattle about Manifest Destiny or the "American Century"— all those visions that have so richly commended themselves to Americans of all generations since, and even before, the foundation of our country. We are, for the love of God, only human beings, the descendants of human beings, the bearers, like our ancestors, of all the usual human frailties. Divine hands . . . may occasionally reach down to support us in our struggles, as individuals, with our divided nature; but no divine hand has ever reached down to make us, as a national community, anything more than what we are, or to elevate us in that capacity over the remainder of mankind. We have great military power—yes; but there is, as Reinhold Niebuhr so brilliantly and persuasively argued, no power, individual or collective, without some associated guilt. And if there were any qualities that lie within our ability to cultivate that might set us off from the rest of the world, these would be the virtues of modesty and humility; and of these we have never exhibited any exceptional abundance. The discussion that follows is predicated on the rejection of such illusions.

We saw, in the preceding chapters, some examples of the failures and unsolved problems of our society. There are others that could have been mentioned. Until these inadequacies have been overcome, the task of overcoming them will have to have first claim on our resources. Comprehensive programs of reform in several areas of our life will have to be devised, put in motion, and carried through. Until this is done, we will not know what resources we can spare for foreign policy; and those we find it imperative to continue to devote to that purpose will have to be cut to the bone. What we should want, in these circumstances, is the minimum, not the maximum, of external involvement.

All of this seems to me to call for a very modest and restrained foreign policy, directed to the curtailment of external undertakings and involvements wherever this is in any way possible, and to the avoidance of any assumption of new ones. This means a policy far less pretentious in word and deed than the ones we have been following in recent years. It means, in particular, a rejection of the tempting but fatuous assumption that we can find, in our relations with other countries or other parts of the world, relief from the painful domestic confrontation with ourselves.

There will no doubt be those who will be quick to label what has just been suggested as a policy of isolationism. The term is not very meaningful; but if it means what I think it does, I could only wish that something of that sort were possible; for most foreign involvements are burdens we should be happy to be without. But unfortunately, as will be seen shortly, whatever possibilities may exist for the curtailment of our external commitments and obligations, there will always be a goodly number that cannot be eliminated—not, at least, in any short space of time—and of which we must acquit ourselves as best we can. . . . The value of any policy purporting to reflect the national interests of the United States cannot be greater than the ability of the U.S. government to carry it out. And that will depend, in turn, on the extent to which the policymaker is free to address himself to that particular problem—the extent, that is, to which his field of vision and his energies are not preempted by competing undertakings in which the national interest is not a factor at all.

First of all, let us note the manner in which our government is at present set up for the conduct of foreign policy. In recent decades, the power to make foreign policy decisions has been scattered all over the vast panorama of Washingtonian bureaucracy. The process is theoretically under the ultimate control of the president, in the sense that anytime he decides to put in his word, that word is the controlling one. But the president is a very busy man. The time he has to devote to this sort of thing is limited. It was pointed out in an earlier chapter of this disquisition that under the American system of government, but not under many others, the president has to be both chief of state and prime minister, not to mention his responsibilities in party leadership. This puts great strain on him. The number of decisions, great and small, that enter daily into the conduct of American foreign policy are multitudinous. The State Department alone, we are told, receives, and is obliged to respond to, more than seven hundred telegrams a day. The president cannot possibly occupy himself personally with more than the tiniest fraction of such demands. The vast majority have to be delegated.

In recent years, this process of delegation has occurred in such a way that the power to take the necessary decisions has been fragmented, and is, as I say, farmed out all over the governmental pasture. In addition to the Department of State, the National Security Council, the Pentagon, the CIA, the Treasury, the Department of Commerce, and no end of legislators, legislative committees, and staffs all have their fingers in this pie. Parochial bureaucratic outlooks, interests, and competitive aspirations clash at every point. The result is, for obvious reasons, a very messy business. In this confusion, such a thing as a clear, firm, and prompt decision—and particularly one where all the relevant aspects of national interest are brought together, calmly weighed, and collectively taken into account—is rare indeed. It would do little good to have, here or there, at one place or another in the Washington scene, clear concepts of long-term national interest, so long as the power to make decisions remains thus fragmentized. As things now stand, many of the decisions taken are the results of long, labored, and tortuous compromises among endless numbers of individuals and committees, each of whom or of which has a different idea of the interests to be served. The result, not surprisingly, is everything else than a coherent, concise, thoughtfully formed, or clearly articulated foreign policy. . . .

Plainly, of course, there would always likewise be Congress to be taken into account. It, too, has its constitutional place in the designing of foreign policy. Decisions taken in the executive branch will always have to be compromised with the views and wishes of individual legislators and congressional committees. But here is where politics come in. Here, the president and the secretary of state, both political figures, are the ones whose responsibility it is to make the unavoidable decisions as to the extent to which congressional views and wishes, very often the reflection of lobbyist pressures, should be deferred to, compromised with, or defied in the designing of foreign policy.

In the days of my directorship at the State Department's Policy Planning Staff, I was sometimes urged to take into account, in our recommendations to the secretary of state, the domestic-political aspects of the recommendation in question. "Should you not warn the secretary," it would be asked of me, "of the domestic-political problems this recommendation would present, and make suggestions as to how they might be met?" I resisted firmly all such pressures. Our duty, I insisted, was to tell the president and the secretary what, in our view, was in the national interest. It was their duty, if they accepted the force of our recommendations, to see how far these could be reconciled with domestic-political realities. This was a duty that they were far better fitted to perform than were we. And if we did not give them, as a starter, a view of the national interest in its pure form, as we saw it, no one else would, and they would not be able to judge its importance relative to the domestic-political pressures by which they were confronted. . . .

In the behavior in recent decades of the American political establishment in matters of foreign policy, I see reflected a number of persistent motivations, most of them illustrated in what has been said in this chapter. I see, thus reflected, remnants of the astigmatism and the corruption of understanding that marked the Cold War period. I see the impulse to cater to the demands and desiderata of powerful special domestic-political interests. I see a great deal (some of it contradictory) of what I think of as diplomacy before the flattering mirror: the desire to appear as the gracious and high-minded lady bountiful (the many aid programs), as the thrilling military adventurer—the knight in shining armor, rushing to the aid of the threatened and the downtrodden (Vietnam, Panama, the Persian Gulf War)—and as the unbending champion of democracy and human rights. I see the addiction to established habit, and the ponderous inertia, of entrenched bureaucracies. And in all of this I see the never-ending compulsion of successive administrations to present themselves, for the popularity polls, in postures that feed the American public's favorite wish-images of itself. All this I see. What I do not see is any marked concern for the national interest in the narrow sense, on the one hand, or for the wider interests of the threatened planet, on the other.

The reader may recall the observation . . . to the effect that every political regime, in all places and all times, speaks with two voices: one for the interests of its people as a whole, the other for its own interests as one of the contenders in the inevitable domestic-political competition. And it strikes me that in the behavior of the American political establishment, as noted above, there is a decided, and undue, predominance of the second of those two voices. I am not arguing that it should not be heard at all. I know that this distortion of priorities is one of the prices we pay for the advantages of our form of government. I have no doubt that most of our politicians, confronted with this reproach, would say, "Don't you realize that in order to have the ability to act in the national interest, we first have to gain power; and that to gain that power requires precisely the sort of compromises and pretensions that you are professing to deplore?" But to this I would have to reply, "Yes, within limits. But I don't see any great difference in your behavior before and after an election. One electoral test successfully surmounted, you at once begin thinking of the next one; and the domestic-political considerations again crowd out the interests of the nation as a whole."

Still, I see this situation as the fault not so much of the individuals who command, at one time or another, the seats of power but rather of the political system that installs them in those positions. Is there not, I wonder, some serious structural defect that puts so great a premium on one sort of political motivation, and so little on the other? . . .

Is it a dark and despairing view of the human predicament that emerges? The writer's answer is no—it could not be. No one—neither this writer nor anyone else who undertakes to comment on the human scene—can profess to stand outside the subject on which he is commenting. There is no detached Archimedean platform from which the subject could be viewed. Just as the scientist's observation of an experiment affects the very material on which he is experimenting, the humanist, too, makes himself a part of the problem he examines; and he assumes thereby at least a small share of responsibility for the image he describes. His words, after all, may be expected to have *some* consequences, however trivial; otherwise, they would not be worth uttering. But the measure and quality of this effect is never predictable; and, that being the case, the responsibility of the writer is all the greater.

I cannot too strongly emphasize the seriousness of this responsibility. If the commentator's words sow despair, particularly among younger people whose ability to act upon life has not yet exhausted itself or even reached its peak, he may, by his despairing words, have given discouragement where courage was needed. He may have created hopelessness where, even if he could not himself see this, there was no reason not to hope.

And that, as I see it, would be the unpardonable sin. The hour may be late, but there is nothing that says that it is too late. There is nothing in man's plight that his vision, if he cared to cultivate it, and his will, if he dared to exercise it, could not alleviate. The challenge is to see what could be done, and then to have the heart and the resolution to attempt it. Anything in the way of a comment on the human condition that weakened that heart or undermined that resolution would be an inexcusable abuse of the responsibility of the speaker.

The observations brought forward in this book are offered, then, however severe some of them may seem, with a view to encouraging others to take heart—not to lose it. But to take heart is to act. It is the writer's hope that this book itself, in its own small way, is an action, and will be received accordingly.

PERMISSIONS
ACKNOWLEDGMENTS

1. From *Democracy in America* by Alexis de Tocqueville, translated by Henry Reeve, published by Schoeken Books, 1961. Originally published in 1835.
2. From *The American Commonwealth* by James Bryce. Published by Macmillan, 1888.
3. Excerpts from *The Liberal Tradition in America: An Interpretation of American Political Thought Since the Revolution*, by Louis Hartz, copyright © 1955 and renewed 1983 by Louis Hartz, reprinted by permission of Harcourt, Inc.
4. Reprinted with the permission of Simon & Schuster Adult Publishing Group, from *Bowling Alone: The Collapse and Revival of American Community* by Robert D. Putnam. Copyright © 2000 by Robert D. Putnam.
5. Reprinted with the permission of The Free Press, a Division of Simon & Schuster Adult Publishing Group, from *The Ladd Report* by Everett Carll Ladd. Copyright © 1999 by Everett Carll Ladd.
6. From *Race Matters*, by Cornel West. Copyright © 1993, 2001 by Cornel West. Reprinted by permission of Beacon Press, Boston.
7. From *People of Paradox* by Michael Kammen. Copyright © 1972 by Michael Kammen. Reprinted by permission of Alfred A. Knopf, Inc., a Division of Random House, Inc.
8. From *Habits of the Heart: Individualism and Commitment in American Life* by Robert Bellah, et al. Copyright © 1985, 1996 The Regents of the University of California. Reprinted by permission of The University of California Press.
9. From *The American Political Tradition* by Richard Hofstadter. Copyright © 1948 by Alfred A. Knopf, Inc. and renewed 1976 by Beatrice Hofstadter. Reprinted by permission of Alfred A. Knopf, Inc., a Division of Random House, Inc.
10. *The Federalist* 10, by James Madison, 1787.
11. From *A Machine That Would Go of Itself* by Michael Kammen. Copyright © 1986 by Michael Kammen. Reprinted by permission of Alfred A. Knopf, Inc., a Division of Random House, Inc.
12. From *The Power Elite, New Edition* by C. Wright Mills. Copyright © 1956, 2000 by Oxford University Press. Used by permission of Oxford University Press.
13. From Richard Zweigenhaft and G. William Domhoff, *Diversity in the Power Elite*. Copyright © 1998 by Richard Zweigenhaft and G. William Domhoff. Reprinted by permission of Yale University Press.

14. From *Who Governs* by Robert Dahl. Copyright © 1961 by Yale University Press. Reprinted by permission of Yale University Press. From *A Preface to Democratic Theory* by Robert Dahl. Copyright © 1956 by The University of Chicago Press. Reprinted by permission of The University of Chicago Press.

15. *The Federalist* 51, by James Madison, 1787.

16. From *Congressional Government* by Woodrow Wilson. Published by Peter Smith publishers. Originally published 1885.

17. From *The Washington Community: 1800–1828* by James Young, Copyright © 1966, Columbia University Press. Reprinted with permission of the Publisher.

18. From *Revolving Gridlock: Politics and Policy from Carter to Clinton* by David W. Brady and Craig Volden. Copyright © 1998 by Westview Press, Inc. Reprinted by permission of Westview Press, a member of Perseus Books , L.L.C.

19. *The Federalist* 39 and 46, by James Madison, 1787.

20. From *American Federalism: A View from the States*, 3rd Edition by Daniel J. Elazar. Copyright © 1984 by Harper & Row Publishers, Inc. Reprinted by permission of Pearson Education, Inc.

21. From *Laboratories of Democracy*, by David Osborne. Copyright © 1991 by David Osborne. Reprinted by permission of International Creative Management, Inc.

22. Excerpt from *United States v. Lopez* 115 S.Ct. 1624 (1995).

23. From *Congress: The Electoral Connection* by David Mayhew, published by Yale University Press. Copyright © 1974 by Yale University Press. Reprinted by permission of Yale University Press.

24. From *Home Style: House Members in Their Districts* by Richard F. Fenno, Jr. Copyright © 1978 by Little, Brown and Company. Reprinted by permission of Addison–Wesley Educational Publishers, Inc.

25. From *The Web of Politics: The Internet's Impact on the American Political System* by Richard Davis, copyright © 1999 by Oxford University Press, Inc. Used by permission of Oxford University Press, Inc.

26. From *Congressional Women: Their Recruitment, Integration, and Behavior*, Second Edition, Revised and Updated by Irwin N. Gertzog. Copyright © 1995 by Praeger Publishers. Reprinted by permission of Greenwood Publishing Group, Inc. Westport, CT.

27. From *Hispanics in Congress: A Historical and Political Survey* by Maurilio E. Vigil. Copyright © 1996 by Maurilio E. Vigil. Reprinted by permission of University Press of America, Inc.

28. "Pork: A Time-Honored Tradition Lives On" by Paul Starobin from *Congressional Quarterly Weekly Report*, Oct. 24, 1987. Copyright © 1987 by Congressional Quarterly, Inc. Reprinted by permission.

29. From "In Praise of Pork," by John Ellwood and Eric Patashnik, from *The Public Interest*, Number 110, Winter 1993, pp. 19–23, 31. © 1993 by National Affairs, Inc. Reprinted by permission of the authors and *The Public Interest*.

30. From *Unorthodox Lawmaking* by Barbara Sinclair [CQ Press: 2000]. Copyright © 2000 by Congressional Quarterly, Inc. Reprinted by permission of Congressional Quarterly, Inc.

31. From *The Congressional Experience*, by David Price, Copyright © 1992 by Westview Press Inc. Reprinted by permission of Westview Press, a member of Perseus Books, L.L.C.

49. Excerpts from *Miranda v. Arizona*, 384 U.S. 436, 86 S.Ct. 1602 (1966).

50. From "Security Versus Civil Liberties," by Judge Richard A. Posner, in *The Atlantic Monthly*, Vol. 288, No. 5 (December, 2001), copyright © 2001 by The Atlantic Monthly. Reprinted by permission of the author.

51. From *Simple Justice* by Richard Kluger. Copyright © 1975 by Richard Kluger. Reprinted by permission of Alfred A. Knopf, Inc., a division of Random House Inc.

52. Selected excerpts from *The Rage of the Privileged Class*, by Ellis Cose. Copyright © 1993 by Ellis Cose. Reprinted by permission of HarperCollins Publishers, Inc.

53. Excerpts from *Affirmative Action At Work: Law, Politics, and Ethics*, by Bron Raymond Taylor, © 1991 by University of Pittsburgh Press. Reprinted by permission of the University of Pittsburgh Press.

54. From *PGA Tour, Inc. v. Casey Martin*, 532 U.S. _____ (2001).

55. From "Gay and Lesbian Issues in the Congressional Arena" by Colton Campbell and Roger Davidson, in *The Politics of Gay Rights*, edited by Craig A. Rimmerman, Kenneth D. Wald, and Clyde Wilcox. Copyright © 2000 by The University of Chicago. Used by permission of the University of Chicago Press.

56. Eight pages from *In Our Defense* by Ellen Alderman and Caroline Kennedy. Copyright © 1991 by Ellen Alderman and Caroline Kennedy. By permission of William Morrow & Company, Inc.

57. From *Girls Lean Back Everywhere*, by Edward DeGrazia. Copyright © 1992 by Edward DeGrazia. Published by Random House, Inc.

58. Adapted with the permission of The Free Press, a Division of Simon & Schuster, Inc. from *Rights Talk: The Impoverishment of Political Discourse* by Mary Ann Glendon. Copyright © 1991 by Mary Ann Glendon.

59. From *The American Commonwealth* by James Bryce. Published by Macmillan, 1888.

60. From *The Phantom Public* by Walter Lippmann. Copyright © 1925 and renewed 1953 by Walter Lippmann. Published by Simon and Schuster.

61. From *Public Opinion and American Democracy* by V. O. Key, published by Alfred Knopf, 1961. Permission granted by the executors of the Key Estate.

62. From *Politicians Don't Pander: Political Manipulation and the Loss of Democratic Responsiveness* by Lawrence R. Jacobs and Robert Y. Shapiro. Copyright © 2000 by The University of Chicago. Used by permission of the University of Chicago Press.

63. From *Direct Democracy: The Politics of Initiative, Reform, and Recall*, by Thomas Cronin, pp. 1–3, 5, 6, 10–12, 196–199, 222, Cambridge, Mass.: Harvard University Press, © 1989 by the Twentieth Century Fund, Inc. Reprinted by permission of Harvard University Press.

64. From *Democracy in America* by Alexis de Tocqueville, translated by Henry Reeve, published by Schoeken Books, 1961. Originally published 1835.

65. Excerpts from *The Semisovereign People: A Realist's View of Democracy in America*, 1st Edition, by E. E. Schattschneider. Copyright © 1961. Reprinted by permission of Wadsworth, a division of Thompson Learning: www.thompsonrights.com. FAX 800 730-2215.

66. From *The End of Liberalism: The Second Republic of the United States*, Second Edition, by Theodore J. Lowi. Copyright © 1979, 1969 by W. W. Norton & Company, Inc. Used by permission of W. W. Norton & Company, Inc.